real world MACRO

twenty-sixth edition

edited by
**Daniel Fireside, John Miller, Bryan Snyder
and the *Dollars & Sense* Collective**

REAL WORLD MACRO
TWENTY-SIXTH EDITION

Copyright 1983, 1984, 1986, 1987, 1989, 1990, 1991, 1992, 1993, 1994, 1995, 1996, 1997, 1998, 1999, 2000, 2001, 2002, 2003, 2004, 2005, 2006, 2007, 2008, 2009 by the Economic Affairs Bureau, Inc. All rights reserved. No portions of this book may be reproduced except by prior permission from the Economic Affairs Bureau.

ISBN: 978-1-878585-96-7

Published by:
Economic Affairs Bureau, Inc.
Dollars and Sense
29 Winter Street
Boston, MA 02108
tel: 617-447-2177
dollars@dollarsandsense.org
www.dollarsandsense.org

Real World Macro is edited by the *Dollars & Sense* collective, publishers of *Dollars & Sense* magazine and *Real World Micro, Real World Globalization, Current Economic Issues, Real World Banking, The Environment in Crisis, Grassroots Journalism, Introduction to Political Economy, Striking a Balance, Unlevel Playing Fields, Real World Latin America,* and *The Wealth Inequality Reader*.

The 2009 Collective: Arpita Banerjee, Amy Benjamin, Eric Benjamin, Heather Boersma, Ben Collins, Daniel Fireside, Ben Greenberg, Amy Gluckman, Mary Jirmanus, James McBride, John Miller, Larry Peterson, Smriti Rao, Alejandro Reuss, Bryan Snyder, Chris Sturr, Ramaa Vasudevan, and Jeanne Winner.

Production: Chris Sturr and David Gerratt (NonprofitDesign.com)

Printed in U.S.A.

INTRODUCTION

CHAPTER 1: MEASURING ECONOMIC PERFORMANCE

Introduction

1.1	What's in a Name? Crisis, Recession, Depression *John Miller*	7
1.2	The Real Unemployment Rate *John Miller*	11
1.3	CPI Blues *Joshua Holland*	13
1.4	The Growth Consensus Unravels *Jonathan Rowe*	14
1.5	Gender and Recession *Heather Boushey*	18
1.6	Wages for Housework: The Movement and the Numbers *Lena Graber and John Miller*	20
1.7	War Spending Placed Above Domestic Priorities *Monique Morrissey*	22

CHAPTER 2: WEALTH, INEQUALITY, AND POVERTY

Introduction

2.1	Slicing Up at the Long Barbeque *James M. Cypher*	27
2.2	What's Good for Wal-Mart *John Miller*	32
2.3	Measures of Poverty *Ellen Frank*	35
2.4	Access to Paid Sick Days Vastly Unequal *Elise Gould*	36
2.5	The Death of Horatio Alger *Paul Krugman*	37
2.6	America's Growing Fringe Economy *Howard Karger*	38
2.7	Geese, Golden Eggs, and Traps: Why Inequality is Bad for the Economy *Chris Tilly*	43
2.8	Transforming the Engines of Inequality *William Greider*	46
2.9	Rich and Poor in the Global Economy *Interview with Bob Sutcliffe*	49

CHAPTER 3: SAVINGS AND INVESTMENT

Introduction

3.1	Boosting Investment: The Overrated Influence of Interest Rates *Gretchen McClain and Randy Albelda*	55
3.2	The Dow High and Stock Ownership *Sylvia Allegretto*	57
3.3	Who Decides Stock Prices? *Ellen Frank*	58
3.4	Private Equity Exposed *Orlando Segura, Jr.*	59
3.5	From Tulips to Mortgage-Backed Securities *Gerald Friedman*	62
3.6	Who Gets Those Trillions? *Arthur MacEwan*	63
3.7	The Homeownership Myth *Howard Karger*	64
3.8	How to Stop the Foreclosures *Fred Moseley*	69

CHAPTER 4: CAPITALISM IN CRISIS

Introduction

4.1	Inequality, Power, and Ideology *Arthur MacEwan*	75
4.2	Derivatives and Deregulation *Marty Wolfson*	81
4.3	Crisis and Neoliberal Capitalism *David Kotz*	83
4.4	Capitalism Hits the Fan *Rick Wolff*	84
4.5	The Greed Fallacy *Arthur MacEwan*	87
4.6	Top Ten Ways to Recognize the Next Great Depression *John Miller*	88
4.7	Financialization: A Primer *Ramaa Vasudevan*	90

CHAPTER 5: FISCAL POLICY, DEFICITS, AND DEBT

Introduction

5.1	A New WPA? *Ryan A. Dodd*	95
5.2	Stimulus Whining *John Miller*	99
5.3	Bail Out the Safety Net *Randy Albelda*	100
5.4	War Spending, Deficits, and Economic Stimulus *Arthur MacEwan*	101
5.5	The Tax Cut Con *Paul Krugman*	102
5.6	One-Quarter of Large U.S. Corporations Don't Pay Profit Taxes—Why Should the Rest? *John Miller*	106
5.7	Social Security Isn't Broken *Doug Orr*	108
5.8	The Opposite of Insurance *James Woolman*	111

CHAPTER 6: MONETARY POLICY AND FINANCIAL MARKETS

Introduction

6.1	What is Money? *Doug Orr*	114
6.2	Focus on the Fed *Doug Orr and Ellen Frank*	116
6.3	How do Fiscal and Monetary Policy Compare? *Arthur MacEwan*	119
6.4	Pushing on Strings *Gerald Friedman*	120
6.5	The Fed and the International Banking Conspiracy *Arthur MacEwan*	121
6.6	(Mis) Understanding a Banking Industry in Transition *William K. Black*	123
6.7	Dealing with a "Rotten Tooth" *Arthur MacEwan*	129
6.8	The Bear Stearns Bailout *Arthur MacEwan*	130
6.9	When a Hedge Fund Makes $3 Billion, Who Loses $3 Billion? *Arthur MacEwan*	131
6.10	The Bailout of Fannie Mae and Freddie Mac *Fred Moseley*	133
6.11	Time for Permanent Nationalization *Fred Moseley*	136
6.12	Transforming the Fed *Robert Pollin*	138

CHAPTER 7: UNEMPLOYMENT AND INFLATION

Introduction

7.1	The "Natural Rate" of Unemployment: It's All About Class Conflict *Robert Pollin*	143
7.2	Raw Deal for Workers *Chris Tilly*	146
7.3	Coming Clean on Class Conflict *John Miller*	148
7.4	Outsized Offshore Outsourcing *John Miller*	150
7.5	The Relationship of Unemployment and Inflation *Ramaa Vasudevan*	155
7.6	Hot Commodities, Stuffed Markets, and Empty Bellies *Ben Collins*	157

CHAPTER 8: PERSPECTIVES ON MACROECONOMIC POLICY

Introduction

8.1	The Revenge of the Classics *John Miller and Gina Neff*	163
8.2	What's Wrong with Neoliberalism? The Marx, Keynes, and Polanyi Problems *Robert Pollin*	165
8.3	Keynes and the Limits of Monetary Policy *Alejandro Reuss*	168
8.4	Fiscal Policy and the "Treasury View" *Alejandro Reuss*	171
8.5	Opening Pandora's Box: The Basics of Marxist Economics *Alejandro Reuss*	173
8.6	Under the Margins: Feminist Economists Look at Gender and Poverty *Randy Albelda*	176

CHAPTER 9: INTERNATIONAL TRADE AND FINANCE

Introduction

9.1	What is Globalization? *Arthur MacEwan*	*185*
9.2	The Gospel of Free Trade: The New Evangelists *Arthur MacEwan*	*189*
9.3	Comparative Advantage *Ramaa Vasudevan*	*192*
9.4	Free, Free at Last *John Miller*	*193*
9.5	The Specter of Capital Flight *Marie Duggan*	*195*
9.6	The Global Oil Market *Paul Cummings*	*201*
9.7	Measures of Global Poverty *Arthur MacEwan*	*205*
9.8	Inequality Worsens Across Asia *John Miller*	*206*
9.9	The Social Cost of Neoliberalism in China *Stephen Philion*	*211*
9.10	Remittances to the Rescue? *Alissa Thuotte*	*217*
9.11	Women of NAFTA *Martha A. Ojeda*	*219*
9.12	International Labor Standards *Arthur MacEwan*	*222*
9.13	Nike to the Rescue? *John Miller*	*223*

Contributors   227

INTRODUCTION

THE TWO ECONOMIES

It sometimes seems that the United States has not one, but two economies. The first economy exists in economics textbooks and in the minds of many elected officials. It is an economy in which no one is unemployed for long, families are rewarded with an ever-improving standard of living, and anyone who works hard can live the American Dream. In this economy, people are free and roughly equal, and each individual carefully looks after him- or herself, making voluntary choices to advance their own economic interests. Government has some limited roles in this world, but it is increasingly marginal, since the macroeconomy is a self-regulating system of wealth generation.

The second economy is described in the writings of progressives, environmentalists, union supporters, and consumer advocates—as well as honest business writers who recognize that the real world does not always conform to textbook models. This second economy features vast disparities of income, wealth, and power. It is an economy where economic instability and downward mobility are facts of life. Jobs disappear, workers suffer long spells of unemployment, and new jobs seldom afford the same standard of living as those lost. And, periodically, market economies unravel, much like today. As for the government, it sometimes adopts policies that ameliorate the abuses of capitalism, and other times does just the opposite, but it is always an active and essential participant in economic life.

If you are reading this introduction, you are probably a student in an introductory college course in macroeconomics. Your textbook will introduce you to the first economy, the harmonious world of self-regulating stability. *Real World Macro* will introduce you to the second.

WHY "REAL WORLD" MACRO?

A standard economics textbook is full of powerful concepts. It is also, by its nature, a limited window on the economy. What is taught in most introductory macroeconomics courses today is a relatively narrow set of concepts. Inspired by classical economic theory, most textbooks depict an inherently stable economy in little need of government intervention. But fifty years ago, textbooks were very different. Keynesian economic theory, which holds that government action can and must stabilize modern monetized economies, occupied a central place in introductory textbooks. Even Marxist economics, with its piercing analysis of class structure and instability in capitalism, appeared regularly on the pages of those textbooks. The contraction of economics education has turned some introductory courses into little more than celebrations of today's economy as "the best of all possible worlds."

Real World Macro, designed as a supplement to a standard macroeconomics textbook, is dedicated to widening the scope of economic inquiry. Its articles rub mainstream theory up against reality by providing vivid, real-world illustrations of economic concepts. And where most texts uncritically present the key assumptions and propositions of traditional macroeconomic theory, *Real World Macro* asks provocative questions: What are alternative propositions about how the economy operates and who it serves? What difference do such propositions make? What might *actually* constitute the best of all possible macroeconomic worlds?

For instance, *Real World Macro* questions the conventional wisdom that economic growth lifts all boats or benefits all of us. While mainstream textbooks readily allow that economic growth has not benefited us all to the same degree, we go further and ask "Who benefits from economic growth and by how much?" "Who has been left behind by the economic growth of the last two decades?" The answers are quite disturbing. Today, economic growth, when it occurs, benefits far fewer of us than just a few decades ago. The most recent recovery did more to boost profits and less to lift wages than any economic upswing since World War II. The truth is that spreading the benefits of economic growth more widely, through public policy intended to improve the lot of most people in the work-a-day world, would not only make our economy more equitable, but would start to resolve today's economic crisis.

No one needs to be told that today's economy is mired in the worst crisis since the Great Depression, but you might not know that the day-to-day operation of the market economy, left to its own devices, brought on that crisis. Unregulated financial markets, the concentration of political and social power in the hands of an oligarchy of capitalists, and gaping inequality pushed most people into debt at the same time that it fueled speculative excesses sparking the crisis. Explaining how and why that happened and what to do about it is every responsible economist's job.

Today, with unemployment at its highest levels in seven decades, government needs to step up and become the economy's employer of last resort. Similarly, with our financial system shaken to the core, the government needs to step in and properly regulate financial markets and institutions. Those two steps will go a long way toward improving the lot of those who have fallen on hard times and will reduce the likelihood of a future crisis. Finally, genuine and sustained full employment, with unemployment rates as low as 2%, will lead to "a major reduction in the incidence of poverty, homelessness, sickness, and crime," as William Vickery, the Nobel-prize winning economist, once argued. We think that policies like this, and the alternative propositions that lie behind them, are worth debating—and that requires hearing a range of views.

WHAT'S IN THIS BOOK

Real World Macro is organized to follow the outline of a standard economics text. We have specifically keyed our table of contents to David Colander's *Economics* (8th edition) and its *Macroeconomics* "split." However, since the topics covered by all major texts are similar, this reader is a good fit with any other standard textbook. Each chapter leads off with a brief introduction, including study questions for the chapter, and then provides several short articles from *Dollars & Sense* magazine that illustrate the chapter's key concepts—76 articles in all. In many cases, the articles have been updated or otherwise edited to heighten their relevance.

Here is a quick walk through the chapters.

Chapter 1, Measuring Economic Performance, starts off the volume by taking a critical look at the standard measures of economic activity. What do those measures actually tell us about the quality of life in today's economy, and what crucial aspects of economic life do they leave uncounted? This chapter also asks why the latest ups and downs of the business cycle, the current crisis and the anemic economic expansion that preceded it, left so many in dire straits.

Chapter 2, Wealth, Inequality, and Poverty, examines these three end products of economic growth. *Dollars & Sense* authors show who is accumulating wealth and who isn't, and argue that inequality is not a prerequisite to economic growth, but rather a major contributor to today's economic crisis.

Chapter 3, Savings and Investment, peers inside the pump house of economic growth and comes up with some probing questions. How are stock prices determined? Who owns them and who doesn't? What caused the mortgage crisis and what can be done about it? In addition, we ask what public policies have proven track records of encouraging investment and promoting stable and functional housing and financial markets.

Chapter 4, Capitalism in Crisis, is about just that. The chapter's authors uncover the causes of the crisis, rooted in the inequalities of the real economy and the unregulated excesses of the housing and financial markets. In everyday language they explain how arcane financial instruments spread the crisis. Finally they argue that economic policies that bring those practices under control and promote a more equitable economy are our best bet for resolving the crisis and preventing its reoccurrence.

Chapter 5, Fiscal Policy, Deficits, and Debt, assesses current government spending and tax policy. The chapter's authors assess the Obama stimulus package and argue that more needs to be done and that unprecedented peacetime deficits should not be an impediment to government action. But pro-rich tax cuts, the military buildup, and failed health care policy that helped get us into this fiscal and economic mess will not get us out of it. Nor will privatizing Social Security. Rather what is needed, according to our authors, are stronger social programs, expanded and greener infrastructure investment, and the government's commitment to be the economy's employer of last resort.

Chapter 6, Monetary Policy and Financial Markets, explains how the Federal Reserve Board (aka "the Fed") conducts monetary policy and how its actions contributed to today's financial crisis. It details the Fed's efforts to bail out investment banks and other financial institutions brought down in the crisis. The chapter asks whose interests the Fed serves: those who hold financial assets, or the rest of us? The authors also address how the Fed and our financial institutions can be transformed to better serve our needs.

Chapter 7, Unemployment and Inflation, reveals how macroeconomic policy that prioritizes price stability over employment puts the interests of owners and bondholders ahead of the interests of workers. The chapter begins with a critique of the "natural rate" of unemployment. It also looks at the effects of unemployment, inflation, and productivity growth on workers' bargaining power and living standards. In addition, it discusses how stock market fundamentals and the spread of offshore outsourcing stand in the way of most workers getting ahead.

KEY TO COLANDER

In each chapter introduction, we provide a key that links our text to David Colander's *Economics*, 8th edition, and its macroeconomics "split," *Macroeconomics*, 8th edition. Professors and students using other textbooks should, of course, feel free to ignore these keys.

Here is the summary key for the entire table of contents. In the individual chapter keys, *Economics* Chapter 1 is abbreviated "E1," and *Macroeconomics* Chapter 1 is abbreviated "M1."

- Chapter 1—Colander chapters E2, E24, E25; or M2, M7, M8.
- Chapter 2—Colander chapters E24-E26 or M7-M9.
- Chapter 3—Colander chapters E24-E26 E29, E30, M3, M4 or M8-M10, M15.
- Chapter 4—Colander chapters E25-E26, E30-E31, E32; or M9-M10, M14-M15, M19.
- Chapter 5—Colander chapters E27-E29, E35; or M11- M15, M18.
- Chapter 6—Colander chapter E30-E32 or M13-M15.
- Chapter 7—Colander chapters E24, E26, E27, E30-E33; or M7, M9, M13-M16.
- Chapter 8—Colander chapters E6, E29, E32, E35; or M6, M10, M12, M15, M16-M18.
- Chapter 9—Colander chapters E2, E9, E36, E37, E38 or M2, M19, M20, M21, M22

Chapter 8, Perspectives on Macroeconomic Policy, introduces alternatives to classical-inspired macroeconomic theory. It begins with a critical analysis of the New Classical economics' claim that the macroeconomy is inherently stable, and then discusses what Keynes *actually* said about the practice of monetary and fiscal policy in an economic crisis. The chapter also develops Marxist and feminist perspectives on macroeconomic theory and policy, and neoliberal economic policymaking.

Chapter 9, International Trade and Finance, critically assesses the prevailing neoliberal policy prescriptions for the global economy. The articles criticize globalization based on "free trade" and financial liberalization, looking closely at its effects on economic growth, global inequality and poverty, and "economic freedom." They also look at the role of China in today's global economy, the global oil market, and the U.S. economy's dependence on foreign capital. Finally, the articles look critically at the effects of remittances and global trade agreements on workers in the developing world and assess proposals to improve international labor standards and to eliminate sweatshop conditions.

CHAPTER 1
MEASURING ECONOMIC PERFORMANCE

INTRODUCTION

Most macroeconomics textbooks begin with a snapshot of today's economy as seen through the lens of the standard measures of economic performance. This chapter provides a different view of today's economy, one far more critical of current economic policy and performance, that asks what the standard measures of economic performance really tell us.

In "What's In a Name," economist John Miller takes the measure of today's disastrous downturn, the worst since the Great Depression. Miller traces the course of this decade's business cycle. It moves from a feeble expansion, which did little to improve the standard of living of most people, to a housing crisis, financial panic, and economic collapse that has left millions of people in dire straits. Miller argues that undoing the repressive and deregulatory policies that brought on the crisis is the key to getting the economy going again in a way that will improve the lot of most people, not just economic elites (Article 1.1).

Miller's next article shows how the official unemployment rate understates the extent of unemployment. Correcting the official rate for the underemployed and those not counted by the official rate, the unemployment rate reaches a 68-year high (Article 1.2). Job losses have hit male-dominated jobs especially hard, as economist Heather Boushey documents. She calls for more support for female workers who increasingly find themselves in the role of chief breadwinners of their families (Article 1.5).

Economists' measures of inflation also suffer from serious deficiencies. Joshua Holland documents how recent changes in the Consumer Price Index, the best-known inflation measure, dramatically reduced the "official" rate of inflation. Those changes spruced up reported economic performance and reduced the cost of living adjustments of seniors on Social Security and others (Article 1.3).

Real GDP, or Gross Domestic Product adjusted for inflation, is the economist's measure of the value of economic output. Increases in real GDP define economic growth, and for economists, rising real GDP per capita shows that a nation's standard of living is improving. Our authors are not convinced. Jonathan Rowe argues that GDP actually counts environmental destruction, worsening health, and ruinous overconsumption as contributions to economic growth and national well-being (Article 1.4). While Rowe worries that GDP includes the wrong things, Lena Graber and John Miller discuss what it excludes: work in the home that is essential to economic well-being. They report that counting home-based work—from cleaning to child care—would add 33% to 112% to the GDP of industrialized economies and even more to the GDP of developing economies (Article 1.6).

Of course, macroeconomics textbooks examine not only the ups and downs of the business cycle, but also trade-offs in economies whose resources are fully employed. Many present the famed trade-off between "guns" and "butter." Economists use a production possibilities curve to demonstrate the opportunity cost of devoting economic resources to certain kinds of production. For example, the opportunity cost of producing arms ("guns") is the set of social goods ("butter") that society must forego. That trade-off is being made today in the United States, and Monique Morrissey presents a vivid depiction of its staggering social cost (Article 1.7).

DISCUSSION QUESTIONS

1. (Article 1.1) How does the expansion of this decade's business cycle compare to the typical postwar expansion? How does the current contraction compare to the typical postwar recession?
2. (Article 1.1) According to Miller, "The Repression" is the right name for the current economic crisis. Why does he choose that name? In your opinion, what is the right name for today's economic crisis? Why?
3. (Article 1.2) What are the shortcomings of the official (U-3) unemployment rate? Using the data in Table 2, calculate the more comprehensive U-6 unemployment rate for May 2009. Be sure to show each step of the conversion from the U-3 unemployment rate to the U-6 rate.
4. (Article 1.3) How did the changes in the Consumer Price Index in the 1990s lower the reported rate of inflation? Which of those changes, if any, were justified?

KEY TO COLANDER

E = Economics   M = Macroeconomics

This chapter is designed to be used with chapters E2 and E24, E25 or M2 and M7, M8.

Chapters E24 and M7 contain sections on dating business cycles and economic performance. Article 1.2 concerns measuring unemployment rates.

Article 1.4 and 1.6 complement the section "Some Limitations of National Income Accounting" in chapter E25 and M8. Both Rowe and Colander discuss the Genuine Progress Indicator.

Article 1.4 and 1.7 go with the discussion of production possibilities curves in E2 and M2.

5. (Article 1.4) How is GDP measured, and what does it represent? What are Rowe's criticisms of GDP? Do you find them convincing?
6. (Article 1.4) Rowe discusses the Genuine Progress Indicator (GPI) as an alternative measure of economic progress. What are the differences between GDP per capita and the GPI? Which do you think provides a better measure of economic progress and why?
7. (Article 1.5) Why has men's unemployment increased more quickly than women's unemployment in the current economic contraction? What are some possible policy responses that could address this gender disparity in unemployment levels?
8. (Article 1.6) Wages for housework might sound outlandish, but there are several economic justifications for valuing work in the home. What are they? Do you find them persuasive?
9. (Article 1.6) Suppose we decided that home-based work should be included in macroeconomic measures. How should it be counted? Should this work be paid? If so, by whom?
10. (Article 1.7) After reviewing Morrisey's article, describe the opportunity cost of today's military buildup. Now identify where the U.S. economy is today on a production possibilities curve.

WHAT'S IN A NAME?

BY JOHN MILLER

A frightening financial panic, a virulent housing bust, and plummeting economic output have left global capitalism facing its worst crisis since the Great Depression.

Economies across the globe are in trouble. The European and Japanese economies shrank at double-digit rates in the first three months of this year; even China's growth rate is slowing precipitously. U.S. autoworkers, European and U.S. finance workers, Japanese electronics workers, Chinese garment workers, and Indian software workers are losing their jobs as their economies slow and world export markets dry up.

In the United States, where the crisis hit first, the downturn that began in December 2007 is now the longest since World War II, with the greatest job losses and, by some measures, the highest unemployment of the postwar period.

Housing prices, the fountainhead of the crisis, have now fallen more than they did during the housing bust of the Great Depression. Record levels of mortgage defaults and foreclosures have spread panic through a rickety global financial system. In a six-month span, three of the five largest U.S. investment banks disappeared. Leading U.S. mortgage company Countrywide bit the dust. Washington Mutual collapsed, the largest commercial bank failure in U.S. history.

The stock market has crashed as well. Stock prices fell to below one-half of their peak value in most indices, matching the initial declines in 1929.

In brief, the current contraction is no run-of-the-mill recession. But neither, at least at this point, is it comparable to the decade-long Great Depression, in which output fell by one-quarter and more than one-quarter of the U.S. workforce went without work.

So what is it? A recession or a depression? Truth is, economists make no precise distinction between the two other than that recessions are mild and depressions are more severe.

Even with their imprecision, neither term properly fits our current economic decline at this point, although it may yet become inarguably a depression. What term would fit? "The Great Recession," the name favored by former Fed chair Paul Volcker among others, is one candidate. "The Panic of 2008-2009" is another.

But better yet is "The Repression," a name suggested by University of Massachusetts economist (and *D&S* Dr. Dollar) Arthur MacEwan. Part recession, part depression, today's economic meltdown is very much a product of the large dose of economic repression that preceded it. Deregulatory, pro-rich, anti-labor public policy guaranteed that the benefits of economic growth, at least what we had of it this decade, went almost exclusively to the most well-to-do among us, leaving many vulnerable. The latest business cycle, both its expansion beginning in 2001 and its catastrophic downturn now underway, make those consequences clear for all to see. In a very real way, the Repression of 2008 and 2009 has now pushed many people out of the frying pan and into the fire. And not only does the term "repression" describe the causes of the current crisis; it also points us toward its consequences, and toward prospective cures for today's economic woes.

THE FRYING PAN: THE EXPANSION OF 2001–07

Economic expansions are supposed to improve our life chances, not just swell the economy. For some time now, however, economic upswings have done less to improve the lot of most people than they used to.

During the first two decades after World War II, the U.S. economy grew rapidly, lifted incomes and wages, reduced inequality, and alleviated poverty. With its global dominance, the U.S. economy grew an average of 5.0% a year during the expansions between 1950 and 1969. Strong trade unions and expanding government programs helped to protect workers, fight poverty, and spread the benefits of economic growth widely, at least by today's standards.

No subsequent expansion has met those standards. But in this decade the capacity of economic growth to make most people better off all but evaporated. First off, the U.S. economy has grown more slowly in this decade than in any of the earlier postwar decades, even before accounting for the current crisis. Beginning in November 2001, the economy grew for 73 months or just over six years, reaching a peak in December 2007. That is longer than the 57-month average duration of postwar expansions. But GDP grew at an anemic annual rate of 2.5% in the 2001–07 expansion, far below the 4.3% average for postwar expansions. (See Table 1.)

Along with slower growth that failed to engage the productive capacity of the U.S. economy, successive economic expansions have created fewer and fewer jobs. In the last three business cycles, the economy has continued to lose jobs even after an economic recovery was underway. On top of that, recoveries have taken longer and longer

---

*Dates denote when the article appeared in *Dollars & Sense* magazine.

TABLE 1: **Sizing Up the 2001–2007 Expansion**

	2001–07 Expansion	Average Postwar Expansion
Length of Expansion	73 Months	57 Months
GDP Growth	2.5%	4.3%
Employment Gains	0.9%	2.5%
Wage and Salary Growth	1.8%	3.8%
Corporate Profits	10.8%	7.4%

Notes: GDP, employment, wages and salaries, and corporate profits are all measured as annual rates of change and corrected for inflation. The average for postwar expansions is calculated for the six expansions from 1961 to 2001.

Sources: Bureau of Economic Analysis, Bureau of Labor Statistics, and Federal Reserve Board.

TABLE 2: **Job Market Decline and Recovery in Six Postwar Recessions** (numbers in months)

Recession	Length of Recession	Months of Job Losses	Months until Jobs Recovery
Nov. 1969 – Nov. 1970	12	14	19
Dec. 1973 – March 1975	16	16	25
Jan. 1980 – July 1980	6	6	11
July 1981 – Nov. 1982	16	19	29
July 1990 – March 1991	8	11	30
March 2001 – Nov. 2001	8	32	48

Source: Bureau of Labor Statistics.

to replace the jobs lost in the downturn. (See Table 2.)

In this decade, "the great American jobs machine" truly met its maker. Shockingly, the economy continued to lose jobs *for the first two and half years* of this last expansion. A full four years passed before the economy had added back the jobs lost during the 2001 recession, more than twice as long as in the average expansion since 1970.

The economic expansion from 2001 to the end of 2007 added jobs more slowly than any other expansion since World War II. The number of jobs in the economy increased by just 0.9% a year, about one-third of the 2.5% rate posted by the average postwar expansion.

Sluggish economic growth left employers with little need for new hires. Another drain on U.S. job creation was the increasing number of jobs lost to global outsourcing. Not only manufacturing jobs went abroad, but so did white collar work from backroom office operations (bookkeeping, customer service, and marketing) to engineering and computer software design.

All told, during the eight years of the Bush administration, job growth averaged a meager 0.28% annually. That's just 378,000 new jobs a year, a total we would expect a growing economy to add in a single month.

EXPANSION AND REPRESSION

The sluggish economic growth of the first six years of this decade not only created fewer jobs than earlier postwar expansions, it also, not surprisingly, did less to lift incomes, alleviate poverty, or improve the economic well-being of all but the best-off. Those lopsided results are easily documented:

- For the first time in the postwar period, median household income (corrected for inflation) at the peak of this expansion was still below its level at the previous peak in 2000.
- By 2007, 5.9 million more people were without health insurance than when the expansion began in 2001.
- For the first time in a postwar expansion, the poverty rate failed to decline. In 2007 at the peak of this expansion, the U.S. poverty rate stood at 12.5%, well above the 11.7% rate when the expansion began.
- After correcting for inflation, wages and salaries grew just 1.8% a year during this expansion, less half the 3.8% rate during the average postwar expansion.
- At the same time, real corporate profits skyrocketed, increasing 10.8% a year, after adjusting for inflation, compared to the 8.3% average growth rate in other postwar growth periods.

Not surprisingly, inequality, which by 2001 was already unprecedented by postwar standards, continued to worsen during the decade. But just how much of the population missed out on the benefits of economic growth was astonishing. The average real income of the poorest 20% of households declined, but so did that of the best-off 20% of households. The incomes of the three quintiles in between stagnated; none grew by more than 1.1% over the entire period. Even the average income of the richest 5% declined during this expansion.

The top one percent of households, on the other hand, continued to make out like bandits. Their real income grew by 10.9% each year from 2002 to 2006, reports economist Emmanuel Saez using the most recent data available. That small sliver of the population monopolized 73% of the income growth during those years. In contrast, the bottom 99% of households saw their real incomes grow just 1.0% in each of those years.

As these figures make clear, the combination of sluggish economic growth, few new jobs, stagnant wages and incomes, and extreme inequality left many people behind long before the economy collapsed in 2008.

BUBBLES BURSTING

The economic collapse, however, began before 2008 with the bursting of the housing bubble. Despite spanning the 2001 recession, that ten-year bubble, from 1996 to 2006, drove up housing prices further and for longer than in any period since 1890. According to Yale economist Robert Shiller's long-term U.S. home price index, real (i.e., inflation-adjusted) housing prices increased an unprecedented 84.5% in that period.

Skyrocketing housing prices allowed homeowners to use their homes as ATMs, as economics journalist Doug Henwood first put it, taking out loans on the rising value of their houses. The volume of these so-called mortgage equity withdrawals more than doubled from 2000 to the peak of the housing bubble in 2005-6 and financed about one-third of the growth in consumption over those years.

U.S. housing prices are now down by more than one-quarter from their peak in late 2005. That is not only the sharpest decline of the postwar period, it is the biggest drop in housing prices since the 32.3% drop from 1914 to 1921—including the housing bust during the Great Depression. The collapse of housing prices put the kibosh on consumer spending, precipitated a crisis of mortgage defaults and foreclosures, and punched a hole in the financial system.

The crash of the stock market is unprecedented by postwar standards as well. By March 2, 2009, the Dow Jones Industrial Average of 30 blue-chip stocks had fallen 53.2% from its October 2007 peak. Broader stock indices, such as the Standard & Poor's 500, had registered even sharper declines. In comparison, the high-tech stock market crash earlier this decade had knocked 35.2% off the price of blue-chip stocks at its low point; the bear market of 1973, 42.2%. Only the Great Depression took more out of stock prices. At their low point in June 1932, stocks had lost a stunning 88.8% of their October 1929 value. While the stock market lately has shown some life, the turnaround in stock prices is unlikely to be rapid even if the stock market has already seen its bottom. It took 6 years, 9 years, and 25 years respectively for the stock market to replace the value lost in the 2001, 1973, and 1929 crashes.

THE FIRE: INCREASED REPRESSION IN 2007–09

Dismal labor market conditions were the cutting edge of the economic downturn proper. The economy began shedding jobs long before economic growth plummeted. Even the National Bureau of Economic Research (NBER), which determines the turning points of U.S. business cycles, took notice. In 2008 the economy lost jobs every month of the year for the first time since the Great Depression. The mounting monthly job losses convinced the NBER to declare the recession's start-date December 2007, even though at that point the economy had not yet suffered two consecutive quarters of negative economic growth—the standard definition of a recession.

In other words, in this downturn job losses are no lagging indicator. But don't expect employment to be a leading indicator of the recovery either. Job losses will almost certainly continue even after economic growth returns. Before things are over, the labor market downturn and the suffering endured by all those looking for work will have persisted far longer than the contraction of economic output.

The U.S. economy is losing jobs as never before in the postwar period. Seventeen months into the downturn, the economy has lost more jobs than in any previous downturn and has lost nearly twice the share of its employment base as in the typical postwar recession. (See Table 3.) Construction, manufacturing of all sorts, and the financial industry, all male-dominated employments, have been especially hard hit. But even software giant Microsoft and major law firms are now laying off workers.

The fact that the 2001–2007 economic expansion created so few jobs heightens the effects of this extreme job loss. With few new jobs, especially full-time ones, workers' connection to the labor force is ever more tenuous. By the first quarter of 2009, marginally attached workers (those who want a job and have looked for work in the last year but not in the last month, hence are not counted as unemployed) formed a larger share of the labor force than in the 2001 recession. (Data are available only from 1994 on.) Also, the proportion of the labor force forced to work part-time because they could not find full-time jobs was higher than in any recession since 1970, including the severe 1974–75 and 1982 recessions. (Data are available from 1968 on.) By April 2009, forced part-time workers made up twice the share of the labor force as in the 2001 recession. (See "The *Real* Unemployment Rate," p. 29, for a closer look at the unemployment picture.)

The failure of the 2001 expansion to lift incomes is also intensifying the suffering in this crisis. In the nearly decade-long expansion of the 1960s, the income of the median household, corrected for inflation, rose nearly 4% a year. But the 2001 to 2007 expansion added a measly 0.2% a year to real median incomes.

As income stagnated with increasingly repressive economic growth, households went deeper into debt. In the 1982 recession, 10.7% of U.S. households' disposable income went to service debt payments. In December 2007, at the onset of this downturn, that figure had reached 14.3%. It dipped slightly in 2008 as worried households began to cut back on their borrowing, but it is no longer dropping as mounting unemployment has pushed down households' disposable income.

This downturn has already gone on longer than even the two longest postwar downturns, in 1973–75 and 1981–1982, both of which lasted 16 months. Even if the economy begins to recover in the last quarter of 2009, the downturn would have lasted 22 months, more than twice as long as the 10-month average length of postwar recessions.

To date, the loss of output has not matched that in the worst postwar recessions. Through its first five quarters, inflation-adjusted GDP in the current downturn has fallen 2.4%—more than the average loss of output during all postwar recessions of 2.05% but less than the steeper declines in output during the 1974–75 and 1982 recessions. In the first half of 2008 the economy continued to grow slowly even as it shed jobs. Then the contraction began; output fell at annual rates of over 6% in the last quarter of 2008 and the first quarter of 2009. Even the most optimistic forecasts do not see a return to economic growth until the last quarter of 2009. By that time the loss of output over the last two years will surely have outdistanced that of any postwar downturn.

In specific sectors the current loss of output has already outdistanced all postwar recessions. Industrial production, which includes hard-hit manufacturers of automobiles, home electronics, and construction supplies, has fallen off at double-digit rates—more than three times its decline in the average postwar recession. Today's loss of industrial output has already matched the shredding of industry in the 1982 recession, the worst previous case (see Table 3).

Retail sales have been decimated as well. In the typical postwar recession, retail sales dropped off by about 3.5%, stabilizing within half a year after the onset of the downturn. But this time, retail sales have dropped 12.9% and are still falling. Circuit City, the electronics giant, closed its doors; Filene's Basement, the venerable department store, laid off workers; and even eBay, the internet retailer, issued pink slips.

FIGHTING REPRESSION

The cure to the Repression is to fight repressive policies. Public policy must make the fight by promoting genuine full employment, legalizing card check union drives by passing the Employee Free Choice Act, enforcing labor laws already on the books by expanding the workplace inspection staff of the Department of Labor, and extending health insurance to all. Reducing payroll taxes, the bulk of most people's federal tax bill, will help, along with letting the Bush tax cuts targeted at the wealthy expire in 2010. Those policies would do much to enhance workers' bargaining power, lessen labor abuse, and arrest today's worsening inequality—or if you will, to undo repression.

Realizing those goals would take active and progressive government intervention into the labor markets and substantial funding for government programs that will put people to work repairing our decaying infrastructure and making it greener, restoring the social services cut out of state budgets in the crisis, and providing relief to those who have lost their homes or their jobs. And that spending would also get the economy going and counteract the Repression.

None of that will happen without massive public pressure. The Obama administration must not succumb to the calls of deficit hawks to slash government spending. Their do-nothing strategy, or worse yet more tax cuts for the wealthy, would saddle the federal government with even larger deficits as the economy and tax revenues fell through the floor. And unlike a program of progressive government spending, which holds the potential to spark a period of economic growth that could pay the public debt, a do-nothing strategy would likely lead us into a depression that would impose costs far more serious than a rise in government debt.

In addition, the Obama administration will need to impose strict controls on a financial industry to which it has close ties: one of its most senior economic advisors played a key role in deregulation. It will also have to convert its stress tests of troubled banks into a lever to take over any distressed bank, mortgage house, or insurer that is too big to fail and then run them as mutual savings banks for the benefit of the public.

Those steps will help to end the Repression by getting the economy going and to disable the drivers that have shaped economic growth so lopsidedly in favor of so few while repressing so many. Without them we will see either a return of the kind of economic growth that creates few jobs and does little to alleviate economic repression, or worst yet a decade-long period of economic stagnation and worsening economic suffering.

Resources: Kelly Evans and Robert Guy Matthews, "Manufacturing Tumbles Globally," *Wall Street Journal*, Jan. 3, 2009; *Left Business Observer* #118, Dec. 22, 2008; Josh L. Bivens and John Irons, "A Feeble Recovery: The Fundamental Economic Weaknesses of the 2001-2007 Expansion," Economic Policy Institute Briefing Paper #214, May 1, 2008; Jon Hilsenrath and Kelly Evans, "Mixed Economic Data Show a Changing Business Cycle," *Wall Street Journal*, September 8, 2008; National Bureau of Economic Research, "Determination of the 2007 Peak in Economic Activity," December 11, 2008; John Schmitt and Dean Baker, "What We're In For: Projected Economic Impact of the Next Recession," Center for Economic and Policy Research, January 2008; Marcus Walker et al., "Global Slump Seen Deepening," *Wall Street Journal*, Jan. 1, 2009; Tom Lauricella and Annelena Lobb, "Stocks Hit '97 Level, Signaling Long Slump," *Wall Street Journal*, March 3, 2009; Sudeep Reedy, "Jobless Rate Hits 8.5%," *Wall Street Journal*, April 4, 2009; Charles Gascon, "The Current Recession: How Bad Is It?" Economic Synopsis No. 4, St. Louis Federal Reserve Bank, 2009; Kevin Klieson, "Recession or Depression," *Economic Synopsis* No. 15, St. Louis Federal Reserve Bank, 2009; Robert Shiller, "Online Data," at www.econ.yale.edu/~shiller/data.htm.

THE *REAL* UNEMPLOYMENT RATE HITS A 68-YEAR HIGH

BY JOHN MILLER

Although you have to dig into the statistics to know it, unemployment in the United States is now worse than at any time since the end of the Great Depression.

From December 2007, when the recession began, to May of this year, 6.0 million U.S. workers lost their jobs. The big three U.S. automakers are closing plants and letting white-collar workers go too. Chrysler, the worst off of the three, will lay off one-quarter of its workforce. Heavy equipment manufacturer Caterpillar and giant banking conglomerate Citigroup have both laid off thousands of workers. Alcoa, the aluminum giant, has let workers go. Computer maker Dell and express shipper DHL have both canned many of their workers. Circuit City, the leading electronics retailer, went out of business, costing its 40,000 workers their jobs. Lawyers in large national firms are getting the ax. Even on Sesame Street, workers are losing their jobs.

The official unemployment rate hit 9.4% in May—already as high as the peak unemployment rates in all but the 1982 recession, the worst since World War II. And topping the 1982 recession's peak rate of 10.8% is now distinctly possible. The current downturn has pushed up unemployment rates by more than any previous postwar recession (see figure).

Some groups of workers are already facing official unemployment rates in the double digits. As of May, unemployment rates for black, Hispanic, and teenage workers were already 14.9%, 12.7% and 22.7%, respectively. Workers without a high-school diploma confronted a 15.5% unemployment rate, while the unemployment rate for workers with just a high-school degree was 10.0%. Nearly one in five (19.2%) construction workers were unemployed. In Michigan, the hardest hit state, unemployment was at 12.9% in April. Unemployment rates in seven other states were at double-digit levels as well.

As bad as they are, these figures dramatically understate the true extent of unemployment. First, they exclude anyone without a job who is ready to work but has not actively looked for a job in the previous four weeks. The Bureau of Labor Statistics classifies such workers as "marginally attached to the labor force" so long as they have looked for work within the last year. Marginally attached workers include so-called discouraged workers who have given up looking for job-related reasons, plus others who have given up for reasons such as school and family responsibilities, ill health, or transportation problems.

Second, the official unemployment rate leaves out part-time workers looking for full-time work: part-time workers are "employed" even if they work as little as one hour a week. The vast majority of people working part time involuntarily have had their hours cut due to slack or unfavorable business conditions. The rest are working part time because they could only find part-time work.

To its credit, the BLS has developed alternative unemployment measures that go a long way toward correcting the shortcomings of the official rate. The broadest alternative measure, called "U-6," counts as unemployed "marginally attached workers" as well as those employed "part time for economic reasons."

When those adjustments are taken into account for May 2009, the unemployment rate soars to 16.4%. That is the

Rise in the Official Unemployment Rate in Six Recessions
(monthly rates, seasonally adjusted)

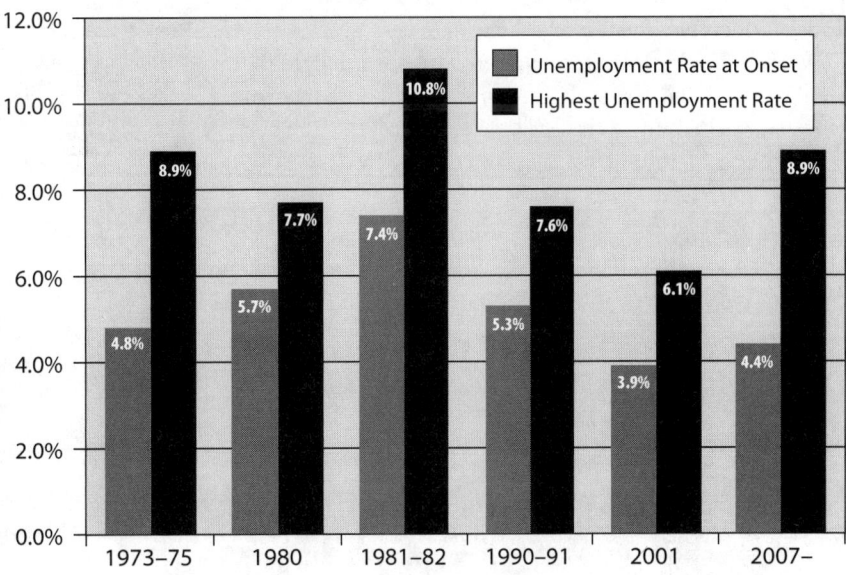

Source: Table A-1, Bureau of Labor Statistics, U.S. Labor Department, at *www.bls.gov*.

CALCULATING THE REAL UNEMPLOYMENT RATE

The BLS calculates the official unemployment rate, U-3, as the number of unemployed as a percentage of the civilian labor force. The civilian labor force consists of employed workers plus the officially unemployed, those without jobs who are available to work and have looked for a job in the last 4 weeks. Applying the data found in the table yields an official unemployment rate of 9.1%, or a seasonally adjusted rate 9.4% for April 2009.

The comprehensive U-6 unemployment rate adjusts the official rate by adding marginally attached workers and workers forced to work part time for economic reasons to the officially unemployed. To find the U-6 rate the BLS takes that higher unemployment count and divides it by the official civilian labor force plus the number of marginally attached workers. (No adjustment is necessary for forced part-time workers since they are already counted in the official labor force as employed workers.)

Accounting for the large number of marginally attached workers and those working part-time for economic reasons raises the count of unemployed to 24.0 million workers for May 2009. Those numbers push up the U-6 unemployment rate to 15.9% or a seasonally adjusted rate of 16.4%.

The May 2009 Unemployment Picture
(data in thousands, not seasonally adjusted)

Civilian Labor Force	**154,336**
Employed	140,363
Unemployed	13,973
Marginally Attached Workers	**2,210**
Discouraged workers	792
Reasons other than discouragement	1,418
Part-time for Economic Reasons	**8,785**
Slack work or business conditions	6,647
Could only find part-time work	1,898

Sources: Bureau of Labor Statistics, Tables A-1, A-5. A-12, A-13. Data are not seasonally adjusted because seasonally adjusted data for marginally attached workers are not available.

highest rate since the BLS began calculating the U-6 rate in 1994. While not exactly comparable, it is also higher than the BLS's earlier and yet broader adjusted unemployment rate called the U-7. The BLS began calculating the U-7 rate in 1976 but discontinued it in 1994 in favor of the U-6 rate. In the 1982 recession, the U-7 reached 15.3%, its highest level. In fact, no bout of unemployment since the last year of the Great Depression in 1941 would have produced an adjusted unemployment rate as high as today's.

Why is the real unemployment rate so much higher than the official, or U-3, rate? First, forced part-time work has reached its highest level ever, going all the way back to 1956 and including the 1982 recession. In May 2009, 8.8 million workers were forced to work part time for economic reasons. Forced part-timers are concentrated in retail, food services, and construction; about a quarter of them are young workers between 16 and 24. The number of discouraged workers is high today as well. In May, the BLS counted 2.2 million "marginally attached" workers. That matches the highest number since 1994, when the agency introduced this measure.

With the economy in the throes of a catastrophic downturn, unemployment, no matter how it's measured, will rise dramatically and impose yet more devastating costs on society and on those without a job or unable to find full-time work.

Resources: U.S. Dept. of Labor, "The Unemployment Rate and Beyond: Alternative Measures of Labor Underutilization," *Issues in Labor Statistics,* June 2008; John E. Bregger and Steven E. Haugen, "BLS introduces new range of alternative unemployment measures," *Monthly Labor Review,* October 1995.

CPI BLUES

CHANGES TO THE CONSUMER PRICE INDEX DRAMATICALLY REDUCED THE "OFFICIAL" RATE OF INFLATION.

BY JOSHUA HOLLAND

Think about economic conditions in the 1970s, and you're likely to have visions of gas lines snaking around corners, a weary Jimmy Carter look-ing droopy and forlorn in the Oval Office, and the general sense of "malaise" (Carter's word) that Ronald Reagan exploited so adroitly to give rise to the new conservative movement. You're also likely to think of high rates of inflation.

Over the last few years, even as the prices of food, energy, and other goods have soared, the mainstream media have maintained that today's inflation does not compare to those unhappy years. This past July, *Newsweek* reassuringly noted that "the Consumer Price Index is rising at a 3% annual rate, compared with 13% in 1979." (More recently, in the wake of the global economic turmoil, some commentators are even talking about the danger of *de*flation.) But talk of inflation rarely mentions that the measures of inflation commonly discussed today bear little resemblance to the stats used in the 1970s.

In large part, that's because the Consumer Price Index (CPI)—the measure most frequently cited in media reports—is used to determine government benefits like Social Security, federal and state pensions, and Medicare payments. Recalculating inflation downward was a back-door way of keeping the growth of these entitlements in check without pissing off veterans' groups or the AARP.

The CPI was historically based on a relatively simple formula. Officials took a theoretical "basket of goods" that "typical" consumers required and averaged their current prices. Beginning in the early 1990s, however, conservative economists were unhappy that increases in the CPI kept increasing entitlement payments to government employees, vets, and the elderly—whiners and greedy gray-hairs. Through some impressive intellectual contortions, they came up with a number of proposals for adjusting how inflation is measured.

They began by weighting items in the basket differently. Federal Reserve Chair Alan Greenspan argued that it was wrong to compare the price of a pound of steak one year to the price of a pound of steak the next because when steak gets too expensive, people start eating hamburger—they lead more frugal lives when prices rise, and the measure of inflation should reflect their decisions. But as economist

Annual Consumer Inflation Through Aug 2008: Two Measures

Sources: ShadowStats.com; Bureau of Labor Statistics.

John Williams, author of the *Shadow Government Statistics* newsletter, notes:

> Replacing hamburger for steak in the calculations would reduce the inflation rate, but it represented the rate of inflation in terms of *maintaining a declining standard of living*. Cost of living was being replaced by the cost of survival. The old system told you how much you had to increase your income in order to keep buying steak. The new system promised you hamburger, and then dog food, perhaps, after that. [emphasis mine]

In the same vein, conservative economists argued that the CPI wasn't taking into account the increased enjoyment people got from buying shiny new consumer goods. That new toaster may have cost you 60% more than the one you bought just five years ago, but the new one has a computer chip that monitors the internal temperature, and that makes it harder to burn the toast. Therefore, they argued, your happiness at having perfect toast every morning should be factored into the CPI.

In 1995, under Bill Clinton, the Boskin Commission—led by a former economic adviser to the first President Bush—was formed to "fix" the way we measure the CPI by applying these economists' views. Changes were quietly made, with little Congressional oversight. Ostensibly designed to improve accuracy, their net result was a dramatic reduction of the official rate of inflation.

While the mainstream media tout our 3% annual rate of inflation (5% since this spring), the reality is that inflation, using the CPI as it was calculated before the Clinton-era changes went into effect, was more than 8% in July. And that's not including a whole other set of methodological changes made in 1983.

Until 1983, the CPI included the cost of owning a house—it factored in home prices, mortgage rates, and real estate taxes. But then the Bureau of Labor Statistics—the agency that crunches all these numbers—decided to replace the cost of home ownership with rents (actually, a rental equivalent) as the key housing component in the CPI. But while home prices increased dramatically between 1995 and 2005, the "owners' equivalent rent" used to calculate inflation actually declined by a few points. As a result, the rising housing costs many U.S. families have faced over the past decade have not been reflected in the CPI. (That rents did not rise along with home prices, argued economists like Dean Baker, was evidence that the housing boom was in fact a "bubble," untethered from the basic laws of supply and demand.)

The average rate of inflation during the 1970s was just over 7% (and 9.75% during the Carter years). Williams estimates that today's CPI understates the inflation rate as it was calculated before the Reagan era by about seven percentage points. The figure above shows the CPI from 1980 to August 2008 as it is measured today compared with Williams' calculation of the inflation rate using the earlier methodologies.

It's a controversial claim, but if Williams is right, inflation in the first eight years of the 21st century has averaged around 9.5%—or two percentage points *higher* than it averaged during the 1970s. Compare that with the official inflation rate, which averaged 2.4% over that period.

Even more misleading is the "core" inflation rate, used by the Federal Reserve. The "core" rate simply excludes certain "volatile" goods from the basket —little things like energy and food. In recent years it's become increasingly popular among pundits to cite the core rate, but with energy and food costs making up about a quarter of most household expenses (and significantly more for low-income households), it's a poor measure of the economic pain most Americans have been feeling. In just the last year (ending in June), food prices increased by more than 5%, and energy costs skyrocketed by almost 25%.

To gauge what most of us are really experiencing on a day-to-day basis, one might imagine economic reporters relying on a monthly "pizza index" instead of the Consumer Price Index. According to a February report by Al Olson of MSNBC, "Pizza makers have seen their cheese costs soar this year from $1.30 a pound to $1.76 a pound. Even worse, the flour used to make the dough has gone from $3 to $7 a bushel to $25 a bushel in less than a year." Between the second quarters of 2007 and 2008, even the cost of the paperboard used to make pizza boxes increased by 8%. (Several years of rising to-mato prices—for the sauce—were blunted by the salmonella scare.)

The same is true for a host of items that working America buys every day. According to Olson, "If you're looking for a sure sign the U.S. economy is headed in the wrong direction, all you need to do is look at the skyrocketing price of 'recession-proof' foods: pizza, hot dogs, bagels and beer." But those items, and other costs that have a significant impact on ordinary people, are under-counted in the Consumer Price Index.

Resources: Daniel Gross, "Why Its Worse Than You Think," *Newsweek.* June 16, 2008; John Williams, "Consumer Price Index," *Government Economic Reports: Things You've Suspected But Were Afraid To Ask,* October 1, 2006; Al Olson, "Pizza and Beer Now Cost an Arm and a Leg," *MSNB*, Feb 29, 2008; Bureau of Labor Statistics, "Consumer Price Index Summary," July 2008 (www.bls.gov); Dean Baker, "Bush's House of Cards," *The Nation*, August 9, 2004.

ARTICLE 1.4

September/October 2002

THE GROWTH CONSENSUS UNRAVELS

BY JONATHAN ROWE

Economics has been called the dismal science, but beneath its gray exterior is a system of belief worthy of Pollyanna.

Yes, economists manage to see a dark cloud in every silver lining. Downturn follows uptick, and inflation rears its ugly head. But there's a story within that story—a gauzy romance, a lyric ode to Stuff. It's built into the language. A thing produced is called a "good," for example, no questions asked. The word is more than just a term of art. It suggests the automatic benediction which economics bestows upon commodities of any kind.

By the same token, an activity for sale is called a "service." In conventional economics there are no "dis-services," no actions that might be better left undone. The bank that gouges you with ATM fees, the lawyer who runs up the bill—such things are "services" so long as someone pays. If a friend or neighbor fixes your plumbing for free, it's not a "service" and so it doesn't count.

The sum total of these products and activities is called the Gross Domestic Product, or GDP. If the GDP is greater this year than last, then the result is called "growth." There is no bad GDP and no bad growth; economics does not even have a word for such a thing. It does have a word for less growth. In such a case, economists say growth is "sluggish" and the economy is in "recession." No matter what is growing—more payments to doctors because of worsening health, more toxic cleanup—so long as there is more of it, then the economic mind declares it "good."

This purports to be "objective science." In reality it is a rhetorical construct with the value judgments built in, and this rhetoric has been the basis of economic debate in the United States for the last half century at least. True, people have disagreed over how best to promote a rising GDP. Liberals generally wanted to use government more, conservatives less. But regarding the beneficence of a rising GDP, there has been little debate at all.

If anything, the Left traditionally has believed in growth with even greater fervor than the Right. It was John Maynard Keynes, after all, who devised the growth-boosting mechanisms of macroeconomic policy to combat the Depression of the 1930s; it was Keynesians who embraced these strategies after the War and turned the GDP into a totem. There's no point in seeking a bigger pie to redistribute to the poor, if you don't believe the expanding pie is desirable in the first place.

Today, however, the growth consensus is starting to unravel across the political spectrum and in ways that are both obvious and subtle. The issue is no longer just the impact of growth upon the environment—the toxic impacts of industry and the like. It now goes deeper, to what growth actually consists of and what it means in people's lives. The things economists call "goods" and "services" increasingly don't strike people as such. There is a growing disconnect between the way people experience growth and the way the policy establishment talks about it, and this gap is becoming an unspoken subtext to much of American political life.

The group most commonly associated with an antigrowth stance is environmentalists, of course. To be sure, one faction, the environmental economists, is trying to put green new wine into the old bottles of economic thought. If we would just make people pay the "true" cost of, say, the gasoline they burn, through the tax system for example, then the market would do the rest. We'd have benign, less-polluting growth, they say, perhaps even more than now. But the core of the environmental movement remains deeply suspicious of the growth ethos, and probably would be even if the environmental impacts somehow could be lessened.

In the middle are suburbanites who applaud growth in the abstract, but oppose the particular manifestations they see around them—the traffic, sprawl and crowded schools.

On the Right, meanwhile, an anti-growth politics is arising practically unnoticed. When social conservatives denounce gambling, pornography, or sex and violence in the media, they are talking about specific instances of the growth that their political leaders rhapsodize on other days.

Environmentalists have been like social conservatives in one key respect. They have been moralistic regarding growth, often scolding people for enjoying themselves at the expense of future generations and the earth. Their concern is valid, up to a point—the consumer culture does promote the time horizon of a five year old. But politically it is not the most promising line of attack, and conceptually it concedes too much ground. To moralize about consumption as they do is to accept the conventional premise that it really is something chosen—an enjoyable form of self-indulgence that has unfortunate consequences for the earth.

That's "consumption" in the common parlance—the sport utility vehicle loading up at Wal-Mart, the stuff piling up in the basement and garage. But increasingly that's not what people actually experience, nor is it what the term really means. In economics, consumption means everything people spend money on, pleasurable or not. Wal-Mart is just one dimension of a much larger and increasingly unpleasant whole. The lawyers' fees for the house settlement or divorce; the repair work on the car after it was rear-ended; the cancer treatments for the uncle who was a three-pack-a-day smoker; the stress medications and weight loss regimens—all these and more are "consumption." They all go into the GDP.

Cancer treatments and lawyer's fees are not what come to mind when environmentalists lament the nation's excess consumption, or for that matter when economists applaud America's "consumers" for keeping the world economy afloat. Yet increasingly such things are what consumption actually consists of in the economy today. More and more, it consists not of pleasurable things that people choose, but rather of things that most people would gladly do without.

Much consumption today is addictive, for example. Millions of Americans are engaged in a grim daily struggle with themselves to do less of it. They want to eat less, drink less, smoke less, gamble less, talk less on the telephone—do less buying, period. Yet economic reasoning declares as growth and progress, that which people themselves regard as a tyrannical affliction.

Economists resist this reality of a divided self, because it would complicate their models beyond repair. They cling instead to an 18th century model of human psychology—the "rational" and self-interested man—which assumes those complexities away. As David McClelland, the Harvard psychologist, once put it, economists "haven't even discovered Freud, let alone Abraham Maslow." (They also haven't discovered the Apostle Paul, who lamented that "the good that I would I do not, but the evil that I would not, that I do.")

Then too there's the mounting expenditure that sellers foist upon people through machination and deceit. People don't choose to pay for the corrupt campaign finance system or for bloated executive pay packages. The cost of these is hidden in the prices that we pay at the store. As I write this, the *Washington Post* is reporting that Microsoft has hired Ralph Reed, former head of the Christian Coalition, and Grover Norquist, a right-wing polemicist, as lobbyists in Washington. When I bought this computer with Windows 95, Bill Gates never asked me whether I wanted to help support a bunch of Beltway operators like these.

This is compulsory consumption, not choice, and the economy is rife with it today. People don't choose to pay some $40 billion a year in telemarketing fraud. They don't choose to pay 32% more for prescription drugs than do people in Canada. ("Free trade" means that corporations are free to buy their labor and materials in other countries, but ordinary Americans aren't equally free to do their shopping there.) For that matter, people don't choose to spend $25 and up for inkjet printer cartridges. The manufacturers design the printers to make money on the cartridges because, as the *Wall Street Journal* put it, that's "where the big profit margins are."

Yet another category of consumption that most people would gladly do without arises from the need to deal with the offshoots and implications of growth. Bottled water has become a multibillion dollar business in the United States because people don't trust what comes from the tap. There's a growing market for sound insulation and double-pane windows because the economy produces so much noise. A wide array of physical and social stresses arise from the activities that get lumped into the euphemistic term "growth."

The economy in such cases doesn't solve problems so much as create new problems that require more expenditure to solve. Food is supposed to sustain people, for example. But today the dis-economies of eating sustain the GDP instead. The food industry spends some $21 billion a year on advertising to entice people to eat food they don't need. Not coincidentally there's now a $32 billion diet and weight loss industry to help people take off the pounds that inevitably result. When that doesn't work, which is often, there is always the vacuum pump or knife. There were some 110,000 liposuctions in the United States last year; at five pounds each that's some 275 tons of flab up the tube.

It is a grueling cycle of indulgence and repentance, binge and purge. Yet each stage of this miserable experience, viewed through the pollyanic lens of economics, becomes growth and therefore good. The problem here goes far beyond the old critique of how the consumer culture cultivates feelings of inadequacy, lack and need so people will buy and buy again. Now this culture actually makes life worse, in order to sell solutions that purport to make it better.

Traffic shows this syndrome in a finely developed form. First we build sprawling suburbs so people need a car to go almost anywhere. The resulting long commutes are daily torture but help build up the GDP. Americans spend some $5 billion a year in gasoline alone while they sit in traffic and go nowhere. As the price of gas increases this growth sector will expand.

Commerce deplores a vacuum, and the exasperating hours in the car have spawned a booming subeconomy of relaxation tapes, cell phones, even special bibs. Billboards have 1-800 numbers so commuters can shop while they stew. Talk radio thrives on traffic-bound commuters, which accounts for some of the contentious, get-out-of-my-face tone. The traffic also helps sustain a $130 billion a year car wreck industry; and if Gates succeeds in getting computers into cars, that sector should get a major boost.

The health implications also are good for growth. Los Angeles, which has the worst traffic in the nation, also leads—if that's the word—in hospital admissions due to respiratory ailments. The resulting medical bills go into the GDP. And while Americans sit in traffic they aren't walking or getting exercise. More likely they are entertaining themselves orally with a glazed donut or a Big Mac, which helps explain why the portion of middle-aged Americans who are clinically obese has doubled since the 1960s.

C. Everett Koop, the former Surgeon General, estimates that some 70% of the nation's medical expenses are lifestyle induced. Yet the same lifestyle that promotes disease also produces a rising GDP. (Keynes observed that traditional virtues like thrift are bad for growth; now it appears that health is bad for growth too.) We literally are growing ourselves sick, and this puts a grim new twist on the economic doctrine of "complementary goods," which describes the way new products tend to spawn a host of others. The automobile gave rise to car wash franchises, drive-in restaurants, fuzz busters, tire dumps, and so forth. Television produced an antenna industry, VCRs, soap magazines, ad infinitum. The texts present this phenomenon as the wondrous perpetual motion machine of the market—goods beget more goods. But now the machine is producing complementary ills and collateral damages instead.

Suggestive of this new dynamic is a pesticide plant in Richmond, California, which is owned by a transnational corporation that also makes the breast cancer drug tamoxifen. Many researchers believe that pesticides, and the toxins created in the production of them, play a role in breast cancer. "It's a pretty good deal," a local physician told the *East Bay Express*, a Bay Area weekly. "First you cause the cancer, then you profit from curing it." Both the alleged cause and cure make the GDP go up, and this syndrome has become a central dynamic of growth in the U.S. today.

Mainstream economists would argue that this is all beside the point. If people didn't have to spend money on such things as commuting or medical costs, they'd simply spend it on something else, they say. Growth would be the same or even greater, so the actual content of growth should be of little concern to those who promote it. That view holds sway in the nation's policy councils; as a result we try continually to grow our way out of problems, when increasingly we are growing our way in.

To the extent conventional economics has raised an eyebrow at growth, it has done so mainly through the concept of "externalities". These are negative side effects suffered by those not party to a transaction between a buyer and a seller. Man buys car, car pollutes air, others suffer that "externality." As the language implies, anything outside the original transaction is deemed secondary, a subordinate reality, and therefore easily overlooked. More, the effects upon buyer and seller—the "internalities" one might say—are assumed to be good.

Today, however, that mental schema is collapsing. Externalities are starting to overwhelm internalities. A single jet ski can cause more misery for the people who reside by a lake, than it gives pleasure to the person riding it.

More importantly, and as just discussed, internalities themselves are coming into question, and with them the assumption of choice, which is the moral linchpin of market thought.

If people choose what they buy, as market theory posits, then—externalities aside—the sum total of all their buying must be the greatest good of all. That's the ideology behind the GDP. But if people don't always choose, then the model starts to fall apart, which is what is happening today. The practical implications are obvious. If growth consists increasingly of problems rather than solutions, then scolding people for consuming too much is barking up the wrong tree. It is possible to talk instead about ridding our lives of what we don't want as well as forsaking what we do want—or think we want.

Politically this is a more promising path. But to where? The economy may be turning into a kind of round robin of difficulty and affliction, but we are all tied to the game. The sickness industry employs a lot of people, as do ad agencies and trash haulers. The fastest-growing occupations in the country include debt collectors and prison guards. What would we do without our problems and dysfunctions?

The problem is especially acute for those at the bottom of the income scale who have not shared much in the apparent prosperity. For them, a bigger piece of a bad pie might be better than none.

This is the economic conundrum of our age. No one has more than pieces of an answer, but it helps to see that much growth today is really an optical illusion created by accounting tricks. The official tally ignores totally the cost side of the growth ledger—the toll of traffic upon our time and health for example. In fact, it actually counts such costs as growth and gain. By the same token, the official tally ignores the economic contributions of the natural environment and the social structure; so that the more the economy destroys these, and puts commoditized substitutes in their places, the more the experts say the economy has "grown." Pollute the lakes and oceans so that people have to

> ## MEASURING PROGRESS
>
> Far from being a true measure of economic (and human) progress, the GDP thrives on bad news. The GDP soars when the government spends millions to clean up a toxic waste site or to treat those suffering from cancer who lived nearby. And the GDP can drop from some very good news. For instance, it is good news for a family if a parent can afford to cut back on work and devote more hours at home. But because she is working less, spending less money on day care, and earning less, the GDP measures it as a drop in economic activity.
>
> In the mid-1990s, the San Francisco group Redefining Progress created an alternative GDP that measures the costs as well as the benefits of economic growth. The "Genuine Progress Indicator," or GPI, accounts for how production and consumption create social ills like inequality, and creates environmental problems that threaten future generations, such as global warming and the depletion of natural resources. It adjusts the GDP downward to account for each of these aspects of economic activity, along with underemployment and the loss of leisure time. It would adjust the GDP upward if there had been more leisure time and social progress.
>
> The result: while the GPI rose somewhat between 1950 and the early 1970s, it has been falling ever since. By 1994 the GPI was 26% lower than in 1973. During the same period, the GDP was growing.

join private swim clubs and the economy grows. Erode the social infrastructure of community so people have to buy services from the market instead of getting help from their neighbors, and it grows some more. The real economy—the one that sustains us—has diminished. All that has grown is the need to buy commoditized substitutes for things we used to have for free.

So one might rephrase the question thus: how do we achieve real growth, as opposed to the statistical illusion that passes for growth today? Four decades ago, John Kenneth Galbraith argued in *The Affluent Society* that conventional economic reasoning is rapidly becoming obsolete. An economics based upon scarcity simply doesn't work in an economy of hyper-abundance, he said. If it takes a $200 billion (today) advertising industry to maintain what economists quaintly call "demand," then perhaps that demand isn't as urgent as conventional theory posits. Perhaps it's not even demand in any sane meaning of the word.

Galbraith argued that genuine economy called for shifting some resources from consumption that needs to be prodded, to needs which are indisputably great: schools, parks, older people, the inner cities and the like. For this he was skewered as a proto-socialist. Yet today the case is even stronger, as advertisers worm into virtually every waking moment in a desperate effort to keep the growth machine on track.

Galbraith was arguing for a larger public sector. But that

brings dysfunctions of its own, such as bureaucracy; and it depends upon an enlarging private sector as a fiscal base to begin with. Today we need to go further, and establish new ground rules for the economy, so that it produces more genuine growth on its own. We also need to find ways to revive the nonmarket economy of informal community exchange, so that people do not need money to meet every single life need.

In the first category, environmental fiscal policy can help. While the corporate world has flogged workers to be more productive, resources such as petroleum have been in effect loafing on the job. If we used these more efficiently the result could be jobs and growth, even in conventional terms, with less environmental pollution. If we used land more efficiently—that is, reduced urban sprawl—the social and environmental gains would be great.

Another ground rule is the corporate charter laws. We need to restore these to their original purpose: to keep large business organizations within the compass of the common good. But such shifts can do only so much. More efficient cars might simply encourage more traffic, for example. Cheap renewable power for electronic devices could encourage more noise. In other words, the answer won't just be a more efficient version of what we do now. Sooner or later we'll need different ways of thinking about work and growth and how we allocate the means of life.

This is where the social economy comes in, the informal exchange between neighbors and friends. There are some promising trends. One is the return to the traditional village model in housing. Structure does affect content. When houses are close together, and people can walk to stores and work, it encourages the spontaneous social interaction that nurtures real community. New local currencies, such as Time Dollars, provide a kind of lattice work upon which informal nonmarket exchange can take root and grow.

Changes like these are off the grid of economics as conventionally defined. It took centuries for the market to emerge from the stagnation of feudalism. The next organizing principle, whatever it is, most likely will emerge slowly as well. This much we can say with certainty. As the market hurdles towards multiple implosions, social and environmental as well as financial, it is just possible that the economics profession is going to have to do what it constantly lectures the rest of us to do: adjust to new realities and show a willingness to change.

ARTICLE 1.5

May 2009

GENDER AND THE RECESSION
RECESSION HITS TRADITIONALLY MALE JOBS HARDEST

HEATHER BOUSHEY

A woman is now the primary breadwinner in millions of families across the United States because her husband has lost his job. Three out of four jobs lost during our Great Recession, which began in December 2007, have been men's jobs. This has left women to support their families nationwide—a task made more challenging since women typically earn only 78 cents compared to the male dollar.

Men have lost more jobs than women because the industries with the largest job losses so far during the recession have been ones dominated by men. New Bureau of Labor Statistics Current Establishment Survey data for March 2009 shows that since the recession began men have lost 75.0 percent of all nonfarm jobs and 72.7 percent of all private-sector jobs.

Women have become a larger share of payroll employees. As of March 2009, the latest data available, women made up nearly half the labor force: 49.7 percent of all workers employed in the United States are women, up from 48.7 percent when the recession began in December 2007.

The recession is playing out differently by gender because men and women tend to work in very different industries and occupations. Women especially predominate in financial activities—mostly because they are the majority of real estate agents, not because they are the majority of bankers—as well as in government, education, and health. (See Chart 1.) Men predominate in transportation, construction, and manufacturing, as well as in certain retail professions, such as the sale of automobiles and electronic appliances.

Larger job losses among men have occurred because the recession is hitting traditionally male working-class jobs. Half of the job losses during this recession so far have occurred in either construction or manufacturing. Another quarter of the total job losses have occurred in professional and business services, mostly among temporary workers. Even though it is the financial sector which is driving the economic crisis, the financial activities industry only accounts for 7.4 percent of the jobs lost so far in this recession.

FIGURE 1: **The Recession By Gender**
Total Change in Employment, December 2007 to April 2009 (000s)

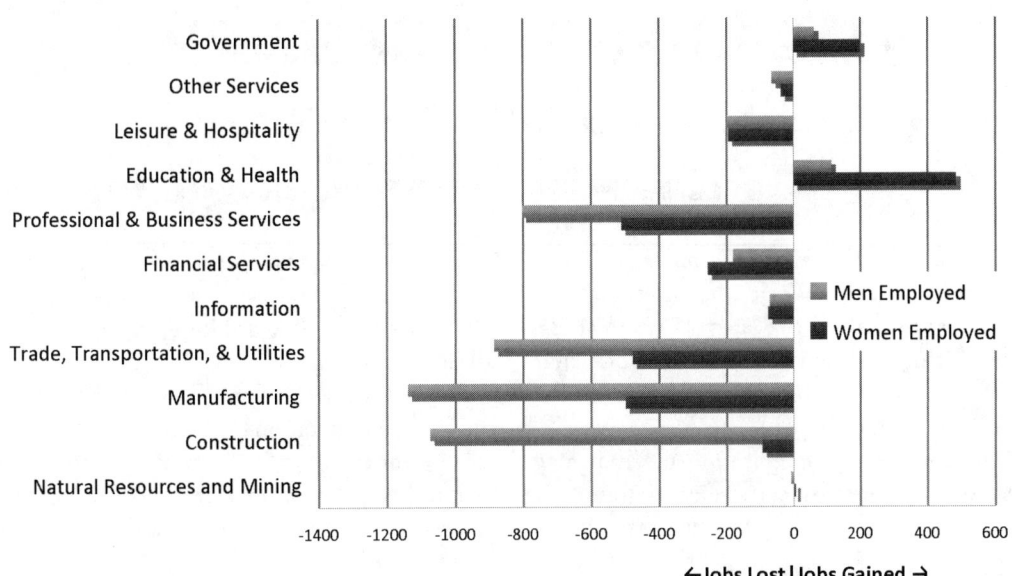

Source: Center for American Progress and the BLS

Yet, it is not just that men work in industries hardest hit by the recession. Within a number of hard-hit industries, men are also losing a disproportionate share of the jobs. For example, within retail, although men accounted for half (49.8 percent) of all workers at the beginning of the recession, they held two-thirds (64.5 percent) of the jobs lost. In finance and insurance, men accounted for over a third (36.7 percent) of the jobs at the beginning of the recession, but have lost half (50.6 percent) of the jobs.

It is not unique for blue-collar workers to bear the brunt of job losses in a recession. What is notable in this recession is that while manufacturing and construction accounted for a larger share of total job losses than in prior recessions, the industries that are seeing jobs gains—education, health, and government—are seeing smaller gains than during prior recessions. This does not bode well for women's jobs moving forward, since women are concentrated in these industries.

Notably, during the 1980s recession—when the unemployment rate went above 10 percent—women actually gained jobs on net because of continued hiring in women-dominated industries. Clearly, that is not the case during the current recession. Women's employment is already 98.5 percent of its level from December 2007.

As of April 2009 the unemployment rate for adult men was 9.4 percent—more than double what it was in December 2007. The unemployment rate for adult women was 7.1 percent in April. The male unemployment rate is now 2.3 percentage points higher than women's—larger than at any other time since 1949.

Women are also less likely than men to be unemployed in married families. The unemployment rate for married men is 6.3 percent—higher than at any time since 1983. The unemployment rate for married women is 5.5 percent—the highest since 1986.

That means more and more women in millions of families across the United States will be supporting their families.

Ensuring that those women, and every woman, earn a fair day's pay could not be a more pressing issue for families. A good—and fast—place to start would be for the Obama administration to devote its efforts to simply enforcing the laws already on the books and implementing better monitoring of equal pay. That would be a down payment to help families make ends meet while the labor market is getting back on track.

This article combines two "infographics" written by Heather Boushey, ""Gender and The Recession," May 8, 2009, and "The Importance of Women Breadwinners," April 30, 2009. Both are available at the Center for American Progress: http://www.americanprogress.org/issues/2009/05/gender_recession.htm and http://www.americanprogress.org/issues/2009/04/women_breadwinners.html.

WAGES FOR HOUSEWORK
THE MOVEMENT AND THE NUMBERS

BY LENA GRABER AND JOHN MILLER

The International Wages for Housework Campaign (WFH), a network of women in Third World and industrialized countries, began organizing in the early 1970s. WFH's demands are ambitious—"for the unwaged work that women do to be recognized as work in official government statistics, and for this work to be paid."

Housewives paid wages? By the government? That may seem outlandish to some, but consider the staggering amount of unpaid work carried out by women. In 1990, the International Labor Organization (ILO) estimated that women do two-thirds of the world's work for 5% of the income. In 1995, the UN Development Programme's (UNDP) Human Development Report announced that women's unpaid and underpaid labor was worth $11 trillion worldwide, and $1.4 trillion in the United States alone. Paying women the wages they "are owed" for unwaged work, as WFN puts it, would go a long way toward undoing these inequities and reducing women's economic dependence on men.

Publicizing information like this, WFH—whose International Women Count Network now includes more than 2,000 non-governmental organizations (NGOs) from the North and South—and other groups have been remarkably successful in persuading governments to count unwaged work. In 1995, the UN Fourth World Conference on Women, held in Beijing, developed a Platform for Action that called on governments to calculate the value of women's unpaid work and include it in conventional measures of national output, such as Gross Domestic Product (GDP).

So far, only Trinidad & Tobago and Spain have passed legislation mandating the new accounting, but other countries—including numerous European countries, Australia, Canada, Japan, and New Zealand in the industrialized world, and Bangladesh, the Dominican Republic, India, Nepal, Tanzania, and Venezuela in the developing world—have undertaken extensive surveys to determine how much time is spent on unpaid household work.

THE VALUE OF HOUSEWORK

Producing credible numbers for the value of women's work in the home is no easy task. Calculating how many hours women spend performing housework—from cleaning to childcare to cooking to shopping—is just the first step. The hours are considerable in both developing and industrialized economies. (See Table 1.)

What value to place on that work, and what would constitute fair remuneration—or wages for housework—is even more difficult to assess. Feminist economists dedicated to making the value of housework visible have taken different approaches to answering the question. One approach, favored by the UN's International Research and Training Institute for the Advancement of Women (INSTRAW), bases the market value of work done at home on the price of market goods and services that are similar to those produced in the home (such as meals served in restaurants or cleaning done by professional firms). These output-based evaluations estimate that counting unpaid household production would add 30-60% to the GDP of industrialized countries, and far more for developing countries. (See Table 2.)

A second approach evaluates the inputs of household production—principally the labor that goes into cooking, cleaning, childcare, and other services performed in the home, overwhelmingly by women. Advocates of this approach use one of three methods. Some base their calculations on what economists call opportunity cost—the wages women might have earned if they had worked a similar number of hours in the market economy. Others ask what it would cost to hire someone to do the work—either a general laborer such as a domestic servant (the generalist-

---

TABLE 1
WOMEN'S TIME SPENT PER DAY PERFORMING HOUSEHOLD LABOR, BY ACTIVITY, IN HOURS:MINUTES

	Childcare Time	Cleaning Time	Food Prep Time	Shopping Time	Water/Fuel Collection	Total Country Time[a]
Australia (1997[b])	2:27	1:17	1:29	0:58	n.a.	3:39
Japan (1999)	0:24	2:37	n.a.	0:33	n.a.	3:34
Norway (2000)	0:42	1:16	0:49	0:26	0:01	3:56
U.K. (2000)	1:26	1:35	1:08	0:33	n.a.	4:55
Nepal (1996)	1:28	2:00	5:30	0:13	1:10	11:58

Note: Some activities, especially childcare, may overlap with other tasks
[a] Totals may include activities other than those listed.
[b] Only some percentage of the population recorded doing these activities. Averages are for that portion of the population. Generally, figures represent a greater number of women than men involved. *Sources:* Australia: <www.abs.gov.au/ausstats>; Japan: <www.unescap.org/stat>; Norway: <www.ssb.no/tidsbruk_en>; United Kingdom: <www.statistics.gov.uk/themes/social_finances/TimeUseSurvey>; Nepal: INSTRAW, *Valuation of Household Production and the Satellite Accounts* (Santo Domingo: 1996), 34-35; <www.cbs.nl/isi/iass>.

replacement method) or a specialist such as a chef (the specialist-replacement method)—and then assign those wages to household labor. Ann Chadeau, a researcher with the Organization for Economic Cooperation and Development, has found the specialist-replacement method to be "the most plausible and at the same time feasible approach" for valuing unpaid household labor.

These techniques produce quite different results, all of which are substantial in relation to GDP. With that in mind, let's look at how some countries calculated the monetary value of unpaid work.

UNPAID WORK IN CANADA, GREAT BRITAIN, AND JAPAN

In Canada, a government survey documented the time men and women spent on unpaid work in 1992. Canadian women performed 65% of all unpaid work, shouldering an especially large share of household labor devoted to preparing meals, maintaining clothing, and caring for children. (Men's unpaid hours exceeded women's only for outdoor cleaning.)

The value of unpaid labor varied substantially, depending on the method used to estimate its appropriate wage. (See Table 3.) The opportunity-cost method, which uses the average market wage (weighted for the greater proportion of unpaid work done by women), assigned the highest value to unpaid labor, 54.2% of Canadian GDP. The two replacement methods produced lower estimates, because the wages they assigned fell below those of other jobs. The specialist-replacement method, which paired unpaid activities with the average wages of corresponding occupations—such as cooking with junior chefs, and childcare with kindergarten teachers—put the value of Canadian unpaid labor at 43% of GDP. The generalist-replacement method, by assigning the wages of household servants to unpaid labor, produced the lowest estimate of the value of unpaid work: 34% of Canadian GDP. INSTRAW's output-based measure, which matched hours of unpaid labor to a household's average expenditures on the same activities, calculated the value of Canada's unpaid work as 47.4% of GDP.

In Great Britain, where unpaid labor hours are high for an industrialized country (see Table 1), the value of unpaid labor was far greater relative to GDP. The British Office for National Statistics found that, when valued using the opportunity cost method, unpaid work was 112% of Britain's GDP in 1995! With the specialist-replacement method, British unpaid labor was still 56% of GDP—greater than the output of the United Kingdom's entire manufacturing sector for the year.

In Japan—where unpaid labor hours are more limited (see Table 1), paid workers put in longer hours, and women perform over 80% of unpaid work—the value of unpaid labor is significantly smaller relative to GDP. The Japanese Economic Planning Agency calculated that counting unpaid work in 1996 would add between 15.2% (generalist-replacement method) and 23% (opportunity-cost method) to GDP. Even at those levels, the value of unpaid labor still equaled at least half of Japanese women's market wages.

HOUSEWORK NOT BOMBS

While estimates vary by country and evaluation method, all of these calculations make clear that recognizing the value of unpaid household labor profoundly alters our perception of economic activity and women's contributions to production. "Had household production been included in the system of macro-economic accounts," notes Ann Chadeau, "governments may well have implemented quite different economic and social policies."

For example, according to the UNDP, "The inescapable implication [of recognizing women's unpaid labor] is that the fruits of society's total labor should be shared more equally." For the UNDP, this would mean radically altering property and inheritance rights; access to credit; entitlement to social security benefits, tax incentives, and child care; and terms of divorce settlements.

For WFH advocates, the implications are inescapable as well: women's unpaid labor should be paid—and "the money," WFH insists, "must come first of all from military spending."

Here in the United States, an unneeded and dangerous military buildup begun last year has already pushed up military spending from 3% to 4% of GDP. Devoting just the additional 1% of GDP gobbled up by the military budget to wages for housework—far from being outlandish—would be an important first step toward fairly remunerating women who perform much-needed and life-sustaining household work.

TABLE 2
VALUE OF UNPAID HOUSEHOLD LABOR AS % OF GDP, USING OUTPUT-BASED EVALUATION METHOD

Country	% of GDP
Canada (1992)	47.4%
Finland (1990)	49.1%
Nepal (1991)	170.7%

Source: INSTRAW, *Valuation of Household Production and the Satellite Accounts* (Santo Domingo, 1996), 62, 229.

TABLE 3
VALUE OF UNPAID HOUSEHOLD LABOR IN CANADA AS % OF GDP, 1992

Evaluation Method	% of GDP
Opportunity Cost (before taxes)	54.2 %
Specialist-Replacement	43.0%
Generalist-Replacement	34.0%
Output-Based	47.4%

Source: INSTRAW, *Valuation of Household Production and the Satellite Accounts* (Santo Domingo: 1996), 229.

Resources: Ann Chadeau, "What is Households' Non-Market Production Worth?" *OECD Economic Studies* No. 18 (Spring 1992); Economic Planning Unit, Department of National Accounts, Japan, "Monetary Valuation of Unpaid Work in 1996" <unstats.un.org/unsd/methods/timeuse/tusresource_papers/japanunpaid.htm>; INSTRAW, *Measurement and Valuation of Unpaid Contribution: Accounting Through Time and Output* (Santo Domingo: 1995); INSTRAW, *Valuation of Household Production and the Satellite Accounts* (Santo Domingo: 1996); Office of National Statistics, United Kingdom, "A Household Satellite Account for the UK," by Linda Murgatroyd and Henry Neuberger, *Economic Trends* (October 1997) <www.statistics.gov.uk/hhsa/hhsa/Index.html>; Hilkka Pietilä, "The Triangle of the Human Ecology: Household-Cultivation-Industrial Production," *Ecological Economics Journal* 20 (1997); UN Development Programme, Human Development Report (New York: Oxford University Press, 1995); Wages For Housework <ourworld.compuserve.com/homepages/crossroadswomenscentre/WFH.html>

ARTICLE 1.7

November/December 2007

WAR SPENDING PLACED ABOVE DOMESTIC PRIORITIES

BY MONIQUE MORRISSEY

Claiming the mantle of fiscal discipline, President Bush has threatened to veto domestic spending bills for fiscal year 2008 that exceed his budget request. His threat cannot be justified by a claim that Congress is being unusually profligate: Congress's non-defense appropriations bills approximately keep pace with economic growth, and earmarks are down sharply.

Meanwhile, the administration has asked for significant increases in both war appropriations and regular defense appropriations for FY08: $524 billion for defense, military construction, and veterans' affairs, and $193 billion (so far) for war funding. If Congress agrees to these requests, defense spending, which rose from 3.0% of GDP when Bush came into office in 2001 to 4.0% in 2005, 2006, and 2007, will resume its upward climb to between 4.3% and 5.0% of GDP in 2008. (The 4.3% estimate assumes that the ratio of actual outlays to appropriations, as measured by the Congressional Budget Office, is the same in FY08 as in FY07. The 5.0% estimate assumes that all moneys appropriated are actually spent.)

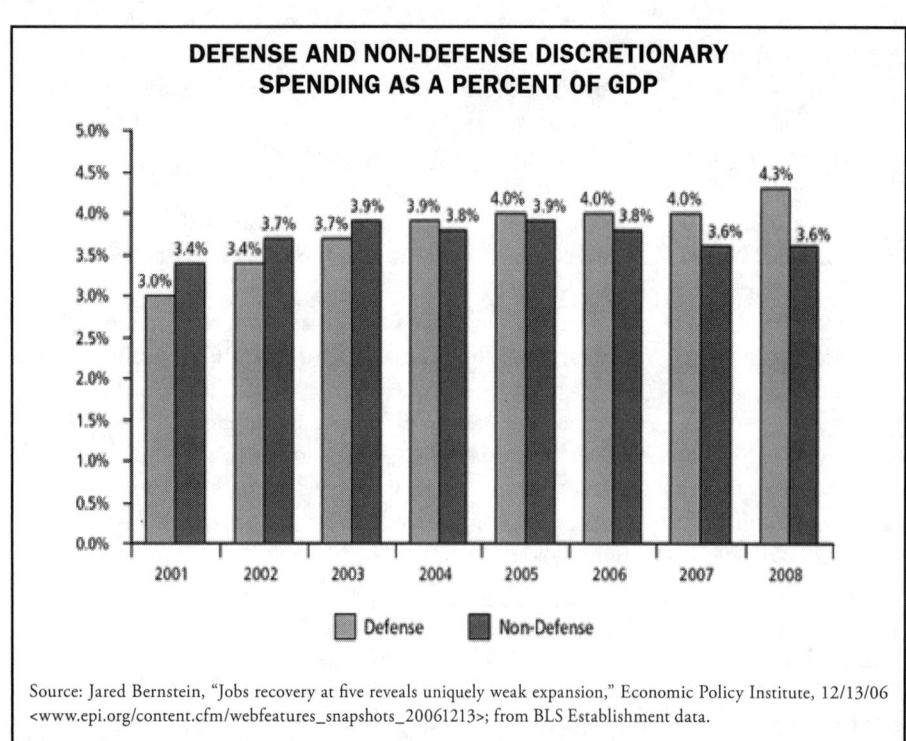

Source: Jared Bernstein, "Jobs recovery at five reveals uniquely weak expansion," Economic Policy Institute, 12/13/06 <www.epi.org/content.cfm/webfeatures_snapshots_20061213>; from BLS Establishment data.

*Current recovery figures include benchmark revision.

Note: Where they differ, Senate and House appropriations bills are averaged. The chart assumes that the ratio of outlays to appropriations is the same in FY07 and FY08. In the case of defense spending, the difference between outlays and appropriations reflects the fact that war funds are not necessarily spent within a fiscal year, and appropriations bills are not cleanly split along functional lines. In the case of non-defense spending, the discrepancy is due to spending from the Highway Trust Fund and the Airport and Airway Trust Fund, which is not included in appropriations bills.

The chart on the opposite page illustrates what happens if the president gets his way on military spending. It shows that even if Congress gets its way on domestic spending, the entire increase in discretionary spending as a share of GDP since 2002 (the first year President Bush had any input on the budget) will be due to growth in defense spending rather than domestic initiatives. ("Discretionary spending" refers to budget items appropriated by Congress each year, as opposed to mandatory spending, authorized by permanent laws, on programs such as Medicare and Social Security.) The chart actually understates the full cost of the "war on terror," because Homeland Security, State Department, and Foreign Operations funding is counted under non-defense spending. Plus, the figures shown do not include significant long-term war costs, for veterans' health care, for example.

The proposed $70 billion increase in defense appropriations for FY08 would be more than enough to fund the $35 billion expansion of the State Children's Health Insurance Program that the president just vetoed. In addition, it would make up the $21 billion difference between the president and Congress on the domestic appropriations bills that the president has threatened to veto. Polls show that voters are concerned that defense spending—especially on the Iraq war—is placed above government spending on health care, education, and other domestic priorities. The voters are right.

Resources: Author's calculations, based on Congressional Budget Office (CBO), www.cbo.gov/budget/historical.shtml; CBO, *The Budget and Economic Outlook: An Update,* August 2007; *CongressDaily,* "Dems Lay Groundwork for Challenging Bush over Vetoes," September 28, 2007; Center on Budget and Policy Priorities, *The Fight over Appropriations: Myths and Reality,* June 21, 2007.

CHAPTER 2
WEALTH, INEQUALITY, AND POVERTY

INTRODUCTION

Wealth and inequality are both end products of today's economic growth. But while all macroeconomics textbooks investigate wealth *accumulation*, most give less attention to wealth *disparities*. The authors in this chapter fill in the gap by looking at who makes out, and who doesn't, with the accumulation of wealth.

"Slicing Up at the Long Barbeque" (Article 2.1) starts the discussion by providing hard numbers on today's income and wealth gaps. Economist Jim Cypher documents the alarming increase in U.S. inequality, which has reached levels not seen since the Great Depression. This holds for both income (how much you or your family makes in a year) and wealth (the assets you or your family own minus your debts). Today, the top 1% of households own nearly two-fifths of the nation's wealth and the richest 20% get nearly three-fifths of our national income. Median household income (after adjusting for inflation) is declining. For Cypher, these numbers define who gorged, who served, and who got roasted during the last thirty years.

All told, greater wealth hasn't made for greater equality or social mobility. As Paul Krugman reports, it is not just left-wing critics who say so, but the business press as well. The number of people who go from rags to riches—while always so few as to be near-mythical—has decreased since 1980 (Article 2.5). In addition, low-wage workers are five times less likely to have sick days at their job than workers at the top of the wage scale (Article 2.4). On top of that, poverty rates, which according to most experts badly underestimate the extent of poverty in the U.S. economy, continue to rise in the current economic recovery (Article 2.3)

Rising inequality and declining social mobility have led to more people seeking employment at Wal-Mart—where wages are lower, benefits poorer, and working conditions worse than at other big-box retailers, such as Costco, as Esther Cervantes and John Miller document (Article 2.2). Wal-Mart's low prices seem to come at the cost of an ill-paid workforce that cannot afford to shop anywhere else. Many are stuck in what economist Howard Karger describes as "the fringe economy of the United States," where poorly paid and heavily indebted consumers are subjected to predatory financial practices, such as excessive interest rates, super-high fees, and exorbitant prices (Article 2.6).

It doesn't have to be this way. Chris Tilly debunks the myth that inequality is necessary for economic growth, showing that among both developing and industrial economies and across regions within countries, there is no correlation between higher inequality and faster economic growth. He argues that greater equality actually supports economic growth by bolstering spending, promoting agricultural and industrial productivity, and reducing social conflict (Article 2.7). William Greider provides a blueprint for how the engines of inequality of today's economy can be transformed through workplace democracy, strategic investment of public and union-managed pension funds, and shareholder activism (Article 2.8).

What has happened to world income inequality is a matter of intense debate. Many analysts claim that world incomes have converged, leading to a sharp reduction in world inequality in the second half of the twentieth century. Many others report that the gaps between the poorest and the richest people and between countries have continued to widen over the last two decades. Economist Bob Sutcliffe has taken a close look at these studies. In his *Dollars & Sense* interview, Sutcliffe reports that "the wide range of different results of respected studies of world inequality in the last two decades casts doubt on the idea that world inequality has sharply and unambiguously declined or increased during the epoch of neoliberalism" (Article 2.9).

DISCUSSION QUESTIONS

1. (General) The authors in this chapter believe that the distribution of wealth is as important as wealth itself, and consider greater economic equality an important macroeconomic goal. What are some arguments for and against this position? Where do you come down in the debate?
2. (Articles 2.1, 2.4, 2.5) Who benefited from the wealth accumulation of the 1990s? How did stockholders fare versus wage earners? How did the concentration of wealth—holding by income group and by race—change during the decade?
3. (Articles 2.1, 2.3, 2.4, 2.5) "A rising tide lifts all boats," proclaimed John F. Kennedy as he lobbied for pro-business tax cuts in the early 1960s. Did the 1990s boom and the current economic recovery lift all boats? What do the changes in income, wealth, and poverty suggest?

KEY TO COLANDER

E = Economics   M = Macroeconomics

This chapter fits with chapters E24-E26 or M7-M9. Inequality and wealth accumulation are also important topics in chapters on monetary policy E31, M14, inflation, unemployment, and growth E33, M14.

4. (Article 2.3) What are the shortcomings of the federal poverty threshold? How should the United States change the way it calculates the poverty threshold to get a more accurate measure of the incidence of poverty?

5. (Article 2.5) The "New Economy" fed the myth that anyone can get rich quick in this country, but Paul Krugman says it just ain't so. What evidence does he present to argue that social mobility is declining? Do you find his evidence compelling?

6. (Articles 2.2) Wal-Mart is now the largest employer in the United States and the trendsetter for U.S. labor relations. What has been the effect of the Wal-Mart low-prices, low-cost, low-wage strategy on the U.S. economy? Has it been for the better or the worse? For retail workers? Other workers in the United States and around the globe? U.S. consumers? Corporate America?

7. (Article 2.6) How does Karger define the fringe economy? How big is it? How important is the fringe economy for today's new economy, which we usually think of as a high-productivity, high-consumption economy?

8. (Article 2.7) Why do conservatives argue that inequality is good for economic growth? What counterarguments does Tilly use to challenge this traditional view of the tradeoff between inequality and growth? What evidence convinces Tilly that equality is good for economic growth? Does that evidence convince you?

9. (Article 2.8) Why, in Greider's opinion, is transforming the workplace the key to making the U.S. economy more egalitarian and democratic?

10. (Article 2.9) If Sutcliffe is correct and world inequality has neither sharply declined or increased during the epoch of neoliberalism, what does his reading of the world inequality data suggest about the convergence hypothesis—the hypothesis that per capita income in countries with similar institutional structures will converge to the higher level?

SLICING UP AT THE LONG BARBEQUE:
WHO GORGES, WHO SERVES, AND WHO GETS ROASTED?

BY JAMES M. CYPHER

Economic inequality has been on the rise in the United States for 30-odd years. Not since the Gilded Age of the late 19th century—during what Mark Twain referred to as "the Great Barbeque"—has the country witnessed such a rapid shift in the distribution of economic resources.

Still, most mainstream economists do not pay too much attention to the distribution of income and wealth—that is, how the value of current production (income) and past accumulated assets (wealth) is divided up among U.S. households. Some economists focus their attention on theory for theory's sake and do not work much with empirical data of any kind. Others who are interested in these on-the-ground data simply assume that each individual or group gets what it deserves from a capitalist economy. In their view, if the share of income going to wage earners goes up, that must mean that wage earners are more productive and thus deserve a larger slice of the nation's total income—and vice versa if that share goes down.

Heterodox economists, however, frequently look upon the distribution of income and wealth as among the most important shorthand guides to the overall state of a society and its economy. Some are interested in economic justice; others may or may not be, but nonetheless are convinced that changes in income distribution signal underlying societal trends and perhaps important points of political tension. And the general public appears to be paying increasing attention to income and wealth inequality. Consider the strong support voters have given to recent ballot questions raising state minimum wages and the extensive coverage of economic inequality that has suddenly begun to appear in mainstream news outlets like the *New York Times*, the *Los Angeles Times*, and the *Wall Street Journal*, all of which published lengthy article series on the topic in the past few years. Just last month, news outlets around the country spotlighted the extravagant bonuses paid out by investment firm Goldman Sachs, including a $53.4 million bonus to the firm's CEO.

By now, economists and others who do pay attention to the issue are aware that income and wealth inequality in the United States rose steadily during the last three decades of the 20th century. But now that we are several years into the 21st, what do we know about income and wealth distribution today? Has the trend toward inequality continued, or are there signs of a reversal? And what can an understanding of the entire post-World War II era tell us about how to move again toward greater economic equality?

The short answers are: (1) Income distribution is even more unequal that we thought; (2) The newest data suggest the trend toward greater inequality continues, with no signs of a reversal; (3) We all do better when we all do better. During the 30 or so years after World War II the economy boomed and every stratum of society did better—pretty much at the same rate. When the era of shared growth ended, so too did much of the growth: the U.S. economy slowed down and recessions were deeper, more frequent, and harder to overcome. Growth spurts that did occur left most people out: the bottom 60% of U.S. households earned only 95 cents in 2004 for every dollar they made in 1979. A quarter century of falling incomes for the vast majority, even though average household income rose by 27% in real terms. Whew!

THE CLASSLESS SOCIETY?

Throughout the 1950s, 1960s, and 1970s, sociologists preached that the United States was an essentially "classless" society in which everyone belonged to the middle class. A new "mass market" society with an essentially affluent, economically homogeneous population, they claimed, had emerged. Exaggerated as these claims were in the 1950s, there was some reason for their popular acceptance. Union membership reached its peak share of the private-sector labor force in the early 1950s; unions were able to force corporations of the day to share the benefits of strong economic growth. The union wage created a target for non-union workers as well, pulling up all but the lowest of wages as workers sought to match the union wage and employers often granted it as a tactic for keeping unions out. Under these circumstances, millions of families entered the lower middle class and saw their standard of living rise markedly. All of this made the distribution of income more equal for decades until the late 1970s. Of course there were outliers—some millions of poor, disproportionately blacks, and the rich family here and there.

Something serious must have happened in the 1970s as the trend toward greater economic equality rapidly reversed. Here are the numbers. The share of income received by the bottom 90% of the population was a modest 67% in 1970, but by 2000 this had shrunk to a mere 52%, according to a detailed study of U.S. income distribution conducted by Thomas Piketty and Emmanuel Saez, published by the prestigious National Bureau of Economic Research in 2002. Put another way, the top 10% increased their overall share of the nation's

**FIGURE 1
INCOME SHARE BY QUINTILE:
SELECTED YEARS 1979-2003**

Source: "Further Analysis Of The Distribution Of Income And Taxes, 1979-2002," Michael Strudler and Tom Petska, Statistics of Income Division, Internal Revenue Service, and Ryan Petska, Quantitative Economics and Statistics, Ernst and Young LLP. Accompanying Excel files include data to 2003. Available at www.irs.gov/taxstats/article/0,,id=131260,00.ht

total income by 15 percentage points from 1970 to 2000. This is a rather astonishing jump—the *gain* of the top 10% in these years was equivalent to more than the *total income received* annually by the bottom 40% of households.

To get on the bottom rung of the top 10% of households in 2000, it would have been necessary to have an adjusted gross income of $104,000 a year. The real money, though, starts on the 99th rung of the income ladder—the top 1% received an unbelievable 21.7% of all income in 2000. To get a handhold on the very bottom of this top rung took more than $384,000.

The Piketty-Saez study (and subsequent updates), which included in its measure of annual household income some data, such as income from capital gains, that generally are not factored in, verified a rising *trend* in income inequality which had been widely noted by others, and a *degree* of inequality which was far beyond most current estimates.

The Internal Revenue Service has essentially duplicated the Piketty-Saez study. They find that in 2003, the share of total income going to the "bottom" four-fifths of households (that's 80% of the population!) was only slightly above 40%. (See Figure 1.) Both of these studies show much higher levels of inequality than were previously thought to exist based on widely referenced Census Bureau studies. The Census studies still attribute 50% of total income to the top fifth for 2003, but this number appears to understate what the top fifth now receives—nearly 60%, according to the IRS.

A BRAVE NEW (GLOBALIZED) WORLD FOR WORKERS

Why the big change from 1970 to 2000? That is too long a story to tell here in full. But briefly, we can say that beginning in the early 1970s, U.S. corporations and the wealthy individuals who largely own them had the means, the motive, and the opportunity to garner a larger share of the nation's income—and they did so.

Let's start with the motive. The 1970s saw a significant slowdown in U.S. economic growth, which made corporations and stockholders anxious to stop sharing the benefits of growth to the degree they had in the immediate postwar era.

Opportunity appeared in the form of an accelerating globalization of economic activity. Beginning in the 1970s, more and more U.S.-based corporations began to set up production operations overseas. The trend has only accelerated since, in part because international communication and transportation costs have fallen dramatically. Until the 1970s, it was very difficult—essentially unprofitable—for giants like General Electric or General Motors to operate plants offshore and then import their foreign-made products into the United States. So from the 1940s to the 1970s, U.S. workers had a geographic lever, one they have now almost entirely lost. This erosion in workers' bargaining power has undermined the middle class and decimated the unions that once managed to assure the working class a generally comfortable economic existence. And today, of course, the tendency to send jobs offshore is affecting many highly trained professionals such as engineers. So this process of gutting the middle class has not run its course.

Given the opportunity presented by globalization, companies took a two-pronged approach to strengthening their hand vis-à-vis workers: (1) a frontal assault on unions, with decertification elections and get-tough tactics during unionization attempts, and (2) a debilitating war of nerves whereby corporations threatened to move offshore unless workers scaled back their demands or agreed to givebacks of prior gains in wage and benefit levels or working conditions.

A succession of U.S. governments that pursued conservative—or pro-corporate—economic policies provided the means. Since the 1970s, both Republican and Democratic administrations have tailored their economic policies to benefit corporations and shareholders over workers. The laundry list of such policies includes

- new trade agreements, such as NAFTA, that allow companies to cement favorable deals to move offshore to host nations such as Mexico;
- tax cuts for corporations and for the wealthiest households, along with hikes in the payroll taxes that represent the largest share of the tax burden on the working and middle classes;
- lax enforcement of labor laws that are supposed to protect the right to organize unions and bargain collectively.

EXPLODING MILLIONAIRISM

Given these shifts in the political economy of the United States, it is not surprising that economic inequality in 2000 was higher than in 1970. But at this point, careful readers may well ask whether it is misleading to use data for the year 2000, as the studies reported above do, to demonstrate rising inequality. After all, wasn't 2000 the year the NASDAQ peaked, the year the dot-com bubble reached its maximum volume? So if the wealthiest households received an especially large slice of the nation's total income that year, doesn't that just reflect a bubble about to burst rather than an underlying trend?

To begin to answer this question, we need to look at the trends in income and wealth distribution *since* 2000. And it turns out that after a slight pause in 2000–2001, inequality has continued to rise. Look at household income, for example. According to the standard indicators, the U.S. economy saw a brief recession in 2000-2001 and has been in a recovery ever since. But the median household income has failed to recover.* In 2000 the median household had an annual income of $49,133; by 2005, after adjusting for inflation, the figure stood at $46,242. This 6% drop in median household income occurred while the inflation-adjusted Gross Domestic Product *expanded* by 14.4%.

When the Census Bureau released these data, it noted that median household income had gone up slightly between 2004 and 2005. This point was seized upon by Bush administration officials to bolster their claim that times are good for American workers. A closer look at the data, however, revealed a rather astounding fact: Only 23 million households moved ahead in 2005, most headed by someone aged 65 or above. In other words, subtracting out the cost-of-living increase in Social Security benefits and increases in investment income (such as profits, dividends, interest, capital gains, and rents) to the over-65 group, workers again suffered a *decline* in income in 2005.

Another bit of evidence is the number of millionaire households—those with net worth of $1 million or more excluding the value of a primary residence and any IRAs. In 1999, just before the bubbles burst, there were 7.1 million millionaire households in the United States. In 2005, there were 8.9 million, a record number. Ordinary workers may not have recovered from the 2000-2001 rough patch yet, but evidently the wealthiest households have!

Many economists pay scant attention to income distribution patterns on the assumption that those shifts merely reflect trends in the productivity of labor or the return to risk-taking. But worker productivity *rose* in the 2000-2005 period, by 27.1% (see Figure 2). At the same time, from 2003 to 2005 average hourly pay fell by 1.2%. (Total compensation, including all forms of benefits, rose by 7.2% between 2000 and 2005. Most of the higher compensation spending merely reflects rapid increases in the health insurance premiums that employers have to pay just to maintain the same levels of coverage. But even if benefits are counted as part of workers' pay—a common and questionable

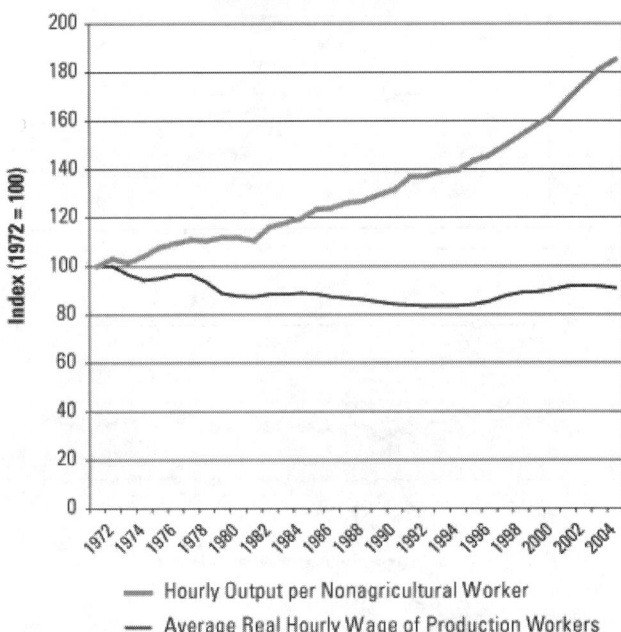

FIGURE 2
REAL WAGES AND PRODUCTIVITY OF U.S. PRODUCTION WORKERS, 1972-2005

— Hourly Output per Nonagricultural Worker
— Average Real Hourly Wage of Production Workers

Source: Economic Report of the President 2006, Tables B-47 and B-49.

practice—productivity growth outpaced this elastic definition of "pay" by 50% between 1972 and 2005.)

And at the macro level, recent data released by the Commerce Department demonstrate that the share of the country's GDP going to wages and salaries sank to its lowest postwar level, 45.4%, in the third quarter of 2006 (see Figure 3). And this figure actually overstates how well ordinary workers are doing. The "Wage & Salary" share includes all income of this type, not just production workers' pay. Corporate executives' increasingly munificent salaries are included as well. Workers got roughly 65% of total wage and salary income in 2005, according to survey data from the U.S. Department of Labor; the other 35% went to salaried professionals—medical doctors and technicians, managers, and lawyers—who comprised only 15.6% of the sample.

Moreover, the "Wage & Salary" share shown in the National Income and Product Accounts includes bonuses, overtime, and other forms of payment not included in the Labor Department survey. If this income were factored in, the share going to nonprofessional, nonmanagerial workers would be even smaller. Bonuses and other forms of income to top employees can be ma*ny times* base pay in important areas such as law and banking. Goldman Sachs's notorious 2006 bonuses are a case in point; the typical

---

*Whenever possible, medians should be used here instead of averages (means): if some in the population have exceedingly high incomes (or wages, or wealth), then the mean fails to accurately depict the situation of the "average household."

**FIGURE 3
WAGES/SALARIES VS. CORPORATE PROFITS
AS SHARES OF U.S. INCOME, 1972–2006**

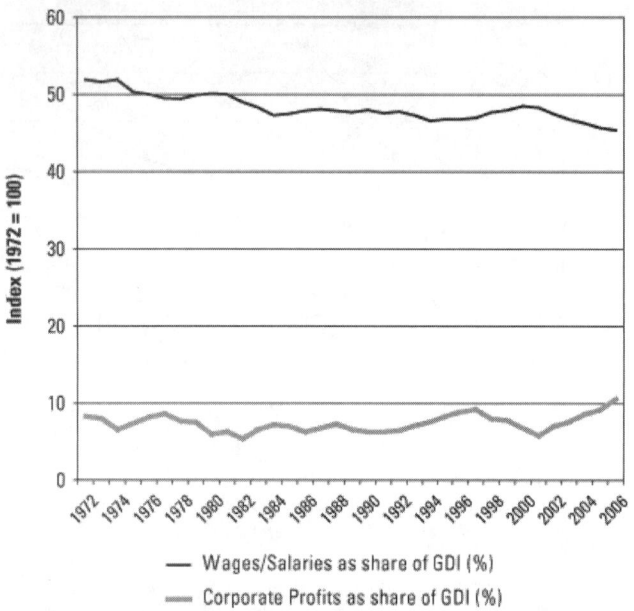

Source: U.S. Dept. of Commerce, Bureau of Economic Analysis, *National Income and Product Accounts 2006*, Table 1.10.

managing director on Wall Street garnered a bonus ranging between $1 and $3 million.

So, labor's share of the nation's income is falling, as Figure 3 shows, but it is actually falling much faster than these data suggest. Profits, meanwhile, are at their highest level as a share of GDP since the booming 1960s.

These numbers should come as no surprise to anyone who reads the paper: story after story illustrates how corporations are continuing to squeeze workers. For instance, workers at the giant auto parts manufacturer Delphi have been told to prepare for a drop in wages from $27.50 an hour in 2006 to $16.50 an hour in 2007. In order to keep some of Caterpillar's manufacturing work in the United States, the union was cornered into accepting a contract in 2006 that limits new workers to a maximum salary of $27,000 a year—no matter how long they work there—compared to the $38,000 or more that long-time Caterpillar workers make today. More generally, for young women with a high school diploma, average entry-level pay fell to only $9.08 an hour in 2005, down by 4.9% just since 2001. For male college graduates, starter-job pay fell by 7.3% over the same period.

AIDING AND ABETTING

And the federal government is continuing to play its part, facilitating the transfer of an ever-larger share of the nation's income to its wealthiest households. George W. Bush once joked that his constituency was "the haves and the have-mores"—this may have been one of the few instances in which he was actually leveling with his audience. Consider aspects of the four tax cuts for individuals that Bush has implemented since taking office. The first two cut the top *nominal* tax rate from 39.6% to 35%. Then, in 2003, the third cut benefited solely those who hold wealth, reducing taxes on dividends from 39.6% to 15% and on capital gains from 20% to 15%. (Bush's fourth tax cut—in 2006—is expected to drop taxes by 4.8% percent for the top one tenth of one percent of all house-holds, while the median household will luxuriate with an extra nickel per day.)

So, if you make your money by the sweat of your brow and you earned $200,000 in 2003, you paid an *effective* tax rate of 21%. If you earned a bit more, say another $60,500, you paid an effective tax rate of 35% on the additional income. But if, with a flick of the wrist on your laptop, you flipped some stock you had held for six months and cleared $60,500 on the transaction, you paid the IRS an effective tax rate of only 15%. What difference does it make? Well, in 2003 the 6,126 households with incomes over $10 million saw their taxes go down by an average of $521,905 from this one tax cut alone.

These tax cuts represent only one of the many Bush administration policies that have abetted the ongoing shift of income away from most households and toward the wealthiest ones. And what do these top-tier households do with all this newfound money? For one thing, they save. This is in sharp contrast to most households. While the top fifth of households by income has a savings rate of 23%, the bottom 80% as a group dissave—in other words, they go into debt, spending more than they earn. Households headed by a person under 35 currently show a negative savings rate of 16% of income. Today *overall* savings—the savings of the top fifth minus the dis-savings of the bottom four-fifths—are slightly negative, for the first time since the Great Depression.

Here we find the crucial link between income and wealth accumulation. Able to save nearly a quarter of their income, the rich search out financial assets (and sometimes real assets such as houses and businesses) to pour their vast funds into. In many instances, sometimes with inside information, they are able to generate considerable future income from their invested savings. Like a snowball rolling downhill, savings for the rich can have a turbo effect—more savings generates more income, which then accumulates as wealth.

LIFESTYLES OF THE RICH

Make the rich even richer and the creative forces of market capitalism will be unleashed, resulting in more savings and consequently more capital investment, raising productivity and creating abundance for all. At any rate, that's the supply-side/neoliberal theory. However—and reminiscent of the false boom that defined the Japanese economy in the late 1980s—the big money has not gone into productive investments in the United States. Stripping out the money pumped into the residential real estate bubble, inflation-adjusted investment in machinery, equipment, technology, and structures increased only 1.4% from 1999 through 2005—an average of 0.23% per year. Essentially, productive investment has stagnated since the close of the dot-com boom.

Instead, the money has poured into high-risk hedge funds. These are vast pools of unregulated funds that are now generating 40% to 50% of the trades in the New York Stock Exchange and account for very large portions of trading in many U.S. and foreign credit and debt markets.

And where is the income from these investments going? Last fall media mogul David Geffen sold two paintings at record prices, a Jasper Johns ($80 million) and a Willem de Kooning ($63.5 million), to two of "today's crop of hedge-fund billionaires" whose cash is making the art market "red-hot," according to the *New York Times*.

Other forms of conspicuous consumption have their allure as well. Boeing and Lufthansa are expecting brisk business for the newly introduced 787 airplane. The commercial version of the new Boeing jet will seat 330, but the VIP version offered by Lufthansa Technik (for a mere $240 million) will have seating for 35 or fewer, leaving room for master bedrooms, a bar, and the transport of racehorses or Rolls Royces. And if you lose your auto assembly job? It should be easy to find work as a dog walker: High-end pet care services are booming, with sales more than doubling between 2000 and 2004. Opened in 2001, Just Dogs Gourmet expects to have 45 franchises in place by the end of 2006 selling hand-decorated doggie treats. And then there is Camp Bow Wow, which offers piped-in classical music for the dogs (oops, "guests") and a live Camper Cam for their owners. Started only three years ago, the company already has 140 franchises up and running.

According to David Butler, the manager of a premiere auto dealership outside of Detroit, sales of Bentleys, at $180,000 a pop, are brisk. But not many $300,000 Rolls Royces are selling. "It's not that they can't afford it," Butler told the New York Times, "it's because of the image it would give." Just what is the image problem in Detroit? Well, maybe it has something to do with those Delphi workers facing a 40% pay cut. Michigan's economy is one of the hardest-hit in the nation. GM, long a symbol of U.S. manufacturing prowess, is staggering, with rumors of possible bankruptcy rife. The best union in terms of delivering the goods for the U.S. working class, the United Auto Workers, is facing an implosion. Thousands of Michigan workers at Delphi, GM, and Ford will be out on the streets very soon. (The top three domestic car makers are determined to permanently lay off three-quarters of their U.S. assembly-line workers—nearly 200,000 hourly employees. If they do, then the number of autoworkers employed by the Big Three—Ford, Chrysler, and GM—will have shrunk by a staggering 900,000 since 1978.) So, this might not be the time to buy a Rolls. But a mere $180,000 Bentley—why not?

HAD ENOUGH OF THE "HAVES"?

In the era Twain decried as the "great barbeque," the outrageous concentration of income and wealth eventually sparked a reaction and a vast reform movement. But it was not until the onset of the Great Depression, decades later, that massive labor/social unrest and economic collapse forced the country's political elite to check the growing concentration of income and wealth.

Today, it does not appear that there are, as yet, any viable forces at work to put the brakes on the current runaway process of rising inequality. Nor does it appear that this era's power elite is ready to accept any new social compact. In a recent report on the "new king of Wall Street" (a co-founder of the hedge fund/private-equity buyout corporation Blackstone Group) that seemed to typify elite perspectives on today's inequality, the *New York Times* gushed that "a crashing wave of capital is minting new billionaires each year." Naturally, the *Times* was too discreet to mention is that those same "crashing waves" have flattened the middle class. And their backwash has turned the working class every-which-way while pulling it down, down, down.

But perhaps those who decry the trend can find at least symbolic hope in the new boom in yet another luxury good. Private mausoleums, in vogue during that earlier Gilded Age, are back. For $650,000, one was recently constructed at Daytona Memorial Park in Florida—with matching $4,000 Medjool date palms for shade. Another, complete with granite patio, meditation room, and doors of hand cast bronze, went up in the same cemetery. Business is booming, apparently, with 2,000 private mausoleums sold in 2005, up from a single-year peak of 65 in the 1980s. Some cost "well into the millions," according to one the nation's largest makers of cemetery monuments. Who knows: maybe the mausoleum boom portends the ultimate (dead) end for the neo-Gilded Age.

Resources: Jenny Anderson, "As Lenders, Hedge Funds Draw Insider Scrutiny," *NY Times* 10/16/06; Steven Greenhouse, "Many Entry-Level Workers Feel Pinch of Rough Market," *NY Times* 9/4/06; Greenhouse and David Leonhardt, "Real Wages Fail to Match a Rise in Productivity," *NY Times* 8/28/06; Paul Krugman, "Feeling No Pain," *NY Times* 3/6/06; Krugman, "Graduates vs. Oligarchs," *NY Times* 2/27/06; David Cay Johnston, *Perfectly Legal* (Penguin Books, 2003); Johnston, "Big Gain for Rich Seen in Tax Cuts for Investments," *NY Times* 4/5/06; Johnston, "New Rise in Number of Millionaire Families," *NY Times* 3/28/06; Johnston, "'04 Income in US was Below 2000 Level," *NY Times* 11/28/06; Leonhardt, "The Economics of Henry Ford May Be Passé," *NY Times* 4/5/06; Rick Lyman, "Census Reports Slight Increase in '05 Incomes," *NY Times* 8/30/06; Micheline Maynard and Nick Bunkley, "Ford is Offering 75,000 Employees Buyout Packages," *NY Times* 9/15/06; Jeremy W. Peters, "Delphi Is Said to Offer Union a One-Time Sweetener," *NY Times* 3/28/06; Joe Sharky, "For the Super-Rich, It's Time to Upgrade the Old Jumbo Jet," *NY Times* 10/17/06; Guy Trebay, "For a Price, Final Resting Place that Tut Would Find Pleasant" *NY Times* 4/17/06.

WHAT'S GOOD FOR WAL-MART

BY JOHN MILLER

"Is Wal-Mart Good for America?"
It is a testament to the public relations of the anti-Wal-Mart campaign that the question above is even being asked.

By any normal measure, Wal-Mart's business ought to be noncontroversial. It sells at low costs, albeit in mind-boggling quantities....

The company's success and size ... do not rest on monopoly profits or price-gouging behavior. It simply sells things people will buy at small markups and, as in the old saw, makes it up on volume.... You may believe, as do service-workers unions and a clutch of coastal elites—many of whom, we'd wager, have never set foot in Wal-Mart—that Wal-Mart "exploits" workers who can't say no to low wages and poor benefits. You might accept the canard that it drives good local businesses into the ground, although both of these allegations are more myth than reality.

But even if you buy into the myths, there's no getting around the fact that somewhere out there, millions of people are spending billions of dollars on what Wal-Mart puts on its shelves. No one is making them do it.... Wal-Mart can't make mom and pop shut down the shop anymore than it can make customers walk through the doors or pull out their wallets.

What about the workers? ... Wal-Mart's average starting wage is already nearly double the national minimum of $5.15 an hour. The company has also recently increased its health-care for employees on the bottom rungs of the corporate ladder.

—Wall Street Journal *editorial, December 3, 2005*

Who's Number One? The Customer! Always!" The last line of Wal-Mart's company cheer just about sums up the *Wall Street Journal* editors' benign view of the behemoth corporation. But a more honest answer would be Wal-Mart itself: not the customer, and surely not the worker.

The first retail corporation to top the Fortune 500, Wal-Mart trailed only Exxon-Mobil in total revenues last year. With 1.6 million workers, 1.3 million in the United States and 300,000 offshore, Wal-Mart is the largest private employer in the nation and the world's largest retailer.

Being number one has paid off handsomely for the family of Wal-Mart founder Sam Walton. The family's combined fortune is now an estimated $90 billion, equal to the net worth of Bill Gates and Warren Buffett combined.

But is what's good for the Walton family good for America? Should we believe the editors that Wal-Mart's unprecedented size and market power have redounded not only to the Walton family's benefit but to ours as well?

LOW WAGES AND MEAGER BENEFITS

Working for the world's largest employer sure hasn't paid off for Wal-Mart's employees. True, they have a job, and others without jobs line up to apply for theirs. But that says more about the sad state of today's labor market than the quality of Wal-Mart jobs. After all, less than half of Wal-Mart workers last a year, and turnover at the company is twice that at comparable retailers.

Why? Wal-Mart's oppressive working conditions surely have something to do with it. Wal-Mart has admitted to using minors to operate hazardous machinery, has been sued in six states for forcing employees to work off the books (i.e., unpaid) and without breaks, and is currently facing a suit brought by 1.6 million current and former female employees accusing Wal-Mart of gender discrimination. At the same time, Wal-Mart workers are paid less and receive fewer benefits than other retail workers.

Wal-Mart, according to its own reports, pays an average of $9.68 an hour. That is 12.4% below the average wage for retail workers even after adjusting for geography, according to a recent study by Arindrajit Dube and Steve Wertheim, economists at the University of California's Institute of Industrial Relations and long-time Wal-Mart researchers. Wal-Mart's wages are nearly 15% below the average wage of workers at large retailers and about 30% below the average wage of unionized grocery workers. The average U.S. wage is $17.80 an hour; Costco, a direct competitor of Wal-Mart's Sam's Club warehouse stores, pays an average wage of $16 an hour (see box on p. 32).

Wal-Mart may be improving its benefits, as the *Journal*'s editors report, but it needs to. Other retailers provide health care coverage to over 53% of their workers, while Wal-Mart covers just 48% of its workers. Costco, once again, does far better, covering 82% of its employees. Moreover, Wal-Mart's coverage is far less comprehensive than the plans offered by other large retailers. Dube reports that according to 2003 IRS data, Wal-Mart paid 59% of the health care costs of its workers and dependents, compared to the 77% of health care costs for individuals and 68% for families the average retailer picks up.

A recent internal Wal-Mart memo leaked to the *New York Times* confirmed the large gaps in Wal-Mart's health care coverage and exposed the high costs those gaps impose on government programs. According to the memo, "Five percent of our Associates are on Medicaid compared to an average for national employees of 4 percent. Twenty-seven percent of Associates' children are on such programs, compared to a national average of 22 percent. In total, 46 percent of Associates' children are either on Medicaid or are uninsured."

A considerably lower 29% of children of all large-retail workers are on Medicaid or are uninsured. Some 7% of the children of employees of large retailers go uninsured, compared to the 19% reported by Wal-Mart.

Wal-Mart's low wages drag down the wages of other retail workers and shutter downtown retail businesses. A 2005 study by David Neumark, Junfu Zhang, and Stephen Ciccarella, economists at the University of California at Irvine, found that Wal-Mart adversely affects employment and wages. Retail workers in a community with a Wal-Mart earned 3.5% less because Wal-Mart's low prices force other businesses to lower prices, and hence their wages, according to the Neumark study. The same study also found that Wal-Mart's presence reduces retail employment by 2% to 4%. While other studies have not found this negative employment effect, Dube's research also reports fewer retail jobs and lower wages for retail workers in metropolitan counties with a Wal-Mart. (Fully 85% of Wal-Mart stores are in metropolitan counties.) Dube figures that Wal-Mart's presence costs retail workers, at Wal-Mart and elsewhere, $4.7 billion a year in lost earnings.

In short, Wal-Mart's "everyday low prices" come at the expense of the compensation of Wal-Mart's own employees and lower wages and fewer jobs for retail workers in the surrounding area. That much remains true no matter what weight we assign to each of the measures that Wal-Mart uses to keep its costs down: a just-in-time inventory strategy, its ability to use its size to pressure suppliers for large discounts, a routinized work environment that requires minimal training, and meager wages and benefits.

HOW LOW ARE WAL-MART'S PRICES?

Even if one doesn't subscribe to the editors' position that it is consumers, not Wal-Mart, who cause job losses at downtown retailers, it is possible to argue that the benefit of Wal-Mart's low prices to consumers, especially low-income consumers, outweighs the cost endured by workers at Wal-Mart and other retailers. Jason Furman, New York University economist and director of economic policy for the 2004 Kerry-Edwards campaign, makes just such an argument. Wal-Mart's "staggering" low prices are 8% to 40% lower than people would pay elsewhere, according to Furman. He calculates that those low prices on average boost low-income families' buying power by 3% and more than offset the loss of earnings to retail workers. For Furman, that makes Wal-Mart "a progressive success story."

But exactly how much savings Wal-Mart affords consumers is far from clear. Estimates vary widely. At one extreme is a study Wal-Mart itself commissioned by Global Insight, an economic forecasting firm. Global Insight estimates Wal-Mart created a stunning savings of $263 billion, or $2,329 per household, in 2004 alone.

At the other extreme, statisticians at the U.S. Bureau of Labor Statistics found no price savings at Wal-Mart. Relying on Consumer Price Index data, the BLS found that Wal-Mart's prices largely matched those of its rivals, and that instances of lower prices at Wal-Mart could be attributed to lower quality products.

Both studies, which rely on the Consumer Price Index and aggregate data, have their critics. Furman himself allows that the Global Insight study is "overly simplistic" and says he "doesn't place as much weight on that one." Jerry Hausman, the M.I.T. economist who has looked closely at Wal-Mart's grocery stores, maintains that the CPI data that the Bureau of Labor Statistics relies on systematically miss the savings offered by "supercenters" such as Wal-Mart. To show the difference between prices at Wal-Mart and at other grocers, Hausman, along with Ephraim Leibtag, USDA Economic Research Service economist, used supermarket scanner data to examine the purchasing patterns of a national sample of 61,500 consumers from 1988 to 2001. Hausman and Leibtag found that Wal-Mart offers many identical food items at an average price about 15%-25% lower than traditional supermarkets.

While Hausman and Leibtag report substantial savings from shopping at Wal-Mart, they fall far short of the savings alleged in the Global Insight study. The Hausman and Leibtag study suggests a savings of around $550 per household per year, or about $56 billion in 2004, not $263 billion. Still, that is considerably more than the $4.7 billion a year in lost earnings to retail workers that Dube attributes to Wal-Mart.

But if "Wal-Mart hurts wages, not so much in retail, but across the whole country," as economist Neumark told *Business Week*, then the savings to consumers from Wal-Mart's everyday low prices might not outweigh the lost wages to all workers. (Retail workers make up just 11.6% of U.S. employment.)

Nor do these findings say anything about the sweatshop conditions and wages in Wal-Mart's overseas subcontractors. One example: A recent Canadian Broadcasting Corporation investigative report found that workers in Bangladesh were being paid less than $50 a month (below even the United Nation's $2 a day measure of poverty) to make clothes for the Wal-Mart private label, Simply Basic. Those workers included 10- to 13-year-old children forced to work long hours in dimly lit and dirty conditions sewing "I Love My Wal-Mart" t-shirts.

MAKING WAL-MART DO BETTER

Nonetheless, as Arindrajit Dube points out, the relevant question is not whether Wal-Mart creates more savings for consumers than losses for workers, but whether the corporation can afford to pay better wages and benefits.

Dube reasons that if the true price gap between Wal-Mart and its retail competitors is small, then Wal-Mart might not be in a position to do better—to make up its wage and benefit gap and still maintain its price advantage. But if Wal-Mart offers consumers only minor price savings, then its lower wages and benefits hardly constitute a progressive success story that's good for the nation.

If Wal-Mart's true price gap is large (say, the 25% price advantage estimated by Hausman), then Wal-Mart surely is in a position to do better. For instance, Dube calculates that closing Wal-Mart's 16% overall compensation gap with other large retailers would cost the company less than 2% of sales. Raising prices by two cents on the dollar to cover those increased compensation costs would be "eminently absorbable," according to Dube, without eating away much of the company's mind-boggling $10 billion profit (2004).

Measures that set standards to force Wal-Mart and all big-box retailers to pay decent wages and provide benefits are beginning to catch on. Chicago, New York City, and the state of Maryland have considered or passed laws that would require big-box retailers to pay a "living wage" or to spend a minimum amount per worker-hour for health benefits. The Republican board of Nassau County on Long Island passed an ordinance requiring that all big-box retailers pay $3 per hour toward health care. Wal-Mart's stake in making sure that such proposals don't become law or spread nationwide goes a long way toward explaining why 80% of Wal-Mart's $2 million in political contributions in 2004 went to Republicans.

Henry Ford sought to pay his workers enough so they could buy the cars they produced. Sam Walton sought to pay his workers so little that they could afford to shop nowhere else. And while what was good for the big automakers was probably never good for the nation, what is good for Wal-Mart, today's largest employer, is undoubtedly bad for economic justice.

Resources: "Is Wal-Mart Good for America?" *Wall Street Journal*, 12/3/05; "Gauging the Wal-Mart Effect," *WSJ*, 12/03/05; Arindrajit Dube & Steve Wertheim, "Wal-Mart and Job Quality—What Do We Know, and Should We Care?" 10/05; Jason Furman, "Wal-Mart: A Progressive Success Story," 10/05; Leo Hindery Jr., "Wal-Mart's Giant Sucking Sound," 10/05; A. Bernstein, "Some Uncomfortable Findings for Wal-Mart," *Business Week Online*, 10/26/05, and "Wal-Mart: A Case for the Defense, Sort of," *Business Week Online*, 11/7/05; Dube, Jacobs, and Wertheim, "The Impact of Wal-Mart Growth on Earnings throughout the Retail Sector in Urban and Rural Counties," *Institute of Industrial Relations Working Paper*, U-C Berkeley, 10/05; Dube, Jacobs, and Wertheim, "Internal Wal-Mart Memo Validates Findings of UC Berkeley Study," 11/26/05; Jerry Hausman and Ephraim Leibtag, "Consumer Benefits from Increased Competition in Shopping Outlets: Measuring the Effect of Wal-Mart," 10/05; Hausman and Leibtag, "CPI Bias from Supercenters: Does the BLS Know that Wal-Mart Exists?" *NBER Working Paper No. 10712*, 8/04; David Neumark, Junfu Zhang, and Stephen Ciccarella, "The Effects of Wal-Mart on Local Labor Markets," *NBER Working Paper No. 11782*, 11/05; Erin Johansson, "Wal-Mart: Rolling Back Workers' Wages, Rights, and the American Dream," (American Rights at Work, 11/05); Wal-Mart Watch, "Spin Cycle"; CBC News, "Wal-Mart to cut ties with Bangladesh factories using child labour," 11/30/05; National Labor Committee, "10 to 13-year-olds Sewing 'I Love My Wal-Mart' Shirts," 12/05; Global Insight. "The Economic Impact of Wal-Mart," 2005.

THE COSTCO ALTERNATIVE? WALL STREET PREFERS WAL-MART

In an April 2004 online commentary, *BusinessWeek* praised Costco's business model but pointed out that Costco's wages cause Wall Street to worry that the company's "operating expenses could get out of hand."

Average Hourly Wage		Percentage of U.S. Workforce in Unions		Employees Covered by Company Health Insurance		Employees Who Leave After One Year	
Wal-Mart	Costco	Wal-Mart	Costco	Wal-Mart	Costco	Sam's Club*	Costco
$9.68	$16.00	0.0%	17.9%	48%	82%	21%	6%

* Sam's Club is the Wal-Mart unit that competes directly with Costco.

How does Costco compare to low-wage Wal-Mart on overhead expenses? At Costco, overhead is 9.8% of revenue; at Wal-Mart, it is 17%. Part of Costco's secret is that its better paid workers are also more efficient: Costco's operating profit per hourly employee is $13,647; each Wal-Mart employee only nets the company $11,039. Wal-Mart also spends more than Costco on hiring and training new employees: each one, according to Rutgers economist Eileen Appelbaum, costs the company $2,500 to $3,500. Appelbaum estimates that Wal-Mart's relatively high turnover costs the company $1.5 to $2 million per year.

Despite Costco's higher efficiency, Wall Street analysts like Deutsche Bank's Bill Dreher complain that "Costco's corporate philosophy is to put its customers first, then its employees, then its vendors, and finally its shareholders. Shareholders get the short end of the stick." Wall Street prefers Wal-Mart's philosopy: executives first, then shareholders, then customers, then vendors, and finally employees.

In 2004, Wal-Mart paid CEO Lee Scott $5.3 million, while a full-time employee making the average wage would have received $20,134. Costco's CEO Jim Senegal received $350,000, while a full-time average employee got $33,280. And *Business Week* intimates that the top job at Costco may be tougher than at Wal-Mart. "Management has to hustle to make the high-wage strategy work. It's constantly looking for ways to repackage goods into bulk items, which reduces labor, speeds up Costco's just-in-time inventory, and boosts sales per square foot. Costco is also savvier … about catering to small shop owners and more affluent customers, who are more likely to buy in bulk and purchase higher-margin goods."

Costco's allegedly more affluent clientele may be another reason that its profit per employee is higher than Wal-Mart's and its overhead costs a lower percentage of revenue. However, Costco pays its employees enough that they could afford to shop there. As the *Business Week* commentary noted, "the low-wage approach cuts into consumer spending and, potentially, economic growth." —*Esther Cervantes*

MEASURES OF POVERTY

BY ELLEN FRANK

Dear Dr. Dollar:

Can you explain how poverty is defined in government statistics? Is this a realistic definition?

—Susan Balok, Savannah, Ga.

Each February, the Census Bureau publishes the federal poverty thresholds—the income levels for different sized households below which a household is defined as living "in poverty." Each August, the bureau reports how many families, children, adults, and senior citizens fell below the poverty threshold in the prior year. As of 2008, the federal poverty thresholds were as follows:

Household Size	Federal Poverty Threshold
1 person	$11,201
2 people	14,417
3 people	17,330
4 people	21,834
5 people	25,694

Using these income levels, the Census Bureau reported that 12.5% percent of U.S. residents and 18.0% of U.S. children lived in poverty in 2007. Black Americans experience poverty at nearly double these rates: 24.5% of all Blacks and 34.5% of Black children live in households with incomes below the poverty line.

The poverty threshold concept was originally devised by Social Security analyst Mollie Orshansky in 1963. Orshansky estimated the cost of an "economy food plan" designed by the Department of Agriculture for "emergency use when funds are low." Working from 1955 data showing that families of three or more spent one-third of their income on food, Orshansky multiplied the food budget by three to calculate the poverty line. Since the early 1960s, the Census Bureau has simply recalculated Orshansky's original figures to account for inflation.

The poverty line is widely regarded as far too low for a household to survive on in most parts of the United States. For one thing, as antipoverty advocates point out, since 1955 the proportion of family budgets devoted to food has fallen from one-third to one-fifth. Families expend far more on nonfood necessities such as child care, health care, transportation, and utilities today than they did 50 years ago, for obvious reasons: mothers entering the work force, suburbanization and greater dependence on the auto, and soaring health care costs, for example. Were Orshansky formulating a poverty threshold more recently, then, she would likely have multiplied a basic food budget by five rather than by three.

Furthermore, costs—particularly for housing and energy—vary widely across the country, so that an income that might be barely adequate in Mississippi is wholly inadequate in Massachusetts. Yet federal poverty figures make no adjustment for regional differences in costs.

A number of state-level organizations now publish their own estimates of what it takes to support a family in their area, in conjunction with the national training and advocacy group Wider Opportunities for Women. Using local data on housing costs, health care premiums, taxes, and child care costs as well as food, transportation and other necessities, these "self-sufficiency standards" estimate that a two-parent two-child family needs between $40,000 and $70,000 a year, depending on the region, to cover basic needs.

State and federal officials often implicitly recognize that official poverty thresholds are unrealistically low by setting income eligibility criteria for antipoverty programs higher than the poverty level. Households with incomes of 125%, 150%, or even 185% of the federal poverty line are eligible for a number of federal and state programs. In addition, the Census Bureau publishes figures on the number of households with incomes below 200% of the federal poverty line—a level many social scientists call "near poor" or "working poor."

Poverty calculations also have critics on the right. Conservative critics contend that the official poverty rate overstates poverty in the United States. While the Census Bureau's poverty-rate calculations include Social Security benefits, public assistance, unemployment and workers' compensation, SSI (disability) payments, and other forms of cash income, they exclude noncash benefits from state and federal antipoverty programs like Food Stamps, Medicaid, and housing subsidies. If the market value of these benefits were counted in family income, fewer families would count as "poor." On the other hand, by not counting such benefits, policy makers have a better grasp of the numbers of Americans in need of such transfer programs.

Resources: For background information on poverty thresholds and poverty rate calculations, see aspe.hhs.gov/poverty/papers/hptgssiv.htm. Self-sufficiency standards for different states can be found at www.sixstrategies.org/states/states.cfm. In addition, the Economic Policy Institute has calculated family budgets for the 435 metropolitan areas: www.epi.org/content/budget_calculator.

ACCESS TO PAID SICK DAYS

BY ELISE GOULD

Just 57% of private-industry workers in the United States have access to paid sick leave; 43% have no paid sick days. When these workers get sick, they are forced either to stay home, without pay and, in many cases, with some risk of losing their job, or else to go to work.

What this number masks, however, is how vastly unequal access to paid sick leave is for workers at different wage levels. Workers at the bottom of the wage scale, those making less than $7.38 an hour, are five times less likely to have sick days than workers at the top of the scale, those making greater than $29.47 an hour. As the figure reveals, only 16% of low-wage workers have access to paid sick days, versus 79% of high-wage workers.

In recent months, legislation has been introduced that would level the playing field and provide much needed paid leave for all workers who are sick. Such legislation—as exists in other advanced economies—would not only give workers an important benefit. Universal paid sick leave could increase productivity by strengthening worker loyalty, decreasing turnover, and cutting down on the number of sick employees who show up to work and infect others.

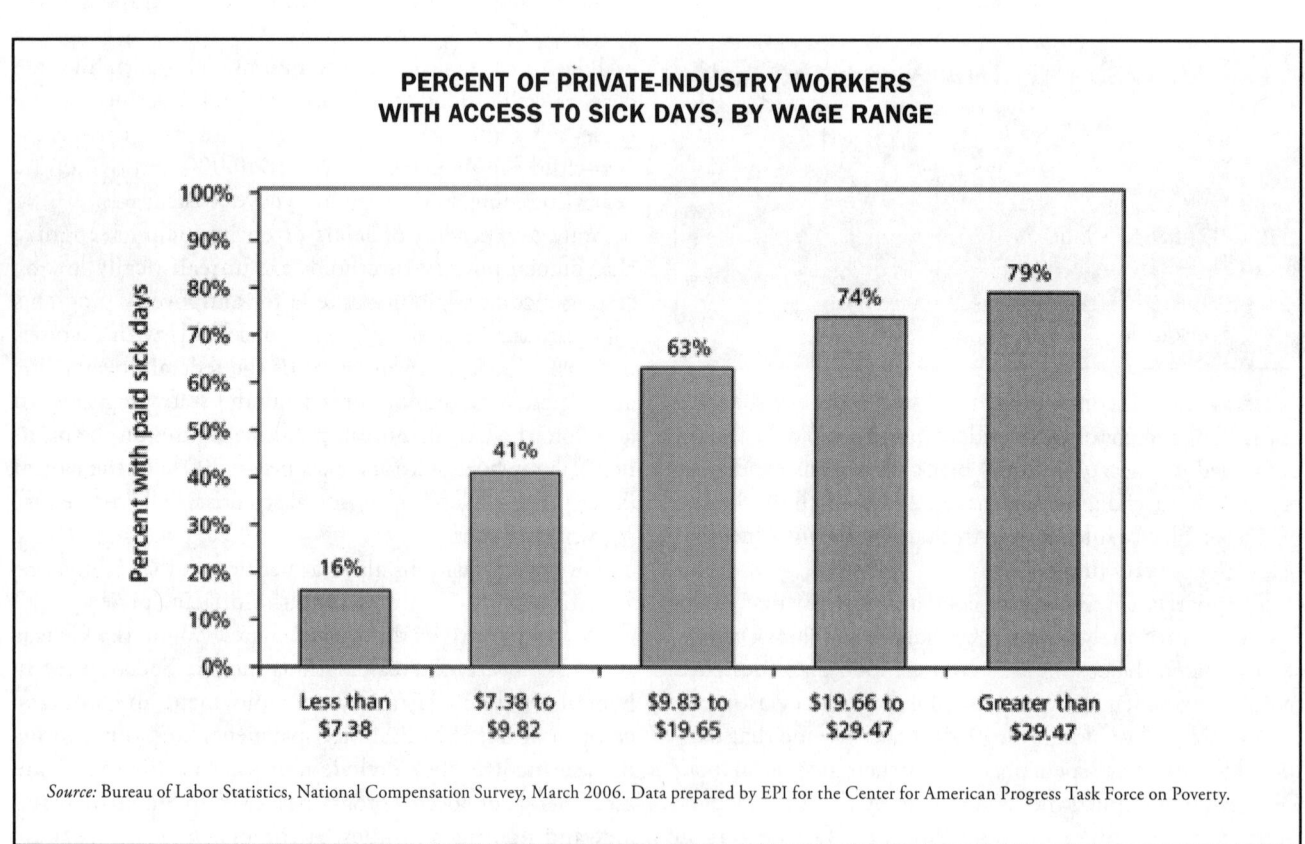

Source: Bureau of Labor Statistics, National Compensation Survey, March 2006. Data prepared by EPI for the Center for American Progress Task Force on Poverty.

ARTICLE 2.5

THE DEATH OF HORATIO ALGER

BY PAUL KRUGMAN

The other day I found myself reading a leftist rag that made outrageous claims about America. It said that we are becoming a society in which the poor tend to stay poor, no matter how hard they work; in which sons are much more likely to inherit the socioeconomic status of their fathers than they were a generation ago.

The name of the leftist rag? *Business Week*, which published an article titled "Waking Up From the American Dream." The article summarizes recent research showing that social mobility in the United States (which was never as high as legend had it) has declined considerably over the past few decades. If you put that research together with other research that shows a drastic increase in income and wealth inequality, you reach an uncomfortable conclusion: America looks more and more like a class-ridden society.

And guess what? Our political leaders are doing everything they can to fortify class inequality, while denouncing anyone who complains—or even points out what is happening—as a practitioner of "class warfare."

Let's talk first about the facts on income distribution. Thirty years ago we were a relatively middle-class nation. It had not always been thus: Gilded Age America was a highly unequal society, and it stayed that way through the 1920s. During the 1930s and '40s, however, America experienced what the economic historians Claudia Goldin and Robert Margo have dubbed the Great Compression: a drastic narrowing of income gaps, probably as a result of New Deal policies. And the new economic order persisted for more than a generation. Strong unions, taxes on inherited wealth, corporate profits and high incomes, and close public scrutiny of corporate management all helped to keep income gaps relatively small. The economy was hardly egalitarian, but a generation ago the gross inequalities of the 1920s seemed very distant.

Now they're back. According to estimates by the economists Thomas Piketty and Emmanuel Saez—confirmed by data from the Congressional Budget Office—between 1973 and 2000 the average real income of the bottom 90% of American taxpayers actually fell by 7%. Meanwhile, the income of the top 1% rose by 148%, the income of the top 0.1% rose by 343% and the income of the top 0.01% rose 599%. (Those numbers exclude capital gains, so they're not an artifact of the stock-market bubble.) The distribution of income in the United States has gone right back to Gilded Age levels of inequality.

Never mind, say the apologists, who churn out papers with titles like that of a 2001 Heritage Foundation piece, "Income Mobility and the Fallacy of Class-Warfare Arguments." America, they say, isn't a caste society—people with high incomes this year may have low incomes next year and vice versa, and the route to wealth is open to all. That's where those commies at *Business Week* come in. As they point out (and as economists and sociologists have been pointing out for some time), America actually is more of a caste society than we like to think. And the caste lines have lately become a lot more rigid.

The myth of income mobility has always exceeded the reality. As a general rule, once they've reached their 30s, people don't move up and down the income ladder very much. Conservatives often cite studies like a 1992 report by Glenn Hubbard, a Treasury official under the elder Bush who later became chief economic adviser to the younger Bush, that purport to show large numbers of Americans moving from low-wage to high-wage jobs during their working lives. But what these studies measure, as the economist Kevin Murphy put it, is mainly "the guy who works in the college bookstore and has a real job by his early 30s." Serious studies that exclude this sort of pseudo-mobility show that inequality in average incomes over long periods isn't much smaller than inequality in annual incomes.

It is true, however, that America was once a place of substantial intergenerational mobility—sons often did much better than their fathers. A classic 1978 survey found that among adult men whose fathers were in the bottom 25% of the population as ranked by social and economic status, 23% had made it into the top 25%. In other words, during the first thirty years or so after World War II, the American dream of upward mobility was a real experience for many people.

Now for the shocker: The *Business Week* piece cites a new survey of today's adult men, which finds that this number has dropped to only 10%. That is, over the past generation upward mobility has fallen drastically. Very few children of the lower class are making their way to even moderate affluence. This goes along with other studies indicating that rags-to-riches stories have become vanishingly rare, and that the correlation between fathers' and sons' incomes has risen in recent decades. In modern America, it seems, you're quite likely to stay in the social and economic class into which you were born.

Business Week attributes this to the "Wal-Martization" of the economy, the proliferation of dead-end, low-wage jobs and the disappearance of jobs that provide entry to the middle class. That's surely part of the explanation. But public policy plays a role—and will, if present trends continue, play an even bigger role in the future.

Put it this way: Suppose that you actually liked a caste society, and you were seeking ways to use your control of the government to further entrench the advantages of the haves against the have-nots. What would you do?

One thing you would definitely do is get rid of the estate tax, so that large fortunes can be passed on to the next generation. More broadly, you would seek to reduce tax rates both on corporate profits and on unearned income such as dividends and capital gains, so that those with large accumulated or inherited wealth could more easily accumulate even more. You'd also try to create tax shelters mainly useful for the rich. And more broadly still, you'd try to reduce tax rates on people with high incomes, shifting the burden to the payroll tax and other revenue sources that bear most heavily on people with lower incomes.

Meanwhile, on the spending side, you'd cut back on healthcare for the poor, on the quality of public education and on state aid for higher education. This would make it more difficult for people with low incomes to climb out of their difficulties and acquire the education essential to upward mobility in the modern economy.

And just to close off as many routes to upward mobility as possible, you'd do everything possible to break the power of unions, and you'd privatize government functions so that well-paid civil servants could be replaced with poorly paid private employees.

IT ALL SOUNDS SORT OF FAMILIAR, DOESN'T IT?
Where is this taking us? Thomas Piketty, whose work with Saez has transformed our understanding of income distribution, warns that current policies will eventually create "a class of rentiers in the U.S., whereby a small group of wealthy but untalented children controls vast segments of the US economy and penniless, talented children simply can't compete." If he's right—and I fear that he is—we will end up suffering not only from injustice, but from a vast waste of human potential.

Goodbye, Horatio Alger. And goodbye, American Dream.

Reprinted with permission from the January 5, 2004 issue of *The Nation*. For subscription information call 1-800-333-8536. Portions of each week's *Nation* Magazine can be accessed at www.thenation.com

---

ARTICLE 2.6

November/December 2006

AMERICA'S GROWING FRINGE ECONOMY

BY HOWARD KARGER

Ron Cook is a department manager at a Wal-Mart store in Atlanta. Maria Guzman is an undocumented worker from Mexico; she lives in Houston with her three children and cleans office buildings at night. Marty Lawson works for a large Minneapolis corporation.* What do these three people have in common? They are all regular fringe economy customers.

The term "fringe economy" refers to a range of businesses that engage in financially predatory relationships with low-income or heavily indebted consumers by charging excessive interest rates, superhigh fees, or exorbitant prices for goods or services. Some examples of fringe economy businesses include payday lenders, pawnshops, check-cashers, tax refund lenders, rent-to-own stores, and "buy-here/pay-here" used car lots. The fringe economy also includes credit card companies that charge excessive late payment or over-the-credit-limit penalties; cell phone providers that force less credit worthy customers into expensive prepaid plans; and subprime mortgage lenders that gouge prospective homeowners.

The fringe economy is hardly new. Pawnshops and informal high-interest lenders have been around forever. What we see today, however, is a fringe-economy sector that is growing fast, taking advantage of the ever-larger part of the U.S. population whose economic lives are becoming less secure. Moreover, in an important sense the sector is no longer "fringe" at all: more and more, large mainstream financial corporations are behind the high-rate loans that anxious customers in run-down storefronts sign for on the dotted line.

THE PAYDAY LENDING TRAP
Ron and Deanna Cook have two children and a combined family income of $48,000—more than twice the federal poverty line but still $10,000 below Georgia's median income. They are the working poor.

To make ends meet, the Cooks borrow from payday lenders. When Ron and Deanna borrow $300 for 14 days they pay $60 in interest—an annual interest rate of 520%! If they can't pay the full $360, they pay just the $60 interest fee and roll over the loan for another two weeks. The original $300 loan now costs $120 in interest for 30 days. If they roll over

---

*The names have been changed to protect the privacy of the individuals.

the loan for another two-week cycle, they pay $180 in interest on a $300 loan for 45 days. If the payday lender permits only four rollovers, the Cooks sometimes take out a payday loan from another lender to repay the original loan. This costly cycle can be devastating. The Center for Responsible Lending tells the tale of one borrower who entered into 35 back-to-back payday loans over 17 months, paying $1,254 in fees on a $300 loan.

The Cooks take out about ten payday loans a year, which is close to the national average for payday loan customers. Although the industry claims payday loans are intended only for emergencies, a 2003 study of Pima County, Ariz., by the Southwest Center for Economic Integrity found that 67% of borrowers used their loans for general non-emergency bills. The Center for Responsible Lending found that 66% of borrowers initiate five or more loans a year, and 31% take out twelve or more loans yearly. Over 90% of payday loans go to borrowers with five or more loans a year. Customers who take out 13 or more loans a year account for over half of payday lenders' total revenues.

THE UNBANKED

Maria Guzman and her family are part of the 10% of U.S. households—more than 12 million—that have no relationship with a bank, savings institution, credit union, or other mainstream financial service provider. Being "unbanked," the Guzmans turn to the fringe economy for check cashing, bill payment, short-term pawn or payday loans, furniture and appliance rentals, and a host of other financial services. In each case, they face high user fees and exorbitant interest rates.

Without credit, the Guzmans must buy a car either for cash or through a "buy-here/pay-here" (BHPH) used car lot. At a BHPH lot they are saddled with a 28% annual percentage rate (APR) on a high-mileage and grossly overpriced vehicle. They also pay weekly, and one missed payment means a repossession. Since the Guzmans have no checking account, they use a check-casher who charges 2.7% for cashing their monthly $1,500 in payroll checks, which costs them $40.50 a month or $486 a year.

Like many immigrants, the Guzmans send money to relatives in their home country. (Money transfers from the United States to Latin America are expected to reach $25 billion by 2010.) If they sent $500 to Mexico on June 26, 2006, using Western Union's "Money in Minutes," they would have paid a $32 transfer fee. Moreover, Western Union's exchange rate for the transaction was 11.12 pesos for the U.S. dollar, while the official exchange rate that day was 11.44. The difference on $500 was almost $14, which raised the real costs of the transaction to $46, or almost 10% of the transfer amount.

Without a checking account, the Guzmans turn to money orders or direct bill pay, both of which add to their financial expenses. For example, ACE Cash Express charges 79 cents per money order and $1 or more for each direct bill payment.

If the Guzmans use money orders to pay six bills a month, the fees total nearly $57 a year; using direct bill pay, they would pay a minimum of $72 in fees per year.

All told, the Guzmans spend more than 10% of their income on alternative financial services, which is average for unbanked households. To paraphrase James Baldwin, it is expensive to be poor and unbanked in America.

The Cooks and the Guzmans, along with people like Marty Lawson caught in a cycle of credit card debt (see sidebar on next page), may not fully appreciate the economic entity they are dealing with. Far from a mom-and-pop industry, America's fringe economy is largely dominated by a handful of large, well-financed multinational corporations with strong ties to mainstream financial institutions. It is a comprehensive and fully formed parallel economy that addresses the financial needs of the poor and credit-challenged in the same way as the mainstream economy meets the needs of the middle class. The main difference is the exorbitant interest rates, high fees, and onerous loan terms that mark fringe economy transactions.

THE SCOPE OF THE FRINGE ECONOMY

The unassuming and often shoddy storefronts of the fringe economy mask the true scope of this economic sector. Check-cashers, payday lenders, pawnshops, and rent-to-own stores alone engaged in at least 280 million transactions in 2001, according to Fannie Mae Foundation estimates, generating about $78 billion in gross revenues. By comparison, in 2003 combined state and federal spending on the core U.S. social welfare programs—Temporary Aid to Needy Families (AFDC's replacement), Supplemental Security Income, Food Stamps, the Women, Infants and Children (WIC) food program, school lunch programs, and the U.S. Department of Housing and Urban Development's (HUD) low-income housing programs—totaled less than $125 billion. Revenues in the combined sectors of the fringe economy—including subprime home mortgages and refinancing, and used car sales—would inflate the $78 billion several times over and eclipse federal and state spending on the poor.

There can be no doubt that the scope of the fringe economy is enormous. The Community Financial Services Association of America claims that 15,000 payday lenders extend more than $25 billion in short-term loans to millions of households each year. According to Financial Service Centers of America, 10,000 check-cashing stores process 180 million checks with a face value of $55 billion.

The sheer number of fringe economy storefronts is mind-boggling. For example, ACE Cash Express—only one of many such corporations—has 68 locations within 10 miles of my Houston zip code. Nationwide there are more than 33,000 check-cashing and payday loan stores, just two parts of the fringe economy. That's more than the all the McDonald's and Burger King restaurants and all the Target, J.C. Penney, and Wal-Mart retail stores in the United States combined.

CREDIT CARDS, COLLEGE STUDENTS, AND THE FRINGE ECONOMY

Marty Lawson is one of the growing legions of the credit poor. Although he earns $65,000 a year, his $50,000 credit card debt means that he can buy little more than the essentials. This cycle of debt began when Marty received his first credit card in college.

Credit cards are the norm for today's college students. A 2005 Nellie Mae report found that 55% of college students get their first credit card during their freshman year; by senior year, 91% have a credit card and 56% carry four or more cards.

College students are highly prized credit card customers because of their high future earnings and lifetime credit potential. To ensnare them, credit card companies actively solicit on campus through young recruiters who staff tables outside university bookstores and student centers. Students are baited with free t-shirts, frisbees, candy, music downloads, and other come-ons. Credit card solicitations are stuffed into new textbooks and sent to dormitories, electronic mailboxes, and bulletin boards. According to Junior Achievement, the typical college freshman gets about eight credit card offers in the first week of the fall semester. The aggressiveness of credit card recruiters has led several hundred colleges to ban them from campus.

Excited by his newfound financial independence, Marty overlooked the fine print explaining that cash advances carried a 20% or more APR. He also didn't realize how easily he could reach the credit limit, and the stiff penalties incurred for late payments and over-the-credit-limit transactions. About one-third of credit card company profits come from these and other penalties.

Marty applied for a second credit card after maxing out his first one. The credit line on his second card was exhausted in only eight months. Facing $4,000 in high-interest credit card bills, Marty left college to pay off his debts. He never returned. Dropping out to repay credit card debt is all too common, and according to former Indiana University administrator John Simpson, "We lose more students to credit card debt than academic failure." Not coincidentally, by graduation the average credit card debt for college seniors is almost $3,000. Credit card debt worsens the longer a student stays in school. A 2004 Nellie Mae survey found the average credit card debt for graduate students was a whopping $7,831, a 59% increase over 1998. Fifteen percent of graduate students carry credit card balances of $15,000 or more.

ACE Cash Express is the nation's largest check-casher and exemplifies the growth and profitability of the fringe economy. In 1991 ACE had 181 stores; by 2005 it had 1,371 stores with 2,700 employees in 37 states and the District of Columbia. ACE's revenues totaled $141 million in 2000 and by 2005 rose to $268.6 million. In 2005 ACE:

- cashed 13.3 million checks worth approximately $5.3 billion (check cashing fees totaled $131.6 million);
- served more than 40 million customers (3.4 million a month or 11,000 an hour) and processed $10.3 billion in transactions;
- processed over 2 million loan transactions (worth $640 million) and generated interest income and fees of $91.8 million;
- added a total of 142 new locations (in 2006 the company anticipates adding 150 more);
- processed over $410 million in money transfers and 7.6 million money orders with a face value of $1.3 billion;
- processed over 7.8 million bill payment and debit card transactions, and sold approximately 172,000 prepaid debit cards.

Advance America is the nation's leading payday lender, with 2,640 stores in 36 states, more than 5,500 employees, and $630 million this year in revenues. Dollar Financial Corporation operates 1,106 stores in 17 states, Canada, and the United Kingdom. Their 2005 revenues were $321 million. Check-into-Cash has more than 700 stores; Check N' Go has 900 locations in 29 states. Almost all of these are publicly traded NASDAQ corporations.

There were 4,500 pawnshops in the United States in 1985; now there are almost 12,000, including outlets owned by five publicly traded chains. In 2005 the three big chains—Cash America International (a.k.a Cash America Pawn and SuperPawn), EZ Pawn, and First Cash—had combined annual revenues of nearly $1 billion. Cash America is the largest pawnshop chain, with 750 locations; the company also makes payday loans through its Cash America Payday Advance, Cashland, and Mr. Payroll stores. In 2005, Cash America's revenues totaled $594.3 million.

The Association of Progressive Rental Organizations claims that the $6.6 billion a year rent-to-own (RTO) industry serves 2.7 million households through 8,300 stores in 50 states. Many RTOs rent everything from furniture, electronics, major appliances, and computers to jewelry. Rent-A-Center is the largest RTO corporation in the world. In 2005 it employed 15,000 people; owned or operated 3,052 stores in the United States and Canada; and had revenues of $2.4 billion. Other leading RTO chains include Aaron Rents (with 1,255 stores across the United States and Canada and gross revenues of $1.1 billion in 2005) and RentWay (with 788 stores in 34 states and revenues of almost $516 million in 2005).

These corporations represent the tip of the iceberg. Low-income consumers spent $1.75 billion for tax refund loans in 2002. Many lost as much as 16% of their tax refunds because of expensive tax preparation fees and/or interest incurred in tax refund anticipation loans. The interest and fees on such loans can translate into triple-digit annualized interest rates, according to the Consumer Federation of America, which has also reported that 11 million tax filers received refund anticipation loans in 2000, almost half through H&R Block. According to a Brookings Institution report, the nation's largest tax preparers earned about $357 million from fringe economy "fast cash" products in 2001, more than double their earnings in 1998. All for essentially lending people their own money!

The fringe economy plays a big role in the housing market, where subprime home mortgages rose from 35,000 in 1994 to 332,000 in 2003, a 25% a year growth rate and a tenfold increase in just nine years. (A subprime loan is a loan extended to less creditworthy customers at a rate that is higher than the prime rate.) According to Edward Gramlich, former member of the Board of Governors of the Federal Reserve System, subprime mortgages accounted for almost $300 billion or 9% of all mortgages in 2003.

While the fringe economy squeezes its customers, it is generous to its CEOs. According to Forbes, salaries in many fringe economy corporations rival those in much larger companies. In 2004 Sterling Brinkley, chairman of EZ Corp, earned $1.26 million; ACE's CEO Jay Shipowitz received $2.1 million on top of $2.38 million in stocks; Jeffrey Weiss, Dollar Financial Group's CEO, earned $1.83 million; Mark Speese, Rent-A-Center's CEO, made $820,000 with total stock options of $10 million; and Cash America's CEO Daniel Feehan was paid almost $2.2 million in 2003 plus the $9 million he had in stock options.

Fringe-economy corporations argue that the high interest rates and fees they charge reflect the heightened risks of doing business with an economically unstable population. While fringe businesses have never made their pricing criteria public, some risks are clearly overstated. For example, ACE assesses the risk of each check-cashing transaction and reports losses of less than 1%. Since tax preparers file a borrower's taxes, they are reasonably assured that refund anticipation loans will not exceed refunds. To further guarantee repayment, they often establish an escrow account into which the IRS directly deposits the tax refund check. Pawnshops lend only about 50% of a pawned item's value, which leaves them a large buffer if the pawn goes unclaimed (industry trade groups claim that 70% of customers do redeem their goods). The rent-to-own furniture and appliance industry charges well above the "street price" for furniture and appliances, which is more than enough to offset any losses. Payday lenders require a post-dated check or electronic debit to assure repayment. Payday loan losses are about 6% or less, according to the Center for Responsible Lending.

Much of the profit in the fringe economy comes from financing rather than the sale of a product. For example, if a used car lot buys a vehicle for $3,000 and sells it for $5,000 cash, their profit is $2,000. But if they finance that vehicle for two years at a 25% APR, the profit jumps to $3,242. This dynamic is true for virtually every sector of the fringe economy. A customer who pays off a loan or purchases a good or service outright is much less profitable for fringe economy businesses than customers who maintain an ongoing financial relationship with the business. In that sense, profit in the fringe economy lies with keeping customers continually enmeshed in an expensive web of debt.

FUNDING AND EXPORTING AMERICA'S FRINGE ECONOMY

Fringe economy corporations require large amounts of capital to fund their phenomenal growth, and mainstream financial institutions have stepped up to the plate. ACE Cash Express has a relationship with a group of banks including Wells Fargo, JP Morgan Chase Bank, and JP Morgan Securities to provide capital for acquisitions and other activities. Advance America has relationships with Morgan Stanley, Banc of America Securities LLC, Wachovia Capital Markets, and Wells Fargo Securities, to name a few. Similar banking relationships exist throughout the fringe economy.

The fringe economy is no longer solely a U.S. phenomenon. In 2003 the HSBC Group purchased Household International (and its subsidiary Beneficial Finance) for $13 billion. Headquartered in London, HSBC is the world's second largest bank and serves more than 90 million customers in 80 countries. Household International is a U.S.-based consumer finance company with 53 million customers and more than 1,300 branches in 45 states. It is also a predatory lender. In 2002, a $484 million settlement was reached between Household and all 50 states and the District of Columbia. In effect, Household acknowledged it had duped tens of thousands of low-income home buyers into loans with unnecessary hidden costs. In 2003, another $100 million settlement was reached based on Household's abusive mortgage lending practices.

HSBC plans to export Household's operations to Poland, China, Mexico, Britain, France, India, and Brazil, for starters. One shudders to think how the fringe economy will develop in nations with even fewer regulatory safeguards than the United States. Presumably, HSBC also believes that predatory lending will not tarnish the reputation of the seven British lords and one baroness who sit on its 20-member board of directors.

WHAT CAN BE DONE?

The fringe economy is one of the few venues that credit-challenged or low-income families can turn to for financial help. This is especially true for those facing a penurious welfare system with a lifetime benefit cap and few mechanisms for emergency assistance. In that sense, enforcing strident usury and banking laws to curb the fringe economy while providing no legal and accessible alternatives would hurt the very people such laws are intended to help by driving these transactions into a criminal underground.

A GLOSSARY OF THE FRINGE ECONOMY

Payday loans are small, short-term loans, usually of no more than $1,500, to cover expenses until the borrower's next payday. These loans come with extremely high interests rates, commonly equivalent to 300% APR. The Center for Responsible Lending conservatively estimates that predatory payday lending practices cost American families $3.4 billion annually.

Refund anticipation loans (RALs), provided by outlets of such firms as H&R Block, Western Union, and Liberty Tax Service, are short-term loans, often with high interest rates or fees, secured by an expected tax refund. Interest rates can reach over 700% APR-equivalent.

Check cashing stores (ACE Cash Express is the biggest chain) provide services for people who don't have checking accounts. These stores are most often located in low-income neighborhoods and cash checks for a fee, which can vary greatly but is typically far higher than commercial banks charge for the same service. Check cashing fees have steadily increased over the past ten years.

Money transfer companies (outlets of such companies as Western Union, Moneygram, and Xoom) allow people to make direct bill payments and send money either to a person or bank account for a fee, typically 10% of the amount being sent, not including the exchange rate loss for money sent internationally. the total cost can reach up to 25% of the amount sent.

Pawnshops give loans while holding objects of value as collateral. The pawnbroker returns the object when the loan is repaid, usually at a high interest rates. If the borrower doesn't repay the loan within a specified period, the pawnbroker sells the item. For example, the interest charge on a 30-day loan of $10 could be $2.20, equivalent to a 264% APR. Most pawnshops are individually owned but regional chains are now appearing.

Rent-to-own (RTO) stores—two leading chains are Rent-A-Center and Aaron Rents—rent furniture, electronics, and other consumer goods short-term or long-term. The consumer can eventually own the item after paying many times the standard retail price through weekly rental payments with an extremely high interest rate, commonly around 300% APR. If the consumer misses a payment, the item is repossessed.

Buy here/pay here (BHPH) car lots offer car loans on used cars on-site, with interest rates much higher than auto loans issued by commercial banks. Customers are often saddled with high-interest loans for high-mileage, overpriced vehicles. If a customer misses one payment, the car is repossessed. The largest BHPH company is the J.D. Byrider franchise, with 124 dealerships throughout the country.

—Barbara Sternal

Instead of ending up in court, non-paying debtors would wind up in the hospital. Simply outlawing a demand-driven industry is rarely successful.

One strategy to limit the growth of the fringe economy is to develop more community-based lending institutions modeled on the Grameen Bank or on local cooperatives. Although community banks might charge a higher interest rate than commercial banks charge prime rate customers, the rates would still be significantly lower than in the existing fringe sector.

Another policy option is to make work pay, or at least make it pay better. In other words, we need to increase the minimum wage and the salaries of the lower middle class and working poor. One reason for the rapid growth of the fringe economy is the growing gap between low and stagnant wages and higher prices, especially for necessities like housing, health care, pharmaceuticals, and energy.

Stricter usury laws, better enforcement of existing banking regulations, and a more active federal regulatory system to protect low-income consumers can all play a role in taming the fringe economy. Concurrently, federal and state governments can promote the growth of non-predatory community banking institutions. In addition, commercial banks can provide low-income communities with accessible and inexpensive banking services. As the "DrillDown" studies conducted in recent years by the Washington, D.C., non-profit Social Compact suggest, low-income communities contain more income and resources than one might think. If fringe businesses can make billions in low-income neighborhoods, less predatory economic institutions should be able to profit there too. Lastly, low and stagnant wages make it difficult, if not impossible, for the working poor to make ends meet without resorting to debt. A significant increase in wages would likely result in a significant decline in the fringe economy. In the end, several concerted strategies will be required to restrain this growing and out-of-control economic beast.

Resources: "2003 Credit Card Usage Analysis" (2004) and "Undergraduate Students and Credit Cards in 2004" (2005) (Nellie Mae); Alan Berube, Anne Kim, Benjamin Forman, and Megan Burns, "The Price of Paying Taxes: How Tax Preparation and

Refund Loan Fees Erode the Benefits of the EITC" (Brookings Institution and Progressive Policy Institute, May 2002); James H. Carr and Jenny Shuetz, "Financial Services in Distressed Communities: Framing the Issue, Finding Solutions," Financial Services in Distressed Communities: Issues and Answers (2001, Fannie Mae Foundation); "Making the Case for Financial Literacy: A Collection of Current Statistics Regarding Youth and Money" (Junior Achievement); Amanda Sapir and Karen Uhlich, "Pay Day Lending in Pima County Arizona" (Southwest Center for Economic Integrity, 2003); Keith Urnst, John Farris, and Uriah King, "Quantifying the Economic Cost of Predatory Payday Lending" (Center for Responsible Lending, 2004).Organizations working on these issues include U.S. Public Interest Research Group, www.uspirg.org; Association of Community Organizations for Reform Now (ACORN), www.acorn.org; Coalition for Responsible Credit Practices, www.responsible-credit.net; Community Financial Services Association of America, www.cfsa.net; Consumer Federation of America, www.consumerfed.org; Harvard University, Joint Center for Housing Studies, www.jchs.harvard.edu; National Consumer Law Center, www.consumerlaw.org.

ARTICLE 2.7

GEESE, GOLDEN EGGS, AND TRAPS
WHY INEQUALITY IS BAD FOR THE ECONOMY

BY CHRIS TILLY

Whenever progressives propose ways to redistribute wealth from the rich to those with low and moderate incomes, conservative politicians and economists accuse them of trying to kill the goose that lays the golden egg. The advocates of unfettered capitalism proclaim that inequality is good for the economy because it promotes economic growth. Unequal incomes, they say, provide the incentives necessary to guide productive economic decisions by businesses and individuals. Try to reduce inequality, and you'll sap growth. Furthermore, the conservatives argue, growth actually promotes equality by boosting the have-nots more than the haves. So instead of fiddling with who gets how much, the best way to help those at the bottom is to pump up growth.

But these conservative prescriptions are absolutely, dangerously wrong. Instead of the goose-killer, equality turns out to be the goose. Inequality stifles growth; equality gooses it up. Moreover, economic expansion does not necessarily promote equality—instead, it is the types of jobs and the rules of the economic game that matter most.

INEQUALITY: GOOSE OR GOOSE-KILLER?

The conservative argument may be wrong, but it's straightforward. Inequality is good for the economy, conservatives say, because it provides the right incentives for innovation and economic growth. First of all, people will only have the motivation to work hard, innovate, and invest wisely if the economic system rewards them for good economic choices and penalizes bad ones. Robin Hood-style policies that collect from the wealthy and help those who are worse off violate this principle. They reduce the payoff to smart decisions and lessen the sting of dumb ones. The result: people and companies are bound to make less efficient decisions. "We must allow [individuals] to fail, as well as succeed, and we must replace the nanny state with a regime of self-reliance and self-respect," writes conservative lawyer Stephen Kinsella in The Freeman: Ideas on Liberty (not clear how the free woman fits in). To prove their point, conservatives point to the former state socialist countries, whose economies had become stagnant and inefficient by the time they fell at the end of the 1980s.

If you don't buy this incentive story, there's always the well-worn trickle-down theory. To grow, the economy needs productive investments: new offices, factories, computers, and machines. To finance such investments takes a pool of savings. The rich save a larger fraction of their incomes than those less well-off. So to spur growth, give more to the well-heeled (or at least take less away from them in the form of taxes), and give less to the down-and-out. The rich will save their money and then invest it, promoting growth that's good for everyone.

Unfortunately for trickle-down, the brilliant economist John Maynard Keynes debunked the theory in his *General Theory of Employment, Interest, and Money* in 1936. Keynes, whose precepts guided liberal U.S. economic policy from the 1940s through the 1970s, agreed that investments must be financed out of savings. But he showed that most often it's changes in investment that drive savings, rather than the other way around. When businesses are optimistic about the future and invest in building and retooling, the economy booms, all of us make more money, and we put some of it in banks, 401(k)s, stocks, and so on. That is, saving grows to match investment. When companies are glum, the process runs in reverse, and savings shrink to equal investment. This leads to the "paradox of thrift": if people try to save too much, businesses will see less consumer spending, will invest less, and total savings will end up diminishing rather than growing as the economy spirals downward. A number of Keynes's followers added the next logical step: shifting money from the high-saving rich to the high-spending rest of us, and not the other way around, will spur investment and growth.

Of the two conservative arguments in favor of inequality, the incentive argument is a little weightier. Keynes himself agreed that people needed financial consequences to steer their actions, but questioned whether the differences in payoffs needed to be so huge. Certainly state socialist countries' attempts to replace material incentives with moral exhortation have often fallen short. In 1970, the Cuban government launched the Gran Zafra (Great Harvest), an attempt to reap 10 million tons of sugar cane with (strongly encouraged) volunteer labor. Originally inspired by Che Guevara's ideal of the New Socialist Man (not clear how the New Socialist Woman fit in), the effort ended with Fidel Castro tearfully apologizing to the Cuban people in a nationally broadcast speech for letting wishful thinking guide economic policy.

But before conceding this point to the conservatives, let's look at the evidence about the connection between equality and growth. Economists William Easterly of New York University and Gary Fields of Cornell University have recently summarized this evidence:

- Countries, and regions within countries, with more equal incomes grow faster. (These growth figures do not include environmental destruction or improvement. If they knocked off points for environmental destruction and added points for environmental improvement, the correlation between equality and growth would be even stronger, since desperation drives poor people to adopt environmentally destructive practices such as rapid deforestation.)
- Countries with more equally distributed land grow faster.
- Somewhat disturbingly, more ethnically homogeneous countries and regions grow faster—presumably because there are fewer ethnically based inequalities.

In addition, more worker rights are associated with higher rates of economic growth, according to Josh Bivens and Christian Weller, economists at two Washington think tanks, the Economic Policy Institute and the Center for American Progress.

These patterns recommend a second look at the incentive question. In fact, more equality can actually *strengthen* incentives and opportunities to produce.

EQUALITY AS THE GOOSE

Equality can boost growth in several ways. Perhaps the simplest is that study after study has shown that farmland is more productive when cultivated in small plots. So organizations promoting more equal distribution of land, like Brazil's Landless Workers' Movement, are not just helping the landless poor—they're contributing to agricultural productivity!

Another reason for the link between equality and growth is what Easterly calls "match effects," which have been highlighted in research by Stanford's Paul Roemer and others in recent years. One example of a match effect is the fact that well-educated people are most productive when working with others who have lots of schooling. Likewise, people working with computers are more productive when many others have computers (so that, for example, e-mail communication is widespread, and know-how about computer repair and software is easy to come by). In very unequal societies, highly educated, computer-using elites are surrounded by majorities with little education and no computer access, dragging down their productivity. This decreases young people's incentive to get more education and businesses' incentive to invest in computers, since the payoff will be smaller.

Match effects can even matter at the level of a metropolitan area. Urban economist Larry Ledebur looked at income and employment growth in 85 U.S. cities and their neighboring suburbs. He found that where the income gap between those in the suburbs and those in the city was largest, income and job growth was slower for everyone.

"Pressure effects" also help explain why equality sparks growth. Policies that close off the low-road strategy of exploiting poor and working people create pressure effects, driving economic elites to search for investment opportunities that pay off by boosting productivity rather than squeezing the have-nots harder. For example, where workers have more rights, they will place greater demands on businesses. Business owners will respond by trying to increase productivity, both to remain profitable even after paying higher wages, and to find ways to produce with fewer workers. The CIO union drives in U.S. mass production industries in the 1930s and 1940s provide much of the explanation for the superb productivity growth of the 1950s and 1960s. (The absence of pressure effects may help explain why many past and present state socialist countries have seen slow growth, since they tend to offer numerous protections for workers but no right to organize independent unions.) Similarly, if a government buys out large land-holdings in order to break them up, wealthy families who simply kept their fortunes tied up in land for generations will look for new, productive investments. Industrialization in Asian "tigers" South Korea and Taiwan took off in the 1950s on the wings of funds freed up in exactly this way.

INEQUALITY, CONFLICT, AND GROWTH

Inequality hinders growth in another important way: it fuels social conflict. Stark inequality in countries such as Bolivia and Haiti has led to chronic conflict that hobbles economic growth. Moreover, inequality ties up resources in unproductive uses such as paying for large numbers of police and security guards—attempts to prevent individuals from redistributing resources through theft.

Ethnic variety is connected to slower growth because, on the average, more ethnically diverse countries are also more likely to be ethnically divided. In other words, the problem isn't ethnic variety itself, but racism and ethnic conflict that can exist among diverse populations. In nations like Guatemala, Congo, and Nigeria, ethnic strife has crippled growth—a problem alien to ethnically uniform Japan and South Korea. The reasons are similar to some of the reasons that large class divides hurt growth. Where ethnic divisions (which can take tribal, language, religious, racial, or regional forms) loom large, dominant ethnic groups seek to use government power to better themselves at the expense of other groups, rather than making broad-based investments in education and infrastructure. This can involve keeping down the underdogs—slower growth in the U.S. South for much of the country's history was linked to the Southern system of white supremacy. Or it can involve seizing the surplus of ethnic groups perceived as better off—in the extreme, Nazi Germany's expropriation and genocide of the Jews, who often held professional and commercial jobs.

Of course, the solution to such divisions is not "ethnic cleansing" so that each country has only one ethnic group—in addition to being morally abhorrent, this is simply impossible in a world with 191 countries and 5,000 ethnic groups. Rather, the solution is to diminish ethnic inequalities. Once the 1964 Civil Rights Act forced the South to drop racist laws, the New South's economic growth spurt began. Easterly reports that in countries with strong rule of law, professional bureaucracies, protection of contracts, and freedom from expropriation—all rules that make it harder for one ethnic group to economically oppress another—ethnic diversity has no negative impact on growth.

If more equality leads to faster growth so everybody benefits, why do the rich typically resist redistribution? Looking at the ways that equity seeds growth helps us understand why. The importance of pressure effects tells us that the wealthy often don't think about more productive ways to invest or reorganize their businesses until they are forced to. But also, if a country becomes very unequal, it can get stuck in an "inequality trap." Any redistribution involves a tradeoff for the rich. They lose by giving up part of their wealth, but they gain a share in increased economic growth. The bigger the disparity between the rich and the rest, the more the rich have to lose, and the less likely that the equal share of boosted growth they'll get will make up for their loss. Once the gap goes beyond a certain point, the wealthy have a strong incentive to restrict democracy, and to block spending on education which might lead the poor to challenge economic injustice—making reform that much harder.

DOES ECONOMIC GROWTH REDUCE INEQUALITY?

If inequality isn't actually good for the economy, what about the second part of the conservatives' argument—that growth itself promotes equality? According to the conservatives, those who care about equality should simply pursue growth and wait for equality to follow.

"A rising tide lifts all boats," President John F. Kennedy famously declared. But he said nothing about which boats will rise fastest when the economic tide comes in. Growth does typically reduce poverty, according to studies reviewed by economist Gary Fields, though some "boats"—especially families with strong barriers to participating in the labor force—stay "stuck in the mud." But inequality can increase at the same time that poverty falls, if the rich gain even faster than the poor do. True, sustained periods of low unemployment, like that in the late 1990s United States, do tend to raise wages at the bottom even faster than salaries at the top. But growth after the recessions of 1991 and 2001 began with years of "jobless recoveries"—growth with inequality.

For decades the prevailing view about growth and inequality within countries was that expressed by Simon Kuznets in his 1955 presidential address to the American Economic Association. Kuznets argued that as countries grew, inequality would first increase, then decrease. The reason is that people will gradually move from the low-income agricultural sector to higher-income industrial jobs—with inequality peaking when the workforce is equally divided between low- and high-income sectors. For mature industrial economies, Kuznets's proposition counsels focusing on growth, assuming that it will bring equity. In developing countries, it calls for enduring current inequality for the sake of future equity and prosperity.

But economic growth doesn't automatically fuel equality. In 1998, economists Klaus Deininger and Lyn Squire traced inequality and growth over time in 48 countries. Five followed the Kuznets pattern, four followed the reverse pattern (decreasing inequality followed by an increase), and the rest showed no systematic pattern. In the United States, for example:

- incomes became more equal during the 1930s through 1940s New Deal period (a time that included economic decline followed by growth)
- from the 1950s through the 1970s, income gaps lessened during booms and expanded during slumps
- from the late 1970s forward, income inequality worsened fairly consistently, whether the economy was stagnating or growing.

The reasons are not hard to guess. The New Deal introduced widespread unionization, a minimum wage, social security, unemployment insurance, and welfare. Since the late 1970s, unions have declined, the inflation-adjusted value of the minimum wage has fallen, and the social safety net has been shredded. In the United States, as elsewhere, growth only promotes equality if policies and institutions to support equity are in place.

TRAPPED?

Let's revisit the idea of an inequality trap. The notion is that as the gap between the rich and everybody else grows wider, the wealthy become more willing to give up overall growth in return for the larger share they're getting for themselves.

The "haves" back policies to control the "have-nots," instead of devoting social resources to educating the poor so they'll be more productive.

Sound familiar? It should. After two decades of widening inequality, the last few years have brought us massive tax cuts that primarily benefit the wealthiest, at the expense of investment in infrastructure and the education, child care, and income supports that would help raise less well-off kids to be productive adults. Federal and state governments have cranked up expenditures on prisons, police, and "homeland security," and Republican campaign organizations have devoted major resources to keeping blacks and the poor away from the polls. If the economic patterns of the past are any indication, we're going to pay for these policies in slower growth and stagnation unless we can find our way out of this inequality trap.

ARTICLE 2.8

TRANSFORMING THE ENGINES OF INEQUALITY

BY WILLIAM GREIDER

American politics has always involved a struggle between "organized money" and "organized people." It's a neglected truth that has resurfaced with ironic vengeance in our own time—ironic because the 20th century produced so much progress toward political equality among citizens, and because the emergence of a prosperous and well-educated middle class was expected to neutralize the overbearing political power of concentrated wealth. Instead, Americans are reminded, almost any time they read a newspaper, that the rich do indeed get richer and that our political system is, as Greg Palast put it, "the best democracy money can buy."

What should we make of this retrogressive turn—a nation of considerable abundance still ruled by gilded-age privilege? A cynic would say it was ever thus, end of story. Political commentators argue it's a sign of the country's maturation that its citizens now accept what they once resisted—gross and growing inequalities of wealth. And many economists simply avert their gaze from the troubling consequences of maldistribution for economic progress and the well-being of society.

I stake out a contrary claim: The United States remains an unfinished nation—stunted in its proclaimed values—so long as it fails to confront the enduring contradictions between wealth and democracy. That is not a utopian lament for radical change, but simply an observation of what our own era has taught us.

Inequality retains its crippling force over society and politics and the lives of citizens, despite the broader distribution of material comforts. We are not the nation of 80 or 100 years ago, when most Americans struggled in very modest circumstances, often severe deprivation. Yet, despite the nation's wealth (perhaps also because of it), the influence of concentrated economic power has grown stronger and more intimate in our lives. Today the social contract is determined more by the needs and demands of corporations and finance than by government or the consensual will of the people.

The federal government and several generations of liberal and labor reformers did achieve great, life-improving gains during the last century. But those reforms and redistributive programs did not succeed in altering the root sources of economic inequality, much less taming them. On the contrary, the U.S. economic system recreates and even expands the maldistribution of incomes and wealth in each new generation.

The root sources of inequality are located within the institutions of advanced capitalism—in the corporation and financial system—with their narrow operating values and the peculiar arrangements that consign enormous decision-making power to a remarkably small number of people. The problem of inequality is essentially a problem of malformed power relationships: Advanced capitalism deprives most people of voice and influence, while it concentrates top-down authority among the insiders of finance and business. Ameliorative interventions by government (for example, through regulation, taxation, and reform) have never succeeded in overcoming the tendency within capitalism toward increased concentrations of economic power.

The drive for greater equality must involve governmental actions, of course, but it cannot succeed unless it also confronts the engines of inequality within the private realm and forces deep changes in how American capitalism functions. The challenge is nothing less than to rearrange power relationships within the corporation and finance capital.

Who has the power to restructure capitalist institutions? In my view, ordinary people do—at least potentially—acting collectively as workers, investors, consumers, managers or owners and, above all, as citizens, to force change.

Many are, in small and different ways, already at work on the task of reinventing capitalism.

TRANSFORMING THE WORKPLACE

The workplace is perhaps the most effective engine of inequality, since it teaches citizens resignation and subservience, while it also maldistributes the returns of enterprise. For most Americans, the employment system functions on the archaic terms of the master-servant relationship inherited from feudalism. The feudal lord commanded the lives and livelihoods of serfs on his land and expelled those who disobeyed. The corporate employer has remarkably similar powers, restrained only by the limited prohibitions in law or perhaps by the terms of a union contract. Elaine Bernard, director of Harvard's trade union studies program, described the blunt reality:

> As power is presently distributed, workplaces are factories of authoritarianism polluting our democracy. Citizens cannot spend eight hours a day obeying orders and being shut out of important decisions affecting them, and then be expected to engage in a robust, critical dialogue about the structure of our society.

Where did people learn to accept their powerlessness? They learned it at work. Nor is this stunted condition confined to assembly lines and working-class occupations. The degradation of work now extends very far up the job ladder, including even well-educated professionals whose expert judgments have been usurped by distant management systems.

In most firms, only the insiders at the top of a very steep command-and-control pyramid will determine how the economic returns are distributed among the participants. Not surprisingly, the executives value their own work quite generously while regarding most of the employees below as mere commodities or easily interchangeable parts. More importantly, these insiders will harvest the new wealth generated by an enterprise, while most workers will not. In the long run, this arrangement of power guarantees the permanence of wealth inequalities.

Joseph Cabral, CEO of Chatsworth Products Inc., a successful employee-owned computer systems manufacturer in California, is an accountant, not a political philosopher, but he understands the wealth effects of closely held control in private businesses. "The wealth that's created ends up in too few hands," he said. "The entrepreneur who's fortunate enough to be there at the start ends up really receiving a disproportionate amount of wealth. And the working folks who enabled that success to take place share in little of that wealth. At some point, capitalism is going to burst because we haven't done right for the folks who have actually created that wealth."

But there are other, more democratic, ways to structure the work environment. At Chatsworth, where the workers collectively purchased the enterprise, "Everyone is sharing in the wealth they're creating. ... We're not just doing this for some outside shareholder. We're doing it because we are the shareholders."

Employee ownership, worker-management, and other systems of worker self-organization provide a plausible route toward reforming workplace power relations and spreading financial wealth among the many instead of the few.

TRANSFORMING FINANCE CAPITAL

The top-down structure of how Wall Street manages "other people's money" ensures the maldistribution of financial returns. As wealthy people know, those who bring major money to the table are given direct influence over their investments and a greater return on their risk-taking. The rank-and-file investors—because their savings are modest and they lack trustworthy intermediaries to speak for them—are regarded as passive and uninformed, treated more or less like "widows and orphans," and blocked from exerting any influence over how their wealth is invested. To put the point more crudely, the stock market is a casino, and the herd of hapless investors is always the "mark."

Nevertheless, finance capital is, I predict, the realm of capitalism most vulnerable to reform pressures. That's mainly because it operates with other people's money, and most of that money belongs not to the wealthiest families but to the broad ranks of ordinary working people. A historic shift in the center of gravity has occurred in U.S. finance over the past decade: Fiduciary institutions like pension funds and mutual funds have eclipsed individual wealth as the largest owner of financial assets. Their collectivized assets now include 60% of the largest 1,000 corporations. Because these funds invest across the broad stock market, they literally own the economy.

Public pension funds, union-managed pension funds, and shareholder activists are already working to forge an engaged voice for the individuals whose wealth is in play, and to force the fiduciary institutions to take responsibility for the social and environmental effects of how these trillions in savings are invested. The collapse of the stock-market bubble and subsequent corporate scandals have accelerated these reform efforts.

Some of the largest public-employee pension funds including the California Public Employees' Retirement System and the New York State public employees fund, joined by state officials who sit on supervisory boards, are aggressively leading the fight for corporate-governance reform and for stricter social accountability on urgent matters like workers' rights and global warming. The labor movement is organizing proxy battles to press for corporate reforms at individual companies including the Disney Corporation and Royal Dutch Shell, while the AFL's Office of Investment won a victory for mutual-fund investors in early 2003 when it persuaded the Securities and Exchange Commission to require mutual funds to disclose their proxy votes in corporate-governance shareholder fights. (The mutual fund industry is working to resist the measure, and for good reason. Investment firms regularly vote against the interests of their own rank-and-file investors in order to curry favor with the corporations that hire them to manage corporate-run pension funds and 401(k) plans.)

The major banks and brokerages cannot brush aside these new critics as easily as corporate directors often do. Wall Street will respond to fiduciary concerns because it must. It needs the rank-and-file's capital to operate. When six or seven major funds, collectively holding nearly $1 trillion, speak to Wall Street, things do change. Their unspoken threat to scorn companies or financial firms that ignore larger social obligations and shift their money elsewhere sends broad shockwaves across both financial markets and corporate boardrooms.

The more profound tasks are to challenge fraudulent economic valuations (think Enron) and to account for (and internalize) the true costs of products and production processes. Both steps would refocus capital investing toward creating real, long-term value and away from the transient thrill of quarterly returns. The fiduciary funds have the potential power to enforce this new economic perspective, though it is not yet widely understood or accepted by them. As universal owners of the economy, their own portfolios are the losers when individual corporations throw off externalities in order to boost their bottom lines. The costs will be borne by every other firm, by the economy as a whole, or by taxpayers who have to clean up the mess. The compelling logic of this new economic argument is this: what is bad for society cannot be good for future retirees or for their communities and their families.

Citizens, in other words, have more power than they imagine. If they assert influence over these intermediaries, they have the power to punish rogue corporations for anti-social behavior and block the low-road practices that have become so popular in business circles. In coalition with organized labor, environmentalists, and other engaged citizens, they have the capacity to design—and enforce—a new social contract that encourages, among other things, participatory management systems and worker ownership, loyalty to community, and respect for our deeper social values.

While none of this promises a utopian outcome of perfect equality, the redistribution of power within capitalism is certainly a predicate for the creation of a more equitable society.

My conviction is that we are on the brink of a broad new reform era, in which reorganizing capitalism becomes the principal objective. What I foresee is a long, steady mobilization of people attempting to do things differently, often in small and local settings, trying out new arrangements, sometimes failing, then trying again. As these inventive departures succeed, others will emulate them. In time, an alternative social reality will emerge with different values, alongside the archaic and destructive system that now exists. When that begins to happen and gains sufficient visibility, the politics is sure to follow. If all this sounds too remote to the present facts, too patient for our frenetic age, remember that this is how deep change has always occurred across American history.

This article is adapted from *The Soul of Capitalism* (Simon & Schuster, 2003).

RICH AND POOR IN THE GLOBAL ECONOMY

INTERVIEW WITH BOB SUTCLIFFE

Whether economic inequality is rising or falling globally is a matter of intense debate, a key question in the larger dispute over how three decades of intensified economic globalization have affected the world's poor. Bob Sutcliffe is an economist at the University of the Basque Country in Bilbao, Spain, and the author of 100 Ways of Seeing an Unequal World. *He has been analyzing both the statistical details and the broader political-economic import of the debate and shared some of his insights in a recent interview with* Dollars & Sense.

DOLLARS & SENSE: If someone asked you whether global inequality has grown over the past 25 years, I assume you'd say, "It depends—on how inequality is defined, on what data is used, on how that data is analyzed." Is that fair?

BOB SUTCLIFFE: Yes, it's fair, but it's not enough. First, the most basic fact about world inequality is that it is monstrously large; that result is inescapable, whatever the method or definition. As to its direction of change in the last 25 years, to some extent there are different answers. But also there are different questions. Inequality is not a simple one-dimensional concept that can be reduced to a single number. Single overall measures of world inequality (where all incomes are taken into account) give a different result from measures of the relation of the extremes (the richest compared with the poorest). Over the last 25 years, you find that the bottom half of world income earners seems to have gained something in relation to the top half (so, in this sense, there is less inequality), but the bottom 10% have lost seriously in comparison with the top 10% (thus, more inequality), and the bottom 1% have lost enormously in relation to the top 1% (much more inequality). None of these measures is a single true measure of inequality; they are all part of a complex structure of inequalities, some of which can lessen as part of the same overall process in which others increase.

We do have to be clear about one data-related question that has caused huge confusion. To look at the distribution of income in the world, you have to reduce incomes of different countries to one standard. Traditionally it has been done by using exchange rates; this makes inequality appear to change when exchange rates change, which is misleading. But now we have data based on "purchasing power parity" (the comparative buying power, or real equivalence, of currencies). Using PPP values achieves for comparisons over space what inflation-adjusted index numbers have achieved for comparisons over time. Although many problems remain with PPP values, they are the only way to make coherent comparisons of incomes between countries. But they produce estimates that are astonishingly different from exchange rate-based calculations. For instance, U.S. income per head is 34 times Chinese income per head using exchange rates, but only 8 times as great using PPP values. (And, incidentally, on PPP estimates the total size of the U.S. economy is now only 1.7 times that of China, and is likely to be overtaken by it by 2011.) So when you make this apparently technical choice between two methods of converting one currency to another, you come up not only with different figures on income distribution but also with two totally different world economic, and thus political, perspectives.

D&S: So even if some consensus were reached on the choices of definition, data, and method, you're urging a complex, nuanced portrait of what is happening to global inequality, rather than a yes or no answer. Could you give a brief outline of what you think that portrait looks like?

BS: Most integral measures—integral meaning including the entire population rather than comparing the extremes—that use PPP figures suggest that overall income distribution at the global level during the last 25 years has shown a slight decline in inequality, though there is some dissent on this. In any event this conclusion is tremendously affected by China, a country with a fifth of world population which has been growing economically at an unprecedented rate. Second, there seems to me little room for debate over the fact that the relative difference between the very rich and the very poor has gotten worse. And the smaller the extreme proportions you compare, the greater the gap. So the immensely rich have done especially well in the last 25 years, while the extremely poor have done very badly. The top one-tenth of U.S. citizens now receive a total income equal to that of the poorest 2.2 billion people in the rest of the world.

There have also been clear trends within some countries. Some of the fastest growing countries have become considerably more unequal. China is an example, along with some other industrializing countries like Thailand. The most economically liberal of the developed countries have also become much more unequal—for instance, the United States, the United Kingdom, and Australia—and so have the post-communist countries. The most extreme figures for inequality are found in a group of poor countries including Namibia and Botswana in southern Africa and Paraguay and Panama in Latin America.

Finally, the overall index of world inequality (measured by the Gini coefficient, a measure of income distribution) is about the same as that for two infamously unequal countries, South Africa and Brazil. And in the last few years it has shown no signs of improvement whatsoever.

D&S: People use the terms "unimodal" and "bimodal" to describe the global distribution of income. Can you explain what these mean? Also, you have referred elsewhere to a possible trimodal distribution—what does that refer to?

BS: The mode of a distribution is its most common value. In many countries there is one level of income around which a large proportion of the population clusters; at higher or lower levels of income there are progressively fewer people, so the distribution curve rises to a peak and then falls off. That is a unimodal distribution. But in South Africa, for example, due to the continued existence of entrenched ethnic division and economic inequality, the curve of distribution has two peaks—a low one, the most common income received by black citizens, and another, higher one, the the most common received by whites. This is a bimodal distribution because there are two values that are relatively more common than those above or below them. Because of its origins you could call it the "Apartheid distribution." The world distribution is in many respects uncannily like that of South Africa. It could be becoming trimodal in the sense that the frequency distribution of income has three peaks—one including those in very poor countries which have not been growing economically (e.g., parts of Africa), one in those developing countries which really have been developing (e.g., in South and East Asia), and one in the high-income industrialized countries. It's a kind of "apartheid plus" form of distribution.

D&S: In 2002, you wrote that many institutions, like the United Nations and the World Bank, were not being exactly honest in this debate—for example, emphasizing results based on data or methods that they elsewhere acknowledged to be poor. Has this changed over the past few years? Has the quality of the debate over trends in global income inequality improved?

BS: The most egregious pieces of statistical opportunism have declined. But I think there is a strong tendency in general for institutions to seize on optimistic conclusions regarding distribution in order to placate critics of the present world order. This increasingly takes the form of putting too much weight on measures of welfare other than income, for instance, life expectancy, for which there has been more international convergence than in the case of income. But there has been very little discussion of the philosophical basis for using life expectancy instead of or combined with income to measure inequality. If poor people live longer but in income terms remain as relatively poor as ever, has the world become less unequal?

The problem of statistical opportunism is not confined to those who are defending the world economic order; it also exists on the left. So, on the question of inequality, there is a tendency to accept whatever numerical estimate shows greatest inequality on the false assumption that this confirms the wickedness of capitalism. But capitalist inequality is so great that the willful exaggeration of it is not needed as the basis of anti-capitalist propaganda. It is more important for the left to look at the best indicators of the changing state of capitalism, including indicators of inequality, in order to intervene more effectively.

Finally, the quality of the debate, regardless of the intentions of the participants, is still greatly restricted by the shortage of available statistics about inequalities. That has improved somewhat in recent years although there are many things about past and present inequalities which we shall probably never know.

D&S: Do you see any contexts in which it's more important to focus on absolute poverty levels and trends in those levels rather than on inequality?

BS: The short answer is no, I do not. Plans for minimum income guarantees or for reducing the number of people lacking basic necessities can be important. But poverty always has a relative as well as an absolute component. It is a major weakness of the Millenium Development Goals, for example, that they talk about halving the number of people in absolute extreme poverty without a single mention of inequality. [The Millenium Development Goals is a U.N. program aimed at eliminating extreme poverty and achieving certain other development goals worldwide by 2015. —*Eds*.] And there is now a very active campaign on the part of anti-egalitarian, pro-capitalist ideologues in favor of the complete separation of the two. That is wrong not only because inequality is what partly defines poverty but more importantly because inequality and poverty reduction are inseparable. To separate them is to say that redistribution should not form part of the solution to poverty. Everyone is prepared in some sense to regard poverty as undesirable. But egalitarians see riches as pathological too. The objective of reducing poverty is integrally linked to the objective of greater equality and social justice.

D&S: Can you explain the paradox that China's economic liberalization since the late 1970s has increased inequality within China and at the same time reduced global inequality? Some researchers and policymakers interpret China's experience over this period as teaching us that it may be necessary for poor countries to sacrifice some equality in order to fight poverty. Do you agree with this—if not, how would you respond?

BS: When you measure *global* inequality, you are not just totalling the levels of inequality in individual countries. In theory all individual countries could become more unequal and yet the world as a whole become more equal, or vice versa. In China, a very poor country in 1980, average incomes have risen much faster than the world average and this has reduced world inequality. But different sections of the population have done much better than others so that inequality within China has grown. If and when China becomes on average a richer country than it is now, further unequal growth there may contribute to increasing rather than decreasing world inequality.

China's growth has been very inegalitarian, but it has been very fast. And the proportion of the population in poverty seems to have been reduced. But it is possible to envisage a more egalitarian growth path which would have been slower in aggregate but which would have reduced the number of poor people at least as much if not more than China's actual record. So I do not think it is right to say that higher inequality is the cause of reduced poverty, though it may for a time be a feature of the rapid growth which in turn creates employment and reduces poverty.

This does not mean that all increases in inequality are necessarily pathological. The famous Kuznets curve sees inequality first rising and then falling during economic growth as an initially poor population moves by stages from low-income, low-productivity work into high-income, high-productivity work, until at the end of the process 100% of the population is in the second group. If you measure inequality during such a process, it does in fact rise and then fall again to its original level—in this example at the start everyone is equally poor, at the end everyone is equally richer. That might be called transitional inequality; many growth processes may include an element of it. In that case equality is not really being "sacrificed" to reduce poverty—poverty is reduced by a process which increases inequality and then eliminates it again. But at the same time inequality may be growing for many other reasons which are not, like the Kuznets effect, self-eliminating, but rather cumulative. When inequality grows, this malign variety tends to be more important than the self-eliminating variety. But many economists are far too ready to see growing inequality as the more benign, self-eliminating variety.

D&S: Where do you think the question of what is happening to global income inequality fits into the broader debate over neoliberalism and globalization?

BS: Many people say that since some measures of inequality started to improve in about 1980 and that is also when neoliberalism and globalization accelerated, it is those processes which have produced greater equality. There are many problems with this argument, among them the fact that at least on some measures global inequality has grown since 1980. In any case, measures which show global inequality falling in this period are, as we have seen, very strongly influenced by China. China's extraordinary growth has, of course, in part been expressed in and permitted by greater globalization (its internationalization has grown faster than its production), and it is also clear that liberalization of economic policy has played a role, though China hardly has a neoliberal economy. But to permit is not to cause. The real cause is surely to be found not so much in economic policy as in a profound social movement in which a new and highly dynamic capitalist class (combined with a supportive authoritarian state) has once again become an agent of massive capitalist accumulation, as seen before in Japan, the United States, and Western Europe. So, an important part of what we are observing in figures which show declining world inequality is not any growth of egalitarianism, but the dynamic ascent of Chinese and other Asian capitalisms.

This interview also appears on the website of the Political Economy Research Institute at the University of Massachusetts-Amherst, along with Bob Sutcliffe's working paper "A More or Less Unequal World? World Income Distribution in the 20th Century." See <www.umass.edu/peri>.

CHAPTER 3
SAVINGS AND INVESTMENT

INTRODUCTION

Never a slip from the savings cup to the investment lip. That is the orderly world of classical macroeconomics, where every cent of household savings is neatly transferred to corporate investment. In the classical world, savings markets—governed by all-powerful interest rates—work seamlessly to assure that savings are matched by investments, fueling growth in the private economy, which in turn guarantees full employment. Should the flow of savings exceed the uptake of corporate investment, falling interest rates automatically solve the problem.

In the real world, macroeconomies are far messier than classical macroeconomists suggest—a proposition no one doubts today. Keynes argued that there is no neat connection, or nexus, between savings and investment in a modern financial economy. Savings often sit, hoarded and uninvested. And interest rates, no matter how low, seldom coax balky investors to lay out their money in a weak economy. In the Keynesian world, economies regularly suffer from investment shortfalls that lead to recessions and cost workers their jobs.

In this chapter, Gretchen McClain and Randy Albelda report on one critical test of the classical and Keynesian visions, conducted by economist Steven Fazzari. In a massive study of 5,000 manufacturing firms, Fazzari rated the influence of interest rates, business cycle conditions, and firms' financial conditions on their investment in plant and equipment. He concluded that the influence of interest rates is overrated, putting him squarely in the Keynesian camp (Article 3.1).

According to conventional wisdom, the stock market boom of the last decade should have benefited most people in the United States who own corporate stock either directly or indirectly through mutual funds or retirement accounts. But, as Sylvia Allegretto shows, the number of households that own stock has been *falling* in recent years, and the wealthiest Americans own the great bulk of stock by value (Article 3.2). Also, as Ellen Frank explains, there is no logical connection between rising stock prices and rising investment. Stock prices are based on traders' guesses about which stocks are likely to catch the eye of other traders—guesses that can have little to do with actual economic conditions (Article 3.3).

But residential investment, a housing boom followed by a mortgage crisis and housing bust, is the root cause of the instability and uncertainty in today's economic crisis. The housing crisis hit the subprime mortgage market and low-income homeowners first. Howard Karger throws into sharp relief the downsides that come with the well-known benefits of homeownership for low-income households (Article 3.7). As Karger shows, a low income often affords these buyers no more than rundown houses located in distressed neighborhoods and leaves them just a heartbeat away from financial disaster if their wages decline, property taxes or insurance rates rise, or if expensive repairs are needed.

The housing crisis then spread to engulf the entire mortgage market and the new financial instruments derived from mortgages, eventually threatening the entire financial system. Economist Gerald Friedman provides a succinct history of financial bubbles in the U.S. economy that demonstrates why financial markets need to be regulated (Article 3.5).

Just where do the trillions of dollars lost in the stock market crash and the bursting of the housing bubble go? Economist Arthur MacEwan explains how they are lost (Article 3.6). Finally, management consultant Orlando Segura, Jr. gives readers a peak into the notoriously secretive private equity industry. Segura describes how these firms realize huge profits, uber-profit in his words, from "leveraged buyouts," and how their buying and selling of private corporations neither foster innovation nor creates output and jobs (Article 3.4).

There are several policies the federal government could implement to stop the spread of foreclosures if it was as dedicated to supporting everyday homeowners as it is to propping up mega banks and insurance companies. Economist Fred Moseley reviews the anti-foreclosure policy alternatives from *bailout polices* in which the government aids lenders or homeowners to *workout policies* in which judges modify mortgage contracts to make monthly payments affordable for homeowners (Article 3.7).

KEY TO COLANDER

E = Economics   M = Macroeconomics

This chapter takes up topics in chapters E24-E26 E29, E30, M3, M4 or M8-M10, M15.
Article 3.1 discusses investment, the subject of chapter E24 & 26 or M7 & 9.
Articles 3.2 and 3.3 fit with the discussion of growth in chapter E24 or M7 & 9.

DISCUSSION QUESTIONS

1. (Article 3.1) Keynes argued that savings and investment were not balanced by the interest rate but by changes in the level of aggregate output. How does the essay by McClain and Albelda support this claim?
2. (Article 3.1) According to McClain and Albelda, how did Fazzari rate the influence of interest rates, business cycle conditions, and firms' financial conditions on corporate

investment? What do his findings suggest about Keynesian and classical theories of investment? Based on his findings, what stabilization policies might be appropriate to promote investment?

3. (Article 3.2) If nearly one half of U.S. households own stock either directly or indirectly, why would a rise in the Dow index be inconsequential for them?

4. (Article 3.3) During the 1930s, Keynes compared the stock market to a newspaper beauty contest that asked readers to pick the photo of the contestant that other readers would pick as the prettiest. Frank suggests that Keynes' analogy still holds for today's stock market. How does Frank's explanation of stock prices compare with those in your textbook? Do you find it convincing?

5. (Article 3.7) Is homeownership a good investment for low-income households? What is the upside? What is the downside?

6. (Article 3.5) What aspects of financial assets make them subject to speculative manias and panics? And what does this pattern suggest about the proper public policy for overseeing financial markets?

7. (Article 3.6) If the increased value of stocks and houses accrue to their owners during booms, explain what happens to the value of those assets in a crash and where it ends up.

8. (Article 3.4) How do corporations that buy and sell corporations make their mega profits and how does their activity affect the economy?

9. (Article 3.9) Explain how bailouts and workouts of home mortgages work and who benefits from them. Should the federal government pursue those policies? Why?

BOOSTING INVESTMENT
THE OVERRATED INFLUENCE OF INTEREST RATES

BY GRETCHEN MCCLAIN AND RANDY ALBELDA

Few economists or politicians would disagree that an economy's prospects for long-term growth depend on the productive capacity of its people and its physical equipment. But what to invest in—and how to get the appropriate economic actors to invest—is a matter of much debate.

All economies face a choice between using their productive resources to produce goods and services to be consumed now, and forsaking today's consumption to produce more goods for the future. While catering to consumption today may be more satisfying for wealthier countries and absolutely vital for poor countries, it fails to provide for future growth.

Investing in new plant and equipment can stimulate growth over time, as it provides the physical capacity for new production. Moreover, new plant and equipment tend to be better designed than the existing capital stock, and the improvement usually helps to boost output per worker. If this new productivity translates into higher wages, investment can also increase a country's standard of living and improve employment possibilities. In turn, improving human productive capacity—through training and education—can lead to growth and increased productivity in the long run.

Investment, and the consequent increase in productivity, is critical for international economic success. The more efficiently a country can produce a product, the more competitive that country will be in the world market. Since international markets provide an avenue of demand for our goods, the more domestically produced products and services we can sell abroad, the more jobs we can support here.

Investment can also help stimulate the economy in the short run. During an economic downturn, increased investment will yield more jobs and income for workers who would otherwise be unemployed. They will then return their income to the market when they purchase goods and services, which will boost demand for those products. Economists call this the "multiplier effect." The increase in demand in turn encourages firms to invest more so that they can meet that demand—known to economists as the "accelerator effect." All in all, such a cycle creates more jobs, income, and spending.

While few economists dispute the importance of investment, many disagree on what type is needed, which sectors of the economy are best able to provide it, and what are the best ways to encourage investment. Typically, these debates have revolved around the government's role in encouraging private investment in new plant and equipment. But the role that public investment in infrastructure and education plays in promoting not only our economic well-being and growth, but also in encouraging private investment, could and should widen the terms of the debate.

THE BACKDROP

The traditional economic argument about investment—and the prevailing conservative line espoused by elected officials at the federal and state levels—has been that the most important fiscal policies to encourage privately owned firms to invest are those which boost profits. If the government helps provide the conditions for profitability, the argument goes, firms will be encouraged to make the right types of investment.

Government tax-and-spend policies during the 1980s and 1990s have often tried to promote investment by reducing corporate taxes, in order to boost profits and stimulate savings. Such measures were supposed to leave firms with a bigger bottom line, in the hope that they would turn profits into new plant and equipment. Cuts in personal income tax rates—especially for the wealthiest—were intended to leave people with more after-tax income that they could save. Higher savings, according to this logic, translates into lower interest rates which in turn lead to more investment. While such policies have been very effective in redistributing money from the poor to the wealthy, they did not do much for investment. For example, the amount of new fixed investment (i.e., new plant and equipment) relative to the total amount of plant and equipment actually sank to its lowest post-World War II mark between 1989 and 1991.

Merely providing the conditions for profit-making does not mean that private firms will plow those profits back into new plant and equipment. Speculation on real-estate markets, the value of foreign currencies, or the price of silver and gold could easily eat up new profits. Much of the money generated for investment in the 1980s financed mergers and acquisitions, which generally resulted in less employment and little new physical productive capacity. And, perhaps even more important, new investment by U.S. firms may not take place in the United States. Investing abroad has been the trend since the 1970s. Finally, even if there is domestic investment and it increases productivity, unless workers share in those gains it may not promote robust growth or increase the standard of living of the country as a whole.

In the face of the failure of the 1980s policies to promote investment, conservatives came up with a new explanation of why the economy was so sluggish: the deficit. Ironically, the conservative policies mentioned above were largely responsible for the public debt, but nonetheless Republicans, along with many Democrats galvanized by billionaire Ross Perot, latched onto deficit reduction as the most important fiscal policy of the 1990s.

The deficit, they argued, kept long-term interest rates high because it created competition for precious funds. The result was that federal borrowing, necessitated by debt-financed government spending and tax cuts, "crowded out" private investment. The best solution, they said, was to reduce the deficit and bring down long-term interest rates so that private investment would thrive.

IDENTIFYING INFLUENCE

Economist Steven Fazzari tackled these assumptions in a study of the influence of the federal government's taxing and spending policies on private investment. Using a large data base from Standard and Poor on over 5,000 manufacturing firms from 1971 to 1990, Fazzari tested three different factors for their effects on levels of investment in plant and equipment: interest rates, the business cycle, and the financial conditions of the firms.

According to Fazzari, these three "channels of influence" shape patterns of investment. First, he takes on the traditionalists, by addressing the costs associated with investment: the price of borrowing money (i.e., interest rates), depreciation (how fast the new piece of equipment or building will lose its value), and taxes affecting both corporate profits and dividends. To measure this channel, Fazzari employs the interest rate on one type of corporate bond.

Next, he considers the influence of the business cycle by looking at sales growth. Traditional economic theory tends to assume a ready market, but Fazzari suggests instead that firms make investment decisions based on their perception of their ability to sell their products. The more robust current sales are and are expected to be, the more likely firms will be willing to risk new investment—regardless of the interest rate. Since the general condition of the economy influences sales levels, it also has an impact on investment.

In Fazzari's examination of the third channel of influence—the financial condition of firms—he again questions conventional wisdom, this time about the supply and demand for loans. Most economists assume that if the expected return on an investment exceeds the interest rate, then the project is profitable and will be undertaken. This is most likely to be true when the firm in question has enough cash on hand from prior profits to make the investment without asking a bank for a loan. Many firms, though, need to borrow money, and some are unable to persuade banks to loan it to them. Banks often refuse loan applications from new businesses with few assets, or charge them prohibitively high interest rates. Even if a young firm finds a potentially profitable investment, severe constraints on raising capital may prevent the firm from pursuing it. A firm's financial condition—not the projected rate of return on the new investment—can thus end up determining whether or not investment takes place.

PERFECTING POLICY

After looking at the importance of interest rates, the business cycle, and the financial conditions of firms in determining investment, Fazzari found that interest rates exert the weakest influence of the three factors. He concludes that there is no evidence that interest rates significantly affect investment for the fastest growing firms in his sample. Based on these findings, Fazzari claims that "it would be speculative to base policy on the assumption that interest rates drive investment to an important extent, especially for growing firms."

So, what kinds of fiscal policies should we adopt? If we believe Fazzari's results, we should be looking for those that attend to the financial conditions of firms and stimulate demand for products.

A tax cut targeted not at the very rich but at the "middle class" would probably give investment at least a temporary boost by generating increased consumption. Increased sales from a temporary tax cut create the illusion of a permanent increase in demand, and the multiplier and accelerator effects discussed earlier come into play. In order to meet what firms believe is a permanent increase in demand for their goods, they make investments in more equipment, more factories, and more employees.

Another means of encouraging investment that Fazzari evaluates is cutting corporate income taxes. Such cuts increase firms' after-tax profits, leaving them with a larger pool of funds to invest if they so choose. Since there is no guarantee that they will invest the savings from reduced taxes, though, Fazzari prefers investment tax credits (ITCs) to cuts in taxes for all firms. Only if firms invested would they be able to reduce their corporate tax bills. In Fazzari's view, ITCs will effectively encourage investment whether it is sensitive to interest rates or not.

The most important lesson from Fazzari's analysis is that concerns about investment should not stand in the way of policy initiatives that are important for society, such as spending on education and job training, simply because they may increase the federal budget deficit and cause interest rates to rise. Government investments in public works and education will likely increase productivity in the long run, and this can only be good for investment. Moreover, if investment is not sensitive to interest rates, then the much-discussed "crowding out" effect of deficit spending on private business is bound to be very small. And as Fazzari points out, when unemployment is high, the stimulative effects of deficit spending on sales may far outweigh the impacts of increased interest rates.

The focus on balanced budgets should be tempered by a thorough analysis of what this policy implies for society's immediate and long-term welfare. When we underinvest in the economy during a recession by eliminating educational and social investments, the foregone technical innovation resulting from this underinvestment may lead to less efficient workers, and lower productivity, for many years.

Fazzari's results not only repudiate the traditional answer to lagging investment—tax cuts for the wealthy and the lowering of interest rates. Instead, the government should be trying to stimulate the economy through improved physical and social infrastructure, which will boost not only sales but investment and incomes.

ARTICLE 3.2   March/April 2007

THE DOW HIGH AND STOCK OWNERSHIP

BY SYLVIA ALLEGRETTO

In April [2007] the Dow Jones Industrial Average rose above 13,000 for the first time ever, an event marked with great fanfare in some quarters. "Dow 13,000" may be a milestone on Wall Street, but it is a relatively insignificant blip on the radar screen of average working families. Fostered by the constant focus and widespread attention given to the performance of the stock market, conventional wisdom has it that everyone in the United States is heavily invested in the stock market—and so is poised to benefit when stock prices rise. However, the data tell a different story.

In recent decades the share of U.S. households owning any stock, whether directly (owning shares in a particular company) or indirectly (owning shares through a mutual fund or a retirement account) has indeed increased. But the most recent triennial data from the Survey of Consumer Finances show that this trend has actually reversed course: just over half of households (51.9%) owned any stock in 2001, but just under half (48.6%) in 2004—the first such decline on record (see Figure 1). In 2004, only about a third of U.S. households had stock holdings valued at more than $5,000.

The distribution of stocks by value is heavily tilted to the wealthiest Americans, as shown in Figure 2. In 2004, the wealthiest 1% of households owned 36.9% of the value of all stocks, while the next 9% owned 41.9%. Hence, the wealthiest 10% owned about 80% of all wealth in stocks. Between 2001 and 2004, while the wealthiest 1% of households increased their share of total stock value, the share held by the bottom 80% fell from just above 10% (10.7%) to just below (9.4%).

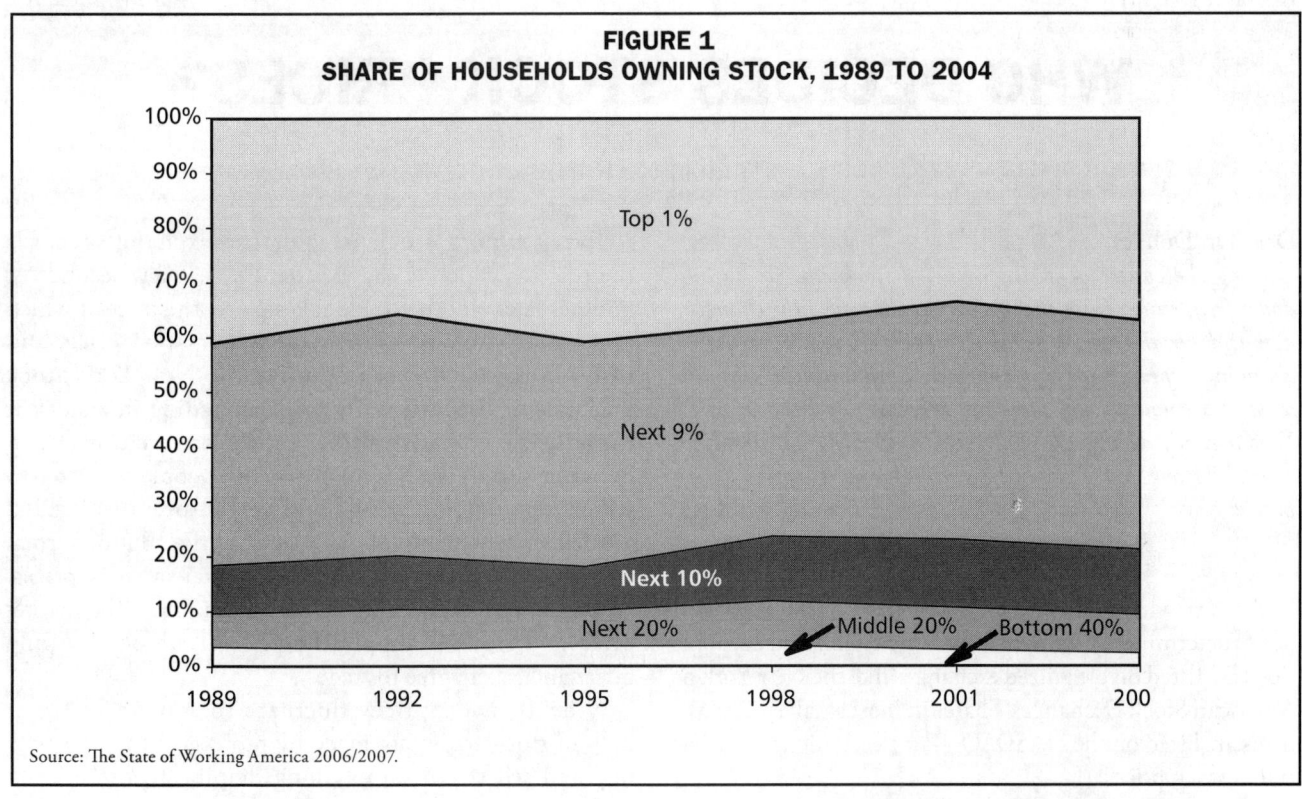

Source: The State of Working America 2006/2007.

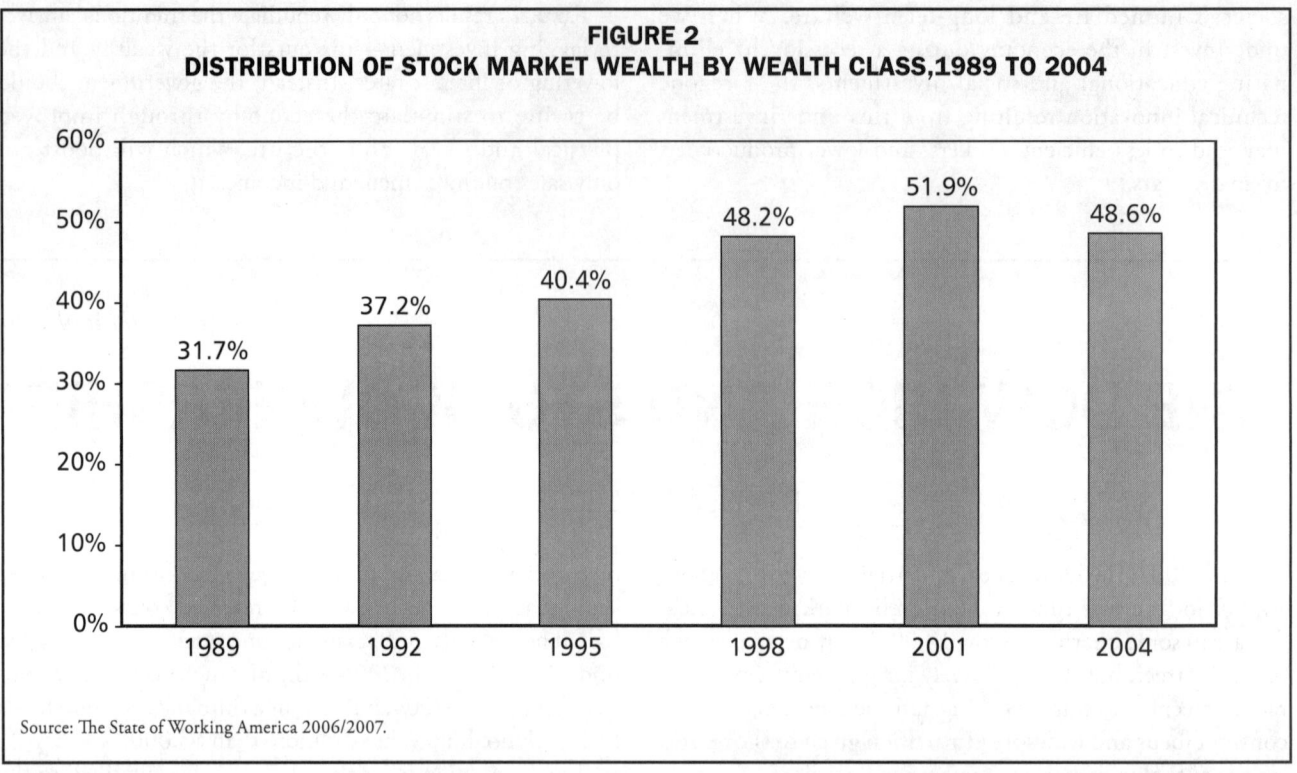

**FIGURE 2
DISTRIBUTION OF STOCK MARKET WEALTH BY WEALTH CLASS, 1989 TO 2004**

Source: The State of Working America 2006/2007.

For the most part, lower-, middle-, and even upper-middle-income working-age households depend on their paychecks, not stock portfolios, to meet their everyday needs. Typical working families that own stock do so in retirement plans that are costly to turn into cash. So higher stock prices do little to help them make ends meet at a time when inflation-adjusted wages for most workers have been stagnant for many years now.

ARTICLE 3.3　　　　　　　　　　　　　　　　　　　　　　　　　　　*May/June 2002*

WHO DECIDES STOCK PRICES?

BY ELLEN FRANK

Dear Dr. Dollar:
During the course of a single day, a stock can go up and down frequently. These changes supposedly reflect the changing demand for that stock (and its potential resale value) or changing expectations of a company's profitability. But this seems too vague to me. How can these factors be so volatile? Who actually decides, or what is the mechanism for deciding, when a stock price should go up or down and by how much?

　　　　　　—Joseph Balszak, Muskegon, Michigan

Let's start with your last question first—how are stock prices determined? Shares in most large established corporations are listed on organized exchanges like the New York or American Stock Exchanges. Shares in most smaller or newer firms are listed on the NASDAQ—an electronic system that tracks stock prices.

Every time a stock is sold, the exchange records the price at which it changes hands. If, a few seconds or minutes later, another trade takes place, the price at which that trade is made becomes the new market price, and so on. Organized exchanges like the New York Stock Exchange will occasionally suspend trading in a stock if the price is excessively volatile, if there is a severe mismatch between supply and demand (many people wanting to sell, no one wanting to buy) or if they suspect that insiders are deliberately manipulating a stock's price. But in normal circumstances, there is no official arbiter of stock prices, no person or institution that "decides" a price. The market price of a stock is simply the price at which a willing buyer and seller agree to trade.

Why then do prices fluctuate so much? The vast bulk of stock trades are made by professional traders who buy and sell shares all day long, hoping to profit from

58　Real World Macro, Twenty-Sixth Edition

small changes in share prices. Since these traders do not hold stocks over the long haul, they are not terribly interested in such long-term considerations as a company's profitability or the value of its assets. Or rather, they are interested in such factors mostly insofar as news that would affect a company's long-term prospects might cause *other traders* to buy the stock, causing its price to rise. If a trader believes that others will buy shares (in the expectation that prices will rise), then she will buy as well, hoping to sell when the price rises. If others believe the same thing, then the wave of buying pressure will, in fact, *cause* the price to rise.

Back in the 1930s, economist John Maynard Keynes compared the stock market to a contest then popular in British tabloids, in which contestants had to look at photos and choose the faces that *other contestants* would pick as the prettiest. Each contestant had to look for photos "likeliest to catch the fancy of the other competitors, all of whom are looking at the problem from the same point of view." Similarly, stock traders try to guess which stocks other traders will buy. The successful trader is the one who anticipates and outfoxes the market, buying before a stock's price rises and selling before it falls.

Financial firms employ thousands of market strategists and technical analysts who spend hours poring over historical stock data, trying to divine the logic behind these price changes. If they could unlock the secret of stock prices, they could arm their traders with the ability to always buy low and sell high. So far, no one has found this particular holy grail. And by continuing to guess and gamble, traders send prices gyrating.

For small investors, who do hold stock for the long term and will need to cash in their stocks at some point to finance their retirements, the volatility of the market can be a source of constant anxiety. Every time a share in, say, General Electric is traded, the new price is used to revalue *all* outstanding shares—just as the value of your home appreciates when the house down the block sells for more than a similar house sold last week. But the value of your home wouldn't be so high if every house on your block were suddenly put up for sale. Similarly, if all ten billion outstanding shares of General Electric—or even a small fraction of them—were put up for sale, they wouldn't fetch anywhere near the current market price. Small investors need to keep in mind that the gains and losses on their 401(k) statements are just hypothetical paper gains and losses. You won't know the true value of your stocks until you actually try to sell them.

ARTICLE 3.4

July/August 2008

PRIVATE EQUITY EXPOSED
AN INSIDER GIVES A PEEK AT A NOTORIOUSLY SECRETIVE INDUSTRY.

BY ORLANDO SEGURA

Today, private equity seems to be everywhere. Enter a Dunkin' Donuts, and you experience private equity. Scan your radio dial, and you're likely to encounter private equity. Purchase gifts for your children at Toys "R" Us, and you engage with private equity. The private equity industry, like other alternative investment industries that have risen to prominence over the last two decades, exerts tremendous economic and political influence in the United States and globally. It is important, then, to understand how this industry works and thrives. For the past three years, I have had the opportunity to see firsthand the inner workings of the industry—first as a consultant to large buyout firms, and then as a financial analyst for one of the firms themselves. Drawing on these experiences, I will try to shed some light on this notoriously secretive industry and answer three important questions: How do private equity firms make money? How do private equity firms affect the distribution of financial risk in society as a whole? And how does the regulatory landscape in the United States give private equity firms an advantage in the market?

HOW DO PRIVATE EQUITY FIRMS MAKE MONEY?

Specialized transactions called leveraged buyouts are central to what private equity firms do, and it is important to be familiar with the mechanics of these transactions in order to understand how these firms generate profit. Private equity firms are private partnerships that raise money from large investors—pension funds, other investment funds, and wealthy individuals (often the same people who are running the private equity firms)—and use that money to purchase other companies. This is the "buyout" part.

The "leveraged" part is the more important one, however. Private equity firms do not simply employ the money they raise on their own to buy companies. They borrow money from investment banks to complete the transactions. In most instances, this borrowed money constitutes the majority of the funding needed to pay for the company. At one point in the industry's infancy, firms were able to borrow 90% or more of the purchase price of the "target" companies. Today, as credit markets have tightened, that number is lower, but on average it still exceeds 50% of purchase price. When the buyout transaction is completed, the payback for this debt becomes the responsibility of the acquired company and is placed on its balance sheet as a liability. Most private equity firms retain ownership of the businesses they buy for three to five years and then sell them for a profit, often to other private equity firms.

The ability to use such leverage vastly increases the potential returns on private equity firms' investments. A simple analogy helps show how this works. Imagine you decide to buy a house that costs $100,000 in a neighborhood where property values are appreciating. You put a very small $1,000 down payment on the house and borrow the other $99,000 from the bank. In three years' time, the house has doubled in value and you are now able to sell it for $200,000. After you repay the loan, you have $100,000 in profit—a return of 100 times your original $1,000 investment. Now, imagine if you had only been able to borrow $1,000 from the bank; you would have had to make a $99,000 down payment. The house still appreciates to a value of $200,000, but in this scenario you have turned your original $99,000 investment into a $100,000 profit, generating only a return roughly equal to your original investment. In the first scenario, you put much less of your own equity at risk, yet you generate the same absolute profit as in the second scenario. This simple example illustrates the power of leverage, and why private equity firms would want to maximize the share of borrowed money they invest.

Why have investment banks been willing to lend private equity firms so much money? Part of the reason is that they are able to pass the debt along by selling, or "syndicating," it. Banks package the debt into securities called collateralized debt obligations, or CDOs, which they sell on the open market. CDOs have existed since 1987, but did not achieve prominence in the markets until 2001, when banks began devising sophisticated models that allowed them to rapidly price and sell these securities.

The benefit banks derive from their ability to segment and distribute the risks associated with the debt they underwrite for private equity firms cannot be overstated. They lower their downside risk associated with default on these loans because they only hold onto a small portion of the entire loan package, or "facility." So banks can underwrite more debt than they would be able to if they held onto the loans in full. And they can take in more lucrative fees, too. The banks get most of their revenues from fees for originating the loans, generally 2% to 3% of the amount of the loan.

All told, such large amounts of capital being used to purchase companies creates hefty profits for the investment banks and the private equity firms, not to mention the ancillary professional service industries required to complete the deals, including accountants, lawyers, and consultants.

This is simply the tip of the profit iceberg for private equity firms, however. The real money comes in what is called "carry"—the share of profits that the funds' managers are entitled to when they sell a business. Remember, the more these firms borrow for a transaction—the more they "leverage" —the more any increase in value translates into equity profit. The industry norm is for private equity partnerships to keep 20% of the profit that they make when they sell a company.

And apart from the über-profits they "earn" from selling the highly leveraged businesses they own, private equity firms charge hefty management fees to *both* the investors in the fund and to the companies they buy. The "market" management fee that private equity firms charge their investors ranges between 2% and 2.5% of the total fund size. The companies they purchase must likewise pay a quarterly "management fee," usually around 2% of the purchase price of the company. Effectively, private equity firms earn money in return for being given money *and* for spending money. As the value of many of the companies that private equity firms buy can soar into the hundreds of millions, or even billions, of dollars, this represents a low-risk, assured stream of income. On a fund of $10 billion, these fees alone can translate into hundreds of millions of dollars in revenue a year.

HOW DO PRIVATE EQUITY FIRMS AFFECT THE DISTRIBUTION OF FINANCIAL RISK IN SOCIETY?

The profits that financial players like private equity firms and investment banks enjoy come at a price. Today, there are hundreds of billions of dollars in CDOs that are spread throughout the economy, most owned by individual investors. Of course, it is the businesses private equity firms own that are carrying the underlying loans that were bundled to create the CDOs. These businesses risk default if they are not able to make the payments on these debts. And the more the private equity firm was able to borrow to purchase the company, the greater the risk the business faces because it will have to manage larger debt payments on an ongoing basis. An ordinary business downturn that the business might have been able to weather may now thrust it into default if it cannot manage the high debt payments resulting from the leveraged buyout. And if enough of these businesses get into trouble, the holders of the CDOs will see the value of their investments tumble. We are seeing this happen now with the subprime crisis, which was fueled by devaluation in mortgage-backed securities.

The ability of banks and private equity firms to siphon the benefits while distributing the risks of leverage is rooted in the legal frameworks that "incentivize" such behavior (to use the industry jargon). Private equity firms are shielded from the extreme downside financial risks because of their peculiar form of corporate governance. Private equity firms set up each company they buy as a separate corporation with limited liability. This means that if one of the highly leveraged businesses experiences a downturn and is unable to pay its loans, the only equity that is at stake is what was used to purchase that business. Thus, a private equity fund can still post healthy returns even if some businesses in its portfolio go bankrupt.

As we've seen, private equity firms have an incentive to leverage their business buyouts as much as possible. But this increases the risk of default for the individual businesses they own because they are forced to pay such large principal and interest payments to support the debt that has been placed on their shoulders. Thus, not only do private equity firms increase the systemic risk across the economy by issuing publicly traded CDOs that provide their leverage, they also increase the more immediate risk for those who work for the businesses they own by saddling them with heavy debt obligations.

The "loosening" of the credit markets, fueled partly through the ascendance of CDOs, predictably led private equity firms to execute ever-larger transactions. In 2007, the Blackstone Group purchased Equity Office Properties for $39 billion and in one fell swoop became one of the largest holders of real estate in the world. Currently, Bain Capital is in the process of completing the purchase of Clear Channel Communications, the largest owner of radio stations in the United States. These are but two of many multi-billion dollar transactions by private equity firms that have occur-red over the past decade, and which until now have largely gone unnoticed by the general public. These colossal companies, like all businesses bought up by private equity firms, are now at an increased risk should their profit margins weaken or interest rates rise in a cyclical downturn of the economy. To ensure that their requisite loan payments are made, the new managers of these companies, appointed by and acting on behalf of the private equity firm owner, may cut costs by simply laying off workers and offshoring certain functions. The market implications of contractions in the economy are thus amplified by the actions of private equity firms.

HOW DOES THE REGULATORY LANDSCAPE GIVE PRIVATE EQUITY FIRMS A MARKET ADVANTAGE?

With the profits that can be earned in private equity, it is no surprise that the industry has grown as much as it has recently, and it is no surprise that private equity firms are able to attract some of the brightest business minds in the market. Predictably, self-interested individuals are drawn to these firms, aiming to maximize the amount of money they can earn. But that is not the whole story. The regulatory landscape in the United States has given private equity firms a number of advantages in the market—limited transparency into the business dealings of the firms and the businesses they own, capital-gains tax advantages, a lack of consumer protection in the credit markets, lax antitrust law enforcement, among others. In effect, the legal landscape is ripe for private equity firms to thrive.

Since private equity firms have at their disposal all these levers for generating profit so seamlessly, one would imagine that the government would tax their earnings at an effectively higher tax rate than normal business earnings. This could not be further from the truth. Owners of corporations in the United States are afforded numerous tax breaks and incentives from writing off "losses" or deducting "business expenses" from taxable earnings. On this front, private equity firms have cleverly found ways to go above and beyond the call of duty. Virtually all private equity firms are structured as limited liability partnerships, or LLPs. This confers two explicit benefits to the partners. First, they are protected from any downside in their equity investments, meaning that if one of their investments goes bust, they will only lose the equity that they put into that specific business. Second, they are protected under a tax shelter that allows the majority of their profits to be taxed at a very low rate. Because they are partnerships that technically earn "capital gains" on the profitable sale of a business, they are taxed at a flat 15% rate, as opposed to the 28% to 33% income tax rate that ordinary individuals pay. Thanks to this loophole, private equity managers are taxed at lower rates than their secretaries and administrative assistants who make as much money in a year as their bosses make in a day.

Many European countries have recently instituted laws in recognition of the legal and regulatory advantages that private equity owners have enjoyed since the industry's inception. In the UK this past year, for example, Parliament passed a law that took away private equity firms' tax advantages, which incidentally were very similar to what currently exists in the United States. Here, House Democrats recently introduced a bill to do away with the capital gains tax structure for private equity firms and tax them at ordinary income tax rates. This would have raised private equity firms' tax rates on their carry from a flat 15% to a flat 35%. But Charles Schumer (D-N.Y.), head of the Senate Finance Committee, came out against the bill, killing it for now.

It is no coincidence that, as a senator from New York, Schumer receives tens of thousands of dollars from private equity bosses and relies on their support for an ever-increasing portion of his campaign funding. Of course, he is not alone. The private equity industry created its own PAC in 2007, the Private Equity Council, to lobby against efforts to increase taxes on the industry. To date, they have succeeded; there is every reason to believe they will continue to succeed. Schumer's fellow senator from New York, Hillary Clinton, is a loyal recipient of private equity money and joined him in opposing the bill. On the Republican side, former New York City mayor Rudy Giuliani has taken a predictable pro-private-equity stance, as did his competitor in the Republican presidential primaries, Mitt Romney, who made hundreds of millions of dollars as a partner of Bain Capital, one of the leading private equity firms in the world. The political muscle of the industry is as strong as its economic success.

The legal framework that actively encourages this industry to thrive has spawned a new breed of capitalism, one in which businesses are treated as assets to be bought and sold rather than as social institutions that are sources of people's livelihood. Perhaps we should ask: What value do these firms confer upon the economy, and through it, on society? Private equity firms do not foster innovation in the economy, they do not create jobs, and for the most part they do not actively manage the businesses they own. Rather, they redirect the benefits of equity ownership to a small and insular group of people instead of creating social value for everyone. It is time to learn more about how and why these institutions exert their power and, at the very least, to demand more transparency, thoughtful regulation, and fairer taxation in return for the privilege of being able to operate in our economy.

Resources: Tomas Krüger Andersen, "Legal Structure of Private Equity and Hedge Funds," 2007 (available at isis.ku.dk/kurser/blob.aspx?feltid= 155330); Martin Arnold, "Doubt Cast on Buy-Out Firms' Huge Profits," *Financial Times*, November 23, 2007; Neil Hodge, "Private Equity: A Debt to Society?" *Financial Management*, September 2007.

ARTICLE 3.5

January/February 2008

FROM TULIPS TO MORTGAGE-BACKED SECURITIES

BY GERALD FRIEDMAN

Thirty years ago, economist Charles Kindleberger published a little book, *Manias, Panics, and Crashes* (New York, 1978), describing the normal tendency of capitalist financial markets to fluctuate between speculative excess (or "irrational exuberance" in the words of a recent central banker) and panic. Kindleberger describes about 40 of these panics over the nearly 260 years from 1720–1975, or one every seven years. Following Kindleberger's arithmetic, we were due for a panic because it had been seven years since the high-tech bubble burst and the stock market panic of 2000–1. And the panic came, bringing in its wake a tsunami of economic woe, liquidity shortages, cancelled investments, rising unemployment, and economic distress.

Of course, more than mechanics and arithmetic are involved in the current financial panic. But there is a sense of inevitability about the manias and panics of capitalist financial markets, a sense described by writers from Karl Marx to John Maynard Keynes, Hyman Minsky, John Kenneth Galbraith, and Robert Shiller. The problem is that financial markets trade in unknown and unknowable future returns. Lacking real information, they are inevitably driven by the madness of crowds.

Unlike tangible commodities whose price should reflect its real value and real cost of production, financial assets are not priced according to any real returns, nor even according to some *expected* return, but rather according to *expectations of what others will pay in the future, or, even worse, expectations of future expectations that others will have of assets' future return*. Whether it is Dutch tulips in 1637, the South Sea Bubble of 1720, Florida real estate in the 1920s, or mortgage-backed securities today, it is always the same story of financial markets floating like a manic-depressive from euphoria to panic to bust. When unregulated, this process is made still worse by market manipulation, and simple fraud. Speculative markets like these can make some rich, and can even be exciting to watch, like a good game of poker; but this is a dangerous and irresponsible way to manage an economy.

There was a time when governments understood. Learning from past financial disasters, the United States established rules to limit the scope of financial euphoria and panic by strictly segregating different types of banks, by limiting financial speculation, and by requiring clear accounting of financial transactions. While they were regulated, financial markets contributed to the best period of growth in American history, the "glorious thirty" after World War II. To be sure, restrictions on speculative behavior and strict regulations made this a boring time to be a banker, and they limited earnings in the financial services sector. But, limited to a secondary role, finance served a greater good by providing liquidity for a long period of steady and relatively egalitarian economic growth.

Of course, over time we forgot why we had regulated financial markets, memory loss helped along by the combined efforts of free-market economists and self-interested bankers and others on Wall Street. To promote "competition," we lowered the barriers between different types of financial institutions, widening the scope of financial markets. We moved activities such as home mortgage lending onto national markets and allowed a rash of bank mergers to create huge financial institutions too large to be allowed to fail, but never too large to operate irresponsibly. Despite the growing scope and centralization of financial activity, the government accepted arguments that we could trust financial firms to self-regulate because it was in their interest to maintain credible accounting.

So we reap the whirlwind with a market collapse building to Great Depression levels. Once again, we learn history's lesson from direct experience: capitalist financial markets cannot be trusted. It is time to either re-regulate or move beyond.

ARTICLE 3.6

January/February 2008

WHO GETS THOSE TRILLIONS?

BY ARTHUR MACEWAN

Dear Dr. Dollar:

As housing prices have fallen, it seems that people have lost a huge amount in terms of the value of their homes. We are told that, over the whole country, trillions of dollars in home equity have been lost. Who gets those trillions? And, likewise, what about the trillions lost in the stock market?

—Carlos Rafael Alicea Negrón, Bronx, N.Y.

The simple answer to your question is that no one gets the lost trillions; they are simply gone. But, like all simple answers, this one doesn't explain very much.

Suppose that seven years ago, you bought your house for $200,000. Housing prices continued to rise, and at the beginning of 2007 you saw that other people in your neighborhood were selling houses similar to yours for $400,000. So you, quite reasonably, figured that your house was worth $400,000.

But now the housing bubble has burst. Similar houses in your neighborhood are selling for "only" $300,000 and thus it is now quite reasonable to figure that the value of your house has dropped by $100,000 as compared to the beginning of 2007. (Multiply this $100,000 by roughly 75 million homes across the country, and you have losses of $7.5 trillion.)

Your house, however, was not involved in any actual transaction at this lower value. So no one has gained the value you lost. If, for example, last year one of your neighbors had sold an equivalent house for $400,000 and now buys your house for $300,000 this neighbor would have gained what you lost. But most houses are not bought and sold in any given year. Their value is determined by those equivalent (or similar) houses that are actually bought and sold.

Moreover, even if someone bought your house at $300,000, that person would gain the value you lost only in the special case of the example above, where the person was lucky enough to have sold an equivalent house at $400,000. If instead that person was a new entrant to the housing market or a person who had just sold a similar house elsewhere for $300,000, then no one would be gaining what you lost.

Thus in the great majority of cases, the $100,000 value would simply be gone, and no one would have gotten it.

The situation on the stock market is similar. The values of stocks are determined by the sales that actually take place. When we hear that today the value of Mega Corporation's stock fell from $100 a share to $75 dollars a share, this means that the price of shares that were traded today were selling at $75 while those that were traded yesterday were selling for $100. But most shares of Mega Corporation were not actually traded either day. Their value fell—just like the value of your house fell when neighbors sold their houses—but no one gained this lost value. As in the housing market, the values of stocks have declined by trillions, but the trillions are simply gone.

Of course as with the situation in the housing market, some actual gains of value can take place when stock prices fall. If someone sold a share of Mega Corporation yesterday for $100 and bought it today for $75, this person obtained a gain. But with most of the declines in stock values, no one gets a gain.

To understand what has happened recently, it is useful to keep in mind that the high housing values of recent years were the result of a speculative bubble. The values increased not because there was some real change in the houses themselves. The houses were not providing more living services to the degree that their prices rose. The prices of housing rose because people expected them to rise more. The situation was a speculative bubble, and housing prices rose far above their historical trend.

And just as, in general, the loss of value when prices fell was not balanced by a gain, the gains that people saw when the bubbles expanded were not balanced by losses. As the bubble grew and the value of your house rose from $200,000 to $400,000, no one experienced an equivalent loss. Virtually all home buyers and owners were winners.

But speculative bubbles do not last.

THE HOMEOWNERSHIP MYTH

BY HOWARD KARGER

Anyone who has given the headlines even a passing glance recently knows the subprime mortgage industry is in deep trouble. Since 2006 more than 20 subprime lenders have quit the business or gone bankrupt. Many more are in serious trouble, including the nation's number two subprime lender, New Century Financial. The subprime crisis is also hitting Wall Street brokerages that invested in these loans, with reverberations from Tokyo to London. And the worst may be yet to come. At least $300 billion in subprime adjustable-rate mortgages will reset this year to higher interest rates. CNN reports that one in five subprime mortgages issued in 2005-2006 will end up in foreclosure. If these dire predictions come true, it will be the equivalent of a nuclear meltdown in the mortgage and housing industries.

What's conspicuously absent from the news reports is the effect of the subprime lending debacle on poor and working-class families who bought into the dream of homeownership, regardless of the price. Sold a false bill of goods, many of these families now face foreclosure and the loss of the small savings they invested in their homes. It's critical to examine the housing crisis not only from the perspective of the banks and the stock market, but also from the perspective of the families whose homes are on the line. It is also critical to uncover the systemic reasons for the recent burst of housing-market insanity that saw thousands upon thousands of families getting signed up for mortgage loans that were highly likely to end in failure and foreclosure.

Like most Americans, I grew up believing that buying a home represents a rite of passage in U.S. society. Americans widely view homeownership as the best choice for everyone, everywhere and at all times. The more people who own their own homes, the common wisdom goes, the more robust the economy, the stronger the community, and the greater the collective and individual benefits. Homeownership is the ticket to the middle class through asset accumulation, stability, and civic participation.

For the most part, this is an accurate picture. Homeowners get a foothold in a housing market with an almost infinite price ceiling. They enjoy important tax benefits. Owning a home is often cheaper than renting. Most important, homeownership builds equity and accrues assets for the next generation, in part by promoting forced savings. These savings are reflected in the data showing that, according to the National Housing Institute's Winton Picoff, the median wealth of low-income homeowners is 12 times higher than that of renters with similar incomes. Plus, owning a home is a status symbol: homeowners are seen as winners compared to renters.

Homeownership may have positive effects on family life. Ohio University's Robert Dietz found that owning a home contributes to household stability, social involvement, environmental awareness, local political participation and activism, good health, low crime, and beneficial community characteristics. Homeowners are better citizens, are healthier both physically and mentally, and have children who achieve more and are better behaved than those of renters.

Johns Hopkins University researchers Joe Harkness and Sandra Newman looked at whether homeownership benefits kids even in distressed neighborhoods. Their study concluded that "[h]omeownership in almost any neighborhood is found to benefit children. ... Children of most low-income renters would be better served by programs that help their families become homeowners in their current neighborhoods instead of helping them move to better neighborhoods while remaining renters." (Harkness and Newman also found, however, that the positive effects of homeownership on children are weaker in unstable low-income neighborhoods. Moreover, the study cannot distinguish whether homeownership leads to positive behaviors or whether owners were already predisposed to these behaviors.)

Faith in the benefits of homeownership—along with low interest rates and a range of governmental incentives—have produced a surge in the number of low-income homeowners. In 1994 Bill Clinton set—and ultimately surpassed—a goal to raise the nation's overall homeownership rate to 67.5% by 2000. There are now 71 million U.S. homeowners, representing close to 68% of all households. By 2003, 48% of black households owned their own homes, up from 34.5% in 1950. Much of this gain has been among low-income families.

Government efforts to increase homeownership for low-income families include both demand-side (e.g., homeowner tax credits, housing cost assistance programs) and supply-side (e.g., developer incentives) strategies. Federal housing programs insure more than a million loans a year to help low-income homebuyers. Fannie Mae and Freddie Mac—the large, federally chartered but privately held corporations that buy mortgages from lenders, guarantee the notes, and then resell them to investors—have increasingly turned their attention to low-income homebuyers as the upper-income housing market becomes more saturated. Banking industry regulations such as the Community Reinvestment Act and the Home Mortgage Disclosure Act encourage homeownership by reducing lending discrimination in underserved markets.

The Housing and Urban Development department (HUD) has adapted some of its programs originally designed to help renters to focus on homeownership. For instance, cities and towns can now use the federal dollars they receive through HOME (the Home Investment Partnerships Act) and Community Development Block Grants to provide housing grants, down payment loans, and closing cost assistance. The American Dream Downpayment Initiative, passed by Congress in 2003, authorized up to $200 million a year for down payment assistance to low-income families. Private foundations have followed suit. The Ford Foundation is currently focusing its housing-related grants on homeownership rather than rental housing; the foundation views homeownership as an important form of asset-building and the best option for low-income people.

While homeownership has undeniable benefits, that doesn't mean it is the best option for everyone. For many low-income families, buying a home imposes burdens that end up outweighing the benefits. It is time to re-assess the policy emphasis on homeownership, which has been driven by an honest belief in the advantages of homeownership, but also by a wide range of business interests who stand to gain when a new cohort of buyers is brought into the housing market.

THE DOWNSIDES OF HOMEOWNERSHIP

Low-income families can run into a range of pitfalls when they buy homes. These pitfalls may stem from the kinds of houses they can afford to buy (often in poor condition, with high maintenance costs); the neighborhoods they can afford to buy in (often economically distressed); the financing they can get (often carrying high interest rates, high fees, and risky gimmicks); and the jobs they work at (often unstable). Taken together, these factors can make buying a home a far riskier proposition for low-income families than it is for middle- and upper-income households.

Most low-income families only have the financial resources to buy rundown houses in distressed neighborhoods marked by few jobs, high crime rates, a dearth of services, and poor schools. Few middle-class homebuyers would hitch themselves to 30-year mortgages in these kinds of communities; poor families, too, have an interest in making the home-buying commitment in safe neighborhoods with good schools.

Homeownership is no automatic hedge against rising housing costs. On the contrary: lower-end affordable housing stock is typically old, in need of repair, and expensive to maintain. Low-income families often end up paying inflated prices for homes that are beset with major structural or mechanical problems masked by cosmetic repairs. A University of North Carolina study sponsored by the national nonprofit organization NeighborWorks found that almost half of low-income homebuyers experienced major unexpected costs due to the age and condition of their homes. If you rent, you can call the landlord; but a homeowner can't take herself to court because the roof leaks, the plumbing is bad, or the furnace or hot water heater quits working.

Besides maintenance and repairs, the expenses of homeownership also include property taxes and homeowners insurance, both of which have skyrocketed in cost in the last decade. Between 1997 and 2002 property tax rates rose nationally by more than 19%. Ten states (including giants Texas and California) saw their property tax rates rise by 30% or more during that period. In the suburbs of New York City, property tax rates grew two to three times faster than personal income from 2000 to 2004.

Nationally, the average homeowner's annual insurance premiums rose a whopping 62% from 1995 to 2005—twice as fast as inflation. Low-income homeowners in distressed neighborhoods are hit especially hard by high insurance costs. According to a Conning and Co. study, 92% of large insurance companies run credit checks on potential customers. These credit checks translate into insurance scores that are used to determine whether the carrier will insure an applicant at all, and if so, what they will cover and how much they will charge. Those with poor or no credit are denied coverage, while those with limited credit pay high premiums. Needless to say, many low-income homeowners do not have stellar credit scores. Credit scoring may also partly explain why, according to HUD, "Recent studies have shown that, compared to homeowners in predominantly white-occupied neighborhoods, homeowners in minority neighborhoods are less likely to have private home insurance, more likely to have policies that provide less coverage in case of a loss, and are likely to pay more for similar policies."

With few cash reserves, low-income families are a heartbeat away from financial disaster if their wages decline, property taxes or insurance rates rise, or expensive repairs are needed. With most—or all—of their savings in their homes, these families often have no cushion for emergencies. HUD data show that between 1999 and 2001, the only group whose housing conditions worsened—meaning, by HUD's definition, the only group in which a larger share of households spent over 30% of gross household income on housing in 2001 than in 1999—were low- and moderate-income homeowners. The National Housing Conference reports that 51% of working families with critical housing needs (i.e., those spending more than 50% of gross household income on housing) are homeowners.

Most people who buy a home imagine they will live there for a long time, benefiting from a secure and stable housing situation. For many low-income families, this is not what happens. Nationwide data from 1976 to 1993 reveal that 36% of low-income homeowners gave up or lost their homes within two years and 53% exited within five years, according to a 2005 study by Carolina Katz Reid of the University of Washington. Reid found that very few low-income families ever bought another house after returning to renting. A 2004 HUD research study by Donald Haurin and Stuart Rosenthal reached similar conclusions. Following a national sample of African Americans from youth (ages 14 to 21) in 1979 to middle age in 2000, the researchers found that 63% of the sample owned a home at some point, but only 34% still did in 2000.

Low-income homeowners, often employed in unstable jobs with stagnant incomes, few health care benefits, limited or no sick days, and little vacation time, may find it almost impossible to keep their homes if they experience a temporary job loss or a change in family circumstances, such as the loss of a wage earner. Homeownership can also limit financial opportunities. A 1999 study by economists Richard Green (University of Wisconsin) and Patric Hendershott (Ohio State University) found that states with the highest homeownership rates also had the highest unemployment rates. Their report concluded that homeownership may constrain labor mobility since the high costs of selling a house make unemployed homeowners reluctant to relocate to find work.

Special tax breaks have been a key selling point of homeownership. If mortgage interest and other qualifying expenses come to less than the standard deduction ($10,300 for joint filers in 2006), however, there is zero tax advantage to owning. That is one reason why only 34% of taxpayers itemize their mortgage interest, local property taxes, and other deductions. Even for families who do itemize, the effective tax saving is usually only 10 to 35 cents for every dollar paid in mortgage interest. In other words, the mortgage deduction benefits primarily those in high income brackets who have a need to shelter their income; it means little to low-income homeowners.

Finally, homeownership promises growing wealth as home prices rise. But the homes of low-income, especially minority, homeowners generally do not appreciate as much as middle-class housing. Low-income households typically purchase homes in distressed neighborhoods where significant appreciation is unlikely. Among other reasons, if financially-stressed property owners on the block can't afford to maintain their homes, nearby property values fall. For instance, Reid's longitudinal study surveyed low-income minority homeowners from 1976 to 1994 and found that they realized a 30% increase in the value of their homes after owning for 10 years, while middle- and upper-income white homeowners enjoyed a 60% jump.

"FUNNY MONEY" MORTGAGES AND OTHER TRAVESTIES

Buying a home and taking on a mortgage are scary, and people often leave the closing in a stupor, unsure of what they signed or why. My partner and I bought a house a few years ago; like many buyers, we didn't retain an attorney. The title company had set aside one hour for the closing. During that time more than 125 single-spaced pages (much of it in small print) were put in front of us. More than 60 required our signature or initials. It would have been difficult for us to digest these documents in 24 hours, much less one. When we asked to slow down the process, we were met with impatience. After the closing, Anna asked, "What did we sign?" I was clueless.

Yet buying a home is the largest purchase most families will make in their lifetimes, the largest expenditure in a family budget, and the single largest asset for two-thirds of homeowners. It's also the most fraught with danger.

For low-income families in particular, homeownership can turn out to be more a crushing debt than an asset-building opportunity. The primary reason for this is the growing chasm between ever-higher home prices and the stagnant incomes of millions of working-class Americans. The last decade has seen an unprecedented surge in home prices, which have risen 35% nationally. While the housing bubble is largely confined to specific metropolitan areas in the South, the Southwest, and the two coasts (home prices rose 50% in the Pacific states and 60% in New England), there are also bubbles in midwestern cities like Chicago and Minneapolis. And although the housing bubble is most pronounced in high-end properties, the prices of low-end homes have also spiked in many markets.

Current incomes simply do not support these inflated home prices. For example, only 18% of Californians can afford the median house in the state using traditional loan-affordability calculations. Even the fall in mortgage interest rates in the 1990s and early 2000s was largely neutralized by higher property taxes, higher insurance premiums, and rising utility costs.

This disparity might have put a dent in the mortgage finance business. But no: in 2005, Americans owed $5.7 trillion in mortgages, a 50% increase in just four years. Over the past decade the mortgage finance industry has developed creative schemes designed to squeeze potential homebuyers, albeit often temporarily, into houses they cannot afford. It is a sleight of hand that requires imaginative and risky financing for both buyers and financial institutions.

Most of the "creative" new mortgage products fall into the category of subprime mortgages—those offered to people whose problematic credit drops them into a lower lending category. Subprime mortgages carry interest rates ranging from a few points to ten points or more above the prime or market rate, plus onerous loan terms. The subprime mortgage industry is growing: lenders originated $173 billion in subprime loans in 2005, up from only $25 billion in 1993. By 2006 the subprime market was valued at $600 billion, one-fifth of the $3 trillion U.S. mortgage market.

Subprime lending can be risky. In the 37 years since the Mortgage Bankers Association (MBA) began conducting its annual national mortgage delinquency survey, 2006 saw the highest share of home loans entering foreclosure. In early 2007, according to the MBA, 13.5% of subprime mortgages were delinquent (compared to 4.95% of prime-rate mortgages) and 4.5% were in foreclosure. By all accounts, this is just the tip of the iceberg. However, before the current collapse the rate of return for subprime lenders was spectacular. *Forbes* claimed that subprime lenders could realize returns up to six times greater than the best-run banks.

In the past there were two main kinds of home mortgages: fixed-rate loans and adjustable-rate loans (ARMs). In a fixed-rate mortgage, the interest rate stays the same throughout the 15- to 30-year loan term. In a typical ARM the interest rate varies over the course of the loan, although there is usually a cap. Both kinds of loans traditionally required borrowers to provide thorough documentation of their finances and a down payment of at least 10% of the purchase price, and often 20%.

Adjustable-rate loans can be complicated, and a Federal Reserve study found that fully 25% of homeowners with ARMs were confused about their loan terms. Nonetheless, ARMs are attractive because in the short run they promise a home with an artificially low interest rate and affordable payments.

Even so, traditional ARMs proved inadequate to the tasks of ushering more low-income families into the housing market and generally keeping home sales up in the face of skyrocketing home prices. So in recent years the mortgage industry created a whole range of "affordability" products with names like "no-ratio loans," "option ARMS," and "balloon loans" that it doled out like candy to people who were never fully apprised of the intricacies of these complicated loans. (See box for a glossary of the new mortgage products.) These new mortgage options have opened the door for almost anyone to secure a mortgage, whether or not their circumstances auger well for repayment. They also raise both the costs and risks of buying a home—sometimes steeply—for the low- and moderate-income families to whom they're largely marketed.

Beyond the higher interest rates (at some point in the loan term if not at the start) that characterize the new "affordability" mortgages, low-income homebuyers face other costs as well. For instance, predatory and subprime lenders often require borrowers to carry credit life insurance, which pays off a mortgage if the homeowner dies. This insurance is frequently sold either by the lender's subsidiary or else by a company that pays the lender a commission. Despite low payouts, lenders frequently charge high premiums for this insurance.

As many as 80% of subprime loans include prepayment penalties if the borrower pays off or refinances the loan early, a scam that costs low-income borrowers about $2.3 billion a year and increases the risk of foreclosure by 20%. Prepayment penalties lock borrowers into a loan by making it difficult to sell the home or refinance with a different lender. And while some borrowers face penalties for paying off their loans ahead of schedule, others discover that their mortgages have so-called "call provisions" that permit the lender to accelerate the loan term even if payments are current.

And then there are all of the costs outside of the mortgage itself. Newfangled mortgage products are often sold not by banks directly, but by a rapidly growing crew of mortgage brokers who act as finders or "bird dogs" for lenders. There are approximately 53,000 mortgage brokerage companies in the United States employing an estimated 418,700 people, according to the National Association of Mortgage Brokers; *BusinessWeek* notes that brokers now originate up to 80% of all new mortgages.

Largely unregulated, mortgage brokers live off loan fees. Their transactions are primed for conflicts of interest or even downright corruption. For example, borrowers pay brokers a fee to help them secure a loan. Brokers may also receive kickbacks from lenders for referring a borrower, and many brokers steer clients to the lenders that pay them the highest kickbacks rather than those offering the lowest interest rates. Closing documents use arcane language ("yield spread premiums," "service release fees") to hide these kickbacks. And some hungry brokers find less-than-kosher ways to make the sale, including fudging paperwork, arranging for inflated appraisals, or helping buyers find co-signers who have no intention of actually guaranteeing the loan.

Whether or not a broker is involved, lenders can inflate closing costs in a variety of ways: charging outrageous document preparation fees; billing for recording fees in excess of the law; "unbundling," whereby closing costs are padded by duplicating charges already included in other categories.

All in all, housing is highly susceptible to the predations of the fringe economy. Unscrupulous brokers and lenders have considerable latitude to ply their trade, especially with vulnerable low-income borrowers.

TIME TO CHANGE COURSE

Despite the hype, homeownership is not a cure-all for low-income families who earn less than a living wage and have poor prospects for future income growth. In fact, for some low-income families homeownership only leads to more debt and financial misery. With mortgage delinquencies and foreclosures at record levels, especially among low-income households, millions of people would be better off today if they had remained renters. Surprisingly, rents are generally more stable than housing prices. From 1995 to 2001 rents rose slightly faster than inflation, but not as rapidly as home prices. Beginning in 2004 rent increases began to slow—even in hot markets like San Francisco and Seattle—and fell below the rate of inflation.

In the mid-1980s, low- and no-downpayment mortgages led to increased foreclosures when the economy tanked. Today, these mortgages are back, along with a concerted effort to drive economically marginal households into homeownership and high levels of unsustainable debt. To achieve this goal, the federal government spends $100 billion a year for homeownership programs (including the $70-plus billion that the mortgage interest deduction costs the Treasury).

Instead of focusing exclusively on homeownership, a more progressive and balanced housing policy would address the diverse needs of communities for both homes and rental units, and would facilitate new forms of ownership such as community land trusts and cooperatives. A balanced policy would certainly aim to expand the stock of affordable rental units. Unfortunately, just the opposite is occurring: rental housing assistance is being starved to feed low-income homeownership programs. From 2004 to 2006, President Bush and the Congress cut federal funding for public housing alone by 11%. Over the same period, more than 150,000 rental housing vouchers were cut.

And, of course, policymakers must act to protect those consumers who do opt to buy homes: for instance, by requiring mortgage lenders to make certain not only that a borrower is eligible for a particular loan product, but that the loan is suitable for the borrower.

The reason the United States lacks a sound housing policy is obvious if we follow the money. Overheated housing markets and rising home prices produce lots of winners. Real estate agents reap bigger commissions. Mortgage brokers, appraisers, real estate attorneys, title companies, lenders, builders, home remodelers, and everyone else with a hand in the housing pie does well. Cities raise more

THE NEW WORLD OF HOME LOANS

The new home loan products, marketed widely in recent years but especially to low- and moderate-income families, are generally adjustable-rate mortgages (ARMs) with some kind of twist. Here are a few of these "creative" (read: confusing and risky) mortgage options.

Option ARM: With this loan, borrowers choose each month which of three or four different—and fluctuating—payments to make:

- full (principal+interest) payment based on a 30-year or 15-year repayment schedule.
- interest-only payment—does not reduce the loan principal or build homeowner equity. Borrowers who pay only interest for a period of time then face a big jump in the size of monthly payments or else are forced to refinance.
- minimum payment—may be lower than one month's interest; if so, the shortfall is added to the loan balance. The result is "negative amortization": over time, the principal goes up, not down. Eventually the borrower may have an "upside down" mortgage where the debt is greater than the market value of the home.

According to the credit rating firm Fitch Ratings, up to 80% of all option ARM borrowers choose the minimum monthly payment option. So it's no surprise that in 2005, 20% of option ARMs were "upside down." When a negative amortization limit is reached, the minimum payment jumps up to fully amortize the loan for the remaining loan term. In other words, borrowers suddenly have to start paying the real bill.

Even borrowers who pay more than the monthly minimums can face payment shocks. Option ARMs often start with a temporary super-low teaser interest rate (and correspondingly low monthly payments) that allows borrowers to qualify for "more house." The catch? Since the low initial monthly payment, based on interest rates as low as 1.25%, is not enough to cover the real interest rate, the borrower eventually faces a sudden increase in monthly payments.

Balloon Loan: This loan is written for a short 5- to 7-year term during which the borrower pays either interest and principal each month or, in a more predatory form, interest only. At the end of the loan term, the borrower must pay off the entire loan in a lump sum—the "balloon payment." At that point, buyers must either refinance or lose their homes. Balloon loans are known to real estate pros as "bullet loans," since if the loan comes due—forcing the owner to refinance—during a period of high interest rates, it's like getting a bullet in the heart. According to the national organizing and advocacy group ACORN, about 10% of all subprime loans are balloons.

Balloon loans are sometimes structured with monthly payments that fail to cover the interest, much less pay down the principal. Although the borrower makes regular payments, her loan balance increases each month: negative amortization. Many borrowers are unaware that they have a negative amortization loan until they have to refinance.

Shared Appreciation Mortgage (SAM): These are fixed-rate loans for up to 30 years that have easier credit qualifications and lower monthly payments than conventional mortgages. In exchange for a lower interest rate, the borrower relinquishes part of the future value of the home to the lender. Interest rate reductions are based on how much appreciation the borrower is willing to give up. SAMs discourage "sweat equity" since the homeowner receives only some fraction of the appreciation resulting from any improvements. Not surprisingly, these loans have been likened to sharecropping.

Stated-Income Loan: Aimed at borrowers who do not draw regular wages from an employer but live on tips, casual jobs that pay under the table, commissions, or investments, this loan does not require W-2 forms or other standard wage documentation. The trade-off: higher interest rates.

No-Ratio Loan: The debt-income ratio (the borrower's monthly payments on debt, including the planned mortgage, divided by her monthly income) is a standard benchmark that lenders use to determine how large a mortgage they will write. In return for a higher interest rate, the no-ratio loan abandons this benchmark; it is aimed at borrowers with complex financial lives or those who are experiencing divorce, the death of a spouse, or a career change.   —Amy Gluckman in property taxes, and insurance companies enroll more clients at higher premiums. Although housing accounts for only 5% of GDP, it has been responsible for up to 75% of all U.S. job growth in the last four years, according to the consulting firm Oxford Analytica. Housing has buffered the economy, and herding more low-income families into homes, regardless of the consequences, helps keep the industry ticking in the short run. The only losers? Renters squeezed by higher rents and accelerating conversion of rental units into condos. Young middle-income families trying to buy their first house. And, especially, the thousands of low-income families for whom buying a home turns into a financial nightmare.

Resources: Carolina Katz Reid, *Studies in Demography and Ecology: Achieving the American Dream? A Longitudinal Analysis of the Homeownership Experiences of Low-Income Households,* Univ. of Washington, CSDE Working Paper No. 04-04; Dean Baker, "The Housing Bubble: A Time Bomb in Low-Income Communities?" *Shelterforce Online,* Issue #135, May/June 2004, www.nhi.org/online/issues/135/bubble.html; Howard Karger, *Shortchanged: Life and Debt in the Fringe Economy* (Berrett-Koehler, 2005); National Multi Housing Council (www.nmhc.org).

ARTICLE 3.8   September/October 2007

HOW TO STOP THE FORECLOSURES?
A REVIEW OF THE POLICY PROPOSALS

BY FRED MOSELEY

Over one million U.S. homeowners have already lost their homes due to foreclosures since the mortgage crisis began last summer. Another one million homeowners are 90 days past due on their mortgages (foreclosure notices usually go out after 90 days) and two million more are 30 days past due, so three million more households may face foreclosure in the months ahead. If current policies do not change, it is estimated that up to five million homeowners would lose their homes due to foreclosure over the next few years. Five million is roughly 10% of the total number of homes U.S. with mortgages. This is clearly the worst housing crisis since the Great De-pression, and will wreak havoc in the lives of millions of families unless something is done. A high foreclosure rate also has a deteriorating effect on surrounding neighborhoods, further depressing housing prices and quality of life.

Many of those facing foreclosure are low- to middle-income homeowners who were enticed into buying houses by fraudulent mortgage companies and low "teaser" interest rates that are adjusted up ("reset") after two to three years. As long as housing prices were increasing, homeowners could always refinance their mortgages and get a new teaser rate for another few years. However, now that house prices are falling, these homeowners can no longer refinance, and many of them cannot afford to pay the higher interest rates when they are reset. Falling prices also mean that many of these homeowners owe more on their mortgage than the current value of their house (i.e. they have "negative equity" in their house). The recession is also resulting in declining employment and income, meaning even more homeowners are struggling to make their monthly mortgage payments. The further housing prices decline, and the worse the recession is, the worse the foreclosures will be, in a vicious cycle.

Clearly, the federal government must take some positive actions to stop the spreading foreclosures, especially for low- and middle-income families, who would suffer the most. But what should those actions be? At a minimum, policies should apply only to owner-occupied homes, and not to "investor" or "speculative" homeowners (those who buy houses in order to sell them later at a higher price). But beyond this, various policies have been proposed, and not all of them would truly help homeowners at risk.

WORKOUTS, NOT BAILOUTS

There are two main types of anti-foreclosure policies: *bailouts* and *workouts*. In bailouts, the government gives aid either to lenders (e.g., by purchasing bad mortgages at their full original value) or to homeowners (e.g., by giving them loans so they can repay their lenders). Of course, aid to homeowners indirectly bails out the lenders as well. In *workouts*, the terms of the original mortgage contract are modified, either by reducing the rate of interest or reducing the principal owed, or both, in order to make the loan more affordable. So far, most of the proposals to deal with the foreclosure crisis have been workouts more than bailouts, although there are elements of bailout in some of them as well. The lenders made fortunes on these risky mortgages during the housing bubble, so if someone has to suffer losses now, it should be the lenders. There should be no bailouts of the lenders in any way.

LENDER-INITIATED WORKOUTS

There are two types of workouts, depending on whether they are initiated by the lenders or the homeowners. Most of the policies proposed and enacted so far have been *initiated by the lenders*, i.e., they are voluntary on the part of the lenders. The main policy of the Bush administration is called "Hope Now," in which the lenders voluntarily postpone the resets of interest rates that are scheduled to take place in the months ahead, and leave the principal of the loan unchanged (or sometimes the foregone interest is added to the principal). The Bush administration claims that over 500,000 mortgages have been modified in this way in recent months, and estimates that another 500,000 mortgages will be modified in the months ahead. However, critics argue that these numbers are exaggerated and that many of these modifications have been simply allowing homeowners more time to make the same payments. It is likely that in the months ahead, many of these homeowners still will not be able to make their payments, and many of them will be foreclosed on, which has led some critics to call this the "No Hope" plan. The only lasting solution is to reduce the mortgage principal owed to more affordable levels. The main problem now is not the reset of interest rates, but rather declining housing prices, which has the effect that more and more homeowners now owe more money on their mortgage than their house is worth.

The House and Senate have recently passed two versions of a similar bill that is primarily a workout, but also is potentially part bailout, and is also lender-initiated. The bill would replace existing mortgages with new mortgages that would have a value of 85% of the *current* market value of the houses, and these refinanced mortgages would be guaranteed by the Federal Housing Administration (how this "current market value" is to be determined is a crucial detail which so far has not been specified). For example, a homeowner with an original mortgage of $300,000 would have the principal reduced to $225,000, and the monthly payments reduced by a similar proportion. This 15% "write-down" of the principal, plus the prior 10% decline of prices, means that the total write-down for lenders will be a maximum of approximately 25% (and less to the extent that the borrower made a down payment or has accumulated equity through monthly payments). The bill would permit FHA to guarantee up to $300 billion in new mortgages, which it estimates could help up to 1.5 million homeowners. President Bush initially threatened a veto, but has since promised to sign the bill. In any case, it remains unclear how many lenders will voluntarily implement this refinancing.

Another problem with this bill is that housing prices in some areas are likely to fall more than an additional 15%. Mortgages on these houses are likely to be the ones that the lenders will voluntarily refinance, and any further losses would be borne by the government (i.e., by the taxpayers). This will be a partial bailout of the lenders.

HOMEOWNER-INITIATED WORKOUTS

Another bill has been introduced into the House (H.R. 3609) and Senate (S. 26360) that would provide workouts that would be *initiated by the homeowners* and would be mandatory for the lenders. These bills would allow bankruptcy judges to modify mortgage contracts (by reducing the principal and/or by reducing the interest rate) in order to make monthly payments more affordable for homeowners. It used to be possible for bankruptcy judges to modify mortgage contracts, but this was explicitly prohibited in a 1993 bankruptcy law. One can see the hand of the mortgage bankers in the writing of that provision. Modifications on other types of loans are allowed: for investment properties, for vacation homes, and even for boats, but no modifications allowed for primary residences! So all that needs to be done is to delete this one phrase in the law which prohibits modifications for primary residences. A significant advantage of this plan is that it would not cost taxpayers anything.

One problem with this bill is that homeowners would have to declare bankruptcy, which is expensive (about $2,000) and would hurt their credit rating in the future. But at least they would still have their home, with an affordable mortgage, and thus would have the chance to restore their credit rating.

This bill is supported by the AFL-CIO, SEIU, NAACP, ACORN, the Center for Responsible Lending, and many other consumer protection groups. It is of course strongly opposed by the Mortgage Bankers Association, and does not seem to have enough support for passage at the present time.

Another homeowner-initiated plan has been proposed by Dean Baker of the Center for Economic and Policy Research. According to this "own-to-rent" plan, homeowners faced with foreclosure would have the option to stay in their houses as tenants, rather than as owners, and would pay the prevailing rental rates, which are generally much lower than mortgage payments. Eligibility for the plan would be capped at the median house price in a metropolitan area and thus would not benefit high-income homeowners. This plan also would not cost taxpayers anything. A bill along these lines was recently introduced in the House (H.R. 6116).

LOOKING AHEAD

The presidential candidates have had disappointingly little to say about the foreclosure crisis and anti-foreclosure policies. Senator Barack Obama has expressed support for the FHA guarantee bill, but not yet for the bankruptcy modification bill. In good Republican tradi-tion, McCain advocates "no government intervention." But the foreclosure crisis is likely to worsen in the coming months, and the public may well demand more policies to address this growing problem. The homeowner-initiated policies are preferable because they provide the most protection for homeowners against foreclosure. Both of these options should be available to homeowners facing foreclosure, especially for those with low or moderate incomes.

The guiding principles of government anti-foreclosure policies should be: (1) homeowners should be allowed to stay in their homes; and (2) there should be no bailouts for the lenders. And the long-run objective of government housing policies should be: decent affordable housing for all.

Resources: For more information about H.R. 3609 and S. 26360, visit the website of the Center for Responsible Lending (www.responsiblelending.org). For more information about Dean Baker's "own-to-rent" plan (introduced in the House as H.R. 6116), visit the website of the Center for Economic and Policy Research (www.cepr.net).

CHAPTER 4
CAPITALISM IN CRISIS

INTRODUCTION

A frightening financial panic, a virulent housing bust, and plummeting economic output have left global capitalism facing its worst crisis since the Great Depression.

Economies across the globe are in trouble. The economies of the United States, Western Europe, and Japan are contracting as a group in 2009 for the first time since 1945. Even the once red-hot Chinese economy has slowed. European and U.S. finance workers, Japanese electronics workers, Chinese garment workers, and Indian software workers are losing their jobs as their economies slow and world export markets dry up.

In the United States, where the crisis hit first, the downturn is now the longest since World War II. Job losses already surpass those in the 1982 recession, the most severe recession of the postwar period. As consumers scrimped, retail sales sank, prices fell, and construction, major retailers, the U.S. automobile industry unraveled, and the stock market crashed.

Housing prices, the fountainhead of the crisis, fell by more from their late-2005 peak than during the housing bust of the Great Depression. Record levels of mortgage defaults and foreclosures spread panic through a rickety global financial system. Banks held mortgage loans that will never be repaid, while many kinds of securities, based on packaging and repackaging these mortgage loans (e.g. credit-default swaps), were rendered worthless. In a six-month span, three of the five largest U.S. investment banks disappeared. Leading mortgage companies, large commercial banks, and mammoth insurers all bit the dust.

Just what are we to make of this crisis? That is the topic of this chapter. Economist Arthur MacEwan identifies three root causes of the crisis—growing economic and social power in the hands of the wealthy, free market ideology, and rising inequality. He argues that addressing these causes of the crisis through better social programs, stronger unions, and market regulation are all crucial steps to making the economy more egalitarian, and will go a long way toward resolving capitalism's current problems (Article 4.1).

In a series of short articles, economists Marty Wolfson, David Kotz, and Rick Wolff delve into different aspects of the crisis and what can be done about them. Wolfson gives a down-to-earth description of the financial instruments and deregulatory measures at the heart of the crisis. He calls for a regulatory structure that puts limits on financial risk and manipulation (Article 4.2). Kotz traces the effects of the housing bubble on the real economy through the destruction of wealth and a credit crunch that put the kibosh on investment and consumer spending. The crisis has forced a restructuring of neoliberal capitalism, but the outcome of that restructuring is in doubt and popular movements could have a powerful influence on that outcome (Article 4.3). For Wolff, the long term widening difference between rising productivity and stagnating wages brought on the current crisis by forcing workers to borrow more and more to maintain their standard of living and leaving capitalists gorged with profits that they invested ever more recklessly. Wolff would have these abuses regulated and he also calls for fundamental changes in the economic system beginning with democratizing the workplace and corporations (Article 4.4).

In the remaining articles in the chapter, MacEwan make the case that irresponsible deregulation and the failure to regulate our financial system and not greed are the immediate causes of today crisis (Article 4.5). Economist John Miller provides readers with a top-ten list for recognizing if today's crisis is morphing into the next Great Depression (Article 4.6). Finally, economist Ramaa Vasudevan provides a primer on the increased importance of financial markets, financial institutions, and financial elites in today's economy and its governing institutions. That failed financial corporations have received massive bailouts, for Vasudevan, only underlines the power they wield in the era of financialization (Article 4.7).

DISCUSSION QUESTIONS

1. (Article 4.1) According to MacEwan, how did inequality, power, and ideology lead to the current crisis? In what ways would addressing these causes alleviate the crisis?
2. (Article 4.2) What are derivatives? What role did derivatives and their deregulation play in the current crisis? What rules would you put in place to regulate these assets?

KEY TO COLANDER

E = Economics   M = Macroeconomics

Colander chapters E25-E26, E30-E31, E32; Or M9-M10, M14-M15, M19.
   The chapter "Financial Crises, Panics, and Macroeconomic Policy" E32 & M15 is particularly good background for essays 4.1, 4.2, 4.3, 4.4, 4.5, and 4.6.
   What would also be good here is E35 & M18 on "The Modern Fiscal Policy Dilemma."

3. (Article 4.3) How did the financial crisis drive the real economy into crisis? And why does Kotz conclude that the financial sector cannot be operated on a profit and loss basis? Do you agree with him?
4. (Article 4.4) Why does Wolff identify the growing gap between rising productivity and stagnating wages as the root cause of the crisis? How has that widening gap driven the economy into crisis? What would Wolff do to address that widening gap and the current crisis?
5. (Article 4.5) Why is MacEwan convinced that greed is not the root cause of the current crisis? If MacEwan is right, what does that suggest about which policies would best resolve the crisis?
6. (Article 4.6) Are we in for the next Great Depression? Which of Miller's top ten indicators, written in November of 2008, still hold or are even more true now?
7. (Article 4.7) What is financialization? How does it manifest itself in today's economy and the current crisis?

INEQUALITY, POWER, AND IDEOLOGY
GETTING IT RIGHT ABOUT THE CAUSES OF THE CURRENT ECONOMIC CRISIS

BY ARTHUR MACEWAN

It is hard to solve a problem without an understanding of what caused it. For example, in medicine, until we gained an understanding of the way bacteria and viruses cause various infectious diseases, it was virtually impossible to develop effective cures. Of course, dealing with many diseases is complicated by the fact that germs, genes, diet and the environment establish a nexus of causes.

The same is true in economics. Without an understanding of the causes of the current crisis, we are unlikely to develop a solution; certainly we are not going to get a solution that has a lasting impact. And determining the causes is complicated because several intertwined factors have been involved.

The current economic crisis was brought about by a nexus of factors that involved: a growing concentration of political and social power in the hands of the wealthy; the ascendance of a perverse leave-it-to-the-market ideology which was an instrument of that power; and rising income inequality, which both resulted from and enhanced that power. These various factors formed a vicious circle, reinforcing one another and together shaping the economic conditions that led us to the present situation. Several other factors were also involved—the growing role of credit, the puffing up of the housing bubble, and the increasing deregulation of financial markets have been very important. However, these are best understood as transmitters of our economic problems, arising from the nexus that formed the vicious circle.

What does this tell us about a solution? Economic stimulus, repair of the housing market, and new regulation are all well and good, but they do not deal with the underlying causes of the crisis. Instead, progressive groups need to work to shift each of the factors I have noted—power, ideology, and income distribution—in the other direction. In doing so, we can create a *virtuous* circle, with each change reinforcing the other changes. If successful, we not only establish a more stable economy, but we lay the foundation for a more democratic, equitable, and sustainable economic order.

A crisis by its very nature creates opportunities for change. One good place to begin change and intervene in this "circle"—and transform it from vicious to virtuous—is through pushing for the expansion and reform of social programs, programs that directly serve social needs of the great majority of the population (for example: single-payer health care, education programs, and environmental protection and repair). By establishing changes in social programs, we will have impacts on income distribution and ideology, and, perhaps most important, we set in motion *a power shift* that improves our position for preserving the changes. While I emphasize social programs as a means to initiate social and economic change, there are other ways to intervene in the circle. Efforts to re-strengthen unions would be especially important; and there are other options as well.

CAUSES OF THE CRISIS: A LONG TIME COMING

Sometime around the early 1970s, there were some dramatic changes in the U.S. economy. The twenty-five years following World War II had been an era of relatively stable economic growth; the benefits of growth had been widely shared, with wages rising along with productivity gains, and income distribution became slightly less unequal (a good deal less unequal as compared to the pre-Great Depression era). There were severe economic problems in the United States, not the least of which were the continued exclusion of African Americans, large gender inequalities, and the woeful inadequacy of social welfare programs. Nonetheless, relatively stable growth, rising wages, and then the advent of the civil rights movement and the War on Poverty gave some important, positive social and economic character to the era—especially in hindsight!

In part, this comparatively favorable experience for the United States had depended on the very dominant position that U.S. firms held in the world economy, a position in which they were relatively unchallenged by international competition. The firms and their owners were not the only beneficiaries of this situation. With less competitive pressure on them from foreign companies, many U.S. firms accepted unionization and did not find it worthwhile to focus on keeping wages down and obstructing the implementation of social supports for the low-income population. Also, having had the recent experience of the Great Depression, many wealthy people and business executives were probably not so averse to a substantial role for government in regulating the economy.

A POWER GRAB

By about 1970, the situation was changing. Firms in Europe and Japan had long recovered from World War II, OPEC

ALAN GREENSPAN, SYMBOL OF AN ERA

One significant symbol of the full rise of the conservative ideology that became so dominant in the latter part of the 20th century was Alan Greenspan, who served from 1974 through 1976 as chairman of the President's Council of Economic Advisers under Gerald Ford and in 1987 became chairman of the Federal Reserve Board, a position he held until 2006. While his predecessors had hardly been critics of U.S. capitalism, Greenspan was a close associate of the philosopher Ayn Rand and an adherent of her extreme ideas supporting individualism and laissez-faire (keep-the-government-out) capitalism.

When chairman of the Fed, Greenspan was widely credited with maintaining an era of stable economic growth. As things fell apart in 2008, however, Greenspan was seen as having a large share of responsibility for the non-regulation and excessively easy credit (see article) that led into the crisis.

Called before Congress in October of 2008, Greenspan was chastised by Rep. Henry Waxman (D-Calif.), who asked him: "Do you feel that your ideology pushed you to make decisions that you wish you had not made?" To which Greenspan replied: "Yes, I've found a flaw. I don't know how significant or permanent it is. But I've been very distressed by that fact."

And Greenspan told Congress: "Those of us who have looked to the self-interest of lending institutions to protect shareholders' equity, myself included, are in a state of shocked disbelief."

Greenspan's "shock" was reminiscent of the scene in the film "Casablanca," where Captain Renault (Claude Rains) declares: "I'm shocked, shocked to find that gambling is going on in here!" At which point, a croupier hands Renault a pile of money and says, "Your winnings, sir." Renault replies, sotto voce, "Thank you very much."

---

was taking shape, and weaknesses were emerging in the U.S. economy. The weaknesses were in part a consequence of heavy spending for the Vietnam War combined with the government's reluctance to tax for the war because of its unpopularity. The pressures on U.S. firms arising from these changes had two sets of consequences: slower growth and greater instability; and concerted efforts—a power grab, if you will—by firms and the wealthy to shift the costs of economic deterioration onto U.S. workers and the low-income population.

These "concerted efforts" took many forms: greater resistance to unions and unionization, battles to reduce taxes, stronger opposition to social welfare programs, and, above all, a push to reduce or eliminate government regulation of economic activity through a powerful political campaign to gain control of the various branches and levels of government. The 1980s, with Reagan and Bush One in the White House, were the years in which all these efforts were solidified. Unions were greatly weakened, a phenomenon both demonstrated and exacerbated by Reagan's firing of the air traffic controllers in response to their strike in 1981. The tax cuts of the period were also important markers of the change. But the change had begun earlier; the 1978 passage of the tax-cutting Proposition 13 in California was perhaps the first major success of the movement. And the changes continued well after the 1980s, with welfare reform and deregulation of finance during the Clinton era, to say nothing of the tax cuts and other actions during Bush Two.

IDEOLOGY SHIFT

The changes that began in the 1970s, however, were not simply these sorts of concrete alterations in the structure of power affecting the economy and, especially, government's role in the economy. There was a major shift in ideology, the dominant set of ideas that organize an understanding of our social relations and both guide and rationalize policy decisions.

Following the Great Depression and World War II, there was a wide acceptance of the idea that government had a major role to play in economic life. Less than in many other countries but nonetheless to a substantial degree, at all levels of society, it was generally believed that there should be a substantial government safety net and that government should both regulate the economy in various ways and, through fiscal as well as monetary policy, should maintain aggregate demand. This large economic role for government came to be called Keynesianism, after the British economist John Maynard Keynes, who had set out the arguments for an active fiscal policy in time of economic weakness. In the early 1970s, as economic troubles developed, even Richard Nixon declared: "We are all Keynesians now."

The election of Ronald Reagan, however, marked a sharp change in ideology, at least at the top. Actions of the government were blamed for all economic ills: government spending, Keynesianism, was alleged to be the cause of the inflation of the 1970s; government regulation was supposedly crippling industry; high taxes were, it was argued, undermining incentives for workers to work and for businesses to invest; social welfare spending was blamed for making people dependent on the government and was charged with fraud and corruption (the "welfare queens"); and so on and so on.

On economic matters, Reagan championed supply-side economics, the principal idea of which was that tax cuts yield an increase in government revenue because the cuts lead to more rapid economic growth through encouraging more work and more investment. Thus, so the argument went, tax cuts would reduce the government deficit. Reagan, with the cooperation of Democrats, got the tax cuts—and, as the loss of revenue combined with a large increase in military spending, the federal budget deficit grew by leaps and bounds, almost doubling as a share of GDP over the course of the 1980s. It was all summed up in the idea of keeping the government out of the economy; let the free market work its magic.

GROWING INEQUALITY

The shifts of power and ideology were very much bound up with a major redistribution upwards of income and wealth. The weakening of unions, the increasing access of firms to low-wage foreign (and immigrant) labor, the refusal of government to maintain the buying power of the minimum wage, favorable tax treatment of the wealthy and their corporations, deregulation in a wide range of industries and lack of enforcement of existing regulation (e.g., the authorities turning a blind eye to off-shore tax shelters) all contributed to these shifts.

Many economists, however, explain the rising income inequality as a result of technological change that favored more highly skilled workers; and changing technology has probably been a factor. Yet the most dramatic aspect of the rising inequality has been the rapidly rising share of income obtained by those at the very top (see figures below), who get their incomes from the ownership and control of business, not from their skilled labor. For these people the role of new technologies was most important through its impact on providing more options (e.g., international options) for the managers of firms, more thorough means to control labor, and more effective ways—in the absence of regulation—to manipulate finance. All of these gains that might be associated with new technology were also gains brought by the way the government handled, or didn't handle (failed to regulate), economic affairs.

Several sets of data demonstrate the sharp changes in the distribution of income that have taken place in the last several decades. Most striking is the changing position of the very highest income segment of the population. In the mid-1920s, the share of all pre-tax income going to the top 1% of households peaked at 23.9%. This elite group's share of income fell dramatically during the Great Depression and World War II to about 12% at the end of the war and then slowly fell further during the next thirty years, reaching a low of 8.9% in the mid-1970s. Since then, the top 1% has regained is exalted position of the earlier era, with 21.8% of income in 2005. Since 1993, more than one-half of all income gains have accrued to this highest 1% of the population.

Figures 1 and 2 show the gains (or losses) of various groups in the 1947 to 1979 period and in the 1979 to 2005 period. The difference is dramatic. For example, in the earlier era, the bottom 20% saw its income in real (inflation-adjusted) terms rise by 116%, and real income of the top 5% grew by only 86%. But in the latter era, the bottom 20% saw a 1% decline in its income, while the top 5% obtained a 81% increase.

THE EMERGENCE OF CRISIS

These changes, especially these dramatic shifts in the distribution of income, set the stage for the increasingly large reliance on credit, especially consumer and mortgage credit, that played a major role in the emergence of the current economic crisis. Other factors were involved, but rising inequality was especially important in effecting the increase in both the demand and supply of credit.

CREDIT EXPANSION

On the demand side, rising inequality translated into a growing gap between the incomes of most members of society and their needs. For the 2000 to 2007 period, average weekly earnings in the private sector were 12% below their average for the 1970s (in inflation-adjusted terms). From 1980 to 2005 the share of income going to the bottom 60% of families fell from 35% to 29%. Under these circum-

FIGURE 1: **Change in Real Family Income by Quintile and Top 5%, 1949–1979**

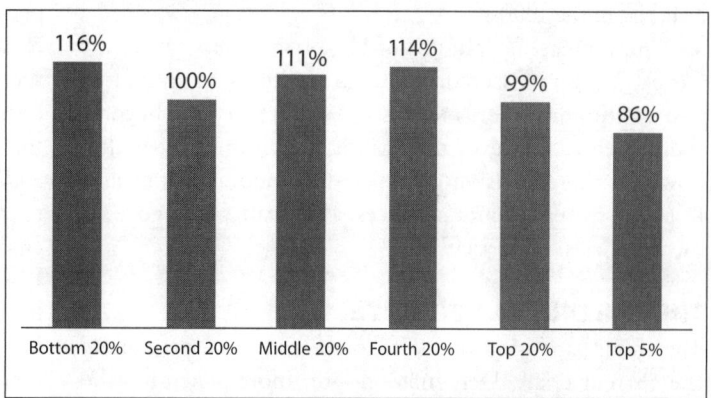

Source: Analysis of U.S. Census Bureau data in Economic Policy Institute, *The State of Working America 1994–95* (1994) p. 37.

FIGURE 2: **Change in Real Family Income by Quintile and Top 5%, 1979–2005**

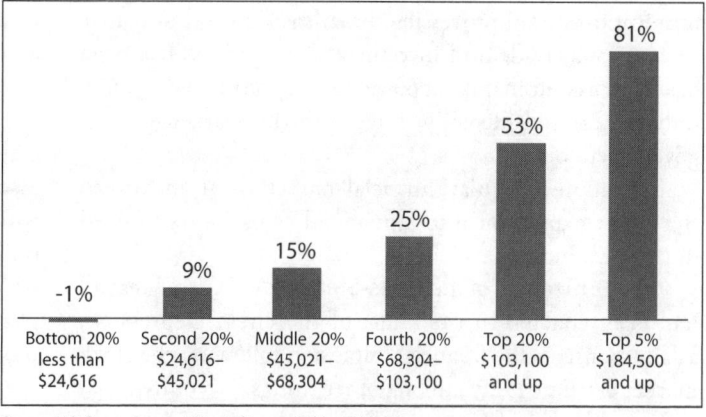

Source: U.S. Census Bureau, Historical Income Tables, Table F-3.

stances, more and more people relied more and more heavily on credit to meet their needs—everything from food to fuel, from education to entertainment, and especially housing.

While the increasing reliance of consumers on credit has been going on for a long time, it has been especially marked in recent decades. Consumer debt as a share of after-tax personal income averaged 20% in the 1990s, and then jumped up to an average of 25% in the first seven years of the new millennium. But the debt expansion was most marked in housing, where mortgage debt as a percent of after-tax personal income rose from 89% to 94% over the 1990s, and then ballooned to 140% by 2006 as housing prices skyrocketed.

On the supply side, especially in the last few years, the government seems to have relied on making credit readily available as a means to bolster aggregate demand and maintain at least a modicum of economic growth. During the 1990s, the federal funds interest rate averaged 5.1%, but fell to an average of 3.4% in the 2000 to 2007 period—and averaged only 1.4% in 2002 to 2004 period. (The federal funds interest rate is the rate that banks charge one another for overnight loans and is a rate directly affected by the Federal Reserve.) Corresponding to the low interest rates, the money supply grew twice as fast in the new millennium as it had in the 1990s.

The increasing reliance of U.S. consumers on credit has often been presented as a moral weakness, as an infatuation with consumerism, and as a failure to look beyond the present. Whatever moral judgments one may make, however, the expansion of the credit economy has been a response to real economic forces—inequality and government policies, in particular.

THE FAILURE TO REGULATE

The credit expansion by itself, however, did not precipitate the current crisis. Deregulation—or, more generally, the failure to regulate—is also an important part of the story. The government's role in regulation of financial markets has been a central feature in the development of this crisis, but the situation in financial markets has been part of a more general process—affecting airlines and trucking, telecommunications, food processing, broadcasting, and of course international trade and investment. The process has been driven by a combination of power (of large firms and wealthy individuals) and ideology (leave it to the market, get the government out).

The failure to regulate financial markets that transformed the credit expansion into a financial crisis shows up well in three examples:

The 1999 repeal of the Glass-Steagall Act. Glass-Steagall had been enacted in the midst of the Great Depression, as a response to the financial implosion following the stock market crash of 1929. Among other things, it required that different kinds of financial firms—commercial banks, investment banks, insurance companies—be separate. This separation both limited the spread of financial problems and reduced conflicts of interest that could arise were the different functions of these firms combined into a single firm. As perhaps the most important legislation regulating the financial sector, the repeal of Glass-Steagall was not only a substantive change but was an important symbol of the whole process of deregulation.

The failure to regulate mortgage lending. Existing laws and regulations require lending institutions to follow prudent practices in making loans, assuring that borrowers have the capacity to be able to pay back the loans. And of course fraud—lying about the provisions of loans—is prohibited. Yet in an atmosphere where regulation was "out," regulators were simply not doing their jobs. The consequences are illustrated in a December 28, 2008, *New York Times* story on the failed Washington Mutual Bank. The article describes a supervisor at a mortgage processing center as having been "accustomed to seeing baby sitters claiming salaries worthy of college presidents, and schoolteachers with incomes rivaling stockbrokers'. He rarely questioned them. A real estate frenzy was under way and WaMu, as his bank was known, was all about saying yes."

One may wonder why banks—or other lending institutions, mortgage firms, in particular—would make loans to people who were unlikely to be able to pay them back. The reason is that the lending institutions quickly combined such loans into packages (i.e., a security made up of several borrowers' obligations to pay) and sold them to other investors in a practice called "securitization."

Credit-default swaps. Perhaps the most egregious failure to regulate in recent years has been the emergence of credit-default swaps, which are connected to securitization. Because they were made up of obligations by a diverse set of borrowers, the packages of loans were supposedly low-risk investments. Yet those who purchased them still sought insurance against default. Insurance sellers, however, are regulated—required, for example, to keep a certain amount of capital on hand to cover possible claims. So the sellers of these insurance policies on packages of loans called the policies "credit-default swaps" and thus were allowed to avoid regulation. Further, these credit-default swaps, these insurance policies, themselves were bought and sold again and again in unregulated markets in a continuing process of speculation.

The credit-default swaps are a form of derivative, a financial asset the value of which is derived from some other asset—in this case the value of packages of mortgages on which they were the insurance policies. When the housing bubble began to collapse and people started to default on their mortgages, the value of credit-default swaps plummeted and their future value was impossible to determine. No one would buy them, and several banks that had speculated in these derivatives were left holding huge amounts of these "toxic assets."

BUBBLE AND BUST

The combination of easy credit and the failure to regulate together fueled the housing bubble. People could buy expensive houses but make relatively low monthly payments. Without effective regulation of mortgage lending, they could get the loans even when they were unlikely to be able to make payments over the long run. Moreover, as these pressures pushed up housing prices, many people bought houses simply to resell them quickly at a higher price, in a process called "flipping." And such speculation pushed the prices up further. Between 2000 and 2006, housing prices rose by 90% (as consumer prices generally rose by only 17%).

While the housing boom was in full swing, both successful housing speculators and lots of people involved in the shenanigans of credit markets made a lot of money. However, as the housing bubble burst—as all bubbles do—things fell apart. The packages of loans lost value, and the insurance policies on them, the credit-default swaps, lost value. These then became "toxic" assets for those who held them, assets not only with reduced value but with unknown value. Not only did large financial firms—for example, Lehman Brothers and AIG—have billions of dollars in losses, but no one knew the worth of their remaining assets. The assets were called "toxic" because they poisoned the operations of the financial system. Under these circumstances, financial institutions stopped lending to one another—that is, the credit markets "froze up." The financial crisis was here.

The financial crisis, not surprisingly, very quickly shifted to a general economic crisis. Firms in the "real" economy rely heavily on a well-functioning financial system to supply them with the funds they need for their regular operations—loans to car buyers, loans to finance inventory, loans for construction of new facilities, loans for new equipment, and, of course, mortgage loans. Without those loans (or with the loans much more difficult to obtain), there has been a general cut-back in economic activity, what is becoming a serious and probably prolonged recession.

WHAT IS TO BE DONE?

So here we are. The shifts in power, ideology, and income distribution have placed us in a rather nasty situation. There are some steps that will be taken that have a reasonable probability of yielding short-run improvement. In particular, a large increase in government spending—deficit spending—will probably reduce the depth and shorten the length of the recession. And the actions of the Federal Reserve and Treasury to inject funds into the financial system are likely, along with the deficit spending, to "unfreeze" credit markets (the mismanagement and, it seems, outright corruption of the bailout notwithstanding). Also, there is likely to be some re-regulation of the financial industry. These steps, however, at best will restore things to where they were before the crisis. They do not treat the underlying causes of the crisis—the vicious circle of power, ideology, and inequality.

JOSEPH STIGLITZ ON THE WAR AND THE ECONOMY

On October 2, 2008, on the Pacifica radio program Democracy Now!, Amy Goodman and Juan Gonzalez interviewed Joseph Stiglitz about the economic situation. Stiglitz was the 2001 winner of the Nobel Prize in Economics, former chief economist at the World Bank, and former chair of President Clinton's Council of Economic Advisers. He is a professor at Columbia University. Following is an excerpt from that interview:

AMY GOODMAN: Joseph Stiglitz, you're co-author of *The Three Trillion Dollar War: The True Cost of the Iraq Conflict*. How does the bailout [of the financial sector] connect to war?

JOSEPH STIGLITZ: Very much. Let me first explain a little bit how the current crisis connects with the war. One of the reasons that we have this crisis is that the Fed flooded the economy with liquidity and had lax regulations. Part of that was this ideology of regulations were bad, but part of the reason was that the economy was weak. And one of the reasons the economy was weak was oil prices were soaring, and part of the reason oil prices were soaring is the Iraq war. When we went to war in 2003, before we went, prices were $23 a barrel. Futures markets thought they would remain at that level. They anticipated the increase in demand, but they thought there would be a concomitant increase in supply from the low-cost providers, mainly in the Middle East. The war changed that equation, and we know what happened to the oil prices.

Well, why is that important? Well, we were spending—Americans were spending hundreds of millions—billions of dollars to buy—more, to buy imported oil. Normally, that would have had a very negative effect on our economy; we would have had a slowdown. Some people have said, you know, it's a mystery why we aren't having that slowdown; we repealed the laws of economics. Whenever anybody says that, you ought to be suspect.

It was actually very simple. The Fed engineered a bubble, a housing bubble to replace the tech bubble that it had engineered in the '90s. The housing bubble facilitated people taking money out of their . . . houses; in one year, there were more than $900 billion of mortgage equity withdrawals. And so, we had a consumption boom that was so strong that even though we were spending so much money abroad, we could keep the economy going. But it was so shortsighted. And it was so clear that we were living on borrowed money and borrowed time. And it was just a matter of time before, you know, the whole thing would start to unravel.

OPPORTUNITY FOR CHANGE

Fortunately, the crisis itself has weakened some aspects of this circle. The cry of "leave it to the market" is still heard, but is now more a basis for derision than a guide to policy. The ideology and, to a degree, the power behind the ideology, have been severely weakened as the role of "keeping the government out" has shown to be a major cause of the financial mess and our current hardships. There is now widespread support among the general populace and some support in Washington for greater regulation of the financial industry.

Whether or not the coming period will see this support translated into effective policy is of course an open question. Also an open question is how much the turn away from "leaving it to the market" can be extended to other sectors of the economy. With regard to the environment, there is already general acceptance of the principle that the government (indeed, many governments) must take an active role in regulating economic activity. Similar principles need to be recognized with regard to health care, education, housing, child care, and other support programs for low-income families.

The discrediting of "keep the government out" ideology provides an opening to develop new programs in these areas and to expand old programs. Furthermore, as the federal government revs up its "stimulus" program in the coming months, opportunities will exist for expanding support for these sorts of programs. This support is important, first of all, because these programs serve real, pressing needs—needs that have long existed and are becoming acute and more extensive in the current crisis.

BREAKING THE CIRCLE

Support for these social programs, however, may also serve to break into the vicious power-ideology-inequality circle and begin transforming it into a virtuous circle. Social programs are inherently equalizing in two ways: they provide their benefits to low-income people and they provide some options for those people in their efforts to demand better work and higher pay. Also, the further these programs develop, the more they establish the legitimacy of a larger role for social control of—government involvement in—the economy; they tend to bring about an ideological shift. By affecting a positive distributional shift and by shifting ideology, the emergence of stronger social programs can have a wider impact on power. In other words, efforts to promote social programs are one place to start, an entry point to shift the vicious circle to a virtuous circle.

There are other entry points. Perhaps the most obvious ones are actions to strengthen the role of unions. The Employee Free Choice Act may be a useful first step, and it will be helpful to establish a more union-friendly Department of Labor and National Labor Relations Board. Raising the minimum wage—ideally indexing it to inflation—would also be highly desirable. While conditions have changed since the heyday of unions in the middle of the 20th century, and we cannot expect to restore the conditions of that era, a greater role for unions would seem essential in righting the structural conditions at the foundation of the current crisis.

SHIFTING CLASS POWER

None of this is assured, of course. Simply starting social programs will not necessarily mean that they have the wider impacts that I am suggesting are possible. No one should think that by setting up some new programs and strengthening some existing ones we will be on a smooth road to economic and social change. Likewise, rebuilding the strength of unions will involve extensive struggle and will not be accomplished by a few legislative or executive actions.

Also, all efforts to involve the government in economic activity—whether in finance or environmental affairs, in health care or education, in work support or job training programs—will be met with the worn-out claims that government involvement generates bureaucracy, stifles initiative, and places an excessive burden on private firms and individuals. We are already hearing warnings that in dealing with the financial crisis the government must avoid "over-regulation." Likewise, efforts to strengthen unions will suffer the traditional attacks, as unions are portrayed as corrupt and their members privileged. The unfolding situation with regard to the auto firms' troubles has demonstrated the attack, as conservatives have blamed the United Auto Workers for the industry's woes and have demanded extensive concessions by the union.

Certainly not all regulation is good regulation. Aside from excessive bureaucratic controls, there is the phenomenon by which regulating agencies are often captives of the industries that they are supposed to regulate. And there are corrupt unions. These are real issues, but they should not be allowed to derail change.

The current economic crisis emerged in large part as a shift in the balance of class power in the United States, a shift that began in the early 1970s and continued into the new millennium. Perhaps the present moment offers an opportunity to shift things back in the other direction. Recognition of the complex nexus of causes of the current economic crisis provides some guidance where people might start. Rebuilding and extending social programs, strengthening unions, and other actions that contribute to a more egalitarian power shift will not solve all the problems of U.S. capitalism. They can, however, begin to move us in the right direction.

DERIVATIVES AND DEREGULATION

BY MARTY WOLFSON

It has become commonplace to describe the current financial crisis as the most serious since the Great Depression. Although we have more tools now to avoid a depression, the current crisis presents in some ways more significant challenges than did the banking crises of the 1930s.

And it's not over.

The form of the current crisis is similar to others we have seen in the past: a speculative increase in asset prices, overly optimistic expectations, and an expansion of debt sustainable only if the speculative bubble continues. Then the bubble pops, debt can't be repaid, and losses mount at financial institutions. The risk of bank failures rises and lenders get scared. They panic, refuse to lend to anyone that seems at all risky, and seek safety in cash or super-safe assets.

In the early 1930s, there was no federal deposit insurance and little federal government intervention. Depositor runs took down the banking system.

In more recent crises, though, the Federal Reserve successfully developed and used its powers as a lender of last resort. Deposit insurance helped to reassure small depositors and, if needed, the Federal Deposit Insurance Corporation stepped in and bailed out threatened banks. It could guarantee all liabilities of a failing bank and arrange mergers with healthier banks. These tools generally worked to reduce panicked reactions and prevent the freezing up of credit.

But this time, after the collapse of the speculative bubble in housing prices, the course of events has been different. The Federal Reserve was forced to expand the concept of a lender of last resort in unprecedented ways. It has lent to investment banks and insurance companies, not just regulated depository institutions. It has taken all kinds of assets as collateral for its loans, not just the high-grade securities it traditionally accepted. It has even lent to nonfinancial corporations (by buying their commercial paper).

What is surprising is that these dramatic actions and expensive bailouts of financial institutions, such as American International Group (AIG) and even Fannie Mae and Freddie Mac, were insufficient to reassure lenders about the ability of financial institutions to honor their repayment commitments. Treasury Secretary Paulson's plan to use $700 billion to buy "toxic assets" from financial institutions, signed into law by President Bush on October 3rd, failed to stop what had become by then a generalized panic and freeze-up of credit. It took a coordinated global initiative to inject capital directly into financial institutions, plus a federal guarantee on bank debt and unlimited FDIC insurance on non-interest-bearing (mostly business) accounts at banks, announced on October 12th, to begin to have an effect on unfreezing credit markets.

The "TED spread," a widely watched measure of credit risk that had spiked sharply during the panic, began to reverse its path following the October 12 announcement. The TED spread measures the difference between an interest rate that banks charge when lending to each other (the London Interbank Offered Rate, or LIBOR) and the interest rate on U.S. Treasury bills. Because the Treasury is assumed to be "risk-free," the difference between it and LIBOR measures the perceived relative risk of lending to banks.

Why has this panic been so much more difficult to control? The answer has to do with the widespread use of complicated and opaque securities, known as derivatives, in a deregulated, interconnected, and global financial system.

A derivative is a financial contract that derives its value from something else, such as an asset or an index. At the root of the current crisis are derivatives known as mortgage-backed securities (MBSs). MBSs are claims to payments from an underlying pool of mortgages. The ability of MBS issuers to repay their debt, and thus the value of the MBS, is derived from the ability of homeowners to meet their mortgage payments.

In the process leading up to the crisis, a mortgage broker typically extended a mortgage to a borrower, and then turned to a commercial bank to fund the loan. The bank might sell the loan to Fannie Mae, which would pool a group of mortgages together and sell the resulting MBS to an investment bank like Lehman Brothers. Lehman, in turn, repackaged the MBS in various ways, and issued even more complicated derivatives called collateralized debt obligations (CDOs). Buyers of the CDOs might be other banks, hedge funds, or other lenders.

At the base of this complicated pyramid of derivatives might be a subprime borrower whose lender did not explain an adjustable-rate loan, or another borrower whose ability to meet mortgage payments depended on a continued escalation of home prices. As subprime borrowers' rates reset, and especially as housing price speculation collapsed, the whole house of cards came crashing down.

Why were mortgage loans made that could not be repaid? And why did supposedly sophisticated investors buy MBSs and CDOs based on these loans? First of all, the mortgage brokers and commercial banks that made and funded these loans quickly sold them off and no longer had any responsibility for them. Second, rating agencies like Moody's and Standard & Poor's gave these derivatives stellar AAA ratings, signifying a credit risk of almost zero. Recent Congressional hearings have highlighted the conflict of interest that these rating agencies had: they were being paid by the issuers of the derivatives they were rating. Third, financial institutions up and down the line were making money and nobody was limiting what they could do. In the deregulated financial environment, federal regulators stood aside as housing speculation spun out of control and did little to regulate, or even document, the growth of complicated derivatives.

Finally, financial institutions' concerns about the creditworthiness of the derivatives they held were eased because they thought they could protect themselves against possible loss. For example, by using another type of derivative known as a credit default swap, holders of MBSs and CDOs could make periodic premium payments to another financial institution, like American International Group (AIG), to insure themselves against default by the issuers of the MBSs and CDOs. (This insurance contract was technically classified as a derivative rather than insurance in order to escape regulation.) However, if an insurer like AIG is unable to honor all its insurance contracts, then the protection against loss is illusory.

The total value of all the securities insured by credit default swaps at the end of 2007 was estimated by the Bank of International Settlements to be $58 trillion, and by the International Swaps and Derivatives Association to be $62 trillion. (The estimates could vary by as much as $4 trillion because unregulated credit default swaps do not have to be officially reported to regulatory agencies. Moreover, even greater ambiguity surrounds these contracts because insurers can transfer their liability to other parties, and the insured party may be unaware of the creditworthiness or even the identity of the new insurer.)

Surprisingly, though, the value of the actual securities that form the basis of these credit default swaps was only about $6 trillion. How could $6 trillion worth of assets be insured at ten times that amount? The discrepancy is due to the fact that it is possible to speculate on the likelihood of default of a security without actually owning the security: all the speculator has to do is enter into a credit default swap contract with an insurer. The total volume of "insured securities" can thus escalate dramatically.

Because derivatives are so complex, because so much speculation and debt are involved, and because it is so hard to know how much is at risk (and exactly who is at risk), regulators are unsure of the implications of the failure of a particular financial institution. That is why they have been so fearful of the consequences of letting a troubled institution fail.

The exception that did indeed prove the rule was Lehman Brothers. The Federal Reserve and Treasury did not bail it out, and its failure led to an intensification of the problems in credit markets. A money market fund, the Reserve Primary Fund, announced that it would only pay 97 cents on the dollar to its investors, because its investments in Lehman Brothers could not be redeemed. The Treasury moved quickly to announce that it would insure money market funds, in order to prevent a run on the funds. However, the Lehman failure raised further concerns that lenders had about the derivatives portfolios of other banks, and about the possibility that the banks would not have enough capital to cover potential losses.

Secretary Paulson's initial plan to buy "toxic" assets (including MBSs and CDOs) from financial institutions was designed to address these concerns about bank capital. However, his plan was probably also negatively affected by uncertainty. Because these "toxic" assets are complex and nobody wants to buy them, there is no market for them and their value is uncertain. And because the Paulson plan's unstated objective was to boost bank capital by overpaying for these assets, the difficulties in pricing the assets raised the prospects of long delays and questions about whether the plan to increase bank capital would be successful. Lenders continued to hold back. They may also have hesitated because of concern about a political backlash against a taxpayer subsidy for the very banks that many people blamed for the crisis.

By injecting capital directly into the banks, the global initiative announced on October 12th raised the prospect of returns on the capital investment for taxpayers. It also avoided the uncertainties of buying individual assets and helped to reduce the panic.

But the crisis isn't over. Reducing the panic is only the first step. There is now likely to be a longer-term credit crunch that will continue to threaten the broader economy. Banks and other lenders will be wary for quite some time. Losses on mortgage-related assets will continue as years of housing speculation—financed with heaps of borrowed money—continues to unwind. Bank lending will lag as banks rebuild their capital and overcome their pessimistic expectations.

It will be up to the federal government to pick up the slack that the banks will leave. We will need programs to enable people to stay in their homes and stabilize their communities. We will need to create jobs by investing in infrastructure, renewable energy, and education. We will need a "trickle-up" approach that puts people first and raises living standards and opportunities.

At the same time, we need a regulatory structure for the financial system that puts limits on risk and manipulation. It is clear that deregulation, and the entire neoliberal model that has dominated economic policy for the past 30 years, has run aground. It has sown the seeds of financial crisis, and this crisis has led us to the edge of an abyss. Only by dramatically reorienting our economic and financial structure can we avoid the abyss and create the kind of society that meets our needs. The nature of that new structure should be the subject of intensive democratic discussion and debate in the days to come.

CRISIS AND NEOLIBERAL CAPITALISM

BY DAVID KOTZ

THE FINANCIAL CRISIS AND THE REAL ECONOMY

It is impossible to predict the course of the financial crisis. The effects of the crisis on the real economy could be very large, especially if it engulfs more and more of the financial sector. But even if the financial crisis is contained, the bursting of the housing bubble—which began in 2007 and is bound to continue for some time—will have a powerful downward impact on the economy.

A speculative "bubble" arose in the housing sector of the U.S. economy starting around 2002. By the summer of 2007, housing prices had risen by 70% since 1995 corrected for inflation. Yet since 2002 the real value of home rents had been flat. By 2006 the ratio of the Housing Price Index to the Homeowners Equivalent Rent had risen sharply to an all-time high of 168.3, compared to 110.0 in 1995. This is clear evidence of a huge asset bubble in the U.S. housing market. This bubble created an estimated $8 trillion in inflated new wealth, which was about 38% of the peak total housing wealth of $21 trillion. When this bubble started to collapse in 2007, it set the stage for both a financial crisis and a recession in the "real" economy.

There are two ways in which the collapsing housing bubble affects the real economy. First, there is a downward wealth effect on housing investment and consumer spending. The collapse of the bubble in the housing sector has led to a sharp drop in residential investment. Since the second quarter of 2007, it has been falling at 21.6% annual rate. Second, falling home values are causing a reduction in consumer spending. Since 2002 households had been borrowing against their homes to get funds for consumer spending. One study estimated that during 2004-06 Americans took $840 billion per year from their home equity through borrowing and capital gains from the sale of housing. This was almost 10% of disposable personal income in the United States.

Suddenly, in 2007, people could no longer supplement their income with funds borrowed against their home, which has now led to a large drop in consumer spending, at a 3.1% per year rate in the third quarter of 2008. This happened *before* the financial crisis had begun to affect consumer spending. If all of the estimated $8 trillion of inflated home value disappears, the estimated effect on aggregate consumption would be a reduction of about $320 billion to $480 billion per year, or about 5% of total consumption. Dean Baker, co-director of the Center for Economic and Policy Research and a respected analyst of the financial crisis, estimated the total effect of the collapsing housing bubble to be a decline of between 3.1% and 7.0% of GDP.

The collapse of the bubble also affects investment in new plant and equipment by business. After several quarters of little growth, business investment fell at a 1% annual rate in the first quarter of 2008. The bubble-propelled and debt-financed expansions of 1991-2000 and 2001-2007 produced a growing amount of productive capacity, relative to ordinary income. As the current crash develops, industry will find it has substantial excess productive capacity. As a result, the incentive for business investment may be depressed for some time. In the last recession in the United States, in 2001, business fixed investment fell for two consecutive years, at an accelerating rate, for this reason.

A severe recession was averted in 2001–2002 by the start of the housing bubble. It does not seem possible for a new bubble to arise and avert a serious recession this time. Also, the financial crisis is likely to make the coming recession more severe. One way this happens is that banks' reluctance to lend to business due to the financial crisis will worsen the recession. Secondly, the stock market collapse precipitated by the financial crisis will have effects similar to the effects of the housing price collapse—it will tend to reduce consumer and investment demand. The only bright spot for the U.S. economy has been exports, but they are not likely to continue to do well in the face of a spreading global recession.

THE RESTRUCTURING IS JUST BEGINNING

Every form of capitalism has contradictions that eventually bring about a structural crisis of that form of capitalism. In the 1970s the system of state-regulated capitalism, having produced rapid growth and high profits for a few decades, stopped working effectively and went into structural crisis. The predominant form of capitalism changed to the "neoliberal" form, which means a type of capitalism in which the state plays a limited role in the economy, particularly withdrawing from activities that benefit ordinary people. It now appears that neoliberal capitalism can no longer overcome two key problems and is entering a structural crisis of its own. First, the high and rising inequality it generates means that the majority has insufficient income to buy the growing output of the economy without relying on an unsustainable buildup of household debt. Second, the deregulated financial system of neoliberal capitalism is inherently unstable, as we have so clearly seen in recent months.

From 1945 to 1973, a regulated form of capitalism predominated in the world, including in the United States. Regulated capitalism here included extensive government regulation of business and finance, regulation of the macro-economy (aimed partly at achieving a relatively low unemployment rate), social programs that amounted to a modest welfare state, relatively cooperative relations between big business and trade unions, restrained competition between big corporations, and trade and capital flows regulated by governments and international institutions.

The shift to neoliberal capitalism in the United States involved the deregulation of business and finance, the reduction of active government macroeconomic policy (and a shift of aim to assuring low inflation, not low unemployment), sharply reduced social programs, a big business and government attack against labor unions, unrestrained ("cutthroat") competition among large corporations, and relatively free movement of goods, services, and capital across national boundaries. This neoliberal transformation of capitalism was relatively thorough in the United States, the United Kingdom, and in international financial institutions such as the International Monetary Fund and World Bank.

As neoliberal capitalism enters a period of crisis, we can see the rapid loss of legitimacy of the previously reigning dominant "free market" ideology. This is similar to the sudden demise of the previously dominant Keynesian ideology of regulated capitalism in the 1970s. Capitalism is going to be restructured, in the United States and globally, during the coming years. The outcome of this restructuring process, however, is not pre-determined.

So far the bankers have led the initial stage of restructuring. Treasury Secretary Henry Paulson, the former CEO of Wall Street giant Goldman Sachs, has been succeeding so far in getting the government to rescue the banks in ways that mainly benefit the bankers. This process has encouraged rapidly growing concentration of the financial sector, as the largest banks merge with one another and get big cash infusions and new federal backing.

However, the restructuring is just beginning. We can fight for changes that would benefit the majority rather than the bankers. First, the underlying reason for the financial crisis is all those people unable to make the payments on their mortgages. The government should pass an emergency measure to ease mortgage terms to reflect the declining values of homes and the declining economy. This would impose a one-time loss on the financial institutions that invested in the risky new mortgage-based securities, but it would also make it easier to know the value of the mortgage-backed securities, eliminating a source of great uncertainty in the financial system.

Second, millions of people have learned the important lesson that banks and other financial institutions are not ordinary private companies. If General Mills loses money, or even goes bankrupt, it harms its shareholders and workers—but its competitors gain. But if a few major banks lose money and are in danger of going under, this threatens the entire financial system, and with it the economy as a whole.

The obvious conclusion is that the financial sector cannot be operated on a profit and loss basis. Instead, it should become part of the public sector, operated to serve the public interest. If banks, which are granted the power to create our money supply, and whose credit is essential to the welfare of the entire public, were made public institutions, then public policy aims could guide their actions. They could be directed to stay away from speculative activities and instead make loans for socially valuable purposes. This would include steering credit into renewable energy technologies, fuel-efficient vehicles, low cost housing, and other good purposes. An advantage of public ownership of the banks over another cycle of government regulation of private banks is that reregulated private banks would simply press for the elimination of the regulations—as they did successfully starting in the early 1980s.

The developing financial and economic crises have exposed the high-flying financial operators for what they always were—thieves who got rich without doing anything productive. This has also exposed their fallacious free-market ideology. This is a promising time to build popular movements that can fight for progressive changes in our economy.

ARTICLE 4.4

November/December 2008

CAPITALISM HITS THE FAN

BY RICK WOLFF

Let me begin by saying what I think this crisis is not. It is not a *financial* crisis. It is a systemic crisis whose first serious symptom happened to be finance. But this crisis has its economic roots and its effects in manufacturing, services, and, to be sure, finance. It grows out of the relation of wages to profits across the economy. It has profound social roots in America's households and families and political roots in government policies. The current crisis did not start with finance, and it won't end with finance.

From 1820 to around 1970, 150 years, the average productivity of American workers went up each year. Average workers produced more stuff every year than they had the year before. They were trained better, they had more machines, and they had better machines. So productivity went up every year.

And, over this period of time, the wages of American workers rose every decade. Every decade, real wages—the amount of money you get in relation to the prices you pay for the things you use your money for—were higher than the decade before. Profits also went up.

The American working class enjoyed 150 years of rising consumption, so it's not surprising that it would choose to define its own self-worth, measure its own success in life, according to the standard of consumption. Americans began to think of themselves as successful if they lived in the right neighborhood, drove the right car, wore the right outfit, went on the right vacation.

But in the 1970s, the world changed for the American working class in ways that it hasn't come to terms with—at all. Real wages stopped going up. As U.S. corporations moved operations abroad to take advantage of lower wages and higher profits and as they replaced workers with machines (and especially computers), those who lost their jobs were soon willing to work even if their wages stopped rising. So real wages trended down a little bit. The real hourly wage of a worker in the 1970s was higher than what it is today. What you get for an hour of work, in goods and services, is less now that what your parents got.

Meanwhile, productivity kept going up. If what the employer gets from each worker keeps going up, but what you give to each worker does not, then the difference becomes bigger, and bigger, and bigger. Employers' profits have gone wild, and all the people who get their fingers on employers profits—the professionals who sing the songs they like to hear, the shareholders who get a piece of the action on each company's profits—have enjoyed a bonanza over the last thirty years.

The only thing more profitable than simply making the money off the worker is handling this exploding bundle of profits—packaging and repackaging it, lending it and borrowing it, and inventing new mechanisms for doing all that. That's called the finance industry, and they have stumbled all over themselves to get a hold of a piece of this immense pot of profit.

What did the working class do? What happens to a population committed to measuring people's success by the amount of consumption they could afford when the means they had always had to achieve it, rising wages, stop? They can go through a trauma right then and there: "We can't anymore—it's over." Most people didn't do that. They found other ways.

Americans undertook more work. People took a second or third job. The number of hours per year worked by the average American worker has risen by about 20 percent since the 1970s. By comparison, in Germany, France, and Italy, the number of hours worked per year per worker has dropped 20 percent. American workers began to work to a level of exhaustion. They sent more family members—and especially women—out to work. This enlarged supply of workers meant that employers could find plenty of employees without having to offer higher pay. Yet, with more family members out working, new kinds of costs and problems hit American families. The woman who goes out to work needs new outfits. In our society, she probably needs another car. With women exhausted from jobs outside and continued work demands inside households, with families stressed by exhaustion and mounting bills, interpersonal tensions mounted and brought new costs: child care, psychotherapy, drugs. Such extra costs neutralized the extra income, so it did not solve the problem.

The American working class had to do a second thing to keep its consumption levels rising. It went on the greatest binge of borrowing in the history of any working class in any country at any time. Members of the business community began to realize that they had a fantastic double opportunity. They could get the profits from flat wages and rising productivity, and then they could turn to the working class traumatized by the inability to have rising consumption, and give them the means to consume more. So instead of paying your workers a wage, you're going to lend them the money—so they have to pay it back to you! With interest!

That solved the problem. For a while, employers could pay the workers the same or less, and instead of creating the usual problems for capitalism—workers without enough income to buy all the output their increased productivity yields—rising worker debt seemed magical. Workers could consume ever more; profits exploding in every category. Underneath the magic, however, there were workers who were completely exhausted, whose families were falling apart, and who were now ridden with anxiety because their rising debts were unsustainable. This was a system built to fail, to reach its end when the combination of physical exhaustion and emotional anxiety from the debt made people unable to continue. Those people are, by the millions, walking away from those obligations, and the house of cards comes down.

If you put together (a) the desperation of the American working class and (b) the efforts of the finance industry to scrounge out every conceivable borrower, the idea that the banks would end up lending money to people who couldn't pay it back is not a tough call. The system, however, was premised on the idea that that would not happen, and when it happened nobody was prepared.

The conservatives these days are in a tough spot. The story about how markets and private enterprise interact to produce wonderful outcomes is, even for them these days, a cause for gagging. Of course, ever resourceful, there are conservatives who will rise to the occasion, sort of like dead fish. They rattle off twenty things the government did over the last twenty years, which indeed it did, and draw a line from those things the government did to this disaster now, to reach the conclusion that the reason we have this problem now is too much government intervention. These days they get nowhere. Even the mainstream press has a hard time with this stuff.

What about the liberals and many leftists too? They seem to favor regulation. They think the problem was that the banks weren't regulated, that credit-rating companies weren't regulated, that the Federal Reserve didn't regulate better, or differently, or more, or something. Salaries should be regulated to not be so high. Greed should be regulated. I find this astonishing and depressing.

In the 1930s, the last time we had capitalism hitting the fan in this way, we produced a lot of regulation. Social Security didn't exist before then. Unemployment insurance didn't exist before then. Banks were told: you can do this, but you can't do that. Insurance companies were told: you can do that, but you can't do this. They limited what the board of directors of a corporation could do ten ways to Sunday. They taxed them. They did all sorts of things that annoyed, bothered, and troubled boards of directors because the regulations impeded the boards' efforts to grow their companies and make money for the shareholders who elected them.

You don't need to be a great genius to understand that the boards of directors encumbered by all these regulations would have a very strong incentive to evade them, to undermine them, and, if possible, to get rid of them. Indeed, the boards went to work on that project as soon as the regulations were passed. The crucial fact about the regulations imposed on business in the 1930s is that they did not take away from the boards of directors the freedom or the incentives or the opportunities to undo all the regulations and reforms. The regulations left in place an institution devoted to their undoing. But that wasn't the worst of it. They also left in place boards of directors who, as the first appropriators of all the profits, had the *resources* to undo the regulations. This peculiar system of regulation had a built-in self-destruct button.

Over the last thirty years, the boards of directors of the United States' larger corporations have used their profits to buy the president and the Congress, to buy the public media, and to wage a systematic campaign, from 1945 to 1975, to evade the regulations, and, after 1975, to get rid of them. And it worked. That's why we're here now. And if you impose another set of regulations along the lines liberals propose, not only are you going to have the same history, but you're going to have the same history faster. The right wing in America, the business community, has spent the last fifty years perfecting every technique that is known to turn the population against regulation. And they're going to go right to work to do it again, and they'll do it better, and they'll do it faster.

So what do we do? Let's regulate, by all means. Let's try to make a reasonable economic system that doesn't allow the grotesque abuses we've seen in recent decades. But let's not reproduce the self-destruct button. This time the change has to include the following: The people in every enterprise who do the work of that enterprise, will become collectively their own board of directors. For the first time in American history, the people who depend on the survival of those regulations will be in the position of receiving the profits of their own work and using them to make the regulations succeed rather than sabotaging them.

This proposal for workers to collectively become their own board of directors also democratizes the enterprise. The people who work in an enterprise, the front line of those who have to live with what it does, where it goes, how it uses its wealth, they should be the people who have influence over the decisions it makes. That's democracy.

Maybe we could even extend this argument to democracy in our political life, which leaves a little to be desired—some people call it a "formal" democracy, that isn't real. Maybe the problem all along has been that you can't have a real democracy politically if you don't have a real democracy underpinning it economically. If the workers are not in charge of their work situations, five days a week, 9 to 5, the major time of their adult lives, then how much aptitude and how much appetite are they going to have to control their political life? Maybe we need the democracy of economics, not just to prevent the regulations from being undone, but also to realize the political objectives of democracy.

THE GREED FALLACY
YOU CAN'T EXPLAIN A CHANGE WITH A CONSTANT

BY ARTHUR MACEWAN

Various people explain the current financial crisis as a result of "greed." There is, however, no indication of a change in the degree or extent of greed on Wall Street (or anywhere else) in the last several years. Greed is a constant. If greed were the cause of the financial crisis, we would be in financial crisis pretty much all the time.

But the financial markets have not been in perpetual crisis. Nothing close to the current crisis has taken place since 1929. Yes, there was 1987 and the savings-and-loan debacle of that era. But, the current crisis is already more dramatic—and threatens to get a good deal worse. This crisis emerged over the last decade and appeared full-blown only at the beginning of 2008 (though, if you were looking, it was moving up on the horizon a year or two earlier). The current mess, therefore, is a change, a departure from the normal course of financial markets. So something has to have changed to have brought it about. The constant of greed cannot be the explanation.

So what changed? The answer is relatively simple: the extent of regulation changed.

As a formal matter, the change in regulation is most clearly marked by the Gramm-Leach-Bliley Act of 1999, passed by the Republican-dominated Congress and signed into law by Bill Clinton. This act in large part repealed the Glass-Steagall Act of 1933, which had imposed various regulations on the financial industry after the debacle of 1929. Among other things, Glass-Steagall prohibited a firm from being engaged in different sorts of financial services. One firm could not be both an investment bank (organizing the funding of firms' investment activities) and a commercial bank (handling the checking and savings accounts of individuals and firms and making loans); nor could it be one of these types of banks and an insurance firm.

However, the replacement of Glass-Steagall by Gramm-Leach-Bliley was only the formal part of the change that took place in recent decades. Informally, the relation between the government and the financial sector has increasingly become one of reduced regulation. In particular, as the financial sector evolved new forms of operation—hedge funds and private equity funds, for example—there was no attempt on the part of Washington to develop regulations for these activities. Also, even where regulations existed, the regulators became increasingly lax in enforcement.

The movement away from regulation might be seen as a consequence of "free market" ideology, the belief as propounded by its advocates that government should leave the private sector alone. But to see the problem simply as ideology run amok is to ignore the question of where the ideology comes from. Put simply, the ideology is generated by firms themselves because they want to be as free as possible to pursue profit-making activity. So they push the idea of the "free market" and deregulation any way they can. But let me leave aside for now the ways in which ideas come to dominate Washington and the society in general; enough to recognize that deregulation became increasingly the dominant idea from the early 1980s onward. (But, given the current presidential campaign, one cannot refrain from noting that one way the firms get their ideas to dominate is through the money they lavish on candidates.)

When financial firms are not regulated, they tend to take on more and more risky activities. When markets are rising, risk does not seem to be very much of a problem; all—or virtually all—investments seem to be making money. So why not take some chances? Furthermore, if one firm doesn't take a particular risk—put money into a chancy operation—then one of its competitors will. So competition pushes them into more and more risky operations.

The danger of risk is not simply that one investment—one loan, for example—made by a financial firm will turn out bad-ly, or even that a group of loans will turn out badly. The danger arises in the relation between its loans (obligations to the firm), the money it borrows from others (the firm's obligations to its creditors) and its capital (the funds put in by investors, the stockholders). If some of the loans it has made go bad (i.e., if the debtors default), it can still meet its obligations to its creditors with its capital. But if the firm is unregulated, it will tend to make more and more loans and take on more and more debt. The ratio of debt to capital can become very high, and, then, if trouble with the loans develops, the bank cannot meet its obligations with its capital.

In the current crisis, the deflation of the housing bubble was the catalyst to the general crumbling of financial structures. The housing bubble was in large part a product of the Federal Reserve Bank's policies under the guidance of the much-heralded Alan Greenspan, but let's leave that issue aside for now.

When the housing bubble burst, many financial institutions found themselves in trouble. They had taken on too much risk in relation to their capital. The lack of regulation had allowed them to get in this trouble.

But the trouble is much worse than it might have been because of the repeal of the provisions of Glass-Steagall that prevented the merging of investment banks, commercial banks, and insurance companies. Under the current circumstances, when trouble develops in one part of a firm's operations, it is immediately transmitted throughout the other segments of that firm. And from there, the trouble spreads to all the other entities to which it is connected—through credits, insurance deals, deposits, and a myriad set of complicated (unregulated) financial arrangements.

AIG is the example *par excellence*. Ostensibly an insurance company, AIG has morphed into a multi-faceted financial institution, doing everything from selling life insurance in rural India to speculating in various esoteric types of investments on Wall Street. Its huge size, combined with the extent of its intertwining with other financial firms, meant that its failure would have had very large impacts around the world.

The efforts of the U.S. government may or may not be able to contain the current financial crisis. Success would not breathe life back into the Lehman Brothers, Bear Stearns, and who knows how many other major operators that are on their deathbeds. But it would prevent the financial crisis from precipitating a severe general depression; it would prevent a movement from 1929 to 1932.

The real issue, however, is what is learned from the current financial mess. One thing should be evident, namely that greed did not cause the crisis. The cause was a change in the way markets have been allowed to operate, a change brought on by the rise of deregulation. Markets, especially financial markets, are never very stable when left to themselves. It turns out that the "invisible hand" does some very nasty, messy things when there is no visible hand of regulation affecting the process.

The problem is that maintaining some form of regulation is a very difficult business. As I have said, the firms themselves do not want to be regulated. The current moment may allow some re-imposition of financial regulation. But as soon as we turn our backs, the pressure will be on again to let the firms operate according to the "free market." Let's not forget where that leads.

ARTICLE 4.6   *November/December 2008*

TOP TEN WAYS TO RECOGNIZE THE NEXT GREAT DEPRESSION

BY JOHN MILLER

Maybe it is just a professional liability, but I have spent much of the last few months thinking about when someone would have known they were living through the Great Depression. Would you have known as early as the October 1929 stock market crash that an economic collapse was in the making? If not, then would the seizing up of commerce by 1931 have convinced you that the economic doom was inescapable? Or perhaps the magnitude of the situation would not have become clear until 1933, when the economy hit its low point and more than a quarter of the U.S. workforce was without work?

Without meaning to suggest that we already are in the midst of the next Great Depression—although a prolonged economic malaise is surely possible—I have put together a list of the top ten ways to know whether today's economic crisis is morphing into the next Great Depression.

10. EXTREME INEQUALITY

In 1928, on the eve of the stock market crash, 23.9% of all income went to the richest one percent of Americans. Depression then brought about a shift in income distribution: by 1931, the top one percent saw their income share plunge to 15.5%.

In 2005, at the peak of the housing bubble, the richest one percent of U.S. households received 21.8% of all income; in 2007 their share was an estimated 23% to 24%. That was the greatest concentration of income since 1928, and more than double the figure in the 1970s. But economist Emmanuel Saez predicts that the share of income held by the top one percent will drop to 18% or 19% in the next two years.

9. REPORTS OF PANIC-STRICKEN WALL STREET INVESTORS JUMPING TO THEIR DEATHS

In October 1929 the stock market collapsed from its peak, beginning with panic selling on Black Thursday, October 24, followed by a 12.8% drop in stock prices four days later and another 11.7% drop the next day. The London tabloids reported rumors that 11 investors had leaped to their deaths, and Will Rogers, the Depression-era humorist, hyped the story. But it wasn't true. A few high-roller investors did commit suicide. Gas or guns, however, were the usual methods.

Initial losses in the current stock market slide have been nearly comparable to those in October and November 1929, save the single-day double-digit percentage drops; however, we have not read reports of the bloody spectacle of investors jumping out of skyscraper windows. But the element of dark wishful thinking in those Depression-era reports was evident recently when protesters on Wall Street carried signs that read, "Jump you f***ers."

8. DEAD CAT BOUNCE

Like even a dead cat will do, stocks will bounce if they fall from a great height. On November 13, 1929, the stock market reached a floor 47% below its October peak. The market then recovered; by April 1930, bargain hunters had driven stock prices back up to just 25% below their peak level. But the rally faltered, and the dead cat bounce gave way to a downward spiral that went on for over two years until June of 1932 when stock prices hit the real floor, 89% below their peak value.

When stock market prices plummeted by 40% this October, bargain hunters then bid up the stock prices on the Dow Jones by 10.9% in a single day. But with plenty of bad economic news on the horizon, including reports of declining output, slumping retail sales, and massive job losses, the stock market will be hard pressed to bounce much higher than a dead cat.

7. UNDERWATER INVESTORS

Today, according to one report, one-fifth of U.S. homeowners are "under water," owing more on their mortgage than the current value of their home. That was true in 1930s as well, but with a few striking differences. First, during the 1920s, not just houses and stocks lost value, but almost all financial assets, leaving investors across the board holding debt that exceeded the value of their assets—the essence of a depression. Second, while the run-up in stock prices during the 1920s was comparable to that in the 1990s, increasing 17.0% a year between 1923 and 1929 and 18.9% a year between 1994 and 2000, the Depression-era housing bubble can't measure up to this one. Housing prices in the first half of the 1920s, fueled in part by interest-only mortgages much like today, jumped up about one-fifth. But from 1998 to 2006 housing prices nearly doubled, increasing an unprecedented 8.0% a year. That makes today's mortgage crisis proper more dangerous than the Depression-era housing crisis. At the end of 2008, housing prices are down 20.3% from their peak, already wiping out about $5 trillion of the $8 trillion in housing-bubble wealth. But to restore a historically normal ratio of housing prices to median household income, home prices will have to fall another 10% from their peak value.

6. WIDESPREAD BANK FAILURES

Since August 2007, 14 banks, three major investment houses, and a giant insurance company have gone belly up, leaving the financial system "shaken to the core," according to even the *Wall Street Journal*.

But almost 10,000 commercial banks failed from 1929 to 1934. In 1930 the New York-based Bank of the United States, one of the nation's largest banks, failed, and 4,000 banks failed in 1933 alone. That precipitated a national bank holiday and prompted FDR's first fireside radio chat in which he promised listeners that their money would be safer "in a bank than under a mattress." Later in 1933 Congress established the Federal Deposit Insurance Corporation to back up FDR's promise.

5. LIQUIDITY TRAP

During the mid-1930s, short-term interest rates were continuously close to zero. That left the Fed with no room to further cut interest rates in an attempt to get investment spending going again. This September, when the financial crisis hit, the interest rate, or yield, on three-month Treasury bills, among the safest of all assets, plunged to 0.06%. That convinced Keynesian economist and *New York Times* columnist Paul Krugman that "we're quite close to liquidity trap territory"—the point where, once again, monetary policy would no longer be able to lower interest rates. Because the current problem is not a lack of funds but solvency, banks are reluctant to lend, even to other banks, when they don't know much of the economy's bad mortgage debt their customers are holding. When the Fed adds liquidity to the system, banks, like everyone else, buy safe Treasury bills— the functional equivalent of hoarding, since the Treasury returns their money three months later with next to no interest. With few willing to buy other bonds, long-term interest rates, or the yields on those bonds, have not dropped. And that keeps lending prohibitively expensive, for banks and Josephine the Plumber alike, and the economy in check.

4. DEFLATION

During the Great Depression, not just asset prices, but prices across the economy dropped precipitously as goods went unsold. By 1933 prices had fallen 25% from their level at the onset of the depression in 1929.

Today we have seen the price of oil, driven up by speculation earlier in the year, fall by half in just three months. The prices of 13 raw materials including copper, cotton, and rubber are down 29% from their August levels. The consumer price index, the most widely reported measure of inflation, didn't rise in August or September, and is likely to remain flat through 2009 as the economy slows. Should a widespread deflation take hold, sharp cuts in production and employment will surely follow.

3. A WORLDWIDE ECONOMIC DOWNTURN

Capitalist economies across the globe collapsed during the 1930s, not just in the United States. From 1929 to 1932, Gross Domestic Product, the broadest measure of national output, dropped 28% in the United States, 16% in Germany, 8% in Japan, and 6% in Britain.

In the third quarter of this year, U.S economic growth turned negative—in other words, the economy shrank—as consumer spending fell more sharply than at any time since the 1982 recession. And the International Monetary Fund now predicts that the 31 advanced economies of the world, including the United States, Western Europe, and Japan, will contract by a combined 0.3% in 2009. That would be the first time these economies as a group have shrunk since the IMF was founded in 1945.

2. PROMISES TO BALANCE THE BUDGET AS THE ECONOMY GOES TO HELL IN A HANDCART

In the summer of 1932, nearly three years into the Great Depression, candidate Roosevelt promised that he would slash federal expenditures by 25% and balance the budget. But upon taking office in the midst of a banking crisis, he relented and initiated the New Deal. He later famously declared that "to balance the budget in 1933, or 1934, or 1935 would be a crime against the American people." Still, only the massive government spending associated with World War II brought the Great Depression to a close.

This year, even after the financial crisis had struck, Congress had passed a $700 billion bailout package, and the economy had shed jobs every month of the year, both major party presidential candidates continued to promise to balance the federal budget. Without a commitment of massive government spending and without the political will to brand balancing the budget as a "crime against the American people," today's crisis might also drag on for a decade.

1. BREADLINES

We haven't seen a return of the breadlines that formed in major cities across the country during the 1930s. But Suze Orman, a popular financial advisor, recently told a television audience that the economy would be in "intensive care for a year to 18 months" and was facing "five years of decline" that "could mean breadlines." And in Massachusetts the number of families in homeless shelters reached record levels in September.

ARTICLE 4.7

November/December 2008

FINANCIALIZATION: A PRIMER

BY RAMAA VASUDEVAN

You don't have to be an investor dabbling in the stock market to feel the power of finance. Finance pervades the lives of ordinary people in many ways, from student loans and credit card debt to mortgages and pension plans.

And its size and impact are only getting bigger. Consider a few measures:

- U.S. credit market debt—all debt of private households, businesses, and government combined—rose from about 1.6 times the nation's GDP in 1973 to over 3.5 times GDP by 2007.
- The profits of the financial sector represented 14% of total corporate profits in 1981; by 2001-02 this figure had risen to nearly 50%.

These are only a few of the indicators of what many commentators have labeled the "financialization" of the economy—a process University of Massachusetts economist Gerald Epstein succinctly defines as "the increasing importance of financial markets, financial motives, financial institutions, and financial elites in the operation of the economy and its governing institutions."

In recent years, this phenomenon has drawn increasing attention. In his latest book, pundit Kevin Phillips writes about the growing divergence between the real (productive) and financial economies, describing how the explosion of trading in myriad new financial instruments played a role in polarizing the U.S. economy. On the left, political economists Harry Magdoff and Paul Sweezy had over many years pointed to the growing role of finance in the operations of capitalism; they viewed the trend as a reflection of the rising economic and political power of "rentiers"—those whose earnings come from financial activities and from forms of income arising from ownership claims (such as interest, rent, dividends, or capital gains) rather than from actual production.

FROM FINANCE TO FINANCIALIZATION

The financial system is supposed to serve a range of functions in the broader economy. Banks and other financial institutions mop up savings, then allocate that capital, according to mainstream theory, to where it can most productively be used. For households and corporations, the credit markets facilitate greatly increased borrowing, which should foster investment in capital goods like buildings and machinery, in turn leading to expanded production. Finance, in other words, is supposed to facilitate the growth of the "real" economy—the part that produces useful goods (like bicycles) and services (like medical care).

In recent decades, finance has undergone massive changes in both size and shape. The basic mechanism of financialization is the transformation of future streams of income (from profits, dividends, or interest payments) into a tradable asset like a stock or a bond. For example, the future earnings of corporations are transmuted into equity stocks that are bought and sold in the capital market. Likewise, a loan, which involves certain fixed interest payments over its duration, gets a new life when it is converted into marketable bonds. And multiple loans, bundled together then "sliced and diced" into novel kinds of bonds ("collateralized debt obligations"), take on a new existence as investment vehicles that bear an extremely complex and opaque relationship to the original loans.

The process of financialization has not made finance more effective at fulfilling what conventional economic theory views as its core function. Corporations are not turning to the stock market as a source of finance for their investments, and their borrowing in the bond markets is often not for the purpose of productive investment either. Since the 1980s, corporations have actually spent more money buying back their own stock than they have taken in by selling newly issued stock. The granting of stock options to top executives gives them a direct incentive to have the corporation buy back its own shares—often using borrowed money to do so—in order to hike up the share price and allow them to turn a profit on the sale of their personal shares. More broadly, instead of fostering investment, financialization reorients managerial incentives toward chasing short-term returns through financial trading and speculation so as to generate ballooning earnings, lest their companies face falling stock prices and the threat of hostile takeover.

What is more, the workings of these markets tend to act like an upper during booms, when euphoric investors chase the promise of quick bucks. During downturns these same mechanisms work like downers, turning euphoria into panic as investors flee. Financial innovations like collateralized debt obligations were supposed to "lubricate" the economy by spreading risk, but instead they tend to heighten volatility, leading to amplified cycles of boom and bust. In the current crisis, the innovation of mortgage-backed securities fueled the housing bubble and encouraged enormous risk-taking, creating the conditions for the chain reaction of bank (and other financial institution) failures that may be far from over.

FINANCIALIZATION AND POWER

The arena of finance can at times appear to be merely a casino —albeit a huge one—where everyone gets to place her bets and ride her luck. But the financial system carries a far deeper significance for people's lives. Financial assets and liabilities represent claims on ownership and property; they embody the social relations of an economy at a particular time in history. In this sense, the recent process of financialization implies the increasing political and economic power of a particular segment of the capitalist class: rentiers. Accelerating financial transactions and the profusion of financial techniques have fuelled an extraordinary enrichment of this elite.

This enrichment arises in different ways. Financial transactions facilitate the reallocation of capital to high-return ventures. In the ensuing shake-up, some sectors of capital profit at the expense of other sectors. More important, the capitalist class as a whole is able to force a persistent redistribution in its favor, deploying its newly expanded wealth to bring about changes in the political-economy that channel even more wealth its way.

The structural changes that paved the way for financialization involved the squashing of working-class aspirations during the Reagan-Thatcher years; the defeats of the miners' strike in England and of the air traffic controllers' (PATCO) strike in the United States were perhaps the most symbolic instances of this process. At the same time, these and other governments increasingly embraced the twin policy mantras of fighting inflation and deregulating markets in place of creating full employment and raising wages. Corporations pushed through legislation to dismantle the financial regulations that inhibited their profitmaking strategies.

Financialization has gathered momentum amid greater inequality. In the United States, the top 1% of the population received 14.0% of the national after-tax income in 2004, nearly double its 7.5% share in 1979. In the same period the share of the bottom fifth fell from 6.8% to 4.9%.

And yet U.S. consumption demand has been sustained despite rising inequality and a squeeze on real wages for the majority of households. Here is the other side of the financialization coin: a massive expansion of consumer credit has played an important role in easing the constraints on consumer spending by filling the gap created by stagnant or declining real wages. The credit card debt of the average U.S. family increased by 53% through the 1990s. About 67% of low-income families with incomes less than $10,000 faced credit card debt, and the debt of this group saw the largest increase—a 184% rise, compared to a 28% increase for families with incomes above $100,000. Offered more and more credit as a privatized means of addressing wage stagnation, then, eventually, burdened by debt and on the edge of insolvency, the working poor and the middle class are less likely to organize as a political force to challenge the dominance of finance. In this sense, financialization becomes a means of social coercion that erodes working-class solidarity.

As the structures created by financial engineering unravel, the current economic crisis is revealing the cracks in this edifice. But even as a growing number of U.S. families are losing their homes and jobs in the wake of the subprime meltdown, the financial companies at the heart of the crisis have been handed massive bailouts and their top executives have pocketed huge payouts despite their role in abetting the meltdown—a stark sign of the power structures and interests at stake in this era of financialization.

Sources: Robin Blackburn, "Finance and the Fourth Dimension," *New Left Review* 39 May-June 2006; Robert Brenner, "New Boom or Bubble," *New Left Review* 25 Jan-Feb 2004; Tamara Draut and Javier Silva, "Borrowing to make ends meet," *Demos*, Sept 2003; Gerald

Epstein, "Introduction" in G. Epstein, ed., *Financialization and the World* Economy, 2006; John Bellamy Foster, "The Financialization of Capitalism," *Monthly Review*, April 2007; Gretta Krippner, "The financialization of the US economy," *Socio-Economic Review* 3, Feb. 2005; Thomas Palley, "Financialization: What it is and why it matters," Political Economy Research Institute Working Paper #153, November 2007; A. Sherman and Arin Dine, "New CBO data shows inequality continues to widen," Center for Budget Priorities, Jan. 23, 2007; Kevin Phillips, *Bad Money: Reckless Finance, Failed Politics, and the Global Crisis of American Capitalism*, 2008.

CHAPTER 5
FISCAL POLICY, DEFICITS, AND DEBT

INTRODUCTION

Most textbooks depict a macroeconomy stabilized by government intervention. Reflecting the influence of Keynes, they look at ways the government can use fiscal policy—government spending and taxation—to bolster a flagging economy. Today's economy, mired in the worst economic crisis since the Great Depression, is surely flagging. Worse yet, that crisis comes on the heels of a feeble economic expansion that created fewer jobs and did less to raise wages than any other economic expansion since World War II (see Article 1.1).

What is the role of fiscal policy in this context? As the crisis worsened in the fall of 2008, the federal government dramatically increased government spending. Congress passed the Troubled Asset Recovery Program (TARP), which bailed out giant investment banks and insurance companies. Congress then passed a second stimulus package and the Obama budget, which provided some much-needed domestic spending but also boosted military spending. At the same time, the Bernanke Federal Reserve and the Federal Deposit Insurance Corporation (which insures bank deposits) issued loans, lines of credit, and loan guarantees and pledged an emergency fund to clean up losses on Wall Street. All told, the federal government, the Fed, and the FDIC have sunk $12.8 trillion of taxpayer money, nearly the value of a year's national output, into propping up the failed financial sector and rescuing the economy. (See chapter 4 and chapter 6 for more on the financial bailout.)

Only some of those commitments appear in the federal budget. All of this spending has been enough to push government spending far above tax revenues, ringing up a deficit of $1.7 trillion, or 12 percent of GDP in the 2009 fiscal year, according to the latest estimates. This year's deficit and those in the next few years will likely swell federal government debt to 70 percent of GDP early in the next decade. Those are indeed record "peacetime" deficits.

Our coverage of the federal government's attempts to revive the economy begins with the Obama stimulus package. Economist John Miller argues that the stimulus package provided much-needed domestic spending but fell well short of what is needed to turn the economy around and relieve the suffering of those enduring today's economic hard times. He also takes on the crowding-out argument, the conservative argument that government spending will not provide economic stimulus (Article 5.2). Economist Randy Albelda takes a close look at gaping holes in the social safety net for the poor. She argues that stimulus spending needs to repair the safety net, not just bridges and highways (Article 5.3). Economist Ryan Dodd makes the case for the government acting as the economy's employer of last resort, arguing that direct job creation is the ultimate cure to catastrophic economic slumps (Article 5.1).

Today's massive federal budget deficits are not just a product of stimulus spending and declining tax revenues as the economy slows. Arthur MacEwan's article reminds us that the Bush tax cuts and war spending had already blown a sizeable hole in the federal budget when the crisis struck. Also, tax cuts for the rich, the hallmark of Bush's fiscal policy, did remarkably little to add to economic growth (Article 5.4). Paul Krugman's article explains that the 2001–2003 tax cuts can only be sustained by shredding the social safety net, the kind of spending which had added far more to economic growth than the Bush tax cuts. Unfortunately, as Krugman shows, that was exactly the point (Article 5.5). Finally, Miller examines the *Wall Street Journal* editor's complaint that U.S corporations are overtaxed. Riddled with loopholes, effective tax rates on U.S. corporations are below those on corporations in most industrialized countries (Article 5.6).

With record budget deficits, attention has turned to the long-term solvency of Social Security. Conservatives are once again issuing calls to privatize social security. Economist Doug Orr examines the merits of the privatization proposals and finds them wanting. Orr shows that, left alone, Social Security is unlikely to suffer a shortfall in revenues, let alone a crisis. He argues that proposals to privatize social security are not designed to make the system solvent, but are actually aimed at propping up the prices of financial assets (Article 5.7).

Health care programs, whose fate will likely be determined in Congress this year, also suffered under the slash-and-burn approach of privatization. James Woolman looks into Health Savings Accounts (HSAs), created by Congress in 2003 and backed by the Bush Administration.

KEY TO COLANDER

E = Economics   M = Macroeconomics

These readings complement E27-E29, E34, E35 or M11-M15, M17, M18.

Colander's chapter E35, M18 "The Modern Fiscal Policy Dilemma," provides good background to articles 5.1, 5.2, 5.3, and 5.4, which cover recent issues on governmental stimulus spending.

Chapters E34 and M17 on "Deficits and Debt" are also covered in **essays 5.4, 5.5, and 5.6**.

Woolman finds that HSAs are putting consumers with families, health problems, or low incomes at risk of large out-of-pocket expenditures, while awarding high-income, healthy purchasers with tax breaks (Article 5.8).

DISCUSSION QUESTIONS

1. (Article 5.1) What is the case for making the federal government the economy's employer of last resort? Why is Dodd convinced a modern WPA program will work?
2. (Article 5.2) Does private or public spending do more to stimulate economic growth in a collapsing economy? What evidence supports your answer? Given that evidence, what do you think would be the most effective stimulus package for the U.S. economy?
3. (Article 5.3) How have changes over the last two decades left the social safety net in tatters? How might the stimulus package both repair the social safety net and get the economy going again? What is the basis of Albelda's claim that the tax code treats investment income more favorably than wage income?
4. (Article 5.4) According to MacEwan, are military spending and tax cuts effective economic stimuli? What evidence does MacEwan use to make his case?
5. (Article 5.5) What does Krugman think is the hidden agenda of those currently pushing for tax cuts? Do you agree with his analysis? Explain why or why not.
6. (Article 5.6) How have one-quarter of large U.S. corporations gotten away with not paying taxes on their profits? And how do effective corporate tax rates in the United States compare with those in Europe and other industrialized economies?
7. (Article 5.7) What convinces Orr that the Social Security system is not suffering a crisis? What is the looming bond market crisis that Orr says is the real concern of those who want to privatize Social Security?
8. (Article 5.8) According to Woolman, what has been the track record of Health Savings Accounts? Have they worked for employees? Which ones? Have HSAs worked for employers?

A NEW WPA?

NATIONAL GOVERNMENTS, BY SERVING AS "EMPLOYERS OF LAST RESORT," COULD GUARANTEE FULL EMPLOYMENT BY PROVIDING A JOB FOR ANYONE READY, WILLING AND ABLE TO WORK.

BY RYAN A. DODD

Dark clouds are now looming over America's economic future. As first the stock market boom and then the housing boom have come to an end, along with the fountains of cheap credit that were their mainspring, the perennial gale of unemployment is blowing in. The president and Congress have addressed the downturn with tax rebates and talk of "debt relief." Meanwhile, public infrastructure is crumbling. Workers' wages are stagnating while their work hours are rising. Health insurance is becoming less and less affordable for the typical family. And as U.S. military spending escalates, government spending on essential services is drastically reduced.

All of these facts serve to remind us that capitalist economies are inherently unstable and structurally incapable of creating full employment at decent wages and benefits. While tax rebates and debt relief may provide some minor protection from the coming economic storm, these measures are temporary—and inadequate—responses to a perpetual problem. As an alternative to these ad hoc policies or, worse yet, the free-market fundamentalism still widely preached in Washington, some economists and policymakers, in the United States and abroad, are touting a policy that seeks to end unemployment via a government promise to provide a job to anyone ready, willing, and able to work.

ARGENTINA'S EXPERIMENT IN DIRECT JOB CREATION

In early December 2001, following nearly two decades of neoliberal restructuring, the Argentine economy collapsed. Apparently, two decades of privatization, liberalization, and government austerity, ushered in by Argentina's brutal military junta (in power from 1976 to 1983), were not enough to sate the appetites of global financial capital: earlier that year the International Monetary Fund had withheld $1.3 billion in loans the country needed to service its $142 billion external debt. In response to the IMF's action, the government froze all bank accounts (although many wealthy Argentines managed to relocate their funds abroad before the freeze) and drastically cut government spending. As a consequence, the economy experienced a severe depression as incomes and expenditures fell through the floor. The unemployment rate shot up to a record 21.5% by May 2002, with over 50% of the population living in poverty.

The popular response to the crisis was massive. Protests and demonstrations erupted throughout the country. The government went through five presidents in the course of a month. Workers eventually reclaimed dozens of abandoned factories and created democratically run cooperative enterprises, many of which are still in operation today and are part of a growing coop movement.

Reclaiming factories was a lengthy and difficult process, however, and the immediate problem of unemployment remained. In response, in April 2002 the Argentine government put into place a direct job creation program known as *Plan Jefes de Hogar* ("Heads-of-Household Plan"), which promised a job to all heads of households satisfying certain requirements. In order to qualify, a household had to include a child under the age of 18, a person with a disability, or a pregnant woman; the household head had to be unemployed; and each household was generally limited to only one participant in the program. The program provided households with 150 pesos a month for four hours of work a day, five days a week. Program participants mainly engaged in the provision of community services and/or participated in worker training programs administered by local nonprofits.

While limited in scope and viewed by many in the government as an emergency measure, the program was incredibly successful and popular with its workers. It provided jobs and incomes to roughly two million workers, or 13% of Argentina's labor force, as well as bringing desperately needed goods and services—from community gardens to small construction projects—to severely depressed neighborhoods. The entry of many women into the program, while their husbands continued to look for jobs in the private sector, had a liberating effect on traditional family structures. And by some accounts, the program helped facilitate the cooperative movement that subsequently emerged with the takeover of abandoned factories. Not surprisingly, as Argentina's economy has recovered from the depths of the crisis, the government has recently made moves to discontinue this critical experiment in direct job creation.

"EMPLOYER OF LAST RESORT"

The Argentine experience with direct job creation represents a real-world example of what is often referred to as the *employer of last resort* (ELR) proposal by a number of left academics and public policy advocates. Developed over the course of the past two decades, the ELR proposal is based on a rather simple idea. In a capitalist economy, with most people dependent on private employment for their livelihoods, the government has a unique responsibility to guarantee full employment. This responsibility has been affirmed in the U.N. Universal Declaration of Human Rights, which includes a right to employment. A commitment to full employment is also official U.S. government policy as codified in the Employment Act of 1946 and the Humphrey-Hawkins Act of 1976.

Although many versions of the ELR proposal have been put forward, they all revolve around the idea that national governments could guarantee full employment by providing a job to anyone ready, willing, and able to work. The various proposals differ mainly on the wage and benefit packages they would provide to participants. The most common proposal calls for paying all participants a universal basic wage and benefit package, regardless of skills, work experience, or prior earnings. This wage and benefit package would then form the effective minimum for both the public and private sectors of the economy. After fixing a wage and benefit package, the government would allow the quantity of workers in the program to float, rising and falling in response to cyclical fluctuations in private-sector employment.

As with Argentina's program, ELR proposals typically call for participants to work in projects to improve their local communities—everything from basic infrastructure projects to a Green Jobs Corps. Most ELR proponents also advocate a decentralized approach similar to Argentina's, with local public or nonprofit institutions planning and administering the projects, though it is essential that the program be funded at the national level.

This raises an important question: How will governments pay for such a large-scale program? Wouldn't an ELR program require significantly raising taxes or else result in exploding budget deficits? Can governments really afford to employ everyone who wants a job but cannot find one in the private economy? Advocates of ELR address the issue of affordability in different ways, but all agree that the benefits to society vastly outweigh the expense. Many ELR advocates go even further, arguing that any talk of "costs" to society misrepresents the nature of the problem of unemployment. The existence of unemployed workers represents a net cost to society, in terms of lost income and production as well as the psychological and social stresses that result from long spells of unemployment. Employing them represents a net benefit, in terms of increased incomes *and* enhanced individual and social well-being. The real burden of an ELR program, from the perspective of society, is thus effectively zero.

Most estimates of the direct cost of an ELR program are in the range of less than 1% of GDP per year. For the United States, this was less than $132 billion in 2006, or about 5% of the federal budget. (By way of comparison, in 2006 the U.S. government spent over $120 billion on the wars in Iraq and Afghanistan—and that figure does not include the cost of lives lost or ruined or the future costs incurred, for example, for veterans' health care.) Furthermore, an ELR program provides benefits to society in the form of worker retraining, enhanced public infrastructure, and increased social output (e.g., cleaner parks and cities, free child care, public performances, etc.). By increasing the productivity of those participants who attend education or training programs, an ELR program would also decrease real costs throughout the economy. Estimates of program costs take into account a reduction in other forms of social assistance such as food stamps, cash assistance, and unemployment insurance, which would instead be provided to ELR participants in the form of a wage and benefit package. Of course, those who cannot work would still be eligible for these and other forms of assistance.

Today, the ELR idea is mostly confined to academic journals and conferences. Still, proponents can point to a number of little known real-world examples their discussions have helped to shape. For example, the Argentine government explicitly based its *Jefes de Hogar* program on the work of economists associated with the Center for Full Employment and Price Stability (CFEPS) at the University of Missouri-Kansas City. Daniel Kostzer, an economist at the Argentine Ministry of Labor and one of the main architects of the program, had become familiar with the CFEPS proposal and was attempting to create such a program in Argentina a few years before the collapse provided him with the necessary political support. Similar experiments are being considered or are currently underway in India, France, and Bolivia. Advocates of ELR proposals can also be found at the Levy Economics Institute (U.S.), the Center for Full Employment and Equity (Australia), and the National Jobs for All Coalition (U.S.).

THE CASE FOR DIRECT JOB CREATION

Involuntary unemployment is a fundamental and inherent feature of a capitalist economy left to its own devices. In a society where most people depend on employment in the private sector for their livelihood, the inability of a capitalist economy to consistently create enough jobs for all who seek work is deeply troubling, pointing to the need for intervention from outside of the private sector. ELR advocates view national governments—with their unique spending abilities, and with their role as, in principle, democratically accountable social institutions—as the most logical institutions for collective action to bring about full employment. In addition, government job creation is viewed as the simplest and most direct means for overcoming the problem of involuntary unemployment in a capitalist economy.

The standard mainstream response to the problem of unemployment is to blame the victims of capitalism for lacking the necessary talents, skills, and effort to get and keep a job. Hence, the mainstream prescription is to promote policies aimed at enhancing the "human capital" of workers in order to make them more "competitive" in a rapidly globalizing economy. The response of ELR advocates is that such policies, if they accomplish anything at all, simply redistribute unemployment and poverty more equitably. For example, according to the Bureau of Labor Statistics, the number of unemployed workers (including so-called "discouraged" and "underemployed" workers) in August 2007 was 16.4 million, while the number of job vacancies was 4.1 million. No amount of investment in human capital is going to change the fact that there simply aren't enough jobs to go around.

Advocates of ELR also consistently reject the Keynesian rubric, with its focus on demand-management strategies—that is, policies aimed at increasing aggregate demand for the output of the economy. This approach has been pursued either directly, through government spending on goods and services (including transfer payments to households), or indirectly, largely through policies intended to increase private investment. Such an approach exacerbates inequality by biasing policy in favor of the already well-to-do, through tax cuts and investment credits to wealthy individuals and powerful corporations. These policies also tend to privilege the more highly skilled and better-paid workers found in the industries that generally benefit from the government's largesse (often arms manufacturers and other military-related companies). For example, much of the increase in government spending during the Cold War era went into the high-tech, capital-intensive, and oligopolized sectors of the economy. Capital-intensive industries require relatively small amounts of labor, and, thus, produce little employment growth per dollar of government expenditure. Under this policy approach, the most that lower-paid or unemployed workers could hope for would be to snatch a few crumbs from the great corporate feast as the economy expanded over time.

In contrast to both the human-capital and demand-management approaches, ELR provides a means for rapidly achieving zero involuntary unemployment. By definition, anyone who is unemployed and chooses not to accept the ELR offer would be considered voluntarily unemployed. Many individuals with sufficient savings and decent job prospects may forgo the opportunity to participate in the ELR program, but ELR always provides them with a backup option.

In addition to the immediate effects of ELR on employment, the program acts as an "automatic stabilizer" in the face of cyclical fluctuations in the private sector of the economy. During a recession, the number of participants in the program can be expected to grow as people are laid off and/or find it increasingly difficult to find private-sector employment. The opposite happens during the recovery phase of the business cycle, as people find it easier to find private-sector employment at wages above the ELR minimum. As a result, ELR advocates argue, the existence of such a program would dampen fluctuations in private-sector activity by setting a floor to the decline in incomes and employment.

A final and less discussed benefit of the program is its socializing effect. The example of Argentina is instructive in this respect. The nature of employment in the *Jefes* program, oriented as it was toward community rather than market imperatives, created a sense of public involvement and responsibility. Participants reported increases in morale and often continued to work beyond the four hours a day for which they were getting paid; they appreciated the cooperative nature of most of the enterprises and their focus on meeting essential community needs as opposed to quarterly profit targets. By expanding the public sphere, the *Jefes* program created a spirit of democratic participation in the affairs of the community, unmediated by the impersonal relations of market exchange. These are the kinds of experiences that are essential if capitalist societies are to move beyond the tyranny of the market and toward more cooperative and democratic forms of social organization.

Some economists and advocates have pressed for a similar proposal, the *basic income guarantee* (BIG). Instead of guaranteeing jobs, under this proposal the government would guarantee a minimum income to everyone by simply giving cash assistance to anyone earning below that level, in an amount equal to the gap between his or her actual income and the established basic income. (Hence this proposal is sometimes referred to as a "negative income tax.") BIG is an important idea deserving wider discussion than it has so far received. But ELR advocates have a number of concerns. One is that a BIG program is inherently inflationary: by providing income without putting people to work, it creates an additional claim on output without directly increasing the production of that output. Another is that BIG programs are less politically palatable—and hence less sustainable—than ELR schemes, which benefit society at large through the provision of public works and other social goods, and which avoid the stigma attached to "welfare" programs. Finally, a job offers social and psychological benefits that an income payment alone does not: maintaining and enhancing work skills, keeping in contact with others, and having the satisfaction of contributing to society. When, for instance, participants in Argentina's *Jefes* program were offered an income in place of a job, most refused; they preferred to work. Consequently, ELR programs meet the same objectives as basic income guarantee schemes and more, without the negative side effects of inflation and stigmatization. Nonetheless, a BIG program may be appropriate for those who should not be expected to work.

LEARNING FROM THE PAST

The idea that the government in a capitalist economy should provide jobs for the unemployed is not new. In the United States, the various New Deal agencies created during the Great Depression of the 1930s offer a well-known example. Organizations such as the Works Progress Administration and the Civilian Conservation Corps were designed to deal with the massive unemployment of that period.

Unemployment peaked at almost 25% of the civilian labor force in 1933 and averaged over 17% for the entire decade. These programs were woefully inadequate, largely due to their limited scale. It ultimately took the massive increases in government expenditure precipitated by the Second World War to pull the U.S. economy out of depression.

The onset of the postwar "Golden Age" and the dominance of Keynesian economics sounded the death knell of direct job creation as a solution to unemployment. The interwar public employment strategy was replaced with a "demand-management" strategy—essentially a sort of trickle-down economics in which various tax incentives and government expenditure programs, mainly military spending, were used to stimulate private investment. Policymakers believed that this would spur economic growth. The twin problems of poverty and unemployment would then be eliminated since, according to President Kennedy's famous aphorism, "a rising tide lifts all boats."

In the mid-1960s, the civil rights movement revived the idea of direct job creation as a solution to the problems of poverty and unemployment. Although the Kennedy and Johnson administrations had declared a so-called War on Poverty, the movement's call for direct job creation fell on deaf ears as the Johnson administration, at the behest of its Council of Economic Advisers, pursued a more conservative approach based on the standard combination of supply-side incentives to increase private investment and assorted strategies to "improve" workers' "human capital" so as to make them more attractive to private employers.

The rise to dominance of neoliberalism since the mid-1970s has resulted in a full-scale retreat from even the mildly social democratic policies of the early postwar period. While a commitment to full employment remains official U.S. policy, the concerns of central bankers and financial capitalists now rule the roost in government circles. This translates into a single-minded obsession with fighting inflation at the expense of all other economic and social objectives. Not only is fighting inflation seemingly the only concern of economic policy, it is seen to be in direct conflict with the goal of full employment (witness the widespread acceptance among economists and policymakers of the NAIRU, or "non-accelerating inflation rate of unemployment" theory, which posits that the economy has a set-point for unemployment, well above zero, below which rapidly rising inflation must occur). Whenever falling unemployment leads to concerns about "excessive" wage growth, central banks are expected to raise interest rates in an attempt to force slack on the economy and thereby decrease inflationary pressures. The resulting unemployment acts as a kind of discipline, tempering the demands of working-class people for higher wages or better working conditions in favor of the interests of large commercial and financial institutions. The postwar commitment to full employment has finally been sacrificed on the altar of price stability.

ELR AND CAPITALISM

As demonstrated by the history of public employment programs in the United States and the example of Argentina, direct job-creation programs do not happen absent significant political pressure from below. This is the case whether or not those calling for change explicitly demand an ELR program. Given the hegemonic position of neoliberal ideology, there are many powerful forces today that would be hostile to the idea of governments directly creating jobs for the unemployed. These forces represent a critical barrier to the implementation of an ELR program. In fact, these forces represent a critical barrier to virtually any project for greater social and economic justice. The purpose of initiating a wider discussion of ELR proposals is to build them into more comprehensive programs for social and economic justice. As is always the case, this requires the building of mass-based social movements advocating for these and other progressive policies.

A significant objection to the ELR proposal remains: it's capitalism, stupid. If you don't like unemployment, poverty, and inequality—not to mention war, environmental destruction, and alienating and exploitative work—then you don't like capitalism, and you should seek alternatives instead of reformist employment policies. ELR advocates would not disagree. In the face of the overlapping and myriad problems afflicting a capitalist economy, the achievements of even a full-scale ELR program would be limited. The political difficulties involved in establishing an ELR program in the first place, in the face of opposition from powerful elements of society, would be immense. And certainly, the many experiments in non-capitalist forms of economic and social organization currently being carried out, for example, in the factories of Argentina and elsewhere, should be championed. But it is fair to ask: shouldn't we also champion living wage laws, a stronger social safety net for those who cannot or should not be expected to work, and universal health care—as well as an end to imperialist wars of aggression, environmentally unsustainable practices, and the degradation of work? In sum, shouldn't we seek to alleviate all of the symptoms of capitalism, even as we work toward a better economic system?

Sources: Joseph Halevi, "The Argentine Crisis," *Monthly Review*, (April 2002); Pavlina Tcherneva, "Macroeconomic Stabilization Policy in Argentina: A Case Study of the 2002 Currency Collapse and Crisis Resolution through Job Creation," (Bard College Working Paper, 2007); L. Randall Wray, *Understanding Modern Money: The Key to Full Employment and Price Stability*, (Edward Elgar, 1998); Congressional Research Service, "The Cost of Iraq, Afghanistan and Other Global War on Terror Operations Since 9/11," (www.fas.org/sgp/crs/natsec/RL33110.pdf, update 7/07); National Jobs for All Coalition, "September 2007 Unemployment Data," www.njfac.org/jobnews.html); Nancy Rose, "Historicizing Government Work Programs: A Spectrum from Workfare to Fair Work," (Center for Full Employment and Price Stability, Seminar Paper No. 2, March 2000); Judith Russell, *Economics, Bureaucracy and Race: How Keynesians Misguided the War on Poverty*, (Columbia Univ. Press, 2004); Fadhel Kaboub, "Employment Guarantee Programs: A Survey of Theories and Policy Experiences," (Levy Econ. Inst., Working Paper No. 498, May 2007).

STIMULATING WHINING
THE PROSPECT OF BIGGER GOVERNMENT SETS SOME IN THE BUSINESS PRESS HOWLING.

BY JOHN MILLER

"Bridges to Everywhere: Making Ted Stevens jealous" (12/26/08)

"Feel Like a Trillion Bucks: Only WWII was pricier than Obama's stimulus plans" (1/5/09)

"States of Distress: Our local politicians want $200 billion without any shaping up" (1/26/09)

"A 40-Year Wish List: You won't believe what's in that stimulus bill" (1/28/09)

"The Entitlement Stimulus: More giant steps toward government health care" (1/29/09)

"The Real Stimulus Burden: We'll be paying for this in many ways, for many years" (2/12/09)

—recent *Wall Street Journal* editorials opposing the Obama stimulus package

If former Senator Phil Gramm had been talking about the editors of the *Wall Street Journal*, he might have had a point when he dismissed those complaining about the recession as whiners.

To be fair, it is not the recession proper, but the prospect of a massive economic stimulus package that has set the *Journal*'s editors to whining in editorial after editorial, some seventeen and counting since December.

This two-month-long crying jag seems to boil down to two central claims. First, that the package will expand public spending too much and leave us too deep in debt. Second, that government spending, inevitably wasteful, will also be ineffectual as economic stimulus when compared to tax cuts. Both these claims are misleading and at some points just plain wrong.

TOO BIG AND TOO MUCH IN DEBT?
At $789 billion, the final economic stimulus bill *is* big. But it's smaller than the $1.3 trillion Bush tax cut of 2001, wholeheartedly endorsed at the time by the *Journal* and other business publications. And making the Bush 2001 and 2003 tax cuts permanent, a *Journal* editorial-page mantra if there is one, would open a far larger hole in the federal budget than the stimulus package: it would cost the federal government $889 billion in lost tax revenues from 2010 to 2014, and $2.4 trillion by 2020.

If anything, the Obama stimulus package is too small. With over 3.6 million jobs already lost during the recession and more job losses sure to follow—and with over a million new entrants into the job market each year—the plan will need to provide more than its promised 3.5 million jobs.

The editors are also wringing their hands over the record federal budget deficit. Without the stimulus package, the Congressional Budget Office was already projecting the 2009 deficit to reach $1.2 trillion, or 8.4% of GDP. With the stimulus package, the deficit could reach 11% of GDP. Those are indeed record numbers for "peacetime" deficits. The Reagan deficits in their worst year reached 6% of GDP. Only World War II spending pushed the federal deficit to qualitatively different levels—30.3% of GDP in the midst of the war.

But those numbers must be viewed in context. A do-nothing strategy would saddle the federal budget with yet larger deficits as the economy and federal tax revenues fell through the floor. "Without fast action," worries Allen Sinai, chief economist at Decision Economics, "federal debt levels could soon reach 100% of GDP." And unlike World War II spending, which sparked a quarter-century boom that helped pay down that debt, a do-nothing strategy today would be followed by a depression that would impose costs far more serious than a rise in government debt.

PORK, STIMULUS, AND MULTIPLIERS
What is really bugging the *Journal* editors is the *content* of the stimulus package, which they describe as a 40-year Democratic Party pork wish list. Of course, pork is in the eye of the beholder. Replacing the current fleet of government vehicles with more energy-efficient ones may look to some like pure pork, as one *Journal* editorial labeled it, but to others it's worth-while spending.

More important, these editorials claim, the spending side of the package will just not provide a stimulus. Government spending, or so the argument goes, cannot result in net economic growth because the money the government spends has to come from somewhere and that somewhere is the private sector: "For every $1 the government 'injects,' it must take $1 away from someone else—either in taxes or by issuing a bond. In either case this leaves $1 less available for private investment or consumption."

The truth of the matter is far different. Government spending, pork or otherwise, *is* stimulus.

Now, the editors are correct that the money for such spending comes from the private sector. And, private spending could provide much-needed stimulus in today's economy. What they fail to mention is that in a period of economic distress, especially one accompanied by a financial crisis, that private spending is seldom forthcoming. Workers are unemployed but so too is capital. Factories, stores, and businesses of all kinds are cutting back or shutting their doors. With the economy in dire straits, the financial system teetering, and economic anxiety widespread, businesses balk at investing, and consumers are so cautious they are retiring debt for the first time in decades.

With capital and labor standing idle, government taxing or borrowing will not create a drag on private spending. On the contrary, government spending compensates for the lack of private spend-ing and provides the jolt necessary to bring the coding economy back to life. The real issues are how much stimulus any spending program (or tax cut) provides and how quickly it kicks in.

The amount of stimulus is exactly what is measured by Keynesian multipliers, which estimate the bang for each buck of government spending or tax cuts in terms of what it will add to GDP within a year. The multipliers above were submitted to Congress last summer by Mark Zandi, chief economist at Moody's Economy.com and an informal advisor to the McCain campaign—hardly a "tax-and-spend liberal."

Zandi's figures show that the very items championed by the *Journal*, such as making the Bush tax cuts permanent or reducing the corporate income tax, would do the least to stimulate economic growth. It's a tall order to get a corporation to invest in a crumbling economy. And personal income tax cuts, especially the Bush ones, go overwhelmingly to wealthy families who can and likely will save, rather than spend, the extra cash.

It is the programs the editors inveigh against, such as aid to state and local governments, that have the highest multipliers. These programs have the additional advantage of quick start-up and can immediately stem job losses. Sadly, it is this timely and effective spending, including on health care for the unemployed and on education, that the "centrist" Senators demanded be cut from the stimulus package, with the result that 35% of the final version is tax cuts rather than actual spending.

In addition to their disastrous social consequences, these cuts fly in the face of the lessons from Japan's prolonged economic stagnation in the 1990s. There, every dollar spent on social services like elder care and pension payments added $1.64 in additional output and every dollar of financing for schools and education delivered an even bigger $1.74 boost in output, according to a 1998 Japanese think-tank report.

The evidence is clear: Doing good—expanding health care spending, improving schools, and reducing the payroll tax burden on workers—is good for a flagging economy.

Much more needs to be done to stimulate economic justice and not just economic growth. But that surely would be life-threatening for the *Journal* editors and their ilk, whose blood pressure is already spiking from the few important but ultimately disappointing steps in that direction included in the stimulus package.

Sources: Mark Zandi, "A Second Quick Boost From Government Could Spark Recovery," testimony before the U.S. House Committee on Small Business, July 24, 2008; Martin Fackler, "Japan offers lessons on stimulus spending," *New York Times*, Feb. 6, 2009; "Budget and Economic Outlook," Congressional Budget Office, Jan. 9, 2009; "Preliminary Analysis of Obama's Stimulus Tax Cuts: Could Be Worse, Could Be a Lot Better," Citizens For Tax Justice, Jan. 9, 2009.

ARTICLE 5.3   January/February 2009

BAIL OUT THE SAFETY NET

BY RANDY ALBELDA

Even before the financial crisis and the recession, a substantial proportion of working families were not making it in America. In 2007, 20% of the population in a family with a breadwinner—that's 41 million people—did not have enough income, including any Food Stamps, Medicaid, housing and child care subsidies, or other public support they received, to pay their basic living expenses.

The good news for this bottom 20%: in the current crisis, their plight of working hard but not making enough to pay the bills is becoming much more common, so the pressure to address this problem should be growing too. The bad news, of course, is the recession itself. The hardships these families face are growing by the day. More and more households are falling toward the social safety net.

And what about that safety net? In the 1990s, the Clinton administration ended "welfare as we know it," but at the same time promised work supports as low-wage workers moved up the ladder. Since then, employment rates for poor and low-income mothers have indeed soared, and so has the demand for affordable housing and child care assistance. But funding for them has not, with long waiting lists for both. As a result, by the early 2000s, these government work supports helped only 10% of the population in working families that couldn't meet their basic needs to actually meet them. Despite expansions in the Earned Income Tax Credit and public health insurance for children in the 1990s, the public support programs for low-income families provide inadequate help, and even that to only a fraction of those who need it. And for workers who lose their jobs, only about a third of all unemployed workers receive unemployment benefits today.

The safety net is not only tattered; it is nearly obsolete.

Rising unemployment is beginning to take its toll, as are draconian state budget cuts. Congress and President Obama appear ready to enact a large stimulus package to spur the economy and create jobs. Their focus so far is mostly on infrastructure, on "rebuilding our crumbling roads and bridges, modernizing schools...,building wind farms and solar panels," as Obama has said.

But bridge repair and even green jobs are not enough. Our physical infrastructure needs work, but so does our social infrastructure. And it's not just the safety net. Quality care for children and long-term care for disabled and elderly people are in short supply—and unaffordably expensive for many families. Moreover, women are disproportionately employed in these sectors, many at low wages that barely enable them to support their own families. In contrast, the construction and green-energy jobs that often pay decent wages with benefits are overwhelmingly filled by men.

So let's enact a bold recovery plan that promotes employment but also reconstructs the safety net and jumpstarts the process of upgrading our social infrastructure. Here are four suggestions:

First, provide federal funding to states to prevent reductions in essential services. Now is not the time to reduce public health investments, stop transportation projects, cut higher education or lay off K–12 and early-education teachers.

Second, recreate our housing infrastructure. In exchange for buying up bad loans, secure foreclosed properties and develop an affordable housing stock.

Third, expand help for families who are struggling to pay for care for children and elders. Doing so will not only help the families struggling to care for their loved ones. It will also provide the job-creation stimulus for women workers that bridge-repair funding will provide for men.

Fourth, replace our outdated and arbitrary poverty measure with a realistic measure of what it takes to afford basic needs and participate fully in society. This measure should be used to gauge whether the eventual economic recovery is reaching all Americans.

Economic recovery will require bold, public action. Such action isn't limited to reforming our financial system or to traditional stimulus spending. It also means upgrading our social infrastructure in ways that ensure our economy works for all.

ARTICLE 5.4

March/April 2008

WAR SPENDING, DEFICITS, AND ECONOMIC STIMULUS

BY ARTHUR MACEWAN

Dear Dr. Dollar:
Doesn't all the war spending stimulate the economy? And shouldn't the Bush tax cuts do the same? So why are we falling into recession?

—Caitlin Young, Whitehall, N.Y.

Neither war spending nor the tax cuts are able to overcome serious weaknesses in the U.S. economy.

Yes, this combination of war spending and tax cuts has created a federal budget deficit—a situation in which the federal government is spending more than it is taking in as taxes. And in times of weak economic growth, a deficit does tend to promote expansion because the government is increasing demand for goods and services with its spending more than it is reducing private demand through taxes. The use of a federal budget deficit to counteract an economic slowdown is the central policy insight of Keynesian economics and has been a generally accepted practice since the 1930s.

But the size of the deficit has not been large in recent years, as war spending has been balanced by little or no growth of spending on social programs. And the tax cuts have not been of the sort that would lead to a large expansion of private purchases of goods and services.

First of all, the size of the deficit. In the years 2002 to 2007, on average the federal government's budget deficit (the excess of spending over taxes) was 2.4% of gross domestic product (GDP—the value of all goods and services produced in the country). The main reason this looked large was that between 1998 and 2001 there was no deficit at all; in those years the federal government ran small surpluses (taxes greater than spending). However, for the period 1990 through 1997, the deficit averaged 3% of GDP, and during the 1980s the deficit averaged almost 4% of GDP.

As to the tax cuts, they have very much favored the rich. That's nice if you are among the rich, but the trouble is that rich people do not spend as large a share of their incomes as do people with lower incomes. Thus not as large a share of the money they save by paying lower taxes gets spent. So directing tax cuts to the rich does not lead to a large increase in purchases of goods and service and thus not to a large increase in production, employment and incomes.

Perhaps the federal budget deficit and some (not much) extra consumer spending coming from the tax cuts did bolster the economy a bit in recent years. But what really pushed the economy along was high and rising consumer spending. This consumer spending was based heavily on debt. Consumer debt as a share of after-tax personal income averaged 20% in the 1990s, and then jumped up to an average of 25% in the first seven years of the new millennium. But the debt expansion was most marked in housing, where mortgage debt as a percent of after-tax personal income rose from 89% to 94% over the 1990s, and then ballooned to 140% by 2006 as housing prices skyrocketed—the housing bubble.

Then the housing bubble burst. As many homeowners have gone into default, financial problems have spread. Excessive lending/borrowing in housing, it turns out, was just one aspect of a highly unstable financial system. Financial markets appear to have been operating like a casino on Saturday night, including the illicit as well as the unadvisable. This mess in the financial sector was not bad luck. It was the predictable result of deregulation and the whole sweep of pro-business policies of recent U.S. governments—policies that began well before Bush II. Financial markets when unregulated—now as in the past—generate crises.

The crisis in the financial system is now spreading, disrupting the rest of the economy as credit is increasingly tight and as worried consumers curtail their debt expansion and thus their spending. The mess in finance and the heavy consumer debt are a couple of the serious problems plaguing the U.S. economy. They have been combined with high oil prices, a long term poor performance of real investment, and slow growth of employment. All of these weaknesses are pushing the economy toward recession. Against the set of forces that these weaknesses generate, the mild stimulus of war spending and tax cuts for the rich is of little avail.

ARTICLE 5.5

THE TAX-CUT CON

BY PAUL KRUGMAN

Bruce Tinsley's comic strip, "Mallard Fillmore," is, he says, "for the average person out there: the forgotten American taxpayer who's sick of the liberal media." In June 2003, that forgotten taxpayer made an appearance in the strip, attacking his TV set with a baseball bat and yelling: "I can't afford to send my kids to college, or even take 'em out of their substandard public school, because the federal, state and local governments take more than 50% of my income in taxes. And then the guy on the news asks with a straight face whether or not we can 'afford' tax cuts."

Nobody likes paying taxes, and no doubt some Americans are as angry about their taxes as Tinsley's imaginary character. But most Americans also care a lot about the things taxes pay for.

All politicians say they're for public education; almost all of them also say they support a strong national defense, maintaining Social Security and, if anything, expanding the coverage of Medicare. When the "guy on the news" asks whether we can afford a tax cut, he's asking whether, after yet another tax cut goes through, there will be enough money to pay for those things. And the answer is no.

But it's very difficult to get that answer across in modern American politics, which has been dominated for 25 years by a crusade against taxes.

I don't use the word "crusade" lightly. The advocates of tax cuts are relentless, even fanatical. An indication of the movement's fervor—and of its political power—came during the Iraq war. War is expensive and is almost always accompanied by tax increases. But not in 2003. "Nothing is more important in the face of a war," declared Tom DeLay, the House majority leader, "than cutting taxes." And sure enough, taxes were cut, not just in a time of war but also in the face of record budget deficits.

A result of the tax-cut crusade is that there is now a fundamental mismatch between the benefits Americans expect to receive from the government and the revenues government collect. This mismatch is already having profound effects at the state and local levels: teachers and policemen are being laid off and children are being denied health insurance. The federal government can mask its problems for a while by running huge budget deficits, but it, too, will eventually have to decide whether to cut services or raise taxes. And we are not talking about minor policy adjustments. If taxes stay as low as they are now, government as we know it cannot be maintained. In particular, Social Security will have to become far less generous; Medicare will no longer be able to guarantee comprehensive medical care to older Americans; Medicaid will no longer provide basic medical care to the poor.

How did we reach this point? What are the origins of the antitax crusade? And where is it taking us?

SUPPLY-SIDERS, STARVE-THE-BEASTERS, AND LUCKY DUCKIES

It is often hard to pin down what antitax crusaders are trying to achieve. The reason is not, or not only, that they are disingenuous about their motives—though as we will see, disingenuity has become a hallmark of the movement in recent years. Rather, the fuzziness comes from the fact that today's antitax movement moves back and forth between two doctrines. Both doctrines favor the same thing: big tax cuts for people with high incomes. But they favor it for different reasons.

One of those doctrines has become famous under the name "supply-side economics." It's the view that the government can cut taxes without severe cuts in public spending. The other doctrine is often referred to as "starving the beast," a phrase coined by David Stockman, Ronald Reagan's budget director. It's the view that taxes should be cut precisely in order to force severe cuts in public spending. Supply-side economics is the friendly, attractive face of the tax-cut movement. But starve-the-beast is where the power lies.

The starting point of supply-side economics is an assertion that no economist would dispute: taxes reduce the incentive to work, save and invest. A businessman who knows that 70 cents of every extra dollar he makes will go to the IRS is less willing to make the effort to earn that extra dollar than if he knows that the IRS will take only 35 cents. So reducing tax rates will, other things being the same, spur the economy.

This much isn't controversial. But the government must pay its bills. So the standard view of economists is that if you want to reduce the burden of taxes, you must explain what government programs you want to cut as part of the deal. There's no free lunch.

What the supply-siders argued, however, was that there was a free lunch. Cutting marginal rates, they insisted, would lead to such a large increase in gross domestic product that it wouldn't be necessary to come up with offsetting spending cuts. What supply-side economists say, in other words, is, "Don't worry, be happy and cut taxes." And when they say cut taxes, they mean taxes on the affluent: reducing the top marginal rate means that the biggest tax cuts go to people in the highest tax brackets.

The other camp in the tax-cut crusade actually welcomes the revenue losses from tax cuts. Its most visible spokesman today is Grover Norquist, president of Americans for Tax Reform, who once told National Public Radio: "I don't want to abolish government. I simply want to reduce it to the size where I can drag it into the bathroom and drown it in the bathtub." And the way to get it down to that size is to starve it of revenue. "The goal is reducing the size and scope of government by draining its lifeblood," Norquist told *U.S. News & World Report*.

What does "reducing the size and scope of government" mean? Tax-cut proponents are usually vague about the details. But the Heritage Foundation, ideological headquarters for the movement, has made it pretty clear. Edwin Feulner, the foundation's president, uses "New Deal" and "Great Society" as terms of abuse, implying that he and his organization want to do away with the institutions Franklin Roosevelt and Lyndon Johnson created. That means Social Security, Medicare, Medicaid—most of what gives citizens of the United States a safety net against economic misfortune.

The starve-the-beast doctrine is now firmly within the conservative mainstream. George W. Bush himself seemed to endorse the doctrine as the budget surplus evaporated: in August 2001 he called the disappearing surplus "incredibly positive news" because it would put Congress in a "fiscal straitjacket."

Like supply-siders, starve-the-beasters favor tax cuts mainly for people with high incomes. That is partly because, like supply-siders, they emphasize the incentive effects of cutting the top marginal rate; they just don't believe that those incentive effects are big enough that tax cuts pay for themselves. But they have another reason for cutting taxes mainly on the rich, which has become known as the "lucky ducky" argument.

Here's how the argument runs: to starve the beast, you must not only deny funds to the government; you must make voters hate the government. There's a danger that working-class families might see government as their friend: because their incomes are low, they don't pay much in taxes, while they benefit from public spending. So in starving the beast, you must take care not to cut taxes on these "lucky duckies." (Yes, that's what the *Wall Street Journal* called them in a famous editorial.) In fact, if possible, you must raise taxes on working-class Americans in order, as the *Journal* said, to get their "blood boiling with tax rage."

So the tax-cut crusade has two faces. Smiling supply-siders say that tax cuts are all gain, no pain; scowling starve-the-beasters believe that inflicting pain is not just necessary but also desirable. Is the alliance between these two groups a marriage of convenience? Not exactly. It would be more accurate to say that the starve-the-beasters hired the supply-siders—indeed, created them—because they found their naive optimism useful.

A look at who the supply-siders are and how they came to prominence tells the story. The supply-side movement likes to present itself as a school of economic thought like Keynesianism or monetarism—that is, as a set of scholarly ideas that made their way, as such ideas do, into political discussion. But the reality is quite different. Supply-side economics was a political doctrine from Day 1; it emerged in the pages of political magazines, not professional economics journals.

That is not to deny that many professional economists favor tax cuts. But they almost always turn out to be starve-the-beasters, not supply-siders. And they often secretly—or sometimes not so secretly—hold supply-siders in contempt. N. Gregory Mankiw, now chairman of George W. Bush's Council of Economic Advisers, is definitely a friend to tax cuts; but in the first edition of his economic-principles textbook, he described Ronald Reagan's supply-side advisers as "charlatans and cranks."

TO STARVE THE BEAST, YOU MUST MAKE VOTERS HATE THE GOVERNMENT.

It is not that the professionals refuse to consider supply-side ideas; rather, they have looked at them and found them wanting. A conspicuous example came earlier this year when the Congressional Budget Office tried to evaluate the growth effects of the Bush administration's proposed tax cuts. The budget office's new head, Douglas Holtz-Eakin, is a conservative economist who was hand-picked for his job by the administration. But his conclusion was that unless the revenue losses from the proposed tax cuts were offset by spending cuts, the resulting deficits would be a drag on growth, quite likely to outweigh any supply-side effects.

But if the professionals regard the supply-siders with disdain, who employs these people? The answer is that since the 1970s almost all of the prominent supply-siders have been aides to conservative politicians, writers at conservative publications like *National Review*, fellows at conservative policy centers like Heritage or economists at private companies with strong Republican connections. Loosely speaking, that is, supply-siders work for the vast right-wing conspiracy. What gives supply-side economics influence is its connection with a powerful network of institutions that want to shrink the government and see tax cuts as a way to achieve that goal.

Supply-side economics is a feel-good cover story for a political movement with a much harder-nosed agenda.

A PLANNED CRISIS

Right now, much of the public discussion of the Bush tax cuts focuses on their short-run impact. Critics say that the 2.7 million jobs lost since March 2001 prove that the administration's policies have failed, while the administration says that things would have been even worse without the tax cuts and that a solid recovery is just around the corner.

But this is the wrong debate. Even in the short run, the right question to ask isn't whether the tax cuts were better than nothing; they probably were. The right question is whether some other economic-stimulus plan could have achieved better results at a lower budget cost. And it is hard to deny that, on a jobs-per-dollar basis, the Bush tax cuts have been extremely ineffective. According to the Congressional Budget Office, half of this year's $400 billion budget deficit is due to Bush tax cuts. Now $200 billion is a lot of money; it is equivalent to the salaries of four million average workers. Even the administration doesn't claim its policies have created four million jobs. Surely some other policy—aid to state and local governments, tax breaks for the poor and middle class rather than the rich, maybe even WPA-style public works—would have been more successful at getting the country back to work.

Meanwhile, the tax cuts are designed to remain in place even after the economy has recovered. Where will they leave us?

Here's the basic fact: partly, though not entirely, as a result of the tax cuts of the last three years, the government of the United States faces a fundamental fiscal shortfall. That is, the revenue it collects falls well short of the sums it needs to pay for existing programs. Even the U.S. government must, eventually, pay its bills, so something will have to give.

The numbers tell the tale. This year and next, the federal government will run budget deficits of more than $400 billion. Deficits may fall a bit, at least as a share of gross domestic product, when the economy recovers. But the relief will be modest and temporary. As Peter Fisher, undersecretary of the treasury for domestic finance, puts it, the federal government is "a gigantic insurance company with a sideline business in defense and homeland security." And about a decade from now, this insurance company's policyholders will begin making a lot of claims. As the baby boomers retire, spending on Social Security benefits and Medicare will steadily rise, as will spending on Medicaid (because of rising medical costs). Eventually, unless there are sharp cuts in benefits, these three programs alone will consume a larger share of GDP than the federal government currently collects in taxes.

Alan Auerbach, William Gale, and Peter Orszag, fiscal experts at the Brookings Institution, have estimated the size of the "fiscal gap"—the increase in revenues or reduction in spending that would be needed to make the nation's finances sustainable in the long run. If you define the long run as 75 years, this gap turns out to be 4.5% of GDP. Or to put it another way, the gap is equal to 30% of what the federal government spends on all domestic programs. Of that gap, about 60% is the result of the Bush tax cuts. We would have faced a serious fiscal problem even if those tax cuts had never happened. But we face a much nastier problem now that they are in place.

And more broadly, the tax-cut crusade will make it very hard for any future politicians to raise taxes.

So how will this gap be closed? The crucial point is that it cannot be closed without either fundamentally redefining the role of government or sharply raising taxes.

Politicians will, of course, promise to eliminate wasteful spending. But take out Social Security, Medicare, defense, Medicaid, government pensions, homeland security, interest on the public debt and veterans' benefits—none of them what people who complain about waste usually have in mind—and you are left with spending equal to about 3% of gross domestic product. And most of that goes for courts, highways, education and other useful things. Any savings from elimination of waste and fraud will amount to little more than a rounding-off error.

So let's put a few things back on the table. Let's assume that interest on the public debt will be paid, that spending on defense and homeland security will not be compromised and that the regular operations of government will continue to be financed. What we are left with, then, are the New Deal and Great Society programs: Social Security, Medicare, Medicaid and unemployment insurance. And to close the fiscal gap, spending on these programs would have to be cut by around 40%.

It's impossible to know how such spending cuts might unfold, but cuts of that magnitude would require drastic changes in the system. It goes almost without saying that the age at which Americans become eligible for retirement benefits would rise, that Social Security payments would fall sharply compared with average incomes, that Medicare patients would be forced to pay much more of their expenses out of pocket—or do without. And that would be only a start.

All this sounds politically impossible. In fact, politicians of both parties have been scrambling to expand, not reduce, Medicare benefits by adding prescription drug coverage. It's hard to imagine a situation under which the entitlement programs would be rolled back sufficiently to close the fiscal gap.

Yet closing the fiscal gap by raising taxes would mean rolling back all of the Bush tax cuts, and then some. And that also sounds politically impossible.

For the time being, there is a third alternative: borrow the difference between what we insist on spending and what we're willing to collect in taxes. That works as long as lenders believe that someday, somehow, we're going to get our fiscal act together. But this can't go on indefinitely.

Eventually—I think within a decade, though not everyone agrees—the bond market will tell us that we have to make a choice.

In short, everything is going according to plan.

For the looming fiscal crisis doesn't represent a defeat for the leaders of the tax-cut crusade or a miscalculation on their part. Some supporters of President Bush may have really believed that his tax cuts were consistent with his promises to protect Social Security and expand Medicare; some people may still believe that the wondrous supply-side effects of tax cuts will make the budget deficit disappear. But for starve-the-beast tax-cutters, the coming crunch is exactly what they had in mind.

WHAT KIND OF COUNTRY?

The astonishing political success of the antitax crusade has, more or less deliberately, set the United States up for a fiscal crisis. How we respond to that crisis will determine what kind of country we become.

If Grover Norquist is right—and he has been right about a lot—the coming crisis will allow conservatives to move the nation a long way back toward the kind of limited government we had before Franklin Roosevelt. Lack of revenue, he says, will make it possible for conservative politicians—in the name of fiscal necessity—to dismantle immensely popular government programs that would otherwise have been untouchable.

In Norquist's vision, America a couple of decades from now will be a place in which elderly people make up a disproportionate share of the poor, as they did before Social Security. It will also be a country in which even middle-class elderly Americans are, in many cases, unable to afford expensive medical procedures or prescription drugs and in which poor Americans generally go without even basic health care. And it may well be a place in which only those who can afford expensive private schools can give their children a decent education.

But that's a choice, not a necessity. The tax-cut crusade has created a situation in which something must give. But what gives—whether we decide that the New Deal and the Great Society must go or that taxes aren't such a bad thing after all—is up to us. The American people must decide what kind of a country we want to be.

THE LOOMING FISCAL CRISIS ISN'T A DEFEAT FOR THE LEADERS OF THE TAX-CUT CRUSADE. IT'S EXACTLY WHAT THEY HAD IN MIND.

Excerpted from the *New York Times* Magazine, September 14, 2003.

ONE-QUARTER OF LARGE U.S. CORPORATIONS DON'T PAY PROFIT TAXES—WHY SHOULD THE REST?

BY JOHN MILLER

AMERICA THE UNCOMPETITIVE
Our political class has managed to maintain America's rank with the second highest corporate tax rate in the world at 39.3% (average combined federal and state). Only Japan is slightly higher overall.

In Washington, meanwhile, Senator Byron Dorgan of North Dakota waved around a new politically generated study by the Government Accountability Office (GAO) finding that 28% of large U.S. corporations paid no income tax in 2005. "It's time for big corporations to pay their fair share," Mr. Dorgan roared.

Among the large companies that paid no taxes, 85% of them also made no profits that year. American Airlines and General Motors escaped income tax for 2005 through the clever tax dodge of losing $862 million and $10.5 billion, respectively.

The GAO data only add to the case for cutting U.S. corporate rates. America now has the worst of all worlds: high corporate tax rates, but also lots of loopholes passed by Congress at the behest of favored businesses to avoid the confiscatory rate.

The average European nation has tax rates on corporate income 10 percentage points lower than the U.S., but those countries on average raise 50% more as a share of GDP in corporate taxes than does the U.S.

John McCain has proposed cutting the 35% federal corporate tax rate to 25%. That's a good start, but even that would leave the U.S. with a combined state and federal rate nearly five percentage points above the global average. With corporate tax rates falling around the world, and with its damage to investment increasingly obvious, abolishing the U.S. corporate income tax should be on the table.

—Wall Street Journal *editorial, August 15, 2008*

You have to hand it to the *Wall Street Journal* editors: They don't embarrass easily. The Government Accountability Office (GAO) reports that one-quarter of large U.S corporations paid no income taxes in 2005, and the editors whine that high corporate taxes have rendered the United States uncompetitive and call once again for abolishing the corporate income tax.

Let's start with the title. The editors surely know that U.S. competitiveness has been improving, not worsening, due to the decline in the value of dollar (something they regularly lament). According to KPMG, the international accounting and consulting firm, the cost of doing business in the United States dropped from 2006 to 2008 and is now lower than that in much of Europe, including Germany, Italy, France, and the U.K., as well as in Japan.

Such inaccuracy is a problem. But it pales next to the profound illogic the *Journal* editors are trying to purvey here. The editorial acknowledges that U.S. corporations pay less in corporate income taxes than the average across industrialized countries—despite the higher U.S. "nominal" tax rate. It recognizes that European countries collect 50% *more* in corporate income taxes as a share of GDP than does the United States. Nonetheless, the editors still want to argue that high U.S. corporate income taxes are driving investment away to other countries.

But they can't have it both ways. The editors are right that it is myriad tax loopholes that account for the difference between the nominal and effective tax rates on U.S. corporations. If they find loopholes objectionable, then they should propose simplifying the corporate tax code in a revenue-neutral way, with a lower rate and fewer loopholes. But that's entirely different from what they actually propose here: that U.S. corporations should pay less in corporate income taxes altogether. And that is an awfully hard case to make when you have already admitted that U.S. corporations pay less than their counterparts in other industrialized countries.

LOOPHOLES OR LOSSES?
The GAO report does need to be read carefully. It never said that profitable corporations typically avoid federal corporate income taxes, nominally 35% of all taxable income or profits above $10 million. Nonetheless, the report did offer some deservedly headline-grabbing news: 55% of large U.S corporations reported no tax liability for at least one of the eight years from 1998 to 2005, and 25% paid no corporate income taxes in 2005 alone. That last figure was actually down from its peak of 38% in 2001. But that shift must be viewed in context: corporate profits more than doubled from 2001 to 2005, so it's not surprising that the share of corporations managing to avoid income tax liability entirely declined somewhat over the period.

Why did so many large U.S. corporations pay no corporate income taxes? Was it because they suffered massive losses, as the editors maintain? Or was it because they took advantage of loopholes in the tax code to eliminate *on paper* any taxable income or profits?

The GAO report is silent on that question, but other studies point to the key role that loopholes played in allowing these corporations to escape taxation. For instance, Citizens for Tax Justice (CTJ) conducted a detailed study of the tax liability of 275 of the largest U.S. corporations from 2001 to 2003. Eighty-two of those 275 major corporations, or nearly one-third, paid no corporate income taxes in at least one of those three years. Far from losing money, these 82 corporations made a total of $102 billion in pre-tax U.S. profits in the years for which they paid no taxes. But thanks to tax breaks, these corporations actually *got $12.6 billion back* from the U.S. Treasury. In other words, as a group their effective tax rate —the share of their pre-tax profit they paid in corporate income taxes—was -12.6% (yes, that's a minus sign). Among the rebate recipients were Pepco Holdings, Prudential Financial, ITT Industries, Boeing, Unisys, Fluor, and CSX.

Taken together, all 275 corporations in the CTJ study paid from 21.4% (in 2001) to 17.4% (in 2003) of their pre-tax profits in corporate income taxes, not much more than half the nominal rate of 35%. Other measures also peg the effective tax rate on U.S. corporate profits far below 35%. For instance, using Treasury Department data, tax analyst Martin Sullivan found that the effective tax rate on U.S. corporate profits reached a ten-year low of 22.2% in 2006.

HOW TO AVOID CORPORATE TAXES

What accounts for the stark difference between the effective rates of taxation paid by U.S. corporations and the 35% rate specified in the tax code?

Corporate income taxes are levied against reported corporate profits. Corporations use a variety of mechanisms to inflate their reported costs and thereby reduce their taxable profits, including:

• *Accelerated Depreciation.* This provision allows corporations to write off machinery and equipment or other assets more quickly than those assets actually deteriorate. Enacted in the 1980s and expanded by the Bush administration and Congress, it dramatically lowered the effective tax rate on U.S. corporations. Accelerated depreciation generated $70.9 billion of tax savings from 2001 to 2003 for the 275 corporations in the CTJ study. Fully two-thirds of those savings went to just 25 corporations, including Verizon, ExxonMobil, and Wachovia. In fiscal year 2006, accelerated deprecation of machinery and equipment cost the federal government $36.5 billion in lost tax revenues.

• *Stock Options.* Most big corporations give their executives the option to buy the company's stock at a favorable price. Corporations can then take a tax deduction for the difference between what the employee pays for the stock and its market price. Of the 275 corporations in the CTJ study, 269 received stock-option benefits between 2001 and 2003 worth a total of $32 billion in reduced taxes over the period.

• *Debt Financing.* When corporations finance new investment by issuing stock, the dividends they pay to stockholders are not counted as costs, and so do not reduce their taxable profits. But when corporations borrow capital to invest (typically by issuing bonds), the interest payments on that debt do count as costs. This tax advantage that the U.S. tax code grants to debt financing is unusually generous; other countries typically treat debt financing less favorably. Interest deductions accounted for 15% of the total deductions taken by corporations in the GAO study.

The result of these and other corporate tax loopholes is that effective corporate tax rates in the United States are no higher, and in some cases lower, than rates across the Organization for Economic Cooperation and Development (OECD), the group of the world's most industrialized countries. For instance, a Congressional Budget Office study found that effective U.S. corporate income tax rates in 2003 were close to the OECD average for profits derived from equity-financed investments and substantially below the average for profits derived from debt-financed investments.

The U.S. rates, in other words, are hardly prohibitive or non-competitive.

WHAT TO DO WITH $166 BILLION?

Closing loopholes could boost U.S. corporate income tax revenues to the OECD average of 3.4% of GDP. In 2007, that would have added $166 billion to federal government revenues—enough to just restore U.S. infrastructure spending to its level four decades ago, and a large down payment toward the $1.6 trillion of investments over the next five years called for by the American Society of Civil Engineers to repair levees, bridges, schools, and power grids, as well as to build high speed transit and modern sewerage systems and to make many other desperately needed infrastructure investments.

That would do far more to improve U.S. economic competitiveness than the editors' proposal to let the other three-quarters of large U.S. corporations go tax-free. At the same time it would satisfy the demand—not just from Senator Dorgan, but from many Americans—that "big corporations pay their fair share."

Sources: "America the Uncompetitive," *Wall Street Journal*, August 15, 2008; "AP Makes Serious Error in Story on Corporate Income Tax," Tax Foundation, August 12, 2008; "Corporate-Tax Reporting Draws GAO Scrutiny," *WSJ*, August 13, 2008; "Comparison of the Reported Tax Liabilities of Foreign and U.S.-Controlled Corporations, 1998-2005," GAO, July 2008; "Corporate Income Tax Rates: International Comparisons," CBO, Nov. 2005; Joel Friedman, "The Decline of Corporate Income Tax Revenues," Center on Budget and Policy Priorities, October 23, 2003; Robert McIntyre and T.D. Nguyen, "Corporate Income Taxes in the Bush Years," Citizens for Tax Justice, September 2004; "Treasury Conference on Business Taxation and Global Competitiveness: Background Paper," U.S. Treas. Dept., July 23, 2007; "Tax and Economic Growth," OECD, July 11, 2008; Mark Sullivan, "The Effective Corporate Tax Rate is Falling," Tax Analysts, January 22, 2007; Peter Merrill, "The Corporate Tax Conundrum," Tax Analysts, 2007; "U.S. Leaps over Europe as a Cost-Effective Business Cost Location," KPMG in Canada, March 27, 2008; American Society of Civil Engineers, "Report Card for America's Infrastructure," 2005 (updated for 2008).

SOCIAL SECURITY ISN'T BROKEN
SO WHY THE RUSH TO "FIX" IT?

BY DOUG ORR

Federal Reserve Chairman Alan Greenspan told Congress earlier this year that everyone knows there's a Social Security crisis. That's like saying "everyone knows the earth is flat."

Starting with a faulty premise guarantees reaching the wrong conclusion. The truth is there is no Social Security crisis, but there is a potential crisis in retirement income security and there may be a crisis in the future in U.S. financial markets. It's this latter crisis that Greenspan actually is worried about.

Social Security is the most successful insurance program ever created. It insures millions of workers against what economists call "longevity risk," the possibility they will live "too long" and not be able to work long enough, or save enough, to provide their own income. Today, about 10% of those over age 65 live in poverty. Without Social Security, that rate would be almost 50%.

Social Security was originally designed to supplement, and was structured to resemble, private-sector pensions. In the 1930s, all private pensions were defined-benefit plans. The retirement benefit was based on a worker's former wage and years of service. In most plans, after 35 years of service the monthly benefit, received for life, would be at least half of the income received in the final working year.

Congress expected that private-sector pensions eventually would cover most workers. But pension coverage peaked at 40% in the 1960s. Since then, corporations have systematically dismantled pension systems. Today, only 16% of private-sector workers are covered by defined-benefit pensions. Rather than supplementing private pensions, Social Security has become the primary source of retirement income for almost two-thirds of retirees. Thus, Congress was forced to raise benefit levels in 1972.

What has happened to private-sector defined benefit pensions? They've been replaced with defined-contribution (DC) savings plans such as 401(k)s and 403(b)s. These plans provide some retirement income but offer no real protection from longevity risk. Once a retiree depletes the amount saved in the plan, their retirement income is gone.

In a generous DC plan, a firm might match the worker's contribution up to 3% of his or her pay. With total contributions of 6%, average wage growth of 2% a year, and an average return on the investment portfolio of 5%, after 35 years of work, a retiree would exhaust the plan's savings in just 8.5 years even if her annual spending is only half of her final salary. If she restricts spending to just one-third of the final salary, the savings can stretch to 14 years.

At age 65, life expectancy for women today is about 20 years, and for men about 15 years, so DC savings plans will not protect the elderly from longevity risk. The conversion of defined-benefit pensions to defined-contribution plans is the source of the real potential crisis in retirement income. Yet Greenspan did not mention this in his testimony to Congress.

NO CRISIS

Opponents of Social Security have hated it since its creation in 1935. The first prediction of a Social Security crisis was published in 1936! The Heritage Foundation and Cato Institute are home to many of the program's opponents today, and they fixate on the concept of a "demographic imperative." In 1960, the United States had 5.1 workers per retiree, in 1998 we had 3.4, and by 2030 we will have only 2.1. Opponents claim that with these demographic changes, revenues will eventually be insufficient to pay Social Security retirement benefits.

The logic is appealingly simple, but wrong for two reasons. First, this "old-age dependency" ratio in itself is irrelevant. No amount of financial manipulation can change this fact: all current consumption must come from current physical output. The consumption of all dependents (non-workers) must come from the output produced by current workers. It's the overall dependency ratio—the number of workers relative to all non-workers, including the aged, the young, the disabled, and those choosing not to work—that determines whether society can "afford" the baby boomers' retirement years. In the 1960s we had only 0.62 workers for each dependent, and we were building new schools and the interstate highway system and getting ready to put a man on the moon. No one bemoaned a demographic crisis or looked for ways to cut the resources allocated to children; in fact, the living standards of most families rose rapidly. In 2030, we will have 0.98 workers per dependent. We'll have more workers per dependent in the future than we did in the past. While it is true a larger share of total output will be allocated to the aged, just as a larger share was allocated to children in the 1960s, society will easily produce adequate output to support all workers and dependents, and at a higher standard of living.

Second, the "demographic imperative" ignores productivity growth. Average worker productivity has grown by about 2% per year, adjusted for inflation, for the past half-century. That means real output per worker doubles every 36 years. This productivity growth is projected to continue, so by 2040, each worker will produce twice as much as today. Suppose each of three workers today produces $1,000 per week and one retiree is allocated $500 (half of his final salary)—then each worker gets $833. In 2040, two such workers will produce $2,000 per week each (after adjusting for inflation). If each retiree gets $1,000, each worker still gets $1,500. The incomes of both workers and retirees go up. Thus, paying for the baby boomers' retirement need not decrease their children's standard of living. A larger share of output going to retirees does not imply that the standard of living of those still working will be lower. Those still working will have a slightly smaller share of a much larger pie.

So why the talk of a Social Security crisis? Social Security always has been a pay-as-you-go system. Current benefits are paid out of current tax revenues. But in the 1980s, a commission headed by Greenspan recommended raising payroll taxes to expand the trust fund in order to supplement tax revenues when the baby boom generation retires. Congress responded in 1984 by raising payroll taxes significantly. As a result, the Social Security trust fund, which holds government bonds as assets, has grown every year since. As the baby boom moves into retirement, these assets will be sold to help pay their retirement benefits.

Each year, Social Security's trustees must make projections of the system's status for the next 75 years. In 1996, they projected the trust fund balance would go to zero in 2030. In 2000, they projected a zero balance in 2036 and today they project a zero balance in 2042. The projection keeps changing because the trustees continue to make unrealistic assumptions about future economic conditions. The current projections are based on the assumption that annual GDP growth will average 1.8 % for the next 75 years. In no 20-year period, even including the Great Depression, has the U.S. economy grown that slowly. Each year the economy grows faster than 1.8%, the zero balance date moves further into the future. But the trustees continue to suggest that if we return to something like the Great Depression, the trust fund will go to zero.

Opponents of Social Security claim the system will then be "bankrupt." Bankruptcy implies ceasing to exist. But if the trust fund goes to zero, Social Security will not shut down and stop paying benefits. It will simply revert to the pure pay-as-you-go system that it was before 1984 and continue to pay current benefits using current tax revenues. Even if the trustees' worst-case assumptions come true, the payroll tax paid by workers would need to increase by only about 2% points, and only in 2042, not today.

If the economy grows at 2.4%—which is still slower than the stagnant growth of the 1980s—the trust fund never goes to zero. The increase in real output and real incomes will generate sufficient revenues to pay promised benefits. By 2042, we will need to lower payroll taxes or raise benefits to reduce the surplus.

The claim that benefits of future retirees must be reduced in order to not reduce the standard of living of future workers is simply wrong. It is being used to drive a wedge between generations and panic younger workers into supporting Bush's plan to destroy Social Security. Under the most likely version of his privatization proposal, according to Bush's own Social Security Commission, the guaranteed benefits from Social Security of a 20-year-old worker joining the labor force today would be reduced by 46%. That Commission also admitted that private accounts are unlikely to make up for this drop in benefits. An estimate made by the Goldman-Sacks brokerage firm suggests that even with private accounts, retirement income of younger workers would be reduced by 42% compared to what they would receive if nothing is done to change the Social Security system. Private accounts are a losing proposition for younger workers.

THE REAL FEAR: AN OVERSUPPLY OF BONDS

So why did Greenspan claim cutting benefits would become necessary? To understand the answer, we need to take a side trip to look at how bonds and the financial markets affect each other. It turns out that rising interest rates reduce the selling price of existing financial assets, and falling asset prices push up interest rates (see box "How Does the Bond Market Work?").

For example, in the 1980s, President Reagan cut taxes and created the largest government deficits in history up to that point. This meant the federal government had to sell lots of bonds to finance the soaring government debt; to attract enough buyers, the Treasury had to offer very high interest rates. During the 1980s, real interest rates (rates adjusted for inflation) were almost four times higher than the historic average. High interest rates slow economic growth by making it more expensive for consumers to buy homes or for businesses to invest in new infrastructure. The GDP growth rate in the 1980s was the slowest in U.S. history apart from the Great Depression.

But high interest rates also depress financial asset prices. A five percentage point rise in interest rates reduces the selling price of a bond (loan) that matures in 10 years by 50%. It was the impact of the record-high interest rates of the 1980s on the value of the loan portfolios of the savings and loan industry that caused the S&L crisis and the industry's collapse.

Greenspan is worried because he sees history repeating itself in the form of President Bush's tax cuts. In his testimony, Greenspan expressed concern over a potentially large rise in interest rates. This is his way of warning about an excess supply of bonds. Starting in 2020, Social Security will have to sell about $150 billion (in 2002 dollars) in trust fund bonds each year for 22 years. At the same time, private-sector pension funds will be selling $100 billion per year of financial assets to make their pension payments. State and local governments will be selling $75 billion per year to cover their former employees' pension expenses, and holdings in

> ## HOW DOES THE BOND MARKET WORK?
>
> A bond is nothing more than an IOU. A company or government borrows money and promises to pay a certain amount of interest annually until it repays the loan. When you buy a newly issued bond, you are making a loan. The amount of the loan is the "face value" of the bond. The initial interest rate at which the bond is issued, the "face rate," multiplied by this face value determines the amount of interest paid each period. Until the debt is paid back, events in the financial markets affect the bond's value.
>
> If market interest rates fall, prices of existing bonds rise. Why? Suppose you buy a bond with a face value of $100 that pays 10%. You then collect $10 per year. If the current interest rate falls to 5%, newly issued bonds will pay that new rate. Since your bond pays 10%, people would rather buy that one than one paying 5%. They are willing to pay more than the face value to get it, so the price will be bid up until interest rates equalize. The price at which you could sell your bond will rise to $200, since $10 is 5% of $200.
>
> But changes in bond prices also affect interest rates. If more people are selling bonds than buying them, an excess supply exists, and prices will fall. If you need to sell your bond to get money to pay your rent, you might have to lower the price of the bond you hold to $50. Because the bond still pays $10 per year to the owner, the new owner gets a 20% return on the $50 purchase. Anyone trying to issue new bonds will have to match that return, so the new market interest rate becomes 20%.

private mutual funds will fall by about $50 billion per year as individual retirees cash in their 401(k) assets. Private firms will still need to issue about $100 billion of new bonds a year to finance business expansion. Combined, these asset sales could total $475 billion per year.

This level of bond sales is more than double the record that was set in the 1980s following the Reagan tax cuts. But back then, the newly issued bonds were being purchased by "institutional investors" such as private-sector pension funds and insurance companies. After 2020, these groups will be net sellers of bonds. The financial markets will strain to absorb this level of asset sales. It's unlikely they will be able to also absorb the extra $400 billion per year of bond sales needed to cover the deficit spending that will occur if the new Bush tax cuts are made permanent. This oversupply of bonds will drive down the value of all financial assets.

In a 1994 paper, Sylvester Schieber, a current advisor to President Bush on pension and Social Security reform, predicted this potential drop in asset prices. After 2020, the value of assets held in 401(k) plans, already inadequate, will be reduced even more. More importantly, at least to Greenspan, the prices of assets held by corporations to fund their defined benefit pension promises will fall. Thus, pension payments will need to come out of current revenues, reducing corporate profits and, in turn, driving down stock prices.

It's this potential collapse in the prices of financial assets that worries Greenspan most. In order to reduce the run-up of long-term interest rates, some asset sales must be eliminated. Greenspan said, "You don't have the resources to do it all." But rather than rescinding Bush's tax cuts, Greenspan favors reducing bond sales by the Social Security trust fund. Doing that requires a reduction in benefits and raising payroll taxes even more.

Framing a question incorrectly makes it impossible to find a solution. The problem is not with Social Security, but rather with blind reliance on financial markets to solve all economic problems. If the financial markets are likely to fail us, what is the solution? The solution is simple once the question is framed correctly: where will the real output that baby boomers are going to consume in retirement come from?

The federal budget surplus President Bush inherited came entirely from Social Security surpluses resulting from the 1984 payroll tax increase. Bush gave away revenues meant to provide for workers' retirement as tax cuts for the wealthiest 10% of the population.

We should rescind Bush's tax cuts and use the Social Security surpluses to really prepare for the baby boom retirement. Public investment or targeted tax breaks could be used to encourage the building of the hospitals, nursing homes, and hospices that aging baby boomers will need. Such investment in public and private infrastructure would also stimulate the real economy and increase GDP growth. Surpluses could be used to fund the training of doctors, nurses and others to staff these facilities, and of other high skilled workers more generally. The higher wages of skilled labor will help generate the payroll tax revenues needed to fund future benefits. If baby boomers help to fund this infrastructure expansion through their payroll taxes while they are still working, less output will need to be allocated when they retire. These expenditures will increase the productivity of the real economy, which will help keep the financial sector solvent to provide for retirees.

Destroying Social Security in order to "save" it is not a solution.

Sources: Dean Baker and Mark Weisbrot, *Social Security: The Phony Crises*, University of Chicago Press, 1999; William Wolman and Anne Colamosca, *The Great 401(k) Hoax*, Perseus Publishing, 2002; Sylvester J. Schieber and John B. Shoven, "The Consequences of Population Aging on Private Pension Fund Saving and Asset Markets," National Bureau of Economic Research, Working Paper No. 4665, 1994.

THE OPPOSITE OF INSURANCE
UNLESS YOU'RE RICH, HEALTHY, OR BOTH, HEALTH SAVINGS ACCOUNTS ARE BAD NEWS.

BY JAMES WOOLMAN

Congress created Health Savings Accounts (HSAs) in 2003 as tax-advantaged savings accounts linked to the purchase of a high-deductible health plan. But the scheme is not a new idea. HSA proponents, including many health economists, have long argued that standard "comprehensive" insurance policies are too generous, sheltering consumers from the true cost of medical care. "Empowering" consumers to decide for themselves how much money to save for medical expenses, the theory goes, will unleash the magic of the market; costs will decline and quality will improve as doctors, hospitals, and other providers compete for discriminating customers.

New research on consumer and employer experiences with HSAs, however, confirms many of the fears cited by critics of the plans. The evidence shows that these plans attract relatively high-income, healthy people who are attracted to the tax benefits, while they place other consumers—including those with families, health problems, or low incomes—at risk for steep increases in out-of-pocket spending.

THE MECHANICS OF HSAS

Workers can contribute pre-tax income to an HSA and can withdraw from it at any time for health-related spending. Employers may also contribute to employees' HSAs. Any money remaining at the end of the year stays in the account, enjoys tax benefits, and can be invested just like money in an Individual Retirement Account.

To open an HSA, however, you must have a high-deductible health insurance plan, and you *cannot* have ordinary health coverage. To qualify, a plan must have a deductible of at least $1,050 for an individual or $2,100 for a family. (HSA-qualified plans are allowed to cover some preventive care without a deductible.) Actual deductibles are much higher: in 2006 HSA-qualified plans had average deductibles of around $2,000 (individual) or $4,000 (family). Under the HSA scheme, in other words, a family typically has to pay the first $4,000 in medical bills each year out of pocket; their insurance plan kicks in—with all of the usual co-pays, exclusions, etc.—only after annual medical expenses exceed that amount.

The funds in the HSA are supposed to cover a portion of these out-of-pocket expenses, but workers are wholly responsible for any gap between the amount in their HSA and the amount of the deductible. The gap can be sizeable. A national survey by the Kaiser Family Foundation found the average deductible for a family HSA plan was $4,008, while the average employer HSA contribution was $1,139. Enrollees are fully responsible for the $2,869 gap, in addition to their premium payments and additional co-pays (see Figure 1).

FIGURE 1
THE HEALTH SAVINGS ACCOUNT/HIGH DEDUCTIBLE HEALTH PLAN SCHEME: WORKERS PAY MORE, EMPLOYERS PAY LESS

Annual Worker Contribution Comparison	Single		Family	
	All Plans	HDHP	All Plans	HDHP
Worker Premium Contribution	$624	$467	$2,976	$2,115
Deductible	$508	$2,011	$1,099	$4,008
Employer HSA Contribution		($988)		($1,139)
Total Employer Spending	$1,132	$1,490	$4,075	$4,984

Annual Worker Contribution Comparison	Single		Family	
	All Plans	HDHP	All Plans	HDHP
Employer Premium Contribution	$4,248	$2,709	$7,756	$6,400
Employer HSA Contribution		$988		$1,139
Total Employer Spending	$1,132	$1,490	$4,075	$4,984

* Totals do not include coinsurance.
Source: The Kaiser Family Foundation and The Health Research and Education Trust 2006 Employer Benefits Survey.

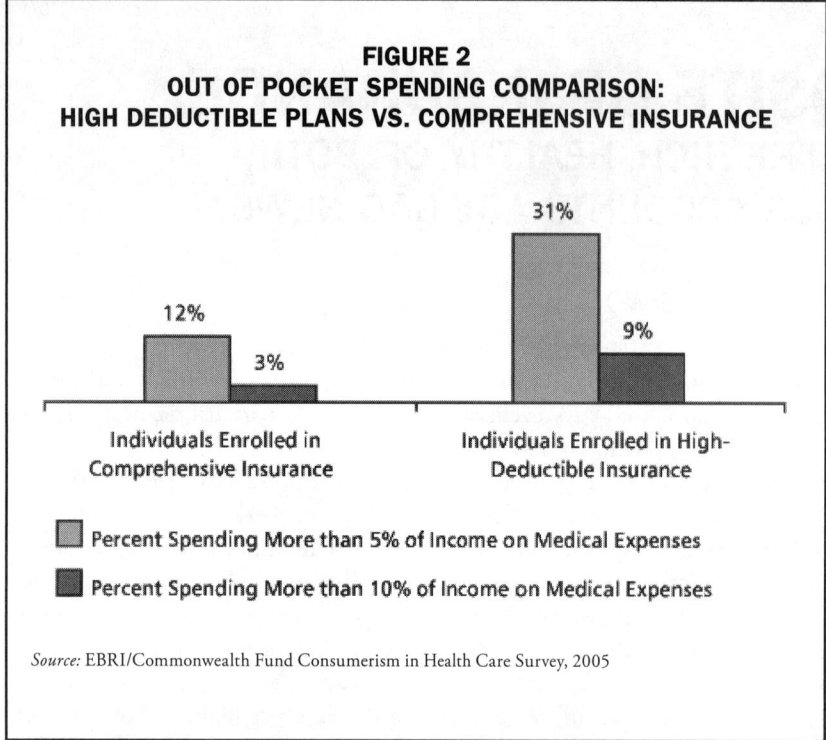

FIGURE 2
OUT OF POCKET SPENDING COMPARISON:
HIGH DEDUCTIBLE PLANS VS. COMPREHENSIVE INSURANCE

- Percent Spending More than 5% of Income on Medical Expenses
- Percent Spending More than 10% of Income on Medical Expenses

Source: EBRI/Commonwealth Fund Consumerism in Health Care Survey, 2005

By reducing employers' premium costs, limiting the amount of services employees are likely to use, and increasing the likelihood that employees will pay more out of pocket for health care, high-deductible plans shift financial risk from employers onto employees. Monthly premiums are lower under these plans than for comprehensive insurance, but high-deductible plan enrollees are still much more likely to spend a substantial amount of their income on health expenses than people enrolled in comprehensive plans. For instance, 31% of enrollees in HSA-type plans spent over 5% of their income on medical expenses, including premiums, compared with only 12% of enrollees in comprehensive plans, according to a recent survey conducted by the Employee Benefits Research Institute and the Commonwealth Fund (see Figure 2).

FLAWED PLAN

Proponents of HSAs would say this shifting of risk is a good thing: a market-based reform to address escalating health care costs. But this is a deeply flawed view.

For one thing, high-deductible plans are unlikely to have much impact on overall health care spending, most of which results from expensive treatments for serious illnesses whose costs exceed the high deductibles. One recent study found that more than 95% of medical expenditures by working-age households with health insurance were made by those who spend above the minimum HSA deductibles, and that overall, nearly 79% of total medical expenditures occurred above the minimum HSA deductibles. In fact, the only type of spending HSAs are likely to reduce is the kind we want to encourage: primary and preventive care.

According to the Commonwealth Fund, enrollees with deductibles over $1,000 were twice as likely as enrollees with deductibles under $500 to avoid seeing the doctor for a medical problem, avoid seeing a specialist, or skip a recommended treatment due to cost.

Moreover, people do not and cannot shop for health care services as they do for other goods. Most people do not have adequate information on the cost and quality of care to make informed purchasing decisions. Nor are they inclined to do so when they are sick or in distress, which is when health care decisions are typically made. Most people enrolled in high-deductible plans do not, in fact, shop for less expensive care, although many shop for better prescription drug prices, according to a 2006 Government Accountability Office (GAO) report.

The GAO found that current HSA participants are disproportionately high income, healthy people who will benefit from the tax advantages and are unlikely to need much health care. Although generally satisfied with their own experience, HSA enrollees polled by the GAO said they would *not* recommend high-deductible plans for people with families, health problems, maintenance medications, or moderate incomes—in other words, most people.

So HSAs represent a double-edged sword. If large numbers of people are forced to switch from comprehensive health coverage to high-deductible plans, they will likely face significantly higher out-of-pocket costs. On the other hand, if HSAs continue to attract the healthiest enrollees, the exit of this healthy segment from the comprehensive coverage pool will likely drive up health insurance costs for everyone else.

HSAs and high-deductible plans appeal to employers looking to cut health care costs, high-income earners looking for more tax breaks, and younger workers willing to gamble they won't get sick. For most people, however, they are the opposite of insurance: they concentrate the financial risk of illness instead of spreading it, and they increase the likelihood of incurring medical debt instead of reducing it.

Resources: "Consumer-Directed Health Plans: Early Enrollee Experiences with Health Savings Accounts and Eligible Health Plans," GAO, 8/06; Kaiser Family Foundation and Health Research and Educational Trust, "Employer Health Benefits: 2006 Annual Survey," 9/06; Paul Fronstin and Sara R. Collins, "Early Experience With High-Deductible and Consumer-Driven Health Plans," Employee Benefits Research Institute and the Commonwealth Fund, 12/05; Edwin Park and Robert Greenstein, "Latest Enrollment Data Still Fail to Dispel Concerns about Health Savings Accounts," Center on Budget and Policy Priorities, 1/30/06.

CHAPTER 6
MONETARY POLICY AND FINANCIAL MARKETS

INTRODUCTION

Ben Bernanke has replaced Alan Greenspan as the man behind the curtain of the Federal Reserve Board, just in time to oversee the worst financial crisis since the Great Depression.

Bernanke will need all the wizard-like powers the business press sometimes attributed to Greenspan if he is going to pull the economy's fat out of the fire. And those wizard-like powers were in awfully short supply when Greenspan himself confessed before Congress in October 2008 that the financial crisis had left him "in a state of shocked disbelief." and that he had "made a mistake in presuming that banks … were capable of protecting their own shareholders."

Even if Bernanke does somehow right the economy and get a handle on the nearly intractable mortgage debt crisis, it is doubtful that working people will fare any better under Bernanke than they did on under maestro Greenspan. Even before the financial crisis, Greenspan worried that, under his tenure, inequality had worsened to levels that threatened our democratic institutions, and that the unprecedented level of U.S. reliance on foreign borrowing had become unsustainable. Bernanke has acknowledged the seriousness of both problems as well, but seems just as incapable as his predecessor at remedying them.

But why should it matter who chairs the Federal Reserve Board? The Fed is charged with using monetary policy to keep inflation in check and provide liquidity to keep the economy going, or bolster a flagging economy. The Fed is supposed to use its three tools—the reserve requirement, the discount and federal funds rates, and open market operations—to manipulate banking activity, control the money supply, and direct the economy to everyone's benefit.

It all sounds value-free. But what the Fed really does is serve those who hold financial assets. And that is just what's wrong with Fed monetary policy. When it comes to making monetary policy, the Fed puts the interests of bondholders first, well before those of job seekers and workers. Investors look to the Fed to protect the value of their stocks and bonds by keeping inflation low—and if that means keeping a cap on employment growth, so be it.

That is why monetary policy is not just a matter for financial market junkies, but for anyone concerned with the social policies it holds hostage. As Doug Orr and Ellen Frank argue in this chapter, "Whenever any policy is proposed, be it in health care, housing or transportation, the first question politicians ask is, 'What will the bond market think about it?'"

The authors go on to show just how monetary policy under Greenspan has worked against most of us and even helped push the economy into a slowdown in 2000 (Article 6.2).

Other articles in this chapter look closely at diverse aspects of Fed policy making. Doug Orr explains in everyday language what money is and how the Fed attempts to control the money supply (Article 6.1). Arthur MacEwan compares monetary and fiscal policy, highlighting the greater powers of fiscal policy to counteract recessions (Article 6.3). In a second article, MacEwan debunks the notion that a small cabal of bankers runs the world through the operations of the Fed, despite the powerful pro-corporate effect the Fed has on day-to-day economic life (Article 6.5). The explosion in banks excess reserves, as Economist Gerald Friedman shows, confirms that the Fed can do little to get the economy going if banks won't make loans (Article 6.4).

The Fed is also charged with overseeing the regulation of U.S. financial institutions, including the stock market and home mortgages, as well as the banking industry. But with the blessing of most economists, Congress and the Fed have done more to deregulate these institutions than to regulate them in a way that promotes the public interest. In a thoroughgoing article, William K. Black tells the story of how the banking industry became dysfunctional with deregulation, and how that deregulation enabled the current subprime mortgage crisis (Article 6.6).

In a series of articles, the remainder of the chapter tallies up the damage inflicted by the financial crisis spawned by those deregulatory policies. Arthur MacEwan contributes three short articles. The first compares the bailout of the financial sector to having a rotten tooth removed (Article 6.7). The second looks closely at the failure and bailout of the Bear Stearns investment bank (Article 6.8). The third explains who makes out and who loses out when hedge funds

---

KEY TO COLANDER

E = Economics   M = Macroeconomics

This entire chapter is keyed to chapter E30-E32; or M13-15.
  Chapter E32, M15 is also highly relevant here. Essays 6.1, 6.2 and 6.3 in particular are excellent primers on money, banking, the Federal Reserve Bank and the efficacy of monetary policy.

turn huge profits (Article 6.9). Economist Fred Moseley then analyzes the bailout of the public mortgage lending agencies, Fannie Mae and Freddie Mac. He makes the case for a public home mortgage agency whose sole purpose would be to provide affordable housing (Article 6.10).

Moseley and another economist, Robert Pollin, close the chapter with proposals for what to do about the banking industry and the Fed. Moseley argues that if banks and other financial institutions are "too big to fail," then nationalize them—permanently (Article 6.11). Pollin makes the case for transforming the Fed into a democratically-controlled investment bank that serves the interests of all of us (Article 6.12).

DISCUSSION QUESTIONS

1. (Article 6.1) What are the mechanisms the Fed uses to "control" the creation of money by the banking system. Why, according to Orr, is the Fed's control over the creation of money "limited"?
2. (Article 6.2) According to Orr and Frank, monetary policy serves the interests of bondholders at the expense of people seeking work and of everyone who benefits from social spending. What evidence do they provide to demonstrate this? Do you find it convincing?
3. (Article 6.3) What advantage is there in using monetary policy to slow down the economy? Why might fiscal policy be a more effective tool for lifting the economy out of a recession?
4. (Article 6.4) Why do Friedman and others before him liken monetary policy to "pushing on a string" and does Friedman think this analogy is an apt description of monetary policy today?
5. (Article 6.5) Why is MacEwan unconvinced by those who argue that a small cabal of bankers runs the world through the Fed?
6. (Article 6.6) After reading Black's article, describe the measures that have led to the deregulation of the U.S. banking industry and the impact this deregulation has had.
7. (Articles 6.7, 6.8) Is it accurate to liken the collapse and bailout of Bears Stearns to dealing with "a rotten tooth?'
8. (Article 6.9) Who gains and who loses when hedge funds make billions of dollars in profits?
9. (Article 6.10) Who is to blame for the financial troubles of Fannie Mae and Freddie Mac? How should Fannie and Freddie be reformed? Should the provision of affordable housing be their sole focus?
10. (Article 6.11) How does Moseley make the case that nationalizing the big banks labeled "too big to fail" is the right policy for cleaning up today's financial mess?
11. (Article 6.12) What are the chief elements of Pollin's proposal to transform the Fed and how would it affect the focus of the Fed and its decision-making? Do you think his proposals would be effective?

ARTICLE 6.1   *November/December 1993*

WHAT IS MONEY?

BY DOUG ORR

We all use money every day. Yet many people do not know what money actually is. There are many myths about money, including the idea that the government "prints" all of it and that it has some intrinsic value. But actually, money is less a matter of value, and more a matter of faith.

Money is sometimes called the universal commodity, because it can be traded for all other commodities. But for this to happen, everyone in society must believe that money will be accepted. If people stop believing that it will be accepted, the existing money ceases to be money. Recently in Poland, people stopped accepting the zloty, and used vodka as money instead.

In addition to facilitating exchanges, money allows us to "store" value from one point in time to another. If you sell your car today for $4,000, you probably won't buy that amount of other products today. Rather, you store the value as money, probably in a bank, until you want to use it.

The "things" that get used as money have changed over time, and "modern" people often chuckle when they hear about some of them. The Romans used salt (from which we get the word "salary"), South Sea Islanders used shark's teeth, and several societies actually used cows. The "Three Wise Men" brought gold, frankincense and myrrh, each of which was money in different regions at the time.

If money does not exist, or is in short supply, it will be created. In POW camps, where guards specifically outlaw its existence, prisoners use cigarettes instead. In the American colonies, the British attempted to limit the supply of British pounds, because they knew that by limiting the supply of money, they could hamper the development of independent markets in the colonies. Today, the United States uses a similar policy, through the International Monetary Fund, in dealing with Latin America.

To overcome this problem, the colonists began to use tobacco leaves as money. This helped the colonies to develop, but it also allowed the holders of large plots of land to grow their own money! When the colonies gained independence, the new government decreed gold to be money, rather than tobacco, much to the dismay of Southern plantation owners. Now, rather than growing money, farmers had to find or buy it.

To aid the use of gold as money, banks would test its purity, put it in storage, and give the depositor paper certificates of ownership. These certificates, "paper money," could then be used in place of the gold itself. Since any bank could store gold and issue certificates, by the beginning of the Civil War, over 7,000 different types of "paper money" were in circulation in the United States, none of it printed by the government.

While paper money is easier to use than gold, it is still risky to carry around large amounts of cash. It is safer to store the paper in a bank and simply sign over its ownership to make a purchase. We sign over the ownership of our money by writing a check. Checking account money became popular when the government outlawed the printing of paper money by private banks in 1864.

HOW BANKS CREATE MONEY

Banks are central to understanding money, because in addition to storing it, they help to create it. Bankers realize that not everyone will withdraw their money at the same time, so they loan out much of the money that has been deposited. It is from the interest on these loans that banks get their profits, and through these loans the banking system creates new money.

If you deposit $100 cash in your checking account at Chase Manhattan Bank, you still have $100 in money to use, because checks are also accepted as money. Chase must set aside some of this cash as "reserves," in case you or other depositors decide to withdraw money as cash. Current regulations issued by the Federal Reserve Bank (the Fed) require banks to set aside three cents out of each dollar. So Chase can make a loan of $97, based on your deposit. Chase does not make loans by handing out cash but instead by putting $97 in the checking account of the person, say Emily, taking out the loan. So from your initial deposit of $100 in cash, the economy now has $197 in checking account money.

The borrower, Emily, pays $97 for some product or service by check, and the seller, say Ace Computers, deposits the money in its checking account. The total amount of checking account money is still $197, but its location and ownership have changed. If Ace Computer's account is at Citibank, $97 in cash is transferred from Chase to Citibank. This leaves just $3 in cash reserves at Chase to cover your original deposit. However, Citibank now has $97 in "new" cash on hand, so it sets aside three cents on the dollar ($2.91) and loans out the rest, $94.09, as new checking account money. Through this process, every dollar of "reserves" yields many dollars in total money.

If you think this is just a shell game and there is only $100 in "real" money, you still don't understand money. Anything that is accepted as payment for a transaction is "real" money. Cash is no more real than checking account money. In fact, most car rental companies will not accept cash as payment for a car, so for them, cash is not money!

Today, there is $292 billion of U.S. currency, i.e. "paper money," in existence. However, somewhere between 50% to 70% of it is held outside the United States by foreign banks and individuals. The vast majority of all money actually in use in the United States is not cash, but rather checking account money. This type of money, $726 billion, was created by private banks, and was not "printed" by anyone. In fact, this money exists only as electronic "bits" in banks' computers. (The less "modern" South Sea Islanders could have quite a chuckle about that!)

The amount of money that banks can create is limited by the total amount of reserves, and by the fraction of each deposit that must be held as reserves. Prior to 1914, bankers themselves decided what fraction of deposits to hold as reserves. Since then, this fraction has been set by the main banking regulator, the Fed.

Until 1934, gold was held as reserves, but the supply of gold was unstable, growing rapidly during the California and Alaska "gold rushes," and very slowly at other times. As a result, at times more money was created than the economy needed, and at other times not enough money could be created. Starting in 1934, the U.S. government decided that gold would no longer be used as reserves. Cash, now printed by the Fed, could no longer be redeemed for gold, and cash itself became the reserve asset.

Banks, fearing robberies, do not hold all of their cash reserves in their own vaults. Rather, they store it in an account at a regional Fed bank. These accounts count as reserves. What banks do hold in their vaults is their other assets, such as Treasury bonds and corporate bonds.

THE FED AND BANK RESERVES

The only role of the government in creating money is through the Fed. If the Fed wants to expand the money supply, it must increase bank reserves. To do this, the Fed buys Treasury bonds from a bank, and pays with a check drawn on the Fed itself. By depositing the check in its reserve account at the Fed, the bank now has more reserves, so the bank can now make more loans and create new checking account money.

By controlling the amount of reserves, the Fed attempts to control the size of the money supply. But as recent history has shown, this control is limited. During the recent recession, the Fed created reserves, but many banks were afraid to make loans, so little new money was created. During the late 1970s, the Fed tried to limit the amount of money banks could create by reducing reserves, but banks simply created new forms of money, just like the POW camp prisoners. In 1979, there was only one form of checking account money. Today, there are many, with odd names such as NOWs, ATSs, repos, and money market deposit accounts.

These amorphous forms of money function only because we believe they will function, which is why the continued stability of the banking system is so critical. Banks do not have cash reserves to cover all checking account money. If, through a replay of the savings & loan debacle, we lose faith in the commercial banking system and all try to take out our "money" as cash, the banks will become insolvent (fail), and the money they have created will simply disappear. This would create a real crisis, since no market economy can function without its money.

ARTICLE 6.2

October 1999

FOCUS ON THE FED
THE BOND MARKET VERSUS THE REST OF US

BY DOUG ORR AND ELLEN FRANK

Why should anyone involved in environmental issues, or education reform efforts, or efforts to house the homeless, or anyone else, care about monetary policy? After all, it only affects the financial markets, right? *Wrong.* Monetary policy is holding all other social policy hostage, and is part of the cause of the rapid increase in income inequality in the United States. Whenever any policy change is proposed, be it in health care, housing, or transportation, the first question politicians ask is, "What will the bond market think about this?"

"The bond market" is a euphemism for the financial sector of the U.S. economy and the Federal Reserve Bank (the Fed), which regulates that sector. The Fed is the central bank of the U.S. government. It controls monetary policy, and has been using its power to help the banking industry and the holders of financial assets, while thwarting government attempts to deal with pressing social problems.

Since 1979, the Fed has had an unprecedented degree of independence from government control. This independence had put it in a position to veto any progressive fiscal policy that the Congress might propose. To understand how this situation developed, we must understand the function of banks, the structure of the Fed, and the role of monetary policy.

BANKS AND INSTABILITY
Government regulates the banking industry because private sector, profit-driven banking is inherently unstable. Banks do more than just store money—they help create it. If you deposit a dollar in the bank, you still have that dollar. Commercial banks will set aside three cents as "reserves" to "cover" your deposit, and the remaining 97 cents is loaned out to someone else who now has "new money." By making loans, banks create new money and generate profit. The drive to maximize profits often leads banks to become overextended: making too many loans and holding too few reserves. This drive for profits can undermine a bank's stability.

If depositors think the bank is holding too few reserves, or is making overly speculative loans, they might try to withdraw their money as cash. Large numbers of depositors withdrawing cash from a bank at the same time is called a "run on the bank." Since banks only hold 3% of their deposit liabilities as cash, even a moderate-sized "run" would be enough to drain the bank of its cash reserves. If a bank has no reserves, it is insolvent and is forced to close. At that point, all remaining deposits in the bank cease to exist, and depositors lose their money.

The failure of a bank affects more than just that bank's depositors. One bank's excesses tend to shake people's faith in other banks. If the run spreads, "bank panics" can occur. During the 1800s, such panics erupted every 10 to 15 years, bankrupting between 10% and 25% of the banks in the United States and creating a recession each time.

THE CREATION OF THE FED
The panic of 1907 bankrupted some of the largest banks and led to demands for bank reforms that would stabilize the system. Reform proposals ranged from doing almost nothing to nationalizing the entire banking industry. As a compromise, the Federal Reserve was created in 1913. The U.S. government saw the Fed as a way for bankers to regulate themselves, and structured the Federal Reserve System so that it could be responsive to its main constituents: banks and other financial-sector businesses that are now called, euphemistically, "the bond market." While ideally it should serve the interests of the general public when it conducts monetary policy, in reality the Fed balances two, occasionally conflicting goals: maintaining the stability of "the bond market" and maximizing financial-sector profits. Over time, Congress and the President have varied the degree of independence that they have given to the Fed to choose between these goals.

Initially, the Fed enjoyed a high degree of independence. Unfortunately, it was more successful in aiding bank profits than in stabilizing the system. During the 1920s, the Fed allowed member banks to engage in highly speculative activities, including using depositor's money to play the stock market. While many banks were very profitable, speculative excesses caused almost 20% of the banks in existence in 1920 to fail during the following decade. With the onset of the Great Depression, between 1929 and 1933, more than 9,000 banks, 38% of the total, failed. Since the Fed had not achieved its first goal, in 1935 Congress responded with laws that put many new regulations on banks, and reduced the Fed's independence.

FED INDEPENDENCE LOST

Under the new regulations, commercial banks were restricted to taking deposits and making commercial loans. Thus, the only opportunity for making a profit was to maintain a "spread" between the interest rate paid on deposits and that charged on loans. Loans are made for relatively long terms, and deposits are not. If the short-term interest rate on deposits varies widely, the spread will grow and shrink, which makes bank profits unstable. In order to stabilize bank profits, during the 30 years after 1935, the Treasury mandated that the Fed keep this rate approximately constant.

Under this arrangement, Congress indirectly controlled monetary policy. If Congress wanted to stimulate the economy it could increase government spending or cut taxes. Both led to an increase in spending and an increase in the demand for money. To keep interest rates, which are the price of money, from rising, the Fed must increase the supply of money. Thus, the Fed "accommodated" fiscal policy decisions made by Congress and the President.

During most of this period, growth was moderate and prices were stable. The Fed went along because this arrangement did not threaten bank profits. Starting in the mid-1960s, however, stimulative fiscal policy started to push up the inflation rate, which did threaten bank profits. A confrontation over Fed independence ensued and grew in intensity throughout the 1970s.

INFLATION'S IMPACT

Contrary to the view commonly propagated by the media, inflation does not affect everyone equally. In fact, there are very clear winners and losers. Inflation is an increase in the average level of prices, but some prices rise faster than average and some rise slower. If the price of something you are selling is rising faster than average, you win. Otherwise, you lose. Inflation redistributes income, but in an arbitrary manner. This uncertainty makes inflation unpopular, even to the winners. However, one industry always loses from unexpected inflation, and that industry is finance.

Banks make loans today that will be repaid, with interest, in the future. If inflation reduces the value of those future payments, the banks' profits will be reduced. So bankers are interested in the "real interest rate," that is, the actual (nominal) interest rate on the loan minus the rate of inflation. If the interest rate on commercial bank loans is 7% and the rate of inflation is 3%, the real rate of interest is 4%. In the early postwar period, real interest rates were relatively stable at about 2%.

From 1965 on, unexpected increases in inflation reduced the real interest rate. This cheap credit was a boon to home buyers, farmers, and manufacturers, but it greatly reduced bank profits. Banks wanted inflation cut. The Keynesian view of monetary policy offered a simple but unpopular solution: raise interest rates enough to cause a recession. High unemployment and falling incomes would take the steam out of inflation.

Putting people out of work to help bankers would be a hard sell. The Fed needed a different story to justify shifting its policy from stabilizing interest rates to fighting inflation. That story was monetarism, a theory that claims that changes in the money supply affect prices, but nothing else in the economy.

THE MONETARIST EXPERIMENT

On October 6, 1979, Fed Chair Paul Volcker, using monetarist theory as a justification, announced that the Fed would no longer try to keep interest rates at targeted levels. He argued that Fed policy should concentrate on controlling inflation, and to do so he would now focus on limiting the money supply growth rate. Since neither Congress nor the President attempted to overrule Volcker, this change ushered in an era of unprecedented independence for Fed monetary policy.

During the next three years, the Fed reduced the rate of growth in the money supply, but this experiment did not yield the results predicted by the monetarists. Instead of a swift reduction in the rate of inflation, the most immediate outcome was a rapid rise in the real interest rate and the start of the worst recession since the Great Depression.

As the Keynesian view predicted, the recession occurred because high interest rates slowed economic growth and increased unemployment. In 1979, the unemployment rate was 5.8%. By 1982 it had reached 10.7%, the first double-digit rate since the Depression. With fewer people working and buying products, the inflation rate, which had been 8.7% in 1979, finally started to slow in 1981 and was approaching 4% by the end of 1982. Tight money policies by the Fed kept nominal interest rates from falling as fast as inflation. This raised real interest rates (nominal rates minus inflation) on commercial loans from 0.5% in 1979 to 10% in 1982.

The Fed's fight against inflation had a severe impact on the entire economy. All businesses, especially farming and manufacturing, run on credit. The rise in interest rates, combined with lower prices, squeezed the profits of farmers and manufacturers.

Both of these industries rely heavily on exports, and so were also hurt by the negative effect of high interest rates on the competitiveness of U.S. exports. Real interest rates in the United States were the highest in the world, thereby attracting financial investment from abroad. In order for foreigners to buy financial assets in the United States, they first had to buy dollars. This demand for dollars drove up their value in international markets. While a "strong" dollar means imports are relatively cheap, it also means that U.S. exports are expensive. Foreign countries could not afford to buy our "costly" agricultural and manufactured exports. As a result, during this period, bankruptcy rates in these two industries were massive, higher than during the 1930s.

Despite its high cost to the rest of the economy, the monetarist experiment did not benefit many banks. Initially, the high real interest rates appeared to help bank profits. Regulations capped the interest rates banks could pay on deposits, but rates charged on loans were not regulated. This increased the profit on loans. Many investors, however, started moving their deposits to less regulated financial intermediaries, such as mutual funds, that could pay higher rates on deposits. In addition, the recession forced many borrowers to declare bankruptcy and default on their loans. Both of these factors pushed banks toward insolvency.

REVERSING COURSE

It was bank losses, rather than the pain in the rest of the economy, that led Volcker to announce in September 1982 that he was abandoning monetarism. His new policy aimed to provide enough reserves to keep most banks solvent and to allow a *slow* recovery from the recession. Unemployment remained high for the next five years, so inflation continued to slow. Real interest rates stayed near 8% through 1986, so interest-sensitive industries, such as farming and manufacturing, did not take part in the recovery.

Volcker made his allegiance to the banking industry very clear during a meeting, in February 1985, with a delegation of state legislators, laborers, and farmers who were demanding easier money and lower interest rates. He told them, "Look, your constituents are unhappy, mine aren't."

Yet by 1985, the crisis in the savings and loan industry was spreading into commercial banking. To provide cash ("liquidity") to the banks, Volcker allowed the money supply to grow by 12% during 1985 and by 17% in 1986. Monetarists raised the specter of a return to double-digit inflation. Instead, the rate of inflation continued to slow, demonstrating that a simple link between the money supply and inflation does not exist.

IN 1995 THE WEALTHIEST 10% OF HOUSEHOLDS OWNED 89.8% OF ALL BONDS, 88.4% OF ALL STOCKS, 88.5% OF FINANCIAL TRUSTS, AND 91% OF OTHER BUSINESS EQUITY.

THE VETO

Despite the failure and subsequent abandonment of monetarist policies, the Fed still uses monetarist *theory* to justify its continued focus on "fighting inflation." The myth that monetary policy only affects inflation provides a convenient "cover" that allows the Fed to serve its narrow constituency: "the bond market." During 1998, nominal interest rates appeared low, but because inflation is so low, real interest rates on commercial loans were 6.8%—3.2 times the post-World War II average. Real interest rates remain high because "the bond market" worries about any possible increase in future inflation.

Fighting inflation benefits the bond market. However, despite the near-depression that monetarism caused in the 1980s and the extremely slow rate of economic growth that has occurred in the 1990s, the Fed continues to claim that fighting inflation serves the interests of the entire country. The public's widespread belief in this myth denies progressives in Congress the support they need to force the Fed back into accommodating fiscal policy. It also provides support for those in Congress that want to block any expansion of social programs.

If Congress decides to spend more for environmental clean-up, housing the homeless, or education, "the bond market" will raise the specter of renewed inflation. The Fed will then raise interest rates, as it did in June 1999, as a "pre-emptive strike" to prevent inflation. The increase in interest rates, if large enough, will slow the economy, increase unemployment, reduce government revenues, and return the federal budget to a deficit. Since Congress is aware of this probable outcome, and knows it will be incorrectly blamed for it, Congress won't pass any legislation "the bond market" doesn't like. This is how the bond market holds Congress hostage. As long as Congress and the President allow the Fed to follow an inflation-fighting policy, the Fed can maintain a veto threat over the elected government.

The Fed has also played a large role in the rapid increase in income and wealth inequality that started in the 1980s and has accelerated in the 1990s. The two decades following World War II are often called the "golden age" of the U.S. economy. On average, Gross Domestic Product (GDP) grew 4.2% each year, unemployment averaged 4.6%, and real commercial interest rates averaged 2.1%. Average real wages, that is, wages adjusted for inflation, grew at an annual rate of 2.1%, rising from $8.34 an hour in 1950 to $12.75 in 1970 (both measured in 1998 dollars). This period saw the creation of a true middle class in the United States.

In the two decades since 1980, GDP growth has averaged 2.6% each year, unemployment has averaged 6.6%, and real interest rates have averaged 5.9%. Average real wages *declined* every year from 1980 to 1996. In fact, the real wage in 1996 was exactly the same as in 1968. If wages had continued to grow at 2.1%, the average wage today would be almost twice what it is. Without the slow growth policies of the Fed and the anti-labor policies started under Reagan, the average income of the majority of the people in the United States would be twice as large. Instead, we've seen a hollowing out of the middle class, and a rapid transfer of wealth and income to those already wealthy.

By focusing on inflation rather than interest rates, the media deflect attention from a critical social issue—how high interest rates transfer income from the indebted middle class to the very rich. The social consequences of high interest rates can be gauged by looking at the share of interest income in total U.S. personal income. Between 1980 and 1989, real interest rates rose from 1.8% to 6.1%. The share of income received as interest rose from 11% to 15.2%. As rates came back down slightly in the mid-1990s, so did the share of income going to interest.

WHERE DO INTEREST PAYMENTS GO?

If ownership of financial assets was evenly distributed among households, the growth in interest income would not be of much importance. When increases in interest rates outstripped wage and salary gains, the typical household would simply gain on the asset side what they were losing on the liability side. An increase in the size of their mortgage payment would be matched by an increase in their interest income.

But ownership of financial assets is heavily concentrated. A mere 7% of families with incomes of $100,000 or more control nearly half of total household net worth. Yet this number understates the concentration of financial wealth. Almost 80% of families in the United States have almost no assets, outside the equity in their homes and vehicles. As a result, despite the massive increase in financial asset values during the 1990s, median net worth was no higher in 1995 than it was in 1989. Almost all of the growth in net worth accrued to the few owners of financial assets.

Detailed studies of wealth data collected by the Fed report that in 1995 the wealthiest 10% of households owned 89.8% of all bonds, 88.4% of all stocks, 88.5% of financial trusts, and 91% of other business equity. Despite the media hype about the "democratization" of the stock market, between 1989 and 1995 the concentration of stock ownership increased. In 1995 only 15.3% of households held stocks directly and only 12% owned shares in mutual funds outside of their retirement accounts.

The "poorest" nine-tenths of the U.S. population—that is, most of us—have virtually no financial assets. Such families gain little from rising interest rates. But the higher mortgage, credit card, and auto payments that result take a real toll on living standards. Each uptick in the real interest rate entails a transfer of income from the lowest 90% of the population to the highest 10%. And most of that income goes to the very, very wealthy who are yet another part of "the bond market" served by the Fed.

Economist James Galbraith has called today's high interest rates a form of taxation without representation. The term is apt. Tax increases are passed by Congress, which has at least some public oversight. Interest rate hikes are decided by the Fed, an institution over which the President, Congress and the public have virtually no control.

Like taxes, rising interest rates are a drain on the resources and income of the vast majority of U.S. households. But unlike tax revenues that can be used to provide education, environmental clean-up, homeless shelters, roads, airports, and other infrastructure, interest payments flow into the pockets of the very rich, who become ever so much richer.

Resources: Arthur B. Kennickell, Martha Starr-McCluer, and Annika E. Sunden, "Family Finances in the U.S.: Recent Evidence from the Survey of Consumer Finances," *Federal Reserve Bulletin* (Jan. 1997); Lawrence Mishel, Jared Bernstein, and John Schmitt, *The State of Working America 1998-99*, 1999.

ARTICLE 6.3

July/August 1997

HOW DO FISCAL AND MONETARY POLICY COMPARE?

BY ARTHUR MACEWAN

The Federal Reserve influences the economy through monetary policy—the actions the Fed takes to affect the cost and availability of credit. For example, in March of this year, the Fed, led by its chairman Alan Greenspan, decided that it was time to slow economic growth. So it induced banks and other lenders to raise their interest rates. Higher interest rates mean fewer businesses and individuals will take out loans and spend the borrowed money. Lower spending means slower economic growth.

The federal government can also influence economic growth and the demand for goods and services through fiscal policy—the way it taxes and spends. If the government wants to slow down the economy, for example, it can raise taxes and reduce its own spending. Less money ends up in people's hands if the government hires fewer construction workers to build roads, or if it cuts back on education programs.

One problem with fiscal policy is that changing the budget takes time—except for programs whose spending levels change automatically when the economy does, like unemployment compensation. To slow down the economy, Congress has to pass new laws raising taxes—certainly a "no no" these days—or cutting spending. Then the President has to accept Congress's new law, which might require negotiations, or more legislative action. All this is to say that the political process involves considerable delays and might result in no action at all.

Monetary policy is different because the Fed does not have to bother with this messy political process that we call democracy. It is "independent" since its members, appointed by the President, serve long terms. They decide whether to ease or tighten the availability of credit, without any role for Congress or the President. To be sure, the "independence" of the Fed is not enshrined in the Constitution. Yet for Congress and the President to pass new laws which directed or restricted the Fed's action would be a serious disruption of well-established policy.

The law governing the Fed says that it should pursue both stable prices (low inflation) and full employment. In fact, the Fed focuses almost exclusively on the goal of stable prices. If unemployment has to rise to meet this goal, well, too bad. It is easy to see why the Fed does its work best when it doesn't have to worry about getting democratic approval.

Fiscal policy is somewhat more constrained by democratic processes than is monetary policy. For example, conservative attacks on Medicare and Social Security have not gotten very far because these programs are very popular.

But the recent mania to balance the budget makes it difficult to use fiscal policy to stimulate economic expansion by increasing spending. This may present some serious problems during economic downturns. The monetary policy of the Fed, it turns out, is not nearly so effective in stimulating economic expansion during a recession as it is in slowing growth during relatively good times. In a recession, the Fed can induce commercial banks to lower their interest rates. But if the recession leads investors to worry that demand for products and services will fall, the lower interest rates might not reignite economic growth. What's the point, for example, in building a new office building when it doesn't look like it will be possible to rent out the space in existing buildings for quite a while?

In a recession, then, trying to use monetary policy to get the economy going can be like pushing on a string. It simply won't do any good. Fiscal policy, however, might directly create demand, present businesses with the reality of a new expansion, and generate a new period of investment and growth.

ARTICLE 6.4　　　　　　　　　　　　　　　　　　　　　　　　　　　　　　　　　　May/June 2009

PUSHING ON STRINGS
THE EXPLOSION OF U.S. BANKS' EXCESS RESERVES SINCE LAST FALL ILLUSTRATES THE DRAMATIC FAILURE OF MONETARY POLICY.

BY GERALD FRIEDMAN

Monetary policy is not working. Since the economic crisis began in July 2007, the Federal Reserve has dramatically cut interest rates and pumped out over a trillion dollars, increasing the money supply by over 15% in less than two years. These vast sums have failed to revive the economy because the banks have been hoarding liquidity rather than lending.

The Federal Reserve requires that banks hold money on reserve to back up deposits and other bank liabilities. In the past, beyond these required reserves, banks would hold very small amounts of excess reserves, holdings that they minimized because reserves earn very little or no interest. Between the 1950s and September 2008, U.S. banks held over $5 billion in total excess reserves only once, after the September 11 attacks. This changed with the collapse of Lehman Brothers. Beginning with less than $2 billion in August 2008, excess reserves soared to $60 billion in September and then to $559 billion in November before peaking at $798 billion in January 2009. (They have since dropped to $644 billion in the last accounting month.)

This explosion of excess reserves represents a signal change in bank policy that threatens the effectiveness of monetary policy in the current economic crisis. Aware of their own financial vulnerability, even insolvency, frightened bank managers responded to the collapse of major investment houses like Lehman Brothers by grabbing and hoarding all the cash that they could get. At the same time, a general loss of confidence and spreading economic collapse persuaded banks that there are few to whom they could lend with confidence that the loans would be repaid. Clearly, our banks have decided that they need, or at least want, the money more than consumers and productive businesses do.

Banks could have been investing this money by lending to businesses needing liquidity to buy inventory or pay workers. Had they done so, monetarist economists would be shouting from the rooftops, or at least in the university halls, about how monetary policy prevented another Great Depression. Instead, even the *Wall Street Journal* is proclaiming that "We're All Keynesians Again" because monetary policy has failed. Monetary authorities, the *Journal* explains, can create money but they cannot force banks to lend or to invest it in productive activities. The Federal Reserve confronts a reality shown in the graph in the accompanying graph: it can't "push on a string," as Fed Chair Marriner Eccles famously put it in testimony before Congress in 1935, in the depths of the Great Depression.

If the banks won't lend, then we need more than monetary policy to get out of the current crisis. No bailout, no TARP program, can revive the economy if banks hoard all the cash they receive. The Obama stimulus was an appropriate response to the failure of string-pushing. But much more government stimulus

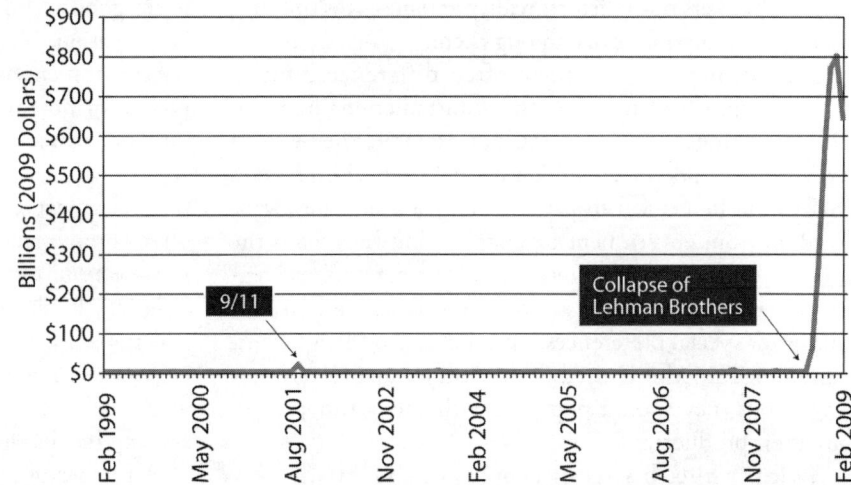

Source: "Excess Reserves of Depository Institutions," Federal Reserve Bank of St. Louis, research.stlouisfed.org.

will be needed to solve a crisis this large, and we will need programs to move liquidity from bank vaults to businesses and consumers. It may be time to stop waiting on the banks, and to start telling them what to do with our money.

ARTICLE 6.5

March/April 2007

THE FED AND THE INTERNATIONAL BANKING CONSPIRACY

BY ARTHUR MACEWAN

Dear Dr. Dollar:

Some of my friends believe that the Federal Reserve and international bankers (Rothschilds, Rockefellers, etc.) run the world. They think the Federal Reserve was formed in secret and is pretty much a conspiracy. This is all hooked up with other conspiracy theories and right-wing views that make me uncomfortable. What do you think? Isn't the banking system part of the whole capitalist system? How does the Federal Reserve work; does it really have so much power?

—Carol Brown, New York, N.Y.

The Federal Reserve is a very powerful institution, and the people who run the world's large banks are a very powerful group of people. No one would claim otherwise. Also, the bankers have common interests, and, like any other group of people with common interests, they do what they can to bring about government policies that favor those interests.

Because the Federal Reserve (the "Fed"), as the central bank of the United States, implements policies that most directly affect the bankers, they of course are quite concerned with what the Fed does, how it is structured, and who runs it. And, like other elite groups, bankers certainly meet in private—in "secret," if one prefers—to figure out how best to get what they want.

With all that said, however, the idea that a small cabal of bankers runs the world through the operations of the Fed is wrong on several counts.

First of all, financial operatives are not the only powerful economic group. There are, for example, the people who run the large oil companies, the Silicon Valley operations, and the pharmaceutical firms, to name a few of the currently important capitalist clusters. These other groups have some common interests with the bankers, and they often all work together, both in private and in public, to achieve their common ends; they do not call in the press every time a few of them meet. (A recent example: when Vice President Cheney held a meeting to formulate the Bush administration's energy policy, the list of attendees —widely assumed to be top energy sector executives—

was kept secret.) But to boil down this large class of people to a few bankers both distorts reality and obscures the conflicts that sometimes exist among them.

Second, not only are there often differences among these groups, but there are often contradictions between different things that they want. For example, they want a well-trained work force, but they do not want the high taxes that would be needed to pay for that training; they want freedom from government regulations, but they want the economic stability that often depends on government regulation; they want free access to international markets, but they want special preferences (as compared to foreign companies) within the United States; they want to pay low wages, but they want a populace with enough income to buy their products.

Third, while this set of people is undoubtedly very powerful in affecting the operation of our economic lives and in shaping history, they do not shape history just as they please. They simply can't control everything—as the problem that the Fed has with long-term interest rates illustrates. They cannot control the economy just as they would like and they cannot control the rest of us just as they would like. Formal democracy, however limited, is a useful device. The power that the rest of us have can be a substantial constraint on the actions of big business—bankers, energy executives, and all the others.

But let's return to the Fed. What does it do, and how? The Fed has a variety of functions involving regulation of the banking system, including influencing the amount of money in circulation and interest rates (the price people pay to use other people's money). Of special importance, the Fed can influence the amount of loans that banks issue. When a bank issues a loan, this creates more spending power. This spending power (usually in the form of increasing the amount in the borrower's checking account) is the same thing as more money in circulation. So by influencing banks' loan actions, the Fed influences the money supply.

Right-wingers who view the Fed and the banks as an evil cabal tend to claim that by allowing banks to increase the money supply, the Fed is debasing our currency. The increased money supply lowers the value of money in relation to other goods, and the money prices of other goods rise—i.e., inflation. Moreover, they view this as a way of allowing the government to engage in excessive spending: the government can borrow from the public, but then, because of inflation, can repay in dollars that have less worth.

This fascination of some right-wingers with inflation and the debasement of the currency is ironic because, in fact, the Fed often (although not always) acts in exactly the opposite manner—*limiting* the growth of the money supply and *restricting* inflation. Banks, and businesses generally, like stable prices and stable interest rates. One reason is that a low-inflation policy keeps unemployment rates higher than they otherwise would be, weakening the bargaining power of workers and shifting the distribution of income in favor of capitalists.

A further irony: the Fed is not as powerful as either its proponents or its critics think. The Fed really has control only over short-term interest rates. Long-term interest rates, however, are more important (as they affect major investment decisions) and are influenced by many forces beyond the Fed's control. The expectations of business about future ups and downs of the economy—and about the myriad events that affect those fluctuations—are the central factors determining long-term interest rates. Neither capitalists' behavior nor capitalist economies are so easily controlled. If they were, then there would never be any stock market crashes, burst financial bubbles, or other serious disruptions.

By the way, the Fed was not formed in secret. The Fed was created by legislative action, formally and publicly. But there were certainly private (secret) meetings that laid the groundwork for it. Of course, the same is true of legislative actions affecting the pharmaceutical industry, Silicon Valley, insurance firms, and the list goes on. Nothing that special about the creation of the Fed.

Finally, while I am sure that there are many decent people who see the Fed and the bankers as the source of the world's problems, this view is often part of a larger anti-Semitism. The focus on "Jewish financiers" (the Rothschilds, for example) as the source of our economic and other problems is as old as it is wrong and offensive.

(MIS)UNDERSTANDING A BANKING INDUSTRY IN TRANSITION

BY WILLIAM K. BLACK

The U.S. financial system is, once again, in crisis. Or, more precisely, twin crises—first, huge numbers of defaults among subprime mortgage borrowers, and second, massive losses for the holders of new-fangled investments comprised of bundles of loans of varying risk, including many of those subprime mortgages.

These crises should shock the nation. Our largest, most sophisticated financial institutions have followed business practices that were certain to produce massive losses—practices so imprudent, in precisely the business task (risk management) that is supposed to be their greatest expertise, that they have created a worldwide financial crisis.

Why? Because their CEOs, acting on the perverse incentives created by today's outrageous compensation systems, engaged in practices that vastly increased their corporations' risk in order to drive up reported corporate income and thereby secure enormous increases in their own individual incomes. And those perverse incentives follow them out the door: CEOs Charles Prince, at Citicorp, and Stanley O'Neal, at Merrill Lynch, had dismal track records of similar failures prior to the latest disasters, but they collected massive bonuses for their earlier failures and will receive obscene termination packages now. Pay and productivity (and integrity) have become unhinged at U.S. financial institutions.

As this goes to print, Treasury Department officials are working with large financial institutions to cover up the scale of the growing losses. This is the same U.S. Treasury that regularly prates abroad about the vital need for transparency. And a former Treasury Secretary, Robert Rubin, who failed utterly in his fiduciary duty as lead board member at Citicorp to prevent the series of recent abuses, will become Citicorp's new CEO.

To even begin to understand events in the U.S. and global banking industries, you have to look back at the seismic shifts in the industry over the past 30 to 40 years, and at the interplay between those shifts and government policy. The story that continues to unfold is one of progressively worse policies that make financial crises more common and more severe.

These policies have their boosters, though. Chief among them are neoclassical banking and finance economists, whose ideology and methodologies lead them into blatant misreadings of the realities of the industry and the causes of its failures. When the history of this crisis-ridden era in global finance is written, the economists will no doubt be given a significant share of the blame.

A NEW ERA OF CRISIS

The changes in the U.S. banking industry in recent decades have been so great that a visitor from the 1950s would hardly recognize the industry. Over two decades of intense merger and acquisition activity has left a far smaller number of banks, with assets far more concentrated in the largest ones. Between 1984 and 2004, the number of banks on the FDIC's rolls fell from 14,392 to 7,511; the share of the U.S. banking industry's assets held by the ten largest banks rose from 21% in 1960 to nearly 60% in 2005. At the same time, nonbank businesses that lend, save, and invest money have proliferated, as have the products they sell: a vast array of new kinds of loans and exotic savings and investment vehicles. And the lines have blurred between all of the different players in the industry—between banks and thrifts (e.g., savings and loans), between commercial banks and investment banks.

These changes were made possible by the deregulation of the industry. Bit by bit, beginning in the 1970s, the banking regulations put into place in the wake of the Great Depression were repealed, culminating in the Gramm-Leach-Bliley Act in 1999, which removed the remaining legal barriers to combining commercial banking, investment banking, and insurance under one corporate roof. The new world of combined financial services is exemplified by the deal, inked (but ostensibly illegal) before the 1999 law was passed, that merged the insurance and investment-banking giant Travelers with Citibank, at the time the nation's number-one commercial bank.

These transformational changes in domestic banking, along with the related effects of economic globalization both in the United States and abroad, have produced recurrent crises in the financial sector. Indeed, the current era has seen over 100 major banking crises, in countries around the globe. Thomas Hoenig, head of the Kansas City Federal Reserve Bank, emphasized the remarkable and disturbing facts in a meeting with fellow heads of supervision:

> A 1996 survey by the IMF [International Monetary Fund] ... found that 73 percent [133 of 181] of their member countries had experienced significant banking problems during the preceding 15 years. Many of these problems led to substantial declines in GDP [and] serious disruptions in credit and capital markets. ...

To date none of these crises has led to a global Great Depression. Only a few were larger in absolute terms than the 1980s S&L debacle in the United States. Yet many imposed a much greater relative cost, measured as a percentage of the country's GDP. Some caused severe, depression-like economic problems in the affected nation. Some produced contagion effects that caused severe crises in other nations. And acute banking crises can cause long-term harm. Japan is a rich nation and can afford a 15-year banking crisis—but the world economy cannot. The crisis cut Japan's economic growth to near-zero for a decade, in turn creating contagion effects in the many countries for whom Japan was a major trading partner or a significant source of capital investment. Tens of millions of people remain in poverty in Asia and Africa as a result.

The recurrent banking crises have come as a shock to the United States, given the dearth of bank failures over the first three decades after World War II. The first severe postwar U.S. banking crisis was stemmed from the large loans that top U.S. banks made to sovereign borrowers (i.e., nations), largely in Latin America. The banks had claimed that sovereign loans offered high returns with minimal default risk because the nation could always repay the loan by printing more money. Citibank head Walter Wriston notoriously implied that countries could not go broke. The claim was absurd. However, banking regulators took no effective action to restrain this lending.

The 1982 Mexican default led to contagion and fears of an international meltdown, but the Federal Reserve and the Bank for International Settlements (BIS) took effective action. Brazil experienced a long economic slowdown that contributed to an imminent default on its loans from major U.S. banks. A Brazilian default could have rendered several of our largest banks insolvent. The banks were rescued by a combination of bailouts to Brazil through the IMF and the World Bank and flawed (albeit permissible under so-called Generally Accepted Accounting Principles, or GAAP) "troubled-debt restructuring" to cover up the losses. Brazil used the bailouts to pay minimal interest on the U.S. bank loans and ultimately recovered; while several U.S. banks took serious losses, none failed.

On the heels of this crisis came the savings and loan crisis, an unprecedented debacle which saw the collapse of some 1,000 S&Ls and which cost U.S. taxpayers about $125 billion dollars—primarily the cost of repaying to depositors money that criminal S&L heads had literally stolen from their institutions.

The causes of these crises are varied. They typically occur, however, when large banks are in essence looted by their owners and managers (a phenomenon known as "control fraud") or when there are financial bubbles in which assets become massively overvalued.

Economists who conduct case studies of banking crises commonly report the existence of substantial control fraud. Looting played a prominent role in the S&L debacle. Here is the conclusion of the National Commission on Financial Institution Reform, Recovery and Enforcement (NCFIRRE):

> The typical large failure was a stockholder-owned, state-chartered institution in Texas or California where regulation and supervision were most lax. ... The failed institution typically had experienced a change of control and was tightly held, dominated by an individual with substantial conflicts of interest. ... In the typical large failure, every accounting trick available was used to make the institution look profitable, safe, and solvent. Evidence of fraud was invariably present as was the ability of the operators to "milk" the organization through high dividends and salaries, bonuses, perks and other means. In short, the typical large failure was one in which management exploited virtually all the perverse incentives created by government policy.

Looting has played a significant role in banking crises around the world. It became so prevalent in the states of the former Soviet Union that it inspired a new term of art, "tunneling," to describe the process of the CEO and owners converting a company's funds to their private benefit.

In addition to the national banking crises, fraud has caused spectacular failures of large banks. The Bank for Credit and Commerce International (BCCI—known informally as the "Bank for Crooks and Criminals International"), Barings Bank, and Continental Bank all stunned the public when they failed. BCCI was the largest bank in the developing world, Barings was England's oldest bank, and Continental was America's third largest bank. Each one collapsed with minimal public warning.

And, of course, more recently control fraud played a role in a number of spectacular business failures outside of the banking industry including Enron, WorldCom, and Tyco. This fact makes it obvious that the conventional economic wisdom, which blames this era's wave of bank failures and banking crises on regulation and deposit insurance (which are specific to the banking industry) is just wrong. Despite this, mainstream economists persist in their diagnosis, rarely scrutinizing the deregulation and privatization that many observers believe in fact triggered these crises.

...THEY FIRST MAKE PROUD

Economists have dominated the creation of public policies to prevent banking crises. Their track record has been abysmal. They designed and implemented the disastrous deregulation that produced the U.S. S&L debacle, they praised Japan's and East Asia's banking structures just before they collapsed, and they designed the IMF's crisis intervention strategy that intensified losses and human misery. They also designed and praised privatization programs in many transition economies that led to banking crises; they planned (and in some cases profited from) the catastrophic failure of "shock therapy" in Russia. The irony is that when financial experts were most confident in their consensus, they erred the most grievously. As Mark Twain remarked: "It's not the things you *don't* know that cause disasters; it's the things you *do* know, *but aren't true.*"

This record of failure is disappointing and has caused great human suffering. Remarkably, the economists' hubris is unaffected by it. They are now engaged in a war against deposit insurance and regulation. At this juncture, they are losing that war, but they are persevering in their effort to reclaim their domination over banking policy.

DEPOSIT INSURANCE SPREADS DESPITE ECONOMISTS' PROTESTS

Banking economists now overwhelmingly criticize deposit insurance. This represents a major change. The prior consensus, shared by Milton Friedman and John Kenneth Galbraith alike, praised deposit insurance for ending the periodic runs on uninsured banks that helped cause the Great Depression. Today, however, the conventional economic wisdom is that deposit insurance may stop runs, but at the expense of encouraging banks to make imprudent loans and take excessive risks. (Neoclassical economists widely view insurance as inherently creating an incentive for insured parties to act in unduly risky ways because of the safety net that insurance provides—a phenomenon termed "moral hazard.")

This claim is dubious: economists do not offer a credible mechanism whereby deposit insurance could lead to the ills they claim it causes. Deposit insurance does not protect the shareholders or the CEO—the two groups (the first, in theory; the second, in practice) that control a bank. It is the depositors who are insured. Thus, they must be the ones who are subject to moral hazard—in other words, the argument against deposit insurance must be based on the claim that it reduces the incentive of depositors to exercise "private market discipline" by pulling their money out of a bank they believe is being poorly run or looted. But there is no credible evidence that depositors are capable of either discerning frauds or avoiding runs on healthy banks based on false rumors. Indeed, studies have shown that even private-sector financial experts who specialize in evaluating the health of banks cannot do so effectively.

Proponents of the view that deposit insurance causes banking failures display an unrecognized logical inconsistency. Their proposed reform is to rely on private market discipline to prevent management from looting the bank or lending imprudently in a bubble. But, if we assume hypothetically that private market discipline is effective against CEOs who would be so inclined, then it should normally be effective despite the presence of deposit insurance. Deposit insurance does not remove private market discipline where the bank is owned by shareholders (unless the CEO owns all the stock) or where the bank issues uninsured subordinated debt. Yet during the S&L crisis, control fraud (the looting of an institution by its own managers or owners) was most common in S&Ls owned in stock form, with the largest losses overwhelmingly among stock S&Ls. In these cases deposit insurance did not preclude private market discipline; market discipline was simply inadequate to prevent control fraud. Some opponents of deposit insurance proclaim the S&L debacle to be their primary example—a flat misreading of the facts.

The empirical evidence economists use to support their critique of deposit insurance is inconsistent. Moreover, even where the adoption of deposit insurance is correlated with a rise in bank failures, the causal relationship may be just the opposite of what economists claim. Nations with early signs of an impending banking crisis may adopt deposit insurance to reduce the risks of runs. Developing nations tend to adopt deposit insurance in conjunction with privatization—which itself often prompts a banking crisis. More broadly, in part because of the fall of the Soviet Union and the rise of the neoliberal "Washington Consensus," the number of nations adopting deposit insurance increased sharply in the last two decades. Banking crises have indeed been far more common over this same period—precisely because these radical transitions have been occurring in nations with weak institutions, too few regulators with too little experience, patterns of bank ownership that maximize conflicts of interest, and substantial corruption.

In addition, empirical studies rely on subjective coding of different countries' deposit insurance policies, often done by economists who oppose deposit insurance. In countries with no formal deposit insurance, implicit government guarantees for banks are common. There are good theoretical and historical reasons to argue that such implicit guarantees—common in crony capitalism and kleptocracies—create greater moral hazard than explicit deposit insurance does because they can be structured to bail out a bank's shareholders and CEO as well as its creditors (as was done in Chile). But there is no way to code accurately for whether there was an implicit guarantee (or whether bank CEOs *believed* there was an implicit guarantee) in a particular country at a particular time.

Despite these weaknesses in both evidence and analysis, World Bank economists draw firm conclusions, opposing the adoption of deposit insurance in any nation and clearly hoping for its elimination. But the world has rejected their advice. By 2006, 95 countries had deposit insurance, over four times the number in 1983. Moreover, economists' suggestions on how to "improve" deposit insurance (require banks to issue subordinated debt, charge variable rates for deposit insurance, or require private insurance of accounts) are rarely adopted and have proven unsuccessful in practice.

Neoclassical banking economists are failing in this arena for three reasons. First, they neither study nor understand fraud mechanisms and the institutions that are essential to limit fraud and corruption. Second, they are shackled by an ideology that *presumes* that unfettered markets always produce the best outcomes and that government intervention is always bad. For instance, in their writings many of the World Bank's banking economists display a passionate contempt for democratic government and banking regulators. Third, they are mono-disciplinary. They rarely cite (and no doubt rarely examine) the literature in other relevant fields such as political science, sociology, and white-collar criminology.

Indeed, although it should be central to their study of crisis prevention, they rarely even cite the work of economist and 2001 Nobel Prize winner George Akerlof. Based on their study of the S&L crisis, which found that looting was a major cause of total S&L losses, Akerlof and Paul Romer developed an economic model of the looting control fraud.

> ## OFFSHORE BANKS
>
> One particularly dark side of globalization is the rise of new offshore banks. While Switzerland now has reasonably workable procedures for tracking the funds of kleptocrats and drug traffickers, several small nations have adopted extreme forms of bank secrecy designed to cater to the needs of criminals and tax evaders. Corporations often incorporate in a tax haven because of the extremely low tax rates. In the late 1990s, the Organisation for Economic Co-operation and Development, an organization of the world's industrialized countries, created an initiative to try to curtail these abuses. Conservative think tanks sought to kill the OECD plan and convinced President Bush to block its implementation as one of his earliest actions. The administration reduced its opposition to the OECD initiative after the 9/11 attacks, when it became clear that terrorists used the offshore banks as their preferred means to move funds.

Looters use accounting fraud to make a company *appear* extraordinarily profitable. Consider the S&L crisis. The worst S&L control frauds were the ones reporting the highest profitability. Moreover, the control frauds were routinely able to get a Big 8 audit firm to give them "clean" GAAP (or Generally Accepted Accounting Principles, the official standard of review in the U.S. accounting industry) opinions for false financial statements.

Economists, in turn, relied on *reported* accounting profits and share prices (which rose along with reported profits) to determine whether a given S&L was well run. But relying on reported accounting earnings or stock prices *must* lead to perverse results when a wave of looting control frauds is expanding. Thanks to their fraudulent accounting, whatever strategies control frauds follow will look profitable, and hence praiseworthy. In the S&Ls, this led economists to praise (1) domination by an owner/CEO; (2) extremely rapid growth; (3) changes of control; and (4) large investments in acquisition, development, and contruction (ADC) loans and direct investments. Lo and behold, these factors turned out to characterize the worst failures. In other words, standard econometrics techniques led economists to praise that which was fraudulent and fatal. The error was so great that they identified the worst S&L in the nation as the best.

Worse, economists persist in the same error. During the recent expansion of the even larger wave of looting control frauds such as Enron, economists touted (1) conflicts of interest at the top audit firms (which they euphemistically restyled as "synergies"); (2) using a top-tier auditor; (3) rapid growth; and (4) granting the CEO greater stock options as positive factors that were leading to increased profits and higher share prices. It was only after the looters began to collapse that variables like these reversed their sign (from a positive to a negative correlation) and displayed their true relationship to business failure. Economists are doomed to repeat these mistakes until they adopt statistical techniques that cannot be gamed by accounting fraud.

THE ECONOMISTS' WAR AGAINST BANKING REGULATION

In keeping with their skewed analysis of the recent wave of bank failures and banking crises, banking economists, including those at the World Bank and the IMF, have been waging a war against banking regulation. It is a curious assault that rests on implicit and false dichotomies between market and regulation and between types of regulation.

The World Bank economists recognize that regulation is vital to mandate accurate disclosure of corporate financial information and aid private market enforcement, but appear to believe that regulatory strength is unnecessary to induce banks to provide accurate information. That view is illogical and incorrect. Obtaining accurate information about banks is the heart of banking examination. Regulators use their powers primarily to pry out accurate information from the fraudulent; control frauds do not cooperate voluntarily.

Economists' rationale for opposing strong banking regulators typically rests on public choice theory, which holds that the actors in political systems act to maximize their own self-interest. This analysis paints politicians as corrupt and regulators as "captured" by the industries they are supposed to be regulating. World Bank economist Thorsten Beck and his colleagues summed up this view in 2003 and 2006 working papers:

> Politicians may induce banks to divert the flow of credit to politically connected firms, or powerful banks may "capture" politicians and induce official supervisors to act in the best interest of banks … .
>
> Government solutions to overcome market failures … have been proven wrong in Bangladesh as across the developed and developing world. … Indeed, powerful regulators are worse than futile—they are corrupt and harmful.

Again, this analysis is nonsensical. If banks can dominate politicians and strong regulators, they can certainly dominate the design of the disclosure standards they face. In that case, pursuant to the economists' own logic, the banks will submit, and politicians beholden to them will permit, deceptive financial reports that grossly overstate banks' value. (This has, in fact, been done in many cases.) Accounting fraud, in turn, renders markets deeply inefficient and causes private market discipline to become perverse. The looters report record profits. Credit is supposed to flow to the most profitable banks. So private markets *aid* the CEOs looting their banks by providing them with the funds to expand rapidly. Again, the failure to understand bank accounting fraud mechanisms, which have been well explained by Akerlof and

Romer, leads to a deeply flawed analysis. (In lieu of Akerlof and Romer, the anti-regulation economists frequently cite work sponsored by Michael Milken's institute. Milken was the notorious junk-bond king and looter who caused large losses during the S&L crisis by recruiting and funding several of the worst control frauds, such as Charles Keating. Today, Milken's institute blames the S&L debacle on regulation and seeks to rehabilitate his reputation.

This overarching logical error, their hostility to democracy, and their view of public officials as inevitably rapacious leads economists to a claim that only *private* parties should exert discipline against banks. The view has a number of problems. First, it is overstated. Regulators in some nations do resist political pressure. In the S&L crisis, many regulators did their job despite intense political pressure and saved over a trillion dollars in the process. On the other hand: if, over time, people are taught to believe that it is normal and rational for public officials to be rapacious, this can become a self-fulfilling prophecy as those who aim to enrich themselves sign on to become officials.

Moreover, the argument proves too much. If the banks (or politicians) are powerful enough to act illegitimately *through* regulators, they are powerful enough to act illegitimately *without* regulators to achieve the same result. The argument is also based on a fundamental misunderstanding of control frauds. It is not the "powerful banks" Beck and his coauthors refer to that put pressure on regulators or politicians—it is the CEOs or their agents who do. They do not coerce regulators "to act in the best interest of banks." They coerce them in an attempt to act to help the CEO loot the bank.

In fact, the evidence shows that private parties are *more* subject to capture than public officials. Looting control frauds are routinely able to get top-tier audit firms to give their blessing to massive accounting fraud. The ratings agencies do no better against control fraud. Our most prestigious law firms have helped CEOs loot and destroy their clients. Private deposit insurance funds for thrifts used to exist in many states. None do now. The Maryland, Ohio, and Utah funds were each destroyed by the very first thrift that collapsed in their state thanks to control fraud. No private insurer made more than a feeble effort to exercise discipline. Instead, they acted as boosters for the CEOs who looted and destroyed their own thrifts and brought down the insurance funds with them.

Finally, the empirical studies on banking regulation rely on coding of data by economists who typically oppose regulation, rendering the results unreliable. The risks of subjective bias are acute. There is no objective measure of "strong" regulation, or capture, or "rent seeking behavior." We know that economists have claimed that the Bank Board under Chairman Edwin Gray was captured during the S&L crisis. Not so. In fact, *private* experts were routinely captured by the S&L control frauds. Plus, the studies focus on formal supervisory power, yet informal banking supervision is widespread and often a regulator's most effective tool.

Overall, empirical studies find that better quality regulation (again, to be fair, a subjective concept) reduces banking losses.

INTERNATIONAL CONVERGENCE

Despite the flawed logic and lack of empirical support for their views, conventional banking economists, including those at the World Bank, continue to voice opposition to the creation of strong supervisory agencies. For now, however, their call has been rejected.

In the 1980s, the U.S. government reacted to Japan's emergence as the new (apparent) dominant financial power by claiming that Japan gained an unfair advantage because its banks were permitted to operate with lower capital reserves. If all other factors are held constant, a bank held to a lower capital reserve requirement can grow more quickly, lend more cheaply, and finance greater economic growth. Complaining that the playing field was not level, the United States insisted on an international agreement to set minimum bank capital standards. The U.S. effort succeeded in 1988, when the largest industrial nations adopted the Basel Accord. More recently, the accord was revised and expanded ("Basel II") to include more closely calibrated minimum capital requirements as well as a supervisory strategy of "prompt corrective action" against banks that fail to meet the capital requirements and a strategy to make private market discipline more effective by requiring banks to disclose more information.

The Basel Accord was a major step towards greater international uniformity of banking regulation ("convergence") among developed nations. The expansion of the European Union is another major force for convergence, as candidate nations must adopt modern banking laws and regulatory structures meeting the EU's minimum standards.

Banks are also subject to an increasing number of international treaties designed to restrict money laundering and bribery. There are, however, very few enforcement actions or prosecutions, so enforcement does not appear to be effective at this time. In addition, offshore banks remain an enormous loophole limiting the effectiveness of convergence.

New banking crises have diminished substantially in nations complying with the Basel accords. Of course, it is too early to judge whether the Basel process is responsible for this success. However, we do have cross-country evidence showing that weak regulation leads to recurrent waves of control fraud. Tests of Basel's effectiveness by one of the World Bank economists find positive relationships between stronger regulation and bank health. (These tests employed a methodology that posed less risk of subjective bias by the economists conducting the studies, but they remain inherently subjective.)

The economists' frustration, however, is understandable. They are skilled research scientists for whom econometric studies are the epitome of proof. Contrary case studies are mere "anecdotal evidence" that are fully encompassed

THEY JUST NEVER LEARN

Today's financial crisis offers a superb example of how their methods lead mainstream economists to endorse both private practices and public policies that are perverse. The current crisis exemplifies a variant of accounting control frauds—one in which the CEO and top managers "skim" rather than loot the company—and demonstrates the unrecognized economic costs of obscenely high CEO pay. The incentives created by typical CEO compensation packages in the financial services industry produce bad investment decisions, decisions that increase the CEO's ability to skim, but that expose the financial institution to losses and the nation and world to recurrent financial crises.

Consider the plight of the honest chief financial officer (CFO) in the modern financial world. His counterparts at rival firms are earning record returns by investing in subprime mortgages. Economists trumpet studies showing that banks' income is boosted by practices he questions, including:

- Making more subprime mortgages
- Making more of the worst mortgages such as "Ninja" loans (no verification of income, job or assets), also known as "liars' loans"
- Making subprime loans at particularly high interest rates—which draws in the riskiest borrowers because only the worst credit risks and frauds will apply
- Making loans as quickly as possible
- Growing as quickly as possible
- Reducing internal controls against fraud
- Making loans in cities known to be "hot spots" for mortgage fraud
- Qualifying borrowers by offering "teaser" interest rates that will soon increase substantially
- Making loans in areas with rapidly inflation housing bubbles
- Purchasing and holding in portfolio high-yield CDOs (collateralized debt obligations, the investment instruments backed by bundles of mortgages and other loans, often of high risk)
- Keeping minimal reserves against losses

When a housing bubble is expanding, these practices dramatically increase fees and other noninterest income, minimize expenses, and produce relatively few losses. (Losses remain low as long as house prices are rising because borrowers who get in trouble can sell their house for more than they owe or else refinance based on its market value.) Note that this pretty income picture requires accounting and securities fraud, though: reserving properly for the future losses inherent in subjecting the financial institution to this vastly increased default risk would remove the fictional accounting gain.

The combination of dramatically increased revenue, moderately reduced expenses, and minimal loss means that financial institutions that invest heavily in subprime mortgages and CDOs must report record profits while the bubble is hyperinflating.

So what is our honest CFO to do? If she does not follow the pack, her company will report substantially lower income. Its stock price will fall relative to its rivals. The CEO's and CFO's compensation and wealth will fall sharply as raises disappear, bonuses decline, and the value of their shares and stock options falls. The CFO may be fired.

The upshot is that modern compensation systems and the short-term perspective of investors and senior managers all result in perverse incentives to make grossly imprudent investments in those assets experiencing the worst bubbles. This creates a destructive cycle in which large numbers of financial institutions follow the same dysfunctional strategy, which in turn extends and inflates the bubble and produces even more accounting control frauds.

---

within their data and, therefore, require no refutation. Moreover, their worldview is shaped by public choice theory. They view banking regulators as corrupt, "rent seeking" parasites who merely pretend to virtue. Alternatively, in their "capture" model, regulators are cowards who roll over to aid the control frauds. They have not been banking regulators, so they are uncontaminated and can see the truth as the empirical data reveal it to them.

Regulators, however, dominate much of the Basel process. They view the economists' disdain as an inaccurate and insulting caricature that indicates their ignorance of the real-world banking business. Regulators tend to believe in their experiences, which overwhelmingly teach that control frauds exploit regulatory weaknesses and that normally honest, sober bankers act like frat boys on spring break during financial bubbles. Imprudent lending is the norm in bubbles. Regulators have seen many econometric "proofs" of propositions they know to be false from experience. Some of them have a reasonably sophisticated understanding of the illusion of precision in empirical work and the many opportunities for subjective coding to lead even the best scholars into error. To date, the regulators have staved off the economists' war against banking regulation, and even the World Bank's economists have had to concede that the *initial* results of the Basel process are extremely positive.

Basel II does have a worrying component. It encourages the large banks to value their assets (which implicitly means evaluating their risk) using their own proprietary models. It is easy for these models to be designed so as to dramatically overstate asset values. The problem is compounded by the nature of proprietary models: they are secret, complex, and (perhaps) subject to frequent adjustment. That makes them a nightmare to try to regulate. And in what is essentially a form of control fraud, modern compensation systems, especially in the United States, create powerful incentives for top managers to overstate banks' asset values in order to puff up their own pay packages. Such abuse is so common that instead of "mark to market," the usual term for bringing the valuation of an asset into line with its market price, the process is often known to insiders as "mark to myth."

In the United States, the word "deregulation" still has a positive ring for many despite the disastrous results of this country's experiment in loosening the reins on the banking industry. So perhaps it is ironic that it was the United States that instigated an international effort to develop convergent banking regulations worldwide. International convergence is moving forward, and for now the pace of new financial crises has slowed. The Basel process is indeed leveling the playing field among financial services companies around the world. But what kind of field will emerge? Does the Basel process offer any hope of reshaping the new world of banking into one that better meets consumer needs and better serves the broader public interest? If the banking economists, with their ideological commitment to oppose any regulation, are kept at bay, then at least we may find out.

Resources: C.E.V Borio and R. Filosa, "The Changing Borders of Banking: Trends and Implications," BIS Working Paper 23, 10/94; Ctr for Intl Private Enterprise, "Financial Reform: Paving the Way for Growth and Democracy," *Econ Reform Today*, 1995; J. Bisignano, "Precarious Credit Equilibria: Reflections on the Asian Financial Crisis," BIS Working Papers, 3/99; W. K. Black, *The Best Way to Rob a Bank is to Own One*, 2005; L.J. White, *The S&L Debacle: Public Policy Lessons for Bank and Thrift Regulation*, 1991; Federal Home Loan Bank Board, *Agenda for Reform: A Report on Deposit Insurance*, 1983; K. Calavita et al., *Big Money Crime: Fraud and Politics in the Savings and Loan Industry*, 1997; W. K. Black et al., "The Savings and Loan Debacle of the 1980's: White-Collar Crime or Risky Business?" *Law & Policy* 17; G. Akerlof and P. M. Romer, "Looting: The Economic Underworld of Bankruptcy for Profit," *Brookings Papers on Econ Activity*, 1993; M. Mayer, *The Greatest-Ever Bank Robbery*, 1990; T. Curry and L. Shibut, "The Cost of the Savings and Loan Crisis: Truth and Consequences," *FDIC Banking Review*, Fall 2000; W. K. Black, "Reexamining the Law-and-Economics Theory of Corporate Governance," *Challenge*, 1993; C-J Lindgren et al., *Bank Soundness and Macroeconomic Policy*, IMF, 1996; T. M. Hoenig, "Exploring the Macro-Prudential Aspects of Financial Sector Supervision," speech to the Meeting for Heads of Supervision, BIS, Basel, Switzerland, 4/27/04; V. A. Atanasov et al., "The Anatomy of Financial Tunneling in an Emerging Market," McCombs School of Business, Research Paper Fin-04-06; N. Passas, "The Genesis of the BCCI Scandal," *J Law and Soc*, 3/66; P. L. Zweig, *Belly Up: The Collapse of the Penn Square Bank*, 1986; R. J. Herring, "BCCI & Barings: Bank Resolutions Complicated by Fraud and Global Corporate Structure"; H.R. Davia et al., *Accountant's Guide to Fraud Detection and Control* (2nd ed.), 2000; P. Blustein, "The Chastening: Inside the Crisis that Rocked the Global Financial System and Humbled the IMF," *Public Aff*, 2001; W. K. Black, "A Tale of Two Crises," *Kravis Leadership Inst Rvw*, Fall 2002; Federal Reserve Bank of San Francisco, *Economic Letter*, 3/06; B. H. Soral et al., "Fraud, banking crisis, and regulatory enforcement: Evidence from micro-level transactions data," *Euro J Law and Econ*, 4/06; J. L. Pierce, *The Future of Banking*, 1991; E. J. Kane, *The Gathering Crisis in Federal Deposit Insurance*, MIT Univ Press, 1985; A. Demirguc-Kunt and E. Detragiache, "Does Deposit Insurance Increase Banking System Stability? An Empirical Investigation," *J Monetary Econ*, 10/02; D. Pyle, review of "The Gathering Crisis in Federal Deposit Insurance" in *J Econ Lit*, 9/86; J. Santos, "Bank Capital Regulation in Contemporary Banking Theory: A review of the literature," in *Financial Markets, Institutions & Instruments*, 2001; A.B. Ashcraft, "Does the Market Discipline Banks? New Evidence from Regulatory Capital Mix," 10/2/06; T. Beck et al., "Bank Supervision and Corporate Finance," World Bank Policy Research Working Paper, 5/03; D. R. Brumbaugh, Jr, *Thrifts Under Siege: Restoring Order to American Banking*, 1988; T. Beck et al., "Bank Supervision and Corruption in Lending," 9/3/05; A. Demirguc-Kunt et al., "Banking on the Principles: Compliance with Basel Core Principles and Bank Soundness," IMF Working Paper 10/06; R. La Porta et al., "Related Lending," *Quarterly J Econ*, 2003; S. Johnson et al., "Tunnelling," *Am Econ Assoc Papers & Proceedings*, 2000; R. Haselmann et al., "How Law Affects Lending," Columbia Law and Economics Working Paper, 9/06; J. D. Edwards and J. H. Godwin, "Why Sound Accounting Standards Count," *Econ Reform Today*, 1995; J. R. Barth, *The Great Savings and Loan Debacle*, 1991.

ARTICLE 6.7

November/December 2008

DEALING WITH A "ROTTEN TOOTH"

BY ARTHUR MACEWAN

Dear Dr. Dollar:
Isn't the "bailout" of Wall Street like having a rotten tooth extracted? The extraction is very unpleasant, but it beats the alternative. Even if the dentist charges an unreasonably high fee, I am still going to pay and have the job done. Later I will worry about taking better care of my teeth. So shouldn't people quit complaining about the bailout, suck it up, and get the job done?

— Peter Wagner, Weston, Mass.

I do like thinking about the mess in the financial markets as a "rotten tooth," for something is certainly "rotten" in the current situation. And there is a way in which the analogy is useful: just as we are heavily dependent on the dentist to deal with our teeth, we are heavily dependent on the banks and other financial institutions for the operation of our economy. But if we are going to use the dentist-finance analogy, we need to take it a bit further.

In particular, if the dentist who tells me I need my tooth yanked out in an emergency extraction is the same dentist who for years has been telling me that my teeth are fine, then I get suspicious. This dentist has been making money from me all along, and now, when the crisis of a rotten tooth emerges, the dentist stands to make more money while I incur the pain. The situation is similar to the bailout of the financial system: the banks keep their profits in good times, but the losses are imposed on the rest of us in bad times. At the very least, when the people responsible for a problem—dentists or bankers—tell me to solve the problem in a way that benefits them, I want to get a second opinion, figure out the options, and proceed with caution.

As we have been learning in recent weeks, there is more than one option for dealing with the "rotten tooth." In part because of public pressure (i.e., complaining), the Treasury shifted away from its initial plan to buy up the bad assets in the financial system and is now taking partial ownership of the banks by providing them with capital. Not only is the second plan more likely to work (in the sense of preventing a breakdown of the financial system), but it is also more likely to cost the rest of us less over the long run (because as the banks recover and start to earn profits, the government will share in those profits).

There are other options that the U.S. government might follow as well. For example, the main reason we care about what happens to the banks is that their failures could spread to the rest of us, causing a severe depression. But instead of working simply from the top down, the U.S. government would do well to work from the bottom up—by focusing on the problems of people losing their homes due to foreclosures and by providing a large economic stimulus program through spending on schools, infrastructure, health care, and other real economic needs.

And, just as with my tooth, if the problem really did arise because of the bad practices of those who were supposed to take care of the situation (wasn't this the dentist who had been telling me all was well?), then we should give some immediate attention to proper regulation. The current financial crisis could have been avoided but for the deregulation craze of recent decades. Fixing the deregulation disaster should not be put off to the distant future.

Regulation is not a panacea. There can certainly be bad regulations, sometimes brought about by the firms themselves in an effort to use regulation to secure their power and profits. Establishing good regulations is a constant battle, as the large firms devote huge amounts of their resources to get deregulation or to shape regulation in their favor. Yet without regulation, markets—especially financial markets—are prone to instability, and at times that instability can have severe impacts on the rest of us.

While the dentist analogy may be incomplete, it does bring out a very important point. Because we are excessively dependent on the operations of a relatively small number of very large firms, when they get in trouble, we can be forced to bail them out. Not a good situation. Indeed, the situation is made worse as the current crisis is leading to more consolidation of the banking industry; with the encouragement of the Federal Reserve and the Treasury, big banks are being taken over by even bigger banks. At the very least, if we are going to allow some firms to become "too big to fail," then we would do well to watch them pretty carefully—that is, to regulate them and thus do all we can to prevent them from operating in ways that put us all at risk.

[Full disclosure: Last month I had a tooth extracted and it wasn't all that bad—certainly not as painful as the current Wall Street bailout! —A.M.]

ARTICLE 6.8   May/June 2008

THE BEAR STEARNS BAILOUT

BY ARTHUR MACEWAN

Dear Dr. Dollar:
Who cares if Bear Stearns fails? Or the Carlyle Group? Or Merrill Lynch? Or one of the other big financial companies? They've made their profits. So what's the problem?
— Julia Willebrand, New York, N.Y.

When Bear Stearns, the large New York investment bank, closed its doors in March, some people lost money. Even with the bailout of Bear Stearns engineered by the Federal Reserve, the stockholders of the company paid dearly.

Of course long-term holders of Bear Stearns stock didn't lose so much relative to what they had invested, perhaps years ago. But they lost a lot relative to what they thought they had one year ago. Then the stock was selling for about seventeen times what they ended up getting when, under the tutelage of the Fed, JPMorgan Chase bought Bear Stearns at $10 a share. Recent buyers of Bear Stearns stock, however, were big losers; if they bought a year ago at $170 a share, they ended up taking losses of 94%. Life is tough.

Then there are the employees of Bear Stearns. Hundreds of people are losing their jobs. And right now is not a good time to be looking for work in the financial industry!

But what about the rest of us? It turns out that the rest of us get hurt too when a large financial firm—or, for that matter, any large firm—goes under. We see the bad impacts of a firm's failure most clearly in a small town where a single employer plays a major role. When the firm fails, people lose their jobs. The fall in their incomes means they buy less, and other firms and other workers in the town feel the pinch. The impact spreads.

When large financial firms like Bear Stearns fail, the impacts can be very far reaching. These firms have extensive financial connections to other firms, which in turn are dependent on payments of obligations from the failing firms to meet their own obligations. If firm A fails, it doesn't meet its payments to firm B, which then can't meet its obligations to firm C, and so on. Any one of these firms that is close to the edge can be pushed over it by this failure of payments.

But the problem goes beyond these very tangible connections. The financial industry works on confidence. People loan money and buy stocks and bonds based on their confidence that these investments will pay off—that the firms to which they provide the money will return their money at a profit. When a large financial firm fails, they start to get worried; they lose their confidence. Not only do they fear the consequences of that firm's failure spreading (from A to B to C). They also worry that the same underlying problems that affected that company will affect others and ultimately their investments. Losing confidence, they are reluctant to supply money.

Loss of confidence is especially understandable when the causes of the problems that afflicted Bear Stearns are so well known and widespread. An era of excessively risky investments—with the sub-prime mortgage mess as the most visible part of the crisis—is now readily apparent.

But loans make the world go round. Without ready access to loans, firms are forced to cut back their investments and home-buyers find it more difficult—or more expensive—to obtain credit for their purchases. Even the student loan market is being affected by the current lack of credit—this "credit crunch." How many students from middle- and low-income families will not go to college next fall because they cannot get the funds?

So the rest of us can pay a dear price when a large financial firm fails. This is the rationale that the Fed offered when it stepped in to arrange for Bear Stearns to avoid actual failure. Its obligations will be taken over by JPMorgan Chase. But the takeover affects confidence roughly like a failure.

Even when the threat to the rest of us is real, this doesn't mean there has to be a bailout—or even a partial bailout as took place with Bear Stearns. For example, early this year, the British government nationalized Northern Rock bank when it could not meet its obligations. The government will run the bank, providing extra funds to the extent needed, and, when it is solvent again, will sell it off to private interests. The original stockholders will get money from the sale of the bank, but only after the government gets all of its money back.

Equally important, because the government, operating through the Fed, has to step in when financial firms fail, the government also has to set rules by which those firms operate. Increasingly, regulations have been removed from the financial sector and new sorts of financial firms have been created to avoid existing regulations. But the financial sector is too important, and too volatile, to be left on its own.

ARTICLE 6.9

July/August 2008

WHEN A HEDGE FUND MAKES $3 BILLION, WHO LOSES $3 BILLION?

BY ARTHUR MACEWAN

Dear Dr. Dollar:

When one hedge fund makes $3 billion, who has lost $3 billion? Where does the money come from that hedge funds capture? Who produced the value?

— Peter Marcuse, Waterbury, Conn.

As with any "winnings" in the financial markets, the money obtained by hedge funds comes directly from some losers who are also operating in the financial markets. On the surface, the situation might appear like a poker game: when one player wins the pot, some other players lose. Those of us not sitting at the table neither win nor lose.

However, while financial markets do involve a lot of gambling, the analogy to a poker game is limited. Those of us who are not sitting in on "the game" do suffer some substantial losses from the operations of hedge funds. Hedge fund operators, along with other operators in the financial system, have taken an active role in increasing the size of their "pot"—that is, in shifting the income distribution upward, moving money from lower-income workers to business owners and high-salaried professionals. So value created by the rest of us becomes the hedge funds' billions.

Contrary to their popular image, however, hedge funds are not making billions and billions of dollars for their investors. In fact, the performance of hedge funds is not significantly better than the performance of other types of investment funds. Nonetheless, although the investors in hedge funds are not doing especially well, the *managers* of the hedge funds are making off with billions.

The key to the incomes of hedge fund managers lies more in the nature of what the funds are than in how well they do. After all, aside from some notable exceptions, hedge funds as a group have not done especially well.

So what are hedge funds? Hedge funds are a category of mutual funds. In all mutual funds, the money of multiple investors is pooled and invested according to the decisions of the funds' managers. Regular mutual funds are subject to various government regulations, as are some other financial institutions, for example, commercial banks. The rationale for these regulations is that they protect the individual investors.

Hedge funds, however, avoid most regulations by limiting participation to a small number of "qualified" individuals and institutions (e.g., pension funds or college endowment funds) with large sums of money. To be "qualified," an investor must have a net worth of at least $5 million, excluding his or her home. Because they have large sums of money, these wealthy investors supposedly do not need the protection that regulation is assumed to provide.

Largely unregulated, hedge funds can undertake highly risky types of investments that would be off limits to regular mutual funds. With these more risky investments, they are *sometimes* able to obtain very high returns. They can also operate with a good deal of secrecy, exempt from the reporting requirements of regular mutual funds.

Like other investment funds, hedge funds charge a fee to the individuals and institutions that provide them with money. But hedge funds have been able to charge relatively high fees, including performance fees on top of the basic management fees. The basic fees run 1.5% to 2% of the total investment, and the performance fees typically run 20% of positive returns—sometimes higher. In some cases, management fees run to 5% combined with performance fees of over 40%. Furthermore, while hedge fund managers get their hefty performance fees when their funds achieve positive returns, they do not lose anything when their funds have negative returns. In effect, they are saying to their investors: If I perform well, we both win; if I perform poorly, you lose.

So it is not difficult to see why the managers of hedge funds do so well.

It is difficult, however, to see why so many investors put their money into hedge funds. Part of the explanation lies in the fact that rich individuals are often not smart investors, and they are drawn in by the popular image, the billions made by some funds, and the aura of success surrounding the stories of hedge fund managers who take home billions. And the institutional investors in hedge funds—local pension funds or college endowment funds, for example—are not especially "smart" either. Perhaps it is also the case that investors with large sums of money are willing to put at least some of their money into hedge funds, looking for the higher returns that the funds do sometimes obtain.

But whatever returns are obtained "sometimes," overall hedge funds do not do significantly better than other types of investment funds. While the secrecy of hedge funds makes it difficult to determine their overall returns, one 2006 study concludes: "…overall performance of hedge funds … is about the same as that of U.S. equities [as measured by the Standard and Poor's Index of 500 equities] … [H]edge funds underperformed the stock market … during the six year, 'bull market' run-up to 1999, while on average they outperformed the stock market during the six year 'bear market' (or lull period) through 2005."

And recently the story has been quite poor: in the period from January 2007 up to May of this year, hedge funds returned on average 3.1% and were out-performed by rich-world corporate bonds. (These figures are only for hedge funds that are open to new investors and thus, presumably, report how they have been doing. Hedge funds that are not accepting new investors are more opaque.) One might conclude that hedge funds are an undistinguished group of investments.

There are, however, some things that distinguish hedge funds—most particularly the huge payments that are often obtained by the people who run the funds. The most outstanding recent example is John Paulson, who in 2007 took in $3.7 billion running his Paulson & Co. hedge funds. Several others did pretty well also: George Soros was number two last year, at $2.9 billion, and James Simons was third at $2.8 billion

The top 25 hedge fund managers got themselves $22.3 billion in 2007, up substantially from a meager $14 billion in 2006. It is, we may assume, the stories of these individuals that generates the aura of success surrounding hedge funds.

How did hedge fund managers do so well when the economy was moving into bad times? In Paulson's case, according to Bloomberg.com, "Paulson & Co., which oversees about $28 billion, made money betting on the collapse of subprime mortgages in 2007. The Paulson Credit Opportunities Fund soared almost sixfold, helped by bets on slumping housing and subprime mortgage prices, according to investor letters obtained by Bloomberg." More generally, the hedge fund managers rely on their fee structure, as described above, to assure that, regardless of bad times, they come out well.

If rich individuals and institutional investors were the only ones to take the hit when the John Paulsons take home their astronomical fees, perhaps the rest of us could shrug it off. If they want to pay excessive fees to take part in the glitter—and possible large returns—of high stakes finance, that's their problem.

But the rest of us do pay a price. First of all, there is the ridiculously favorable tax treatment that hedge fund managers have been able to garner. Most important, they are allowed to classify their payments as capital gains rather than as salaries, and thereby they pay a low tax rate on their incomes—typically only 15%, compared to the top tax rate of 35%.

There is simply no good reason for this favorable treatment of hedge fund managers' incomes—other than the apparent power they are able to wield. The result is that the rest of us either pay more in taxes or get by with fewer public services.

Also important, hedge fund managers are not passive investors. They do not accept as a given the current profit levels of the companies they invest in, and simply try to claim a larger share of those profits. Instead, at least at times (but their secrecy makes it difficult to determine how often and to what extent), they take an active role in attempting to push up their profits. Along with private equity funds, with which the hedge funds are closely associated and sometimes overlap, they can push firms to downsize and reorganize, lay off workers, outsource, or alter their overall investment strategies.

For instance, according to a May 15 report in the "Silicon Alley Insider," John Paulson, who through his funds owns 4% of Yahoo stock, has joined corporate raider Carl Icahn in a proxy fight, an attempt to force Yahoo to accept a Microsoft buy-out offer.

There is no reason to think that any general social interest is served when hedge fund managers attempt to affect the operation of the firms in which they have holdings. In the Yahoo example, the impact on the rest of us may be obscure, but when it comes to layoffs, downsizing, outsourcing, and the like, it is clear that many people outside of the financial markets—people who have no seat at the gambling tables—pay a large price for the gains of hedge funds, and especially of fund managers.

Stagnant wages of workers in recent decades and the increased share of total national income going to corporate profits are the consequence of large, long-run economic forces—the decline of unions, globalization, conservative government policies, and technological shifts to name a few. But the hedge funds are one of the instruments by which these forces have their impact on the rest of us, shifting the value that we create into the financial markets and then taking as large a share as they can.

SOURCES: Andy Baker, "Better than beta? Managers' superior skills are becoming harder to prove," *The Economist*, February 28, 2008; Arindam Bandopadhyaya and James L. Grant, *A Survey of Demographics and Performance In the Hedge Fund Industry*, Working Paper 1011, Financial Services Forum, College of Management, University of Massachusetts Boston, July, 2006; "Hedge-Fund Performance," *The Economist*, May 15, 2008; Tom Cahill and Poppy Trowbridge, "Paulson's $3.7 Billion Top Hedge Fund Pay, Alpha Says," Bloomberg.com, April 16, 2008; Henry Blodget, "Hedge-Fund Mogul Paulson Joins Icahn in Yahoo Siege; 30% of Proxy Vote in Bag," Silicon Alley Insider, May 15, 2008.

ARTICLE 6.10　　　　　　　　　　　　　　　　　　　　　　　　　　　　September/October 2008

THE BAILOUT OF FANNIE MAE AND FREDDIE MAC

BY FRED MOSELEY

On Sunday, September 7, Treasury Secretary Henry Paulson announced that the U.S. government was taking control of Fannie Mae and Freddie Mac, the two giant home mortgage companies, which together either own or guarantee almost half of the mortgages in the United States. This takeover stands in striking contrast to the generally laissez-faire philosophy of the U.S. government, especially the Republican Party. Why did Paulson take this highly unusual action? And what will be the future of Fannie and Freddie? To delve into these questions is to underscore the critical fault line between private profits and public aims—in this case, the aim of making homeownership affordable—a fault line that ran right through the hybrid structure of Fannie and Freddie.

A BRIEF HISTORY

Fannie Mae (short for the Federal National Mortgage Association) was created as an agency of the federal government in 1938 in an attempt to provide additional funds to the home mortgage market and to help the housing industry recover from the Great Depression. Fannie Mae purchased approved mortgages from commercial banks, which could then use the funds to originate additional mortgages. It continued to fulfill this function on a modest scale in the early postwar years.

Fannie Mae was privatized in 1968, in part to help reduce the budget deficit caused by the Vietnam War (a short-sighted goal, if ever there was one). In 1970, Freddie Mac (Federal Home Loan Mortgage Corporation) was created as a private company in order to provide competition for Fannie Mae. Chartered by the federal government, both are (or were, until the takeover) so-called government-sponsored enterprises: private enterprises whose main goal is to maximize profit for the shareholders who own them, but also quasi-public enterprises with a mandated goal of increasing the availability of affordable mortgages to families in the United States. In the end, this dual mandate proved to be untenable.

In order to obtain funds to purchase mortgages, Fannie and Freddie sell short-term bonds. In other words, their business plan involves borrowing short-term and lending long-term, because interest rates are higher on long-term loans than on short-term loans. However, such "speculative finance" is risky because it depends on the willingness of short-term creditors to continue to loan to Fannie and Freddie by rolling over or refinancing their short-term loans. If creditors were to lose confidence in Fannie and Freddie and refuse to do so, then they would be in danger of bankruptcy. This is what almost happened in the recent crisis.

Beginning in the 1970s, Fannie and Freddie began to develop and sell "mortgage-backed securities"—hundreds of mortgages bundled together and sold to investors as a security, similar to a bond. They also guaranteed these securities (so that if a mortgage defaulted, they would repurchase it from the investors) and made money by charging a fee for this guarantee (like an insurance premium). This major financial innovation enabled the two companies to buy more mortgages from commercial banks, thereby increasing the supply of credit in the home mortgage market, which in turn was supposed to push mortgage interest rates lower, making houses more affordable. These early mortgage-backed securities consisted entirely of "prime" mortgages—that is, loans at favorable interest rates, typically made to creditworthy borrowers with full documentation and a substantial down payment.

The securities that Fannie and Freddie sold were widely perceived by investors to carry an implicit government guarantee: if Fannie or Freddie were ever in danger of bankruptcy, then the federal government would pay off their debts (even though this government guarantee was explicitly denied in legislation and in the loan agreements themselves). This perceived guarantee enabled Fannie and Freddie to borrow money at lower interest rates because loans to them were viewed as less risky.

In the 1980s, Wall Street investment banks also began to package and sell mortgage-backed securities. In the 1990s and 2000s, these "private label" mortgage-backed securities expanded rapidly in volume and also in reach, coming to include "subprime" mortgages—loans at higher interest rates with less favorable terms, geared toward less creditworthy borrowers and typically requiring little or no documentation and little or no down payment.

The subprime innovation was entirely the work of the investment banks; as of 2000, Fannie and Freddie owned or guaranteed almost no subprime mortgages. This innovation greatly increased the supply of credit for home mortgages and led to the extraordinary housing boom of the last decade, and also eventually to the crisis. As a result of these changes, the share of mortgage-backed securities sold by Fannie and Freddie fell to around 40% by 2005.

In the recent housing boom, the companies—especially Freddie—began to take greater risks. While continuing to bundle prime mortgages into securities and sell them to investors, Fannie and Freddie began to buy mortgage-backed securities issued by investment banks, including some based on subprime and Alt-A (between prime and subprime) mortgages. Why did they begin buying as well as selling mortgage-backed securities? Buying these private-label securities gave Fannie and Freddie a way to get in on the subprime action—while still avoiding direct purchases of subprime mortgages from the banks and mortgage companies that originated them. It was a way both to increase their profits at the behest of their shareholders, and, in response to pressure from the government, to make more mortgages available to low- and middle-income families. Of course, it also opened them up to the risks of the subprime arena. Moreover, the prime mortgages they continued to buy and guarantee were increasingly at inflated, bubble prices, making them vulnerable to the eventual bust and the decline of housing prices.

ANATOMY OF A CRISIS

When the subprime crisis began in the summer of 2007, Fannie and Freddie at first appeared to be relatively unaffected, and were even counted on to increase their purchases of mortgages in order to support the mortgage market and help overcome the crisis. Congress facilitated this by relaxing some of its regulations on the two companies: the maximum value of mortgages that they could purchase was increased substantially; their reserve capital requirements, already much lower than for commercial banks, were reduced further; and restrictions on their growth were lifted. As a result of these changes and the drying up of private label mortgage-backed securities, the share of all mortgage-backed securities sold by Fannie and Freddie doubled to approximately 80%. Without Fannie and Freddie, the mortgage and housing crises of the last year would have been much worse.

As the overall crisis unfolded, however, the financial situation of Fannie and Freddie deteriorated. Delinquency and foreclosure rates for the mortgages they own or guarantee, while lower than for the industry as a whole, increased rapidly and beyond expectations. The two companies together reported losses of $14 billion in the last year. Their actual losses have been much worse. As of mid-2008, the two had lost about $45 billion due to the decline in the value of their mortgage-backed securities, mostly those backed by subprime and Alt-A mortgages. But by labeling that decline "temporary," they could leave the losses off their balance sheets. If these losses were counted, as they should be, then Freddie's capital would be completely wiped out (a value of -$5.6 billion), and Fannie's would be reduced to a razor-thin margin of $12.2 billion (less than 2% of its assets), likely becoming negative in the coming quarters. In addition, both Fannie and Freddie count as assets "tax deferred losses" that can be used in future years to offset tax bills—if they make a profit. Without this dubious (but legal) accounting trick, the net assets of both Fannie and Freddie would be below zero, -$20 billion and -$32 billion respectively.

The financial crisis of Fannie and Freddie worsened in early July. The price of their stock, which had already fallen by more than half since last summer, declined another 50% in a few weeks, for a total decline of over 80%. Fear spread that Fannie and Freddie's creditors would refuse to roll over their short-term loans to the two. If that were to happen, then the U.S. home mortgage market and the housing construction industry probably would have collapsed completely, and the U.S. economy would have fallen into an even deeper recession. Furthermore, approximately 20% of the mortgage-backed securities and debt of Fannie and Freddie are owned by foreign investors. Mainly these are foreign governments, most significantly China. If these foreign investors became unwilling to continue to lend Fannie and Freddie money, this would have precipitated a steep fall in the value of the dollar which, on top of recent significant declines, would have dealt another blow to the U.S. economy. Clearly, the potential crisis here was serious enough to spur government action.

In late July, Congress passed a law authorizing the Treasury to provide unlimited amounts of money to Fannie and Freddie, either by buying new issues of stock or by making loans, and also to take over the companies in a conservator arrangement if necessary.

GOVERNMENT TAKEOVER

Through August the financial condition of Fannie and Freddie continued to deteriorate (especially Freddie), and confidence in their ability to survive waned. Foreign investors in particular reduced their purchases of the companies' debt, and mortgage rates increased. The Treasury concluded that it had to implement a takeover in order to reassure creditors and restore stability to the home mortgage market.

The Treasury plan has three main components:
- It commits up to $200 billion over the next 15 months for purchases of preferred shares of Fannie and Freddie as necessary to keep the companies solvent;
- It establishes a special lending facility that will provide emergency loans in case of a liquidity crisis;
- It commits to purchase unspecified amounts of Fannie and Freddie's mortgage-backed securities "as deemed appropriate."

The day after Paulson's announcement, William Poole, ex-president of the Federal Reserve Bank of St. Louis, estimated that the total cost to taxpayers would be in the neighborhood of $300 billion.

The top managers and the boards of directors of both companies will be dismissed and replaced by new, government-appointed managers. Other than that, the Treasury hopes that day-to-day operations at Fannie and Freddie will be "business as usual." They will continue to borrow money from creditors, now reassured by the government's intervention and more willing to lend to them, and they will continue to purchase and guarantee prime mortgages. In fact, Treasury Department plans call for the volume of mortgages purchased by the two companies to increase over the next year in order to push the supply of mortgage loans up and mortgage interest rates down.

The Treasury plan is a complete bailout of the creditors of Fannie and Freddie, who will be repaid in full, with taxpayer money if necessary. In contrast, owners of Fannie or Freddie stock will lose to some degree: dividends will be suspended for the foreseeable future, and their stock is now worth very little. But their stock was not expropriated. Nor was it wiped out entirely; it could regain value in the future as the home mortgage market recovers. Without the intervention, both companies would have gone bankrupt and the stockowners would have lost everything. So the intervention does represent at least a modest bailout for shareholders.

The most controversial issue in the months ahead will be the future of Fannie and Freddie. Should they become public enterprises permanently? Should they be re-privatized? Should they be sold off in pieces and cease to exist? Secretary Paulson made it clear that the government's current conservatorship is a holding action, and that decisions about the companies' ultimate status will only be made once the next administration and the next Congress are in office. Paulson said that Fannie and Freddie's current structure is unworkable because of its dual and conflicting goals of making housing affordable and maximizing profit—a radical statement, if you think about it! And he suggested that the two should either be fully public enterprises, or else they should be fully private enterprises without any government backing.

In the upcoming debate, the left should advocate forcefully for a public home mortgage agency, one whose sole purpose is to provide affordable housing without the conflicting purpose of maximizing profit. This would stabilize the home mortgage market and help it avoid the boom/bust cycle of private mortgage markets that has brought on the current crisis.

More fundamentally, because decent affordable housing is a basic economic right, providing credit for home purchases should be a function of the government rather than of private businesses whose primary goal is maximum profit. The provision of credit for housing should not be an arena where enormous profits are made, as has been the case in recent years. Without these huge profits, mortgages would be cheaper and houses more affordable. Plus, the kinds of fraudulent lending practices that played a significant role in the recent housing boom would be minimized.

With the presidential election just weeks away, the crisis of Fannie, Freddie, and the whole home lending market is poised to become a major campaign issue. McCain has said that he wants Fannie and Freddie to "go away"—i.e., to be broken up and disappear, leaving the mortgage market entirely to private enterprises. Obama has emphasized the conflict between the public aim of making housing widely affordable and the private aim of making a profit, but so far he has not come down on one side or the other. Now he will have to decide. I hope that he will be a strong advocate of a public home mortgage agency, and I think this would help him to get elected.

ARTICLE 6.11

March/April 2009

TIME FOR *PERMANENT* NATIONALIZATION!

BY FRED MOSELEY

The Treasury Department's recent bailouts of major U.S. banks will result in a massive transfer of income from taxpayers to those banks' bondholders.

Under the government's current bailout plan, the total sum of money transferred from taxpayers to bondholders will probably be at least several hundred billion dollars and could be as much as $1 trillion, which is about $3,300 for each man, woman, and child in the United States. These bondholders took risks and made lots of money during the recent boom, but now taxpayers are being forced to bail them out and pay for their losses.

This trillion-dollar transfer of income from taxpayers to bondholders is an economic injustice that should be stopped immediately, and it can be stopped—if the government fully and permanently nationalizes the banks that are "too big to fail."

The TARP program ("Troubled Assets Recovery Program") has gone through several incarnations. It was originally intended to purchase high-risk mortgage-backed securities from banks. But this plan floundered because it is very difficult in the current circumstances to determine the value of these risky assets, and thus the price the government should pay for them. The main policy for the first $350 billion spent so far has been to invest government capital into banks by buying preferred stock (which is the equivalent of a loan), which receives a 5% rate of return (Warren Buffet gets a 10% rate of return when he buys preferred stocks these days) and has no voting rights. Managers of the banks are not being replaced, and there are usually cosmetic limits on executive pay, unlikely to be enforced. So these bank managers, who are largely responsible for the banking crisis, will continue to be rewarded with salaries of millions of dollars *per year*, paid for in part with taxpayer money. Existing bank stock loses value as the bank issues stock secured by TARP funds.

But the main beneficiaries of the government bailout money are the bondholders of the banks. In the event of future losses, which are likely to be enormous, the government bailout money will be used directly or indirectly to pay off the bondholders. This could eventually take all of the available TARP money, and perhaps even more. So the government bailout of the banks is ultimately a bailout of the banks' bondholders, paid for by taxpayers.

The Bush administration's rationale for this approach to the bailout was that if the government did not bail out the banks and their bondholders, then the whole financial system in the United States would collapse. Nobody would lend money to anybody, and the economy would seize up (in the memorable words of George W. Bush: "this sucker would go down"). Bush Treasury Secretary Paulson presented us with an unavoidable dilemma—either bail out the bondholders with taxpayers' money or suffer a severe recession or depression.

If Paulson's assertion were correct, it would be a stinging indictment of our current financial system. It would imply that the capitalist financial system, left on its own, is inherently unstable, and can only avoid sparking major economic crises by being bailed out by the government, at the taxpayers' expense. There is a double indictment here: the capitalist financial system is inherently unstable and the necessary bailouts are economically unjust.

But there is a better alternative, a more equitable, "taxpayer friendly" option: *Permanently nationalize banks that are "too big to fail"* and run these banks according to public policy objectives (affordable housing, green energy, etc.), rather than with the objective of private profit maximization. The nationalization of banks, if it's done right, would clearly be superior to current bailout policies because it would not involve a massive transfer of wealth from taxpayers to bondholders.

Besides providing a more equitable response to the current banking crisis, nationalizing the biggest banks will help ensure that a crisis like this never happens again, and we never again have to bail out the banks and their bondholders to "save the economy." Once some banks have become "too big to fail" and everyone understands that the government will always bail out these large banks to avoid a systematic collapse, it follows that these banks should be nationalized. Otherwise, the implicit promise of a bailout gives megabanks a license to take lots of risks and make lots of money in good times, and then let the taxpayers pay for their losses in the bad times. Economists call this dilemma the "moral hazard" problem. In this case, we might instead call it the "economic injustice" problem.

Freed from the need to maximize short-term profit, nationalized banks would also make the economy more stable in the future. They would take fewer risks during an expansion, to avoid debt-induced bubbles, which inevitably burst and cause so much hardship. For example, there would be fewer housing bubbles; instead, the deposits of these megabanks would be invested in decent affordable housing available to all. With housing more affordable, mortgages would be more affordable and less risky.

The newly nationalized banks could also increase their lending to credit-worthy businesses and households, and thereby help stabilize the economy and lessen the severity of the current recession. As things stand, banks do not want to increase their lending, since the crediworthiness of any borrower is difficult to determine, especially that of other banks that may also hold toxic assets. They have suffered enormous losses over the last year, and they fear that more enormous losses are still to come. Banks prefer instead to hoard capital as a cushion against these expected future losses. What the government is doing now is giving money to banks in one way or another, and then begging them to please lend this money to businesses and households.

How would the nationalization of banks work? I suggest the following general principles and guidelines:

The federal government would become the owner of any "systemically significant" bank that asks for a government rescue or goes into bankruptcy proceedings. The value of existing stock would be wiped out, as it would be in a normal bankruptcy.

The government would itself operate the banks. Top management would be replaced by government banking officials, and the managers would not receive "golden parachutes" of any kind.

Most importantly, the banks' long-term bonds would be converted into common stock in the banks. This would restore the banks to solvency, so they could start lending again. The private common stock would be subordinate to the government preferred stock in the capital structure, which would mean that any future losses would be taken out of the private stock before the government stock. Bondholders could also be given the option of converting their stocks back to bonds at a later date, with a significant write-down or discount, determined by bankruptcy judges.

These "bonds-to-stocks" swaps (often called "debt-to-equity" swaps), or partial write-downs if the bondholders so choose, are a crucial aspect of an equitable nationalization of banks. The bondholders lent their money and signed contracts that stipulated that if the banks went bankrupt, they might suffer losses. Now the banks are bankrupt and the bondholders should take the losses.

This process of accelerated bankruptcy and nationalization should be applied in the future to any banks that are in danger of bankruptcy and are deemed to be "systemically significant." This would include the next crises at Citigroup and Bank of America. Other banks in danger of bankruptcy that are not "systemically significant" should be allowed to fail. There should be no more bailouts of the bondholders at the expense of taxpayers. In addition, the banks who received some of the first $350 billion should be subject to stricter conditions along the lines that Congress attached to the second $350 billion—that banks should be required to increase their lending to businesses and consumers, to fully account for how they have spent the government capital, and to follow strict limitations on executive compensation. The government should withdraw its capital from any banks that fail to meet these standards.

There is one other acceptable option: the government could create entirely new banks that would purchase good assets from banks and increase lending to credit-worth borrowers. These government banks are sometimes called "good banks," in contrast to the "bad bank" proposals that have been floated recently, according to which the government would set up a bank to purchase bad ("toxic") assets from banks. The term "good bank" is no doubt more politically acceptable than "government bank," but the meaning is the same. The only difference between the "good bank" proposal and the nationalization proposal I've outlined here is that my proposal would start with existing banks and turn them into government banks.

In mid-February, Treasury Secretary Timothy Geithner announced the Obama administration's plans for the bank bailout—renamed the "Financial Stability Plan." This plan is very similar to Paulson's two versions of TARP: it includes both purchases of high-risk mortgage-backed securities from banks and also investing capital in banks. The main new feature is that government capital is supposed to be invested together with private capital. But in order to attract private capital, the government will have to provide sufficient guarantees, so most of the risks will still fall on taxpayers. So Geithner's Financial Stability Plan has the same fundamental flaw as Paulson's TARP: it bails out the banks and their bondholders at the expense of taxpayers.

The public should demand that the Obama administration should cancel these plans for further bank bailouts and consider other options, including genuine, permanent nationalization. Permanent nationalization with bonds-to-stocks swaps for bondholders is the most equitable solution to the current banking crisis, and would provide a better basis for a more stable and public-oriented banking system in the future.

TRANSFORMING THE FED

BY ROBERT POLLIN

The U.S. financial system faces deep structural problems. Households, businesses, and the federal government are burdened by excessive debts. The economy favors short-term speculation over long-term investment. An unrepresentative and unresponsive elite has extensive control over the financial system. Moreover, the federal government is incapable of reversing these patterns through its existing tools, including fiscal, monetary, and financial regulatory policies.

I propose a dramatically different approach: transforming the Federal Reserve System (the "Fed") into a public investment bank. Such a bank would have substantial power to channel credit in ways that counter financial instability and support productive investment by private businesses. The Fed would use its powers to influence how and for what purposes banks, insurance companies, brokers, and other lenders loan money.

The U.S. government has used credit allocation policies, such as low-cost loans, loan guarantees, and home mortgage interest deductions, extensively and with success. Its primary accomplishment has been to create a home mortgage market that, for much of the period since World War II, provided non-wealthy households with unprecedented access to home ownership.

I propose increasing democratic control over the Federal Reserve's activities by decentralizing power to the 12 district Fed banks and instituting popular election of their boards of directors. This would create a mechanism for extending democracy throughout the financial system.

My proposal also offers a vehicle for progressives to address two separate but equally serious questions facing the U.S. economy:

- how to convert our industrial base out of military production and toward the development and adoption of environmentally benign production techniques; and
- how to increase opportunities for high wage, high productivity jobs in the United States. The U.S. needs such jobs to counteract the squeeze on wages from increasingly globalized labor and financial markets.

Transforming the Federal Reserve system into a public investment bank will help define an economic path toward democratic socialism in the United States.

My proposal has several strengths as a transitional program. It offers a mechanism for establishing democratic control over finance and investment—the area where capital's near-dictatorial power is most decisive. The program will also work within the United States' existing legal and institutional framework. We could implement parts of it immediately using existing federal agencies and with minimal demands on the federal budget.

At the same time, if an ascendant progressive movement put most of the program in place, this would represent a dramatic step toward creating a new economic system. Such a system would still give space to market interactions and the pursuit of greed, but would nevertheless strongly promote general well-being over business profits.

HOW THE FED FAILS

At present the Federal Reserve focuses its efforts on managing short-term fluctuations of the economy, primarily by influencing interest rates. When it reduces rates, it seeks to increase borrowing and spending, and thereby stimulate economic growth and job opportunities. When the Fed perceives that wages and prices are rising too fast (a view not necessarily shared by working people), it tries to slow down borrowing and spending by raising interest rates.

This approach has clearly failed to address the structural problems plaguing the financial system. The Fed did nothing, for example, to prevent the collapse of the savings and loan industry. It stood by while highly speculative mergers, buyouts, and takeovers overwhelmed financial markets in the 1980s. It has failed to address the unprecedented levels of indebtedness and credit defaults of private corporations and households.

NEW ROLES FOR THE FED

Under my proposal, the Federal Reserve would shift its focus from the short to the long term. It would provide more and cheaper credit to banks and other financiers who loan money to create productive assets and infrastructure—which promote high wage, high productivity jobs. The Fed would make credit more expensive for lenders that finance speculative activities such as the mergers, buyouts, and takeovers that dominated the 1980s.

The Fed would also give favorable credit terms to banks that finance decent affordable housing rather than luxury housing and speculative office buildings. It would make low-cost credit available for environmental research and development so the economy can begin the overdue transition to environmentally benign production. Cuts in military spending have idled many workers and productive resources, both of which could be put to work in such transformed industries.

Finally, the Fed would give preferential treatment to loans that finance investment in the United States rather than in foreign countries. This would help counter the trend of U.S. corporations to abandon the domestic economy in search of lower wages and taxes.

The first step in developing the Fed's new role would be for the public to determine which sectors of the economy should get preferential access to credit. One example, suggested above, is industrial conversion from military production to investment in renewable energy and conservation.

Once the public establishes its investment goals, the Fed will have to develop new policy tools and use its existing tools in new ways to accomplish them. I propose that a transformed Federal Reserve use two major methods:

- set variable cash ("asset reserve") requirements for all lenders, based on the social value of the activities the lenders are financing; and
- increase discretionary lending activity by the 12 district Federal Reserve banks.

VARYING BANKS' CASH REQUIREMENTS

The Fed currently requires that banks and other financial institutions keep a certain amount of their assets available in cash reserves. Banks, for example, must carry three cents in cash for every dollar they hold in checking accounts. A bank cannot make interest-bearing loans on such "reserves." I propose that the Fed make this percent significantly lower for loans that finance preferred activities than for less desirable investment areas. Let's say the public decides that banks should allocate 10% of all credit to research and development of new environmental technologies, such as non-polluting autos and organic farming. Then financial institutions that have made 10% of their loans in environmental technologies would not have to hold any cash reserves against these loans. But if a bank made no loans in the environmental area, then it would have to hold 10% of its total assets in reserve. The profit motive would force banks to support environmental technologies without any direct expenditure from the federal budget.

All profit-driven firms will naturally want to avoid this reserve requirement. The Fed must therefore apply it uniformly to all businesses that profit through accepting deposits and making loans. These include banks, savings and loans, insurance companies, and investment brokerage houses. If the rules applied only to banks, for example, then banks could circumvent the rules by redefining themselves as another type of lending institution.

LOANS TO BANKS THAT DO THE RIGHT THING

The Federal Reserve has the authority now to favor some banks over others by making loans to them when they are short on cash. For the most part, however, the Fed has chosen not to exercise such discretionary power. Instead it aids all banks equally, through a complex mechanism known as open market operations, which increases total cash reserves in the banking system. The Fed could increase its discretionary lending to favored banks by changing its operating procedures without the federal government creating any new laws or institutions. Such discretionary lending would have several benefits.

First, to a much greater extent than at present, financial institutions would obtain reserves when they are lending for specific purposes. If a bank's priorities should move away from the established social priorities, the Fed could then either refuse to make more cash available to it, or charge a penalty interest rate, thereby discouraging the bank from making additional loans. The Fed, for example, could impose such obstacles on lenders that are financing mergers, takeovers, and buyouts.

In addition, the Fed could use this procedure to more effectively monitor and regulate financial institutions. Banks, in applying for loans, would have to submit to the Fed's scrutiny on a regular basis. The Fed could more closely link its regulation to banks' choices of which investments to finance.

Implementing this procedure will also increase the authority of the 12 district banks within the Federal Reserve system, since these banks approve the Fed's loans. Each district bank will have more authority to set lending rates and monitor bank compliance with regulations.

The district banks could then more effectively enforce measures such as the Community Reinvestment Act, which currently mandates that banks lend in their home communities. Banks that are committed to their communities and regions, such as the South Shore Bank in Chicago, could gain substantial support under this proposed procedure.

OTHER CREDIT ALLOCATION TOOLS

The Fed can use other tools to shift credit to preferred industries, such as loan guarantees, interest rate subsidies, and government loans. In the past the U.S. government has used these techniques with substantial success. They now primarily support credit for housing, agriculture, and education. Indeed, as of 1991, these programs subsidized roughly one-third of all loans in the United States.

Jesse Jackson's 1988 Presidential platform suggested an innovative way of extending such policies. He proposed that public pension funds channel a portion of their money into a loan guarantee program, with the funds used to finance investments in low cost housing, education, and infrastructure.

There are disadvantages, however, to the government using loan guarantee programs and similar approaches rather than the Fed's employing asset reserve requirements and discretionary lending. Most important is that the former are more expensive and more difficult to administer. Both loan guarantees and direct government loans require the government to pay off the loans when borrowers default. Direct loans also mean substantial administrative costs. Interest subsidies on loans are direct costs to government even when the loans are paid back.

In contrast, with variable asset reserve requirements and discretionary lending policies, the Fed lowers the cost of favored activities, and raises the cost of unfavored ones, without imposing any burden on the government's budget.

INCREASING PUBLIC CONTROL

The Federal Reserve acts in relative isolation from the political process at present. The U.S. president appoints seven members of the Fed's Board of Governors for 14 year terms, and they are almost always closely tied to banking and big business. The boards of directors of the 12 district banks appoint their presidents, and these boards are also composed of influential bankers and business people within each of the districts.

The changes I propose will mean a major increase in the central bank's role as an economic planning agency for the nation. Unless we dramatically improve democratic control by the public over the Fed, voters will correctly interpret such efforts as an illegitimate grasp for more power by business interests.

Democratization should proceed through redistributing power downward to the 12 district banks. When the Federal Reserve System was formed in 1913, the principle behind creating district banks along with the headquarters in Washington was to disperse the central bank's authority. This remains a valuable idea, but the U.S. government has never seriously attempted it. Right now the district banks are highly undemocratic and have virtually no power.

One way to increase the district banks' power is to create additional seats for them on the Open Market Committee, which influences short-term interest rates by expanding or contracting the money supply.

A second method is to shift authority from the Washington headquarters to the districts. The Board of Governors would then be responsible for setting general guidelines, while the district banks would implement discretionary lending and enforcement of laws such as the Community Reinvestment Act.

The most direct way of democratizing the district banks would be to choose their boards in regular elections along with other local, regional, and state-wide officials. The boards would then choose the top levels of the banks' professional staffs and oversee the banks' activities.

HISTORICAL PRECEDENTS

Since World War II other capitalist countries have extensively employed the types of credit allocation policies proposed here. Japan, France, and South Korea are the outstanding success stories, though since the early 1980s globalization and deregulation of financial markets have weakened each of their credit policies. When operating at full strength, the Japanese and South Korean programs primarily supported large-scale export industries, such as steel, automobiles, and consumer electronics. France targeted its policies more broadly to coordinate Marshall Plan aid for the development of modern industrial corporations.

We can learn useful lessons from these experiences, not least that credit allocation policies do work when they are implemented well. But substantial differences exist between experiences elsewhere and the need for a public investment bank in the United States.

In these countries a range of other institutions besides the central bank were involved in credit allocation policies. These included their treasury departments and explicit planning agencies, such as the powerful Ministry of International Trade and Industry (MITI) in Japan. In contrast, I propose to centralize the planning effort at the Federal Reserve.

We could create a new planning institution to complement the work of the central bank. But transforming the existing central banking system rather than creating a new institution minimizes both start-up problems and the growth of bureaucracies.

A second and more fundamental difference between my proposal and the experiences in Japan, France, and South Korea is that their public investment institutions were accountable only to a business-oriented elite. This essentially dictatorial approach is antithetical to the goal of increasing democratic control of the financial system.

The challenge, then, is for the United States to implement effective credit allocation policies while broadening, not narrowing, democracy. Our success ultimately will depend on a vigorous political movement that can fuse two equally urgent, but potentially conflicting goals: economic democracy, and equitable and sustainable growth. If we can meet this challenge, it will represent a historic victory toward the construction of a democratic socialist future.

Resources: Robert Pollin, "Transforming the Federal Reserve into a Public Investment Bank: Why it is Necessary; How it Should Be Done," in G. Epstein, G. Dymski and R. Pollin, eds., *Transforming the U.S. Financial System,* M.E. Sharpe, 1993.

CHAPTER 7
UNEMPLOYMENT AND INFLATION

INTRODUCTION

In June of this year, while the economy was still in the throes of its worst crisis since the Great Depression, supply-side economist Arthur Laffer warned of the threat of inflation. In an op-ed piece in the *Wall Street Journal* Laffer wrote that "we can expect rapidly rising prices over the next four or five years." He argued that the Fed's unprecedented expansion of the money supply during the crisis has the potential to unleash an inflation spiral more virulent than that in the 1970s.

There might be something to Laffer's concerns about price stability over the longer term. But why voice those concerns just three days after the economy had registered its highest unemployment rate in 26 years? Do conservative economists think it is more important to address a threat of inflation that will not manifest itself for another year or more than deal with record-setting unemployment today?

In short, the answer is yes. This is hardly a surprise when considering that investors and stockholders feel precisely the same way because rising prices eat into their real rate of return or profits, after accounting for inflation.

Why is that? The explanation comes down to the tradeoff between inflation and unemployment. Standard macroeconomic textbooks depict that tradeoff as a "Phillips curve" in which rising employment pushes up prices.

Why does this textbook tradeoff affect the returns of stockholders and other investors? The answer, as economist Robert Pollin points out, is "all about class conflict." Wall Street investors, out to protect the value of their assets and their investment profits, are hyper-concerned with price stability, and this pits them against workers on Main Street, who care about employment and wage growth. Higher unemployment rates and fewer jobs eat away at the bargaining power of workers, keeping wage growth and inflation in check, and corporate profit margins wide.

Pollin captures that dynamic in "The 'Natural Rate' of Unemployment." As he sees it, the unemployment rate consistent with price stability: the so-called "natural rate" declined dramatically in the 1990s because workers' economic power eroded during the decade (Article 7.1). John Miller supplements Pollin's class conflict analysis by showing how deteriorating real wages for workers are what make for the "positive fundamentals," such as declining unit labor costs, so valued by Wall Street insiders (Article 7.3).

Economist Ramaa Vasudevan takes a careful look at the macroeconomics between inflation and unemployment and how that tradeoff changed during the stagflation of the 1970s and productivity boom of the 1990s. Like Pollin, she attributes the sustained low inflation and unemployment during the 1990s to the relatively weak bargaining position of workers (Article 7.5).

Economist Chris Tilly attributes the long-term decline in pay, benefits, and working conditions for U.S. workers to slower economic growth, the business offensive against workers' protections, such as unions and the minimum wage, and businesses pushing more risks onto workers in the form of temporary work, mass layoffs, and reduced benefits (Article 7.2).

Perhaps no problem haunts the U.S. labor markets more than offshore outsourcing, which began with shipping manufacturing jobs abroad, and has now spread to back office work and a wide swath of service sector jobs. In his second article, John Miller notes that the alarming estimates of the scope of offshore outsourcing have even given some inveterate free-traders second thoughts (Article 7.4).

Research analyst Ben Collins closes out the chapter by looking at the forces driving the rise of food prices across the globe. Food and other commodities have become the new hot investment as housing and stocks turn sour. The financialization of food, just another in a long list of ills visited upon the global economy by unregulated financial markets, has not only contributed to economic instability but is also changing how people around the world eat and who doesn't (Article 7.6).

DISCUSSION QUESTIONS

1. (Article 7.1) What is the concept of the NAIRU, or natural rate of unemployment? Is there a natural rate? What is it?
2. (Article 7.1) Given the class conflict inherent in the tradeoff between inflation and unemployment, what policies might lead to an improved standard of living in today's economy?

KEY TO COLANDER

E = Economics   M = Macroeconomics

This chapter is keyed to chapters E24, E26, E27, E30-E33; or M7, M9, M10, M13-M16.

Articles 7.1, 7.2, and 7.3 expose the class conflict that underlies the tradeoff between inflation and unemployment, the topic of chapter E33 or M16.

Articles 7.4, 7.5, 7.6 fit squarely with this discussion of unemployment and the "institutional" sources of inflation.

3. (Article 7.2) What forces have led to a raw deal for workers in the long run?
4. (Article 7.2) How have the "paradox of corporate thrift," the "neoliberal paradox," and the "Arkansas paradox" complicated the task of winning a fair deal for workers?
5. (Article 7.3) According to Charles Schwab and the editors of the *Wall Street Journal*, how do higher wages for workers and rising unit labor costs conflict with the interests of investors?
6. (Article 7.4) Just how big of a problem is offshore outsourcing? For whom?
7. (Article 7.4) What policies would best address the negative impacts of offshore outsourcing?
8. (Article 7.5) What are the costs of higher inflation? And according to Vasudevan's evidence, what is the relationship between inflation and growth?
9. (Article 7.1, 7.5) What forces led to the sustained low Inflation and unemployment during the 1990s? How are those conditions changing today?
10. (Article 7.6) What forces have transformed food commodities into a hot speculative investment?
11. (Article 7.6) What steps would you take to regulate speculation in food commodities and its dangerous consequences for the world's food supply?

THE "NATURAL RATE" OF UNEMPLOYMENT
IT'S ALL ABOUT CLASS CONFLICT

BY ROBERT POLLIN

In 1997, the official U.S. unemployment rate fell to a 27-year low of 4.9%. Most orthodox economists had long predicted that a rate this low would lead to uncontrollable inflation. So they argued that maintaining a higher unemployment rate—perhaps as high as 6%—was crucial for keeping the economy stable. But there is a hitch: last year the inflation rate was 2.3%, the lowest figure in a decade and the second lowest in 32 years. What then are we to make of these economists' theories, much less their policy proposals?

Nobel Prize-winning economist Milton Friedman gets credit for originating the argument that low rates of unemployment would lead to accelerating inflation. His 1968 theory of the so-called "natural rate of unemployment" was subsequently developed by many mainstream economists under the term "Non-Accelerating Inflation Rate of Unemployment," or NAIRU, a remarkably clumsy term for expressing the simple concept of a threshold unemployment rate below which inflation begins to rise.

According to both Friedman and expositors of NAIRU, inflation should accelerate at low rates of unemployment because low unemployment gives workers excessive bargaining power. This allows the workers to demand higher wages. Capitalists then try to pass along these increased wage costs by raising prices on the products they sell. An inflationary spiral thus ensues as long as unemployment remains below its "natural rate."

Based on this theory, Friedman and others have long argued that governments should never actively intervene in the economy to promote full employment or better jobs for workers, since it will be a futile exercise, whose end result will only be higher inflation and no improvement in job opportunities. Over the past generation, this conclusion has had far-reaching influence throughout the world. In the United States and Western Europe, it has provided a stamp of scientific respectability to a whole range of policies through which governments abandoned even modest commitments to full employment and workers' rights.

This emerged most sharply through the Reaganite and Thatcherite programs in the United States and United Kingdom in the 1980s. But even into the 1990s, as the Democrats took power in the United States, the Labour Party won office in Britain, and Social Democrats won elections throughout Europe, governments remained committed to stringent fiscal and monetary policies, whose primary goal is to prevent inflation. In Western Europe this produced an average unemployment rate of over 10% from 1990–97. In the United States, unemployment rates have fallen sharply in the 1990s, but as an alternative symptom of stringent fiscal and monetary policies, real wages for U.S. workers also declined dramatically over the past generation. As of 1997, the average real wage for nonsupervisory workers in the United States was 14% below its peak in 1973, even though average worker productivity rose between 1973 and 1997 by 34%.

Why have governments in the United States and Europe remained committed to the idea of fiscal and monetary stringency, if the natural rate theory on which such policies are based is so obviously flawed? The explanation is that the natural rate theory is really not just about predicting a precise unemployment rate figure below which inflation must inexorably accelerate, even though many mainstream economists have presented the natural rate theory in this way. At a deeper level, the natural rate theory is bound up with the inherent conflicts between workers and capitalists over jobs, wages, and working conditions. As such, the natural rate theory actually contains a legitimate foundation in truth amid a welter of sloppy and even silly predictions.

THE "NATURAL RATE" THEORY IS ABOUT CLASS CONFLICT

In his 1967 American Economic Association presidential address in which he introduced the natural rate theory, Milton Friedman made clear that there was really nothing "natural" about the theory. Friedman rather emphasized that: "by using the term 'natural' rate of unemployment, I do not mean to suggest that it is immutable and unchangeable. On the contrary, many of the market characteristics that determine its level are man-made and policy-made. In the United States, for example, legal minimum wage rates ... and the strength of labor unions all make the natural rate of unemployment higher than it would otherwise be."

In other words, according to Friedman, what he terms the "natural rate" is really a social phenomenon measuring the class strength of working people, as indicated by their ability to organize effective unions and establish a livable minimum wage.

Friedman's perspective is supported in a widely-read 1997 paper by Robert Gordon of Northwestern University on what he terms the "time-varying NAIRU." What makes the NAIRU vary over time? Gordon explains that, since the early 1960s, "The two especially large changes in the NAIRU... are the increase between the early and late 1960s and the decrease in the 1990s. The late 1960s were a time of labor militancy, relatively strong unions, a relatively high minimum wage and a marked increase in labor's share in national income. The 1990s have been a time of labor peace, relatively weak unions, a relatively low minimum wage and a slight decline in labor's income share."

In short, class conflict is the spectre haunting the analysis of the natural rate and NAIRU: this is the consistent message stretching from Milton Friedman in the 1960s to Robert Gordon in the 1990s.

Stated in this way, the "Natural Rate" idea does, ironically, bear a close family resemblance to the ideas of two of the greatest economic thinkers of the left, Karl Marx and Michal Kalecki, on a parallel concept—the so-called "Reserve Army of Unemployed." In his justly famous Chapter 25 of Volume I of *Capital*, "The General Law of Capitalist Accumulation," Marx argued forcefully that unemployment serves an important function in capitalist economies. That is, when a capitalist economy is growing rapidly enough so that the reserve army of unemployed is depleted, workers will then utilize their increased bargaining power to raise wages. Profits are correspondingly squeezed as workers get a larger share of the country's total income. As a result, capitalists anticipate further declines in profitability and they therefore reduce their investment spending. This then leads to a fall in job creation, higher unemployment, and a replenishment of the reserve army. In other words, the reserve army of the unemployed is the instrument capitalists use to prevent significant wage increases and thereby maintain profitability.

Kalecki, a Polish economist of the Great Depression era, makes parallel though distinct arguments in his also justly famous essay, "The Political Aspects of Full Employment." Kalecki wrote in 1943, shortly after the 1930s Depression had ended and governments had begun planning a postwar world in which they would deploy aggressive policies to avoid another calamity of mass unemployment. Kalecki held, contrary to Marx, that full employment can be beneficial to the profitability of businesses. True, capitalists may get a smaller share of the total economic pie as workers gain bargaining power to win higher wages. But capitalists can still benefit because the size of the pie is growing far more rapidly, since more goods and services can be produced when everyone is working, as opposed to some significant share of workers being left idle.

But capitalists still won't support full employment, in Kalecki's view, because it will threaten their control over the workplace, the pace and direction of economic activity, and even political institutions. Kalecki thus concluded that full employment could be sustainable under capitalism, but only if these challenges to capitalists' social and political power could be contained. This is why he held that fascist social and political institutions, such as those that existed in Nazi Germany when he was writing, could well provide one "solution" to capitalism's unemployment problem, precisely because they were so brutal. Workers would have jobs, but they would never be permitted to exercise the political and economic power that would otherwise accrue to them in a full-employment economy.

Broadly speaking, Marx and Kalecki do then share a common conclusion with natural rate proponents, in that they would all agree that positive unemployment rates are the outgrowth of class conflict over the distribution of income and political power. Of course, Friedman and other mainstream economists reach this conclusion via analytic and political perspectives that are diametrically opposite to those of Marx and Kalecki. To put it in a nutshell, in the Friedmanite view mass unemployment results when workers demand more than they deserve, while for Marx and Kalecki, capitalists use the weapon of unemployment to prevent workers from getting their just due.

FROM NATURAL RATE TO EGALITARIAN POLICY

Once the analysis of unemployment in capitalist economies is properly understood within the framework of class conflict, several important issues in our contemporary economic situation become much more clear. Let me raise just a few:

1. Mainstream economists have long studied how workers' wage demands cause inflation as unemployment falls. However, such wage demands never directly cause inflation, since inflation refers to a general rise in prices of goods and services sold in the market, not a rise in wages. Workers, by definition, do not have the power to raise prices. Capitalists raise prices on the products they sell. At low unemployment, inflation occurs when capitalists respond to workers' increasingly successful wage demands by raising prices so that they can maintain profitability. If workers were simply to receive a higher share of national income, then lower unemployment and higher wages need not cause inflation at all.

2. There is little mystery as to why, at present, the so-called "time-varying" NAIRU has diminished to a near vanishing point, with unemployment at a 25-year low while inflation remains dormant. The main explanation is the one stated by Robert Gordon—that workers' economic power has been eroding dramatically through the 1990s. Workers have been almost completely unable to win wage increases over the course of the economic expansion that by now is seven years old.

3. This experience over the past seven years, with unemployment falling but workers showing almost no income gains, demonstrates dramatically the crucial point that full employment can never stand alone as an adequate measure of workers' well-being. This was conveyed vividly to me when I was working in Bolivia in 1990 as part of an economic advising team led by Keith Griffin of the University of California-Riverside. Professor Griffin asked me to examine employment policies.

I began by paying a visit to the economists at the Ministry of Planning. When I requested that we discuss the country's employment problems, they explained, to my surprise, that the country *had no employment problems*. When I suggested we consider the situation of the people begging, shining shoes, or hawking batteries and Chiclets in the street just below the window where we stood, their response was that these people *were* employed. And of course they were, in that they were actively trying to scratch out a living. It was clear that I had to specify the problem at hand far more precisely. Similarly, in the United States today, we have to be much more specific as to what workers should be getting in a fair economy: jobs, of course, but also living wages, benefits, reasonable job security, and a healthy work environment.

4. In our current low-unemployment economy, should workers, at long last, succeed in winning higher wages and better benefits, some inflationary pressures are likely to emerge. But if inflation does not accelerate after wage increases are won, this would mean that businesses are not able to pass along their higher wage costs to their customers. Profits would therefore be squeezed. In any case, in response to *either* inflationary pressures or a squeeze in profitability, we should expect that many, if not most, segments of the business community will welcome a Federal Reserve policy that would slow the economy and raise the unemployment rate.

Does this mean that, as long as we live in a capitalist society, the control by capitalists over the reserve army of labor must remain the dominant force establishing the limits of workers' strivings for jobs, security, and living wages? The challenge for the progressive movement in the United States today is to think through a set of policy ideas through which full employment at living wages can be achieved and sustained.

Especially given the dismal trajectory of real wage decline over the past generation, workers should of course continue to push for wage increases. But it will also be crucial to advance these demands within a broader framework of proposals. One important component of a broader package would be policies through which labor and capital bargain openly over growth of wages and profits after full employment is achieved. Without such an open bargaining environment, workers, with reason, will push for higher wages once full employment is achieved, but capitalists will then respond by either raising prices or favoring high unemployment. Such open bargaining policies were conducted with considerable success in Sweden and other Nordic countries from the 1950s to the 1980s, and as a result, wages there continued to rise at full employment, while both accelerating inflation and a return to high unemployment were prevented.

Such policies obviously represent a form of class compromise. This is intrinsically neither good nor bad. The question is the terms under which the compromise is achieved. Wages have fallen dramatically over the past generation, so workers deserve substantial raises as a matter of simple fairness. But workers should also be willing to link their wage increases to improvements in productivity growth, i.e., the rate at which workers produce new goods and services. After all, if the average wage had just risen at exactly the rate of productivity growth since 1973 and not a penny more, the average hourly wage today for nonsupervisory workers would be $19.07 rather than $12.24.

But linking wages to improvements in productivity then also raises the question of who controls the decisions that determine the rate of productivity growth. In fact, substantial productivity gains are attainable through operating a less hierarchical workplace and building strong democratic unions through which workers can defend their rights on the job. Less hierarchy and increased workplace democracy creates higher morale on the job, which in turn increases workers' effort and opportunities to be inventive, while decreasing turnover and absenteeism. The late David Gordon of the New School for Social Research was among the leading analysts demonstrating how economies could operate more productively through greater workplace democracy.

But improvements in productivity also result from both the public and private sector investing in new and better machines that workers put to use every day, with the additional benefit that it means more jobs for people who produce those machines. A pro-worker economic policy will therefore also have to be concerned with increasing investments to improve the stock of machines that workers have at their disposal on the job.

In proposing such a policy approach, have I forgotten the lesson that Marx and Kalecki taught us, that unemployment serves a purpose in capitalism? Given that this lesson has become part of the standard mode of thinking among mainstream economists ranging from Milton Friedman to Robert Gordon, I would hope that I haven't let it slip from view. My point nevertheless is that through changing power relationships at the workplace and the decision-making process through which investment decisions get made, labor and the left can then also achieve a more egalitarian economy, one in which capitalists' power to brandish the weapon of unemployment is greatly circumscribed. If the labor movement and the left neglect issues of control over investment and the workplace, we will continue to live amid a Bolivian solution to the unemployment problem, where full employment is the by-product of workers' vulnerability, not their strength.

Resources: A longer version of this article appears as "The 'Reserve Army of Labor' and the 'Natural Rate of Unemployment': Can Marx, Kalecki, Friedman, and Wall Street All Be Wrong?," *Review of Radical Political Economics*, Fall 1998. Both articles derive from a paper originally presented as the David Gordon Memorial Lecture at the 1997 Summer Conference of the Union for Radical Political Economics. See also Robert Pollin and Stephanie Luce, *The Living Wage: Building A Fair Economy*, 1998; David Gordon, *Fat and Mean*, 1997; David Gordon, "Generating Affluence: Productivity Gains Require Worker Support," *Real World Macro*, 15th ed., 1998.

RAW DEAL FOR WORKERS

BY CHRIS TILLY

Few people have seen the inside of a "secondary meat processor"—a factory where large cuts of beef are turned into hamburger patties, roast beef, and other beef products. The workers who process beef do not have it easy. Many stand for long hours on wet floors. They are in constant contact with raw meat. In a typical plant the temperature ranges from 50° down to 3°F. Some workers rake 30-pound beef slabs from a huge bin onto a scale. Others heave giant roasts from one transmission belt to another. The work is repetitive and boring, but at the same time requires extreme attention to detail because of the potential for injury as well as food safety regulations. At one typical plant, entry-level pay is $7.75 an hour, or $16,000 a year—a poverty-level wage. There is no question that meat processors are getting a raw deal.

But the raw deal for workers is not limited to those workers who deal with raw meat. Pay, opportunities, and job quality have gotten worse for most workers in the United States over the past 30 years, across most sectors of the economy.

Obviously, the 2001 recession and the current jobless recovery have meant two-plus years of severe job shortages. But the deterioration of U.S. labor market conditions is a longer-term phenomenon. The spread of second-class jobs in the past three decades relates to fundamental changes in the economy and society, including sluggish productivity growth and employer assaults on workers' rights and protections.

The strongest evidence for the raw deal comes from looking at how workers were doing at the peak of the 1990s boom, three years ago. It was the longest boom in recorded U.S. history (lasting from March 1991 to March 2001). The expansion drove unemployment down to its lowest level in 30 years and spurred talk about a "new economy" that would turn productivity growth into endless prosperity. It should have been the best of times. But as a glance at the numbers reveals, it was not the best of times for working people.

WHY THE RAW DEAL?

Why are workers getting such a raw deal? First, the economic pie is growing more slowly. Productivity growth during the "new economy" 1990s was only two-thirds as fast as in the "old economy" 1960s. That reflects the fact that companies have not invested as much in upgrading their equipment and training their workers as they once did—although the numbers are up compared to the 1980s, when productivity growth was even slower.

Why are these investments down? Businesses make an investment when they expect a payoff. But total global demand for goods and services grew only about half as fast in the 1980s and 1990s as it did in the 1960s and 1970s, and the increasing globalization of trade and investment meant that businesses were much more likely to face new competitors.

Second, over the last 20 years, businesses have aggressively attacked the protections that workers had built up for themselves. They have busted and blocked unions, shredded the unspoken agreements that governed many non-union workplaces, and lobbied to weaken pro-worker legislation. One consequence of these efforts: private sector workers are now less than one-third as likely to belong to a union now as they were in the mid-1950s. The minimum wage is only worth about two-thirds as much as it was at its high point in the late 1960s (after taking inflation into account). Because the low-wage workforce includes disproportionate numbers of women and people of color, the minimum wage and unions particularly benefit these groups.

Republican presidents have joined in the attacks on these protections. Every Republican administration since Ronald Reagan has doggedly opposed minimum wage increases. When Reagan fired striking air traffic controllers in 1981, he set a precedent for the permanent replacement of strikers. George W. Bush out-did Reagan in 2002 when he demanded that the Department of Homeland Security not have civil service protections and announced plans to privatize half of the federal workforce. Republicans in the White House have also stacked the National Labor Relations Board (NLRB), other federal agencies, and the courts with anti-labor appointees. As a result, these agencies offer at best weak enforcement of labor protections. To provide two recent examples: the NLRB recently ruled that unions have no right to hand out leaflets in company parking lots, and the Supreme Court ruled in 2002 that if a company terminates an undocumented worker, it need not pay the worker his or her back pay. Further, under-funding of the Occupational Safety and Health Administration (OSHA) has reduced inspections in hazardous workplaces—like meat processors. Self-styled New Democrats have backed many of these changes in the name of aiding business.

Of course, at the same time as corporations have attacked rank-and-file workers' protections, they have increased the rewards to top executives and stockholders. CEO pay kept growing through 2001, even while profits and stock values declined.

The third reason for the raw deal is that businesses have pushed more and more risk onto workers. The most extreme example of this is the growth of temporary work, which has expanded more than twenty-fold since the late 1960s.

(Temporary work has been shrinking for the last two years—which of course is exactly the point: you hire temporary workers so you can dump them when the economy goes south.) But beyond the temps themselves, the frequency of mass layoffs highlights the fact that really, almost all jobs are temporary today.

Benefits are another area where workers bear more and more risk. Twenty-five years ago, most workers with pensions had "defined benefit" plans which specified the amount they would be paid upon retirement. Today, fewer than half of all workers are covered by any retirement plan, and fewer than one in five has a defined-benefit pension plan. Businesses prefer to offer defined-contribution plans like 401(k)s which require employee contributions and tie retirement income to market returns. In the last two years, we saw the results for those who had invested their 401(k) savings in Wall Street. Similarly, employers who offer health insurance have made workers take on more and more of the cost of health benefits —with the result that a growing number of workers decide they can't afford their health plan and go without coverage.

BECAUSE THEY CAN

Why are businesses attacking worker protections and demanding that workers bear more risk? The first answer that many people give is "globalization"—and the increased competition that comes with it. Globalization has certainly had an important impact, but it does not offer an adequate explanation for business's newly combative stance. After all, it is the National Restaurant Association—representing an industry that experiences absolutely no global competition—that has fought hardest to keep the minimum wage low. To a large extent, businesses have gone on the offensive not because they *must*, but because they *can*.

Of course, businesses have always had the ability to lobby against the minimum wage, to cut health benefits, and to run anti-union campaigns. What has changed is the social acceptability of such actions. Princeton economist Paul Krugman recently argued that this is what accounts for the stratospheric rise of CEO pay: businesses have torn up the old social contract that placed important restraints on corporate self-seeking. Once a few large companies did this, the pressure mounted for other companies to go along or else face a competitive disadvantage, both in the stock market and in the market for goods and services. And as the social contract got rewritten, the government stopped enforcing the old rules. Cases in point are recent changes by the Supreme Court, the NLRB, and OSHA, mentioned earlier.

What can be done about this raw deal? It's tempting to think about the Arnold Schwarzenegger solution. In the 1986 movie *Raw Deal* ("They gave him a raw deal. *Nobody* gives him a raw deal."), Schwarzenegger used fists, guns, and explosives to wipe out the Chicago mob. But leveling the playing field for workers is no Hollywood action film. Complicating the task of winning a fairer share are three paradoxes.

THREE PARADOXES

The first is the *paradox of corporate thrift*. Again, businesses are spending less on investments in equipment and training, and are also doing their best to keep wages and benefits low, all because the demand for the goods and services they sell is not growing very fast. For any business individually, this kind of thrift makes sense. But the paradox is that for businesses taken as a whole, it's counterproductive. Because if businesses are keeping down their own spending, and giving workers as little as possible, the overall result is to keep down the demand for goods and services. It's a vicious circle.

Handing another million dollars to a CEO is not a good way to stimulate the economy. True, some CEOs, like Tyco's Dennis Kozlowski, found creative ways to spend the money— on art, furniture, boats, and travel. But in general, rich people save most of their income. If you took a million dollars of executive pay and divided it among 1,000 poor families, you would get a lot more economic impact.

The second paradox is what University of Massachusetts economist James Crotty calls the *neoliberal paradox*. With slow global growth and increased global competition, it's become harder for most businesses to keep profits up. But at the same time, changes in the stock market mean that investors now demand consistently high profits. The growth of large institutional investors and the invention of the hostile takeover have made it possible for investors to threaten companies with takeover or destruction unless they generate high returns. Crotty points out that profit for nonfinancial corporations actually peaked in 1997. But corporations knew what would happen if they told their shareholders this bad news. In this context, the pressures for accounting games and even fraud became irresistible.

These first two paradoxes point out that the economy is far too important to let businesses run it. But when we think about how to take more control away from businesses, we run into the third paradox, the *Arkansas Traveler paradox*, named for an old song in which a traveler comes upon a man whose roof is leaking in a rainstorm. When the traveler asks him why he doesn't fix the roof, he says, "I can't fix it when it's raining." Asked why he doesn't then repair the roof when it's sunny, he replies, "When it's sunny, there's no need to fix it."

Similarly, when the economy is booming, workers have more economic leverage. Businesses run up against labor shortages, so they're more willing to make concessions to in order to ensure they can get the workers they need. It's a good time to organize a union, push for a higher minimum wage, or demand that employers provide a training program. Governments have the money to enforce regulations or to help pay for training.

But when the economy is booming, many workers don't see as much need to band together to defend their interests. Why form a union or lobby for a higher minimum wage when you can hop to a better paying job? Why push for a training program when even unskilled workers are getting jobs? The 1990s may not have amounted to a workers' paradise, but employment rates and wages were relatively edenic compared to the two decades that came before.

On the other hand, when the economy crashes, all of a sudden even the corporate media and mainstream politicians begin to focus on all the ways that business falls short. But when businesses are struggling for survival, they will fight desperately against any attempt to give workers a bigger share. The large numbers of unemployed job seekers put a damper on any attempts to organize unions or boost minimum wages. Governments face budget shortfalls, so they are not inclined to take on new activities.

The only way out of this box is not economic, but political. We have to build a movement that sees beyond the current situation in any given year. In the boom years, we have to remember all the problems of a business-dominated economy and use our economic leverage to strengthen institutions and business practices that help workers. In the bust years, like now, we have to keep in mind that economic resources will soon enough be growing again, and put in place rules that will more equitably distribute and effectively use them. We know what rules make a difference: the most important are strong wage floors and collective bargaining protections. By making businesses work under a better set of rules, we can actually help grow those resources by steering the economy out of the paradox of thrift and the neoliberal paradox.

If the problem is a raw deal, the solution is a new New Deal. The New Deal of the 1930s and 1940s saved U.S. capitalism from itself. It looks like we're going to have to do it again.

ARTICLE 7.3

September/October 2007

COMING CLEAN ON CLASS CONFLICT

BY JOHN MILLER

New evidence that American companies are having a hard time keeping labor costs under control raised worries about a pickup in inflation, sending stocks tumbling.

The Labor Department reported that the sum nonfarm businesses pay their workers for each unit of production rose at an annualized rate of 1.8% in the first quarter, sharply exceeding its initial estimate of 0.6%.

The jump in so-called unit labor costs stemmed from a combination of factors: sharper compensation growth, which was revised upward to 2.8% from 2.3%, and lower growth in productivity—or output per hour—which was revised down to 1% from 1.7%.

While strong growth in jobs and wages is good for workers, it raises the possibility that companies, unable to offset higher labor costs by increasing productivity, will try to pass those costs along to consumers, a trend that could fuel inflation and prompt the Federal Reserve to raise interest rates in response.

Concerns that the Fed might ride harder on the economic brakes contributed to yesterday's decline in stocks, market participants said.

The U.S. economy is coming off a decade-long boom in productivity growth. In 2002 and 2003, labor productivity surged at an average annual rate of almost 4%, then slowed to about 2.5% growth in 2004 and 2005. Since then, it has grown at an annualized rate of about 1.5%. Much of that decline is the natural result of the economy's slowdown: When economic growth slows faster than companies cut back on hiring and shifts, output per hour also slows.

—Wall Street Journal, *June 7, 2007*

The degree to which a unit labor costs index meets expectations is typically one of the most influential aspects of the [Bureau of Labor Statistics quarterly] report. ... Bond prices typically fall (yields rise) in reaction to higher-than-expected unit labor costs .... Stock prices may also fall. ... Alternatively, if unit labor costs become subdued, this can give a boost to stock and bond prices. Low growth rates of unit labor costs help reduce inflation pressure while potentially increasing corporate profits, thereby supporting stocks.

—Charles Schwab & Co., *"Guide to Economic Indicators,"* Sept. 28, 2006

Ever had any doubts that class conflict is what drives the economy? Check out the story the *Wall Street Journal* ran this June about how wage gains for workers will puncture the ebullience of the markets.

The *Journal* article describes explicitly how class conflict is driving the reaction of U.S. investors to gains made by ordinary workers:

> While strong growth in jobs and wages is good for workers, it raises the possibility that companies, unable to offset higher labor costs by increasing productivity, will try to pass those costs along to consumers, a trend that could fuel inflation and prompt the Federal Reserve to raise interest rates in response. ... Concerns that the Fed might ride harder on the economic brakes contributed to yesterday's decline in stocks.

This explanation departs entirely from the story found in most mainstream economics reporting: that we are all—workers and investors alike—on the same elevator, moving up or down in concert. Makes you wonder if reporters at the *Journal* have been sneaking off to read Marx's *Capital* on their lunch break.

Or take the "Guide to Economic Indicators" put out by Charles Schwab, one of the largest U.S. financial services corporations, to educate its investor clients. Schwab's document is even more explicit about the fact that deteriorating real wages for workers are what make for the positive fundamentals—rising productivity and declining unit labor costs, improved competitiveness, and low inflation—so prized by the markets. This is a reality that financial industry analysts, unlike many economists, have never felt the need to mask.

The Schwab guide explains the importance of "unit labor costs," the actual dollar costs firms pay for employees to make a unit of output, as follows: "Low growth rates of unit labor costs help reduce inflation pressure while potentially increasing corporate profits, thereby supporting stocks." Schwab's simple chart, reproduced above, could not make the point more clearly: rising wages *bad*; falling wages *good*.

THE REAL STORY

Bare bones, here is the class conflict that drives the story. Economic growth creates jobs, lowering unemployment. Low unemployment gives workers greater bargaining power to press for higher wages and benefits. Businesses can either absorb these higher labor costs by cutting profits, or pass them along by raising prices.

Either way, investors lose out. If their profits decline, corporations may pay their stockholders less in dividends and/or see their share prices fall. If prices rise, that inflation cuts into the real value of investor assets and may provoke the Federal Reserve to hike interest rates, dampening economic growth.

When the Labor Department published its revised first-quarter unit labor cost numbers on June 6, a larger than expected 1.8% jump in the unit labor costs of U.S. nonfarm businesses is what set off the financial alarm bells reported in the *Journal*. That day, the Dow Jones Industrial Average lost 129.7 points, or 1% of its value.

But were investors' fears justified? To the extent their concern was focused on the risk of higher inflation, perhaps not. Labor compensation does make up the largest chunk of business costs. Nonetheless, in recent years unit labor costs have ceased to correlate with inflation. When Jared Bernstein, labor economist at the Washington, D.C.-based Economic Policy Institute, tracked changes in unit labor costs and core inflation (price growth with volatile food and energy prices removed) from 1995 to 2006, he found the two to be "essentially unrelated."

Ironically, the new disconnect between unit labor costs and inflation may itself have something to do with class conflict. More than in the past, recent rises in unit labor costs reflect high-end compensation—those million-dollar bonuses paid out by investment banking firms, for instance. As Bernstein notes, businesses appear to be less likely to pass these bonuses through to consumers in the form of higher prices than they are the costs of wage increases for low- and mid-level workers. Why? No one is sure, but some economists speculate that executives may view oversize compensation packages for themselves and their friends as a kind of profit sharing rather than a wage cost.

LESS THAN MEETS THE EYE

Even with the recent gains in compensation that have rendered investment types apoplectic, most workers are hardly getting rich. Labor's share of national income (64.3%) remains at its lowest level in nearly a decade and well below its level at the start of the expansion in 2001. At the same time, corporate profits as a share of national income are at record levels.

These compensation gains have done little to improve the purchasing power of most workers. Hourly compensation in nonfarm businesses (the compensation measure that the Bureau of Labor Statistics uses to calculate unit labor costs) is up 8.9% after correcting for inflation since the current expansion began in 2001, which may sound impressive. But that measure includes bonuses, stock options, and the value of employee benefits, including health insurance and even employer 401(k) contributions. The Employment Cost Index for private industry, a similar measure that excludes the salaries of self-employed business owners and stock options, is up just 3.3% over the same period after correcting for inflation. And when benefits are excluded, wages and salaries are just a scant 0.6% higher today in real terms than when the expansion began six years ago, according to the Employment Cost Index.

In other words, most of the rise in the wage numbers that so worries Wall Street stems from outsize stock options and from higher health insurance costs—not from genuine wage gains for ordinary Americans.

These numbers not only unmask the class oppression that undergirds financial accumulation. They also reveal the utter unwillingness of the financial powers to share with workers any of the gains of economic growth that come from higher productivity, a mean-spiritedness disturbing even by capitalist standards.

But none of this should really be surprising. For Wall Street remains, as Woody Guthrie once put it, "the street that keeps the rest of us off Easy Street."

OUTSIZED OFFSHORE OUTSOURCING
THE SCOPE OF OFFSHORE OUTSOURCING GIVES SOME ECONOMISTS AND THE BUSINESS PRESS THE HEEBIE-JEEBIES.

BY JOHN MILLER

At a press conference introducing the 2004 *Economic Report of the President*, N. Gregory Mankiw, then head of President Bush's Council of Economic Advisors, assured the press that "Outsourcing is probably a plus for the economy in the long run [and] just a new way of doing international trade."

Mankiw's comments were nothing other than mainstream economics, as even Democratic Party-linked economists confirmed. For instance Janet Yellen, President Clinton's chief economist, told the *Wall Street Journal*, "In the long run, outsourcing is another form of trade that benefits the U.S. economy by giving us cheaper ways to do things." Nonetheless, Mankiw's assurances were met with derision from those uninitiated in the economics profession's free-market ideology. Sen. John Edwards (D-N.C.) asked, "What planet do they live on?" Even Republican House Speaker Dennis Hastert (Ill.) said that Mankiw's theory "fails a basic test of real economics."

Mankiw now jokes that "if the American Economic Association were to give an award for the Most Politically Inept Paraphrasing of Adam Smith, I would be a leading candidate." But he quickly adds, "the recent furor about outsourcing, and my injudiciously worded comments about the benefits of international trade, should not eclipse the basic lessons that economists have understood for more than two centuries."

In fact Adam Smith never said any such thing about international trade. In response to the way Mankiw and other economists distort Smith's writings, economist Michael Meeropol took a close look at what Smith actually said; he found that Smith used his invisible hand argument to favor domestic investment over far-flung, hard-to-supervise foreign investments. Here are Smith's words in his 1776 masterpiece, *The Wealth of Nations*:

> By preferring the support of domestic to that of foreign industry, he [the investor] intends only his own security; and by directing that industry in such a manner as its produce may be of the greatest value, he intends only his own gain, and he is in this, as in many other cases, led by an invisible hand to promote an end, which was no part of his intention.

Outsized offshore outsourcing, the shipping of jobs overseas to take advantage of low wages, has forced some mainstream economists and some elements of the business press to have second thoughts about "free trade." Many are convinced that the painful transition costs that hit before outsourcing produces any ultimate benefits may be the biggest political issue in economics for a generation. And some recognize, as Smith did, that there is no guarantee unfettered international trade will leave the participants better off even in the long run.

KEYNES'S REVENGE

Writing during the Great Depression of the 1930s, John Maynard Keynes, the preeminent economist of the twentieth century, prescribed government spending as a means of compensating for the instability of private investment. The notion of a mixed private/government economy, Keynes's prosthesis for the invisible hand of the market, guided U.S. economic policy from the 1940s through the 1970s.

It is only fitting that Paul Samuelson, the first Nobel Laureate in economics, and whose textbook introduced U.S. readers to Keynes, would be among the first mainstream economists to question whether unfettered international trade, in the context of massive outsourcing, would necessarily leave a developed economy such as that of the United States better off—even in the long run. In an influential 2004 article, Samuelson characterized the common economics wisdom about outsourcing and international trade this way:

> Yes, good jobs may be lost here in the short run. But ... the gains of the winners from free trade, properly measured, work out to exceed the losses of the losers. ... Never forget to tally the real gains of consumers alongside admitted possible losses of some producers. ... The gains of the American winners are big enough to more than compensate the losers.

Samuelson took on this view, arguing that this common wisdom is "dead wrong about [the] *necessary* surplus of winning over losing" [emphasis in the original]. In a rather technical paper, he demonstrated that free trade globalization can sometimes give rise to a situation in which "a productivity gain in one country can benefit that country alone, while permanently hurting the other country by reducing the gains from trade that are possible between the two countries."

Many in the economics profession do admit that it is hard to gauge whether intensified offshoring of U.S. jobs in the context of free-trade globalization will give more in winnings to the winners than it takes in losses from the losers. "Nobody has a clue about what the numbers are," as Robert C. Feenstra, a prominent trade economist, told *Business Week* at the time.

The empirical issues that will determine whether offshore outsourcing ultimately delivers, on balance, more benefits than costs, and to whom those benefits and costs will accrue, are myriad. First, how wide a swath of white-collar workers will see their wages reduced by competition from the cheap, highly skilled workers who are now becoming available around the world? Second, by how much will their wages drop? Third, will the U.S. workers thrown into the global labor pool end up losing more in lower wages than they gain in lower consumer prices? In that case, the benefits of increased trade would go overwhelmingly to employers. But even employers might lose out depending on the answer to a fourth question: Will cheap labor from abroad allow foreign employers to out-compete U.S. employers, driving down the prices of their products and lowering U.S. export earnings? In that case, not only workers, but the corporations that employ them as well, could end up worse off.

BIGGER THAN A BOX

Another mainstream Keynesian economist, Alan Blinder, former Clinton economic advisor and vice-chair of the Federal Reserve Board, doubts that outsourcing will be "immiserating" in the long run and still calls himself "a free-trader down to his toes." But Blinder is convinced that the transition costs will be large, lengthy, and painful before the United States experiences a net gain from outsourcing. Here is why.

First, rapid improvements in information and communications technology have rendered obsolete the traditional notion that manufactured goods, which can generally be boxed and shipped, are tradable, while services, which cannot be boxed, are not. And the workers who perform the services that computers and satellites have now rendered tradable will increasingly be found offshore, especially when they are skilled and will work for lower wages.

Second, another 1.5 billion or so workers—many in China, India, and the former Soviet bloc—are now part of the world economy. While most are low-skilled workers, some are not; and as Blinder says, a small percentage of 1.5 billion is nonetheless "a lot of willing and able people available to do the jobs that technology will move offshore." And as China and India educate more workers, offshoring of high-skill work will accelerate.

Third, the transition will be particularly painful in the United States because the U.S. unemployment insurance program is stingy, at least by first-world standards, and because U.S. workers who lose their jobs often lose their health insurance and pension rights as well.

How large will the transition cost be? "Thirty million to 40 million U.S. jobs are potentially offshorable," according to Blinder's latest estimates. "These include scientists,

> ### OFFSHORED? OUTSOURCED? CONFUSED?
>
> The terms "offshoring" and "outsourcing" are often used interchangeably, but they refer to distinct processes:
>
> Outsourcing—When a company hires another company to carry out a business function that it no longer wants to carry on in-house. The company that is hired may be in the same city or across the globe; it may be a historically independent firm or a spinoff of the first company created specifically to outsource a particular function.
>
> Offshoring or Offshore Outsourcing—When a company shifts a portion of its business operation abroad. An offshore operation may be carried out by the same company or, more typically, outsourced to a different one.

mathematicians and editors on the high end and telephone operators, clerks and typists on the low end."

Blinder arrived at these figures by creating an index that identifies how easy or hard it will be for a job to be physically or electronically "offshored." He then used the index to assess the Bureau of Labor Statistics' 817 U.S. occupational categories. Not surprisingly, Blinder classifies almost all of the 14.3 million U.S. manufacturing jobs as offshorable. But he also classifies more than twice that many U.S. service sector jobs as offshorable, including most computer industry jobs as well as many others, for instance, the 12,470 U.S. economists and the 23,790 U.S. multimedia artists and animators.

In total, Blinder's analysis suggests that 22% to 29% of the jobs held by U.S. workers in 2004 will be potentially offshorable within a decade or two, with nearly 8.2 million jobs in 59 occupations "highly offshorable." Table 1 provides a list of the broad occupational categories with 300,000 or more workers that Blinder considers potentially offshorable.

Mankiw dismissed Blinder's estimates of the number of jobs at risk to offshoring as "out of the mainstream." Indeed, Blinder's estimates are considerably larger than earlier ones. But these earlier studies either aim to measure the number of U.S. jobs that will be outsourced (as opposed to the number at risk of being outsourced), look at a shorter period of time, or have shortcomings that suggest they underestimate the number of U.S. jobs threatened by outsourcing. (See "Studying the Studies.")

GLOBAL ARBITRAGE

Low wages are the reason U.S. corporations outsource labor. Table 2 shows just how large the international wage differentials were for computer programmers in 2002. Programmers in the United States make wages nearly *ten times* those of their counterparts in India and the Philippines, for example.

Today, more and more white-collar workers in the United States are finding themselves in direct competition with the low-cost, well-trained, highly educated workers in Bangalore, Shanghai, and Eastern and Central Europe. These workers often use the same capital and technology and are no less productive than the U.S. workers they replace. They just get paid less.

This global labor arbitrage, as Morgan Stanley's chief economist Stephen Roach calls it, has narrowed international wage disparities in manufacturing, and now in services too, by unrelentingly pushing U.S. wages down toward international norms. ("Arbitrage" refers to transactions that yield a profit by taking advantage of a price differential for the same asset in different locations. Here, of course, the "asset" is wage labor of a certain skill level.) A sign of that pressure: about 70% of laid-off workers in the United States earn less three years later than they did at the time of the layoff; on average, those reemployed earn 10% less than they did before.

And it's not only laid-off workers who are hurt. A study conducted by Harvard labor economists Lawrence F. Katz, Richard B. Freeman, and George J. Borjas finds that every other worker with skills similar to those who were displaced also loses out. Every 1% drop in employment due to imports or factories gone abroad shaves 0.5% off the wages of the remaining workers in that occupation, they conclude.

Global labor arbitrage also goes a long way toward explaining the poor quality and low pay of the jobs the U.S. economy has created this decade, according to Roach. By dampening wage increases for an ever wider swath of the U.S. workforce, he argues, outsourcing has helped to drive a wedge between productivity gains and wage gains and to widen inequality in the United States. In the first four years of this decade, nonfarm productivity in the United States has recorded a cumulative increase of 13.3%—more than double the 5.9% rise in real compensation per hour over the same period. ("Compensation" includes wages, which have been stagnant for the average worker, plus employer spending on fringe benefits such as health insurance, which has risen even as, in many instances, the actual benefits have been cut back.) Roach reports that the disconnect between pay and productivity growth during the current economic expansion has been much greater in services than in manufacturing, as that sector weathers the powerful forces of global labor arbitrage for the first time.

TABLE 1: MAJOR OCCUPATIONS RANKED BY OFFSHORABILITY

Occupation	Category	Index Number	Number of Workers
Computer programmers	I	100	389,090
Telemarketers	I	95	400,860
Computer systems analysts	I	93	492,120
Billing and posting clerks and machine operators	I	90	513,020
Bookkeeping, accounting, and auditing clerks	I	84	1,815,340
Computer support specialists	I and II	92/68	499,860
Computer software engineers: Applications	II	74	455,980
Computer software engineers: Systems software	II	74	320,720
Accountants	II	72	591,311
Welders, cutters, solderers, and brazers	II	70	358,050
Helpers—production workers	II	70	528,610
First-line supervisors/managers of production and operating workers	II	68	679,930
Packaging and filling machine operators and tenders	II	68	396,270
Team assemblers	II	65	1,242,370
Bill and account collectors	II	65	431,280
Machinists	II	61	368,380
Inspectors, testers, sorters, samplers, and weighers	II	60	506,160
General and operations managers	III	55	1,663,810
Stock clerks and order fillers	III	34	1,625,430
Shipping, receiving, and traffic clerks	III	29	759,910
Sales managers	III	26	317,970
Business operations specialists, all other	IV	25	916,290

Source: Alan S. Blinder, "How Many U.S. Jobs Might Be Offshorable?" CEPS Working Paper #142, March 2007, figures from Bureau of Labor Statistics and author's judgments.

DOUBTS IN THE BUSINESS PRESS?!

Even in the business press, doubts that offshore outsourcing willy-nilly leads to economic improvement have become more acute. Earlier this summer, a *Business Week* cover story, "The Real Cost of Offshoring," reported that government statistics have underestimated the damage to the U.S. economy from offshore outsourcing. The problem is that since offshoring took off, *import* growth, adjusted for inflation, has been faster than the official numbers show. That means improvements in living standards, as well as corporate profits, depend more on cheap imports, and less on improving domestic productivity, than analysts thought.

Growing angst about outsourcing's costs has also prompted the business press to report favorably on remedies for the dislocation brought on by offshoring that deviate substantially from the non-interventionist, free-market playbook. Even the most unfazed pro-globalization types want to beef up trade adjustment assistance for displaced workers and strengthen the U.S. educational system. But both proposals are inadequate.

More education, the usual U.S. prescription for any economic problem, is off the mark here. Cheaper labor is available abroad up and down the job-skill ladder, so even the most rigorous education is no inoculation against the threat of offshore outsourcing. As Blinder emphasizes, it is the need for face-to-face contact that stops jobs from being shipped overseas, not the level of education necessary to perform them. Twenty years from now, home health aide positions will no doubt be plentiful in the United States; jobs for highly trained IT professionals may be scarce.

Trade adjustment assistance has until now been narrowly targeted at workers hurt by imports. Most new proposals would replace traditional trade adjustment assistance and unemployment insurance with a program for displaced workers that offers wage insurance to ease the pain of taking a lower-paying job and provides for portable health insurance and retraining. The pro-globalization research group McKinsey Global Institute (MGI), for example, claims that for as little as 4% to 5% of the amount they've saved in lower wages, companies could cover the wage losses of all laid-off workers once they are reemployed, paying them 70% of the wage differential between their old and new jobs (in addition to health care subsidies) for up to two years.

While MGI confidently concludes that this proposal will "go a long way toward relieving the current anxieties," other globalization advocates are not so sure. They recognize that economic anxiety is pervasive and that millions of white-collar workers now fear losing their jobs. Moreover, even if fears of actual job loss are overblown, wage insurance schemes do little to compensate for the downward pressure offshoring is putting on the wages of workers who have not been laid off.

Other mainstream economists and business writers go even further, calling for not only wage insurance but also

---

ATTRIBUTES OF JOBS OUTSOURCED

- No Face-to-Face Customer Servicing Requirement
- High Information Content
- Work Process is Telecommutable and Internet Enabled
- High Wage Differential with Similar Occupation in Destination Country
- Low Setup Barriers
- Low Social Networking Requirement

The McKinsey Global Institute (MGI), a research group known for its unabashedly favorable view of globalization, has done its best to put a positive spin on offshore outsourcing. Its 2003 study, which relied on the Forrester offshoring estimates, concluded that offshoring is already benefiting the U.S. economy. For instance, MGI calculates that for every dollar spent on a business process outsourced to India, the U.S. economy gains at least $1.12. The largest chunk—58 cents—goes back to the original employer in the form of cost savings, almost exclusively in the form of lower wages. In addition, 30% of Indian offshoring is actually performed by U.S. companies, so the wage savings translate into higher earnings for those companies. The study also argues that offshore outsourcing frees up U.S. workers to do other tasks.

A second MGI study, in 2005, surveyed dozens of companies in eight sectors, from pharmaceutical companies to insurers. The study predicted that multinational companies in the entire developed world will have located only 4.1 million service jobs in low-wage countries by 2008—a figure equal to only 1% of the total number of service jobs in developed countries.

But the MGI outsourcing studies have serious limitations. For instance, Blinder points out that MGI's analysis looks at a very short time frame, and that the potential for outsourcing in English-speaking countries such as the United States is higher than elsewhere, a fact lost in the MGI studies' global averages.

In their 2005 book Outsourcing America, published by the American Management Association, public policy professors Ron Hira and Anil Hira argue that MGI's 2003 report "should be viewed as a self-interested lobbying document that presents an unrealistically optimistic estimate of the impact of offshore outsourcing." For instance, most of the data for the report came from case studies conducted by MGI that are unavailable to the public and unsupported by any model. Moreover, the MGI analysis assumes that the U.S. economy will follow its long-term trend and create 3.5 million jobs a year, enough to quickly reemploy U.S. workers displaced by offshoring. But current U.S. job creation falls far short of that trend. A recent White House fact sheet brags that the U.S. economy has created 8.3 million jobs since August 2003. Still, that is less than 2.1 million jobs a year, and only 1.8 million jobs over the last 12 months.

MGI's Farrell is right about one thing. "If the economy were stronger," she says, "there wouldn't be such a negative feeling" about work getting offshored. But merely assuming high job growth doesn't make it so.

> ## STUDYING THE STUDIES
>
> When economist Alan Blinder raised alarm bells in 2006 about the potentially large-scale offshoring of U.S. jobs, his results were inevitably compared to earlier research on offshore outsourcing. Three studies have been especially influential. The 2002 study (revised in 2004) by Forrester Research, a private, for-profit market research firm, which estimated that 3.3 million U.S. service sector jobs would move offshore by 2015, caused perhaps the biggest media stir. It was picked up by Business Week and the Wall Street Journal, and hyped by Lou Dobbs, the CNN business-news anchor and outspoken critic of offshoring.
>
> Forrester researcher John McCarthy developed his estimate by poring over newspaper clippings and Labor Department statistics on 505 white-collar occupations and then making an educated guess about how many jobs would be shipped offshore by 2015.
>
> The Forrester study projects actual offshoring, not the number of jobs at risk of offshoring, so its estimate is rightfully lower than Blinder's. But the ample possibilities for technological change between now and 2015 convince Blinder that the Forrester estimate is nonetheless too low.
>
> A 2003 study by University of California economists Ashok Bardhan and Cynthia Kroll estimated that about 11% of all U.S. jobs in 2001 were vulnerable to offshoring. Bradhan and Kroll applied the "outsourceability attributes" listed in Figure 1 to occupations where at least some outsourcing either has already taken place or is being planned.
>
> Blinder considers the Bardhan and Kroll estimate for 2001 to be comparable to his estimate that 20% to 30% of the employed labor force will be at risk of offshore outsourcing within the next ten to twenty years, especially considering that Bardhan and Kroll do not allow for outsourcing to spread beyond the occupations it is currently affecting. This is like "looking only slightly beyond the currently-visible tip of the iceberg," according to Blinder.

TABLE 2: AVERAGE SALARIES OF PROGRAMMERS

Country	Salary Range
Poland and Hungary	$4,800 to $8,000
India	$5,880 to $11,000
Philippines	$6,564
Malaysia	$7,200
Russian Federation	$5,000 to $7,500
China	$8,952
Canada	$28,174
Ireland	$23,000 to $34,000
Israel	$15,000 to $38,000
USA	$60,000 to $80,000

Source: CIO magazine, November 2002, from Merrill Lynch Smart Access Survey.

taxes on the winners from globalization. And globalization has produced big winners: on Wall Street, in the corporate boardroom, and among those workers in high demand in the global economy.

Economist Matthew Slaughter, who recently left President Bush's Council of Economic Advisers, told the *Wall Street Journal*, "Expanding the political support for open borders [for trade] requires making a radical change in fiscal policy." He proposes eliminating the Social Security-Medicare payroll tax on the bottom half of workers—roughly, those earning less than $33,000 a year—and making up the lost revenue by raising the payroll tax on higher earners.

The goal of these economists is to thwart a crippling political backlash against trade. As they see it, "using the tax code to slice the apple more evenly is far more palatable than trying to hold back globalization with policies that risk shrinking the economic apple."

Some even call for extending global labor arbitrage to CEOs. In a June 2006 *New York Times* op-ed, equity analyst Lawrence Orlowski and NYU assistant research director Florian Lengyel argued that offshoring the jobs of U.S. chief executives would reduce costs and release value to shareholders by bringing the compensation of U.S. CEOs (on average 170 times greater than the compensation of average U.S. workers in 2004) in line with CEO compensation in Britain (22 times greater) and in Japan (11 times greater).

Yet others focus on the stunning lack of labor mobility that distinguishes the current era of globalization from earlier ones. Labor markets are becoming increasingly free and flexible under globalization, but labor enjoys no similar freedom of movement. In a completely free market, the foreign workers would come here to do the work that is currently being outsourced. Why aren't more of those workers coming to the United States? Traditional economists Gary Becker and Richard Posner argue the answer is clear: an excessively restrictive immigration policy.

ONSHORE AND OFFSHORE SOLIDARITY

Offshoring is one of the last steps in capitalism's conversion of the "physician, the lawyer, the priest, the poet, the man of science, into its paid wage laborers," as Marx and Engels put it in the *Communist Manifesto* 160 years ago. It has already done much to increase economic insecurity in the workaday world and has become, Blinder suggests, the number one economic issue of our generation.

Offshoring has also underlined the interdependence of workers across the globe. To the extent that corporations now organize their business operations on a global scale, shifting work around the world in search of low wages, labor organizing must also be global in scope if it is to have any hope of building workers' negotiating strength.

Yet today's global labor arbitrage pits workers from different countries against each other as competitors, not allies. Writing about how to improve labor standards, economists Ajit Singh and Ann Zammit of the South Centre, an Indian nongovernmental organization, ask the question, "On what could workers of the world unite" today? Their answer is that faster economic growth could indeed be a positive-sum game from which both the global North and the global South could gain. A pick-up in the long-term rate of growth of the world economy would generate higher employment, increasing wages and otherwise improving labor standards in both regions. It should also make offshoring less profitable and less painful.

The concerns of workers across the globe would also be served by curtailing the ability of multinational corporations to move their investment anywhere, which weakens the bargaining power of labor both in advanced countries and in the global South. Workers globally would also benefit if their own ability to move between countries was enhanced. The combination of a new set of rules to limit international capital movements and to expand labor mobility across borders, together with measures to ratchet up economic growth and thus increase worldwide demand for labor, would alter the current process of globalization and harness it to the needs of working people worldwide.

Resources: Alan S. Blinder, "Fear of Offshoring," CEPS Working Paper #119, Dec. 2005; Alan S. Blinder, "How Many U.S. Jobs Might Be Offshorable?" CEPS Working Paper #142, March 2007; N. Gregory Mankiw and P. Swagel, "The Politics and Economics of Offshore Outsourcing," Am. Enterprise Inst. Working Paper #122, 12/7/05; "Offshoring: Is It a Win-Win Game?" McKinsey Global Institute, August 2003; Diane Farrell et al., "The Emerging Global Labor Market, Part 1: The Demand for Talent in Services," McKinsey Global Institute, June 2005; Ashok Bardhan and Cynthia Kroll, "The New Wave of Outsourcing," Research Report #113, Fisher Center for Real Estate and Urban Economics, Univ. of Calif., Berkeley, Fall 2003; Paul A. Samuelson, "Where Ricardo and Mill Rebut and Confirm Arguments of Mainstream Economists Supporting Globalization," J Econ Perspectives 18:3, Summer 2004; Alan S. Blinder, "Free Trade's Great, but Offshoring Rattles Me," *Washington Post*, 5/6/07; Michael Mandel, "The Real Cost of Offshoring," *BusinessWeek*, 6/18/07; Aaron Bernstein, "Shaking Up Trade Theory," *BusinessWeek*, 12/6/04; David Wessel, "The Case for Taxing Globalization's Big Winners," *Wall Street Journal*, 6/14/07; Bob Davis, "Some Democratic Economists Echo Mankiw on Outsourcing," *WSJ*; N. Gregory Mankiw, "Outsourcing Redux," gregmankiw.blogspot.com/2006/05/outsourcing-redux; David Wessel and Bob Davis, "Pain From Free Trade Spurs Second Thoughts," *WSJ*, 3/30/07; Ajit Singh and Ann Zammit, "On What Could Workers of the World Unite? Economic Growth and a New Global Economic Order," from *The Global Labour Standards Controversy: Critical Issues For Developing Countries*, South Centre, 2000; Michael Meeropol, "Distorting Adam Smith on Trade," *Challenge*, July/Aug 2004.

ARTICLE 7.5

September/October 2006

THE RELATIONSHIP OF UNEMPLOYMENT AND INFLATION

BY RAMAA VASUDEVAN

Dear Dr. Dollar:
Back in first-year economics we learned that there is a tradeoff between unemployment and inflation, so you can't really have both low inflation and low unemployment at the same time. Do economists still consider that to be true?
—Edith Bross, Cambridge, Mass.

The trade-off between inflation and unemployment was first reported by A. W. Phillips in 1958—and so has been christened the Phillips curve. The simple intuition behind this trade-off is that as unemployment falls, workers are empowered to push for higher wages. Firms try to pass these higher wage costs on to consumers, resulting in higher prices and an inflationary buildup in the economy. The trade-off suggested by the Phillips curve implies that policymakers can target low inflation rates or low unemployment, but not both. During the 1960s, monetarists emphasized price stability (low inflation), while Keynesians more often emphasized job creation.

The experience of so-called stagflation in the 1970s, with simultaneously high rates of both inflation and unemployment, began to discredit the idea of a stable trade-off between the two. In place of the Phillips curve, many economists began to posit a "natural rate of unemployment."

If unemployment were to fall below this "natural" rate, however slightly, inflation would begin to accelerate. Under the "natural rate of unemployment" theory (also called the Non-Accelerating Inflation Rate of Unemployment, or NAIRU), instead of choosing between higher unemployment and higher inflation, policymakers were told to focus on ensuring that the economy remained at its "natural" rate: the challenge was to accurately estimate its level and to steer the economy toward growth rates that maintain price stability, no matter what the corresponding level of unemployment.

The NAIRU has been extremely difficult to pin down in practice. Not only are estimates of it notoriously imprecise, the rate itself evidently changes over time. In the United States, estimates of the NAIRU rose from about 4.4% in the 1960s, to 6.2% in the 1970s, and further to 7.2% in the 1980s. This trend reversed itself in the 1990s, as officially reported unemployment fell. In the latter half of the 1990s, U.S. inflation remained nearly dormant at around 3%, while unemployment fell to around 4.6%. In the later Clinton years many economists warned that if unemployment was brought any lower, inflationary pressures might spin out of control. But growth in these years did not spill over into accelerating inflation. The United States, apparently, had achieved the Goldilocks state—everything just right!

What sustained this combination of low inflation and low unemployment? Explanations abound: a productivity boom, the high rates of incarceration of those who would otherwise fall within the ranks of the unemployed, the openness of the U.S. economy to world trade and competition, among others.

The full story, however, has to do with class conflict and the relatively weak position of workers in the 1990s. Both the breakdown of the Phillips curve in the 1970s and the recent "disappearance" of the natural rate of unemployment are in essence a reflection of institutional and political changes that affect the bargaining strength of working people—in other words, their ability to organize effective unions and establish a decent living wage.

Following the Reagan offensive against trade unions, workers' power fell dramatically. Consequently, unionization rates and the real value of the minimum wage each fell precipitously between the late 1970s and the 1990s. The period of stagflation, in contrast, had been one of labor militancy and rising wages. (Although "stagflation" has a negative ring, by many measures nonsupervisory workers—i.e., the vast majority of the U.S. labor force—fared better in the economy of the early- to mid-1970s than they do today, even after the long 1990s economic expansion.) Labor's weaker position in the 1990s meant that despite low unemployment, workers were not able to win higher wages that would have spurred inflation.

The long period of stable prices and low interest rates in the United States now seems to be coming to a close. The cost of the Iraq War and rising oil prices, among other factors, have fueled expectations of a resurgence of inflation. At the same time, the near jobless recovery from the last recession might suggest that the "natural rate" of unemployment is on the rise again—and that we are witnessing yet another twist in the strange history of the Phillips curve!

With inflation rising (albeit slowly, and still relatively mild at around 4.2%), some business sectors will no doubt begin clamoring for tighter monetary policies that sacrifice job-creation and wage growth by slowing the economy's growth. But these fears of inflation are probably misplaced. A moderate rate of inflation is conducive to the growth of real investment, and in the context of a decades-long squeeze on workers' wage share, there is room to expand employment without setting off a wage-price spiral. What workers need is not greater fiscal and monetary austerity, but rather a revival of a Keynesian program of "employment targeting" that would sustain full employment and empower workers to push for higher wages. It's not likely, however, that the owners of capital and their political allies would sit idly by were such a program to be enacted.

HOT COMMODITIES, STUFFED MARKETS, AND EMPTY BELLIES
WHAT'S BEHIND HIGHER FOOD PRICES?

BY BEN COLLINS

Since 2003, prices of basic agricultural commodities such as corn, wheat, soybeans, and rice have skyrocketed worldwide, threatening to further impoverish hundreds of millions of the world's poor.

Shifts in fundamental supply and demand factors for food grains have undoubtedly contributed to higher food prices. Prominent among these shifts are the increasing diversion of food crops for biofuel production in the United States and Europe; sustained drought and water scarcity in Australia's wheat-growing regions; flooding in the U.S. grain belt; rising prices for oil and fertilizer worldwide; and the adoption of European and American meat-rich diets by the growing middle classes throughout Asia.

On top of these recent developments, long-term threats to worldwide agricultural output have eroded the world food system's resilience in the face of changing supply and demand. Although decades in the making, a loss of agricultural capacity worldwide caused by soil depletion, climate change, water scarcity, and urbanization has begun to take its toll on food production. Moreover, half a century of import restrictions and cheap agricultural exports by wealthy countries has devastated domestic food production capacity in poorer countries, forcing many countries that were once self-sufficient to rely on imported food from the world market.

At the same time, however, the growing presence of buy-and-hold investors in commodity markets has prompted heated debate among commodity traders, economists, and politicians over other possible causes of higher commodity prices apart from supply and demand shifts.

Since 2001, the declining value of the U.S. dollar, low U.S. interest rates, weak stock market returns, and accelerating inflation have drawn investment dollars away from stocks and into non-traditional investments such as commodities. This flight to perceived safety in commodity markets turned into a stampede in 2007 and early 2008, as a credit-induced financial crisis in the United States compounded these existing stresses on global financial markets.

Rising commodity prices and financial speculation on food are not new phenomena. The 1970s saw a similar rise in commodity prices in the United States, and in the 1920s, U.S. investors formed commodity pools to bet on commodity price movements. But the quantity and liquidity of money flowing through today's global markets is unprecedented in human history. The current commodities boom could be a sign of looming agricultural scarcity, or it may prove to be a short-lived speculative bubble that will deflate over the next few months or years. But regardless of where agricultural commodity prices are headed, the boom has already begun to transform how food is financed, grown, and sold, and may dramatically change how people around the world eat (or don't).

COMMODITY INVESTMENT GOES RETAIL

Commodity exchanges exist as a mechanism for the producers and consumers of grains, energy, and livestock to transfer risk to financial institutions and other traders. For example, wheat farmers might seek to reduce the risk of price fluctuations by selling a contract for the future delivery of their wheat crop on a commodity exchange. This futures contract will guarantee a price for the farmer selling the contract, enabling them to pay for their planting costs, and avoid the risk that the price of wheat may decrease between the date they sell the contract and the date they agree to deliver the wheat. Food giants such as Kraft and Nabisco, as well as smaller bakers and grain consumers, typically purchase commodity futures contracts to avoid the opposite risk—that the price of their raw materials may increase in the future. (Commodity markets also trade "spot" contracts, which entitle the purchaser to the immediate delivery of a commodity.)

Because producers and consumers seek to reduce risk, they function as so-called hedgers in commodity markets. In contrast, commercial trading firms and other speculators bet on the price of a commodity rising or falling, buying and selling futures contracts frequently in order to profit from short-term changes in their prices.

Since 2001, commodity funds have gained in popularity as a mechanism for institutions and individuals to profit from increases in commodity prices. These funds purchase commodity futures contracts in order to simulate ownership of a commodity. By periodically rolling over commodity futures contracts prior to their maturity date and reinvesting the proceeds in new contracts, the funds allow investors to gain investment returns equivalent to the change in price of a single commodity, or an "index" of several commodities (hence the name "index investor").

Investors in these commodity index funds include public pension funds, university endowments, and even individual investors, through mutual funds, for example. Although these investors are similar to traditional commodity speculators in that both seek to profit from changes in price, traditional speculators zero in on short-term price shifts, while index investors are almost exclusively long-term buyers betting on higher commodity prices in the future.

Some observers have argued that index investors themselves may have pushed already-high prices of commodities even higher. Hedge fund manager Michael Masters testified to the U.S. Senate that the total holdings of commodity index investors on regulated U.S. exchanges have increased from $13 billion in 2003 to nearly $260 billion as of March 2008. And as of April 2008, index investors owned approximately 35% of all corn futures contracts on regulated exchanges in the United States, 42% of all soybean contracts, and 64% of all wheat contracts, compared to minimal holdings in 2001. As Masters emphasized, these are immense commodity holdings. The wheat contracts, for example, are good for the delivery of 1.3 billion bushels of wheat, equivalent to twice the United States' annual wheat consumption.

Index fund managers have defended against charges that commodity index investment contributes to higher prices, arguing that because index funds never take delivery on their futures contracts, they simulate commodity price shifts for their investors without affecting the price of the underlying commodity. Some economists have also expressed skepticism that investment demand has driven commodity prices higher. Paul Krugman of Princeton University has noted that there is no evidence of "the usual telltale signs of a speculative price boom" such as physical hoarding of commodities. Furthermore, Krugman and others have pointed to non-exchange traded commodities such as iron ore that have also experienced rapid price increases during recent years, arguing that fundamental supply and demand factors, not investors, are to blame for higher commodity prices.

Other economists and commodity market observers have argued that despite price increases in non-exchange traded commodities, and an absence of physical hoarding, the recent flood of money into commodity markets has altered the balance between speculators and hedgers, leading to higher prices and greater price volatility. Mack Frankfurter, a commodities trading advisor at Cervino Capital Management, suggests that the influx of commodity index investors has transformed commodity futures from tools for risk management to long-term investments, "causing a self-perpetuating feedback loop of ever higher prices."

One reason the precise impact of index investors on commodity prices is difficult to determine is that the U.S. commodity trading regulator, the Commodity Futures Trading Commission (CFTC), does not collect data on so-called "over-the-counter" commodity trading—that is, trading on unregulated markets—even though the agency estimated that 85% of commodity index investment takes place on these markets. Because Masters's data on the holdings of commodity index investors only include the 15% of index investor contracts that are held on CFTC-regulated exchanges, total commodity index investor holdings may be much higher than his estimates.

In testimony that warned of the influence of these unregulated markets on commodity prices, Michael Greenberger, the former head of the CFTC's Division of Trading and Markets, estimated that if unregulated trading of energy and agricultural commodities were eliminated, the price of oil would drop by 25% to 50% "overnight." If Greenberger is correct, the effect on food commodity prices would likely be similar. However, index investment is just one of many avenues through which money can enter commodity markets, making it difficult to assess the impact of index investors without taking into account the recent deregulation of U.S. commodity markets that has facilitated the current boom in food and energy investments.

COMMODITY TRADING REGULATION, ENRON-STYLE

Commodity index investment is deeply intertwined with the growth of unregulated commodity trading authorized by the Commodity Futures Modernization Act of 2000. Before 2000, U.S. commodity futures contracts were traded exclusively on regulated exchanges under the oversight of the CFTC. Traders were required to disclose their holdings of each commodity and adhere to strict position limits, which set a maximum number of futures contracts that an individual institution could hold. These regulations were intended to prevent market manipulation by traders who might otherwise attempt to build up concentrated holdings of futures contracts in order to manipulate the price of a commodity.

The 2000 law effectively deregulated commodity trading in the United States by exempting over-the-counter commodity trading outside of regulated exchanges from CFTC oversight. Soon after the bill was passed, several unregulated commodity exchanges opened for trading, allowing investors, hedge funds, and investment banks to trade commodities futures contracts without any position limits, disclosure requirements, or regulatory oversight. Since then, unregulated over-the-counter commodity trading has grown exponentially. The total value of all over-the-counter commodity contracts was estimated to be $9 trillion at the end of 2007, or nearly twice the value of the $4.78 trillion in commodity contracts traded on regulated U.S. exchanges.

Once these unregulated commodity markets were created, energy traders and hedge funds began to use them to place massive bets on commodity prices. Enron famously exploited deregulated electricity markets in 2001, when the firm managed to generate unheard-of profits by using its trading operations to effectively withhold electricity and charge extortionate rates from power grids in California and other western states.

Although Enron went bankrupt later that year, the hedge fund Amaranth later exploited unregulated natural gas markets prior to its 2006 collapse. The fund had been heavily invested in complicated bets on the price of natural gas, borrowing eight times its assets to trade natural gas futures, and lost $6.5 billion when natural gas prices moved in the wrong direction. One month prior to Amaranth's collapse, the New York Mercantile Exchange (NYMEX), which is regulated by the CFTC, asked Amaranth to reduce its huge natural gas position. Amaranth reduced its position at NYMEX's request, but purchased identical positions on the unregulated InterContinental Exchange, where its transactions were invisible to regulators until the fund finally collapsed.

Amaranth's implosion demonstrated the ineffectiveness of regulating some commodity exchanges but not others. Thanks to the Commodity Futures Modernization Act, traders could flout position limits and disclosure rules with impunity, simply by re-routing trades to unregulated exchanges. Although index investment in commodities does not typically involve white-knuckle, leveraged bets on a single commodity's short-term performance, index investment was made possible by the same deregulated environment exploited by Amaranth and Enron. Like Amaranth, commodity index investors commonly purchase futures contracts on unregulated markets when they exceed CFTC position limits on futures contracts for a particular commodity. And other financial actors such as investment banks, hedge funds, or even the sovereign wealth funds of other countries may also be heavily invested in these over-the-counter commodity contracts, but since this trading is unregulated and unreported, the holders of these $9 trillion worth of contracts remain anonymous.

This year, the CFTC has faced intense scrutiny from investors, politicians, farmers, and agricultural traders over the unprecedented volatility and price increases of several agricultural and energy commodities traded on U.S. exchanges. A lively CFTC roundtable on commodity markets in April appeared to confirm arguments made by Frankfurter, Greenberger, Masters, and other critics of commodity index investment. Representatives for farmers, grain elevator operators, and commercial bankers at the hearing repeatedly stressed that commodity markets were "broken," while the only pleas for calm came from CFTC economists and representatives for index investors and the financial industry. Unlike index investors, farmers have not benefited greatly from higher commodity prices, because extremely high levels of market volatility have made it difficult for some farmers to finance crop planting. National Farmers Union president Tom Buis sounded a particularly dire warning about the consequences of tight commodity supplies and burgeoning index investment demand: "We've got a train wreck coming in agriculture that's bigger than anything else we've seen."

Following these warnings from farmers and food producers about the presence of index investors in commodity markets, the CFTC's acting chair publicly acknowledged the ongoing debate over "whether the massive amount of money coming into the markets is overwhelming the system."

Despite this admission, Greenberger, the former CFTC official, remains skeptical of the agency's capacity and willingness to regulate commodity markets effectively. He urged Congress and the Federal Trade Commission to circumvent the CFTC's authority and eliminate unregulated over-the-counter commodity trading. Recently, faced with strong criticism from Congress, the CFTC retreated further from its claim that commodity markets are functioning normally. A CFTC commissioner admitted: "We didn't have the data that we needed to make the statements that we made, and the data we did have didn't support our declarative statements. If we were so right, why the heck are we doing a study now?"

THE CONSEQUENCES OF FINANCIALIZING FOOD

Facing political pressure by constituents over high oil and food prices, several members of Congress have sponsored legislation that would bar index investors from commodity markets. One bill proposed by Sen. Joseph Lieberman (Ind-Conn.) would prohibit public and private pension funds with more than $500 million in assets from trading in commodity futures, and other bills would limit the maximum number of futures contracts an index investor could hold. These bills may stem the flood of money from index investors into commodities, but comprehensive reform is needed to reverse the Commodity Futures Modernization Act's authorization of over-the-counter commodity trading. Absent an outright repeal of this so-called "Enron loophole," energy and agricultural commodities will continue to be traded outside the reach of government regulation, making future Enron- and Amaranth-style market disruptions inevitable.

Ultimately, eliminating unregulated commodity trading cannot address the fundamental causes of higher agricultural prices. Even if speculative buying is curtailed, supply and demand factors such as falling crop yields, destructive trade policies, and the growing use of biofuels have likely brought the age of cheap food to an end. However, if the critics of commodity index investment are correct, then these investors have amplified recent food price shocks and are needlessly contributing to the impoverishment of the world's poorest citizens. Even though commodity market transparency and regulatory oversight will not solve the global food crisis, eliminating unregulated commodity trading can help resolve the debate over the effects of index investors on commodity prices and restore the accountability of commodity markets to the social interests they were originally established to serve.

Sources: Michael Masters, testimony before the Committee on Homeland Security and Government Affairs, United States Senate, May 20, 2008; Daniel P. Collins, "CFTC to up spec limits," *Futures*, May 1, 2005; Paul Krugman, "Fuels on the Hill," *New York Times*, June 27, 2008; Michael Frankfurter, *The Mysterious Case of the Commodity Conundrum, Securitization of Commodities, and Systemic Concerns*, Parts 1-3, www.marketoracle.co.uk; Michael Frankfurter and Davide Accomazzo, "Is Managed Futures an Asset Class? The Search for the Beta of Commodity Futures," December 31, 2007, *Graziadio Business Report*; "Regulator Admits to Futures Tracking Volatility," Associated Press, June 4, 2008; Commodity Futures Trading Commission, *CFTC Announces Agricultural Market Initiatives*. June 3, 2008; Michael Greenberger, testimony before the Committee on Commerce, Science, and Transportation, United States Senate, June 3, 2008; Sinclair Stewart and Paul Waldie. "Who is responsible for the global food crisis?" *Globe and Mail*, May 30, 2008; Commodity Futures Trading Commission, *Agricultural Markets Roundtable*, April 22, 2008; Ann Davis, "Commodities Regulator Under Fire—CFTC Scrutinized As Congress Looks Into Oil-Price Jump," *Wall Street Journal*, July 7, 2008; Ed Wallace, "ICE, ICE, Baby," *Houston Chronicle*, May 19, 2008; Laura Mandaro, "Lieberman plans would bar funds from commodities," *Marketwatch*, June 18, 2008; "Our Confusing Economy, Explained," *Fresh Air*, April 3, 2008, www.npr.org.

CHAPTER 8
PERSPECTIVES ON MACROECONOMIC POLICY

INTRODUCTION

A few years back, political economist Bob Sutcliffe developed a sure-fire economic indicator that he called the Marx/Keynes ratio—the ratio of references to Karl Marx to references to John Maynard Keynes in Paul Samuelson's *Economics*, the best-selling introductory economics textbook during the decades following World War II. In a recession or a period of sluggish economic growth, the Marx/Keynes ratio would climb, as social commentators and even economists fretted over the future of capitalism. In economic booms, however, Marx's predictions of the collapse of capitalism disappeared from the pages of Samuelson's textbook, while the paeans to Keynesian demand-management policies multiplied.

Today Sutcliffe's ratio wouldn't work very well. Marx has been pushed off the pages of most introductory macroeconomics textbooks altogether, and even Keynes has been given only a minor role. Mainstream textbooks now favor the "New Classical" economics, which depicts the private economy as inherently stable and self-regulating, and dismiss Keynesian demand-management policies as ineffectual or counterproductive. Our authors disagree. In this chapter, they reintroduce schools of thought that have been removed from economics textbooks in recent decades and critically assess New Classical economics.

John Miller and Gina Neff start with a down-to-earth account of New Classical "rational expectations" models, in which markets clear instantaneously and bungling government bureaucrats always make a mess of things. Drawing on the writings of Keynesian and New Keynesian economists, Miller and Neff argue that rational expectations models are contradicted by the historical record, which shows that

bigger government has brought milder, not more severe, business cycle fluctuations (Article 8.1).

Robert Pollin (Article 8.2) attacks the underpinnings of the neoliberal policy prescription for the global economy. As he sees it, the unfettered globalization of free markets will be unable to resolve three basic problems: an ever-larger reserve army of the unemployed that reduces the bargaining power of workers in all countries (the Marx problem); the inherent instability and volatility of investment and financial markets (the Keynes problem); and the erosion of the protections of the welfare state (the Polanyi problem).

Alejandro Reuss takes a close look at what Keynes actually had to say about the efficacy of monetary policy and fiscal policy in his most famous book, *The General Theory*. Keynes argued that when short-term interest rates fall to zero, as they did during the Great Depression and again earlier this year, traditional monetary policy could not spark economic growth. But, as Reuss points out, Keynes also allowed that the monetary authorities could overcome those limitations by directly buying up long-term bonds and lowering their interest rates, much as the Bernanke Federal Reserve is now doing (Article 8.3). Nonetheless, Keynes remained a strong advocate of fiscal policy—especially government spending, as Reuss documents in his next article. Keynes challenged "the Treasury view" that government spending could not get the economy going because it would "crowd out" private investment, the same argument today's conservatives have invoked against the Obama stimulus package (Article 8.4).

Reuss also contributes a primer on Marxist economics. Marx rejected the idea of a self-equilibrating economy, and argued that capitalism was inherently dynamic and unstable. Reuss describes some of Marx's key ideas, including the nature of capitalist exploitation, and what Marx saw as two ingredients of an eventual crisis of capitalism: overproduction and the falling rate of profit (Article 8.5).

Randy Albelda offers a feminist analysis of poverty and gender. Feminist economists have illuminated the ways in which having and caring for children alters the economic status of women—including those who are not mothers but are still relegated to poorly paid care-giving jobs. Feminist economists, argues Albelda, provide the best understanding of the obstacles low-income families face and the options that might improve their position in today's economy (Article 8.6).

> **KEY TO COLANDER**
>
> E = Economics   M = Macroeconomics
>
> These articles fit with chapters E6, E26, E29, E32, E35; or M6, M9, M10, M12, M15, M16 - M18.
>
> Articles 8.1 - 8.5 cover some important theoretical issues in Macroeconomics as to Heterodox schools of economic thought.
>
> From a critique of "Lucas Critique" through Keynes, Marx and Feminist Economics there is plenty here to flesh out Colander's text.

DISCUSSION QUESTIONS

1. (Article 8.1) How do classical economists argue that macroeconomies are inherently stable, and that government intervention is ineffective or counterproductive? Are their arguments convincing?
2. (Article 8.1) Why are Keynesians convinced that markets don't clear instantaneously, and that government intervention can and must stabilize market economies? Evaluate the evidence for their position.
3. (Article 8.2) Summarize the Marx, Keynes, and Polanyi problems. Why does Pollin think that neoliberal globalization policies will be unable to resolve them?
4. (Article 8.3) What do the terms "fiscal policy," "automatic stabilizer," "cyclical deficit," and "federal deficit" mean? How do they relate to Keynesian policy-making?
5. (Article 8.3) What is a liquidity trap and how does it render monetary policy ineffective? How might monetary authorities counteract a liquidity trap?
6. (Article 8.4) Why does Keynes think that the crowding-out argument (or the Treasury view) is mistaken? And how might Keynes respond to the arguments today's conservatives have leveled against the Obama stimulus package?
7. (Article 8.5) In Marxist theory, how is a dynamic capitalist economy felled by instability? What roles do a "falling rate of profit," a "reserve army of the unemployed," and "overproduction" play in Marx's theory of how capitalism will fall into a crisis? Do you think today's macroeconomy displays any of those tendencies?
8. (Article 8.6) How does feminist economics' focus on gender challenge other theories of poverty? How are feminist theories of poverty different from Keynesian, Marxist, Institutionalist, and neoclassical analyses?

THE REVENGE OF THE CLASSICS

BY JOHN MILLER AND GINA NEFF

Nineteen ninety-five was not a good year for the welfare state. A Gingrich-led Congress attempted to pull the plug on universal entitlements for the poor, from welfare to Medicaid. And the Royal Swedish Academy of Science awarded the Nobel Prize in economics to Robert Lucas, a 58-year-old University of Chicago economist, for his "insights into the difficulties of using economic policy to control the economy."

Using sophisticated mathematics and economic models, Lucas has persuaded much of the economics profession that the economic policies John Maynard Keynes developed to combat the Great Depression—the economic underpinnings of the welfare state and the mixed economy—are ineffective.

What would Lucas do instead? Forsake those policies, dismantle the welfare state, and embrace the market. That was a job that, back in the mid-1990s, Gingrich and his crowd seemed only too happy to take up. They were glad to join forces with a Federal Reserve Board (the "Fed") already under the influence of the conservative counterrevolution in macroeconomics, led initially by Milton Friedman, another University of Chicago monetary theorist, and then by Lucas.

The Fed has accepted the futility of using monetary policy to promote long-run employment, leaving inflation alone as the ultimate target of its policies. In addition, the Fed's practice of making early announcements of changes in monetary policy, which is probably a good thing, can be directly attributed to Lucas. He has argued that unannounced changes provoke instability in the private sector instead of muting it.

Lucas and his school of followers call themselves New Classical economists. Like the classical economists who predated Keynes, these modern conservatives believe the economy possesses powerful self-correcting forces that guarantee full employment. Their vision of a stable market economy rests on three building blocks: rational expectations, market clearing, and imperfect information.

Let's look first at rational expectations, a notion which does seem rational enough. After all, every one of our economic actions is directed toward the future. Using whatever economic information we can get our hands on about prices, growth, and other economic activity, we predict our economic future. And usually we are good at it. When fellow workers are getting laid off at the company we are employed in, for instance, chances are that buying an expensive house is not at the top of our to-do list.

When we do get things wrong, we reevaluate our predictions. And, says Lucas, we keep up this process of prediction and evaluation until there is no way to improve those predictions, ensuring that we won't consistently make the same forecasting mistakes. In that way we form what Lucas calls "rational expectations." As he sees it, people act much like experienced bettors at the track. They get good at picking horses, but are never able to pick the winning horse every time.

Lucas has made a career out of expressing these ideas in mathematical terms. He argues that predictions about the rates of interest, unemployment, and inflation shape how consumers, workers, and business people decide their economic future. From consumers buying a new home to workers looking for a new job to bosses hiring or laying off employees, rational expectations theory seeks to describe what motivates economic actors.

ADAM SMITH RETURNS

But Lucas does not stop there—with merely a theory of how people make economic decisions. New Classical economic theory also assumes that markets "clear" instantaneously. In the bat of an eye, prices adjust so that how much sellers bring to market just matches whatever buyers take away. For instance, in a labor market, wages (the price of labor) fall quickly enough to guarantee that every worker willing to work (or sell their labor) at the going wage finds a job with an employer (or buyer of labor). For New Classical economists that constitutes full employment. Only workers unwilling to work at the market clearing wage are out of a job. Those workers are voluntarily unemployed—they chose not to work and brought unemployment upon themselves.

The point here is simple: Market capitalism is stable. "Price flexibility" and "market clearing" guarantee a booming full-employment economy—one that does not need economic policymaking to stabilize it. In fact, in Lucas's framework, government attempts to fine tune the economy actually backfire.

Here's why. If people expect the government to change economic policy, they too change their economic actions. That is rational expectations at work. And when prices and wages adjust instantaneously as people scramble to match

WHILE KEYNESIANS MAY ACCEPT THE IDEA OF RATIONALLY FORMED EXPECTATIONS, THEY FIND THE IDEAS OF FLEXIBLE PRICES AND CLEARING MARKETS PREPOSTEROUS.

their economic actions to their new expectations, those adjustments nullify the government's actions.

For instance, suppose the Fed tries to reduce unemployment by increasing the money supply, in the hope of raising spending and putting people to work. Lucas's rational workers anticipate that more spending and hiring will bring not only higher wages but also instantaneously higher prices, leaving their purchasing power unchanged. In this world people are not forced to work to avoid starving, but rather choose to offer their services only when their inflation-adjusted wages are sufficiently high. So no rational worker is lured into the market. The Fed's actions fail to lower unemployment, and succeed only in driving up prices.

As far-fetched as this theory might seem, the stagflation (simultaneous stagnation and inflation) of the 1970s lent these ideas plausibility. New Classical economics gathered adherents as Keynesian policies seemed increasingly ineffectual.

In New Classical economics, meddlesome government is not only ineffective, it is the enemy. Why does Lucas's inherently stable capitalism suffer through the ups and downs of the business cycle? His answer: Washington types trying to fine tune the economy. This is where imperfect information, the third building block of Lucas's theory, enters the model. Even Lucas's rational actors in this market-clearing world possess only limited information and can be fooled by bungling bureaucrats and re-election minded politicians who launch surprise (unannounced) changes in government policy.

People know the economy around them—their own wages or profits, the prices of the products they sell and those that they buy—better than what is going on across the economy. So if the Federal Reserve, without announcing it, increases the money supply in order to beef up spending and lower unemployment, even people with rational expectations can be confounded. They see their prices or wages go up, but don't anticipate prices going up elsewhere in the economy.

And that causes a problem. Corporate managers, for instance, hike up production, thinking that a higher price must signal a soaring demand for their products. Output rises across the economy. But soon inventories pile up, because the price increases were due to general inflation rather than greater demand. Corporate managers realize that the higher production levels were unwarranted, and they order a cutback—below even the initial output. The economy contracts, causing a recession.

What can return stability to the economy? Forsaking government intervention into the economy. In Lucas's world, unannounced changes in government policy cause the ups and downs of the business cycle. And announced changes in government policies are fully anticipated and therefore ineffective. For Lucas, the only rational course of action is to turn our backs on active government attempts to soften the blows of the market economy.

KEYNESIAN CRITICS

Not all economists are convinced by Lucas's arguments or support the draconian policy implications of New Classical economics. The proponents of Keynesian economic policy have been among the most vocal critics. While Keynesians may accept the idea of rationally formed expectations, they find the ideas of flexible prices and clearing markets preposterous. One Nobel laureate, James Tobin, called these ideas a "great myth"—powerful in its effect on how we see the economy, but nonetheless a myth.

Another Keynesian Nobel winner, Franco Modigliani, railed that it is as if "what happened in the United States in the 1930s was a severe attack of contagious laziness." For these dyed-in-the-wool Keynesians, the private economy will not necessarily be driven toward full employment even in the long run and Keynes's fundamental message still holds: "a modern monetized economy needs to be stabilized, can be stabilized, and should be stabilized" by government intervention.

More recently, "New Keynesian" economists have fashioned a different critique of New Classical economics. These modern Keynesians accept not only the idea that people form rational expectations about what will happen in the economy, but also the idea that in the long run the private economy tends toward full employment. Still, they argue that for good economic reasons, wages and prices are "sticky" and much slower to adjust than Lucas suggests. For instance, given the high cost of negotiating a wage settlement, most labor contracts are long term. In the United States, nearly 80% of union contracts are for three years and only about two-fifths of them contain cost-of-living adjustments. Corporations also often rely on long-term pricing agreements to afford them the price stability necessary to bid on contracts.

Thus, while the economy might eventually reach the full employment outcome Lucas's model predicts, the wait is likely to be intolerably long. What's needed is active government intervention designed for the workable policy time frame of three to five years, for as Keynes once wrote, "in the long run we are all dead."

More fundamentally, Lucas's way of thinking exaggerates the amount of power people really have over their economic lives. Economist E. Ray Canterbery writes mockingly that in the New Classical school, "The marginal blue collar worker on his way to the factory anticipates an increase in the money supply then fully anticipates the inflation within his monetarist model ... and a fall in the real interest rates and a fall in real wages. The worker does a U-turn, drives home, and voluntarily disemploys himself." In New Classical economics bosses raise their workers' wages when the economy is doing well rather than pocketing the extra profits. And workers have the power to choose whether or not to work, to ask for higher wages when they expect inflation to go up, or to move into a different industry when they fear the worst for their own job. This is indeed a great myth.

Perhaps the most mythical aspect of New Classical economics is its claim that capitalism is stable—that if only policy makers would cease their interventions, economic stability would be assured and full employment guaranteed.

But the instability of capitalism has been with us since long before Keynesian economic policy, which after all was a response to the Great Depression of the 1930s.

And that instability will worsen if New Classical economics is able to undo what Keynesian policy makers have done to mitigate the instability of capitalism since World War II. Current economic anxiety will heighten as workers struggle with real-life adjustments like stagnant wages and rising layoffs. At the same time, Lucas and his New Classical followers will continue to construct mathematical paeans to the rationality of these adjustments and the inherent stability of capitalism, even if that stability is evident only in their seminar rooms and the the Royal Swedish Academy of Science.

Resources: Robert J. Gordon, *Macroeconomics*, 6th ed., 1994; Robert Lucas, *Studies in Business Cycle Theory*, 1989; N. Gregory Mankiw, "A Quick Refresher Course in Macroeconomics," *Journal of Economic Literature*, December 1990; James Tobin, *Asset Accumulation and Economic Activity*, 1980; *The End of Economic Man*, reviewed by E. Ray Canterbery in *Challenge*, Nov./Dec. 1995.

ARTICLE 8.2

WHAT'S WRONG WITH NEOLIBERALISM?
THE MARX, KEYNES, AND POLANYI PROBLEMS

BY ROBERT POLLIN

During the years of the Clinton administration, the term "Washington Consensus" began circulating to designate the common policy positions of the U.S. administration along with the International Monetary Fund (IMF) and World Bank. These positions, implemented in the United States and abroad, included free trade, a smaller government share of the economy, and the deregulation of financial markets. This policy approach has also become widely known as *neoliberalism*, a term which draws upon the classical meaning of the word *liberalism*.

Classical liberalism is the political philosophy that embraces the virtues of free-market capitalism and the corresponding minimal role for government interventions, especially as regards measures to promote economic equality within capitalist societies. Thus, a classical liberal would favor minimal levels of government spending and taxation, and minimal levels of government regulation over the economy, including financial and labor markets. According to the classical liberal view, businesses should be free to operate as they wish, and to succeed or fail as such in a competitive marketplace. Meanwhile, consumers rather than government should be responsible for deciding which businesses produce goods and services that are of sufficient quality as well as reasonably priced. Businesses that provide overexpensive or low-quality products will then be out-competed in the marketplace regardless of the regulatory standards established by governments. Similarly, if businesses offer workers a wage below what the worker is worth, then a competitor firm will offer this worker a higher wage. The firm unwilling to offer fair wages would not survive over time in the competitive marketplace.

This same reasoning also carries over to the international level. Classical liberals favor free trade between countries rather than countries operating with tariffs or other barriers to the free flow of goods and services between countries. They argue that restrictions on the free movement of products and money between countries only protects uncompetitive firms from market competition, and thus holds back the economic development of countries that choose to erect such barriers.

Neoliberalism and the Washington Consensus are contemporary variants of this longstanding political and economic philosophy. The major difference between classical liberalism as a philosophy and contemporary neoliberalism as a set of policy measures is with implementation. Washington Consensus policy makers are committed to free-market policies when they support the interests of big business, as, for example, with lowering regulations at the workplace. But these same policy makers become far less insistent on free-market principles when invoking such principles might damage big business interests. Federal Reserve and IMF interventions to bail out wealthy asset holders during the frequent global financial crises in the 1990s are obvious violations of free-market precepts.

Broadly speaking, the effects of neoliberalism in the less developed countries over the 1990s reflected the experience of the Clinton years in the United States. A high proportion of less developed countries were successful, just in the manner of the United States under Clinton, in reducing inflation and government budget deficits, and creating a more welcoming climate for foreign trade, multinational corporations, and financial market investors. At the same time, most of Latin America, Africa, and Asia—with China being the one major exception—experienced deepening problems of poverty and inequality in the 1990s, along with slower growth and frequent financial market crises, which in turn produced still more poverty and inequality.

If free-market capitalism is a powerful mechanism for creating wealth, why does a neoliberal policy approach, whether pursued by Clinton, Bush, or the IMF, produce severe difficulties in terms of inequality and financial instability, which in turn diminish the market mechanism's ability to even promote economic growth? It will be helpful to consider this in terms of three fundamental problems that result from a free-market system, which I term "the Marx Problem," "the Keynes problem," and "the Polanyi problem." Let us take these up in turn.

THE MARX PROBLEM

Does someone in your family have a job and, if so, how much does it pay? For the majority of the world's population, how one answers these two questions determines, more than anything else, what one's standard of living will be. But how is it decided whether a person has a job and what their pay will be? Getting down to the most immediate level of decision-making, this occurs through various types of bargaining in labor markets between workers and employers. Karl Marx argued that, in a free-market economy generally, workers have less power than employers in this bargaining process because workers cannot fall back on other means of staying alive if they fail to get hired into a job. Capitalists gain higher profits through having this relatively stronger bargaining position. But Marx also stressed that workers' bargaining power diminishes further when unemployment and underemployment are high, since that means that employed workers can be more readily replaced by what Marx called "the reserve army" of the unemployed outside the office, mine, or factory gates.

Neoliberalism has brought increasing integration of the world's labor markets through reducing barriers to international trade and investment by multinationals. For workers in high-wage countries such as the United States, this effectively means that the reserve army of workers willing to accept jobs at lower pay than U.S. workers expands to include workers in less developed countries. It isn't the case that businesses will always move to less developed countries or that domestically produced goods will necessarily be supplanted by imports from low-wage countries. The point is that U.S. workers face an increased *credible* threat that they can be supplanted. If everything else were to remain the same in the U.S. labor market, this would then mean that global integration would erode the bargaining power of U.S. workers and thus tend to bring lower wages.

But even if this is true for workers in the United States and other rich countries, shouldn't it also mean that workers in poor countries have greater job opportunities and better bargaining positions? In fact, there are areas where workers in poor countries are gaining enhanced job opportunities through international trade and multinational investments. But these gains are generally quite limited. This is because a long-term transition out of agriculture in poor countries continues to expand the reserve army of unemployed and underemployed workers in these countries as well. Moreover, when neoliberal governments in poor countries reduce their support for agriculture—through cuts in both tariffs on imported food products and subsidies for domestic farmers—this makes it more difficult for poor farmers to compete with multinational agribusiness firms. This is especially so when the rich countries maintain or increase their own agricultural supports, as has been done in the United States under Bush. In addition, much of the growth in the recently developed export-oriented manufacturing sectors of poor countries has failed to significantly increase jobs even in this sector. This is because the new export-oriented production sites frequently do not represent net additions to the country's total supply of manufacturing firms. They rather replace older firms that were focused on supplying goods to domestic markets. The net result is that the number of people looking for jobs in the developing countries grows faster than the employers seeking new workers. Here again, workers' bargaining power diminishes.

This does not mean that global integration of labor markets must necessarily bring weakened bargaining power and lower wages for workers. But it does mean that unless some non-market forces in the economy, such as government regulations or effective labor unions, are able to counteract these market processes, workers will indeed continue to experience weakened bargaining strength and eroding living standards.

THE KEYNES PROBLEM

In a free-market economy, investment spending by businesses is the main driving force that produces economic growth, innovation, and jobs. But as John Maynard Keynes stressed, private investment decisions are also unavoidably risky ventures. Businesses have to put up money without knowing whether they will produce any profits in the future. As such, investment spending by business is likely to fluctuate far more than, say, decisions by households as to how much they will spend per week on groceries.

But investment fluctuations will also affect overall spending in the economy, including that of households. When investment spending declines, this means that businesses will hire fewer workers. Unemployment rises as a result, and this in turn will lead to cuts in household spending. Declines in business investment spending can therefore set off a vicious cycle: the investment decline leads to employment declines, then to cuts in household spending and corresponding increases in household financial problems, which then brings still more cuts in business investment and financial difficulties for the business sector. This is how capitalist economies produce mass unemployment, financial crises, and recessions.

Keynes also described a second major source of instability associated with private investment activity. Precisely because private investments are highly risky propositions, financial markets have evolved to make this risk more manageable for any given investor. Through financial markets, investors can sell off their investments if they need or want to, converting their office buildings, factories, and stock of machinery into cash much more readily than they could if they always had to find buyers on their own. But Keynes warned that when financial markets convert long-term assets into short-term commitments for investors, this also fosters a speculative mentality in the markets. What becomes central for investors is not whether a company's products will produce profits over a long term, but rather whether the short-term financial market investors *think* a company's fortunes will be strong enough in the present and immediate future to drive the stock price up. Or, to be more precise, what really matters for a speculative investor is not what they think about a given company's prospects per se, but rather what they think *other investors are thinking*, since that will be what determines where the stock price goes in the short term.

Because of this, the financial markets are highly susceptible to rumors, fads, and all sorts of deceptive accounting practices, since all of these can help drive the stock price up in the present, regardless of what they accomplish in the longer term. Thus, if U.S. stock traders are convinced that Alan Greenspan is a *maestro*, and if there is news that he is about to intervene with some kind of policy shift, then the rumor of Greenspan's policy shift can itself drive prices up, as the more nimble speculators try to keep one step ahead of the herd of Greenspan-philes.

Still, as with the Marx problem, it does not follow that the inherent instability of private investment and speculation in financial markets are uncontrollable, leading inevitably to persistent problems of mass unemployment and recession. But these social pathologies will become increasingly common through a neoliberal policy approach committed to minimizing government interventions to stabilize investment.

THE POLANYI PROBLEM

Karl Polanyi wrote his classic book *The Great Transformation* in the context of the 1930s depression, World War II, and the developing worldwide competition with Communist governments. He was also reflecting on the 1920s, dominated, as with our current epoch, by a free-market ethos. Polanyi wrote of the 1920s that "economic liberalism made a supreme bid to restore the self-regulation of the system by eliminating all interventionist policies which interfered with the freedom of markets."

Considering all of these experiences, Polanyi argued that for market economies to function with some modicum of fairness, they must be embedded in social norms and institutions that effectively promote broadly accepted notions of the common good. Otherwise, acquisitiveness and competition—the two driving forces of market economies—achieve overwhelming dominance as cultural forces, rendering life under capitalism a Hobbesian "war of all against all." This same idea is also central for Adam Smith. Smith showed how the invisible hand of self-interest and competition will yield higher levels of individual effort that increases the wealth of nations, but that it will also produce the corruption of our moral sentiments unless the market is itself governed at a fundamental level by norms of solidarity.

In the post-World War II period, various social democratic movements within the advanced capitalist economies adapted the Polanyi perspective. They argued in favor of government interventions to achieve three basic ends: stabilizing overall demand in the economy at a level that will provide for full employment; creating a financial market environment that is stable and conducive to the effective allocation of investment funds; and distributing equitably the rewards from high employment and a stable investment process. There were two basic means of achieving equitable distribution: relatively rapid wage growth, promoted by labor laws that were supportive of unions, minimum wage standards, and similar interventions in labor markets; and welfare state policies, including progressive taxation and redistributive programs such as Social Security. The political ascendancy of these ideas was the basis for a dramatic increase in the role of government in the post-World War II capitalist economies. As one indicator of this, total government expenditures in the United States rose from 8% of GDP in 1913, to 21% in 1950, then to 38% by 1992. The International Monetary Fund and World Bank were also formed in the mid-1940s to advance such policy ideas throughout the world—that is, to implement policies virtually the opposite of those they presently favor. John Maynard Keynes himself was a leading intellectual force contributing to the initial design of the International Monetary Fund and World Bank.

FROM SOCIAL DEMOCRACY TO NEOLIBERALISM

But the implementation of a social democratic capitalism, guided by a commitment to full employment and the welfare state, did also face serious and persistent difficulties, and we need to recognize them as part of a consideration of the Marx, Keynes, and Polanyi problems. In particular, many sectors of business opposed efforts to sustain full employment because, following the logic of the Marx problem, full employment provides greater bargaining power for workers in labor markets, even if it also increases the economy's total production of goods and services. Greater worker bargaining power can also create inflationary pressures because businesses will try to absorb their higher wage costs by raising prices. In addition, market-inhibiting financial regulations limit the capacity of financial market players to diversify their risk and speculate.

Corporations in the United States and Western Europe were experiencing some combination of these problems associated with social democratic capitalism. In particular, they were faced with rising labor costs associated with low unemployment rates, which then led to either inflation, when corporations had the ability to pass on their higher labor costs to consumers, or to a squeeze on profits, when competitive pressures prevented corporations from raising their prices in response to the rising labor costs. These pressures were compounded by the two oil price "shocks" initiated by the Oil Producing Exporting Countries (OPEC)—an initial fourfold increase in the world price of oil in 1973, then a second four-fold price spike in 1979.

These were the conditions that by the end of the 1970s led to the decline of social democratic approaches to policymaking and the ascendancy of neoliberalism. The two leading signposts of this historic transition were the election in 1979 of Margaret Thatcher as Prime Minister of the United Kingdom and in 1980 of Ronald Reagan as the President of the United States. Indeed, it was at this point that Mrs. Thatcher made her famous pronouncement that "there is no alternative" to neoliberalism.

This brings us to the contemporary era of smaller government, fiscal stringency and deregulation, i.e., to neoliberalism under Clinton, Bush, and throughout the less-developed world. The issue is not a simple juxtaposition between either regulating or deregulating markets. Rather it is that markets have become deregulated to support the interests of business and financial markets, even as these same groups still benefit greatly from many forms of government support, including investment subsidies, tax concessions, and rescue operations when financial crises get out of hand. At the same time, the deregulation of markets that favors business and finance is correspondingly the most powerful regulatory mechanism limiting the demands of workers, in that deregulation has been congruent with the worldwide expansion of the reserve army of labor and the declining capacity of national governments to implement full-employment and macroeconomic policies. In other words, deregulation has exacerbated both the Marx and Keynes problems.

Given the ways in which neoliberalism worsens the Marx, Keynes, and Polanyi problems, we should not be surprised by the wreckage that it has wrought since the late 1970s, when it became the ascendant policy model. Over the past generation, with neoliberals in the saddle almost everywhere in the world, the results have been straightforward: worsening inequality and poverty, along with slower economic growth and far more unstable financial markets. While Margaret Thatcher famously declared that "there is no alternative" to neoliberalism, there are in fact alternatives. The experience over the past generation demonstrates how important it is to develop them in the most workable and coherent ways possible.

ARTICLE 8.3

July/August 2009

THE GENERAL THEORY AND THE CURRENT CRISIS: A PRIMER ON KEYNES' ECONOMICS—PART 1

KEYNES AND THE LIMITS OF MONETARY POLICY

BY ALEJANDRO REUSS

As the United States has plunged into financial crisis and the deepest recession since the Great Depression, the U.S. Federal Reserve (the "Fed") has pursued an aggressively "expansionary" monetary policy. Monetary policy refers to government policies affecting the money supply or interest rates. Expansionary monetary policy is aimed at increasing the money supply or lowering interest rates. The idea is that, by lowering interest rates, the government can stimulate investment (such as firms' purchases of new equipment and construction of new plant). Projects that would not be profitable for a company if it had to borrow at a higher interest rate could be profitable if borrowing were less costly. Fed policymakers hope, then, that lower interest rates will encourage investment and bring about renewed economic growth.

The main interest rate the Fed targets is the "federal funds rate," the interest rate that banks charge each other for overnight loans. For all of 2006 and 2007, the federal funds rate stood at over 4%. In the course of 2008, as the financial crisis and recession grew deeper, the Fed moved aggressively to cut interest rates. By the end of the year, the federal funds rate was 0.0-0.25%, where it remains today. Even with the federal funds rate basically at zero, however, the economy has spiraled deeper into recession. GDP shrank at an annual rate of 6.2% in the fourth quarter of 2008 and the official unemployment rate climbed to 8.5% by March 2009.

ARE INTEREST RATES COMING DOWN?

Firms and consumers cannot borrow at the federal funds rate. Then why does the Fed try to bring down the federal funds rate when it wants to stimulate economic activity? Fed policymakers hope that by pulling down very short-term interest rates that do not directly affect firms and consumers, they can indirectly pull down longer-term interest rates that are important to firms and consumers.

Interest rates on 30-Year Fixed-Rate mortgages *have* declined, reaching historic lows under 5% in March 2009. The low mortgage rates, however, may be deceptive. Mortgage lenders have generally tightened lending standards, and the low rates are only available to borrowers that banks consider very safe. Other borrowers may pay rates several percentage points higher, or be unable to borrow at all. Meanwhile, banks have raised credit-card interest rates and dramatically tightened borrowing limits.

Key corporate interest rates have not come down. Moody's AAA bond rate, an index of the interest rates on long-term bonds for low-risk corporate borrowers, was about the same in March 2009 as in January 2008 (about 5.3%). Moody's Baa bond rate, the equivalent index or higher-risk corporate borrowers, has gone from about 6.5% in January 2008 to over 8% in March 2009. The spreads between these rates and the federal funds rate have increased dramatically as the federal funds rate has fallen.

That would come as no surprise to John Maynard Keynes. Keynes argued, in *The General Theory of Employment, Interest, and Money* (1936), that during boom periods the general estimation of risk by both lenders and borrowers is "apt to become unusually and imprudently low." Lenders loan out money freely, even recklessly, accepting a low rate of interest relative to the risk involved. During crisis periods, on the other hand, lenders often become much more risk-averse, parting with their money less freely, and insisting on a higher rate of interest in exchange for the risk of not being paid back. This is sometimes known as the "flight to liquidity" or "flight to safety."

Keynes' analysis suggests that during economic crises the interest rates on assets that are considered very safe—like government bonds—are apt to go down, since people are looking to avoid losses and willing to accept a low rate of return to do so. But the interest rates on riskier assets may go up. A rise in the interest rates that firms or consumers pay would tend to deepen—rather than correct—an economic downturn.

CAN'T THE FED DO MORE?

If interest rates are not low enough to turn the economy around, then why doesn't the Fed increase the money supply some more—until interest rates *are* low enough? The answer is that nominal interest rates can reach a lower bound below which they cannot decline further. (The "nominal" interest rate, in contrast to the "real" interest rate, does not account for changes in the purchasing power of the dollar due to inflation.) This lower bound can be greater than 0%, but cannot be lower than 0%. The federal funds rate is now about 0%. When interest rates reach this lower limit, the economy is commonly described as being caught in a "liquidity trap."

People hold their wealth in the form of bonds rather than money because they can earn interest on bonds. For example, you may be able to buy a bond for $100 that promises a payment of $110 in one year. That gives you a 10% annual interest rate (you loaned the bond issuer $100 for a year, and at the end of the year get your $100 back plus $10 interest). That is the incentive to buy the bond instead of just holding money.

Suppose the Fed wants to lower interest rates to stimulate spending. It offers to buy government bonds (previously sold to the public) at a higher price, driving down the interest rate. For instance, the Fed might offer $110 for bonds that promise $110 in one year. If you were to buy such a bond at the new price of $110, you would receive the same amount of money back a year later. The interest rate on that bond is now 0%. The idea of the policy is that banks will sell their government bonds to the Fed at the new higher price, take the money and buy other bonds (such as those issued by corporations), driving up their price and lowering the interest rate on those bonds.

Imagine that the Fed, however, decided that an interest rate of 0% was not low enough, and decided instead to pay banks $120 for bonds that promise $110 in a year. The banks would gladly sell their bonds, so the money supply would increase. But they would not loan out the money they received at a *negative* interest rate (paying consumers or firms to borrow from them). They would be better off just keeping the money in their vaults. In other words, once the interest rate reaches 0%, there is nothing more that the government can do with conventional expansionary monetary policy. That is the liquidity trap—any extra liquidity (money) the Fed makes available gets trapped, instead of being loaned out.

MONETARY POLICY AND INTEREST RATES TODAY

Economic journalists and commentators have inaccurately described "interest rates" as being at or near 0% these days. The federal funds rate has hit rock bottom, but other interest rates clearly have not. Keynes was acutely aware that, when monetary authorities limit themselves to buying short-term securities, the "effect may … be mainly confined to the very short-term rate of interest and have but little reaction on the much more important long-term rates of interest."

In a famous passage in *The General Theory*, Keynes notes the possibility that "after the rate of interest has fallen to a certain level … almost everyone prefers cash to holding a debt which yields so low a rate of interest." This passage is often taken to be Keynes' description of the liquidity trap. He goes on to say that he did not know of any case when this had actually happened and notes that it is not likely to happen "owing to the unwillingness of most monetary authorities to deal boldly in debts of long term." It is clear from this passage that Keynes *was not* describing merely a situation in which certain short-term interest rates targeted by the government (such as the federal funds rate) were pushed to their lower limits, but rather one in which *all* interest rates hit rock bottom—a different situation from what is commonly referred to as a "liquidity trap" today.

Keynes viewed monetary policymakers' focus on certain short-run interest rates not as an inherent limitation in monetary policy, but as a limitation in the ways monetary policy was *conventionally* practiced. He notes that governments did not usually buy long-term bonds and drive down long-term interest rates, but that there was no reason they could not. In March, the Fed actually began to do just that, buying billions in *long-term* government securities in an attempt to bring down long-term rates. The 10-Year Treasury Bond Rate dropped dramatically (from about 3% to 2.5%) the day the purchases began. It has increased somewhat since then, but remains lower than it was before November 2008.

Any attempt to revive private investment by manipulating interest rates, however, faces at least two additional barriers:

First, the interest rates consumers and firms pay do not move in lockstep with interest rates on government securities, either short-term or long-term. The contrast between short-term and long-term bonds is not the same as the difference between relatively safe government bonds and riskier corporate bonds or consumer loans. As we have seen, interest rates on corporate bonds have failed to decline, even as rates on long-term government bonds have declined. Banks' consumer lending standards, likewise, have tightened even as the Fed has driven down interest rates on government bonds.

Second, economic activity simply may not change dramatically in response to changes in interest rates, especially during a recession. Expectations of future sales and profits are extremely negative, so firms are dramatically slashing payrolls and investment spending. Total employment has decreased by over half a million people for each of five consecutive months from November 2008 to March 2009. Nonresidential fixed investment decreased by over 20% in the last quarter of 2008; investment in nonresidential structures by nearly 10%. Firms have inventories they cannot sell, are laying off workers, and are producing below their existing productive capacity. Most of them are not going to make large investments in new plant and equipment under such conditions.

For these reasons, Keynesian economists have advocated a very large *fiscal* stimulus. Fiscal policy, in contrast to monetary policy, involves government spending and taxation. A fiscal stimulus program involves increases in government spending or reductions in taxes. Keynesian economists, believing that monetary policy is not adequate to pull the economy out of its current crisis, have argued especially for a dramatic increase in government spending as the surest way to revive overall spending, production, and employment.

Sources: John Maynard Keynes, *The General Theory of Employment, Interest, and Money*, First Harvest/Harcourt, 1964; The Federal Reserve Bank, "Intended federal funds rate, Change and level, 1990 to present," http://www.federalreserve.gov/fomc/fundsrate.htm; Bureau of Economic Analysis, "News Release: Gross Domestic Product (GDP) and Corporate Profits," March 26, 2009, http://www.bea.gov/newsreleases/national/gdp/gdpnewsrelease.htm; Bureau of Labor Statistics, Table A-12. Alternative measures of labor underutilization, http://www.bls.gov/news.release/empsit.t12.htm; Luke Mullins, "Banks Tighten Mortgage Lending Standards," *U.S. News and World Report*, February 2, 2009, http://www.usnews.com/blogs/the-home-front/2009/2/2/banks-tighten-mortgage-lending-standards.html; Jeannine Aversa and Alan Zibel, "Mortgage rates down, but standards remain high," Associated Press, *Press-Telegram* (Long Beach, CA), March 19, 2009, http://www.presstelegram.com/ci_11955917; Bob Tedeschi, "Mortgages: 'Cashing Out' is Now Harder," *New York Times*, March 19, 2009; http://www.nytimes.com/2009/03/29/realestate/29mort.html?_r=1; Kathy Chu, "Changing credit card terms squeeze consumers," *USA Today*, December 16, 2008, http://www.usatoday.com/money/perfi/credit/2008-12-15-credit-card-consumer-squeeze_N.htm; Jane J. Kim, "BofA to Boost Rates on Cards With Balances," *Wall Street Journal*, April 9, 2009, http://online.wsj.com/article/SB123922365800702453.html; Federal Reserve Bank of St. Louis, Moody's Seasoned Aaa Corporate Bond Yield, http://research.stlouisfed.org/fred2/data/AAA.txt; Federal Reserve Bank of St. Louis, Moody's Seasoned Baa Corporate Bond Yield, http://research.stlouisfed.org/fred2/data/BAA.txt; Paul Krugman, "Spreads," January 19, 2009, http://krugman.blogs.nytimes.com/2009/01/19/spreads/; Jon Hilsenrath, *Wall Street Journal*, "Fed in Bond-Buying Binge to Spur Growth," March 19, 2009, http://online.wsj.com/article/SB123739788518173569.html; Paul Krugman, "Return of depression economics," March 4, 2009, http://krugman.blogs.nytimes.com/2009/03/04/return-of-depression-economics/; Federal Reserve Bank of St. Louis, Ten-Year Treasury Constant Maturity Rate, http://research.stlouisfed.org/fred2/data/DGS10.txt; Bureau of Labor Statistics, Payroll Employment, http://www.bls.gov/; Bureau of Economic Analysis, "News Release: Gross Domestic Product (GDP) and Corporate Profits," March 26, 2009, http://www.bea.gov/newsreleases/national/gdp/gdpnewsrelease.htm;

THE GENERAL THEORY AND THE CURRENT CRISIS: A PRIMER ON KEYNES' ECONOMICS—PART 2
FISCAL POLICY AND THE "TREASURY VIEW"

BY ALEJANDRO REUSS

In response to the deepest recession in the United States since the Great Depression, the Obama administration proposed a large fiscal "stimulus" plan. (Fiscal policies involve government spending and taxation. A fiscal stimulus involves increases in government spending or tax cuts, or both.) The current stimulus plan, after some compromises between the Obama administration and Republicans in Congress, included both substantial tax cuts and increases in government spending. Together, they would increase the federal government deficit by over $700 billion.

A fiscal stimulus is a standard "Keynesian" response to a recession. The logic behind these policies is that recessions can be caused by insufficient total demand for goods and services. If saving (a "leakage" from demand) exceeds investment (an "injection" of demand), there will not be enough demand to buy all the goods and services that the economy is capable of producing at the "full employment" level. Some goods will go unsold, and firms will reduce output. They will cut jobs, cancel supply orders, and even close production facilities. The economy will spiral into a recession.

In standard Keynesian models, either tax cuts or increased government spending can increase total demand, and therefore total output and employment. An initial increase in spending (by either the government or the recipients of the tax cuts) results in new income for other individuals, who then go on to spend part (not all) of this income, which results in new income for still other individuals, and so on. Ultimately, this series of additions to income results in a total increase in GDP greater than the original increase in government spending or reduction in taxes. The increase in real GDP divided by the initial spending increase is called the "multiplier." The standard Keynesian view implies a multiplier greater than one.

THE CONSERVATIVE CRITIQUE

Conservative economists, whose intellectual heritage includes decades-old attempts to refute Keynesian theory, disagree with this view. They argue that government spending cannot possibly increase overall economic activity, and that the stimulus plan is therefore doomed to fail. This position is sometimes known as the "Treasury view" (because it mirrors the arguments of the British Treasury Department during the Great Depression) or the theory of "crowding out." The new government spending, these economists argue, "has to come from somewhere," either from higher taxes or increased government borrowing. Either way, the increase in government spending will come at the expense of private spending.

If the spending is financed by tax increases, conservative economists argue, this will reduce individuals' after-tax incomes and therefore reduce their spending. If it is financed through borrowing, the increased government demand for loans will drive up interest rates, and this will "crowd out" private investment. (Some private investment projects that would have been profitable at lower interest rates would not be profitable at the higher rates, and therefore would not be undertaken.) Extreme versions of this theory, known as "dollar-for-dollar" crowding out, argue that the decrease in private investment will exactly offset the increase in government spending, and there will be no change in the overall output of goods and services.

Government intervention is not only incapable of pulling the economy out of a recession, conservative economists argue, it is also unnecessary. If there is more saving than investment, the quantity of funds people are willing to loan out will exceed the quantity that people are willing to borrow at the current interest rate. The surplus of loanable funds will drive down the in-terest rate. People will save less (since the reward to saving is lower) and borrow more and invest more (since the cost of borrowing is lower), until the injection of investment and the leakage of saving are equal. In short, if insufficient demand ever caused a recession, the economy would quickly pull itself back to full employment without any need for government intervention.

KEYNES' REJOINDER

Keynes agreed with the idea that saving equals investment. In his view, however, this is true not only when the economy is producing at its full-employment capacity, but also when it is producing at far less than its capacity. Keynes argued that the "classical" economists (as he called the conservative orthodoxy of his time) had an incorrect view of the relationship between interest rates and savings, and that this was at the heart of their errors about the possibility of prolonged recessions.

The classicals believed that as interest rates increased, savings would increase, and that as interest rates declined, savings would decline. Keynes agreed that this was true at "a given income," but that a change in the interest rate would also affect the amount investment and therefore the level of income. A higher interest rate, he argued, was associated with lower investment, lower incomes, and therefore lower saving; a lower interest rate, with higher investment, higher incomes, and therefore higher saving. (As people's incomes increase, they spend more *and* save more; as their incomes decline, they spend less *and* save less.) In Keynes' view, saving will equal investment whether investment and saving are both high (at or near the full employment level of output) or if investment and saving are both low (in a low-output, high-unemployment economy). In the latter case, Keynes believed, there was no guarantee that the economy would pull itself back to full employment.

Keynes was also well aware, long before his critics, that government borrowing could crowd out some private investment. In *The General Theory* itself, he noted that the effects of the government directly increasing employment on public works may include "increasing the rate of interest and so retarding investment in other directions." This does not imply, however, dollar-for-dollar crowding out. Keynes still believed, and the empirical evidence confirms, that under depression conditions an increase in government spending can result in an increase in total output larger than the initial spending increase (a multiplier greater than one).

OF SPENDING AND MULTIPLIERS

In a recent article in the *Wall Street Journal*, conservative economist Robert Barro declares, as a "plausible starting point," that the multiplier actually equals zero. That's what the dollar-for-dollar crowding-out theory means—an increase in government spending will be matched by equal decreases in private spending, and so will have zero effect on real GDP. When it comes to estimating the multiplier, based on historical data from 1943-1944, however, Barro finds that it is not zero, but 0.8.

First, contrary to Barro's intent, this is actually a disproof of dollar-for-dollar crowding out. It means that increased government spending brought about increased real GDP, though not by as much as the spending increase. It increased the production of public-sector goods by (much) more than it reduced the production of private-sector goods. Unless one views private-sector goods as intrinsically more valuable than public-sector goods, this is not an argument against government spending.

Second, Barro chose to base his study on two years at the height of the U.S. mobilization for World War II. When the economy is at or near full employment, the multiplier is bound to be small. If all resources are already being used, the only way to produce more of some kinds of goods (say, tanks and war planes) is to produce less of some others (say, civilian cars). Keynesian economists certainly understand this. Their point, however, is that government spending creates a large multiplier effect when the economy is languishing in a recession, not when it is already at full employment.

Economist Mark Zandi of Moody's Economy.com reports much higher multipliers for government spending. Zandi estimates multipliers between 1.3 and 1.6 for federal aid to states and for government infrastructure expenditures. The multipliers are even larger for government transfers (such as food stamps or unemployment compensation) to the hardest-hit, who are likely to spend all or almost all of their increase in income. Zandi estimates these multipliers at between 1.6 and 1.8. Tax cuts for high income individuals and corporations, who are less likely to spend their additional disposable income, have the lowest multipliers—between 0.3 and 0.4.

WHY THE GENERAL THEORY?

The conservative case against standard Keynesian fiscal stimulus policy rests on the assumption that all of the economy's resources are already being used to the fullest. Keynes titled his most important work *The General Theory* because he thought that the orthodox economics of his time confined itself to this special case, the case of an economy at full employment. He did not believe that this was generally the case in capitalist economies, and he sought to develop a theory that explained this.

The argument conservatives make against government spending—"it has to come from somewhere"—is actually no less true for private investment. If dollar-for-dollar crowding out were true, therefore, it would be just as impossible for private investment to pull the economy out of a recession. This, of course, would be nonsense unless the economy was already at full employment (and an increase in one kind of production would have to come at the expense of some other kind of production).

If the economy were already operating at full capacity —imagine a situation in which all workers are employed, factories are humming with activity 24/7, and no unused resources would be available to expand production if demand increased—the argument that increased government spending could not increase overall economic output might be plausible. But that is manifestly not the current economic situation.

Real GDP declined at an annual rate of 6.3% in the fourth quarter of 2008. The official unemployment rate surged to 8.5%, the highest rate in 30 years, in March 2009. Over 15% of workers are unemployed, have given up looking for work, or can only find part-time work. Employment is plummeting by more than half a million workers each month. A theory that assumes the economy is already at full employment can neither help us understand how we got into this hole—or how we can get out.

Sources: John Maynard Keynes, The General Theory of Employment, Interest, and Money, First Harvest/Harcourt, 1964; "Obama: Stimulus lets Americans claim destiny," msnbc.msn.com, February

17, 2009; Paul Krugman, "A Dark Age of macroeconomics (wonkish)," January 27, 2009, krugman.blogs.nytimes.com; J. Bradford DeLong, "More 'Treasury View' Blogging," delong.typepad.com, February 5, 2009; J. Bradford DeLong, "The Modern Revival of the 'Treasury View,'" braddelong.posterous.com, January 18, 2009; Robert J. Barro, "Government Spending Is No Free Lunch," Wall Street Journal, January 22, 2009; Paul Krugman, "War and non-remembrance," krugman.blogs.nytimes.com, January 22, 2009; Paul Krugman, "Spending in wartime," krugman.blogs.nytimes.com, January 22, 2009; Mark Zandi, "The Economic Impact of a $750 Billion Fiscal Stimulus Package," Moody's Economy.com, January 6, 2009; Bureau of Economic Analysis, "News Release: Gross Domestic Product (GDP) and Corporate Profits," March 26, 2009, www.bea.gov; Bureau of Labor Statistics, Table A-12: Alternative measures of labor underutilization, www.bls.gov; Bureau of Labor Statistics, Payroll Employment, www.bls.gov.

ARTICLE 8.5

February 2000

OPENING PANDORA'S BOX
THE BASICS OF MARXIST ECONOMICS

BY ALEJANDRO REUSS

In most universities, what is taught as "economics" is a particular brand of orthodox economic theory. The hallmark of this school is a belief in the optimal efficiency (and, it goes without saying, the equity) of "free markets."

The orthodox macroeconomists—who had denied the possibility of general economic slumps—were thrown for a loop by the Great Depression of the 1930s, and by the challenge to their system of thought by John Maynard Keynes and others. Even so, the orthodox system retains at its heart a view of capitalist society in which individuals, each equal to all others, undertake mutually beneficial transactions tending to a socially optimal equilibrium. There is no power and no conflict. The model is a perfectly bloodless abstraction, without all the clash and clamor of real life.

KARL MARX AND THE CRITIQUE OF CAPITALIST SOCIETY

One way to pry open and criticize the orthodox model of economics is by returning to the idiosyncrasies of the real world. That's the approach of most of the articles in this book, which describe real-world phenomena that the orthodox model ignores or excludes. These efforts may explain particular facts better than the orthodoxy, while not necessarily offering an alternative general system of analysis. They punch holes in the orthodox lines but, ultimately, leave the orthodox model in possession of the field.

This suggests the need for a different conceptual system that can supplant orthodox economics as a whole. Starting in the 1850s and continuing until his death in 1883, the German philosopher and revolutionary Karl Marx dedicated himself to developing a conceptual system for explaining the workings of capitalism. The system which Marx developed and which bears his name emerged from his criticism of the classical political economy developed by Adam Smith and David Ricardo. While Marx admired Smith and Ricardo, and borrowed many of their concepts, he approached economics (or "political economy") from a very different standpoint. He had developed a powerful criticism of capitalist society before undertaking his study of the economy. This criticism was inspired by French socialist ideas and focused on the oppression of the working class. Marx argued that wage workers—those working for a paycheck—were "free" only in the sense that they were not beholden to a single lord or master, as serfs had been under feudalism. But they did not own property, nor were they craftspeople working for themselves, so they were compelled to sell themselves for a wage to one capitalist or another. Having surrendered their freedom to the employer's authority, they were forced to work in the way the employer told them while the latter pocketed the profit produced by their labor.

Marx believed, however, that by creating this oppressed and exploited class of workers, capitalism was creating the seeds of its own destruction. Conflict between the workers and the owners was an essential part of capitalism. But in Marx's view of history, the workers could eventually overthrow the capitalist class, just as the capitalist class, or "bourgeoisie," had grown strong under feudalism, only to supplant the feudal aristocracy. The workers, however, would not simply substitute a new form of private property and class exploitation, as the bourgeoisie had done. Rather, they would bring about the organization of production on a cooperative basis, and an end to the domination of one class over another.

This line of thinking was strongly influenced by the ideas of the day in German philosophy, which held that any new order grows in the womb of the old, and eventually bursts forth to replace it. Marx believed that the creation of the working class, or proletariat, in the heart of capitalism was one of the system's main contradictions. Marx studied capitalist economics in order to explain the conditions under which it would be possible for the proletariat to overthrow capitalism and create a classless society. The orthodox view depicts capitalism as tending towards equilibrium (without dynamism or crises), serving everyone's best interests, and lasting forever. Marx saw capitalism as crisis-ridden, full of conflict, operating to the advantage of some but not others, and far from eternal.

CLASS AND EXPLOITATION

Marx studied history closely. Looked at historically, he saw capitalism as only the latest in a succession of societies based on exploitation. When people are only able to produce the bare minimum needed to live, he wrote, there is no room for a class of people to take a portion of society's production without contributing to it. But as soon as productivity exceeds this subsistence level, it becomes possible for a class of people who do not contribute to production to live by appropriating the surplus for themselves. These are the masters in slave societies, the lords in feudal societies, and the property owners in capitalist society.

Marx believed that the owners of businesses and property—the capitalists—take part of the wealth produced by the workers, but that this appropriation is hidden by the appearance of an equal exchange, or "a fair day's work for a fair day's pay."

Those who live from the ownership of property—businesses, stocks, land, etc.—were then a small minority and now are less than 5% of the population in countries like the United States (Marx wrote before the rise of massive corporations and bureaucracies, and did not classify managers and administrators who don't own their own businesses as part of the bourgeoisie.) The exploited class, meanwhile, is the vast majority who lived by earning a wage or salary—not just the "blue collar" or industrial workers but other workers as well.

Marx's view of how exploitation happened in capitalist society depended on an idea, which he borrowed from Smith and Ricardo, called the Labor Theory of Value. The premise of this theory, which is neither easily proved nor easily rejected, is that labor alone creates the value which is embodied in commodities and which creates profit for owners who sell the goods. The workers do not receive the full value created by their labor and so they are exploited.

Students are likely to hear in economics classes that profits are a reward for the "abstinence" or "risk" of a businessperson—implying that profits are their just desserts. Marx would argue that profits are a reward obtained through the exercise of power—the power owners have over those who own little but their ability to work and so must sell this ability for a wage. That power, and the tribute it allows owners of capital to extract from workers, is no more legitimate in Marx's analysis than the power of a slaveowner over a slave. A slaveowner may exhibit thrift and take risks, after all, but is the wealth of the slaveowner the just reward for these virtues, or a pure and simple theft from the slave?

As Joan Robinson, an important 20th-century critic and admirer of Marx, argues, "What is important is that owning capital is not a productive activity. The academic economists, by treating capital as productive, used to insinuate the suggestion that capitalists deserve well by society and are fully justified in drawing income from their property."

THE FALLING RATE OF PROFIT

Marx believed that his theory had major implications for the crises that engulf capitalist economies. In Marx's system, the value of the raw materials and machinery used in the manufacture of a product does not create the extra value that allows the businessman to profit from its production. That additional value is created by labor alone.

Marx recognized that owners could directly extract more value out of workers in three ways: cutting their wages, lengthening their working day, or increasing the intensity of their labor. This need not be done by a direct assault on the workers. Capitalists can achieve the same goal by employing more easily exploited groups or by moving their operations where labor is not as powerful. Both of these trends can be seen in capitalism today, and can be understood as part of capital's intrinsic thirst for more value and increased exploitation.

> **MARX'S DISCUSSIONS OF CAPITALISM'S IRRESISTIBLE EXPANSIVE IMPULSE SEEM AS APT TODAY AS THEY DID 150 YEARS AGO.**

With the mechanization of large-scale production under capitalism, machines and other inanimate elements of production form a larger and larger share of the inputs to production. Marx believed this would result in a long-term trend of the rate of profit to fall as less of production depended on the enriching contribution of human labor. This, he believed, would make capitalism increasingly vulnerable to economic crises.

This chain of reasoning, of course, depends on the Labor Theory of Value (seeing workers as the source of the surplus value created in the production process) and can be avoided by rejecting this theory outright. Orthodox economics has not only rejected the Labor Theory of Value, but abandoned the issue of "value" altogether. After lying fallow for many years, value analysis was revived during the 1960s by a number of unorthodox economists including the Italian economist Piero Sraffa. Marx was not the last word on the subject.

UNEMPLOYMENT, PART I: THE "RESERVE ARMY OF THE UNEMPLOYED"

Marx is often raked over the coals for arguing that workers, under capitalism, were destined to be ground into ever more desperate poverty. That living standards improved in rich capitalist countries is offered as proof that his system is fatally flawed. While Marx was not optimistic about the prospect of workers raising their standard of living very far under capitalism, he was critical of proponents of the "iron law of wages," such as Malthus, who held that any increase in wages above the minimum necessary for survival would simply provoke population growth and a decline in wages back to subsistence level.

Marx emphasized that political and historical factors influencing the relative power of the major social classes, rather than simple demographics, determined the distribution of income.

One economic factor to which Marx attributed great importance in the class struggle was the size of the "reserve army of the unemployed." Marx identified unemployment as the major factor pushing wages down—the larger the "reserve" of unemployed workers clamoring for jobs, the greater the downward pressure on wages. This was an influence, Marx believed, that the workers would never be able to fully escape under capitalism. If the workers' bargaining power rose enough to raise wages and eat into profits, he argued, capitalists would merely substitute labor-saving technology for living labor, recreating the "reserve army" and reasserting the downward pressure on wages.

Though this has not, perhaps, retarded long-term wage growth to the degree that Marx expected, his basic analysis was visionary at a time when the Malthusian (population) theory of wages was the prevailing view. Anyone reading the business press these days—which is constantly worrying that workers might gain some bargaining power in a "tight" (low unemployment) labor market, and that their wage demands will provoke inflation—will recognize its basic insight.

UNEMPLOYMENT, PART II: THE CRISIS OF OVERPRODUCTION

Marx never developed one definitive version of his theory of economic crises (recessions) under capitalism. Nonetheless, his thinking on this issue is some of his most visionary. Marx was the first major economic thinker to break with the orthodoxy of "Say's Law." Named after the French philosopher Jean-Baptiste Say, this theory held that each industry generated income equal to the output it created. In other words, "supply creates its own demand." Say's conclusion, in which he was followed by Smith, Ricardo, and orthodox economists up through the Great Depression, was that while a particular industry such as the car industry could overproduce, no generalized overproduction was possible. In this respect, orthodox economics flew in the face of all the evidence. In his analysis of overproduction, Marx focused on what he considered the basic contradiction of capitalism—and, in microcosm, of the commodity itself—the contradiction between "use value" and "exchange value." The idea is that a commodity both satisfies a specific need (it has "use value") and can be exchanged for other articles (it has "exchange value"). This distinction was not invented by Marx; it can be found in the work of Smith. Unlike Smith, however, Marx emphasized the way exchange value—what something is worth in the market—overwhelms the use value of a commodity. Unless a commodity can be sold, the portion of society's useful labor embodied in it is wasted (and the product is useless to those in need). Vast real needs remain unsatisfied for the majority of people, doubly so when—during crises of overproduction—vast quantities of goods remain unsold because there is not enough "effective demand."

It is during these crises that capitalism's unlimited drive to develop society's productive capacity clashes most sharply with the constraints it places on the real incomes of the majority to buy the goods they need. Marx developed this notion of a demand crisis over 75 years before the so-called "Keynesian revolution" in economic thought (whose key insights were actually developed before Keynes by the Polish economist Michal Kalecki on the foundations of Marx's analysis).

Marx expected that these crises of overproduction and demand would worsen as capitalism developed, and that the crises would slow down more and more the development of society's productive capacities (what Marx called the "forces of production"). Ultimately, he believed, these crises would be capitalism's undoing. He also pointed to them as evidence of the basic depravity of capitalism. "In these crises," Marx writes in the *Communist Manifesto*,

> there breaks out an epidemic that, in all earlier epochs would have seemed an absurdity, the epidemic of overproduction. Society suddenly finds itself put back into a state of momentary barbarism; it appears as if a famine, a universal war of devastation had cut off the supply of every means of subsistence; industry and commerce seem to be destroyed; and why? Because there is too much civilization, too much means of subsistence, too much industry, too much commerce …
>
> And how does the bourgeoisie get over these crises? On the one hand by enforced destruction of productive force; on the other hand, by the conquest of new markets, and by the more thorough exploitation of old ones.

This kind of crisis came so close to bringing down capitalism during the Great Depression that preventing them became a central aim of government policy. While government intervention has managed to smooth out the business cycle, especially in the wealthiest countries, capitalism has hardly become crisis-free.

While the reigning complacency about a new, crisis-free capitalism is much easier to sustain here than in, say, East Asia, capitalism clearly has not yet run up against any absolute barrier to its development. In fact, Marx's discussions (in the *Communist Manifesto* and elsewhere) of capitalism's irresistible expansive impulse—capital breaking down all barriers, expanding into every crevice, always "thirsting

> AS AESTHETICALLY APPEALING AS THE CLOCKWORK HARMONY OF THE ORTHODOX MODEL MAY BE, THIS IS PRECISELY ITS FAILING.

for surplus value" and new fields of exploitation—seem as apt today as they did 150 years ago.

MARX AS PROPHET

Marx got a great deal about capitalism just right—its incessant, shark-like forward movement; its internal chaos, bursting forth periodically in crisis; its concentration of economic power in ever fewer hands. Judged on these core insights, the Marxist system can easily stand toe-to-toe with the orthodox model. Which comes closer to reality? The capitalism that incessantly bursts forth over new horizons, or the one that constantly gravitates towards comfortable equilibrium? The one where crisis is impossible, or the one that lurches from boom to bust to boom again? The one where perfect competition reigns, or the one where a handful of giants towers over every industry?

In all these respects, Marx's system captures the thundering dynamics of capitalism much better than the orthodox system does. As aesthetically appealing as the clockwork harmony of the orthodox model may be, this is precisely its failing. Capitalism is anything but harmonious.

There was also a lot that Marx, like any other complex thinker, predicted incorrectly, or did not foresee. In this respect, he was not a prophet. His work should be read critically, and not, as it has been by some, as divine revelation. Marx, rather, was the prophet of a radical approach to reality. In an age when the "free market" rides high, and its apologists claim smugly that "there is no alternative," Joan Robinson's praise of Marx is apt: "[T]he nightmare quality of Marx's thought gives it … an air of greater reality than the gentle complacency of the orthodox academics. Yet he, at the same time, is more encouraging than they, for he releases hope as well as terror from Pandora's box, while they preach only the gloomy doctrine that all is for the best in the best of all *possible* worlds."

Resources: Joan Robinson, *An Essay on Marxian Economics* (Macmillan, 1952); "Manifesto of the Community Party," and "Crisis Theory (from Theories of Surplus Value)," in Robert C. Tucker, ed., *The Marx-Engels Reader* (W.W. Norton, 1978); Roman Rosdolsky, *The Making of Marx's 'Capital'* (Pluto Press, 1989); Ernest Mandel, "Karl Heinrich Marx"; Luigi L. Pasinetti, "Joan Violet Robinson"; and John Eatwell and Carlo Panico, "Piero Sraffa"; in John Eatwell, Murray Milgate, and Peter Newman, eds., *The New Palgrave: A Dictionary of Economics* (Macmillan, 1987).

ARTICLE 8.6

September/October 2002

UNDER THE MARGINS
FEMINIST ECONOMISTS LOOK AT GENDER AND POVERTY

BY RANDY ALBELDA

For all the hype about welfare-to-work, most former welfare recipients are still living in poverty. It is true that, since the advent of 1990s-style "welfare reform," families no longer on welfare are earning more, on average, than those still on welfare. But more often than not, the jobs that former welfare mothers find don't provide employer-sponsored health insurance, vacation time, sick leave, or wages sufficient to support their families. In fact, the percentage of families who are "desperately" poor (with incomes at or below 50% of the official poverty line) has gone up since the mid-1990s, and so has the percentage of former welfare recipients who report hardships such as difficulty feeding their families or paying bills. And remember: All of this occurred during a so-called economic boom.

So why does the emphasis on work (and now marriage) continue to dominate the welfare debate? In large part, this is because the poverty "story" of the last 20 years—created and perpetuated by conservative ideologues and politicians—blames poor people for their own poverty. Women supposedly have too many children without husbands, poor black urban dwellers exhibit pathological behaviors, and liberal welfare policies—by expanding government spending and providing an attractive alternative to jobs and marriage—have made matters worse.

At least one group of theorists—feminist economists—says it isn't so. It is women's particular economic role in capitalism—as caregiver—that shapes their relationship to the labor market, men, and the state. Feminist economists have shown how having and caring for children affects the economic status of women—including women who are not mothers but are still relegated to poorly paid care-giving jobs. While their voices are largely ignored in research and policy circles, feminist economists' analyses provide the best understanding of the obstacles low-income families face and the range of policy options that might work.

WOMEN AND POVERTY

Almost everywhere, women are the majority of poor adults. Recently, a group of sociologists from several U.S. universities looked at poverty in eight industrialized nations. Using a relative poverty measure (half of median family income), they found that, in the 1990s, women's poverty

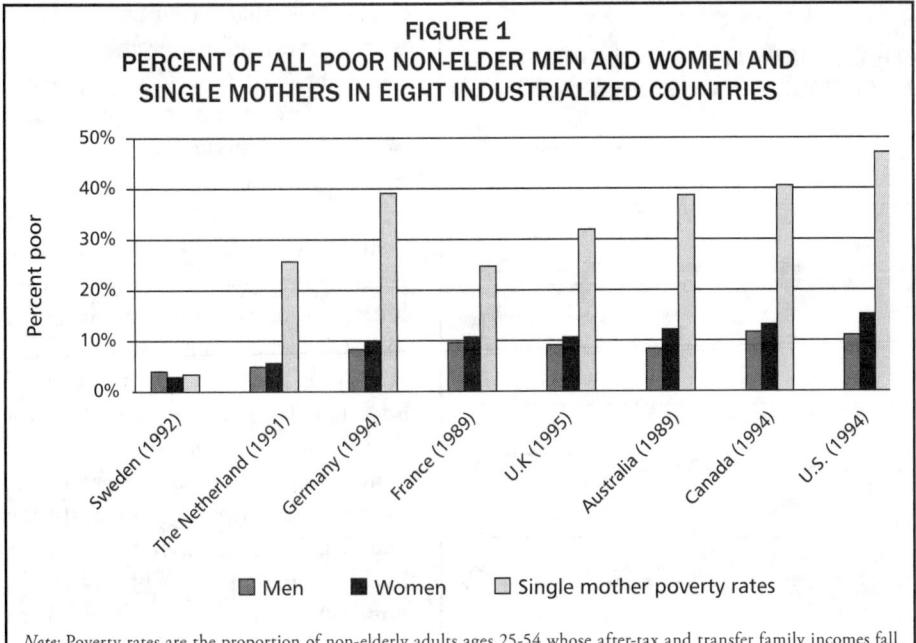

FIGURE 1
PERCENT OF ALL POOR NON-ELDER MEN AND WOMEN AND SINGLE MOTHERS IN EIGHT INDUSTRIALIZED COUNTRIES

Note: Poverty rates are the proportion of non-elderly adults ages 25-54 whose after-tax and transfer family incomes fall below 50% of the median family income.
Source: Table 1, in Karen Christopher et al., "Gender Inequality in Poverty in Affluent Nations: The Role of Single Motherhood and the State," in Karen Vleminckx and Timothy Smeeding, eds., *Child Well-Being, Child Poverty and Child Policy in Modern Nations* (London: Policy Press, 2001).

rates exceeded men's in all countries but Sweden. Further, they found that single-mother poverty rates—even in countries with deep social welfare systems—are exceptionally high. (See Figure 1.)

In the United States in 2000, women comprised just over half of the adult population but constituted 61% of all poor adults. (The U.S. poverty income threshold is based on an absolute dollar figure determined in the 1960s and since indexed for inflation.) Toss in children, and the data are even grimmer; 16.2% of all children were poor, while over one-third of all single-mother families were poor. Together, women and children comprised 76% of the poor in the United States, far surpassing their 62% representation in the population as a whole.

Since the late 1950s (when the data were first collected), single-mother families in the United States have never constituted more than 13% of all families; however, they form just under half of all poor families. Figure 2 depicts the proportion of all families—and all poor families—that are single-mother families. The steepest increase occurred in the late 1960s on the heels of the War on Poverty, as poverty rates for everyone were falling.

ECONOMIC THEORY AND POVERTY

From Adam Smith onward, most economists have understood poverty by looking at labor markets, labor-market inequality, and economic growth. According to this approach, it is underemployment or the lack of employment—and the resulting lack of income—that causes poverty. A brief summary of the dominant economic theories in the last half of the 20th century illustrates the point.

Keynesian economic theory argues that the lack of demand in the economy as a whole leads to unemployment. When investors and consumers can't jumpstart the economy, we need fiscal or monetary economic stimuli to induce demand. It was this wisdom that has guided economists to promote economic growth as a way to reduce poverty, arguing that "a rising tide lifts all boats"—as, for example, during the Kennedy and Johnson administrations.

Marxian theorists say that, under capitalism, unemployment cannot be totally eliminated because it is a necessary component of capitalist production that serves to "discipline" workers. Unless we make radical changes to the economic system, there will always be families that are without employment and therefore poor.

Like Marxian economists, *institutional* economists also believe that economic outcomes aren't simply the result of pure market forces; cultural, social, and political forces also come into play. In the 1970s, economists Peter Doeringer and Michael Piore identified distinct labor-market segments. Younger workers, workers of color, and women tend to end up in what they call the "secondary labor market"—characterized by low wages, few promotional opportunities, and easy-to-acquire skills—more than other workers. These workers are particularly vulnerable to unemployment and hence more likely to be poor. The way to relieve poverty is to help these workers move into better jobs, or to create policies that make their jobs better.

These understandings of poverty offer little or no gender analysis—presumably what ails men is equally applicable to women. Analyses of insufficient (aggregate) demand, unemployment, and labor-market inequality rarely mention women or discuss how and why gender matters—unless feminist scholars provide them.

Neoclassical (mainstream) economists also argue that poverty is caused by lack of employment and low wages—but they consider workers responsible for their own wage levels. Workers who choose not to pursue education, training, or on-the-job experience will participate in the labor force less often than more highly trained and skilled workers, be less productive, and receive lower wages. Unlike the political economy theorists just discussed, many non-feminist economists—the most well known being Nobel Prize winner Gary Becker—have tackled the topic of women's lower wages. But they consistently conclude that women's lack of employment, or employment at low wages,

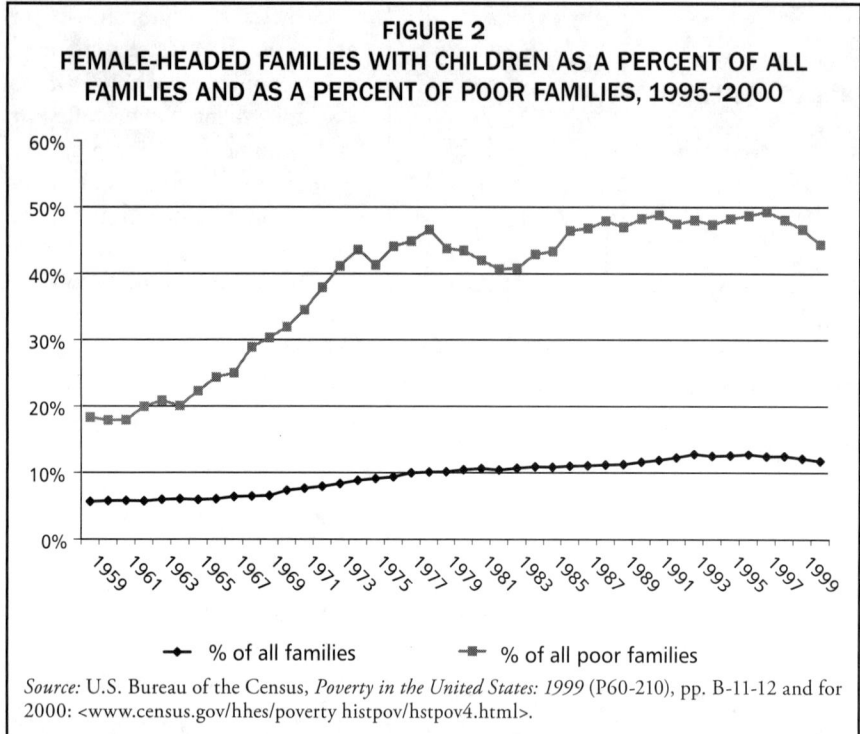

**FIGURE 2
FEMALE-HEADED FAMILIES WITH CHILDREN AS A PERCENT OF ALL FAMILIES AND AS A PERCENT OF POOR FAMILIES, 1995–2000**

Source: U.S. Bureau of the Census, *Poverty in the United States: 1999* (P60-210), pp. B-11-12 and for 2000: <www.census.gov/hhes/poverty histpov/hstpov4.html>.

results from rational individual choice. Only policies that boost incentives for individuals to invest in themselves (like tax credits for education) will alleviate poverty.

GENDER MATTERS

It is true that one reason women are poor is that they are not in the labor force or are underemployed. But while employment is an important underpinning to understanding poverty, it is not the same for women as for men.

Most economists who study labor markets assume that workers in capitalist economies are "unencumbered"—that they don't have significant constraints on their time outside of paid work. Encumbered workers are treated as a "special case"—worthy of examination, but understood and analyzed as an exception rather than the rule.

Since the beginnings of capitalism, however, female workers have almost always been "encumbered." And women's role as caregivers—their main encumbrance—has shaped their participation in the economy, as feminist historians and economic historians have shown. Historically, women's economic opportunities have been severely constricted, with race, age, and marital status sending important market "signals" about where women could or should be employed. For example, until the 1960s, many professional and some clerical jobs had "marriage bars," i.e., employers refused to hire married women on the assumption that they did not need the salaries these jobs paid, and would not stick around once they had children. Similarly, before anti-discrimination laws were enacted, many workers of color could not get jobs as managers in many professions, or even as sales clerks if the business catered to a white clientele.

For more than a century, this labor market "ordering" has given rise to employment, income, and wage policies that reinforce and reproduce women's political and economic dependence on men (and non-whites' inferior status in relation to whites). These policies assume that the standard family is a heterosexual married couple with a lone male breadwinner employed in industrial production. For example, in order to collect unemployment insurance benefits, workers must work a minimum number of hours and receive a minimum amount of earnings. Because many women work part-time and earn low wages, they are much less likely to qualify for benefits than men. Similarly, Social Security benefits are based on previous earnings over a sustained period of employment. Women who have spent most of their adult lives as caregivers are thus ineligible for benefits on their own, and must rely on their husbands' contributions instead.

Men's and women's employment patterns are very different. Women's labor force participation rates are lower than men's, and women's employment experiences in economic downturns often differ from men's. Women's job options and choices are also highly influenced by care-giving responsibilities; mothers are more likely than fathers to trade higher-paying jobs for jobs that are closer to childcare, have more flexible schedules, or require fewer hours.

In addition to shaping women's paid labor-market activities, care work has been economically, socially, and politically undervalued, as feminist economists point out. This is true both when that work is done in the home for free and when others do it for low pay. Among the few jobs immigrant women and women of color can almost always find are low-paying care-work jobs, and they are disproportionately represented in those jobs. For example, in 2001, women were 47% of all workers but 97% of child care workers, 93% of registered nurses, 90% of health aides, and 72% of social workers. Black workers comprised 11% of the workforce but were 33% of health aides, 23% of licensed practical nurses, and 20% of cleaning service workers. This type of occupational "stereotyping" reinforces the care-giving roles that women and people of color fill, and the low pay (relative to jobs with similar skill requirements) reinforces women's dependence on men and racial inequality. Economist Nancy Folbre, in her 2001 book *The Invisible Heart: Economics and Family Values*, calls this the "care penalty."

It is because of their low-paid and unpaid care work, then, that women are particularly economically vulnerable and much more likely to be poor than are men. The role of care giving—as distinct from other factors like employment, economic growth, and labor-market inequality—helps to explain not only women's employment patterns but also women's poverty. So theories of poverty that rely on analyses of employment that assume all people are men—or that women are a special case of men—are not only incomplete, they are wrong.

FEMINIST ANALYSES OF POVERTY

It is no coincidence that, when there has been a viable women's movement—in the early part of the 20th century and in the late 1960s—feminists and women researchers have paid particular attention to poor women.

Documenting poor families: early efforts

In the early 20th century, there was a good deal of concern about how women fit into the capitalist economy. Social scientists living in or near poor communities—often in settlement houses established by women reformers—conducted surveys of women workers, mostly through government-sponsored research. Many of the surveys found that the biggest problems faced by two-parent families were a lack of employment and insufficient wages. Researchers readily recognized that families headed by women were constrained by women's role as caregiver and women's low wages. Instead of advocating more employment for women, they promoted relatively meager levels of public assistance.

In the 1910s and 1920s, women reformers were key players not only in doing research but also in creating policies directed toward poor women and children. These women imposed white middle-class values about child-rearing, hygiene, and education; their construction of "deservingness" replicated and reinforced the ways in which women and men, immigrants and non-immigrants, were supposed to act. At the same time, they successfully implemented income supplement programs for single-mother families at the state level, and they were instrumental in incorporating AFDC (Aid to Families with Dependent Children) into the Social Security Act of 1935. Feminist poverty researchers and reformers did not emerge again until the late 1960s.

Sisterhood may be powerful, but motherhood is not: recent efforts

The women's movement of the late 1960s and 1970s laid some important foundations for understanding women's poverty, even though its main economic strategies were aimed at improving the wages of women who were employed. Feminists fought for affirmative action, which was most successful in creating opportunities for college-educated women. Today, women hold 46% of executive and professional jobs—exactly their representation in all jobs—and comprise just under 30% of all doctors and lawyers. Feminists also organized for comparable worth, which was intended to lift wages for low-income women by recognizing and rewarding the skill level and effort needed to perform low-paying women's jobs (including care-giving ones).

At the same time, feminist scholars called attention to women's "double day" (now called "work/family conflict") and theorized about the role of care work and reproduction in capitalist economies. From the outset, feminist analysts understood that "housework" was work and a vital component of capitalist production. This intellectual work paralleled "wages for housework" campaigns that were launched in Italy, Canada, Great Britain, and the United States.

Using these tools to reinterpret poverty was not hard. Among the first to apply a feminist analysis to women's poverty was sociologist Diana Pearce, in an 1978 article entitled "The Feminization of Poverty: Women, Work, and Welfare." Pearce called attention to the fact that women were disproportionately represented among the poor. Her phrase—"the feminization of poverty"—became very popular in feminist circles as well as in the mainstream press.

Economist Nancy Folbre followed up with a theoretical framework directly linking women's care work as mothers to their poverty. In her 1985 article, "The Pauperization of Motherhood: Patriarchy and Social Policy in the U.S.," she argued that, when the costs of raising children are shifted onto women, women (and children) become dependent on men. Then, when fathers abandon their families, women and children are consigned to poverty. Folbre also argues that public policies around divorce, child support, unemployment insurance, and welfare reinforce this relationship. For example, welfare policies—even before the 1990s reforms—never provided enough income for women to support their families without working "under the table" or getting unreported income, paying a big price for not being married.

Single mothers especially bear the burden of these policies in the form of incredibly high poverty rates. But, Folbre points out, the benefits of care labor—healthy, productive children who become tax-paying adults—are enjoyed by all of society, not merely the mothers who provided the care. If society recognized the value of women's care work and compensated them for it, then fewer women would be poor.

Current trends

Currently, some feminist scholars are addressing the ways that gender influences government allocation of income supports (like pensions, unemployment insurance, and welfare) and non-cash assistance (e.g., education and child care). Sociologist Ann Orloff and political scientists Diane Sainsbury and Jane Lewis argue that state welfare policies (construed broadly) embody deeply gendered notions of citizenship and need. Much of this work is theoretical and does not explicitly address poverty. However, it helps to explain the lack of policies that would correct women's poverty.

Other researchers are focusing on how people's capacity—access to health and education, living conditions, how they are treated in a society—affects their potential to generate income and causes poverty. Building on the work of economist Amartya Sen, feminist economists in the United States have shown that it is unreasonable and unlikely to expect single mothers to "work" their way out of poverty—because women earn lower wages than men, because they have care-giving responsibilities, and because the additional costs associated with caring for children restrict their capacity to be employed even while family needs remain high. For example, Barbara Bergmann and Trudi Renwick developed budgets for low-income families in the 1990s. Chris Tilly and I have demonstrated that the income needs of single-mother families far exceed their earnings possibilities—even with full-time employment. This work refutes the claims of liberals who supported welfare reform in the naïve belief that welfare recipients could easily substitute earnings for public assistance.

Finally, feminist economists are documenting how low-income women—especially single-mother families in which the same adult is both caregiver and breadwinner—relate to the labor market, fathers, and the state. Using longitudinal data, feminist social scientists Roberta Spalter-Roth and Heidi Hartmann found that many poor single-mother families either combine government assistance with wages (under or above the table) or cycle between the two. This research is confirmed and extended by feminist sociologists like Kathryn Edin and Laura Lein, who, through extensive interviews with poor single mothers, documented the particular ways and times that poorly paying jobs as well as men and their incomes drift in and out of women's lives. These studies make it clear that women's employment is not family-sustaining, and that, to survive, single-mother families need a sane combination of earnings, child support, *and* government assistance. In contrast to the narrowly focused, incentive-based literature that characterizes poor women's behavior as pathological, these approaches demonstrate that poor women's lives are dynamic yet fragile, and that the decisions they make are creative, adaptive, and almost always child-centered.

WHO CARES?

Despite their efforts, feminist scholars have not had much impact on the poverty literature—at least not in economics—nor have they influenced policies intended to alleviate poverty. Much (though not all) poverty research is grant-funded, and it tends to focus narrowly on evaluating the individual impact of welfare reform, mostly by looking at welfare "leavers." These factors discourage the use of feminist analysis, since most funding goes either to conservative think tanks with a specific ideological aversion to feminism or to "liberal" think tanks that have made their fortunes in mainstream analysis fitted to their main consumer—the federal government.

Further, these conventional studies often preclude the larger political economy approach taken by feminists. Welfare reform is a mechanism of social control over poor single women—especially women of color—that is part of a larger conservative agenda to justify if not exacerbate economic inequality, assure a large pool of low-wage labor, and silence important political movements. Feminist analysis suggests the need for policies that would not only reduce poverty but also change women's (and people of color's) relationship to the labor market, (white) men, and the state, thus loosening the grip of economic dependence. This isn't in line with the right-wing agenda at all.

However, feminist economic analysis has been very useful to activists who are trying to help poor women. For example, in the mid-1990s, Wider Opportunity for Women (WOW), a feminist group based in Washington, D.C., started conducting family economic self-sufficiency standard projects. Currently, WOW operates projects in 40 states and D.C. The studies demonstrate how much income a single-mother family needs to survive, and are being used as organizing tools in the states.

During the mid-1990s welfare reform debates and now in discussions about reauthorization of Temporary Assistance for Needy Families (TANF), feminist scholars—connected informally through the "Women's Committee of 100"—have argued that raising children is work and that responsible legislation should recognize unpaid work as work. The Committee has called for a caregiver's allowances (see "Wages for Housework," article 1.5, and <www.welfare2002.org>). And while Congress has not embraced these ideas, a TANF reauthorization bill sponsored by Representative Patsy Mink (D-Hawaii) in the spring of 2002 garnered support from close to 90 members of the House.

Feminist economists argue that the role of economists is to understand how societies do or do not provide for people's needs. Through their research and skills, they provide the tools for activists to argue that women's employment status and care-giving responsibilities place many at the bottom of the economic pecking order. At the same time, feminist economists are connecting their work directly to social movements, lending their expertise—and their own voices—to living wage campaigns, efforts to improve compensation for child care workers and home health aides, and efforts to eliminate poverty, not welfare.

Resources: Kathryn Edin and Laura Lein, *Making Ends Meet: How Single Mothers Survive Welfare and LowWage Work* (Russell Sage Foundation, 1997); Nancy Folbre, "The Pauperization of Motherhood: Patriarchy and Social Policy in the U.S.," *Review of Radical Political Economics*, vol. 16, no. 4 (1984): 72-88; Nancy Folbre, *The Invisible Heart: Economics and Family Values* (New York: The New Press, 2001); Jane Lewis, "Gender and the Development of Welfare Regimes," *Journal of European Social Policy* 3 (1992): 159-73; Alice O'Connor, *Poverty Knowledge: Social Science, Social Policy, and the Poor in Twentieth Century U.S. History* (Princeton, N.J.: Princeton University Press, 2001); Ann Orloff, "Gender and the Social Rights of Citizenship: The Comparative Analysis of Gender Relations and Welfare States," *American Sociological Review* 58 (1993): 303-28; Diana Pearce, "The Feminization of Poverty: Women, Work, and Welfare," *Urban and Social Change Review* (February 1978); Trudi Renwick and Barbara Bergmann, "A Budget-based Definition of Poverty with an Application to Single-parent Families," *Journal of Human Resources* 28, no. 1 (1993): 1-24; Diane Sainsbury, *Gender, Equality, and Welfare States* (Cambridge:

Cambridge University Press, 1996); Amartya K. Sen, *Development as Freedom* (New York: Alfred A. Knopf, 1999); Roberta SpalterRoth et al., *Welfare That Works: The Working Lives of AFDC Recipients* (Washington, D.C.: Institute for Women's Policy Research, 1995); Chris Tilly and Randy Albelda, "Family Structure and Family Earnings: The Determinants of Earnings Differences among Family Types," *Industrial Relations* 33, no. 2 (1994): 151-167; U.S. Census, *Current Population Surveys* <www.census.gov/hhes/income/histinc/histpovtb.html>; Bureau of Labor Statistics, *Employment and Earnings*, Table 11 <*www.bls.gov/cps/home.htm#charemp.*>

CHAPTER 9
INTERNATIONAL TRADE AND FINANCE

INTRODUCTION

When it comes to the global economy, most textbooks line up behind the "Washington Consensus"—a package of free trade and financial liberalization policies that the U.S. Treasury Department, the International Monetary Fund (IMF), and the World Bank have spun into the prevailing prescriptions for the world's developing economies. Mainstream textbook discussions of exchange rates, international trade, and economic development policies almost always promote a market-dictated integration into the world economy. Outside the classroom, however, popular discontent with the Washington Consensus has spawned a worldwide movement calling into question the myth of self-regulating markets on which these policies rest.

While the doctrines of free trade and financial liberalization are seldom questioned in mainstream economics textbooks, both are scrutinized here. Arthur MacEwan gives an overview of the process of globalization today, what is new and what continues long-established patterns, and the difficulties opposition groups face coming to grips with the power and the complexity of these forces (Article 9.1). MacEwan's second article shows how industrialized economies developed by protecting their own manufacturing sectors—never preaching the "gospel of free trade" until they were highly developed. Today, he argues, these countries prescribe free trade not because it's the best way for others to develop, but because it gives U.S. corporations free access to the world's markets and resources, which in turn strengthens the power of businesses against workers (Article 9.2).

Economist Ramaa Vasudevan takes a critical look at the doctrine of comparative advantage, the backbone of free trade theory, and shows that it comes up short as a guide for economic development (Article 9.3). John Miller debunks the Economic Freedom Index that the Heritage Foundation and other backers of neoliberal globalization use to argue that economic freedom and prosperity go hand-in-hand. Miller argues that the Index measures neither prosperity nor freedom, but rather corporate freedom from accountability (Article 9.4). In another article, John Miller takes on the *Wall Street Journal*'s editors' claim that policies that promote equality stand in the way of rapid economic growth. Miller argues that, contrary to the claims of the editors, the experience of the East Asian economies shows that poverty reduction depends on both raising a nation's income and reducing its inequality (Article 9.8).

Economist Marie Duggan lays bare the financial flows and policies that lie behind the unprecedented current account deficit of the United States and increased reliance of the U.S. economy on foreign capital, especially from China. She traces the flight of foreign capital from the United States with the onset of current crisis and why it ceased when other economies across the globe fell into crisis (Article 9.5). Two important factors in the huge U.S. current account deficit come from U.S. dependence on foreign oil and the sizable remittance from workers in the United States to their families in the developing world. Environmentalist Paul Cummings looks at who controls the supply and price of the oil market, how the oil market imposes tremendous costs on the environment, and how it ought to be regulated (Article 9.6). Alissa Thuotte looks at the large and growing flow of remittances that have improved the standard of living of families in the developing world but left them vulnerable to far off economic disturbances, as the current crisis illustrates (Article 9.10). Higher remittances are associated with a modest reduction in global poverty. But just is the proper way to measure global poverty? Economist MacEwan accesses the different measures of poverty in the developing world (Article 9.7).

Labor standards are another casualty of neo liberal globalization. In his last article, Arthur MacEwan argues that using trade agreements to pressure governments to allow unhindered union organizing is always a good thing. But when it comes to including other labor standards in trade agreements, from use of child labor to health and safety standards, MacEwan councils first-world activists to take their lead from the workers in the developing world affected by those agreements (Article 9.12). John Miller replies to *New York Times* columnist Nicholas Kristof, who steadfastly maintains that more sweatshops, not fewer, is the key to lifting young men and women in Sub-Saharan Africa out of

---

KEY TO COLANDER

E = Economics   M = Macroeconomics

The articles in this chapter are linked to chapters E2, E9, E36, E37, E38 or M2, M19, M20, M21, M22, which take up macroeconomic policies in International Trade and Finance as well as issues faced by developing countries.

Articles 9.1, 9.2, 9.3 cover the issues of Globalization, Comparative Advantage and Outsourcing. This chapter is a welcome addition to the last three chapters of Colander's "Economics" and four chapters of his "Macroeconomics."

poverty. Miller then offers an alternative set of policies to bring development to the region (Article 9.13). Sociologist Stephen Philion interviews economist Han Deqiang, one of China's leading critics of that country's neoliberal development strategy. Deqiang enumerates the devastating social costs of this strategy, including its toll on China's workers and farmers (Article 9.9). Martha Ojeda, Executive Director of the Coalition for Justice in the Maquiladoras, paints a devastating picture of the effects of the North American Free Trade Agreement (NAFTA) on workers in *maquiladoras*, or border factories, over the last twenty years. In her article, she recounts how women played a central role in the struggle for workers to establish a democratic union at a Sony plant in Nuevo Laredo, a Mexican border town (Article 9.11).

DISCUSSION QUESTIONS

1. (Article 9.1) According to MacEwan, what aspects of today's globalization are new and what continues earlier trends? How might opposition forces best push for a more democratic and equitable globalization process?
2. (Article 9.2) MacEwan claims that the "infant industry" argument for trade protection is much more widely applicable than standard theory suggests. To what countries and industries might it apply in today's world economy? Explain your answer.
3. (Article 9.2) Free trade, MacEwan argues, gives business greater power relative to labor. Why is this so? Is it a good reason to oppose free trade?
4. (Article 9.3) What is the doctrine of comparative advantage? And why, according to Vasudevan, is it not a good guide to successful economic development?
5. (Article 9.4) According to Miller, how is the Economic Freedom Index misleading about the relationship between "free market policies," economic growth, economic income, and political freedom?
6. (Article 9.5) What is a current account deficit and what causes it? What problems does the present U.S. current account deficit create for the U.S. economy and its citizens?
7. (Article 9.5) Why did foreign capital leave the United States with the onset of the current crisis in 2007 and why did it return a year later?
8. (Article 9.6) What forces determine the price of oil? Do they include the supply and demand for oil?
9. (Article 9.6) How do the failures of the oil market affect the environment and what should be done about them?
10. (Article 9.7) What are the standard measures of global poverty? What is a more effective way to measure global poverty?
11. (Article 9.8) What does the experience of the East Asian economies suggest about the relationship between equity, economic growth, and poverty alleviation? Give specific examples from the 22 developing countries studied by the Asian Development Bank.
12. (Article 9.9) According to Philion and Deqiang, what has been the impact of China's neoliberal development policies on Chinese workers in export factories, state-owned enterprises, small shops, and on farms?
13. Article (9.10) How big are remittances? Where do they come from and where do they go? Finally, what sort of effect are they having on families in the developing world?
14. (Article 9.11) What was the role of women workers in organizing the Sony *maquiladora* factory? How has NAFTA impacted the rights of Mexican workers in the *maquiladora* plants?
15. (Article 9.12) What are the pros and cons of including labor standards in trade agreements? Why does MacEwan consider the right to organize unions a special case? Do you agree with MacEwan that first-world activists pressing more stringent labor standards across the global economy should take their cue from workers in the developing world?
16. (Article 9.13) What is the basis of journalist Nicholas Kristof's claim that young men on the streets of Namibia's capital city need the opportunity to work in sweatshops? Why does Miller find Kristof's claim unconvincing? Who do you think is right? Why?

ARTICLE 9.1

WHAT IS GLOBALIZATION?

BY ARTHUR MacEWAN

Ever since Adam and Eve left the garden, people have been expanding the geographic realm of their economic, political, social and cultural contacts. In this sense of extending connections to other peoples around the world, globalization is nothing new. Also, as a process of change that can embody both great opportunities for wealth and progress and great trauma and suffering, globalization at the beginning of the 21st century is following a well established historical path. Yet the current period of change in the international system does have its own distinctive features, not the least important of which is the particular sort of political conflict it is generating.[1]

"GREATEST EVENTS" AND "DREADFUL MISFORTUNES"

We are fond of viewing our own period as one in which great transformations are taking place, and it is easy to recite a list of technological and social changes that have dramatically altered the way we live and the way we connect to peoples elsewhere in the world. Yet, other surges of globalization in the modern era have been similarly disruptive to established practices. The first surge by which we might mark the beginning of modern globalization came with the invasion of the Western Hemisphere by European powers and with their extension of ocean trade around Africa to Asia. Adam Smith, writing *The Wealth of Nations* in 1776, did not miss the significance of these developments:

The discovery of America, and that of a passage to the East Indies by the Cape of Good Hope, are the two greatest and most important events recorded in the history of mankind... By uniting, in some measure, the most distant parts of the world, by enabling them to relieve one another's wants, to increase one another's enjoyments, and to encourage one another's industry, their general tendency would seem to be beneficial.

Alongside of what Adam Smith saw as the great gains of globalization (not his term!), were the slaughter, by battle and disease, of millions of Native Americans, the enslavement and associated deaths of millions of Africans, and the subjugation of peoples in Asia. Smith did recognize the "dreadful misfortunes" that fell upon the peoples of the East and West Indies as a result of these "greatest events" (though he does not mention Africans in this expression of concern). He saw these misfortunes, however, as arising "rather from accident than from any thing in the nature of the events themselves."

The first stage of modern globalization illustrates not only the combined great gains and "dreadful misfortunes" that have characterized globalization but also the vast scope of the process. The political and economic changes that followed from the European conquest of the Americas and forays into Asia are relatively well known. Equally momentous were the huge cultural transformations that were tied to the great expansion of economic contacts among the continents. Peoples moved, or they were moved by force. As they came to new locations and in contact with other peoples, almost every aspect of their lives was altered—from what people eat ("Italian" spaghetti with tomato sauce comes from Asia, the spaghetti, and America, the tomatoes) to their music (jazz is now the best known example, blending the backgrounds of different continents to emerge in America) to religion (the cross accompanied the sword in the era of colonial conquest).

The second great surge of modern globalization came in the 19th century, both as product and cause of the Industrial Revolution. On the one hand, the expansion of industry generated large reductions in transport costs that brought huge increases in international commerce. On the other hand, for the emerging commercial centers of Europe and North America, the opening of foreign markets and access to foreign sources of raw materials fueled (sometimes literally) the expansion of industry. Great Britain, as the "workshop of the world," was at the center of these changes and over the course of the century saw its foreign trade increase three times as rapidly as national income.

Britain during the 19th century provided a foreshadowing of current-day globalization as it officially touted "free trade" as the proper mode of organization for commerce—not just for itself, but for the entire world. The gospel of "free trade" was then carried around the globe by the British navy, and heroic ideological gymnastics allowed a growing

---

[1] We usually measure "the extent of economic connections" by levels of imports and exports relative to total production or by the level of international investment relative to total production. For example, in 1913, US exports were 6% as large as Gross Domestic Product (GDP); the figure had fallen to 4.6% in 1950, but was up to 7.1% in 1973 and 10.6% in 1999. For Europe, the figures are: 22% in 1913, 16.7% in 1950, 21.8% in 1973, and 32.1% in 1999. Interestingly, Japan, for which exports were 20% of GDP in 1913, saw this figure remain relatively stable at around 10% of GDP in the latter half of the 20th century. Figures on foreign investment are harder to come by for the early part of the 20th century, but they seem to show a similar pattern. In recent years, the foreign investment figures show strong increases of economic connections. In the 1985-90 period, for the world as a whole, foreign direct investment (i.e., not including financial investments) were 5.4% of the level of GDP in the countries making the investments and 6.0% of GDP in the countries receiving the investments; in the 1996-98 period, the figures had risen to 8.2% and 8.4%, respectively.

colonial empire to be included under this same rubric. As the British historian E. J. Hobsbawm has commented, "British industry could grow up, by and large, in a protected home market until strong enough to demand free entry into other people's markets, that is 'Free Trade'." In today's globalization it is the United States, a country that also attained its economic power on the foundation of protectionism, that preaches the gospel of "free trade" to the rest of the world.

Current day globalization is, by and large, a continuation of the process that began in the 19th century (which in turn had its roots in the great transformation that began along with the 16th century). Two world wars and the Great Depression disrupted the progress of globalization for some sixty years and shifted its center from Britain to the United States, but it is now back on track. By the 1980s, the extent of economic connections that had been established among the world's national economies by 1913 had been reattained, and in subsequent years international trade and investment have continued to expand their roles in the economies of most nations.

HOMOGENIZATION AND COMPETITION

Change in the world economy today, however, is not simply an extension of what went on in earlier periods, not simply a quantitative extension of well established trends. What distinguishes the current era from earlier phases of globalization is that now capitalism is ubiquitous. Virtually everywhere, production takes place for profit and is based on wage labor. In the 19th century, capitalism may have provided the leading dynamic of the international economy, but in many parts of the world—most everywhere outside of Europe and North America—a great deal of economic activity was organized through families (peasant farms or shops), under semi-feudal conditions, or through slavery. These activities were all connected to markets and to a world capitalist system, but they were not capitalist in themselves. Certainly there are important aspects of life and work today which take place outside of markets and are not directly capitalist—for example, work in the home, interactions within governments, volunteer activity, and some other forms of production. Yet capitalism holds sway, dominating and defining economic relationships in almost all parts of the world.

The ubiquity of capitalism gives a new character to the economic connections among peoples in distant parts of the world. There has, in particular, been a grand homogenization, both of consumer markets and of production activity. Wal-Mart and McDonald's establish themselves in Mexico to sell the same sorts of products in the same way as in the United States. At the same time, Mexican workers at the Ford plant in Hermosillo produce the same cars that are produced in US factories and they do so with equipment and procedures that are among the most "modern" in the world. Also on the production side, plants in Mexico and the United States are sometimes integrated with one another in a "global assembly line," with Mexican workers engaged in the labor intensive aspects of the operation and US workers engaged in the more highly skilled activities; for example, in clothing production, design and cutting is done in the United States while the pieces are stitched together on the Mexican side of the border.

Mexico, because of its proximity to the United States and the reduction of trade restrictions between the two countries, presents an extreme example of the cross-border integration of production. Yet in broad terms, we are presented today with a new international organization of production, as people on different corners of the globe produce the same sorts of products with the same technologies and often for the same employers—though the ultimate employers often operate through local subcontractors.

The homogenization of the world economy creates a new set of relationships, a direct competition, among workers in different parts of the world. Although such competition always existed, it is much more extensive and intense than in the past and, most important, it takes place between workers whose wages are dramatically different from each other. It is one thing when US and Canadian workers, who have very similar wages and standards of living, are in competition with each other. It is quite another thing when the US and Canadian workers are in competition with Mexican workers.

This new relationship among workers in different countries presents obvious problems for the workers in the rich countries: they simply cannot compete with workers who, using the same equipment and methods of production (i.e., the same technology), are paid far, far lower wages. Yet similar, though perhaps less obvious, problems exist for the low-wage workers as well. With wage labor markets existing throughout most of the world, virtually all workers are placed in competition with one another. While workers in Bangladesh may be willing to accept very low wages to assemble clothing for the European market, they are always faced with the prospect that Vietnamese workers may accept even lower wages. Or Indonesian workers, who assemble sports shoes for the US market, may face the prospect of production innovations that will substitute machinery and skilled workers for unskilled workers on an assembly line, making it profitable for the firms to move their production back to the United States.

In a capitalist world, where many different sites around the world provide firms with the labor markets they need, those firms can have a great advantage over workers. That advantage, however, depends upon "free trade," the elimination of government barriers to the movement of goods and funds across national boundaries. Free trade has given firms the option of either moving themselves or moving their sources of supply in response to cost differences (wage differences, but also other cost differences). Free trade, however, does not include the reduction—let alone the elimination—of barriers to the movement of workers. So labor does not enjoy the same freedom in the globalized economy as does capital. Since "freedom" means having alternatives, and having alternatives means having power, a system that enhances the freedom of firms relative to the freedom of labor means giving businesses more power relative to labor. (Even were barriers to migration to be reduced, there are still substantial costs to labor movement compared to capital movement; and capital's advantage, while reduced, would not be eliminated.)

The drive for free trade existed, as pointed out above, in the British-led globalization of the 19th century, but the United States has been able to push the concept to a whole new level. In part, free trade is important for the power it confers on business, but it is also important as ideology. The ideology of free trade has provided the defining rationale for the North American Free Trade Agreement (NAFTA), the Free Trade Agreement of the Americas (FTAA), the World Trade Organization (WTO), and the programs pushed on low income countries by the International Monetary Fund (IMF) and the World Bank. The opening of markets, the opening of sources of supply, the spread of private economic activity—all of this is supposed to provide a new era of rapid economic growth for the world and serve the needs of the poor as well as the rich.

NOT SO FAST

The concept of free trade has a certain intuitive appeal. After all, if the firms and people of a nation are free to buy their supplies from the lowest-cost source of supply, then they will be able to buy more and satisfy their needs more thoroughly than if their government limits the sources from which they can buy those supplies (bans imports) or imposes extra costs (tariffs) on supplies from abroad. For low income countries, desperate for economic growth, it would seem absurd for their governments to place restrictions on imports, forcing firms and people to waste resources on expensive domestic goods. Moreover, it only takes a moment's reflection to note the huge gains we attain from international commerce: not only the banana I eat for breakfast and a good portion of the oil that fuels my car and heats my home, but also the ideas and culture from elsewhere in the world—to say nothing of the competitive pressures from abroad that help drive economic advances in my own country. For a small country, the gains from foreign commerce are a virtual necessity.

Another moment's reflection, however, reveals that things are not so simple. Free trade is not the only way to engage extensively in international commerce. In fact, none of the countries we now denote as "developed" attained their development through free trade, though all engaged extensively in international commerce. There are, it seems, some substantial advantages to having the production of certain kinds of goods take place within a country, as compared to obtaining those same goods from abroad. The US textile industry in the 19th century, the US auto industry through most of the 20th century, the Japanese computer industry in the mid-20th century, the South Korean steel and ship building industries later in the 20th century—all generated broad economic gains in terms of the transformation of technology and the formation of a skilled work force that far surpassed the costs that arose from the government protection they received in their early stages of expansion. None of this provides a justification for protectionism in general; continuing protection of sugar and steel production in the United States imposes costs with no off-setting benefits (except to those directly engaged in the industries). Yet the experience of two centuries of capitalist development does demonstrate the fallacy of the free trade argument. Efforts by the US government to push free trade on low income countries today may make sense from the perspective of the interests of US firms, but it is hardly a prescription for economic advancement in low income countries.

But there is more. Globalization as it is being organized under the banner of free trade is doing nothing to reduce the "development gap," the huge difference in material well-being between the peoples of the rich nations and the peoples of most of the rest of the world. In fact, there is some evidence that under the regime of increasingly open world markets, the "development gap" is increasing. Worse yet: there is a good deal of evidence that free trade globalization is contributing to increasing inequality within nations, not only within the low income countries of the "South" but also within the United States and the other high income countries of the "North."

As the international economy is increasingly organized in a way that enhances the power of firms and tends to undermine the power of labor, it is certainly likely that greater inequality would be the outcome. Unfortunately, available data do not allow us to draw strong conclusions about what has been happening to world income inequality in recent decades. What we do know is that income distribution in today's world is already grossly unequal, with hundreds of millions of people living at the edge of subsistence, while the elites in all countries live in obscene luxury. We also know that, although some low income countries have made substantial gains (South Korea and some other countries of East Asia), the current surge of globalization has provided no general relief for the world's poor. Furthermore, we know that globalization—new patterns of international trade and investment—has disrupted people's lives, pushed people out of their traditional lines of work, shifted the location of economic activity, and forced people to adopt new patterns of consumption. All of this makes many people's lives very unpleasant, regardless of what can be uncovered with the aggregate statistics regarding income distribution and economic growth.

WHAT ELSE IS NEW?

One might well absorb this summary of change in the world economy and respond with the comment: So, what else is new? It does seem that periods of great change in the world economy, whatever immediate benefits they may generate for the elite and whatever their long run benefits for society in general, are accompanied by severe disruptions, hardships and inequalities. Current day experience seems to fit well with the pattern established in the 16th and 19th centuries, to say nothing of earlier eras of imperial expansion. (Many commentators quite reasonably reject the term "globalization" in favor of "imperialism" precisely because the latter term underscores the great inequalities of power and income that are always so important in international affairs.)

Yet perhaps there is something new in the current era in the particular type of political response to globalization that has been generated in recent years. The "dreadful misfortunes" of earlier eras have also generated political responses —sometimes in the form of spontaneous rebellion, sometimes as more organized resistance and revolution, and sometimes as waves of new oppositional organizations and alliances. The political response to globalization at the beginning of the 21st century, however, has some distinguishing characteristics that are worth emphasizing.

Most important, parts of the response to globalization are themselves global. The coming out "party" for the anti-globalization movement in Seattle in the fall of 1999 involved people and organizations from all over the world. As a coordinated effort by groups from many rich countries and many poor countries, the action in Seattle—and the ones that have followed in Washington, Quebec, Prague, Puerto Allegre, and elsewhere—suggest something is different about the nature of political action. Many times, opposition movements based on national identities have, at least implicitly, been in conflict with one another; at other times, organizations in rich countries have opted to "support" groups in poor countries, but not as a joint and coordinated effort. While progressive movements have always talked about their internationalism, this time around the talk may translate more effectively into practice.

Also, the globalization of political opposition to globalization has included steps by labor unions, which have long adhered to highly nationalist positions. So far, more of the new internationalism of the US labor movement has been in the realm of rhetoric rather than practice, but US unions have made some important efforts at cross border organizing—in the form, for example, of supporting efforts of Mexican workers to organize firms in their country that supply the US market. (NAFTA, while allowing corporations, the organizations of capital, to operate in both the United States and Mexico, as well as Canada, makes no parallel provision for unions, the organizations of labor.) The rhetoric of internationalism, too, is important, especially because it marks such a departure from the past practices of the US labor movement. Some critics complain that the new-found interest of the US labor movement in conditions abroad arises from its own immediate concerns, the competition from low-cost imports, instead from a concern for workers elsewhere in the world. But that is just the point. If globalization forces US unions to secure the interests of their own members by pursuing a new internationalism, then that is certainly a change of significance.

The organized opposition to globalization goes far beyond the labor movement, however, involving a wide spectrum of social movements. Environmental and women's organizations, peasant groupings, student-based action committees, and others have all been a part of the actions. In addition, well established non-governmental organizations such as Oxfam, while not engaged in the protest actions in Seattle and elsewhere, have been a part of the general opposition to globalization. Not only is this opposition based on a wide range of social movements, but these different movements have at least begun to work in alliance with one another. Some aspects of this alliance, particularly that between environmental groups and labor unions, suggest a major shift from past conflicts.

Opposition actions have taken place in a wide spectrum of countries. On the one hand, there have been the much publicized actions led by young, often middle-class activists in the United States, focused on meetings of the principal international economic agencies such as the IMF, World Bank, and WTO. On the other hand, there have been actions in India, where peasant organizations have demonstrated against the international pharmaceutical and seed companies that are trying to use the internationalization of patent regulations to secure their control of world markets. While these geographically disparate actions are not coordinated through any cohesive international organization, they are part of an interconnected movement.

The opposition that has developed to globalization is not a cohesive movement, and it is not so well developed that we can have confidence in its lasting impact. Furthermore, it has many problems. Opposition to globalization sometimes is expressed as an opposition to connections with other peoples rather than as an opposition to the way those connections are exacerbating inequalities of power and income. Thus xenophobic protectionism is sometimes just below the surface of protest actions. By and large, however, the opposition to globalization appears to be based on an internationalism that may provide a basis for a progressive, and perhaps lasting, movement.

The more serious problems of this opposition arise from the difficulties in coming to grips with the power and complexity of the globalization process itself. A small example is provided by efforts in the rich countries to respond to the proliferation of imports of goods produced in "sweat shop" conditions in low income countries. Protests against the companies that utilize these shops—firms such as Nike and Gap—are met with the response that workers in these "sweat shops" are eager to obtain their jobs because these jobs are significantly better in terms of pay and working conditions than other available jobs. What's more, the response is often true. A sophisticated movement can come to terms with this reality by emphasizing the need to alter the context that impoverishes workers in low income countries and by stressing that such a context is most effectively transformed through political struggle. Also, by focusing on workers' right to political freedom—in particular, the right to organize unions—rather than on particular aspects of workers' conditions, anti-sweat shop activists can have a positive impact.

The "sweat shop" example helps clarify that globalization is not simply a collection of practices, not simply a peculiar set of connections among peoples around the globe. It is part of the long historical development and spread of capitalism. Within the framework of capitalism, it is difficult to solve problems that are based on the inequality of income and power, because those problems are generated by the system itself. Nonetheless, capitalism is not an immutable system, and it is probably not a permanent system. The oppositional struggles are not only responses to globalization, but they are part of the process of globalization itself. They will play a role in shaping events and in shaping the entire nature of the process. And they will contribute to answering the question: What is globalization?

Reprinted with permission from *Radical Teacher*, Issue 61, 2001.

ARTICLE 9.2

November/December 1991, updated July/August 2002

THE GOSPEL OF FREE TRADE
THE NEW EVANGELISTS

BY ARTHUR MacEWAN

In the early 1990s, the passage of the North American Free Trade Agreement marked a new epoch of U.S. economic expansion into the Americas. Today, the chimes of "free trade" are ringing out even more loudly in corporate America, as neoliberal economic policies—such as the Free Trade Area of the Americas —continue to make their way around the world.

With his article, "The Gospel of Free Trade," published in November 1991, Arthur MacEwan helped Dollars & Sense readers to demystify the role of trade in the development of domestic economies. Drawing on the lessons of economic history, MacEwan shows that "free trade" is not the best route to economic prosperity for nations.

Just as British corporations cheered in favor of free trade in the 19th century, the largest U.S. corporations today are pushing to reduce restraints on trade and investment. The result: downward pressure on wages and social welfare programs in both rich and poor countries, and a reduced capacity of citizens across the globe to control their own economic conditions.

—Darius Mehri

Free trade! It's the cure-all for the 1990s. With all the zeal of Christian missionaries, the U.S. government has been preaching, advocating, pushing, and coercing around the globe for "free trade."

While a Mexico-U.S.-Canada free trade pact is the immediate aim of U.S. policy, George Bush has heralded a future free trade zone from the northern coast of Canada to the southern tip of Chile. For Eastern Europe, U.S. advisers prescribe unfettered capitalism and ridicule as unworkable any move toward a "third way." Wherever any modicum of economic success appears in the Third World, free traders extol it as one more example of their program's wonders.

Free traders also praise their gospel as the proper policy at home. The path to true salvation—or economic expansion, which, in this day and age, seems to be the same thing—lies in opening our markets to foreign goods. Get rid of trade barriers, allow business to go where it wants and do what it wants. We will all get rich.

Yet the history of the United States and other advanced capitalist countries teaches us that virtually all advanced capitalist countries found economic success in protectionism, not in free trade. Likewise, heavy government intervention has characterized those cases of rapid and sustained economic growth in the Third World.

Free trade, does, however, have its uses. Highly developed nations can use free trade to extend their power and their control of the world's wealth, and business can use it as a weapon against labor. Most important, free trade can limit efforts to redistribute income more equally, undermine progressive social programs, and keep people from democratically controlling their economic lives.

A DAY IN THE PARK

At the beginning of the 19th century, Lowell, Massachusetts, became the premier site of the country's textile industry. Today, thanks to the Lowell National Historical Park, you can tour the huge mills, ride through thee canals that redirected the Merrimack River's power to the mills, and learn the story of the textile workers, from the Yankee "mill girls" of the 1820s through the various waves of immigrant laborers who poured into the city over the next century.

During a day in the park, visitors get a graphic picture of the importance of 19th-century industry to the economic growth and prosperity of the United States. Lowell and the other mill towns of the era were centers of growth. They not only created a demand for Southern cotton, they also created a demand for new machinery, maintenance of old machinery, parts, dyes, skills, construction materials, construction machinery, more skills, equipment to move the raw materials and products, parts maintenance for that equipment, and still more skills. The mill towns also created markets —concentrated groups of wage earners who needed to buy products to sustain themselves. As centers of economic activity, Lowell and similar mill towns contributed to U.S. economic growth far beyond the value of the textiles they produced.

The U.S. textile industry emerged decades after the industrial revolution had spawned Britain's powerful textile industry. Nonetheless, it survived and prospered. British linens inundated markets throughout the world in the early 19th century, as the British navy nurtured free trade and kept ports open for commerce. In the United States, however, hostilities leading up to the War of 1812 and then a substantial tariff made British textiles relatively expensive. These limitations on trade allowed the Lowell mills to prosper, acting as a catalyst for other industries and helping to create the skilled work force at the center of U.S. economic expansion.

> **FREE TRADE FORCES DOWN THE GENERAL LEVEL OF WAGES ACROSS THE BOARD, EVEN OF THOSE WORKERS NOT DIRECTLY AFFECTED BY IMPORTS.**

Beyond textiles, however, tariffs did not play a great role in the United States during the early 19th century. Southern planters had considerable power, and while they were willing to make some compromises, they opposed protecting manufacturing in general because that protection forced up the price of the goods they purchased with their cotton revenues. The Civil War wiped out Southern opposition to protectionism, and from the 1860s through World War I, U.S. industry prospered behind considerable tariff barriers.

DIFFERENT COUNTRIES, SIMILAR STORIES

The story of the importance of protectionism in bringing economic growth has been repeated, with local variations, in almost all other advanced capitalist countries. During the late 19th century, Germany entered the major league of international economic powers with substantial protection and government support for its industries. Likewise, in 19th-century France and Italy, national consolidation behind protectionist barriers was a key to economic development.

Only Britain—which entered the industrial era first—might be touted as an example of successful development without tariff protection. Yet, in addition to starting first, Britain built its industry through the expansion of its empire and the British navy, hardly prime ingredients in any recipe for free trade.

Japan provides a particularly important case of successful government protection and support for industrial development. In the post-World War II era, when the Japanese established the foundations for the modern "miracle," the government rejected free trade and extensive foreign investment and instead promoted its national firms.

In the 1950s, for example, the government protected the country's fledgling auto firms from foreign competition. At first, quotas limited imports to $500,000 (in current dollars) each year; in the 1960s, prohibitively high tariffs replaced the quotas. Furthermore, the Japanese allowed foreign investment only insofar as it contributed to developing domestic industry. The government encouraged Japanese companies to import foreign technology, but required them to produce 90% of parts domestically within five years.

The Japanese also protected their computer industry. In the early 1970s, as the industry was developing, companies and individuals could only purchase a foreign machine if a suitable Japanese model was not available. IBM was allowed to produce within the country, but only when it licensed basic patents to Japanese firms. And IBM computers produced in Japan were treated as foreign-made machines.

Today, while Japan towers as the world's most dynamic industrial and financial power, one looks in vain for the role free trade played in its success. The Japanese government provided an effective framework, support, and protection for the country's capitalist development.

Likewise, in the Third World, capitalism has generated high rates of economic growth where government involvement, and not free trade, played the central role. South Korea is the most striking case. "Korea is an example of a country that grew very fast and yet violated the canons of conventional economic wisdom," writes Alice Amsden in *Asia's Next Giant: South Korea and Late Industrialization,* widely acclaimed as the most important recent book on the Korean economy. "In Korea, instead of the market mechanism allocating resources and guiding private entrepreneurship, the government made most of the pivotal investment decisions. Instead of firms operating in a competitive market structure, they each operated with an extraordinary degree of market control, protected from foreign competition."

With Mexico, three recent years of relatively moderate growth, about 3-4% per year, have led the purveyors of free trade to claim it as one of their success stories. Yet Mexico has been opening its economy increasingly since the early 1980s, and most of the decade was an utter disaster. Even if the 1980s are written off as the cost of transition, the recent success does not compare well with what Mexico achieved in the era when its government intervened heavily in the economy and protected national industry. From 1940 to 1980, with policies of state-led economic development and extensive limits on imports, Mexican national output grew at the high rate of about 6% per year.

The recent Mexican experience does put to rest any ideas that free market policies will improve the living conditions for the masses of the people in the Third World. The Mexican government has paved the road for free trade policies by reducing or eliminating social welfare programs. In addition, between 1976 and 1990, the real minimum wage declined by 60%. Mexico's increasing orientation toward foreign trade has also destroyed the country's self-sufficiency in food, and the influx of foreign food grains has forced small farmers off the land and into the ranks of the urban unemployed.

THE USES OF FREE TRADE
While free trade is not the best economic growth or development policy, the largest and most powerful firms in many countries find it highly profitable. As Britain led the cheers for free trade in the early 19th century, when its own industry was already firmly established, so the United States—or at least many firms based in the United States—finds it a profitable policy in the late 20th century.

For U.S. firms, access to foreign markets is a high priority. Mexico may be relatively poor, but with a population of 85 million it provides a substantial market. Furthermore, Mexican labor is cheap; using modern production techniques, Mexican workers can be as productive as workers in the United States. For U.S. firms to obtain full access to the Mexican market, the United States must open its borders to Mexican goods. Also, if U.S. firms are to take full advantage of cheap foreign labor and sell the goods produced abroad to U.S. consumers, the United States must be open to imports.

On the other side of the border, wealthy Mexicans face a choice between advancing their interests through national development or advancing their interests through ties to U.S. firms and access to U.S. markets. For many years, they chose the former route. This led to some development of the Mexican economy but also—due to corruption and the massive power of the ruling party—created huge concentrations of wealth in the hands of a few small groups of firms and individuals. Eventually, these groups came into conflict with their own government over regulation and taxation. Having benefited from government largesse, they now see their fortunes in greater freedom from government control and, particularly, in greater access to foreign markets and partnerships with large foreign companies. National development is a secondary concern when more involvement with international commerce will produce greater riches quicker.

In addition, the old program of state-led development in Mexico ran into severe problems. These problems came to the surface in the 1980s with the international debt crisis. Owing huge amounts of money to foreign banks, the Mexican government was forced to respond to pressure from the International Monetary Fund, the U.S. government, and large international banks. That pressure meshed with the pressure coming from Mexico's own richest elites, and the result has been the move toward free trade and a greater opening of the Mexican economy to foreign investment.

Of course, in the United States, Mexico, and elsewhere, advocates of free trade claim that their policies are in everyone's interest. Free trade, they point out, will mean cheaper products for all. Consumers in the United States, who are mostly workers, will be richer because their wages will buy more. In both Mexico and the United States, they argue, rising trade will create more jobs. If some workers lose their jobs because cheaper imported goods are available, export industries will produce new ones.

Such arguments obscure many of the most important issues in the free trade debate. Stated, as they usually are, as universal truths, these arguments are plain silly. No one, for example, touring the Lowell National Historical Park could seriously argue that people in the United States would have been better off had there been no tariff on textiles. Yes, in 1820, they could have purchased textile goods more cheaply, but the cost would have been an industrially backward, impoverished nation. One could make the same point with the Japanese auto and computer industries, or indeed with numerous other examples from the last two centuries of capitalist development.

In the modern era, even though the United States already has a relatively developed economy with highly skilled workers, a freely open international economy does not serve the interests of U.S. workers, though it will benefit large firms. U.S. workers today are in competition with workers around the globe. Many different workers in many different places can produce the same goods and services. Thus, an international economy governed by the free trade agenda will bring down wages for U.S. workers.

The problem is not simply that of workers in a few industries—such as auto and steel—where import competition is the most obvious and immediate problem. A country's openness to the international economy affects the entire structure of earnings in that country. Free trade forces down the general level of wages across the board, even of those workers not directly affected by imports. The simple fact is that when companies can produce the same products in several different places, it is owners who gain because they can move their factories and funds around much more easily than workers can move themselves around. Capital is mobile, labor is much less mobile. Businesses, not workers, gain from having a larger territory in which to roam.

CONTROL OVER OUR ECONOMIC LIVES
But the difficulties with free trade do not end with wages. Free trade is a weapon in the hands of business when it opposes any progressive social programs. Efforts to place environmental restrictions on firms are met with the threat of moving production abroad. Higher taxes to improve the schools? Business threatens to go elsewhere. Better health and safety regulations? The same response.

Some might argue that the losses from free trade for people in the United States will be balanced by gains for most people in poor countries—lower wages in the United States, but higher wages in Mexico. Free trade, then, would bring about international equality. Not likely. In fact, as pointed out

Chapter 9: International Trade and Finance 191

above, free trade reforms in Mexico have helped force down wages and reduce social welfare programs, processes rationalized by efforts to make Mexican goods competitive on international markets.

Gains for Mexican workers, like those for U.S. workers, depend on their power in relation to business. Free trade and the imperative of international "competitiveness" are just as much weapons in the hands of firms operating in Mexico as they are for firms operating in the United States. The great mobility of capital is business' best trump card in dealing with labor and popular demands for social change—in the United States, Mexico, and elsewhere.

None of this means that people should demand that their economies operate as fortresses, protected from all foreign economic incursions. There are great gains that can be obtained from international economic relations—when a nation manages those relations in the interests of the great majority of the people. Protectionism often simply supports narrow vested interests, corrupt officials, and wealthy industrialists. In rejecting free trade, we should move beyond traditional protectionism.

Yet, at this time, rejecting free trade is an essential first step. Free trade places all the cards in the hands of business. More than ever, free trade would subject us to the "bottom line," or at least the bottom line as calculated by those who own and run large companies.

For any economy to operate in the interest of the great majority, people's conscious choices—about the environment, income distribution, safety, and health—must command the economy. The politics of democratic decision-making must control business. In today's world, politics operates primarily on a national level. To give up control over our national economy—as does any people that accepts free trade—is to give up control over our economic lives.

Resources: The New Gospel: North American Free Trade," *NACLA's Report on the Americas* 24(6), May 1991; Robert Pollin and Alexander Cockburn, "Capitalism and its Specters: The World, the Free Market and the Left," *The Nation*, 25 February 1991; P. Armstrong, A. Glyn, and J. Harrison, *Capitalism Since World War II*, 1984.

ARTICLE 9.3

July/August 2007

COMPARATIVE ADVANTAGE

BY RAMAA VASUDEVAN

Dear Dr. Dollar:

When economists argue that the outsourcing of jobs might be a plus for the U.S. economy, they often mention the idea of comparative advantage. So free trade would allow the United States to specialize in higher-end service-sector businesses, creating higher-paying jobs than the ones that would be outsourced. But is it really true that free trade leads to universal benefits?

—David Goodman, Boston, Mass.

You're right: The purveyors of the free trade gospel do invoke the doctrine of comparative advantage to dismiss widespread concerns about the export of jobs. Attributed to 19th-century British political-economist David Ricardo, the doctrine says that a nation always stands to gain if it exports the goods it produces *relatively* more cheaply in exchange for goods that it can get *comparatively* more cheaply from abroad. Free trade would lead to each country specializing in the products it can produce at *relatively* lower costs. Such specialization allows both trading partners to gain from trade, the theory goes, even if in one of the countries production of *both* goods costs more in absolute terms.

For instance, suppose that in the United States the cost to produce one car equals the cost to produce 10 bags of cotton, while in the Philippines the cost to produce one car equals the cost to produce 100 bags of cotton. The Philippines would then have a comparative advantage in the production of cotton, producing one bag at a cost equal to the production cost of 1/100 of a car, versus 1/10 of a car in the United States; likewise, the United States would hold a comparative advantage in the production of cars. Whatever the prices of cars and cotton in the global market, the theory goes, the Philippines would be better off producing only cotton and importing all its cars from the United States, and the United States would be better off producing only cars and importing all of its cotton from the Philippines. If the international terms of trade—the relative price—is one car for 50 bags, then the United States will take in 50 bags of cotton for each car it exports, 40 more than the 10 bags it forgoes by putting its productive resources into making the car rather than growing cotton. The Philippines is also better off: it can import a car in exchange for the export of 50 bags of cotton, whereas it would have had to forgo the production of 100 bags of cotton in order to produce that car domestically. If the price of cars goes up in the global marketplace, the Philippines will lose out in relative terms—but will still be better off than if it tried to produce its own cars.

The real world, unfortunately, does not always conform to the assumptions underlying comparative-advantage theory. One assumption is that trade is balanced. But many countries are running persistent deficits, notably the United States, whose trade deficit is now at nearly 7% of its GDP. A second premise, that there is full employment within the trading nations, is also patently unrealistic. As global trade intensifies, jobs created in the export sector do not necessarily compensate for the jobs lost in the sectors wiped out by foreign competition.

The comparative advantage story faces more direct empirical challenges as well. Nearly 70% of U.S. trade is trade in similar goods, known as *intra-industry trade*: for example, exporting Fords and importing BMWs. And about one third of U.S. trade as of the late 1990s was trade between branches of a single corporation located in different countries (*intra-firm trade*). Comparative advantage cannot explain these patterns.

Comparative advantage is a static concept that identifies immediate gains from trade but is a poor guide to economic development, a process of structural change over time which is by definition dynamic. Thus the comparative advantage tale is particularly pernicious when preached to developing countries, consigning many to "specialize" in agricultural goods or be forced into a race to the bottom where cheap sweatshop labor is their sole source of competitiveness.

The irony, of course, is that none of the rich countries got that way by following the maxim that they now preach. These countries historically relied on tariff walls and other forms of protectionism to build their industrial base. And even now, they continue to protect sectors like agriculture with subsidies. The countries now touted as new models of the benefits of free trade—South Korea and the other "Asian tigers," for instance—actually flouted this economic wisdom, nurturing their technological capabilities in specific manufacturing sectors and taking advantage of their lower wage costs to *gradually* become effective competitors of the United States and Europe in manufacturing.

The fundamental point is this: contrary to the comparative-advantage claim that trade is universally beneficial, nations as a whole do not prosper from free trade. Free trade creates winners and losers, both within and between countries. In today's context it is the global corporate giants that are propelling and profiting from "free trade": not only outsourcing white-collar jobs, but creating global commodity chains linking sweatshop labor in the developing countries of Latin America and Asia (Africa being largely left out of the game aside from the export of natural resources such as oil) with ever-more insecure consumers in the developed world. Promoting "free trade" as a political cause enables this process to continue.

It is a process with real human costs in terms of both wages and work. People in developing countries across the globe continue to face these costs as trade liberalization measures are enforced; and the working class in the United States is also being forced to bear the brunt of the relentless logic of competition.

Resources: Arthur MacEwan, "The Gospel of Free Trade: The New Evangelists," Dollars & Sense, July/August 2002; Ha-Joon Chang, Kicking away the Ladder: The Real History of Fair Trade, Foreign Policy in Focus, 2003; Anwar Shaikh, "Globalization and the Myths of Free Trade," in Globalization and the Myths of Free Trade: History, Theory, and Empirical Evidence, ed. Anwar Shaikh, Routledge 2007.

ARTICLE 9.4   March/April 2005

FREE, FREE AT LAST
ECONOMIC FREEDOM FOR CORPORATIONS HAS LITTLE TO DO WITH EITHER POLITICAL FREEDOM OR ECONOMIC GROWTH.

BY JOHN MILLER

HAIL ESTONIA!
For the first time in the 11 years that the Heritage Foundation and The Wall Street Journal *have been publishing the Index of Economic Freedom, the U.S. has dropped out of the top 10 freest economies in the world. ...*

The 2005 Index, released today, ranks Hong Kong once again as the world's freest economy, followed by Singapore and Luxembourg. But it is Estonia at No. 4 that makes the point. This former Soviet satellite is a model reformer, setting the standard for how fast countries can move ahead in the realm of economic liberalization. ...

The U.S. ... scores well. But worrying developments like Sarbanes-Oxley in the category of regulation and aggressive use of antidumping law in trade policy have kept it from keeping pace with the best performers in economic freedom. Most alarming is the U.S.'s fiscal burden, which imposes high marginal tax rates for individuals and very high marginal corporate tax rates. ...

Policy makers who pay lip service to fighting poverty would do well to grasp the link between economic freedom and prosperity. This year the Index finds that the freest economies have a per-capita income of $29,219, more than twice that of the "mostly free" at $12,839, and more than four times that of the "mostly unfree." Put simply, misery has a cure and its name is economic freedom.

—Wall Street Journal op-ed by Mary Anastasia O'Grady, January 4, 2005

I must be confused. I somehow thought that an Economic Freedom Index would showcase countries that are reducing the democratic deficits of the global economy by giving people more control over their economic lives and the institutions that govern them. In the hands of the *Wall Street Journal* and the Heritage Foundation, Washington's foremost right-wing think tank, however, an economic freedom index merely measures corporate and entrepreneurial freedom from accountability. Upon examination, the index turns out to be a poor barometer of either freedom more broadly construed or of prosperity.

The index does not even pretend that its definition of economic freedom has anything to do with political freedom. Take the two city-states, Hong Kong and Singapore, which top the index's list of free countries. Both are only "partially free" according to *Freedom in the World*, an annual country-by-country assessment published by the nonpartisan think tank Freedom House, which the *Journal*'s editors themselves have called "the Michelin Guide to democracy's development." Hong Kong is still without direct elections for its legislature or its chief executive, and a proposed internal security law threatens press and academic freedom as well as political dissent. In Singapore, freedom of the press and the right to demonstrate are limited; films, TV, and other media are censored; preventive detention is legal; and you can do jail time for littering.

Moving further down the list of "free" countries, the rankings are no better correlated with any ordinary definition of "freedom," as economic journalist Robert Kuttner pointed out when the index was first published in 1997. For instance, Bahrain (#20), where the king holds an effective veto over parliament and freedom of expression is limited, ranks higher than Norway (#29), whose comprehensive social insurance and strong environmental regulation drag down its score. Likewise, Kuwait, an emirship no one would term free or democratic, is tied (at #54) with Costa Rica, long the most vigorous democracy in Latin America.

These results are not surprising, however, given the index's premise: the less a government intervenes in the economy, the higher its freedom ranking. Specifically, the index breaks "economic freedom" down into 10 components: trade policy; fiscal burden of government; level of government intervention; monetary policy; financial liberalization; banking and finance policies; labor market policies; enforcement of property rights; business, labor, and environmental regulations; and size of the black market. In other words, minimum-wage laws, environmental regulations, or requirements for transparency in corporate accounting make a country less free, whereas low business taxes, harsh debtor laws, and little or no regulation of occupational health and safety make a country more free.

Consider that the index docks the United States' ranking for passing Sarbanes-Oxley, a law that seeks to improve corporate accounting practices and to make CEOs responsible for their corporations' profit reports. The segment of the U.S. population whose economic freedom this law erodes is tiny, but it's obviously that segment—not workers and not even shareholders—whose freedom counts for the folks at the *Journal* and at Heritage.

The rather objective-looking list that results from assessing the 10 components ranks 155 countries from freest (Hong Kong and Singapore) to most repressive (Burma and North Korea). The index then becomes a tool its authors can use to hammer home their message: economic freedom (as they define it) brings prosperity. As they point out, "the freest economies have a per-capita income more than twice that of the 'mostly free' and more than four times that of the 'mostly unfree.'"

Not so fast. For one thing, the index's creators used some oddball methods that compromise its linkage of prosperity to economic freedom.

For instance, according to the index, the fiscal burden of the Swedish and Danish welfare states is smaller than that of the United States, even though U.S. government spending is more than 20 percentage points lower relative to Gross Domestic Product (GDP, or the size of the economy). This bizarre result comes about because the index uses the change in government spending, not its actual level, to calculate fiscal burden.

To measure the tax side of a country's fiscal burden, the index uses the top rate of the personal and corporate income taxes—and that's equally misleading. Besides ignoring the burden of other taxes, these two figures don't get at *effective* tax rates, which also depend on what share of corporate profits and personal income is actually taxed. On paper, U.S. corporate tax rates are higher than those in Europe, as the *Journal* is quick to point out. But nearly half of U.S. corporate profits go untaxed. The average rate of taxation on U.S. corporate profits currently stands at 15%, far below the top corporate tax rate of 35%. And relative to GDP, U.S. corporate income taxes are no more than half those of other OECD countries.

The index's treatment of government intervention is flawed as well, for it fails to count industrial policy as a form of intervention. This is a serious mistake: it means that the index overestimates the degree to which some of the fastest growing economies of the last few decades, such as in Taiwan and South Korea, relied on the market and underestimates the positive role that government played in directing economic development in those countries by guiding investment and protecting infant industries.

The treatment of informal markets is downright strange. The index considers a large informal sector to indicate less economic freedom because government restrictions must have driven that economic activity underground. (Of course, you could take the opposite view: since the informal sector is for the most part unregulated, countries with larger informal sectors are, by the index's definition, more free!) But this way of looking at it biases the index. Developing countries tend to have large informal sectors while developed economies usually have small informal sectors. That means the index systematically lowers the economic freedom index of developing countries while boosting the scores of developed countries, thus artificially correlating income levels with economic freedom. Even right-wing economist Stefan Karlsson of the libertarian Ludwig Von Mises Institute has criticized the index on this point. Thanks in part to this bias, Estonia, Chile, and Bahrain are the only middle-income countries to make it into the top 20.

Whatever the biases in the index do to cement a tight relationship between economic freedom and income, they can't produce a tight correlation between economic freedom and *growth*. The fastest-growing countries are mostly unfree. Take China, India, and Vietnam, three of the fastest-growing countries in the world. They are way down in the rankings, at #112, #118, and #137 respectively. While all three countries have adopted market reforms in recent years that have improved their standing in the index, their trade policies and regulations remain "repressive." And there are plenty of relatively slow growers among the countries high up in the index, including Estonia (#4), the *Journal*'s poster child for economic freedom. How free or unfree a country is according to the index seems to have little to do with how quickly it grows.

An "Economic Freedom Index" that tells us little about economic growth or political freedom is a slipshod measure that would seem to have no other purpose other than to sell the neoliberal policies that stand in the way of most people gaining control over their economic lives and obtaining genuine economic freedom in today's global economy.

Resources: Mary Anastasia O'Grady, "Hail Estonia!" *Wall Street Journal*, 1/4/05; *The 2005 Index of Economic Freedom* (Heritage Foundation, 2005); Johan Fernandez, "Malaysia climbs up economic freedom index," *The Star Online*, 1/25/05; "Freedom & Growth: No Siamese twins," *The Economic Times*, 5/27/02; Robert Kuttner, "A Weird Set of Values," *The American Prospect*, 12/7/97; Stefan M. I. Karlsson, "The Failings of the Economic Freedom Index," (Ludwig Von Mises Institute, 1/21/05); "Freedom in the World 2005: Civic Power and Electoral Politics," (Freedom House, 2005) <www.freedomhouse.org/research/survey2005.htm>.

ARTICLE 9.5

January/February 2009

THE SPECTER OF CAPITAL FLIGHT
HOW LONG WILL THE POWER OF THE DOLLAR PROTECT THE U.S.?

BY MARIE DUGGAN

The depth and scope of the unfolding financial crisis have taken most observers by surprise. Yet there were definite warning signs. One was the United States' growing dependence on foreign capital, an issue that came to my attention in 2005 when I was preparing a lecture on Mexico's mid-1990s financial crisis. This was the so-called Tequila Crisis: foreign investors and wealthy Mexicans abruptly fled dollar-denominated Mexican bonds called Tesebonos as well as Mexican stocks, moving their money into safer U.S. assets. In hindsight, many observers point to Mexico's increased borrowing from abroad in the early 1990s, reflected in its worsening current account deficit, as a sign of impending trouble. (See "Current Account Explained," page 23.)

Curious about where the United States stood, I was shocked to discover that the U.S. current account deficit in 2005, measured as a percent of GDP, was approaching the same level as Mexico's had been in 1993—and getting worse

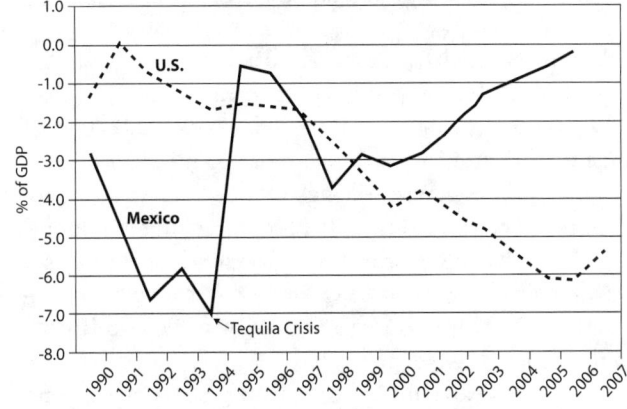

FIGURE 1

CURRENT ACCOUNT AS A PERCENT OF GDP: MEXICO VS. UNITED STATES

Source: World Bank, WDI Online

(see Figure 1). In other words, in the early 2000s the United States became as dependent on foreign financing as Mexico was just prior to its crisis.

Mexico was only the first of many emerging markets to undergo spectacular financial crises in the late 1990s and early 2000s. The list includes Thailand, Indonesia, South Korea, Malaysia, Russia, and Argentina, among others.

The typical financial crisis story in an emerging market begins with capital flight—the sudden withdrawal of money by foreign investors from an economy's stocks, bonds, and banking system. Often locals decide to move their wealth abroad as well. Stock markets crash, banks fail, the local currency drops in value, and governments face default. Interest rates rise as governments try to woo foreign investors and their own citizens back into the home currency with the promise of high returns, but then the high interest rates push domestic borrowers, whether firms or households, toward bankruptcy. Unemployment shoots up and GDP falls. In some emerging markets, the magnitude of these difficulties mirrored those the United States experienced in the Great Depression of the 1930s.

At the time, the United States and the other developed countries were widely viewed as immune from such financial crises.

Now it is clear that the United States is not immune. The current crisis began in the financial sector in the summer of 2007 and hit the real side of the economy in fall 2008, with the unemployment rate rising by more than 26% in just five months, from 5.7% in July to 7.2% in December. Since 1979, the real side of the U.S. economy has suffered (think deindustrialization) while the financial side has thrived. With stagnant or falling real wages coinciding with a lengthy period of low interest rates, many working people went into debt in order to purchase homes and stocks so that they would be able to participate in some modest way in the rise of finance. The collapse of finance, then, is pulling working Americans down with it.

But the United States' crisis is departing from the typical pattern. For one thing, far from dropping in value, the dollar has risen against other currencies in recent months. The factors which were supposed to make the United States immune to financial crisis did not do so, but they are causing the crisis to play out in new and unpredictable ways.

SWIMMING POOL OF SAVINGS

The United States' dependence on foreign financing is one reason the collapse of housing prices has sparked an economy-wide financial crisis.

Imagine the pool of savings in an economy as a giant swimming pool; the water in the pool represents money available to borrowers. Everyone who saves money in a bank account, in the stock market, or in government bonds—whether a U.S. resident or a foreign investor—adds water to the pool.

In recent years an increasingly large share of the water in the United States' pool has been coming from abroad. And when foreign capital is a substantial part of the water in the pool, the sheer volume of capital that can fly in and out of a country's assets is much larger, making its stock market and other asset markets more volatile. Here we are not talking about foreign investment in factories or other economic activity on U.S. soil, termed foreign direct investment, which would take months or years to liquidate. Rather, this is portfolio investment—investment in paper assets such as stocks and bonds—and this money can fly out of a country at the touch of a computer key.

You can see in Figure 1 the moment when foreign investors suddenly stopped putting money into Mexico, forcing the nation to live within its means: Mexico's current account deficit went from 7% of GDP in 1994 to 1% of GDP in 1995. So one might think that foreign investors pulling out of the United States would be a good thing—Americans would finally be forced to live within our means.

But it's not quite that simple. Most Americans with debts—whether student loans, a mortgage, a car loan, or credit card balances—do not think of themselves as borrowing from foreigners. But part of the reason banks were willing to provide all this credit to U.S. consumers at fairly low interest rates was that foreign investors were filling the pool with plenty of water by buying U.S. stocks or bonds or putting their savings into U.S. deposit accounts. It is not only our government that borrows from foreign investors, but U.S. households and firms as well.

As a result, as large numbers of both foreign and domestic investors have pulled out of U.S. stocks and banks over the past 18 months, it has become harder for my students, for small businesses, and even for General Motors to get loans. Without access to student loans, the poorest students are dropping out of college; some colleges may close their doors. Fewer people now qualify for mortgage loans, so houses sell more slowly and at cut prices. Car loans are drying up, so dealerships are laying people off. If the credit crunch pushes credit-card interest rates up, then even consumers who stop making new purchases will be stuck with high interest rates on existing balances. In Mexico in 1995, credit card interest rates of 65% were considered on the low side.

Until 2007, this kind of capital flight and ensuing financial crisis were widely viewed as impossible in the United States. Three factors were supposed to account for U.S. immunity:

- The dollar is the world's reserve currency, so foreign investors will always hold it.
- U.S. debt is denominated in dollars, so the exchange rate depreciation that would result from capital flight would not increase the debt burden on domestic borrowers.
- U.S. political and financial institutions are far more functional and less corrupt than those in emerging markets.

Let's look at how each of these factors has played out in the current crisis.

DOLLARS ARE SPECIAL

Many countries around the world hold onto U.S. Treasury bonds as a so-called reserve asset.

To explore what reserves are, consider a professor suddenly faced with $30,000 in urgent home repairs she cannot cover out of her current income. This is not a problem as long as relatively cheap credit is available; for instance, she may plan to take out a home equity loan to pay for the repairs. But suppose that loan suddenly becomes unavailable. What will she do?

Many people do have other sources of financing, and in a sense, these are their reserves. They resort to liquidating the savings account and the IRA or selling off the wedding ring.

Countries, too, have reserves. Typically, they hoard gold and U.S. Treasury bonds for rainy days. The dollar has been the world's reserve currency since the close of World War II. This means that U.S. Treasury bonds (which are issued by the U.S. government to finance its debt) are the safest, most stable place for countries to park their reserves because the U.S. government has the power to print the reserve currency.

In fact, one reason the United States has been able to run so large a current account deficit has been other countries' desire to hold more reserves.

In 1997, suddenly unable to borrow from abroad, many Asian countries used up their reserves. Then they turned to the International Monetary Fund (IMF) for emergency loans. This is analogous to the professor turning to her parents for an emergency loan. Her parents may well agree to finance the repairs—but only on the condition that she never buy another caffè latte at Starbucks. Likewise, the IMF agreed to these loans, but only if the Asian nations acquiesced to certain conditions, generally much more onerous ones than giving up lattes. For example, then-Treasury Secretary Robert Rubin basically withheld South Korea's IMF rescue package until the country agreed to sell shares of its profitable companies, like Samsung, to U.S. investors. The Asian nations agreed to the IMF's conditions, but they swore "never again," and have since hoarded vast amounts of dollars. Today, about 20% of the United States' total borrowing comes from foreign governments that are buying up dollar assets as reserves.

But it is starting to seem possible that other countries might not want to use the dollar as their reserve currency forever.

By July 2008, China, which alone holds about $1.8 trillion in U.S. assets, admitted that "it has been looking to strike deals with private equity firms in Europe as part of a strategy to reduce its dollar holdings," and "a big sovereign fund in the [Persian] Gulf has cut its dollar denominated holdings from more than 80% a year ago to less than 60% today," the *Financial Times* reported.

The euro is emerging as an alternative, as is gold. Between August 2007, when it became clear that the subprime debacle would cause widespread losses for investors, and March 2008, when fear of a U.S. financial meltdown reached fever pitch, the price of gold jumped by over 45%, breaking the $1,000/ounce mark. Investors in large numbers were evidently selling U.S. assets and buying gold as an alternative safe haven.

DEBT STABLE; NET WORTH DOWN

So maybe the dollar's role as reserve currency cannot prevent capital flight from the United States. But even if it did occur, capital flight was not supposed to hurt the U.S. economy the way it damaged so many emerging markets in the late 1990s and early 2000s.

When other nations borrow in a foreign currency—which is common in many emerging markets—then any devaluation of their home currency automatically swells the size of the debts owed by their citizens, governments, and businesses. Here's an example: In 1995 my landlady in Mexico City owed $1,000 on a dollar-denominated credit card. She earned her income in pesos, so this meant 3,000 pesos of debt prior to January 1995. But that turned into 12,000 pesos of debt a few weeks later, when capital flight from the peso had caused it to devalue from three pesos to the dollar to twelve pesos to the dollar. (Her income, of course, did not quadruple!) In 2001, many Argentineans had taken out mortgage loans in dollars, so that when the Argentine peso devaluated from one to three pesos per dollar, their monthly mortgage payments effectively tripled.

With the debts of U.S. households and businesses denominated in our own currency, a devaluation of the dollar does not affect the size of those debts. But capital flight can damage net worth anyway—by causing asset values to fall.

The current fall in home prices, for instance, is directly tied to the United States' dependence on foreign lending. International buyers were swelling the U.S. housing bubble

---

CURRENT ACCOUNT EXPLAINED

For over 15 years, the United States has been spending more foreign currency annually on imports than the country has earned through its exports—and borrowing from foreign investors every year to cover the difference. The amount a nation's spending on imports differs from its income from exports is called the current account. If imports exceed exports, the current account is negative; in other words, the country has a current account deficit.

Specifically, in 2007 U.S. imports exceeded exports to the tune of $731 billion. That current account deficit was covered by a $774 billion "net financial inflow," i.e., the amount U.S. borrowing from abroad exceeded U.S. lending to foreigners. (The $41 billion difference between the current account deficit and the country's net borrowing is mostly a statistical discrepancy.) Note that the United States's total foreign debt is going to be much higher, the pile of net financial inflows accumulated year after year.

by buying up the now-infamous mortgage-backed securities comprised of bundles of individual mortgage loans. So long as there was international (as well as domestic) demand for these securities, U.S. lenders could not issue new mortgages fast enough. But once foreign investors realized that these securities were not the safe investment they'd been marketed as and dumped them, U.S. banks were much less interested in making mortgages since they could no longer sell them off. With fewer buyers able to get home loans, houses are harder to sell and their prices are falling.

It's a parallel story in the stock market, which has lost close to half its value just since last summer as both foreign and U.S. investors have pulled their money out.

Although data on household wealth trends are not immediately available, this one-two punch almost certainly means that the net worth of U.S. households has taken a big hit. In my case, until recently home equity and pension funds performed the miracle of giving me positive net worth despite my typical debt load. They are not pulling this miracle off today.

The loss of wealth that occurs when assets lose value can in itself cause problems in the real economy. Even though net worth is somewhat intangible, it is disconcerting to watch it fall. Vacations get cancelled, new car purchases delayed, and home improvements put off. This is happening on a massive scale today, resulting in significant layoffs by airlines, car dealerships, and construction firms, with spin-off effects throughout the economy. The pain on the real side of the economy has only just begun.

ARE U.S. INSTITUTIONS MORE SOUND?

In the mid-1990s, one of the major clues that Argentina was heading for crisis was the country's high level of government debt, nearly 40% of GDP. At the time, the IMF opposed new loans to Argentina until the country got its government debt down to 34% of GDP.

By these IMF guidelines, the United States has been in the danger zone since 2003. U.S. central government debt as a percent of GDP jumped from the 30% range in 2002 to the 47% range just a year later—presumably due to the combination of Bush's 2001 tax cut and the wars in Iraq and Afghanistan. It is unusual for a nation to cut taxes while it is entering two wars.

Economist Paul Blustein's description of the Menem regime so resonates with George W. Bush's time in office that it bears repeating here:

Former Argentine policymakers acknowledge that foreign money made the government less concerned than it should have been about its debt burden and more inclined to treat admonitions with indifference. [One Argentine advisor stated,] "You can say to the politicians 'We need fiscal balance.' But if you get the money so easily, as we did, it's very tough to tell the politicians, 'Don't spend more, be more prudent,' because the money was there, and they knew it."

George Bush is a consummate politician. Like Menem, he used money (including big tax cuts for his well-to-do patrons) to build up debts and loyalty. Throwing money around helped keep Menem (and Bush) in power, but it built up debt which hamstrings economic policy in a crunch. Had Bush maintained the surpluses of the Clinton years, the U.S. economy might be in a different place today.

Of course, as recent events have underscored, the government has no monopoly on dysfunction. At first glance, it may seem ludicrous to suggest that U.S. banks could be fragile in a way similar to the banks in, say, Indonesia. In the years leading up to the Asian financial crises, Indonesia's banks held many non-performing loans, often loans made to Pres. Suharto's cronies that no one ever expected would be repaid. Thus, the banking system's net worth on paper was an overstatement, inflated by what were essentially political donations by the banks.

But it turns out that U.S. banks have also been claiming worthless paper as assets. As of March 2008, when U.S. banks had reported only $160 billion in losses, independent analysts argued that their losses were in fact at least $300 billion and possibly as high as $1.2 trillion, according to the *Financial Times*. Clearly, many banks had lost more than they were willing to admit.

U.S. regulatory institutions were slow to force banks to reveal the real magnitude of their losses. However, investors do not rely solely on regulators to verify the value of the financial instruments they buy or hold. They also rely on private credit rating agencies. Here too, though, a kind of institutionalized corruption has crept in. One reason international holders of mortgage-backed securities and other similarly complex investments (broadly known as collateralized debt obligations, or CDOs) began dropping them like hot potatoes in August 2007 was that they realized the AAA credit rating these investments bore was false. A triple-A credit rating was supposed to mean that these securities were a very safe investment. But credit ratings are not what they used to be. Traditionally, it was the buyers of securities who paid agencies such as Moody's to rate them, but today it is the sellers of securities who pay for the ratings. So ratings agencies now have an incentive to please the issuers of CDOs by calling them safe.

Once the credibility of the rating system was put into question, the collapse in the value of CDOs had the potential to spark capital flight from many U.S. assets. International faith in Wall Street as a place of transparent and reasonably honest institutions was shaken—and with it, at least potentially, the dollar's role as key global currency.

A PECULIAR CRISIS

All in all, the factors that were supposed to inoculate the United States against any threat of capital flight turned out to work not quite in the way economists and financial analysts had expected. In the summer of 2007, capital flight struck. The dramatic announcement came two months after the fact, when the data were released:

FIGURE 2

DOLLAR-EURO EXCHANGE RATE, 2007-2008

Source: Federal Reserve System, FRED II

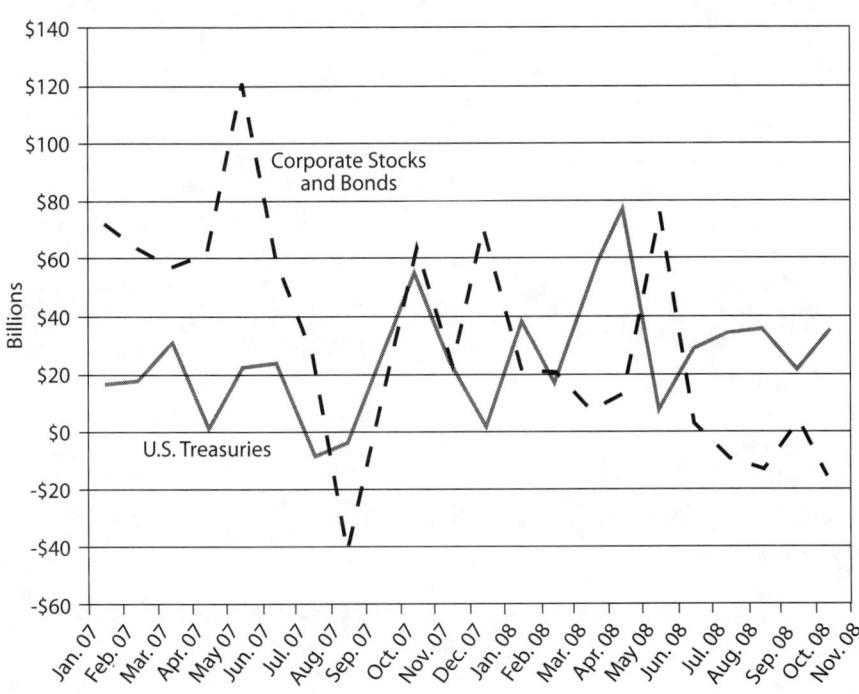

FIGURE 3

SELECTED NET FOREIGN INFLOWS INTO U.S. ASSETS, JANUARY 2007–OCTOBER 2008 (NET FOREIGN INFLOWS INTO U.S. TREASURY BILLS VERSUS STOCKS AND BONDS OF PRIVATE U.S. CORPORATIONS)

Source: U.S. Treasury Department, TIC data

Foreign investors slashed their holdings of US securities by a record amount... The Treasury said net sales of US market assets—including bonds, notes, and equities, were $69.3 billion in August.... The August outflow exceeded the previous record decline of $21.2 billion in March 1990. (*Financial Times*, October 17, 2007)

As in the standard capital-flight scenario, the dollar's value did fall (see Figure 2). Then, in February 2008, the dollar fell further when it turned out that U.S. firms with only $46 billion in assets had sold so-called credit default swaps—a kind of quasi-insurance against financial losses—on $2 trillion worth of securities.

The dollar depreciation that occurred between August 2007 and April 2008 had a silver lining. With foreign investors selling more U.S. assets than they were buying, U.S. borrowing from abroad declined. Plus, a devalued dollar made U.S. products cheaper abroad, so exports rose. Both factors contributed to an improvement in the U.S. current account deficit. At the time, this was hailed as an "orderly" change in trajectory. Many observers breathed a sigh of relief, believing the U.S. current account deficit would shrink gradually, allowing the United States to avoid a severe contraction such as Mexico had experienced.

But then a strange thing happened. Shortly after major investment bank Bear Stearns collapsed, and while the larger financial crisis was far from over, the dollar exchange rate bottomed out and began to rise.

This was probably not on account of foreign investors suddenly renewing their faith in the securities Wall Street was selling. Rather, global investors had fled dollar-denominated assets when they got nervous in the summer of 2007, but when they got a full-blown case of panic around March 2008, they flocked to the safest haven in the financial world: U.S. Treasury bonds. (See Figure 3.) Between January and July 2007, the monthly net inflow of foreign capital into the stocks and bonds of U.S. corporations averaged over $65 trillion, more than four times the net foreign capital flowing into U.S. Treasuries. But from August 2007 to October 2008, the average monthly net inflow from abroad to U.S. stocks and bonds fell by over 75% compared to the earlier period, while the inflow to U.S. Treasuries almost doubled. At this point, almost twice as much foreign capital is flowing into Treasuries per month as into stocks and corporate bonds.

On balance, money was now coming into the United States, so the dollar appreciated. Unfortunately, that makes

Chapter 9: International Trade and Finance   199

U.S. exports more expensive and imports a bargain, and as a result the current account worsens. By April 2008, the current account was already beginning to dive back down (see Figure 4). Hopes for an orderly escape from dependence on foreign capital evaporated.

Capital flight has played out in the United States in an unusual, even perverse way. Capital has been fleeing from U.S. stocks and private banks for over a year now. But as the saying goes, when the United States sneezes, other parts of the world get pneumonia. The U.S. financial crisis has shaken stock markets around the world. As a result, rather than continuing to leave U.S. shores, investment capital from abroad started to be re-routed to U.S. Treasury bonds. And panicky U.S. investors are augmenting the sums flowing into U.S. Treasuries as they repatriate their money from foreign stock markets.

The stampede into Treasury bonds means that money is available to the federal government at extremely low rates, close to 0% interest. The effect is to push the U.S. government to the forefront of all financing, putting it in the driver's seat of the economy whether or not the political leadership believes in laissez-faire. No surprise then that the private sector is seeking financing from the government on a massive scale.

The key to any kind of recovery for working people is going to be persuading the government to use that money to rebuild the real side of the economy, not just the financial sector. Of course, families want to see the value of their houses and 401(k)s go back up. What they really need, though, are jobs that pay enough so they don't have to count on asset bubbles and ballooning debt to meet their expenses. Talk of rebuilding infrastructure is welcome: both the labor market and a lot of bridges need to be strengthened. Stimulus dollars would be welcome in the economy's care sector too—in child care, in education, in elder care.

And yes, the United States needs a functioning financial sector so that small businesses, students, and even GM have access to credit. But not one as large as it was before the crisis. In recent years finance has acted as a weight on the real economy. Foreign investment in U.S. assets was causing the dollar to appreciate to such levels that U.S. products were less and less affordable overseas. So yes, fix the financial sector, but don't let it get awash with cash to the extent that the dollar appreciates U.S. manufacturers out of business, and that Wall Street CEOs pay themselves tens of millions of dollars a year with which to buy political influence. Don't let the financiers use the money that the government is borrowing today to rebuild finance as the primary engine of the U.S. economy.

FIGURE 4

U.S. CURRENT ACCOUNT, QUARTERLY, 1960–2008

Source: U.S. Dept. of Commerce, Bureau of Economic Analysis, "International Economic Accounts."

Sources: Gerard Dumenil & Dominique Levy, *Capital Resurgent*, 2004; Nora Lustig, *Mexico: The Remaking of an Economy*, 1998; Paul Blustein, *And the Money Kept Rolling In (and Out)*, 2005.

THE GLOBAL OIL MARKET
HOW IT OPERATES, WHY IT DOESN'T WORK, AND WHO WANTS TO KEEP IT THAT WAY.

BY PAUL CUMMINGS

Since the United States-led coalition invaded Iraq in March 2003, the price of a barrel of oil has just about quadrupled to around $135. With U.S. oil imports currently totaling 4.5 billion barrels a year, this translates into a staggering $600 billion annual oil bill. Many energy economists predict that oil prices could top $200 a barrel in the near future, particularly if U.S. opposition to Iran's nuclear enrichment program leads to a confrontation, either directly or through surrogate states.

Why are oil prices skyrocketing? Many economists and business analysts like to talk about "the fundamentals": supply (constrained) and demand (strong). They point to rapid economic growth in China and India driving demand. On the supply side, it's the OPEC cartel limiting production while tree-huggers in the United States block the development of new offshore and Alaskan oil supplies.

But other analysts claim the so-called fundamentals tell us little about why oil prices are rising rapidly. Recently the London *Times*'s economy and finance commentator, Anatole Kaletsky, noted that over the past nine months, as the price of oil has doubled, none of the basic determinants of supply or demand has changed much. China's demand growth is in fact slowing, as is the world's demand growth overall. Iraqi oil production is back up to prewar levels. Kaletsky views the current price spikes as symptoms of a classic financial bubble during which, typically, "prices end up bearing almost no relation to the balance of underlying supply and demand."

For now, the experts are displaying a remarkable lack of consensus on whether it's the actions of commodities traders and other financial-market movements or real supply and demand factors that explain the current oil price spike. In any case, the terms "supply" and "demand" are supposed to conjure up images of a free market. But the global oil market is anything but. Even leaving aside the role of financial markets in setting the price of oil, the supply of and demand for oil are heavily shaped by the actions of mammoth multinational oil companies and of governments in both the consuming and producing countries. And while the price of oil is rising fast, causing real pain to consumers, those extra dollars are going straight to the governments of the oil-rich countries and to the major oil companies—*not* to offset the tremendous costs that oil imposes, chiefly on the environment but in multiple other arenas as well.

SUPPLY MANAGEMENT

From the very beginning of the modern oil industry, the supply of oil has been managed by powerful oil companies and the magnates who run them. The first was none other than John D. Rockefeller, who founded Standard Oil in 1870. By 1878 he had gained control of 90% of U.S. oil refining. In the 1880s Rockefeller used his strategic control of refining to build the first vertically integrated oil company, with oil fields, tankers, pipelines, refineries, and retail sales facilities under one corporate roof. By mercilessly undercutting competitors until they were near bankruptcy, and then buying them on the cheap, Standard Oil gained control of over half of the world's then-known oil supply. By the turn of the century Rockefeller had become the richest man in the world, with a fortune valued at around a billion dollars. Then, in 1911, the Supreme Court ruled that Standard Oil was a monopoly and, to create competition, split it into 34 companies, including Esso and Socony, which eventually became Exxon and Mobil, respectively.

Instead of competing, over the next 50 years Exxon, Mobil, and five other giant oil companies (the "majors") essentially formed a cartel. Leveraging their superior technology, production experience, and control of the retail market, the majors engaged in oil colonialism: they pumped and sold oil from a number of developing countries under highly favorable terms, earning vast profits.

In the 1950s, oil-rich countries began nationalizing their oil and training domestic oil technocracies to run the business. The advantages of collusion were no secret to them. In the 1960s Venezuela and Saudi Arabia organized OPEC (the Organization of Petroleum Exporting Countries), a cartel whose explicit purpose was to control the price of oil by regulating supply. By acting together, the oil-rich nations leveled the playing field with the majors and gained a larger share of oil profits.

With this context in mind, let's consider how oil gets to market today. Currently, around 75% of the world's oil is nationalized, managed by state-run oil companies that are monopolies in their own country. These state companies are often their country's largest employer, largest exporter, largest source of hard currency, and largest contributor to state revenue. State oil executives report to political authorities instead of a corporate board, and local political considerations can trump economic factors in their business decisions. For example, state oil companies may site new facilities in poorer communities to spur local economic development. More importantly, nationalized oil earns the money to pay for hospitals, schools, sanitation systems, and roads, projects rarely funded by Western oil corporations. The downside is that oil money all too frequently has been stolen by corrupt rulers or siphoned away to buy expensive weapons—Zaire's Mobutu Sese Seko and Iraq's Saddam Hussein were just two in a long line of oil-funded despots.

State oil ministers set oil production targets taking into consideration both economic and political factors, including current global economic performance, OPEC member production quotas, long-term contracts with oil corporations, International Monetary Fund debt repayment schedules, domestic revenue requirements, the desires of greedy and corrupt rulers, and the cost of oil extraction compared to oil's market price.

Of course, most of the state-owned oil across the globe lies within OPEC, whose policies fundamentally shape supply. The eleven member states of OPEC control over 50% of the world's oil. After both the 1973 Israeli-Arab war and the 1979 Islamic revolution in Iran, OPEC cut oil production, oil prices skyrocketed, cartel members earned hundreds of billions of dollars in windfall profits, and the world economy slid into recession.

Then, in the 1980s, a weak economy and more efficient cars cut oil demand, while newly discovered non-OPEC oil increased supply. OPEC tried to prop up plunging prices by cutting production. In particular, Saudi Arabia cut its output by nearly 8 million barrels per day. When other OPEC members began to cheat on their lower production quotas, the Saudis enforced market discipline by flooding the market with cheap oil, driving many suppliers out of business. With oil supply back under control, prices rose to around $20 a barrel, OPEC's market share was restored, and OPEC production quotas were honored. John D. Rockefeller would have applauded.

In 1990, the first "oil war" was launched when Iraq invaded Kuwait and seized its oil fields. With Iraqi troops poised to attack Saudi Arabia, a U.S.-led coalition drove the Iraqi army out of Kuwait. The Saudis once again demonstrated their market power by pumping enough additional oil to offset the loss of Kuwaiti and Iraqi oil production.

The cartel aims to keep the price of oil high, but it also seeks reasonable stability in the oil market. After all, the lion's share of the petrodollars that OPEC members earn are plowed back into the United States and the other wealthy consuming countries in the form of investments. If oil price volatility begins to damage the U.S. and other industrialized economies, those investments will likely suffer as well. But OPEC's ability to manage supply for the twin goals of profitability and stability is limited. In recent years conflicts in the Middle East, rapidly growing oil demand in China and India, and OPEC's own tendency to overshoot or undershoot planned production levels have all contributed to a more volatile oil market than OPEC perhaps intended.

The remaining 25% of global oil supply comes from fields owned by the majors or by Russia's ostensibly private energy giant Gazprom. This production is more responsive to market signals, but is still influenced by non-price factors such as government tax and environmental policies and Wall Street pressure to report high quarterly earnings.

Perhaps the clearest indicator that the supply of oil is managed and not a simple response to market signals is the curious fact that much of the oil that is brought to market is relatively expensive to produce because of high extraction costs (for instance, deep sea oil), transport costs (Alaskan oil), or refining costs (some of Africa's oil). At the same time, oil that could be brought to market far more cheaply—much of the oil in the Arabian Peninsula, for example—is left in the ground. Saudi oil costs just $1.50 per barrel to produce, while the average production cost of oil outside of the Middle East is $22 per barrel. In a free market, competition would cause the lowest-cost oil to be sold first, since cheap oil can undercut expensive oil. However, in the case of managed supply, producers of cheap oil can hold back their oil, allowing the market price to rise until it exceeds the production price of expensive oil. This means very high profits for the producers of cheap oil, while many energy analysts estimate that consumers are paying twice as much as they would if oil markets were free, Paul Roberts writes in *The End of Oil*.

Retail supplies are influenced by vertically integrated global oil delivery systems—pipelines, supertankers, refineries, delivery tanker trucks, assorted retail sales facilities—which are controlled by the Saudis, Venezuela, and the super-majors (the six largest private oil companies: ExxonMobil, Shell, BP, Chevron, ConocoPhillips, and Total S.A.). Every day 85 million barrels of oil flow to consumers around the world. The massive oil delivery systems are worth a combined $5 trillion dollars and create a large barrier to entry for alternative energy suppliers. Supply can be constrained for other reasons as well, for instance, environmental or other regulations that block expansion or construction of oil pipelines or refineries.

Occasionally a geopolitical or extreme weather event breaks the oil supply system and retail oil prices go through the roof, creating outrageous profits. For example, in the aftermath of Hurricane Katrina, U.S. gasoline prices doubled overnight. The oil industry denied using Katrina to fleece customers, but a 2006 investigation by the Federal Trade Commission found multiple examples of price gouging at the refining, wholesale, and retail levels. Coincidentally, in the last quarter of 2005, the accounting quarter following Katrina, ExxonMobil earned $9.9 billion, the largest quarterly profits ever reported by a U.S. company.

In 2007 oil prices were exploding along with much of Iraq. That year ExxonMobil earned $40.6 billion in profits on $400 billion in revenue, the highest yearly profit ever earned by a public corporation. Amazingly, even this record profit pales in comparison to the 2007 Saudi net oil revenue of $194 billion.

CAPTIVE CONSUMERS

The demand for oil is no more a simple result of free-market forces than is the supply. To begin with, energy demand is not created directly by consumers: we do not desire gasoline the way we might desire a new house or a new pair of shoes. Instead, demand is "pulled" by the economy, whose mix of technologies and rate of growth determine how much energy, from oil and other sources, is required to power it. Oil heats tens of millions of homes, offices, and factories and powers 30% of the world's electric generation. Oil is also used as an input in the manufacture of petrochemicals such as plastics.

And, of course, oil moves mountains of raw materials, tons of finished goods, and billions of people every day. The world's armada of oil-fueled vehicles consists of nearly a billion cars, trucks, buses, tractors, bulldozers, ships and airplanes. The troubling reality is that this armada runs only on oil; there is no viable alternative fuel today, and oil companies intend to keep it that way.

Every year the armada grows, moving more people and more stuff over greater distances. Globalization has spread out the production and sales processes over ever-longer international supply chains. U.S. and Canadian commuters drive more and more miles as suburbanization moves home and work farther apart. And the average fuel efficiency of U.S. passenger vehicles *fell* by 5% during the past 20 years, due to aggressive marketing of SUVs and trucks.

Oil companies use their political clout to stop government efforts to increase fuel efficiency. Over the last 20 years, the oil industry has given $200 million to U.S. politicians, mostly Republicans, who believe in free markets but regularly give an invisible helping hand to the oil companies. During those same 20 years, oil lobbyists have rolled back gas mileage standards and created tax subsidies for buying eight-ton Hummers that inhale gas. Oil lobbyists have redirected funding from alternative energy technology to road and bridge repair.

Oil companies have also used their wealth and political power to crush electric powered transportation systems. In the 1920s city-dwellers commuted on electric trolleys, but oil and auto companies wanted to sell them buses and cars. Standard Oil, General Motors, Mack Truck, and Firestone Tire funded a dummy corporation, National City Lines (NCL), to replace trolleys with buses. It didn't matter if NCL lost money; its goal was to create demand for buses, cars, tires, and oil. If it could do so, its parent companies would make a fortune. By 1929 NCL had established its business model and when the Great Depression deepened, over 100 electric utility companies, located in most major cities, were forced to sell their trolley lines at a sharply discounted price to NCL, the only buyer with cash. Once NCL had control, the trolley systems were sold for scrap and within days a new fleet of buses arrived, followed by a tidal wave of cars. In the late 1940s, NCL had served its purpose and was failing. Government lawyers had been investigating NCL, and in 1949 they successfully prosecuted its parent companies for collusion to destroy the nation's trolley system. Each parent company paid a $5,000 fine, which wasn't too bad considering they had made on the order of $100 million in profits from NCL's illegal actions.

By 1990 the Los Angeles basin faced a serious public health problem due to smog from car exhaust. The state of California issued a mandate requiring car companies to develop a zero emission vehicle, or ZEV. Oil and automobile companies launched a full-fledged political campaign to overturn the ZEV mandate, including TV and magazine ads, direct mail, and thousands of calls from phone banks. The ZEV mandate was never enforced and, in 2003, was replaced with a minimal requirement that car companies sell a few gas-electric hybrid cars by 2008. That same year, in a remarkable episode chronicled in the 2006 documentary "Who Killed the Electric Car?," GM was taking back the hundreds of EV1 electric vehicles it had leased to U.S. drivers beginning in 1996. The carmaker assembled most of the EV1s at a site in Arizona where it proceeded to crush them—despite very positive feedback from EV1 lessees, many of whom wanted to purchase and keep the cars. Explanations for GM's decision to halt the EV1 program and destroy the cars vary. GM says it determined the venture could never be profitable, in part because hoped-for breakthroughs in battery technology did not occur. One thing is certain: the car did become less marketable once California gave in to pressure from the oil and auto industries (including GM) and lifted the ZEV mandate.

In 1994 oil companies attacked Ballard Power Systems for developing a hydrogen fuel cell to power cars. With a game plan similar to the one they'd used to undermine the ZEV mandate, they took out ads decrying the fuel cell, challenged the company's veracity at trade conferences, and questioned its ability to actually bring a viable product to market. Oil companies pointed out that useable hydrogen was in short supply and an entirely new hydrogen refining, delivery, and fueling infrastructure would need to be built at the cost of many billions of dollars. As a result of these attacks Ballard backed off, and further development of its fuel cell was hidden in an internal R&D program for over a decade.

So the demand for oil is driven by economic and social trends far beyond the control of individual consumers, who are stuck, at least in the short term, paying whatever price the oil companies set if they want to fill their tanks and heat their homes.

Finally, it's impossible to get the whole picture of demand for oil without recognizing one very special oil consumer: the U.S. military. Every tank, armored vehicles, truck, humvee, jet, and missile runs on refined oil, as do most ships. In 2007, the U.S. military consumed about 250 million barrels of oil and 2.6 billion gallons of jet fuel, making it the world's single largest fuel-burning entity. Without oil the Army and Marines could not maneuver, the Air Force could not fly, and most of the Navy could not sail. The United States would be a paralyzed superpower, unable to project power throughout the world. Since all the other military forces in the world also run on oil, the ability to cut their oil lifelines is a tremendous strategic advantage in any conflict. These factors make oil more than just another commodity. Oil is a weapon, a strategic commodity, a national security resource; it is not just like wheat or widgets. By the same token, any shift in U.S. foreign policy that reduces the country's military engagements can also represent a sizeable drop in U.S. oil demand.

MULTIPLE MARKET FAILURES

Today's global oil market is working well for the major oil companies, their managers, and their shareholders. It is also working well for the oil-producing countries, at least to the extent that they are garnering vast revenues. (Of course, the extent to which these revenues are benefiting ordinary people in the oil-rich countries varies dramatically.)

But the oil market is characterized by many kinds of market failure: the workings of the market are producing less-than-optimal results on multiple levels. For instance, oil price spikes can lead to "demand shocks" that suck money rapidly out of the economies of the oil-importing nations. If the global financial system cannot get this money re-invested and generating demand quickly, the result can be a drop in global demand followed by an economic downturn. According to energy economist Philip Verleger, over the last 50 years there have been six major oil price spikes, each causing economic losses that have totaled more than $1 trillion. Verleger posits that a 20% increase in the price of a barrel of oil results in a 0.5% decline in global economic growth. Based on that formula, the current $100 spike in the price of oil, if sustained, could wind up causing a reversal in the global economy from a baseline of 2% growth to a 1% contraction.

By and large, Americans have benefited from the fact that the price of oil worldwide is denominated in dollars rather than another currency. Right now, though, the falling value of the dollar against other major currencies is one factor pushing up the price of oil in the United States. Moreover, not only can fluctuations in the value of the dollar affect oil prices; oil market shifts can affect the value of the dollar. Hence, a second type of market failure in the global oil market is the increased "risk premium" that attaches to a whole range of financial transactions when a build-up of petrodollars makes the financial markets worry about an increased risk of either a devaluation of the dollar or a run on the dollar. In both cases the U.S. Federal Reserve may not be able to successfully intervene because trillions of petrodollars are outside of the Fed's control. In general, increased risk is bad for the economy and leads to higher interest rates and slower economic growth.

A third group of oil market failures are environmental. Oil is a dirty business that pollutes the air, water, and earth, often in health-threatening ways. Take oil spills for example.

In Ecuador a pipeline runs over the Andes, connecting Ecuador's eastern jungle oil fields to its Pacific coast refinery. When earthquakes or landslides break the pipeline, all the oil between the break and the shut-off valve simply pours out, contaminating a broad swath of the mountain below.

Six thousand miles to the north, Exxon's supertanker, the Valdez, struck Bligh Reef on March 24, 1989, spilling 11 million gallons of oil into Prince William Sound. The oil contaminated 1,500 miles of Alaskan shoreline; nearly 20 years later, local economies dependent on fishing and tourism have still not entirely recovered. There are thousands of similar cases all over the planet.

The mother of all oil market failures is climate change. When oil is converted to energy, it gives off CO_2 which traps heat in the atmosphere and, in large quantity, can alter the climate. The result is a global, cumulative, and intergenerational problem that an increasing number of climate scientists fear may become a crisis of biblical proportions: higher sea levels flooding coastal cities around the globe; droughts, heat waves, pests, and more frequent extreme weather events affecting food supplies and human health.

No matter where CO_2 originates, it spreads quickly through-out the entire atmosphere, and so makes the problem a global one. The longevity of atmospheric CO_2 creates a cumulative problem. Since 1850, our species has dumped so much carbon into the sky that atmospheric CO_2 levels are at their highest point in a million years. That is 500,000,000,000,000 pounds of carbon stuck in the sky, as if the atmosphere were an open sewer! And that longevity makes the problem intergenerational: it will take the earth 16 generations (400 years) to reabsorb 80% of the CO_2 we emit today, and the remaining 20% will stay in the sky for thousands of years.

Solving climate change begins by realizing that the oil market doesn't have to be managed for the benefit of a small number of extremely rich people. We must also put to rest the canard that oil resources are best allocated by the free market's "invisible hand." Columbia University economist Joseph Stiglitz points out, "the reason that the hand may be invisible is that it is simply not there—or at least that if is there, it is palsied." The public needs to fight to remove the control of oil pricing from the oil corporations and establish an oil market that is more fair and sustainable.

In a sustainable energy market, the price of gasoline and other fossil fuel products should reflect the real costs these energy sources impose—above all, on the environment. That means prices that are higher than what Americans are accustomed to. But a progressive oil agenda would include recapturing that additional revenue and using it to compensate low-income consumers and, especially, to move the economy toward one based on renewable energy. Paying that extra dollar or more a gallon at the pump would feel very different if U.S. consumers knew the money was being spent not to line the pockets of dictators and oil executives, but instead to offset the extra cost for low-income families and, especially, to generously fund myriad projects to put the economy on a green-energy path.

SOURCES: Sohbet Karbuz, "US military energy consumption: facts and figures," *Energy Bulletin*, May 20, 2007; Chalmers Johnson, "The Arithmetic of America's Military Bases Abroad: What Does It All Add Up To?" www.tomdispatch.com, 2004; OPEC, "World Oil Outlook 2007"; Paul Roberts, *The End of Oil* (Houghton Mifflin, 2005); U.S. Federal Trade Comm., "Investigation of Gasoline Price Manipulation and Post-Katrina Gasoline Price Increases: Report to Congress" (Spring 2006); Eric Noe, "For Oil Giants, Pricey Gas Means Big Profits," *ABC News*, Jan. 25, 2006; Steven Mufson, "Exxon-Mobil's Profit in 2007 Tops $40 Billion," *Washington Post*, Feb. 2, 2008; U.S. Energy Information Admin., "OPEC Oil Export Revenues 2007"; Michael Renner, "Five Hundred Million Cars, One Planet—Who's Going to Give?" (Worldwatch Institute, August 2003); Daniel Engber, "How Gasoline Becomes CO_2: A gallon turns into 19 pounds?" *Slate*, Nov. 1, 2006; Matthew Kahn, "The Environmental Impact of Suburbanization," *Jrnl of Policy Analysis and Mgmt* 19:4 (Fall 2000); Philip Verleger, "A Collaborative Policy to Neutralize the Economic Impact of Energy Price Fluctuations," Policy paper, June 10, 2003; "The Real Price of Gasoline: An Analysis of the Hidden External Costs Consumers Pay to Fuel Their Automobiles," Int'l Ctr for Technology Assessment, 1998; Joseph Stiglitz, *Making Globalization Work* (W.W. Norton, 2006); Laura Peterson, "Big Oil Wields Ultra Deep Influence," Ctr for Public Integrity, Dec. 2004.

ARTICLE 9.7

January/February 2008

MEASURES OF GLOBAL POVERTY

BY ARTHUR MACEWAN

Dear Dr. Dollar:

I hear all kinds of views about poverty in the developing world from different corners of the media. One minute you can get the impression that a huge swell is lifting everyone up and that millions of people in Asia are no longer in poverty. Then from a different source you get the impression that poverty is deepening and getting worse—the pictures of the kids with swollen bellies, etc. What's the reality?

—William Chin, Randolph, Mass.

The reality of poverty, like many other "realities," is elusive! There are disputes over how to define poverty, and, even when we can agree on a definition, there are disputes over how to measure poverty. However, one aspect of the poverty reality is fairly clear: there are still a great many very poor people in the world.

One widely used standard used to measure poverty is $2 per day—that is, people whose income is less than $2 per day are considered "in poverty." And people are viewed as in "extreme poverty" if their income is less than $1 per day. By these standards, in 2004 about 2.5 billion people, 39% of the world's 6.4 billion people, were in poverty, and 969 million were in extreme poverty.

This standard, however, requires a bit of explanation. The $2/day and the $1/day are based on what people could buy in 1990. Translated into today's prices, these figures would be about $3.20/day and $1.60/day. Also, these amounts are defined in terms of real purchasing power, not in terms of actual exchange rates. Thus $1.60 per day represents what a person could buy with that amount in the United States, not what could be bought in a low-income country if the $1.60 were exchanged for the local currency. Generally the latter would be substantially more than the former.

The World Bank makes annual attempts to update the figures on how many people are in poverty and how many are in extreme poverty by these standards. According to the Bank, there has been some substantial progress in the last fifteen years. By the Bank's count, the number of people in extreme poverty dropped from 1.25 billion in 1990 to below a billion in 2004—or from 24% of the world's people to its 2004 figure of 15%. The absolute number below $2/day fell only slightly in this period, from 2.6 billion to 2.5 billion, but this was a drop from 49% to 39% of the population (because the population increased).

The World Bank's appraisal of the situation, however, is open to dispute. To begin with, there are always problems in measuring what happens to people's incomes over time, because prices change. While the Bank adjusts for price changes, it does not do so adequately. To measure what happens in a country, the bank uses price changes for that country as a whole. It seems, however, that the prices of the goods that the poor buy have generally risen more rapidly than prices for the society as a whole. Thus the Bank's estimates of poverty reduction are probably overstated.

Furthermore, as the Bank recognizes, its picture of overall progress for the world obscures some very great differences between countries. By the $2/day and $1/day standard, the last fifteen years have seen great progress in China and India, two countries that together account for more than one-third of the world's population and which have grown quite rapidly. Other parts of the world, especially much of sub-Saharan Africa and parts of Latin America, have not done so well.

But there is a bigger difficulty. The $2/day and $1/day definitions of extreme poverty and poverty are, at best, a questionable way to frame the problem. It is misleading to define the poverty line simply in absolute terms, as the value of a certain quantity of goods and services that people must purchase to meet their basic needs (as represented by the $2/day and $1/daycutoffs). Raising people's absolute incomes is important and leads to improvements in nutrition, shelter, longevity, and general well-being. But there is more to poverty than an absolute level of income.

Poverty is a social status, a relation among people, and our standard of what it means to be in poverty varies across societies and over time. As a society's economy grows, its standard of 'need' changes, and thus the meaning of poverty changes. For example, as an economy grows, more work takes place away from the home, and thus people's need for transportation increases. Also, as incomes rise, people's standards of what they need in terms of food, clothing, shelter, and everything else change.

Roughly speaking, we can think of a society's standard of needs as determined by what the people in the middle have. If so, people are in poverty when their level of income is far below what the people in the middle have. This means that poverty is greatly affected by the distribution of income. In two societies where the absolute income of the bottom segment (say the bottom 20%) is the same, poverty will be greater in the society where income distribution is more unequal because in that society the bottom segment will be further from the norm and thus more lacking in that society's socially determined needs.

In China and India, in particular, the countries responsible for large reductions in poverty by the $2/day measure, income inequality has increased dramatically in recent decades. Thus, if we define poverty as a certain distance (in income terms) form the middle, it is possible that there are more people in poverty in China and India than there were twenty years ago, in spite of rapid economic expansion. And China and India are not unusual. Over the last few decades, many countries have seen rising inequality.

Even if one accepts the absolute poverty definition—the $2/day and $1/day standards—rising inequality makes the reduction of poverty with economic growth much less than it would be if, along with growth, income distribution were improving. The problem is that the World Bank and much of the U.N. effort to "make poverty history" largely ignore the issue of income distribution. For example, land redistribution is not on the table in World Bank and U.N. programs, yet unequal land holdings are at the foundation of the lack of income and political power experienced by the poor in many parts of the world. Or another example: the Bank and the United Nations tout education as a cure-all for poverty, but they give no consideration to the ways inequalities of income and political power restrict the emergence of effective school programs.

Whether one emphasizes the absolute or relative concept of poverty—or takes both into account—it is doubtful that much progress can be attained while ignoring the underlying issues of power and social structure that create and maintain poverty.

ARTICLE 9.8

November/December 2007

INEQUALITY WORSENS ACROSS ASIA

BY JOHN MILLER

A report from the Asian Development Bank, comparing more than a decade's worth of data from 22 developing countries, found significant increases in inequality across the region [Asia].

But, as the ADB notes, this doesn't mean the rich are taking food from the mouths of the poor. Rather, the rich are getting richer faster than the poor are. In all but one developing country, per capita incomes for the bottom fifth of the work force increased at least slightly; Pakistan was the only exception.

Poverty remains a serious problem throughout Asia—the ADB estimates 600 million people still live below the $1-a-day line, to use one popular measure. But "fixing" inequality won't fix poverty. As even the ADB recognizes, inequality can be a symptom of economic growth.

While inequality of outcome can be a good thing, inequality of opportunity is another matter.

The ADB worries that too much of the good inequality can lead to the bad variety by entrenching a new set of self-interested elites.

The danger is that all this talk of "inequality" will lead to policies that, in the name of redistributing income, reduce economic growth and thus make it harder for Asia's poor to join the middle class. The Asian "pie" is growing for everyone. The challenge is to keep it that way, instead of quarreling over the relative size of the pieces.

—Wall Street Journal *editorial, 8/21/07*

When ideologues of global capitalism step out of line, who better to let them know about it than the editors of the *Wall Street Journal*, the keepers of the free-market flame?

Just ask the economists and policy wonks at the Asian Development Bank (ADB), financial capital's Manila-based outpost in East Asia, who had the temerity to report in August that increasing inequality was a serious problem for Asia's economies. The *Journal*'s editors let them hear about it. "The danger," scolded the editors, "is that all this talk of 'inequality' will lead to policies that, in the name of redistributing income, reduce economic growth and thus make it harder for Asia's poor to join the middle class."

But the warning issued by the *Journal* editors is not just misleading, it is wrong. The evidence shows that countries that enjoy rapid economic growth are not more unequal than countries that grow slowly. In fact, a more equal distribution of income is not merely *compatible* with rapid growth; there are a number of avenues by which greater equality can actually *promote* growth. Finally, and most important for millions of people across Asia: poverty reduction depends on both raising a nation's income *and* reducing its inequality.

It is not that the ADB's bean counters got the numbers wrong. Of the 22 developing Asian economies in the ADB study, 15 saw inequality worsen since the early 1990s. That includes economic powerhouse China, where inequality worsened more rapidly and to higher levels than in any other country in the study other than Nepal. Even South Korea and Taiwan, once paragons of rapid *and* equitable growth, have seen inequality rise since 1993.

Economists at the ADB tracked changes in the levels of inequality using Gini coefficients, economists' standard measure of economic inequality, in the 22 developing Asian countries for which there are sufficient data. The Gini coefficient ranges from zero to one: zero corresponds to perfect equality (every household has the same income), and one corresponds to maximal inequality (one household gets the entire national income). In the real world, Gini coefficients range from around 0.25 (Sweden, Denmark, Hungary) to nearly 0.60 (South Africa, Brazil, Haiti).

The ADB report found Gini coefficients rising across Asia. China's, for instance, rose from 0.41 in 1993 to 0.47 in 2004; it is now higher than that of the United States, 0.46 in 2004. (See Figure 1, which shows inequality levels by country, and Figure 2, which reports on changes in inequality levels.)

The trend toward a widening gap between the rich and poor in Asia is actually more alarming than even the ADB tables suggest. For one thing, the Asian financial crisis of the late 1990s sucked millions of dollars out of the caches of the continent's economic elites. Had it not been for this hit, Malaysia, Indonesia, and probably Thailand as well would have joined the worsening inequality column of the ADB report. Plus, the ADB tables rely on household expenditure data as opposed to the more difficult-to-obtain income data used in some countries to measure inequality. Inequality levels calculated from expenditure data are normally lower than those calculated from income data for the same population. In the Philippines, for example, where inequality data are available on both measures, the expenditure-based Gini coefficient is 0.40 for 2003, while the income-based figure is about 20% higher at 0.48.

THE EAST ASIAN MIRACLE UNDER THE GUN

While inequality can be a symptom of economic growth in capitalist economies, as the editors argue, what is remarkable

**FIGURE 1
GINI COEFFICIENTS IN DEVELOPING ADB MEMBER COUNTRIES**

Nepal, 2003
PRC, 2004
Philippines, 2003
Turkmenistan, 2003
Thailand, 2002
Malaysia, 2004
Sri Lanka, 2002
Cambodia, 2004
Viet Nam, 2004
Azerbaijan, 2001
India, 2004
Lao PDR, 2002
Indonesia, 2002
Bangladesh, 2005
Taipei,China, 2003
Kazakhstan, 2003
Armenia, 2003
Mongolia, 2002
Tajikistan, 2003
Korea, Rep. of, 2004
Pakistan, 2004
Kyrgyz Republic, 2003

Note: Per-household income distributions are used for Korea (urban wage and salaried households only) and Taipei, China [Taiwan]. Per-capita expenditure distributions are used for the rest.

Source: Asian Development Bank, "Inequality in Asia: Key Indicators 2007 Special Chapter Highlights," August 2007.

about many East Asian economies is that prior to the 1990s they grew rapidly with far lower levels of inequality than elsewhere in the developing world. In some cases they saw inequality decline rather than worsen. For instance, in South Korea inequality declined from 1976 to 1993 even as the country's economy grew rapidly, posting average growth rates of 7.5% a year. Compared to Brazil, Latin America's fastest growing economy of the period, South Korea grew twice as quickly—with about half of Brazil's level of inequality.

The World Bank's famous 1993 "East Asian Miracle" study celebrated East Asia's "remarkable record of high growth *and* declining inequality." (Emphasis in the original.) From 1965 to 1990 the 23 economies of East Asia grew faster than all other regions of the world, three times as fast as the economies of Latin America and the Caribbean. Rapid growth in the region was spearheaded by the miraculous growth of eight high-performance economies—Japan; the "Four Tigers," Hong Kong, South Korea, Singapore, and Taiwan; and the three newly industrializing economies of southeast Asia, Indonesia, Malaysia, and Thailand—in which inequality remained low or improved over the same period. Because they were "unusually successful at sharing the fruits of growth," as the World Bank report put it, poverty declined rapidly and living conditions, from life expectancy to access to clean water and adequate shelter, improved dramatically in these high performance economies. A 1997 World Bank report went so far as to call rapid growth in East Asia "Everyone's Miracle."

"Everyone's" was surely an exaggeration even then. The editors of the *Wall Street Journal* nonetheless contend that today's much more unequal economic growth in Asia should still be considered everyone's miracle. As they read the ADB report, despite widening inequality, at least some of the benefits of the economic growth have trickled down to the poorest 20% of households in these economies. Since 1993 the expenditures of the bottom quintile increased in all of these 22 Asian economies with the exception of Pakistan, albeit by far less than the expenditures of the richest 20%. (See Figure 3.) "These increases in inequality are not a story of the 'rich getting richer and the poor getting poorer'," confirms the ADB report. "Rather it is the rich getting richer faster than the poor."

That is enough to qualify as "pro-poor growth," according to the editors' absolute definition of the term: economic growth that does anything at all to alleviate poverty, no matter now lopsidedly it benefits the well-to-do.

WHAT IS PRO-POOR GROWTH?

It is true that rapid economic growth usually does more to alleviate poverty than slower economic growth. But if inequality grows at the same time, then much of the poverty-fighting potential of rapid economic growth is being lost. In some sense it may be accurate to say that the rich are not taking food from the mouths of the poor—but it's just as

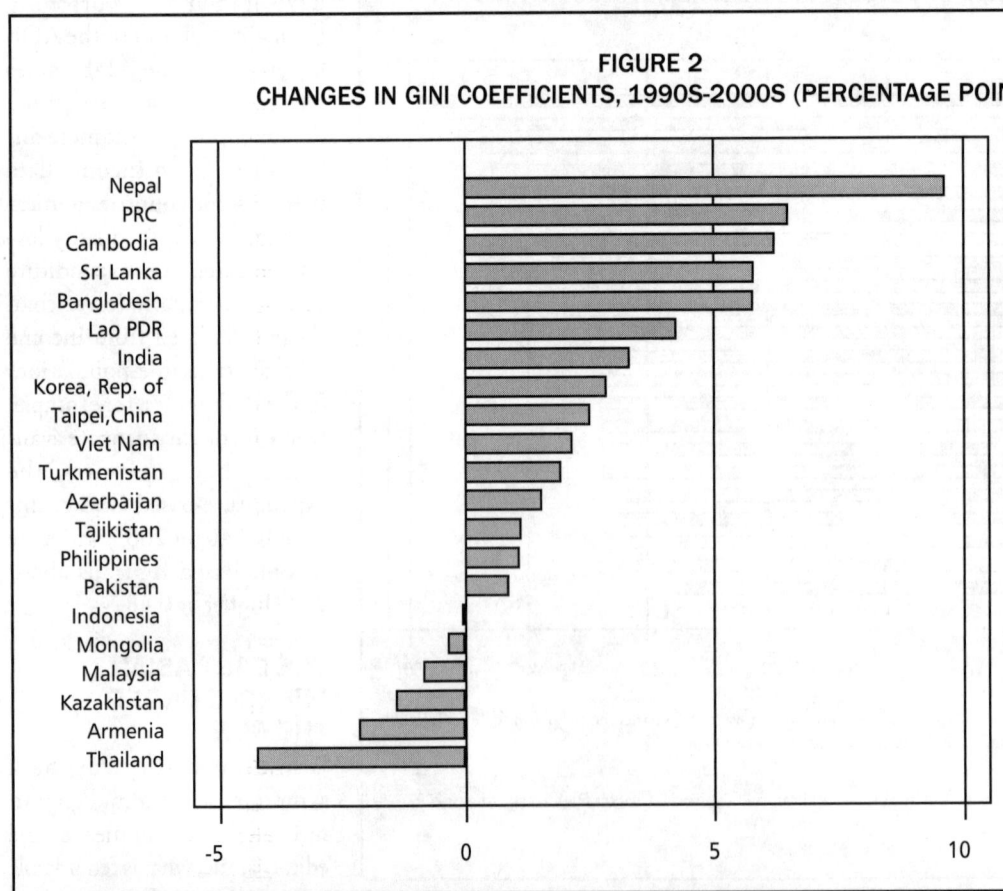

FIGURE 2
CHANGES IN GINI COEFFICIENTS, 1990S-2000S (PERCENTAGE POINTS)

Note: Years over which changes are computed are as follows: Armenia (1998-2003); Azerbaijan (1995-2001); Bangladesh (1991-2005); Cambodia (1993-2004); People's Republic of China (1993-2004); India (1993-2004); Indonesia (1993-2002); Kazakhstan (1996-2003); Republic of Korea (1993-2004); Lao PDR (1992-2002); Malaysia (1993-2004); Mongolia (1995-2002); Nepal (1995-2003); Pakistan (1992-2004); Philippines (1994-2003); Sri Lanka (1995-2002); Taipei,China (1993-2003); Tajikistan (1999-2003); Thailand (1992-2002); Turkmenistan (1998-2003); and Viet Nam (1993-2004). Gini calculated on income distribution for Republic of Korea and Taipei,China; expenditure distribution for all other countries.

Source: Asian Development Bank, "Inequality in Asia: Key Indicators 2007 Special Chapter Highlights," August 2007.

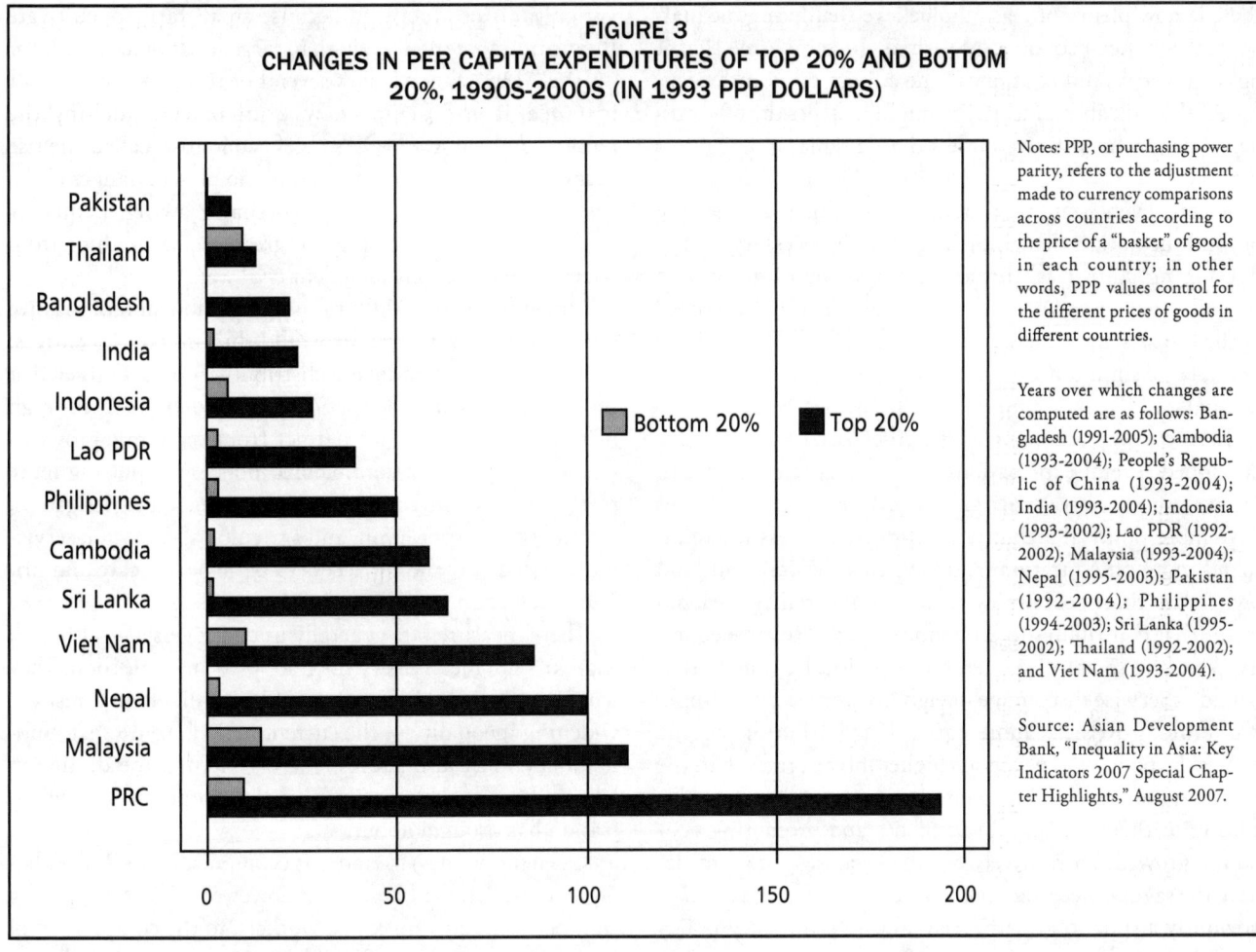

accurate to say that the benefits of economic growth that might otherwise have ended up on the tables of the poor have instead gone to the rich.

The evidence is clear. Had levels of inequality only remained unchanged over the last decade in the 15 countries that suffered worsening inequality, they would have seen a dramatic difference in the numbers of their citizens lifted from poverty. The ADB report documents the large reductions in the percentage of the population living on less than $1 a day (a standard U.N. measure of poverty) that would have occurred had economic inequality not worsened. In China, the number would have been just about halved. (See Figure 4.)

By that standard, economic growth in most of these countries can hardly be considered pro-poor. Each percentage point of economic growth now does less to alleviate poverty than in the past. For instance, economists Hafiz Pasha and T. Palanivel found that national poverty in China fell 9.8% during both the 1980s and 1990s. But the economy needed a 9.0% per capita growth rate in the later decade, as opposed to a 7.8% rate in the earlier one, to effect the same reduction in poverty rates.

And contrary to the claims of the *Journal* editors, a widening difference between rich and poor can be, and at times has been, so great as to bring poverty alleviation to a halt altogether. In Thailand, for instance, the same 1993 World Bank study found that despite growth rates averaging 6.4% a year from 1975 to 1986, poverty rates *increased* over the same period. Rural Thais were hard hit by the falling prices of farm products, and economic differences between urban and rural dwellers widened. Similarly, between 1984 and 1991, rural Chinese suffered worsening poverty as prices for farm products fell and rural output stagnated—even as the national economy was growing at double-digit rates.

While China's agricultural output subsequently picked up and poverty alleviation resumed, the widening gap between the economic standing of rural and urban Chinese continues to sap Chinese growth of its potential to ease poverty. Neglect of agriculture and of rural areas is a common feature that has contributed to rising inequality in many Asian economies; to improve the lot of the poor, the ADB recommends switching some public expenditures from urban to rural areas and from post-secondary education, which favors urban dwellers, to basic education, which is still not available to all, particularly in rural areas.

TACKLING POVERTY AND INEQUALITY

Neglecting to address inequality surely can compromise even the most dynamic economy's ability to fix poverty. That is not to say that fixing inequality alone will fix poverty. But there is now plenty of reason to believe that fixing inequality can enhance economic growth at the same time that it fights poverty. And contrary to the editors' admonishment, the ADB's talk about inequality might help lift the 600 million Asians who still live on less than a dollar a day out of poverty.

Today, even some mainstream economists are moving beyond the notion that rising inequality is necessary during developing countries' initial periods of rapid growth to establish the incentives to work, save, and invest. The record of the East Asian miracle economies provided an important exemplar of simultaneous rapid growth *and* low or declining inequality.

In recent years, economists and other social scientists have developed several explanations of how greater equality can in fact promote economic growth. More equal economies have more political stability, grant greater access to credit, spend more on education, and have more widespread land ownership than economies racked by inequality—each a factor that contributes to economic growth. Relative equality eases the social discontents and political conflicts that would otherwise discourage foreign investment and hamper economic growth. A more equal distribution of income allows the poor, who pay much higher interest rates than the rich in many developing countries, greater access to credit, adding to their personal investments and promoting economic growth. In relatively equal societies, more families have the savings necessary to send their children to school—obviously a spur to growth. And land reform, a key policy for reducing inequality in South Korea and Taiwan, raises agricultural productivity because small farmers cultivate their land more intensively than large landholders.

The ADB acknowledges several of these arguments. For instance, in the Beijing news conference launching the report, Ifzal Ali, the ADB's chief economist, called the rise in inequality in Asia today "a clear and present danger to the sustained growth," and warned that growing inequality could in some countries lead to "greater social conflict, from street demonstrations to violent civil wars."

Nonetheless, the ADB was not about to embrace massive redistribution policies that would dull market incentives. They do, however, endorse redistributive policies targeted at promoting "equality of opportunity" and "funded through mechanisms that do not detract from economic growth." Chief among their recommended polices are putting more public moneys into rural infrastructure including irrigation, electricity, transportation, and agricultural extension services, as well as expanding access to basic health care and primary education.

These measures are generally uncontroversial—although that does not mean they will be adopted any time soon. They would surely help. But they would be unlikely to arrest the widening inequality of the current period. To do that, public policy must also address the big picture: the decline in labor's share of the economic pie that corporate-led globalization has brought about.

Greater openness to trade, as economist Dani Rodrik has argued, erodes the bargaining power of labor by exposing workers, especially unskilled workers, to the competition of having their services replaced by imports from abroad.

Beyond that, export-led growth in many developing economies has failed to bring on the expected boom in manufacturing employment. As manufacturing exports from these countries increased with greater openness, so too did the quantity of manufactured goods imported into their domestic markets. So while export expansion was adding jobs, other jobs were being lost because of import penetration. Moreover, the new export industries are typically less labor-intensive than the older industries they replace. In China, for instance, relatively labor-saving joint ventures and foreign-owned firms in the country's new export zones have taken the place of relatively more labor-intensive state-owned manufacturing firms.

As a result, export promotion has done little to tighten labor markets and thereby improve

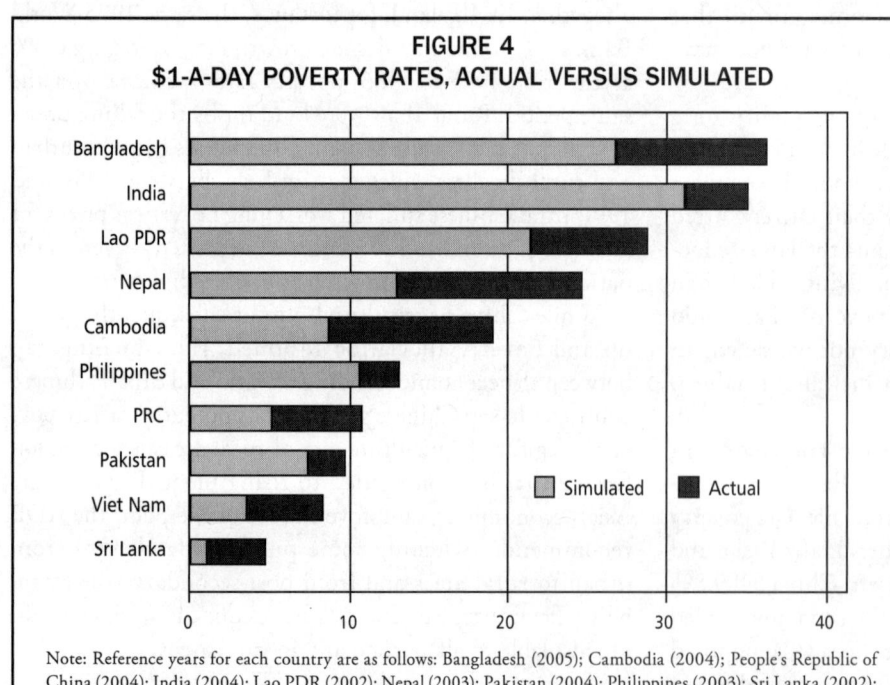

FIGURE 4
$1-A-DAY POVERTY RATES, ACTUAL VERSUS SIMULATED

Note: Reference years for each country are as follows: Bangladesh (2005); Cambodia (2004); People's Republic of China (2004); India (2004); Lao PDR (2002); Nepal (2003); Pakistan (2004); Philippines (2003); Sri Lanka (2002); and Viet Nam (2004). Simulated poverty rates are computed using expenditure/income distribution of initial year and average expenditure/income of recent year.

Source: Asian Development Bank, "Inequality in Asia: Key Indicators 2007 Special Chapter Highlights," August 2007.

labor's bargaining power. In the most detailed study to date, economists J. Felipe and G. Sipin found that in the Philippines, labor's share of national income fell by 6 percentage points from 1980 to 2002 as its economy globalized.

The case of China is also instructive, as economic sociologists Peter Evans and Sarah Staveteig point out. According to official statistics, manufacturing employment in China, the world's workshop, increased steadily from 1978 to 1995, nearly doubling from 53 million to 98 million jobs. But since then Chinese employment in manufacturing has fallen off. Manufacturing's share of Chinese employment has actually declined for nearly two decades now, even as China's share of world manufactured exports has increased more than fivefold.

With the manufacturing share of Chinese employment stagnant, hundreds of millions of people currently dependent on agricultural production for their incomes must either stay in that sector or move to the service sector. Both options suggest increased inequality and a more precarious quality of life for the vast majority of the Chinese population, argue Evans and Staveteig. If they stay in agriculture, the Chinese peasantry are likely to face stagnating incomes. A move into the service sector would allow a few new entrants to gain access to the more lucrative service jobs, but the vast majority will find poorly remunerated, insecure jobs offering personal services as the nannies, maids, drivers, and gardeners that their luckier compatriots will be able to hire.

While this widening inequality in the very countries that not long ago served as exemplars of growth with equality might not present a problem to the editors of the Wall Street Journal, it surely is a serious problem, as even the ADB acknowledges. But genuinely pro-poor economic growth will only come about when public policy confronts the current rules of the global economy—rules that the editors are so dedicated to defending, and that the ADB itself is reluctant to challenge.

Resources: Asian Development Bank, *Key Indicators 2007, Part 1: Inequality in Asia*, August 2007; "Inequality Check," *Wall Street Journal* editorial, 8/21/07; Richard McGregor, "ADB warns on rising inequality in China," *Financial Times*, 8/08/07; Alan Wheatley, "Rising inequality danger for Asia, says ADB," Reuters, 08/08/07; "For whosoever hath, to him shall be given, and he shall have more: Income inequality in emerging Asia is heading towards Latin American levels," *The Economist*, 8/09/07; World Bank, "The East Asian Miracle: Economic Growth and Public Policy," 1993; Vinod Ahuja et al., "Everyone's Miracle," World Bank, 1997; Peter Evans and Sarah Staveteig, "Late 20th Century Industrialization and Changing Employment Structures in the Global South," Univ. of Calif. Berkeley, 8/22/07; Hafiz A. Pasha and T. Palanivel, "Pro-Poor Growth and Policies: The Asian Experience," U.N. Development Programme, 2004; Judith Banister, "Manufacturing Employment in China," *Monthly Labor Review*, July 2005.

ARTICLE 9.9

July/August 2007

THE SOCIAL COST OF NEOLIBERALISM IN CHINA
INTERVIEW WITH ECONOMIST HAN DEQIANG

BY STEPHEN PHILION

Han Deqiang is a prolific economist at the Economics and Management School, Beijing University of Aeronautics and Astronautics, and one of a growing number of Chinese scholars critical of the country's neoliberal development strategy. Han, however, did not just arrive at this stance. He has been critical of neoliberal ideology in China for almost two decades and has written many books and articles on the social crises that rural and urban workers have faced under China's new economic regime.

When I first met Han, in 2000, he was making his way around the country delivering sharp and eloquent lectures to university students refuting the then-dominant faith. At the time, I was conducting research on workers' protests against privatization in Zhengzhou, and most of the labor activists and workers' leaders I met were familiar with Han's devastating critiques of the privatization craze that swept China in the late 1990s and early 2000s. It would not be wrong to characterize him as a Chinese Noam Chomsky, albeit with his own oratorical flair!

In September 2005, I interviewed Han for about three hours. Our discussion focused on the impact of China's 2001 entry into the World Trade Organization and on the social costs, both in and outside of China, of the accelerated neoliberal development that followed that milestone. In January 2007, I followed up with a second interview. What follows is a translated and edited version of both interviews.

STEPHEN PHILION: The last time I met with you was during the height of the East Asian financial crisis. At that time, we discussed the consequences you foresaw for China of entering the World Trade Organization (WTO). Five years later, which of those consequences have come about?

HAN DEQIANG: At the time, I argued the greatest damage would be to China's capacity to control its industrial and technological development autonomously. I think it's safe to say these last five years have more than proven that true. In China, any industry that wants to develop its own technology or markets has encountered increasingly great barriers.

Second, I predicted that unemployment would rise dramatically; this has also shown itself to be a reality. Of course, some say that there has been a shortage of migrant workers from the countryside recently, which allegedly proves that the WTO has not produced greater unemployment. But this requires a more careful analysis. In the late 1990s, agricultural commodity prices fell, and taxes became heavier. Hence the large mass of migrant workers and the ensuing rise in urban unemployment we saw then. However, starting around 2002-2003, the government implemented new tax cuts for farmers and increased education subsidies in poor rural districts. As a result of these new policies, the contradictions in the countryside were mollified some. Also, when the price of rice plummeted, large numbers of farmers stopped producing it. As a result, the price rebounded, improving the livelihood of farmers in 2003 and 2004. So rural dwellers now had less motivation to accept the kind of exploitation that exists in the for-export sector of urban industry, much less migrate to the cities in search of it! However, this doesn't nullify our argument that when foreign companies conquer national industries, greater unemployment results. The opposite actually. When Wal-Mart goes to Gweiyang or Beijing, say, they knock out, in an instant, four or five department stores.[1]

PHILION: And smaller shops?

HAN: Hah! Don't even go there! Medium-size department stores, neighborhood sellers, ones that were supposed to be able to dominate local markets by virtue of their size—they saw those advantages disappear.

Third, I have always acknowledged that WTO entry would provide China certain short-term gains. For example, increases in investment and exports undoubtedly occurred. But I argued that WTO entry was the equivalent of drinking moonshine to deal with thirst. This has two outcomes. One, of course, is the removal of thirst. After all, if there are no other liquids around, I have no choice but to turn to moonshine. But the other result, of course, is your death! So Chinese industry has resolved its investment problem, but that has been accompanied by its death knell.

From what I see, the social crisis facing China will continue to intensify, as will the neglect of China's economic autonomy, in addition to the eventual breakdown of the country's financial system. This is entirely foreseeable; it's only a matter of time before China faces something along the lines of the 1997 East Asian financial crisis. We cannot predict exactly when it will occur, but I suspect it isn't that far off in the future.

PHILION: How has the WTO affected large state-owned enterprises?

HAN: State-owned enterprises (SOEs) fall into two categories. The first are SOEs, like Shenyang Machine Factory or Luoyang Tractor Company, that are subject to competition with private companies. These quickly went bankrupt. Monopoly-sector SOEs, such as petroleum producers, are less directly affected by China's membership in the WTO.

PHILION: The Chinese leadership seems to be working under the assumption that as long as the SOEs that produce the greatest revenues remain vital, Chinese socialism can be sustained.

HAN: First of all, China's not socialist now.

PHILION: Yes, right. I mean in their sense of the phrase, so-called "socialism with Chinese characteristics."

HAN: Not likely either. It is true that in terms of tax contributions and profits, the small and medium-size SOEs are not great, but in the absolute numbers they employ, they are considerable. Their influence on local employment and finances is pretty substantial. So, in the aftermath of the near complete collapse of these small and medium-size SOEs, for the central state to rely on large enterprises alone for maintaining the subsistence of China's population of 1.3 billion becomes extremely difficult.

PHILION: It seems as though the leadership's hope is for local and foreign private capital to replace these small and medium-size companies as the source of investment and to resolve the unemployment problem in the process.

HAN: What I would contend is that for every one job saved by foreign capitalist investment, three to four will be lost unless the foreign investment produces for foreign export alone. This situation does exist, assuredly. Right now 60% of our export is fueled by foreign companies' investment. However, the potential for foreign investment to instigate future Chinese economic growth is weak. It can only largely resolve a segment of the unemployment problem. It can't do much in terms of advancing the upgrading or expansion of China's industrial system.

And its use to resolve the fiscal crisis facing China is even more problematic. From '49 on, we built our nation by using state enterprise to supplement or replace foreign enterprise's contribution to the economy. The idea of doing the opposite is a fantasy.

---

1   *By 2006, there were already more than 50 Wal-Mart stores in China.*

PHILION: China's leaders also seem to believe that as long as the monopoly-based state-owned enterprises are run well, their ability to determine the direction of the economic development will be strong.

HAN: This is a twofold issue. First, whether or not it's possible for the political leadership of a country with no state-owned enterprise to control the direction of the national economy. I think it might be possible. It's the European model, after all, and even in a certain way the American model. In these economies, by and large, control of enterprises is in the hands of private parties. But this doesn't have that much impact on the state's tax receipts and its role in regulating the economy. If the state is powerful, it can play a crucial role in the management of the economy even if it doesn't control much enterprise.

On the other hand, where the state controls a major portion of enterprises but is weak, it has a difficult time managing the economy. And if the collaboration between that weak state and private interests is deep, the result is distortion of policy by capitalists to the point that the state loses more and more capacity to control the economy and the direction of economic development. The key factor here is the strength of the government, not how many companies it controls.

PHILION: Then what is the likelihood of China going in the direction of Japan developmentally?

HAN: I don't think it's possible for China to go that route. The leadership doesn't even have that as a working concept. The Japanese experience is one that greatly emphasizes the role of state planning.

PHILION: Interesting, because the U.S. government complains that China still places too much emphasis on central planning in the economy.

HAN: America likewise is dissatisfied with Japan's level of state planning. America is also dissatisfied with France in this respect. [Laughs.] Is there any country that America is satisfied with? Seriously, today the role of the state and of monopoly SOEs is far greater in Japan than in China. Also, from what I understand of Japanese history, Japan has an elite that has a strong sense of responsibility for the nation's future. But I can't find any such elite in China today. If Japan's leaders lose a war, they feel great shame. They don't send their children off to America.

PHILION: What is your assessment of how different classes view the WTO and liberalization in China?

HAN: Chinese workers and farmers are in a pickle. But is it the damage caused by political power elites or that caused by markets that is greatest? Right now, in their view the pain caused by entry into the WTO is not as great as that caused by the power of government cadres. For example, state workers view layoffs as only indirectly caused by markets; the abuse of power by the Party is viewed as their direct cause.

PHILION: Of course they're interconnected.

HAN: That's right. Domestically it's a matter of a corrupt officialdom; internationally it's a matter of submitting to the will of international capital. The WTO represents international capital's control over China. But of course it is Chinese government policies that make this control possible. So what the masses experience is a problem created by their government, not by the WTO or global monopoly capital.

For example, state workers have to pay income tax once their wages exceed 800 yuan a month. But a worker in a foreign-owned enterprise does not have to pay the tax until after 2,000 or 3,000 yuan a month. This government tax policy results in a positive feeling toward foreign-owned companies on the part of the average Chinese worker. They don't see that the better wages and better profits in the private sector are a product of the government support that sector enjoys. Not to mention many other kinds of special benefits that foreign capitalists enjoy thanks to government policies that simultaneously disadvantage domestic state companies. The ironic result is that many state companies go to Hong Kong and falsely register as foreign companies in order to enjoy these advantageous policies—the so-called fake foreign devil problem.

PHILION: In the past few years, have these views changed at all?

HAN: There has been some change in attitude, yes—especially in terms of recognizing the threat that WTO entry poses to China's future. So the push for economic autonomy is a theme that you now see cropping up in every Chinese web discussion board, far more than five years ago.

PHILION: You've spoken about the kinds of losses that have befallen China upon entering the WTO. In the United States we hear the same concerns, only it's America that is considered to be the victim of China's entry into the WTO! This is so especially in terms of unemployment: it is frequently said that China should be held responsible for America's unemployment problems.

HAN: To be accurate, we should say that America's bosses need to take responsibility for America's unemployment problems. Why? Because since China entered the WTO, both China's workers and America's workers have been hurt. However, in fact, many bosses in China have also suffered losses due to the WTO. The operation of the WTO causes great losses to both workers and bosses in developing countries as well as to workers in developed countries. Broadly speaking, only one group doesn't suffer losses, namely, bosses in developed countries. So to get to the source of the United States' unemployment problem, Americans need to analyze the responsibility of the Bush administration, the bosses at GM and Microsoft, etc.

PHILION: Not to mention the Democratic Party!

HAN: Indeed. Whoever is promoting the WTO is promoting the interests of transnational corporations and doing harm to American and Chinese workers. It's not only developing countries' workers who are hurt by globalization; it's really the world. Globalization gives rise to global recession, not prosperity. Consider a number of indicators that demonstrate this. Globally, debt levels have increased since the 1980s, in terms of both national debt and average citizens' credit overload. Second, the whole world exists in a state of high unemployment. The U.S. unemployment rate is much higher than it was in the 1950s and 1960s. Ditto Europe, whose unemployment rate is even higher! Japan likewise. Third, growth rates have fallen globally compared to those in the 1950s and 1960s. This, of course, is hidden by large rates of credit-fuelled debt, without which growth rates would be even lower. All of this indicates global recession, not global prosperity.

PHILION: What about China's economy? Its promoters argue that liberalization has generated constant growth.

HAN: In the 1990s, China and the United States both grew. However, look at the overall global economic picture. Latin America has seen great declines in growth and serious crises; Africa even worse. The Middle East is in a state of chaos and misfortune, Russia's GDP is only half of what it was in the 1980s, and the East Asian "tigers" have been in a state of recession since the region's financial crisis. Japan's debt in proportion to GDP is the highest in the world, roughly 130%, and its rate of growth has been somewhere near zero. If the government hadn't invested so much in the economy, it's possible Japan's rate of growth would be negative, -4% or -5%! If this isn't depression, what is?

Thus, my definition of globalization is global depression. This departs, of course, from mainstream propaganda. Even many of the anti-globalization movements are fond of arguing that globalization still has its positive points, that it just needs to take into account and protect the interests of developing countries and of workers in developed countries. It's as though if we just removed some of the shortcomings of the process, all would be well. My view is that globalization is nothing short of a massive mistake.

PHILION: In the United States, especially but not solely in the Democratic Party, there's a common notion that the U.S. government must implement economic sanctions against China and pursue higher tariffs in order to protect American jobs. So, for example, Rep. Charles Schumer (D-N.Y.) recently asserted that the conditions China sets for foreign investors aren't as good as those the United States provides for Chinese importers.

HAN: That's quite the exaggeration, eh? Laughable! It's actually the exact opposite. American corporations have enjoyed such high profits in China. Which is in the better position to buy up a company abroad, China or the United States? The benefits China gives to U.S. investments in terms of tax breaks, reductions in land prices, and the like are the kinds of things a Chinese investor in the United States can only dream about. And in terms of volume, Chinese investment in the United States is small in comparison to what it's imagined to be by Schumer types. His words are typical politician rhetoric.

In any event, I welcome America protecting its own markets. Likewise, I can declare American commodities unwelcome in China, along with American investment. If the countries of the world stopped welcoming U.S. investment, watch and see how long America could stand it! Its empire would erode quickly! Its existence is dependent on foreign investment and foreign consumption of its exports in order to maintain a higher standard of living.

PHILION: How much influence will a recession or a worse crisis in the United States have on China? It seems as if China is more and more able to withstand the impact.

HAN: Well, I would say rather that if America catches a cold, China will catch a very serious cold or flu. The United States is still the main market for China's exports. An economic crisis in the United States would definitely result in large numbers of bankruptcies throughout China's coastal regions. And if a U.S. crisis caused the value of the dollar to drop, that would also have a huge impact on the Chinese economy because the real size of the U.S. debt would decrease, as would China's foreign exchange holdings. It would basically mean all our hard work in the service of American profits was a waste.

PHILION: How do you regard the possibility of revaluing the renminbi [the official name of China's currency, abbreviated RMB]?

HAN: To date we haven't seen a real revaluation, only a very small one. The pressure in China against revaluation is huge. Why? If we revalue the RMB upwards, China's exports will be less competitively priced, and the strategy of relying on foreign exports for development will fall apart. I suspect America's leadership wants us to devalue the currency by 20% or 30%. Or at the very least 10%. But even at 10%, the export companies in the coastal provinces would face a crisis of survival.

Of course, U.S. pressure on China to revalue is great. If the U.S. government is not willing to compromise on this issue, Chinese leaders will have a hard time dealing with the political discontent that would result. And if Chinese exports can't go to America, but American imports continue apace, the cycle of trade that makes China's development possible will not last. The United States simultaneously wants to reduce imports in order to protect its markets *and* open up more markets in China that it can export to. Short-term, that's possible; long-term, forget it.

PHILION: But in any case the reliance is mutual, no? The United States is quite reliant on cheap Chinese imports.

HAN: Yes, but American reliance on China is not as great as Chinese reliance on America's economy. Why is that? China's exports are low relative to overall U.S. imports, whereas China's exports to the United States are high in relation to total Chinese exports. Furthermore, American exports to China tend to be those that are less replicable. But what China produces can be produced in almost any country. Thus, when China negotiates, it's from a weaker position.

American politicians are shortsighted. Too much power is concentrated in U.S. hands now, and they don't wish to let other hands in on that control. They don't even take into consideration the needs of foreign leaders who collaborate on behalf of U.S. interests abroad. If American politicians continue like this, they won't have any collaborators left—they'll all be overthrown! What good is that in the eyes of the American ruling class, eh? [Laughs.] So if U.S. leaders really want to extend America's capacity to exploit the world's resources, they're going to have to learn to compromise more.

PHILION: Perhaps from their vantage point there is no alternative. Under this current stage of intensified global competition for profits, perhaps they have little choice but to enforce U.S. hegemony more forcefully and totally.

HAN: But if they really want to reorganize this world economy, they're going to have to increase demand for goods and services in developing countries. That would save the world economy, no? But U.S. politicians and elites won't do this.

PHILION: Has the pace of privatization since WTO entry been faster or slower than you anticipated?

HAN: Privatization has been the basic thrust of China's economic reform policies for the last 20 years. While privatization was already moving along quite rapidly, entering the WTO only added to that.

PHILION: What about privatization of large state-owned companies in China?
HAN: That's underway, but its form differs from other sectors of the state enterprise economy. Small enterprises are subjected to buy-outs or else bankruptcy. Larger companies typically don't need to declare bankruptcy—their profits are still guaranteed because of their monopoly position. And if they were sold off, too much "face" would be lost. However, there are still ways to move in that direction.

One way is to convert state enterprises into stock-holding companies and allow foreign purchase of the stock, thus handing part of the management power over to foreign investors. This mechanism presents an increased threat to the autonomy of the Chinese state—which wouldn't be the case if we were talking about Chinese investors buying up these shares, even though we'd still be talking about privatization. This kind, however, is not only a sell-off of companies, but in effect the sell-off of the country—a re-colonization! A foreign company doesn't even have to buy up an entire state enterprise; a proportion of shares that enables it to dominate production decisions and priorities will do the trick. It's a classic form of imperial control in the economic realm.

PHILION: In 2000, there was a widespread concern in the Chinese media, in academic and business circles, about the problem of insufficient domestic demand—consumers not buying goods, investors not investing, instead waiting to see if prices would go lower. The Chinese government made large investments in public projects to stimulate demand. Have the government's efforts to address the demand problem had any results?

HAN: There are two policies that could be used: expand national demand by reducing the income gap and getting more money into the hands of the masses; or create a bubble. What we're doing is the second one: creating a bubble to cover up the problems spawned by inadequate national demand. Primarily this is seen in real estate bubbles: real estate markets experienced great investment after portions of real estate were subjected to market reforms. Meanwhile, the first strategy has not been employed. In fact, the gap between the incomes of the rich and the poor has grown to a shocking degree, far faster than the growth in GDP.

PHILION: Can you talk about the economic policies of the current government?

HAN: In 2002, with the nomination of Hu Jintao as Party secretary, his apparent commitment to protecting China's national interests, unlike the previous leadership, gave those like myself some hope. He also expresses more concern about the gap between rich and poor, as well as the rights of urban and rural laborers. Our optimism has not been entirely mistaken. But we still feel that his responses to these problems have been inadequate.

The policy of eliminating rural taxes was well received; plainly, taxing the wealthy should come before taxing farmers! Also, the recent arrest of Go Cujun, who represents the pro-privatization wing of the Party, would not likely have taken place without Hu Jintao's support. These actions have contributed to a certain comfort level among critics of privatization in China, as have other developments. For example, recently the National Research Institute published a white paper on the failure of health care reform. This is the first time an official institution has publicly repudiated a particular aspect of economic reform. Also, the Technology Ministry recently took issue publicly with the view of China's head WTO negotiating representative Long Yuantu that China doesn't need its own technology, that we can purchase it all from foreign companies investing in China. This we consider an important event as well.

Naturally, the things that I see as positive, the neoliberal rightwingers in China see as a disaster.

PHILION: There is a neoliberal economist at Peking University who has come under considerable public criticism recently, and you've been a party to that. Five years ago, it would have been hard to imagine so many intellectuals and other comrades in such an open struggle with neoliberal economists in China.

HAN: You're right—now there are more academics who are critical of neoliberalism's price tag in China. Our numbers are better these days, as is our ability to coordinate with each other.

We are not critical of reform. There is obviously a need for reform and for attracting a certain amount of foreign investment in China. We don't at all advocate the closing off of China's market. Our opponents like to accuse us of being against reform. What we are opposed to is their neoliberalism that sees markets as the be-all and end-all. We support socialist reform that improves the social position of workers and farmers and that strengthens the position of China. We're not against that kind of reform at all!

PHILION: Wal-Mart's agreement to allow unions in its facilities in China has been in the news. Will this have any impact, or is it more appearance than substance?

HAN: As I see it, China's requirement that a union be established at Wal-Mart does not mean the situation of Wal-Mart's workers has improved. Nor does it mean that China's workers will be able to create independent unions, free from the official Party-controlled All China Federation of Trade Unions (ACFTU). Instead, we see Wal-Mart creating a union that will be under the control of the employer in order to erode the pressure from unofficial, underground union movements. This ends up making the ACFTU look good and seem able to accomplish something real. At the same time, it can put a pretty face on foreign investors' role in China as being no different from Chinese companies. Look at it this way: Wal-Mart has established a union, so it's become a Chinese company! This suits ACFTU leaders who are sympathetic with such employer-friendly unions as well as many intellectuals who stand by such unions and look at labor issues from the perspective of employers, whether we're talking about state-owned enterprises or domestic or foreign-owned capitalist companies.

PHILION: The government has recently placed some regulations on multinational corporations investing in China—which, tellingly, the corporations have been resisting. Do you think they are likely to be effective?

HAN: Regulations on foreign investors have existed forever, and when concern is expressed in civil society about investors, new regulations are devised. Nonetheless, whether it's central government ministries, or local governments, or state-owned enterprise administrators, none tend to take these regulations too seriously. Attracting business investment and allowing foreign investors access to China's national resources and control over critical industrial sectors remain the central policy directions—ones that are proceeding at a rapid pace.

PHILION: What are the present prospects for household income distribution in terms of developing a viable domestic consumer market for China's future growth?

HAN: In 2006, across sectors, salaries generally increased, especially among lower-level wage earners. The rate of unpaid back wages has also decreased. These are all favorable phenomena. However, consumer goods have seen rapid price inflation, which has hit low-wage workers especially hard, essentially eliminating what wage gains they've experienced. That's in part why income disparities continue to grow.

PHILION: Have there been any improvements in the conditions for workers in the SOEs? Is the SOE sector likely to continue to be a source of labor protests in the future, or do you see it becoming quieter? Why so?

HAN: The policy of mass layoffs that was so widespread in the state sector until recently has basically ended. Also, state workers who are presently employed have more wage security than private-sector workers, so they are less inclined toward conflict. However, those state workers who have been laid off or reassigned remain dissatisfied with the status quo.

REMITTANCES TO THE RESCUE?

BY ALISSA THUOTTE

Remittances—the money sent home to families by migrants living in foreign countries—have been gaining attention in the last few years from international institutions such as the World Bank, the Inter-American Development Bank (IDB), and the International Monetary Fund. These organizations and others have begun to study remittances with an eye to their potential for reducing poverty in the poor and near-poor countries to which most of these funds flow. It turns out that remittances are a mixed blessing. They offer a relatively stable source of incoming funds. At the same time, however, they can create an alarming dependence on behalf of their recipients, heightening their vulnerability to shifting political and economic winds in the host countries over which they have no control.

Remittances have been, until very recently, very much on the rise, with about 10% of the world's population now receiving some remittance income. In 2006, 150 million migrants across the globe sent $300 billion in 1.5 billion transactions. Remittances now represent nearly one-third of total financial flows to the developing world—more than official development assistance and, depending on the country, more even than foreign direct investment. Fifty-nine countries receive more than $1 billion annually in remittances, and 45 receive more than 10% of their GDP. Moreover, remittance flows have tended to be much more stable than foreign direct investment or portfolio (stocks and bonds) investment (see "Remittances versus Other External Financing").

One third of the money sent originates in the United States; most of the rest is sent from Europe and the Middle East. A significant volume of remittance money circulates within the developing world as well, however: so-called "South-South" flows account for 30% to 45% of total remittances, according to the World Bank.

Latin America and the Caribbean is the region receiving the highest level of remittances per capita, averaging $102 annually, and the region's remittance flows have risen tenfold in real terms over the last 20 years. In 2006 the region received $62.3 billion from migrants abroad—five times the amount of "official development assistance" it received—with remittances to Mexico ($24.2 billion) accounting for over a third. After climbing at double-digit rates in the last decade, the flow now appears to be leveling off: a recent survey by an IDB fund estimated 2007 remittances to the region at $66.5 billion, only a 7% increase over the previous year.

Most of the money received in this region is used for everyday living expenses, everything from food and home repairs to school tuition. What interests economists most, though, is the potential for remittances to contribute to economic development—when, for example, recipients put the money toward new small business ventures that may over time provide employment to others and expand local economies. According to a 2007 World Bank report, the data suggest that remittances do tend to increase bank deposits, reflecting at least some potential for such investment.

Research has generally found that higher remittance flows are, to a modest degree, associated with lower poverty, better health, and higher levels of education in the developing world. In ten out of eleven Latin American and Caribbean countries examined in a 2006 World Bank study, children from families receiving remittances were more likely to remain in school than those whose parents were not supported by such funds.

REMITTANCES VERSUS OTHER EXTERNAL FINANCING TO DEVELOPING COUNTRIES

Note: **Private debt and portfolio equity** refers to the net flow of stock and bond purchases by foreign investors plus commercial bank loans from foreign banks. **Foreign direct investment** refers to the net flow of funds invested directly by companies to establish or control business enterprises abroad. **Official development assistance** refers to loans, grants, and other aid given by the governments of developed countries. Remittance figure for 2007 is estimated.

Sources: World Bank: "Global Economic Prospects 2006: Economic Implications of Remittances and Migration," "World Development Indicators 2008," and "Global Development Finance 2008."

> ## WESTERN UNION CALLING
>
> While it has undeniably become easier and more convenient to send money across the border in the last decade, activists charge transfer services, especially Western Union, with taking advantage of their most loyal customers. Remittances represent a nearly $1 billion a year industry for Western Union; global migration is so central to the company's profits that "forecasts of border movements drive the company's stock," according to the *New York Times*. Western Union's huge slice of the industry pie allows the company to charge fees from 4% to as high as 20% of the amount remitted.
>
> The Oakland, Calif.-based Boycott Western Union campaign asserts that the company fails to invest an adequate portion of its earnings in the communities of the customers from which it profits. Its campaign aims to convince Western Union to sign a Transnational Community Benefits Agreement—like the Community Reinvestment Act for banks—that would "ensure community reinvestment of $1 per every transaction while also forcing the company to reduce its fees and establish fairer exchange rates."
>
> In the meantime, experts at the IDB and elsewhere insist that this is a perfect opportunity for banks to get more involved, and are trying to encourage partnerships between U.S. and Latin American banks and to extend networks into Latin America's more rural areas, where access to banking is notoriously scarce. More competition, they argue, would help push transfer fees down and improve customer service.

Yet the increasing remittance flows have a downside: families and national economies that come to rely on the extra income become vulnerable to far-distant events and trends. Take the case of Mexico. One consequence of the current bust in the U.S. housing market is that construction, which employs many Mexican workers, has slowed—and along with it, the flow of money back home. Remittances to Mexico grew only 1% in 2007, and in January of this year *fell* 6% compared to the same period last year, according to the IDB.

And the falloff in construction work is not the only factor depressing Mexican migrants' ability to send money home. Thanks to increasingly visible anti-immigrant sentiment in the United States, stricter border enforcement—including the threat of incarceration, as opposed to just deportation, for undocumented migrants caught crossing the border—and penalties for employers who hire undocumented workers, it has become harder for immigrants to enter the country and find decent jobs. As the dollar falls in value against foreign currencies, those who have been in the United States for some time may have to work longer hours and cut their expenses just to be able to send home the same amounts.

Migration and remittances have certainly transformed many Latin American towns, but not always for the better. So-called "migra-villages" have seen their working-age adult population shrink. Remittance money can help build new homes, but they often remain empty in their owners' absence; new schools get built, but enrollment does not necessarily increase. Family members left behind may stop working and wait month-to-month for money from overseas, weakening local economies—not a sustainable set-up in the long run.

And surprisingly, remittances do not necessarily flow most heavily toward the poorest families that need them the most. In fact, the World Bank's 2006 study found that in the 11 Latin American and Caribbean countries for which data were available, remittance income was actually distributed slightly more unequally than total household income: the top 20% took in 51% of total income, but 54% of remittances. Who receives remittances varies sharply from country to country. Contrast Mexico, for instance, where 61% of the households receiving remittances in 2004 were in the bottom 20% by (non-remittance) income, with Peru, where fewer than 6% were, while 40% were in the top income quintile.

Today, remittance checks are helping millions of households across the global South to keep food on the table and a roof overhead. Although the evidence hardly hails them as a long-term solution to global poverty, as long as remittance flows continue, they should be both facilitated *and* rigorously regulated.

Sources: Jason DeParle, "Migrant Money Flow: A $300 Billion Current," *NY Times*, 11/18/07; Pablo Fajnzylber and J. Humberto Lopez, "Close to Home: The Development Impact of Remittances in Latin America," (World Bank, 2007); "Sending Money Home: Worldwide Remittance Flows to Developing Countries," (IFAD/IDB, 2007); Manuel Orozco, "The Remittance Marketplace: Prices, Policy, and Financial Institutions," (Pew Hispanic Center, 6/7/04); Elisabeth Malkin, "Mexicans Barely Increased Remittances in '07," *NY Times*, 2/26/08; Jason DeParle, "World Banker and His Cash Return Home," *NY Times*, 3/17/08; Donald Greenlees, "As the Dollar Slides, Two Continents Feel the Side Effects in Divergent Ways," *NY Times*, 3/27/08; Jason DeParle, "Western Union Empire Moves Migrant Cash Home," *NY Times*, 11/22/07; Eduardo Porter, "Struggling to Draw Workers Sending Money Back Home," *NY Times*, 6/7/04; Devesh Kapur, "Remittances: the New Development Mantra?" (U.N. Conf. on Trade and Dev't, April 2004); Kevin Plumberg, "Weak Dollar Makes Immigrant Life Tougher," Reuters, 2/11/08; Ami Bonilla, "Mexicans Send Less Cash Home, Bad News for All," New America Media, 8/9/07; Maria Sacchetti, "Beating the Bank," *Boston Globe*, 4/15/08.

WOMEN OF NAFTA

BY MARTHA OJEDA

The outstanding collection *NAFTA From Below: Maquiladora Workers, Farmers, and Indigenous Communities Speak Out on the Impact of Free Trade in Mexico*, combines worker testimony with analytical and historical essays to provide a devastating picture of the effects of neoliberal international trade policies—culminating in the North American Free Trade Agreement (NAFTA)—on workers throughout Mexico. The book, available in both English and Spanish, also offers inspiring accounts of resistance to those policies.

The book's early chapters focus on *maquiladora* workers in the north of the country, addressing key labor issues such as health and safety, environmental concerns, and freedom of association. Later chapters take up organizing by agricultural workers in the south, especially in the state of Chiapas, in response to neoliberal "reforms." That the Zapatista uprising in Chiapas began on January 1, 1994, the very day that NAFTA went into effect, was no accident.

One of the book's achievements is to show how the struggles of industrial workers in the north of Mexico are related to those of agricultural workers in the south. Knitting these struggles together is one of the central aims of the Coalition for Justice in the Maquiladoras, which produced *NAFTA From Below*. The coalition has helped bring *maquila* workers and organizers from the north together with members of grassroots *campesino* and indigenous groups in the south to help strengthen cooperative projects in both regions and to share information about the history of organized struggle in the workplace. Women's strong leadership roles in workplace struggles in the north have been of particular interest to organizers in the south, especially as former agricultural workers from the south migrate to work in *maquiladoras* near the northern border.

Women played a central role in the struggle of workers at a Sony plant in Nuevo Laredo for a democratic union, described in the selections that follow. The events at Sony vividly illustrate the frequent conflicts between Mexico's corrupt official unions and rival independent unions that Chris Tilly and Marie Kennedy describe (pp. 26-30). The Sony workers' struggle was also a key early test of NAFTA's labor side-agreement, the North American Agreement on Labor Cooperation, and the bodies it established, known as National Administrative Offices (NAOs), to investigate violations.

These excerpts include testimony from Martha Ojeda (co-editor of *NAFTA From Below*, with Rosemary Hennessy), a *maquila* worker from 1973 to 1994 who is now executive director of the Coalition for Justice in the Maquiladoras; from Felicitas (Fela) Contreras, an activist with CETRAC (Center for Workers and Communities) in Nuevo Laredo who worked at the Sony plant from 1985 through 1998; and from Yolanda Treviño, a former Sony worker who testified before the NAO as part of the Sony workers' NAFTA complaint.

To order *NAFTA From Below* or for more information, visit www.coalitionforjustice.net write to The Coalition for Justice in the Maquiladoras, 4207 Willowbrook Dr., San Antonio, TX 78228, or call 210-732-8324.

MARTHA A. OJEDA: Official history is always written so that the reality people were living is hidden. If everyone told the part they lived or knew, the truth would be in their collective word.

* * *

In 1979 Sony arrived in my town [Nuevo Laredo].... Sony manually assembled audiocassettes and Beta videocassettes. In 1982, after the first devaluation of the peso, there were more than 1,000 workers working three shifts in five plants, and by then the workers were also producing the VHS videocassette and the 3.5 inch diskette.

They began to bring machines for semiautomatic and automatic assembly of the cassettes. The plastic molding injection plant was providing the plastic cases and the components for the audio and video plants. It was the boom of assembly line production.

In this era children with birth defects began to be born, but the company doctor said that this happened because the parents were alcoholics or because they had genetic problems. By 1993 there were 2,000 employees in seven plants in three shifts. There was a lot of overtime, but still it wasn't enough to meet production quotas.

The molding ingestion plants never stopped working; they were going three shifts seven days a week. For the first time the company proposed 12 hour shifts for four and three days a week. This implied that Sony got their production, because the machines were running around the clock, but they avoided paying overtime. This twelve-hour shift was unknown to workers because it didn't exist in the Federal Labor Law.

It was in this labor and political context that in October 1993 we visited Fidel Velázquez, the CTM national leader, in Mexico City and solicited union elections within the framework of the CTM. All of the *maquilas* were affiliated with this union because it was the only one; if you didn't belong to them there was no other alternative for workers anywhere. But the leaders negotiated the contract with the company even before it was established in the locality.

Fidel told us that he agreed with the elections (but he never said when they would be). We trusted his word and began the process that the Federal Labor Law sets down for forming the union sections.

* * *

On January 1, 1994, we were informed of the Zapatista uprising, but equally surprising to us was to find out in the newspaper on January 4 that Chema Morales had declared that on the order of Fidel Velázquez he would be the new Secretary General of the *maquilas*—without sectionals—and, worst of all, he was already named to the Labor Board at the state level because of his position as Secretary General, not only of the Maquila Union but also of the Workers Federation of Nuevo Laredo.

Shocked, we tried to communicate with Fidel Velázquez, but our efforts were in vain. Then we learned that he was coming to Ciudad Victoria, the capital of Tamaulipas, on January 12. We traveled all night. But when we arrived it was obvious that they would not let us enter. We guessed that Fidel would come in by the side door and we waited there until he arrived with the media.

I demanded publicly that he retract his authorization of Chema Morales as Secretary General. Then I asked for a public debate with him and with Chema. I don't know if I was the only woman from the provinces who had publicly challenged him, but what I do know is that so much corruption repulsed me and gave me the courage to make sure that the two of them, both Chema and Fidel, would be exposed even to the President of the Labor Board of the state who was present. He had authorized naming Chema to be Secretary General even though he had never worked in the *maquilas*, and according to the union by-laws that was one of the requirements.

In the face of the media and all of the evidence, Fidel looked ridiculous and he had no alternative but to accept that there would be union elections. So he declared that he would send a national representative to hold them. When I went to say goodbye to him at the podium he told me, "You are going to eat fire." And I told him, "I'm ready." But I never imagined what he was referring to.

FELICITAS ("FELA") CONTRERAS: In 1993 they began to change the delegates in all of the *maquiladoras* who were not agreed with the CTM. I heard that there were going to be elections in all the *maquilas*, not only in Sony, and we were asking when Sony's turn would be. But before the elections they were changing the delegates. They fired the ones we wanted and after work we had meetings to change the delegates so that they would really be for us. We met in one house and another with Martha because we wanted to change the delegates who were imposed by the CTM. I would get home at 4:00 or 5:00 in the morning. We always were hiding here and there, and that is how we put together a slate, even though they fired our candidates.

Those union delegates who were with Chema Morales (of the CTM) developed their slates with the old delegates from Sony... They preferred Chema instead of our democratic union. In April of 1994 the day arrived for the elections, and Chema's representative from the union and a representative of Fidel Velázquez were set up in the parking lot of Plant #7. We had our slate, but they didn't give us a chance to let our other co-workers know that the voting was taking place.

Representatives of Fidel Velázquez and of the company were there. They told the people to go to the parking lot and they arranged to meet the other shift and take them out to vote. They said on this side go all those in favor of the blue slate, on the other side those in favor of the CTM slate. Our slate won because everyone came to our side. But Fidel's representative said that the other delegates from the CTM won. And so we said, "How is that possible if we are all here, voting for our slate? We were the majority. What are we going to do?" We were really mad! Those who were working came out and we took to the streets to protest that they were doing this fraudulent election, and we made signs that said, "We want democratic elections!!"

YOLANDA TREVIÑO: On Saturday April 16, which was my day off, I went to plant #3 to see what resolution Mayor Horacio Garza had been able to make as to when we would have new elections. The *compañeras* who had spoken with him told us that he wasn't going to help us. That's when we started to hold our protest on the sidewalk in front of the plants, showing our frustration, but in a peaceful manner. We didn't stop anyone who wanted to from going into work and we didn't commit any act of violence.

We continued protesting in this way until Horacio Garza and Maricela López arrived. We had a meeting there with Horacio and he told us to stop the protest and that afterwards he would help us. We answered that the only thing we wanted was Señor Avila's word that they would hold new elections. But he said no. So Horacio Garza left and soon afterward the police and the firemen arrived. The girls were afraid when they saw the police and some of them asked if the were going to take us away, but we told them if we didn't act violently then they shouldn't either.

But that wasn't the case. Francisco Xavier Rios [Vice President of Human Resources at Sony] signaled to the police with a motion of his hand to enter through a side door, and they positioned themselves on the inside lot of the company. Then without any warning the police began to push us with their Plexiglas shields and their billy clubs. They beat us badly; they knocked a *compañera* unconscious, a woman named Alicia Soto, and they pushed the rest of us down with their shields, insulting us all the while, calling us names like "goddamn bitches."

I have been told that the company claims that the police didn't commit any acts of violence and that they only person who acted violently was Alicia who attacked the police with a magazine. I ask you: how is it possible that a 24 year old woman can harm a group of 35 well-armed police agents carrying Plexiglas shields and billy clubs? How is it possible to say they didn't commit acts of violence when my friend Alicia was knocked out by a blow to the head and has had problems ever since? I have here the newspaper *El Mañana*, dated 17 April, which shows very clearly a picture of Alicia unconscious. If they don't want to read the newspapers they should just look at their own videos because they were filming the entire attack.

FELICITAS ("FELA") CONTRERAS: They had pressed charges against us—Martha Ojeda and various others—because Sony had lost millions with the work stoppage. They issued a summons for us to appear at the police department and told us that our lives were not even worth enough to pay for the company's losses.

They wanted us to say that Martha was responsible, and they pitted us against each other. They told Lupe that I had confessed that Martha was doing it all, and they told me that Lupe confessed that Martha told us to stop working. But of the 40 they called to testify all of us said, "We are all responsible, and so you will have to arrest all of us not just Martha." All of our *compañeras* were outside the police department yelling that they would have to arrest everyone. But since there were more than a thousand and we didn't all fit in the cells, after hours of interrogations and threats they let us go.

***

On the fifth day, in the early morning, around 5:00 am the governor —Manuel Cavazos Lerma—ordered that they state police from Reynosa, Matamoros and Cd. Victoria be brought in. The police arrived and the soldiers with machine guns and rifles. And they said to you, "Get out of here or I'll kill you." According to them they came to restore order, and with blows and kicks. They awakened us and ran after those who were sleeping on the sidewalk. You were waking up with a gun pointing in your face and they were yelling, "Get out or we will kill you."

We withdrew, and we were like this for five days and nights. In those days the trucks tried to mow us down because they wanted to take out the production, but we were all sleeping in the main gate so they couldn't cross and take it out.

Unfortunately, we didn't get it. We didn't get our union, and they fired a lot of people without giving them any severance payment because they said that they were leaders of the movement. We stayed there because we wanted an independent union.

***

In 1994 NAFTA was signed, and they said that the rights of workers would not be violated. But they beat us up and violated our rights. With the help of CJM and the lawyers from ANAD a demand was presented to the NAO. In 1995 we had a hearing and we all went to San Antonio to testify. Sony brought lawyers from New York and they said that our testimony was a lie, but we took the newspapers and the evidence, the videos. We won this trial, but we didn't really win anything because they didn't punish or fine Sony and we never had the elections or anything. They just put in these offices [the NAO] just to prop us NAFTA.

***

For me NAFTA was no good. The workers are still just as poor. The only difference is that now there are many settlements, *colonias*, many squatters, a lot of insecurity and a contaminated river. Before I used to drink water from the river and now you cant, and you cant go into it either. Our air is contaminated. There is a lot of sickness. There is a lot of illiteracy. The only one NAFTA helped were the businessmen because they are the ones that have gotten rich. And now they say, "I am going to China; I screwed the Mexicans so now I'm going to screw the Chinese." That is what says with me about NAFTA. We are poor and screwed.

MARTHA A. OJEDA: Each one of my *compañeras* risked her life, her children, and her family. They kidnapped Yolanda and threatened her. They persecuted the others, calling them on the phone and intimidating them. Wherever any of them are, because there were many and I will never forget one, to each of them I render homage and a special tribute to their "*coraje*"—their courage and bravery—for trying to reclaim workers' right to freedom of association. For resisting and never giving up.

That is what NAFTA left me after 20 years in the *maquilas*: it gave me the opportunity to denounce at a global level the failure of this agreement and of the side agreements and to share the rebellion and resistance of my *compañeras*. It taught me that there is a world of solidarity. It clarified the horizon we are looking for, and above all the hope to reach it with a team like this team of women, united until the end.

INTERNATIONAL LABOR STANDARDS

BY ARTHUR MACEWAN

Dear Dr. Dollar:

U.S. activists have pushed to get foreign trade agreements to include higher labor standards. But then you hear that developing countries don't want that because cheaper labor without a lot of rules and regulations is what's helping them to bring industries in and build their economies. Is there a way to reconcile these views? Or are the activists just blind to the real needs of the countries they supposedly want to help?

—Philip Bereaud, Swampscott, Mass.

In 1971, General Emilio Medici, the then military dictator of Brazil, commented on economic conditions in his country with the infamous line: "The economy is doing fine, but the people aren't."

Like General Medici, the government officials of many low-income countries today see the well-being of their economies in terms of overall output and the profits of firms—those profits that keep bringing in new investment, new industries that "build their economies." It is these officials who typically get to speak for their countries. When someone says that these countries "want" this or that—or "don't want" this or that—it is usually because the countries' officials have expressed this position.

Do we know what the people in these countries want? The people who work in the new, rapidly growing industries, in the mines and fields, and in the small shops and market stalls of low-income countries? Certainly they want better conditions—more to eat, better housing, security for their children, improved health and safety. The officials claim that to obtain these better conditions, they must "build their economies." But just because "the economy is doing fine" does not mean that the people are doing fine.

In fact, in many low-income countries, economic expansion comes along with severe inequality. The people who do the work are not getting a reasonable share of the rising national income (and are sometimes worse off even in absolute terms). Brazil in the early 1970s was a prime example and, in spite of major political change, remains a highly unequal country. Today, in both India and China, as in several other countries, economic growth is coming with increasingly severe inequality.

Workers in these countries struggle to improve their positions. They form—or try to form—independent unions. They demand higher wages and better working conditions. They struggle for political rights. It seems obvious that we should support those struggles, just as we support parallel struggles of workers in our own country. The first principle in supporting workers' struggles, here or anywhere else, is supporting their right to struggle—the right, in particular, to form independent unions without fear of reprisal. Indeed, in the ongoing controversy over the U.S.-Colombia Free Trade Agreement, the assassination of trade union leaders has rightly been a major issue.

Just how we offer our support—in particular, how we incorporate that support into trade agreements—is a complicated question. Pressure from abroad can help, but applying it is a complex process. A ban on goods produced with child labor, for example, could harm the most impoverished families that depend on children's earnings, or could force some children into worse forms of work (e.g., prostitution). On the other hand, using trade agreements to pressure governments to allow unhindered union organizing efforts by workers seems perfectly legitimate. When workers are denied the right to organize, their work is just one step up from slavery. Trade agreements can also be used to support a set of basic health and safety rights for workers. (Indeed, it might be useful if a few countries refused to enter into trade agreements with the United States until we improve workers' basic organizing rights and health and safety conditions in our own country!)

There is no doubt that the pressures that come through trade sanctions (restricting or banning commerce with another country) or simply from denying free access to the U.S. market can do immediate harm to workers and the general populace of low-income countries. Any struggle for change can generate short-run costs, but the long-run gains—even the hope of those gains—can make those costs acceptable. Consider, for example, the Apartheid-era trade sanctions against South Africa. To the extent that those sanctions were effective, some South African workers were deprived of employment. Nonetheless, the sanctions were widely supported by mass organizations in South Africa. Or note that when workers in this country strike or advocate a boycott of their company in an effort to obtain better conditions, they both lose income and run the risk that their employer will close up shop.

Efforts by people in this country to use trade agreements to raise labor standards in other countries should, whenever possible, take their lead from workers in those countries. It is up to them to decide what costs are acceptable. There are times, however, when popular forces are denied even basic rights to struggle. The best thing we can do, then, is to push for those rights—particularly the right to organize independent unions—that help create the opportunity for workers in poor countries to choose what to fight for.

NIKE TO THE RESCUE?
AFRICA NEEDS BETTER JOBS, NOT SWEATSHOPS.

BY JOHN MILLER

"IN PRAISE OF THE MALIGNED SWEATSHOP"
WINDHOEK, Namibia—*Africa desperately needs Western help in the form of schools, clinics and sweatshops.*

On a street here in the capital of Namibia, in the southwestern corner of Africa, I spoke to a group of young men who were trying to get hired as day laborers on construction sites.

"I come here every day," said Naftal Shaanika, a 20-year-old. "I actually find work only about once a week."

Mr. Shaanika and the other young men noted that the construction jobs were dangerous and arduous, and that they would vastly prefer steady jobs in, yes, sweatshops. Sure, sweatshop work is tedious, grueling and sometimes dangerous. But over all, sewing clothes is considerably less dangerous or arduous—or sweaty—than most alternatives in poor countries.

Well-meaning American university students regularly campaign against sweatshops. But instead, anyone who cares about fighting poverty should campaign in favor of sweatshops, demanding that companies set up factories in Africa.

The problem is that it's still costly to manufacture in Africa. The headaches across much of the continent include red tape, corruption, political instability, unreliable electricity and ports, and an inexperienced labor force that leads to low productivity and quality. The anti-sweatshop movement isn't a prime obstacle, but it's one more reason not to manufacture in Africa.

Imagine that a Nike vice president proposed manufacturing cheap T-shirts in Ethiopia. The boss would reply: "You're crazy! We'd be boycotted on every campus in the country."

Some of those who campaign against sweatshops respond to my arguments by noting that they aren't against factories in Africa, but only demand a "living wage" in them. After all, if labor costs amount to only $1 per shirt, then doubling wages would barely make a difference in the final cost.

One problem ... is that it already isn't profitable to pay respectable salaries, and so any pressure to raise them becomes one more reason to avoid Africa altogether.

One of the best U.S. initiatives in Africa has been the African Growth and Opportunity Act, which allows duty-free imports from Africa—and thus has stimulated manufacturing there.

—Op-ed by Nicholas Kristof, *New York Times*, June 6, 2006

Nicholas Kristof has been beating the pro-sweatshop drum for quite a while. Shortly after the East Asian financial crisis of the late 1990s, Kristof, the Pulitzer Prize-winning journalist and now columnist for the *New York Times*, reported the story of an Indonesian recycler who, picking through the metal scraps of a garbage dump, dreamed that her son would grow up to be a sweatshop worker. Then, in 2000, Kristof and his wife, *Times* reporter Sheryl WuDunn, published "Two Cheers for Sweatshops" in the *Times Magazine*. In 2002, Kristof's column advised G-8 leaders to "start an international campaign to promote imports from sweatshops, perhaps with bold labels depicting an unrecognizable flag and the words 'Proudly Made in a Third World Sweatshop.'"

Now Kristof laments that too few poor, young African men have the opportunity to enter the satanic mill of sweatshop employment. Like his earlier efforts, Kristof's latest pro-sweatshop ditty synthesizes plenty of half-truths. Let's take a closer look and see why there is still no reason to give it up for sweatshops.

A BETTER ALTERNATIVE?

It is hardly surprising that young men on the streets of Namibia's capital might find sweatshop jobs more appealing than irregular work as day laborers on construction sites.

The alternative jobs available to sweatshop workers are often worse and, as Kristof loves to point out, usually involve more sweating than those in world export factories. Most poor people in the developing world eke out their livelihoods from subsistence agriculture or by plying petty trades. Others on the edge of urban centers work as street-hawkers or hold other jobs in the informal sector. As economist Arthur MacEwan wrote a few years back in *Dollars & Sense*, in a poor country like Indonesia, where women working in manufacturing earn five times as much as those in agriculture, sweatshops have no trouble finding workers.

But let's be clear about a few things. First, export factory jobs, especially in labor-intensive industries, often are just "a ticket to slightly less impoverishment," as even economist and sweatshop defender Jagdish Bhagwati allows.

Beyond that, these jobs seldom go to those without work or to the poorest of the poor. One study by sociologist Kurt Ver Beek showed that 60% of first-time Honduran maquila workers were previously employed. Typically they were not destitute, and they were better educated than most Hondurans.

Sweatshops don't just fail to rescue people from poverty. Setting up export factories where workers have few job alternatives has actually been a recipe for serious worker abuse. In *Beyond Sweatshops,* a book arguing for the benefits of direct foreign investment in the developing world, Brookings Institution economist Theodore Moran recounts the disastrous decision of the Philippine government to build the Bataan Export Processing Zone in an isolated mountainous area to lure foreign investors with the prospect of cheap labor. With few alternatives, Filipinos took jobs in the garment factories that sprung up in the zone. The manufacturers typically paid less than the minimum wage and forced employees to work overtime in factories filled with dust and fumes. Fed up, the workers eventually mounted a series of crippling strikes. Many factories shut down and occupancy rates in the zone plummeted, as did the value of exports, which declined by more than half between 1980 and 1986.

Kristof's argument is no excuse for sweatshop abuse: that conditions are worse elsewhere does nothing to alleviate the suffering of workers in export factories. They are often denied the right to organize, subjected to unsafe working conditions and to verbal, physical, and sexual abuse, forced to work overtime, coerced into pregnancy tests and even abortions, and paid less than a living wage. It remains useful and important to combat these conditions even if alternative jobs are worse yet.

The fact that young men in Namibia find sweatshop jobs appealing testifies to how harsh conditions are for workers in Africa, not the desirability of export factory employment.

Oddly, Kristof's desire to introduce new sweatshops to sub-Saharan Africa finds no support in the African Growth and Opportunity Act (AGOA) that he praises. The Act grants sub-Saharan apparel manufacturers preferential access to U.S. markets. But shortly after its passage, U.S. Trade Representative Robert Zoellick assured the press that the AGOA would not create sweatshops in Africa because it requires protective standards for workers consistent with those set by the International Labor Organization.

ANTISWEATSHOP ACTIVISM AND JOBS

Kristof is convinced that the antisweatshop movement hurts the very workers it intends to help. His position has a certain seductive logic to it. As anyone who has suffered through introductory economics will tell you, holding everything else the same, a labor standard that forces multinational corporations and their subcontractors to boost wages should result in their hiring fewer workers.

But in practice does it? The only evidence Kristof produces is an imaginary conversation in which a boss incredulously refuses a Nike vice president's proposal to open a factory in Ethiopia paying wages of 25 cents a hour: "You're crazy! We'd be boycotted on every campus in the country."

While Kristof has an active imagination, there are some things wrong with this conversation.

First off, the antisweatshop movement seldom initiates boycotts. An organizer with United Students Against Sweatshops (USAS) responded on Kristof's blog: "We never call for apparel boycotts unless we are explicitly asked to by workers at a particular factory. This is, of course, exceedingly rare, because, as you so persuasively argued, people generally want to be employed." The National Labor Committee, the largest antisweatshop organization in the United States, takes the same position.

Moreover, when economists Ann Harrison and Jason Scorse conducted a systematic study of the effects of the antisweatshop movement on factory employment, they found no negative employment effect. Harrison and Scorse looked at Indonesia, where Nike was one of the targets of an energetic campaign calling for better wages and working conditions among the country's subcontractors. Their statistical analysis found that the antisweatshop campaign was responsible for 20% of the increase in the real wages of unskilled workers in factories exporting textiles, footwear, and apparel from 1991 to 1996. Harrison and Scorse also found that "antisweatshop activism did not have significant adverse effects on employment" in these sectors.

Campaigns for higher wages are unlikely to destroy jobs because, for multinationals and their subcontractors, wages make up a small portion of their overall costs. Even Kristof accepts this point, well documented by economists opposed to sweatshop labor. In Mexico's apparel industry, for instance, economists Robert Pollin, James Heintz, and Justine Burns from the Political Economy Research Institute found that doubling the pay of nonsupervisory workers would add just $1.80 to the production cost of a $100 men's sports jacket. A recent survey by the National Bureau of Economic Research found that U.S. consumers would be willing to pay $115 for the same jacket if they knew that it had not been made under sweatshop conditions.

GLOBALIZATION IN SUB-SAHARAN AFRICA

Kristof is right that Africa, especially sub-Saharan Africa, has lost out in the globalization process. Sub-Saharan Africa suffers from slower growth, less direct foreign investment, lower education levels, and higher poverty rates than most every other part of the world. A stunning 37 of the region's 47 countries are classified as "low-income" by the World Bank, each with a gross national income less than $825 per person. Many countries in the region bear the burdens of high external debt and a crippling HIV crisis that Kristof has made heroic efforts to bring to the world's attention.

But have multinational corporations avoided investing in sub-Saharan Africa because labor costs are too high? While labor costs in South Africa and Mauritius are high, those in the other countries of the region are modest by international standards, and quite low in some cases. Take Lesotho, the largest exporter of apparel from sub-Saharan Africa to the United States. In the country's factories that subcontract with Wal-Mart, the predominantly female workforce earns an average of just $54 a month. That's below the United Nations poverty line of $2 per day, and it includes regular forced overtime. In Madagascar, the region's third largest exporter of clothes to the United States, wages in the apparel industry are just 33 cents per hour, lower than those in China and among the lowest in the world. And at Ramatex Textile, the large Malaysian-owned textile factory in Namibia, workers only earn about $100 per month according to the Labour Resource and Research Institute in Windhoek. Most workers share their limited incomes with extended families and children, and they walk long distances to work because they can't afford better transportation.

On the other hand, recent experience shows that sub-Saharan countries with decent labor standards *can* develop strong manufacturing export sectors. In the late 1990s, Francis Teal of Oxford's Centre for the Study of African Economies compared Mauritius's successful export industries with Ghana's unsuccessful ones. Teal found that workers in Mauritius earned ten times as much as those in Ghana—$384 a month in Mauritius as opposed to $36 in Ghana. Mauritius's textile and garment industry remained competitive because its workforce was better educated and far more productive than Ghana's. Despite paying poverty wages, the Ghanaian factories floundered.

Kristof knows full well the real reason garment factories in the region are shutting down: the expiration of the Multifiber Agreement last January. The agreement, which set national export quotas for clothing and textiles, protected the garment industries in smaller countries around the world from direct competition with China. Now China and, to a lesser degree, India, are increasingly displacing other garment producers. In this new context, lower wages alone are unlikely to sustain the sub-Saharan garment industry. Industry sources report that sub-Saharan Africa suffers from several other drawbacks as an apparel producer, including relatively high utility and transportation costs and long shipping times to the United States. The region also has lower productivity and less skilled labor than Asia, and it has fewer sources of cotton yarn and higher-priced fabrics than China and India.

If Kristof is hell-bent on expanding the sub-Saharan apparel industry, he would do better to call for sub-Saharan economies to gain unrestricted access to the Quad markets—the United States, Canada, Japan, and Europe. Economists Stephen N. Karingi, Romain Perez, and Hakim Ben Hammouda estimate that the welfare gains associated with unrestricted market access could amount to $1.2 billion in sub-Saharan Africa, favoring primarily unskilled workers.

But why insist on apparel production in the first place? Namibia has sources of wealth besides a cheap labor pool for Nike's sewing machines. The *Economist* reports that Namibia is a world-class producer of two mineral products: diamonds (the country ranks seventh by value) and uranium (it ranks fifth by volume). The mining industry is the heart of Namibia's export economy and accounts for about 20% of the country's GDP. But turning the mining sector into a vehicle for national economic development would mean confronting the foreign corporations that control the diamond industry, such as the South African De Beers Corporation.

That is a tougher assignment than scapegoating antisweatshop activists.

MORE AND BETTER AFRICAN JOBS

So why have multinational corporations avoided investing in sub-Saharan Africa? The answer, according to international trade economist Dani Rodrik, is "entirely due to the slow growth" of the sub-Saharan economies. Rodrik estimates that the region participates in international trade as much as can be expected given its economies' income levels, country size, and geography.

Rodrik's analysis suggests that the best thing to do for poor workers in Africa would be to lift the debt burdens on their governments and support their efforts to build functional economies. That means investing in human resources and physical infrastructure, and implementing credible macroeconomic policies that put job creation first. But these investments, as Rodrik points out, take time.

In the meantime, international policies establishing a floor for wages and safeguards for workers across the globe would do more for the young men on Windhoek's street corners than subjecting them to sweatshop abuse, because grinding poverty leaves people willing to enter into any number of desperate exchanges. And if Namibia is closing its garment factories because Chinese imports are cheaper, isn't that an argument for trying to improve labor standards in China, not lower them in sub-Saharan Africa? Abusive labor practices are rife in China's export factories, as the National Labor Committee and *Business Week* have documented. Workers put in 13- to 16-hour days, seven days a week. They enjoy little to no health and safety enforcement, and their take-home pay falls below the minimum wage after the fines and deductions their employers sometimes withhold.

Spreading these abuses in sub-Saharan Africa will not empower workers there. Instead it will take advantage of the fact that they are among the most marginalized workers in the world. Debt relief, international labor standards, and public investments in education and infrastructure are surely better ways to fight African poverty than Kristof's sweatshop proposal.r insignia products. They have no system, however, to track apparel production around the world, and often no idea where their production is occurring. Monitoring systems are still in their fledgling stages, so the universities are starting from a difficult position, albeit one they have profited from for years.

What can universities do about this? They should do what they are best at: produce information. They should take the lead in demanding that corporations—beginning with those they do business with—open themselves up to public inspection and evaluation. Universities have done this before, such as during the anti-apartheid campaign for South Africa. By doing this on the sweatshop issue, universities could spur a critical dialogue on labor issues around the world.

To start, the universities could establish a central coordinating office to collect and compare information on factory performance for member universities' licensees. (The WRC has proposed such a model.) This new office would be responsible for keeping records on licensee compliance, for making this information available over the Internet, for registering local NGOs and worker organizations to conduct independent verifications of factory conditions, and for assessing sanctions.

Such a program would allow universities to evaluate different strategies for improving conditions in different parts of the world. This would avoid the danger of locking in one code of conduct or one certification system. In place of sporadic media exposés embarrassing one company at a time, we would have an international system of disclosure and learning—benchmarking good performers, identifying and targeting the worst performers, and motivating improvements.

It is clearly no longer enough to expose one company at a time, or to count on industry-paid consulting firms. The building blocks of a new system depend on information. This fits the mission of universities. Universities should focus on information gathering and dissemination, and most importantly, on learning. If the universities learn nothing else from "Sweatshops 101," they should learn that they still have a lot of homework do to—and that their next test will be coming soon.

Resources: Arthur MacEwan, "Ask Dr. Dollar," *Dollars & Sense*, Sept–Oct 1998; John Miller, "Why Economists Are Wrong About Sweatshops and the Antisweatshop Movement," *Challenge*, Jan–Feb 2003; R. Pollin, J. Burns, and J. Heintz, "Global Apparel Production and Sweatshop Labor: Can Raising Retail Prices Finance Living Wages?" Political Economy Research Institute, Working Paper 19, DATE; N. Kristof, "In Praise of the Maligned Sweatshop,"*New York Times*, June 6, 2006; N. Kristof, "Let Them Sweat," NYT , June 25, 2002; N. Kristof, "Two Cheers for Sweatshops," *NYT* , Sept 24, 2000; N. Kristof, "Asia'[s Crisis Upsets Rising Effort to Confront Blight of Sweatshops," *NYT*, June 15, 1998; A. Harrison and J. Scorse, "Improving the Conditions of Workers? Minimum Wage Legislation and Anti-Sweatshop Activism," Calif. Management Review, Oct 2005; Herbert Jauch, "Africa's Clothing and Textile Industry: The Case of Ramatex in Namibia," in *The Future of the Textile and Clothing Industry in Sub-Saharan Africa*, ed. H. Jauch and R. Traub-Merz (Friedrich-Ebert-Stiftung, 2006); Kurt Alan Ver Beek, "Maquiladoras: Exploitation or Emancipation? An Overview of the Situation of Maquiladora Workers in Honduras," *World Development*, 29(9), 2001; Theodore Moran, *Beyond Sweatshops: Foreign Direct Investment and Globalization in Developing Countries* (Brookings Institution Press, 2002); "Comparative Assessment of the Competitiveness of the Textile and Apparel Sector in Selected Countries," in *Textiles and Apparel: Assessment of the Competitiveness of Certain Foreign Suppliers to the United States Market*, Vol. 1, U.S. International Trade Commission, Jan 2004; S. N. Karingi, R. Perez, and H. Ben Hammouda, "Could Extended Preferences Reward Sub-Saharan Africa's Participation in the Doha Round Negotiations?," World Economy, 2006; Francis Teal, "Why Can Mauritius Export Manufactures and Ghana Can Not?," *The World Economy*, 22 (7), 1999; Dani Rodrik, "Trade Policy and Economic Performance in Sub-Saharan Africa," Paper prepared for the Swedish Ministry for Foreign Affairs, Nov 1997.

CONTRIBUTORS

Randy Albelda, a *Dollars & Sense* Associate, teaches economics at the University of Massachusetts-Boston.

Sylvia Allegretto is currently an economist at the Institute for Research on Labor and Employment at the University of California, Berkeley.

William K. Black is an associate professor of economics and law at the University of Missouri-Kansas City.

Heather Boushey is a Senior Economist at the Center for American Progress.

Esther Cervantes is a former *Dollars and Sense* collective member.

Ben Collins is a member of the *Dollars & Sense* collective and a research analyst at KLD Research & Analytics, a sustainable investment research company.

Paul Cummings is a software engineer with a longstanding interest in environmental and social issues.

James M. Cypher is professor of development economics at the Autonomous University of Zacatecas, Mexico, and a *Dollars & Sense* associate.

Ryan Dodd is a Ph.D. student in economics and a research associate at the Center for Full Employment and Price Stability, both at the University of Missouri-Kansas City.

Marie Duggan is an associate professor of economics at Keene State College in New Hampshire.

Daniel Fireside is the *Dollars & Sense* book editor

Ellen Frank is an economist, author of *The Raw Deal: How Myths and Misinformation about the Deficit, Inflation, and Wealth Impoverish America*, and a *Dollars & Sense* Associate.

Gerald Friedman is a professor of economics at the University of Massachusetts at Amherst

Elise Gould is a staff economist at the Economic Policy Institute.

Lena Graber is a former *Dollars & Sense* intern.

William Greider has been a political journalist for more than 35 years. He is currently the National Affairs Correspondent for the *Nation* magazine.

Joshua Holland is a senior writer and editor with AlterNet.org.

Howard Karger is professor of social policy at the University of Houston.

David Kotz teaches economics at the University of Massachusetts at Amherst.

Paul Krugman teaches economics at Princeton and is a columnist for the *New York Times.*

Arthur MacEwan, a *Dollars & Sense* Associate, teaches economics at the University of Massachusetts-Boston.

Gretchen McClain, a former member of the *Dollars & Sense* collective, is an economic consultant.

John Miller, a *Dollars & Sense* collective member, teaches economics at Wheaton College.

Monique Morrissey is a policy analyst at the Economic Policy Institute.

Fred Moseley is a professor of economics at Mt. Holyoke College.

Gina Neff is the associate director of Economists Allied for Arms Reduction.

Martha A. Ojeda is the Executive Director of the Coalition for Justice in the Maquiladoras.

Doug Orr teaches economics at Eastern Washington University.

Stephen Philion is an assistant professor of sociology in the Department of Sociology and Anthropology at St. Cloud State University.

Robert Pollin teaches economics and is co-director of the Political Economy Research Institute at the University of Massachusetts-Amherst. He is also a *Dollars & Sense* Associate.

Alejandro Reuss is a historian and economist and a member of the *Dollars & Sense* collective.

Jonathan Rowe is a contributing editor at the *Washington Monthly*.

Orlando Segura, Jr. has worked for an Atlanta-based global management consulting company that consults for private equity firms, and for a private equity firm based in Boston.

Bryan Snyder, a *Dollars & Sense* collective member, teaches economics at Bentley University.

Bob Sutcliffe is an economist at the University of the Basque Country in Bilbao, Spain.

Alissa Thuotte is a former *Dollars & Sense* intern.

Chris Tilly is the director of UCLA's Institute for Research on Labor and Employment and a *Dollars & Sense* Associate.

Ramaa Vasudevan is an assistant professor of economics at Colorado State University and a member of the *Dollars & Sense* collective.

Richard Wolff teaches economics at the University of Massachusetts-Amherst.

Marty Wolfson is professor of economics at Mt. Holyoke College.

James Woolman is a health policy analyst and former member of the *Dollars & Sense* collective.

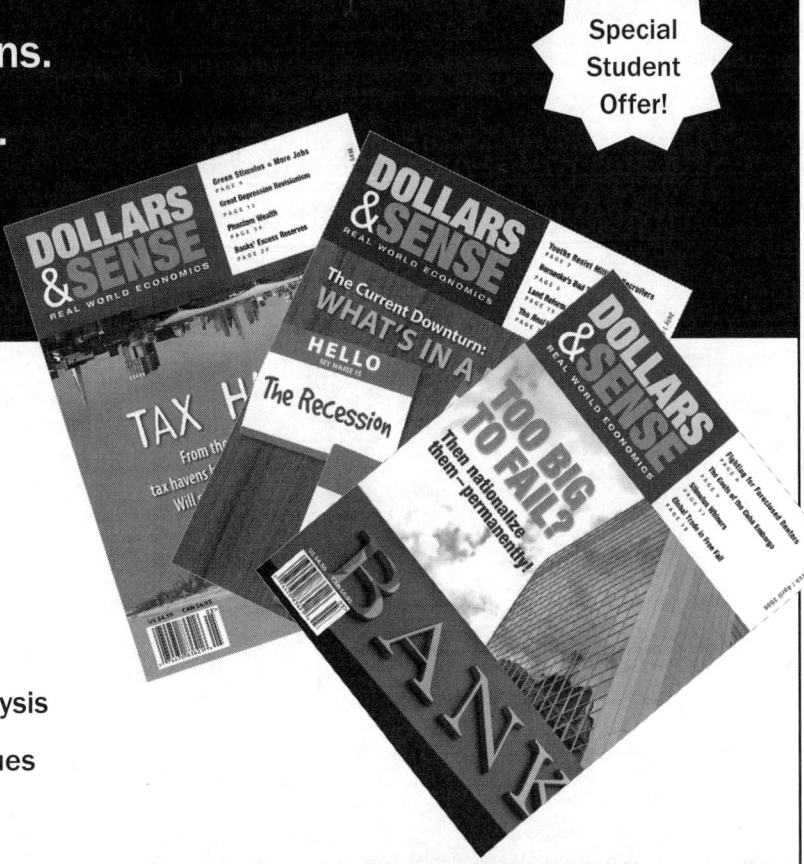